Napoleon & Josephine

AN IMPROBABLE MARRIAGE

KENSINGTON/ 1-57566-056-3
CAN $19.00/ U.S. $16.00

EVANGELINE BRUCE

Critical praise for
NAPOLEON AND JOSEPHINE:

"Evangeline Bruce knows Paris well, and has frequented many of the scenes of Napoleon's and Josephine's glory. She writes of them with style and sympathy. ... This is an extremely readable account of their lives together, and an easy and attractive introduction to Napoleon and his private life."
—*New York Times Book Review*

"A riveting book, full of interesting and colorful detail. ... Bruce's portrayal of the central characters is a masterful one. Deeply moving."
—Alison Weir, author of *The Six Wives of Henry VIII*

"What a saga! Elegant and witty... altogether fascinating."   —Liz Smith

"The book's wealth of detail about the relationship of the ever-intriguing couple offers a rich panorama of the exhilarating and violent time on which they left their mark. The author draws on a multitude of eyewitness accounts and other sources to present a full-bodied Napoleon. ... Josephine is no less distinctive. Vivid portraits abound... and Paris comes alive with its noises, smells, fashions and salons."   —*Publishers Weekly*

"Readers are in for a treat. A vivid narrative written with insight, compassion and wit."   —Nathan Miller, author of *Theodore Roosevelt: A Life*

"For all students of history, NAPOLEON AND JOSEPHINE is a must. Splendid."   —Barbara Cartland

"NAPOLEON AND JOSEPHINE, in an impressive combination of literary elegance and historical sensitivity, sets that fascinating couple in a rich political and social context and splendidly evokes the passion and poignancy of a turbulent marriage and a turbulent age."   —Arthur Schlesinger, Jr.

"An intricate and intimate profile that reveals a charismatic Napoleon obsessed with glory and the all-too-human Josephine desperate for love."
—*Kirkus Reviews*

"After dozens of biographies on both Napoleon and Josephine, running the gamut from love to hate, from scholarly to sensational, author and noted authority on French history Evangeline Bruce has chosen to add to the French history shelf with her own title emphasizing the famous pair's marriage in relation to the turbulent social time in which they lived. Well traveled and well versed in French manners and mores, she adds a graceful, personal, comfortably detailed touch to her topic."   —*Library Journal*

Napoleon and Josephine

AN IMPROBABLE MARRIAGE

EVANGELINE BRUCE

KENSINGTON BOOKS

KENSINGTON BOOKS are published by

Kensington Publishing Corp.
850 Third Avenue
New York, NY 10022

ISBN 1-57566-056-3

First Kensington Trade Paperback Printing: July, 1996
10 9 8 7 6 5 4 3 2 1

Printed in the United States of America

David and Sasha

with constant love.

CONTENTS

Contents

Contents

❧ Tascher de La Pagerie ❧

Gaspard-Joseph m., 1734, Françoise Boureau de la Chevalerie

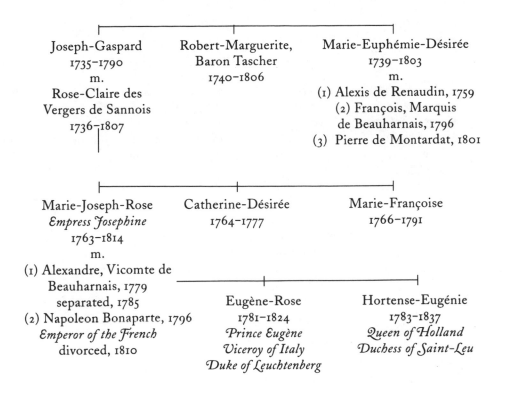

Joseph-Gaspard
1735–1790
m.
Rose-Claire des
Vergers de Sannois
1736–1807

Robert-Marguerite,
Baron Tascher
1740–1806

Marie-Euphémie-Désirée
1739–1803
m.
(1) Alexis de Renaudin, 1759
(2) François, Marquis
de Beauharnais, 1796
(3) Pierre de Montardat, 1801

Marie-Joseph-Rose
Empress Josephine
1763–1814
m.
(1) Alexandre, Vicomte de
Beauharnais, 1779
separated, 1785
(2) Napoleon Bonaparte, 1796
Emperor of the French
divorced, 1810

Catherine-Désirée
1764–1777

Marie-Françoise
1766–1791

Eugène-Rose
1781–1824
Prince Eugène
Viceroy of Italy
Duke of Leuchtenberg

Hortense-Eugénie
1783–1837
Queen of Holland
Duchess of Saint-Leu

❧ Bonaparte ❧

Carlo Maria Buonaparte m., 1764, Letizia Ramolino
1746–1785   1750–1836

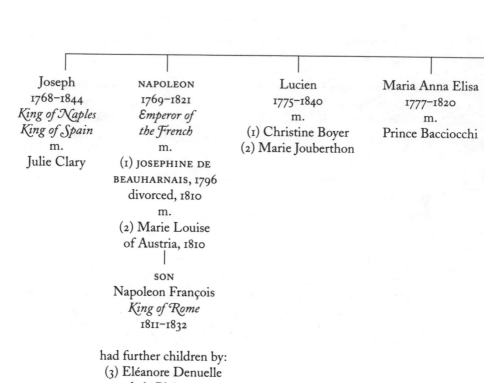

Joseph	NAPOLEON	Lucien	Maria Anna Elisa
1768–1844	1769–1821	1775–1840	1777–1820
King of Naples	*Emperor of*	m.	m.
King of Spain	*the French*	(1) Christine Boyer	Prince Bacciocchi
m.	m.	(2) Marie Jouberthon	
Julie Clary	(1) JOSEPHINE DE		

BEAUHARNAIS, 1796
divorced, 1810
m.
(2) Marie Louise
of Austria, 1810

SON
Napoleon François
King of Rome
1811–1832

had further children by:
(3) Eléanore Denuelle
de la Plaigne:
Léon Denuelle
1806–1881
(4) Comtesse Marie
Walewska:
Alexandre-Florian,
Comte Walewski
1810–1868

Louis
1778–1846
King of Holland
m.
Hortense Beauharnais

CHILDREN
Napoleon Charles
1802–1807
Napoleon Louis
1804–1831
Charles Louis Napoleon
1808–1873
Napoleon III

Paola Maria
(Pauline)
1780–1825
m.
(1) General Victor
Emmanuel Leclerc
(2) Prince Borghese

Maria Annunziata
(Caroline)
1782–1839
Queen of Naples
m.
Joachim Murat
King of Naples

Jérôme
1784–1860
King of Westphalia
m.
(1) Elizabeth Patterson
(2) Princess Catherine
of Württemberg

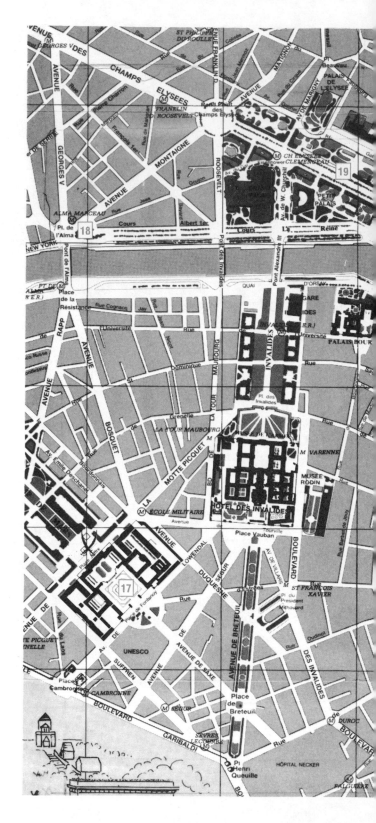

Paris 1995 with Some Revolutionary Milestones

1. Place de le Révolution (Place de la Concorde)
2. Robespierre's lodgings
3. General Bonaparte's headquarters after Vendémiaire
4. Tuileries Riding School, First seat of the Constituent Assembly
5. Jacobin Club
6. Church of St. Roch
7. Tuileries Palace and Gardens
8. Palais Egalité (Palais Royal)
9. Conciergerie Prison
10. Notre Dame
11. Church of St. Sulpice
12. Luxembourg Palace
13. Les Carmes
14. Panthémont
15. Josephine's apartment
16. Swedish Embassy, Mme de Staël's headquarters
17. Royal Military School
18. The Chaumière
19. Champs-Elysées

♠ Liberty cap= revolutionary signposts

⚔ Crossed sabers= massacres, riots

FOREWORD

A CENTURY AND A HALF AGO, STENDHAL WROTE: "IN THE NEXT FIFTY years the history of Napoleon will have to be rewritten each year."[1] Already the Emperor has inspired more studies than there are days since his death, while there are almost sixty biographies of Josephine.

Historical fashions have pursued them both. Napoleon has been seen in as many manifestations as there are ideologies, in turn either as a son of the Revolution, the believer in a united Europe or the archetypal dictator and propagandist. Josephine's reputation has seen nearly as many metamorphoses.

This book does not attempt to emulate the scholarly biographies of their lives, to many of which I am deeply indebted. It was a fascination with the age in which this oddly assorted pair lived, and with their influence on the political, social and cultural life of the period, which led me, in what has necessarily been a highly selective process, to use their marriage as the frame through which to view a time of cataclysmic changes, an era as violent and unpredictable as our own.

I AM MUCH INDEBTED TO MONSIEUR BERNARD CHEVALLIER, CURATOR of the Musée de Malmaison, for enlightening visits to the museum; also to Monsieur Jean-Pierre Samoyault, formerly curator of the Château de Fontainebleau, for sharing with me some of the palace's history. My thanks go also to Mademoiselle Benoit, librarian of the Napoleonic Fonds Masson at the Bibliothèque Thiers and to Monsieur Luc Thévenon, for his courtesy in providing me with photographs of two portraits, the property of the Musée d'Art et d'Histoire, Palais Masséna, Nice.

My warm thanks for their indispensable help and patience go to Pamela McClelland and Trudie Musson; and I owe a special debt of thanks to Elizabeth Johnston, whose skill and quick understanding reduced to order my successive drafts.

I am grateful to all my family for its support, especially to Nicholas Cabell Bruce and to Virginia Surtees. For particular help, advice and encouragement I am immensely indebted to Nicholas Henderson, Priscilla Bruce Jaretzki and Liliane de Rothschild, and I am profoundly grateful to Douglas Matthews, to John Saumarez Smith and to Antonia Till, who kindly read my manuscript, for their perceptive comments, their stimulating observations and especially for their valuable amendments.

Finally my deepest gratitude goes to Liliane Ziegel, who, beyond her immeasurable professional assistance and tireless search for relevant material, has shared with me unstintingly her wide knowledge and her friendship.

✦ 1 ✦

Come with Both Your Daughters, but Hurry

Napoleon's Josephine was born on June 23, 1763, on the family sugar plantation in the French colony of Martinique in the West Indies. She was christened Marie-Joseph-Rose and would be known as Rose for more than half her life, until the day young General Bonparte started his letter: "At seven in the morning: Sweet and incomparable Josephine, I awake full of you and of the memory of our intoxicating night. . . ."

Martinique was one of the island fortresses passed from Britain to France, and back again, in the ceaseless wars for tactical advantage and for possession of the valuable sugar islands of the Caribbean. Only three months before Rose's birth, Martinique had been returned to France after eight years' occupation; she had therefore only narrowly escaped being born a British subject, by as small a margin as Napoleon would avoid being born Italian.

To leave the West Indies, to taste again the pleasures of Paris, was the dream of every Frenchman in the Windward Islands, and Rose's father, bored and in debt on his isolated sugar plantation, lived on nostalgic memories of his years at the court of Versailles. At the age of eighteen Joseph Tascher de La Pagerie had served as a page in the household of the Dauphine, mother of King Louis XVI, and he was forever contrasting his five years there with the provincial life of the island. He spent increasingly long periods at Fort Royal, the island's capital, drinking and gambling in the company, it was said, of his black mistresses.

Rose's birth was a disappointment to both her parents. Her father had hoped for a son who would follow in his footsteps in Paris; her mother, who believed that a son might mend their ailing marriage, wrote:

"Contrary to our hopes, it has pleased God to give us a daughter . . . my own joy has been no less great. Why should we not take a more favorable view of our own sex? I know some who combine so many good qualities that it would seem impossible to find them all in any other person." A second daughter was born, and when Mme de La Pagerie was pregnant for a third time, she wrote to Joseph's sister in Paris: "I hope with all my heart that it will be the little nephew you desire; perhaps that will give his father a little more love for me. . . . He spends his time in his charming Fort Royal where he finds more pleasure than he does with me and his children."[1]

Disappointed by the birth of their daughters and embittered by her husband's repeated absences, Rose-Claire de La Pagerie took over most of the management of the plantation, but it was the white overseer who would go regularly to Fort Royal to purchase oxen for the plough and mules to make the mill run and, most importantly, to sell the plantation sugar and have it loaded on to the ships for France, ships that brought to the West Indies wine, the salted beef and cod eaten on all the plantations, and the bricks and roof slates carried for ballast. They carried other cargo too. These ships were often part of the infamous "triangular" voyages. First, the blacks captured by slave raids in equatorial Africa and sold on the Ivory Coast to slaving captains were shipped to the French ports of Bordeaux, Nantes and Cherbourg; there the same ships took on the foodstuffs required in the West Indies, continued with all their freight for trading in the sugar islands, and then returned to Europe loaded with sugar, tobacco, coffee, cocoa and other tropical produce.

There was no question of buying slaves for Les Trois Ilets, the plantation made over to the couple by the bride's family. The estate overlooked a wide bay and took its name from the three small islands moored in it. Joseph's earlier mismanagement had reduced the sugar harvest to such an extent that fewer than a third of the original 150 slaves now worked the field and the refinery. Running the plantation became still more onerous after the great hurricane of 1766, the worst the island had ever known.

Throughout the terrible night of August 13, three-year-old Rose huddled with her family and all the slaves in the stone sugar refinery. The entire island was devastated; the winds and the tidal wave that followed them had sunk forty-eight ships, killed 440 persons and injured many more. At Les Trois Ilets the slave quarters, the hospital and even the mill built on heavy piles had disappeared; the cane plantations themselves were leveled.

The La Pageries had also lost their big wooden house surrounded by airy verandas. They started by living on the upper floor of the refinery, its walls eight feet thick, and the only building left standing for miles around.* A low gallery was added on two sides of the stone building, and the family's living quarters were provisionally set up above the noisy machinery, the great wheel and the big drums for crushing the sugarcane.

There was always the hope of rebuilding after a good harvest, but the La Pageries were destined never to leave the refinery. The house was not rebuilt and all the family, with the exception of Rose, would die there. But the plantation carpenter did rebuild the slave quarters and the tall wooden bell tower that summoned the field slaves to work at five-thirty—dawn in the West Indies all year round—as well as the slave hospital, the laundry and the dovecote. The flower garden and the slaves' vegetable allotments were replanted. However, the guest house was never replaced. House parties were as common in the Windward Islands as in the antebellum American South, and there had been a time at Les Trois Ilets, too, when stuffed partridge, suckling pig and the local crabs were prepared for guests traveling from one sugar estate to another, often staying for weeks or even months at a time.

Although the estate never recovered from the hurricane, the lack of cash and of certain comforts were barely felt as hardships; the family was screened by the planters' life of apparent ease and the luxury of slave labor. The enervating air, the long siestas, the pace of life in the Caribbean, all appear to have contributed to Rose's native indolence—what she would always prefer to call nonchalance—remarkable even in that climate. She grew up in an affectionate, if not a united family, although in the manner of the day she spent more time as a small child with her wet nurse, Marion, than in the company of her parents.† With her younger sisters,

---

* Only the brick furnace chimney and the refinery itself remain today.

† By an imperial decree of 1807, Napoleon granted "Demoiselle Marion, *mulâtresse libre de Martinique*," an annual pension of twelve hundred francs, in recognition of the care she had bestowed on "our beloved spouse, Empress of the French and Queen of Italy, in her earliest infancy."

Catherine and Manette—two weeks after the hurricane, Mme de La Pagerie had given birth to yet another daughter—and the household slaves and their children, she played in the shade of mango and custard-apple and bread-fruit trees. The memory of the island's brilliant birds and tropical bougainvillea, the jasmine and the orchids, would remain with Rose all her life and be re-created in her greenhouses and aviaries.

At the age of ten Rose—Yéyette to her family and to her wet nurse—was ferried across the bay to Fort Royal. At the convent school where she boarded, instruction was limited to the current demands of a worldly education: deportment and penmanship, music, singing, dancing and court curtsies, subjects considered sufficient for the education of a daughter of the planter aristocracy. Her free days were spent either with old Mme de La Pagerie, her grandmother, or with her father's brother Robert, Baron de Tascher, commander of the port.* The conversation of all the girls centered, as did that of their parents, on Paris, on court gossip, on the names and histories of the personalities at Versailles. And on marriage.

When, at fourteen, Rose returned to Les Trois Ilets, she was at an age when many upper-class girls in the islands were already married. Eleven was a not uncommon age for betrothals between persons of property, both in France and in the colonies. Gentle-mannered and generous, with an equable and loving disposition, Rose harbored one daydream, that of going to Paris, with a tenacity alien to her essentially passive nature. When Aunt Désirée's letter arrived from Paris in October 1777, that dream appeared ready to be fulfilled.

Joseph de La Pagerie would probably not have married without the assistance of his sister Désirée, and her strong family feeling, loyalty and practical sense. Ambitious and determined, she was in every way his opposite. Seeing herself as responsible for the fortunes of his three daughters, she never ceased to advocate their joining her in Paris.

When their father, Gaspard Tascher de La Pagerie, left France in 1726 for Martinique he was dazzled, as were most of his generation, by the

---

* Members of the family did not always use their full name. Josephine usually preferred La Pagerie (or Lapagerie in revolutionary times); her uncle was always known as Baron Tascher.

very idea of "the Americas." The West Indies in particular was the place where fortunes were to be made. The islands exported sugar, coffee and indigo, but it was sugarcane, the only source of sugar until the end of the century, which provided true wealth. Santo Domingo alone, the richest of all the Windward Islands, furnished three-quarters of the world's sugar production and was so important to France that in 1763 the King would, as Voltaire wrote, "sacrifice a few acres of snow in Canada" in exchange for this "pearl of the Antilles." "Rich as a Creole" was a familiar phrase in eighteenth-century France, England, Holland and Denmark, in any country possessing sugar islands in the Caribbean.

The fortunes of the young men in those islands were usually acquired within two generations, after which they returned to France to enjoy a luxurious life in Paris or at the court of Versailles as absentee landlords who never returned to the West Indies and whose plantations were run by stewards, often a family member. Gaspard de La Pagerie had been unable to effect this triumphant return. His shiftless temperament was part of the trouble. Success in the sugar islands depended largely on energy and on sufficient capital to acquire the sugar plantation and the highly priced slaves required to work it, both of which Gaspard lacked. He did not, however, neglect the third indispensable measure—the registering of ample proof of a "certificate of nobility"—without which a planter was deprived of admittance to the political and commercial world of the islands, and was unable to make a suitable marriage.

So incompetent was Gaspard, and so soon in debt, however, that he was reduced to working as a steward for other planters. Unable to support his wife and five children, he managed, thanks to a brother at court, to have his son Joseph, Rose's father, attached as a page at Versailles. Upon his return to Martinique, Joseph, too, ran into debt almost immediately. The situation appeared to be hopeless and would have remained so but for Joseph's sister Désirée, who was herself about to create a resounding scandal in the islands, adding to the already deplorable reputation of the La Pagerie family.

François de Beauharnais, a self-styled marquis, arrived in Fort Royal in 1757 as the newly appointed governor and lieutenant general of "the islands of Martinique, Guadeloupe, Marie Galante, St. Martin, St. Barthélemy, la Désirade, Dominique, Ste. Lucie, la Grenade, les Grenadins, Tobago, St. Vincent, Cayenne and the Windward Islands of America."

Beauharnais's wife took an instant liking to Désirée Tascher de La Pagerie and invited her to live in the governor's house as her companion. Soon Beauharnais himself, a man of forty-two and of many previous liaisons, fell helplessly in love with nineteen-year-old Désirée. By the standards of the day it became imperative for the governor to marry off his mistress. A suitable match was found in the person of one of his aides, Alexis Renaudin of the King's Musketeers, too newly arrived in Martinique to have heard the current rumors of the affair. Renaudin's father, however, a planter in the island of St. Lucia, raised strong objections because of the La Pagerie family's undesirable reputation. While these matrimonial negotiations were continuing, the British fleet appeared off Martinique at the end of 1758, attempted a landing, were repulsed and then sailed on to attack the neighboring French island colony of Guadeloupe.

The King's lieutenant commanding in Guadeloupe appealed to the governor of Martinique for reinforcements. François de Beauharnais had under his command one man-of-war, eight ships of the line and three frigates. But there followed an inexplicable silence from Fort Royal while the inhabitants of Guadeloupe held off the enemy for three months with great loss of life until April 23, 1759, when Beauharnais at last set out with his fleet, arriving off Guadeloupe on April 27 to learn that the commander in chief of the island had finally surrendered the preceding day. Immediately upon receiving this news, and without attempting to recapture the colony, the governor set sail for a rapid return to Fort Royal.

All Martinique knew, and soon Guadeloupe too learned, the reason for the three month delay. The negotiations for Désirée's establishment had filled Beauharnais's time, and only after the Renaudin–La Pagerie marriage on April 19 had he bestirred himself to come to the aid of the besieged island. Still more scandalously, the governor in his report to Paris placed the responsibility for the capitulation of Guadeloupe on its commander and his lieutenants, who were thereupon publicly cashiered and sent to Paris for life imprisonment. When the full extent of the governor's perfidy became known at the Naval Ministry in Paris, Beauharnais was relieved of his command in the West Indies and recalled in disgrace. He refused, however, to leave Martinique and Désirée, and lingered on a full year on the grounds of his wife's pregnancy.

Meanwhile Alexis Renaudin had learned of his wife's liaison with the governor. A violent man, he had first beaten her up and then left for Paris to apply for a legal separation "in view of the notorious misconduct of my wife." Désirée thereupon decided to follow him to France to enter a counterplea to the separation and to establish a claim on Renaudin's income. Before leaving, however, she had arranged the marriage of her shiftless brother Joseph, a far better one than he could have hoped for without her help and that of the former governor.

The bride was Rose-Claire des Vergers de Sannois; the alliance with the La Pageries was said to be unwelcome to the bride's family, one of the oldest and most respected in the islands. It was probably agreed to only because Rose-Claire had reached the almost unmarriageable age of twenty-five. There was also the matter of the bride's mother, Catherine Brown, who was reputedly Irish, but without further identification; this lack of information was a drawback in the island, where each entry in the Nobles' Registry was keenly scrutinized and evaluated in the small circle of planters.

With Joseph settled on the de Sannois plantation of Les Trois Ilets, and pausing only to stand as godmother to the newborn Beauharnais baby, Désirée set sail for France after the christening, accompanied by Charlotte and Arthémise, two freed slaves given her by her mother.

Three-month-old Alexandre de Beauharnais, considered too young to survive the rigors of an Atlantic crossing, was left in the charge of Désirée's mother when the Beauharnais couple followed Mme Renaudin to Paris. Once in France, Mme de Beauharnais retired to her family property in the country and Désirée moved in with the "Marquis." Since Mme de Beauharnais and Désirée continued an affectionate correspondence until the former's death in 1767, there seems to have been no ill feeling between them. The scandal that continued to surround the Beauharnais-Renaudin ménage was not owing to the liaison; eighteenth-century France was shocked only that the couple lived together under the same roof. Matrimony was out of the question. Divorce was virtually nonexistent, and Alexis Renaudin's revenge was to live on for another thirty-five years in excellent health.

When little Alexandre de Beauharnais reached the age of five Rose's grandmother sent him to France, and after his own mother died he was brought up by his godmother, Désirée, under the paternal roof and was as fond of her, he said, "as though she were my own mother."[2]

When Alexandre was seventeen Désirée Renaudin felt how desirable it would be not only to be of use to her improvident brother, but also to consolidate her own position and retain within the family the forty thousand livres* that Alexandre would inherit, for the two Beauharnais sons were to succeed to all their mother's considerable fortune at their majority. The elder had already come into his inheritance and lived an independent life. The marquis was not in financial need, however, for François de Beauharnais' connections at court had finally ensured him, instead of censure, a generous retirement pay as well as the bestowal of the title that he had already conferred upon himself. As one historian has phrased it, "what more indeed could have been done for him, if instead of losing Guadeloupe, he had conquered it, or even simply secured it?"[3]

This was not the first time that Désirée Renaudin had pressed her brother to send her one of his daughters. From the time Rose was five years old she had urged it. The plantation then had shown no sign of recovering from the hurricane, there was no money for two ocean passages, and Rose's de Sannois grandmother was obliged to write to Désirée: "You asked for my eldest granddaughter, but I am truly not in a position to send her."[4]

From her own experience Désirée Renaudin knew how uncultivated a girl raised in the colonies would appear in Paris. The choice of aristocratic families in search of fortunes for their sons was traditionally confined to the daughters of wealthy Paris financiers and the heiresses from the sugar islands. These families usually preferred the latter, of minor but authentic nobility, and readily forgave them their native reckless expenditure. Half of the great families at court were married to Creole ladies (a term then universally applied to white persons born in the colonies) "bringing with them the gracefulness common only to Creoles, their nonchalant speech and the negligé of their customs."[5] They reigned in the capital, remarkable for the "provocative languor of their walk, and for their natural elegance, universally imitated but never surpassed."[6] Their extravagance, indeed, went to inordinate lengths; their influence in Paris on fashion and pleasure was immeasurable.

---

* One livre equaled around three dollars in the 1780s.

But these girls were not only heiresses to vast fortunes; they had usually been sent to France as small children to acquire a fashionable education and a polished tone and bearing. Désirée knew that if she were to arrange a marriage for one of her brother's dowerless daughters, it would be necessary that he send her the girl at an early age. Until October 1777, Désirée had renewed her pleas regularly; now she was in a hurry. One of her nieces, she wrote, should be sent over immediately for a suitable education in France and as a bride for her godson, the twenty-year-old Chevalier Alexandre de Beauharnais, described by her as a paragon of virtue and talents. She had no need to remind her family of his large private income, nor of the miracle of the luck of this match. In families of property, marriage without a dowry was almost inconceivable unless the rank of the proposed partner was more distinguished. The marquis, however, had apparently happily agreed to Désirée's proposal, not in the least put out by the idea of so disadvantageous an alliance for his son.

Rose's hopes were dashed by the next letter from Paris. In it the Marquis de Beauharnais asked for the hand of Catherine, the second La Pagerie daughter, aged twelve. Alexandre, he wrote, felt that Rose at fourteen and a half was too close to his own age. Catherine, however, had died of tuberculosis just one week before the arrival of this letter; Joseph de La Pagerie hastened to inform the Beauharnais ménage of the fact, adding that he himself, with Manette, the youngest daughter, aged eleven, would set sail as soon as the winter storms were over.

But Rose-Claire de La Pagerie and her mother had decided that if either of the girls was to be married into the equally scandalous Beauharnais family, it should not be little Manette. The two women wrote that the fear of leaving home had induced a fever in the girl. There was no dissuading Rose, however, holding fast to her vision, and Joseph made a plea for her. For malleable, sweet-tempered Rose, it appeared, had shed her usual indolence and protested violently and with tears at the vanishing of her dream. "The oldest girl," Joseph wrote, "who has often asked me to take her to France, will I fear be somewhat affected by the preference which I appear to give to her younger sister. She has a very fine skin, beautiful eyes, beautiful arms and a surprising gift for music. She longs to see Paris and has a very sweet disposition. If it were left to me I would bring the two daughters instead of one, but how can one part a mother from both her remaining daughters when death has just deprived her of a third?"[7]

This letter crossed one from the marquis. He, too, was now in a hurry. His health was not good, he wrote, and his son's guardians (presumably the late Mme de Beauharnais' family) would certainly, if he should die, look for a bride elsewhere than in Mme Renaudin's family, it was implied. And Désirée, increasingly impatient, wrote: "We leave you to be guided by Providence which knows better than we do what is good for us . . . but we *must* have one of your children. Come with one of your daughters or with both of them, but hurry."[8] A letter from the marquis quickly followed, enclosing an authorization for the banns to be posted in Martinique. Alexandre's name was filled in, and only the space for the bride's first name was left blank.

And so, by a series of accidents and against all odds, it was Rose after all who was destined for France.

War on the Atlantic had broken out again between Britain and France, the ally of England's former American colony, and Joseph de La Pagerie now objected that it was too dangerous to cross the ocean. Even in peacetime the Atlantic journey was considered so perilous that wills were commonly signed before embarking. But Mme Renaudin, whose fear of the Beauharnais family's intrigues was stronger than that of enemy ships, urged instant departure.

At last, in the hurricane season of September 1779, Joseph obtained passage on the vessel *Ile de France* for himself, Rose and the freed slave Euphémie. They set sail in a convoy escorted by the frigate *La Pomone*, a ship destined to play a role in Rose's later life. Their three months' journey was a nightmare of unending storms and fears of capture by the British fleet. And there was a further danger: only one year earlier, Rose's own cousin Aimée de Buc de Rivery, returning to Martinique from school in France, had been captured by pirates on the same high seas.

M. de La Pagerie took to his bed upon their arrival in the port of Brest. His letter announcing their arrival was the first news that Mme Renaudin had of their departure from Martinique, and she set off immediately from Paris with Alexandre. They found the travelers still shaken by their terrible journey, with Joseph de La Pagerie's state of health so alarming that they delayed their return to Paris for several days.

From Brest, Alexandre de Beauharnais wrote his father a careful letter, dwelling at length on the practical steps taken: a "cabriolet in good condition" hired to accommodate M. de La Pagerie, in no state to travel by public coach, warm clothes for Rose and for Euphémie, shivering in their light colonial dresses, and an account of the money spent. At the very end of the letter he recorded a cool appraisal of his fiancée: "Mademoiselle de La Pagerie may perhaps appear to you less pretty than you had expected, but I think I may assure you that her amiability and the sweetness of her nature will surpass even what you have been told."

2

THE VILEST OF CREATURES

THE LONG JOURNEY FROM BRITTANY TO PARIS WAS UNDERTAKEN IN stages—there was even some doubt as to whether M. de La Pagerie would ever reach their destination—and the party had plenty of leisure to reflect upon the future.

To come into all of his mother's estate while still a minor and to please Mme Renaudin, of whom he was genuinely fond, Alexandre de Beauharnais had been willing to marry this dowerless girl without even a great name as compensation. But he had extracted from his father the promise that he "should not be expected to marry *cette demoiselle* if she and I should feel any mutual aversion."[1]

There was no question of aversion on Rose's side. As she stared entranced at the dashing officer, overwhelmed by his looks and elegance, his white uniform with silver facings and his powdered blond hair, she could not guess at the extent of his vexation.

Whereas Alexandre was considered unusually handsome, he would only note his fiancée's ungainly figure, her nose unfashionably turned up at the end and a face devoid of animation. Neither the caressing expression of her long-lidded eyes nor her later celebrated charm was yet in evidence. Fatuous and conceited, both socially and intellectually snobbish Alexandre could hardly hide his dismay at the appearance of the gentle girl in her provincial clothes. Consumed by a desire to shine in distinguished company, Alexandre saw immediately that it would be impossible to introduce this plump sixteen-year-old into the society he was so eager to impress.

Because he had shared a tutor with the nephews of the Duc de La

Rochefoucauld, he had spent much of his adolescence in the household of this premier liberal grandee of France. A friend of Benjamin Franklin and the translator of the text of the Constitution of the thirteen American States, La Rochefoucauld was the prototype of the disinterested, idealistic men who were to play so decisive a role in the first stages of the Revolution. His house was a center for the liberal young aristocrats educated on the principles of the Enlightenment, an attitude of mind based on the *Encylopédie*, an anthology of "enlightened" opinion on politics and philosophy first published almost thirty years earlier. The *philosophes* who compiled it believed in a more egalitarian and democratic order of society, and Alexandre de Beauharnais had absorbed some of the style, if not the substance, of this circle. He had appropriated the "new ideas" of the Enlightenment without, however, sharing his patron's wish to give up any of the prerogatives of the aristocracy. Certainly he made no move to put into practice, in his inherited estates in Santo Domingo, any of the libertarian principles of the Society of Friends of the Blacks, founded by La Rochefoucauld and dedicated to the abolition of the slave trade.

Just as his father had conferred his title upon himself, Alexandre had exchanged the courtesy title of Chevalier for Vicomte, and at eighteen, in his many successful love affairs, he would always emphasize the rank of his conquests. His friend Louis-Amour de Bouillé, who saw him with the clear eyes of a contemporary, noted that Alexandre's liaisons "flattered his vanity and took up all his time. He even wrote and classified lists of the titles, as well as of the other attributes, of the ladies."[2]

During the months when the La Pagerie marriage was being negotiated and Alexandre himself was with his regiment in Brittany, he kept Mme Renaudin informed of the progress of his conquests, even enclosing a letter from his current mistress so that Désirée "might judge of the choice I have made".[3] The letter also contained references to the lady's expected child, fathered by Alexandre. Her name was Comtesse Laure de la Touche de Longpré, and her influence on Rose's life would be considerable.

Upon their arrival in Paris, Aunt Désirée at once set out to buy the bride's wedding trousseau, to settle the terms of the marriage contract and the bill for the cost of the journey from Brest; this last was to be apportioned by her, Alexandre and M. de La Pagerie, whose share, she informed him, amounted to 1,264 livres, 13 sous.

Joseph de La Pagerie undertook to give his daughter 120,000 livres for her dowry, less the cost of the trousseau; the remaining 100,000 was to be paid "at his discretion." (The meaning of this euphemism, by a man who had been hard-pressed to find funds for three transatlantic passages, was perfectly understood by all.) Meanwhile, Rose was to receive a five percent interest on this sum.

The marriage ceremony in December was small, the company undistinguished. None of the bridegroom's mother's family were present; the bride's father was still too ill to attend. The young couple moved immediately into the house they were to share with Aunt Désirée and the marquis. Very soon Alexandre rejoined his regiment and left the family household for ever-lengthening periods. These absences, which Mme Renaudin described as garrison duties, did not at first concern Rose.

For a while the new Vicomtesse de Beauharnais lived in a daze of happiness, perfectly content with her handsome husband, her wedding trousseau and the three pieces of jewelry he had given her, a bracelet, a pair of earrings and a watch. By her own account never subject to nostalgia, Rose seems not to have missed the color, the noise and the affection of the untidy plantation life. Not even the lack of sun or air, nor of the flowers that were her lifelong passion, seems to have disturbed her.

For Paris was as seductive as she had always known it would be. Even its squalid aspects failed to daunt her. The Beauharnais family house, in the still medieval eastern section of the city, was on a street so narrow that the sun never penetrated the tall houses. Down the center of rue Thévenot ran a stream of foul-smelling mud and sewage. Parisians were known to miss its stench; foreigners came close to fainting when first exposed to it. Blood from the butchers' stalls ran into that central stream, too. In this ancient section of the capital, filth and luxury still existed side by side; there were no totally rich nor totally poor quarters.

Neither was Rose dismayed by the contrast between the casual living in the Trois Ilets sugar refinery and the dark, cold rooms in the Beauharnais house. Even visitors from northern European countries complained of the lack of heat in the drafty Paris mansions. An icy staircase usually preceded an antechamber used as a dining room (such specialized rooms for meals rarely existed), and it, in turn, opened into a salon from which the bedrooms led one into another, as they had in French houses for centuries. These bedrooms were so cold that both men and women commonly kept on their nightcaps until the fires had been lit in the morning.

There was the unaccustomed diversion of the noise and bustle of the Paris streets, starting at dawn with the rattling of carts driving in from the country, carrying produce to the central Halles; with the street cries of the women dispensing coffee to passersby and the whistling of the hairdressers flying from house to house with their curling irons and hair powder. Much later, buildings shook at the passage of heavy, dusty stagecoaches crowded with passengers from the provinces, followed by the carriages of nobles and financiers, their shades lowered, the sedate cabriolets of physicians and lawyers; and the speeding fiacres, or hired cabs. Young men of fashion were perched so high on the huge wheels of their furiously driven whiskies that their heads were level with first-floor windows. All this traffic would sometimes have to make way for a herd of cattle being led to market or even for the sudden eruption of hounds and horses hunting a stag into the heart of the city. The warning cries of the coachmen overtaking at speed, the cracking of their whips and the thunder of wheels over cobblestones were deafening. Pedestrians, in constant fear of being run down, glued themselves to the walls of houses or scuttled into doorways. Their plight worsened in a rainstorm as horses splattered them from the central stream of filth. This activity reached a peak at two in the afternoon, dinnertime for prerevolutionary Europe, and ended only as workers—artisans, stonecutters, carpenters—walked home to the eastern suburbs and the last cafés closed after midnight.

It soon became clear that the street life of Paris would be one of Rose's few distractions, apart from shopping expeditions with Mme Renaudin. (Her aunt would recall that as they drove around the city Rose would play with the jewelry Alexandre had given her and which she carried in her pocket.) Because of their equivocal position Aunt Désirée and the marquis could offer her little social life and Alexandre seemed never to be at home.

Confidently, Rose awaited the invitation from Versailles which required an armor-plated court dress and six-yard train, but when she suggested her presentation at court she was sharply rebuked. The jumped-up "Vicomte" had no right, by the rigorous rules of Versailles, to be granted this honor. Court genealogists even noted that in an earlier generation, too, the Beauharnais family had been fined for "usurping titles not legally theirs."[4] In spite of the egalitarian principles Alexandre proclaimed, "the blow to his pride was so bitter," noted a friend,[5] that it was believed to have inspired much of the particular venom with which he treated Louis XVI and Marie Antoinette during his brief moment of revolutionary power. That Rose's own claims to the honor were a good deal better than her husband's could only aggravate the humiliation; the La Pageries were of more authentic petty nobility, and she had her father's former post at court to prove it.

Alexandre's rare visits home were not successful. He was exasperated when he discovered the extent of Rose's lack of education, although to be "as ignorant as a Creole" was a current expression in Paris. "We all knew great ladies of that origin who scarcely knew how to read," noted Comte de Montgaillard, "much less to write. It was a standing joke; however, few people were surprised, so prevalent was the anomaly."[6]

Alexandre, however, *was* surprised. In letters written to Rose from the country houses of his friends, he recommended the study of Roman history and the learning by heart of contemporary plays. But she appeared unable to concentrate on any subject, and Alexandre complained to Mme Renaudin that it was useless to attempt to educate Rose, whom he described as "an *objet* who has nothing to say to me." How, he asked, could his "tender heart love a woman incapable of filling those long intervals between the effusions of affection?"[7]

But Rose valued these "effusions." She was in love with her husband and frankly enjoyed the physical relationship. When it became clear to her that his "garrison duties" consisted of parties, balls and picnics at friends' houses in the country she exploded in scenes of jealousy, while Alexandre was outraged that his wife should parade an unfashionable—and worse, bourgeois—expectation of conjugal fidelity.

Beauharnais, however, was not in tune with his own era. Although it was only twenty-five years since Lord Chesterfield had informed his son that "in Paris, gallantry is the occupation of every well-bred woman," the promiscuity and heartless love affairs of the preceding age were out of style now in Alexandre's world, replaced by tenderness and *émotions vraies*.

Jean-Jacques Rousseau, idol of this generation, was preaching a new morality based not on abstract reason but on sentiment. Through his political and social writings he was responsible for a revolution in literature, taste, manners, morals and attitudes in relationships. The young had started to react against some of the skeptical teachings of the Enlightenment and adopted Rousseau's cult of sensibility, defined as "the direct expression of powerful feeling." Little personal choice was involved in upper-class arranged marriages, and these men and women felt free to dispose of their hearts. Often involved in a passionate, long-lasting affair conducted with extreme decorum, women of sensibility regarded it as shameful to be unfaithful to the lover they had chosen.

Alexandre's closest circle was made up of the future "constitutionalists," young men determined to honor Rousseau's precept "to be useful to humanity" and already envisaging an ideal state established on the principles of reason, justice and anticlericalism. In the early days of the Revolution they would work toward a constitutional monarchy for France.

Though personal ambition was the incentive for some, with few exceptions they shared a belief in equal rights and social progress. In the early 1780s this group included the economist Pierre Samuel Dupont de Nemours; the orator Mirabeau ("no one knows the power of my ugliness"); Abbé Sieyès, later celebrated as the "mole of the Revolution"; Louis de Narbonne, minister of war during one phase of the Revolution, and the clubfooted Abbé Charles-Maurice de Talleyrand, as celebrated for his wit and his dissolute life as any of his secular friends.

And the "Americans" were part of this circle—the young French volunteers of the American War of Independence, returned from the New World where they believed they had found Rousseau's vision of the ideal republic; they had, they declared, brought back with them "the seeds of human rights." The Marquis de Lafayette was their leader; at thirty the Duc de Castries, who had fought at Yorktown, was one of the oldest members of a group that included Rochambeau, the hero of Saratoga; de Grasse; d'Estaing and the Swedish Count Axel Fersen, another veteran of the American war and reputed to be Marie Antoinette's lover.

They held an idyllic America as their model; Gilbert de Lafayette's own garden was composed of "democratic vegetation," planted with

American seeds and cuttings. The twin centers of the Franco-American relationship were his house and the official residence of the American Minister Thomas Jefferson, who cultivated corn grown from seed from Virginia at his residence off the rural Champs-Elysées.

But it was the women, Rose was to learn, who set the tone of the intellectual and political life of the capital. In this deeply feminized society their authority had been rooted for over a century in the tradition of the salons. Never in French history, however, had their power been greater than it was then as arbiters of ethics and politics and in molding public opinion. The influence of conversation in the years before the Revolution was said to equal that of the increasing flood of pamphlets and brochures. The subjects of politics and "sensibility" occupied these gatherings, in an atmosphere of exhilaration and optimism for the future. There were few social barriers for this feminine elite. The future constitutionalists met as regularly in the drawing rooms of cultivated actresses and courtesans as they did at the houses they considered their headquarters: the Swedish embassy or the Palais Royal. It was to these two salons that Alexandre de Beauharnais is said to have taken his wife. Both hostesses, representing widely differing views, would play roles in the lives of Napoleon and Josephine.

Félicité de Genlis's "Tuesdays" were held in the Palais Royal, the magnificent residence of her lover the Duc d'Orléans, first prince of the blood, cousin of the King. This was no conventional prerevolutionary salon devoted to Rousseau's principles of working "for the development of a social conscience and for the cultivation of sensibility"; its cynical tone appeared to be drawn rather from the contemporary novel *Les Liaisons dangereuses* whose author, Choderlos de Laclos, was Orléans's closest friend. And here the air of opposition to the court was already essentially revolutionary. Money was covertly being spent on disturbances planned to weaken the throne, as the Palais Royal circle worked toward a constitutional monarchy with Orléans at its head.

It was the center of the "Anglomaniacs," too. Although Rousseau could be held directly accountable for the English fashion of extended visits to the country, for English "natural" gardens and for the reading of Samuel Richardson's novels, it was Orléans who had introduced horse racing, the wearing in town of boots and riding coats (ancestor of the redingote) and, complained Horace Walpole, of "betting and whist, the two most boring things in England."[8]

Félicité de Genlis herself was ambitious, cool, prim and pretty, her exaggerated prudery a contrast to the notoriety of her love affair with Orléans. Only a touch of pedantry and her lack of humor—Beauharnais' own weaknesses—were said to impair the subtlety of her conversation.

Rose's second visit was to the true headquarters of the Americans and of the future constitutionalists—the salon of Germaine de Staël at the Swedish embassy. It was the center of political life, the meeting place of all shades of liberal opinion and the very antithesis of the Palais Royal. Its hostess, the daughter of Jacques Necker, the Swiss financial expert, hope of the reformers and idol of the court, was the polar opposite of Félicité de Genlis.

At the age of seventeen Germaine had refused to consider marriage to the young William Pitt, Britain's twenty-four-year-old Prime Minister, unable to contemplate the idea of leaving Paris, particularly to live in a country where, she understood, women retired after dinner while men argued politics. "True pleasure for me," she wrote later, "can be found only in love, in Paris or in power."[*10]

So necessary was Necker's financial acumen believed to be in the country's desperate economic situation that the King himself had joined in the search for a consort for the Protestant Germaine. After seven years of negotiation Eric-Magnus de Staël, attached to the Swedish embassy in Paris, was raised to be his country's ambassador and ennobled by his king; and in order that Necker's daughter should not be exiled from Paris, the marriage contract stipulated that the King of Sweden should never recall his ambassador.

Eric de Staël was happy to have his gambling debts settled by the splendid Necker dowry, while Germaine soon defined her relationship with her husband: "Of all the men I could never love," she said, "he is the one I like the best." The day after her marriage the twenty-year-old wife

---

* No doubt Rose de Beauharnais, too, would have endorsed Germaine's Swiss mother's own pronouncement: "One should, and clearly can be happier elsewhere; however, this is impossible once the magic of Paris has been felt. Without necessarily providing happiness, it poisons forever all other forms of living."[9]

of the ambassador announced that "politics and love"[11] were her twin passions, and in pursuit of both her Thursday salon became central to Paris life.

Although graceless by the standards of her day, stocky and large-featured, "with a lion's muzzle," but with splendid eyes and bosom, she would all of her life be the center of shattering emotional entanglements. Félicité de Genlis might find her ungainly, without malice of dissimulation and "altogether a most embarrassing person," but the most discriminating men admitted that the enchantment of her conversation was as seductive as any physical charms.*

In an age when conversation was an art, when spontaneity, gaiety and humor were prized, Germaine de Staël bewitched her audience by her brilliance, enthusiasm and intellectual vigor. But although, as she would later express it to the Duke of Wellington, "talking politics is my whole life," conversation at the Swedish embassy ranged over literature, history, philosophy, the theater and social gossip.

Talleyrand, Lafayette and Louis de Narbonne, the brilliant heartbreaker and Germaine's first lover, visited her daily in search of news, political direction and advice. Thomas Jefferson, Thomas Paine, author of the *Rights of Man*, the poet-politician André Chénier, men and women of letters and distinguished foreigners, flocked to her Thursdays. There were few women present: the wittiest of those was eighteen-year-old Aimée de Coigny, whose beauty and liberal views would so irritate Napoleon.

That year President George Washington sent a new American envoy, Gouverneur Morris, a large, handsome man with a wooden leg, to check on the official reports of his representatives in England and France. Morris collected much of the material he sent to President Washington from Mme de Staël's Thursdays and, astonished by the role of women in prerevolutionary Paris, marveled in his journal at "their Authority almost unlimited."[12] Morris visited most of these salons, noting the shades of political distinction in each, ranging from houses devoted to the principle of an absolute monarchy like Aglaë de Simiane's (whose transfer of af-

---

* "Ugly" was an adjective never employed by Germaine de Staël. She could not bear to hear it. "She would never describe a woman as pretty or ugly, only as either deprived of or endowed with exterior advantages" (Comtesse de Boigne, *Memoires*).

fections from Lafayette to Philippe of Orléans was said to have been the initial reason for the former's departure for the New World), to the drawing room of Julie Talma, an actress and former courtesan who entertained a more radical group. Guests here like Jacques-Louis David, the painter and future fanatical revolutionary, and half a dozen others would argue so passionately through the night that those who lived at any distance remained to sleep on chairs in her small house, one that would later know such celebrity as the Bonapartes' home. Even here, however, "thinking people," wrote Mme de la Tour du Pin long afterwards, "talked only of abolishing abuses. The word 'Revolution' was never uttered. Had anyone used it, they would have been thought mad."[13] Those salons, Morris noted, offered opportunities unrivaled in Paris for making contacts; he would find them still more useful during the Revolution. Though he visited them all, Morris himself, a little in love with Adèle de Flahaut, was especially faithful to her own "day," centered around Charles-Maurice de Talleyrand. Adèle was, she said, *mariée de coeur* to the thirty-four-year-old abbé; their liaison was to last for ten years and their son was destined to play a role in the Bonapartes' life.

These were the women, Rose learned, who claimed the admiration of her husband, and she was as impressed by their command over opinion as by their rapid, allusive talk.

Her brief view of their ascendancy may well have played some part in her lifelong desire to be associated with those who controlled events; still more in her lasting appetite for the consideration she believed was acquired by having, and by being seen to have, influence over powerful men.

There would be no more of these social rounds, however. "When we are out together," wrote an outraged Alexandre to Mme Renaudin, "she expects me to pay attention only to her. She has become jealous and wants to know what I am doing, what I am writing. . . ."[14] And on his rare visits Rose continued to irritate him with tearful reproaches, while he retaliated with sanctimonious sermons largely on the subject of his own "virtue."*

---

* A key word throughout the Revolution, this favorite term of Rousseau's indicated in the 1780s only some personal sacrifice to the common good.

One of these visits produced their son, Eugène, who was born in September 1781. Shortly after his birth Mme Renaudin persuaded Alexandre to embark upon a Grand Tour of Italy; perhaps she hoped that separation from lovers and social life would help the marriage of her intemperate godson. From there Alexandre's letters to his family alternated between pompous lectures and monumental self-pity. They dwelt largely on the good fortune of those he had left behind who would undoubtedly be enjoying a brilliant social scene in the capital, surely an unlikely circumstance for any of the three. He lamented that his own pleasures would be "of another nature, and achieved with grief. . . . The admiration of paintings and statues will prove an occupation which will console me for an absence which costs me, I swear, more than is believed."[15] The whole man is in the style and content of these letters. We can only speculate upon Alexandre's sentiments had he learned that the Vicomte de Beauharnais' name would be known to history solely because of his graceless wife. Through Rose, future Empress of the French and Queen of Italy, Alexandre would become the ancestor of the royal families of Belgium, Denmark, Norway, Sweden, Luxembourg, Italy, Portugal and Brazil, and the grandfather of Napoleon III, Emperor of the French.

When Alexandre returned to Paris on July 25, 1782, he found his family had moved into a house leased in his name and situated in the newest and most fashionable part of Paris. The street ran parallel to the faubourg St. Honoré, only recently carved out of market gardens and swamps west of today's Place de la Concorde. The aristocracy was moving from the Marais section to the Left Bank of the Seine, while the world of finance occupied the Place Vendôme and built splendid houses of pale limestone along the faubourg St. Honoré, set in the verdure of immense gardens extending down to the Champs-Elysées. When the crenellated walls of the city were pulled down in the 1780s, vast new building possibilities opened up along what had been no more than rides cut through the woods. Whole sections became huge construction sites. Paris broke out of its stone corset and the sound of building continued all night as masons worked for double pay. Mansions were built in two months, the Opéra in seventy-five days, "as though Paris was in haste to enjoy the last hours of calm before the approaching storm."[16]

Alexandre de Beauharnais declared himself delighted with the new house and ready to settle down. Had not Rousseau spoken highly of patriarchal family life, of tranquil joys and domestic happiness? Alexandre, however, had now been promoted to major, thanks to the Duc de La Rochefoucauld's access to court favors, and soon it occurred to him that he had never seen active service. Fellow officers in the Sarre Regiment had been sent to fight overseas, but he had declined to join them—and he feared that this might prove an obstacle to commanding a regiment in the future.

On September 6, Alexandre set out secretly during the night for the port of Brest (Rose had begged him not to leave her again). He had decided, he wrote her from there, to volunteer for service against the British, expected to attack Martinique. The couple exchanged letters as Beauharnais' ship prepared to sail. When Rose told him of her new pregnancy he wrote that he was delighted, decided they were to have another son and chose the name of Scipion. Soon he was raging that his wife had let several couriers leave for Brest without a letter.

"Shall I never taste that precious felicity, the preserve of honorable and delicate beings, which a good man enjoys?" Other officers, he claimed, received more regular letters from their wives, but "only I, who deserve more than they the tenderness of my other half—only I am forsaken." And one letter ends: "I write as a man certain of being loved, of being desired, by many."[17]

Rose wrote almost daily, however, while Alexandre's ship *La Vénus* waited off Brest, first for favorable winds and then for a convoy to assemble. Still, a torrent of his letters arrived in Paris pouring out self-pity, criticism of Rose, affection (he wrote he would have liked to kiss her "plump little cheeks") and bitter denunciation in quick succession. In his last letter before sailing he announced to Mme Renaudin that Laure de Longpré, his former mistress, was sailing to Martinique on the same vessel. Recently widowed, she was traveling to the Windward Islands to claim her late father's inheritance. Airily, he asked the ladies to visit Laure's small children in Paris (one of whom was his own son); also he would like them to send him (and this, he said, was Mme de Longpré's suggestion) a set of the game of lotto to while away the time on board.

At last *La Vénus* set sail. Upon his arrival in Martinique, Alexandre first visited Les Trois Ilets (he wrote that he was disappointed in the run-down condition of the plantation and shocked to note that Joseph de La Pagerie appeared to have been engaged in some manual labor), and then went on to stay with Rose's uncle Baron Tascher in Fort Royal. And in one malicious note he mentioned that during the long voyage he had played lotto with Laure, and although he was "often bored by the game, I was amply rewarded by the pleasure I derived from the company."*[18]

He had not expected a spirited reaction from Rose. Jealous and depressed, and seven months pregnant, she could hardly have been cheered by this letter. She stopped communicating with him directly, but made a point of writing to her family, so it was from them that he learned of the birth on April 10 of their daughter, Hortense. And it was from a letter read aloud to him that he was informed of Rose's angry response. "You do not speak of me," he wrote to her, "except to say that you have cured yourself of the lively feelings I once aroused in you."[19]

When Laure de Longpré heard of the birth, she announced before a large gathering at Fort Royal that Hortense could not be Alexandre's since the child had been born twelve days short of nine months after Beauharnais's return from Italy. Next, with a willing Alexandre, she traveled to the Trois Ilets plantation and attempted to suborn the slaves there, promising to pay them for any information on sexual misconduct by the young Rose. When one of them, Brigitte, swore that her mistress had never been anywhere unaccompanied, Alexandre threatened her life should she tell anyone of their conversation; only the slave Maximin, offered more money than he had ever seen, made what he would later admit to Mme de La Pagerie was a "false confession."[20]

On July 8, Alexandre wrote Rose a violent letter beginning: "Madame, had I written you in my first fit of rage, my pen would have burned the paper. . . . You are in my eyes the vilest of creatures." He had learned, he wrote, that Rose's behavior as a girl had been scandalous, and that she had been found in a lover's arms on the day of her departure "although she was destined for another.

"And what should I think of this last child, born eight months and a few days after my return from Italy? I swear by heaven above that it belongs to another. . . . Have the goodness to take yourself to a convent as soon as you receive this letter."[21] All Rose's friends and acquaintances

---

* This Laure, a character straight out of *Les Liaisons dangereuses*, would nevertheless be the recipient in 1807 of an annuity on the Empress Josephine's purse. "This lady is now very infirm" was written on the request in the Empress's own hand.

were indignant, her mother wrote, except for one Mme du Turon, in whose house Alexandre was now staying in Fort Royal. M. du Turon, she added, certain of his wife's seduction by the vicomte, had locked her up and written a furious letter to Alexandre on the abuse made of his host's hospitality.

With characteristic effrontery Alexandre called on the La Pageries before leaving the West Indies—he had arrived too late to see any military action—and was astonished to be bitterly upbraided by Rose's father: "So this is the only result of the glorious campaign you were to wage against the enemy! All you have done is to make war on the reputation of your wife and bring dishonor on us all."[22]

Secure in his own virtue, oblivious to the poor showing of his military career and alone (Laure had already left for France with a more prestigious lover, carrying with her Alexandre's outrageous letter to his wife), Beauharnais subjected his family to a spate of pompous letters, serenely confident in his own "virtuous conduct."[23]

His self-pity was monumental. He informed Rose that he would be in Paris by October "if my health does not succumb to the fatigue of the journey, added to my terrible state of mind." His grief, he wrote, had forced him to take to his bed in Port Royal—no mention of Mme du Turon. The letter ends: "And believe me, Madame, of the two of us, you are not the more to be pitied."[24]

In Paris, Alexandre's letter was read with disbelief by Aunt Désirée and the marquis, well aware that Rose had been incapable of unfaithfulness if only because she saw virtually no one but their own restricted circle of elderly friends. Mme Renaudin saw the ruin of all her plans. Alexandre had now come into his inheritance; the house they lived in and its contents were his property. They protested in writing. Alexandre was inflexible. Upon landing in France and hearing that Rose was still living in the family house, he wrote angrily from a property belonging to Laure de Longpré's family that he had heard "with astonishment that you are not yet in a convent," and asked her to send him his carriage, which he would need to distract him and to "make up for the extreme weakness of my legs."[25]

Mme de La Pagerie wrote to implore her daughter to return to the plantation; Rose, of course, ignored her family's appeals. She would never again willingly leave Paris; Napoleon's directives to her to do so at the time of his second marriage would be for her among the bitterest consequences of the divorce. On November 27, 1784, she retired to a "convent" and started legal proceedings for a suit for judicial separation. Guided by Aunt Désirée, who had taken similar action against her own husband, Rose drew up a spirited defense, outlining the details of the plot against her in Martinique and listing the dates of the ten months Alexandre had spent with her in the four years of their marriage. Unexpectedly resolute, she insisted that it was "not possible for the petitioner to suffer so many affronts. To do so would be lacking in what she owes herself and her children."[26]

Her answers to the questions put to her in an interview with an official of the King's Counsel imply a change already in Rose's personality. In a letter to his wife that night, the King's counselor *Maître* Joron's secretary wrote that Mme de Beauharnais was "a lady of distinction and elegance, with a perfect manner, endowed with a multitude of graces and with the loveliest of speaking voices"[27]; yet Rose at this time had been at the convent for only a few weeks, and her full emergence from the chrysalis had yet to come.

Alexandre tried several petty methods of revenge. First he had Eugène kidnapped in February 1785—Rose appealed successfully to the Provost of Paris to compel her husband to return the child—then he asked her to return his furniture from the Paris house and all the jewelry he had given her upon her marriage. Rose objected: "Monsieur de Beauharnais must know better than anyone that he sold all the furniture upon his return from Martinique."[28] As for the jewelry, she was, she said, astonished to read the jeweler's account of all the items furnished Alexandre for his marriage. Only three of these had ever come into her possession.

Rose's main concern by now was to regain her liberty and, aroused by a sense of outrage, she was determined to fight. She threatened her husband with a public lawsuit, and by March 1785 the suit was settled out of court. Alexandre, unable to produce any proof whatsoever, made a total retraction of all his accusations, apologized for his letter from Martinique, granted Rose an annual allowance of five thousand livres and recognized the legitimacy of Hortense. Eugène was to stay with his mother until the age of five and thereafter spend his summers with her. Hortense was to remain entirely with Rose. Alexandre even visited his daughter at her wet nurse's house in the country—he seems to have been genuinely fond of both his children—and brought her some toys.

. . .

The winter of 1784 was the true start of Rose's life in France. The "convent" of Penthémont was more accurately an elegant retreat with separate apartments and communal parlors. Aristocratic ladies in situations similar to Rose de Beauharnais' would spend a few months there. It was also a girls' school, and on Sundays Thomas Jefferson would take the ferry across the Seine to visit his daughters boarding there.

At the age of twenty-one Rose proceeded to invent herself. The girl so harshly reprimanded by her husband for lack of application now found the discipline to learn and to retain those lessons that held her attention—the achievement, in this instance, of the manner and appearance of the sophisticated women she met at Penthémont, the ladies admired by Alexandre. Observing their behavior, studying their accents and mannerisms, their intonation and current jargon—even their opinions—she overcame her native nonchalance and was soon expressing herself with elegance, both in conversation and in the apparently spontaneous little notes that were to become her hallmark. And at Penthémont she mastered the essence of her inimitable manner, the art of supreme naturalness, of the appearance of ease in any situation. She perfected a style of her own, of notably graceful movements and gestures and a seductive walk to match her native languorous manner. With a will that would be of iron, she effected a physical transformation too, schooling herself out of her somewhat shapeless body into a new and slender one. The "plump little cheeks" mentioned by Alexandre also disappeared. He had never admired his wife's strong points: the delicate nose turned up at the end, and the slightly slanted, half-closed eyes* fringed with immensely long lashes.

Her arresting voice, with its slight Creole accent filleted of *r*'s, would always be her greatest asset, low and silvery "like a caress," Napoleon would say of it, and that he could not rest until she had read him to sleep with "that melodious voice."[29] His valet Constant would remember that servants passing by the Empress's door at the Tuileries Palace would stop to listen in admiration.

The change in fashions in the mid-eighties could have been expressly

---

* Their color is a mystery; usually described as deep blue, in portraits they most often appear to be dark brown. One passport would describe them as black, another as "orange-colored."

invented for Rose, never suited by the eighteenth-century upper-class uniform of stiff brocade dresses, high heels and elaborate hair styles. The pervasive influence of Rousseau's pastoral dream was reflected in the flimsy white clothes being worn now even in winter. Country living, rural elegance were the fashion, given impetus by Marie Antoinette's rustic village at Trianon and by her portrait hung in the Academy that year. The older generation was scandalized by the white muslin dress in which the Queen was painted by Mme Vigée-Lebrun, instead of in orthodox court clothes. Powdered hair was going out of fashion for both sexes: Rousseau had declared that the poor were deprived of bread because hair powder was made of wheat flour, and the young agreed that long unpowdered curls looked more natural under straw hats, worn with simple dresses tied with a wide sash.

These pale muslins were already known in Paris as *l'habillement américain,* and differed little from what Rose had known in Martinique, where white calico ruffles were worn to protect the ladies' ankles from the dust. It was the Creoles who had, even before Rousseau, brought to France the fashion for muslin and percale dresses, together with their celebrated wastefulness and lack of conventional education.

Although the disappearance of lace and satin might appear to be an economy measure, these deceptively simple muslins were an expensive luxury. It was commonly believed that they could retain their dazzling whiteness only when washed in the West Indies. Versailles and Paris, therefore, "sent their linen to be washed in Santo Domingo, just as they had their shirts made in Curaçao or their porcelain repaired in China."[30]

But questions of economy were never to be of cardinal interest to Rose. Indeed, from the days at Penthémont until her death, she was seldom out of debt. Her intensely personal, invariably becoming style of dress would always be one of her major preoccupations, and an essential element in Parisians' pride in their Empress.

The "little American," as Rose was known—a term used indifferently for anyone either from the Antilles or the American continent—was in no hurry to leave Penthémont and the friends she had made there. However, by September 1785 she decided to join Hortense, Mme Renaudin and the marquis in Fontainebleau; they had moved there for reasons of economy when Alexandre emptied the Paris house of all its contents.

Eugène, now seven, had been returned to his father, as stipulated in the separation contract.

Although in the streets and salons of Paris in 1785, in the influential Masonic lodges and the cafés, the talk was all of constitutional reforms, of the country's financial problems and the hope that M. Necker could solve them, life in Fontainebleau still revolved around the men and women connected with the court. They lived there all year and in the autumn were responsible for organizing the palace functions, and the deer and boar hunts for the regular royal entourage coming from Versailles.

When Alexandre paid a visit to the marquis in Fontainebleau that year, he was not even granted the privilege of following the hunt at a distance. "He was inexpressibly vexed by this," noted his father, "and out of resentment he left immediately."[31] Rose, however, was permitted to take part in the trial hunts before the sovereign's arrival. "The Vicomtesse," wrote the marquis to Mme Renaudin, on a business trip to Paris, "went boar hunting yesterday. She was soaked to the skin but perfectly happy and had a bite to eat after changing her clothes."[32] Afterwards she would watch from a distance for a sight of the King returning to the courtyard of the palace of which she herself would later be mistress; there was no question of Rose, who had not been presented at court, being invited to any of the receptions or balls there. Soon there would be no more of these. By the autumn of 1786, as an economy measure, the King had come without his consort for two or three days only, and for the last time before the Revolution.

The marquis himself was in financial straits. The government had reduced his retirement pay by two-thirds in one of its efforts toward economy, and he received little from his properties in Martinique, which Joseph de La Pagerie managed for him with his usual inefficiency.

During this period Rose found a new role, that of an adroit petitioner. Her letters were successful in obtaining loans from her notary and a rebate on her taxes, although her gentle ones to her father reminding him of her "pressing need" of his promised allowance and for the interest on her dowry were without result.

Rose's financial worries, however, seem not to have weighed on her; the situation had been too familiar since her youth. Neither could Alexandre be counted on for regular payments of her allowance. His family saw little of him that year. As rumors that the King would call the Estates-General became current in 1788, Beauharnais' political ambitions took firmer shape, his activity became obsessive. His time was taken up, too, with new and expensive liaisons.

Rose herself had the reputation of engaging in a number of her own. Her humiliating rejection by her husband appears to have left her with an unending need to be proved desirable. Sensuous, flirtatious and clearly the victim of injustice, she attracted somewhat older men, married and with influence at court. Admittedly, many of the stories of her promiscuity were spread during the Bourbon Restoration that followed the fall of Napoleon's Empire; but then, Napoleon himself would allude with some complacency to his wife's love affair at Fontainebleau with the Duc de Lorge. The Chevalier de Coigny, a fashionable forty-year-old, was mentioned as one of her admirers, too, and there would be gossip at the time of the Consulate when, although believed to be part of a plot against Bonaparte, he was favored with special clemency. Perhaps a liaison with one of these men may have been responsible for what could only be described as Rose's flight from France to Martinique in June 1788.

Aunt Désirée had fallen seriously ill. Eugène was about to arrive at Fontainebleau for the summer. No news, bad or otherwise, had come from Les Trois Ilets.

Yet with an unmistakable air of panic, without word of any vessel bound for the Antilles, almost without baggage, clothes or money, Rose borrowed a thousand livres from Mme Renaudin, sold her harp and, with five-year-old Hortense, left suddenly for Le Havre from which, there being no immediate prospect of a safer vessel, they set sail for Martinique on a merchant ship.

Rose was known to dread another Atlantic crossing. What could have impelled her sudden flight? Although at both the consular and imperial courts her lack of discretion would be legendary, and "with her native Creole immorality"[33] she would recount in detail her nights with the Emperor and other intimate subjects, she was never at any time heard to mention the voyage or its reason. Could she have found that a refuge in those islands was the most secure way in which to terminate an inconvenient pregnancy, one that might also account for her later disastrous sterility? The explanation most often suggested is that she hoped to obtain from her father some of the interest on her dowry. In her *Mémoires,* Hortense, ever defensive of her mother's reputation, would give her own account of the journey to Martinique and its cause, the ill health of the La Pagerie family. (Her mother's position in France at the time of their departure she would touchingly describe as "brilliant."[34])

At Les Trois Ilets, Rose found her mother courageously attempting to keep the plantation going and nursing her youngest daughter, slowly dying of scurvy. Though always affectionate and helpful to her ailing, debt-ridden family, Rose appears to have spent more time at Fort Royal than at Les Trois Ilets. The capital was the naval base for the French fleet of the Antilles, and her presence is mentioned at balls and suppers there, where she danced and flirted with the officers of the warships at anchor. From the house of her uncle Baron Tascher, commander of the port, Rose wrote to Aunt Désirée requesting the dispatch of five pairs of English garters, a dozen fans and a muslin ball gown. Several lovers were ascribed to her; it was considered certain that at least Count Scipion du Roure, a young naval officer, was one of the number.

An illuminating account of Rose's reputation at the time emerged a century later in a naval commander's journal intended for his family only. Writing after the end of Napoleon's Empire, the evidently royalist officer recalled that in 1789 he had met Mme de Beauharnais, "who has since played so great a role during our recent illegitimate splendors. The lady, without being exactly pretty, nevertheless was attractive because of her style, her gaiety and her good heart. . . . She defied public opinion rather openly. . . . As her funds were extremely limited and she loved to spend, she was often forced to draw upon her adorers' purses."[35]

Rose's inability to pay for two passages to France was perhaps the reason for her two year stay on the island. Her departure, however, was precipitated by the beginnings, one year after the fall of the Bastille, of the revolt of the blacks in the French Antilles against colonial oppression and caste discrimination. For months the governor had refused to wear the tricolor cockade obligatory in Paris. (All the white planters were ardent royalists; Rose's own mother would refuse to visit Paris while her son-in-law was Emperor of the French.) By the summer of 1790, the blacks were forming committees and assemblies on the Parisian model, and demanding partial or total equality with the white *Martiniquais.* There were serious revolts when news reached the island that the Society of

Friends of the Blacks founded by La Rochefoucauld had demanded in the Constituent Assembly in Paris the total abolition of slavery.

In June 1790 some of the French troops garrisoned at Fort Royal mutinied and joined forces with slaves, freedmen and underprivileged whites.

That summer Rose, nevertheless, took Hortense to the capital where, as in revolutionary Paris, social life continued unchanged. On the eve of September 3, 1790, Mme de Beauharnais was warned that the mutineers and allied blacks in possession of the surrounding forts were expected to open fire on the city of the following day. Her uncle advised her to leave immediately, and without baggage or money, she fled to the port with Hortense, embarking on the frigate *La Sensible* on which du Roure was serving. A cannonball, Hortense was to relate, landed a few feet from them as they ran across the open fields of the Savane, at the spot where the life-size marble statue of Empress Josephine now stands in the public square.

That night the insurgents in the forts started to fire on the fleet anchored in the bay, and *La Sensible*, with the other ships of the line, escaped only by minutes beyond firing range. After remaining three days under sail and receiving no word from Fort Royal they proceeded to France. Fifty-two days later Rose and Hortense, borrowing their fare from Scipion du Roure, were traveling by coach from the port of Toulon to Paris.

⚜ 3 ⚜

I Am an Amériquaine

OUTWARDLY, THE PARIS OF 1790 WAS NOT GREATLY CHANGED. THE CITY still retained some echoes of the almost universal optimism and belief in the future which had followed the fall of the Bastille on July 14 of the previous year. In the months following Rose's abrupt departure for Martinique, an unparalleled fever had gripped Paris at the news that in response to overwhelming economic pressure, a meeting of the Estates-General was to be called for the summer of 1789 in Versailles.

Without exception, all Beauharnais's circle ran for election as deputies to that meeting, and in May those future constitutionalists, including Lafayette, the Abbé (now Bishop) Talleyrand and Alexandre himself had been elected. They arrived at Versailles confident of introducing political and fiscal reforms, of abolishing the existing system of privileges and inequalities, and determined to press for a limited monarchy with a written constitution.

By June 1789, when the Estates-General had become the National, or Constituent, Assembly and was drafting a written constitution, the hopes of Alexandre's group appeared to be ready for peaceful fulfillment. To these men the unexpected violence of July 14 was little more than an unfortunate event.

Maddened by rumors that the King intended to dissolve the Assembly and to exile Jacques Necker,* an armed mob, 100,000 strong from the eastern districts of Paris, had marched on the Bastille fortress and murdered its governor. Although the dungeon gave up only six "victims of

---

* The man who symbolized the hope of a new order for the French people.

33

tyranny"—five criminals and one madman—it represented royal authority, and the event was an enormous moral victory. At Versailles the deputies threw their hats in the air, and throughout Europe delirious joy greeted the news. In England, the poet William Wordsworth felt that Rousseau's dream of the opening of a new golden age was about to be realized ("Bliss was it in that dawn to be alive . . ." he wrote), and Coleridge declared that the fall of the Bastille made him "feel the heartbeats of humanity." Lafayette handed Thomas Paine the key to the fortress and asked him to place the sacred object in George Washington's own hands.

Jefferson's belief that the French people were not yet prepared for a democratic revolution on the American model appeared to be confirmed when the fall of the Bastille was followed by months of rioting, of human heads and hearts carried through the capital at the end of pikes. And when in November of that year a mob stormed the Palace of Versailles, massacred the guards and brought the royal family back to Paris and to virtual imprisonment in the Tuileries Palace, there was some faltering in optimism and a beginning of emigration, but it was still generally felt that the Revolution of 1789 was over; few dreamed that it had barely begun.

When Rose de Beauharnais returned in October 1790, armed patrols at night and the presence everywhere of the new Paris militia, Lafayette's National Guard, were the only visible effects on the city of the events of the summer of 1789. Coffeehouses remained centers of agitation and discussion, and a man's political allegiance was known by his choice of café: Méot's was the headquarters of advanced liberals, the Café de la Régence was devoted to the more moderate Lafayette. In each of them journals were read aloud, arguments continued from one table to the next, and the noise reached a climax under the arcades of the Palais Royal, which housed the largest number of popular eating houses.

The true life of revolutionary Paris, however, revolved around the nerve center of the National Assembly, charged with the drafting of a written constitution for France and the focus of the passionate interest of the entire country. Its elected president in the month of Rose's return was Alexandre de Beauharnais, and in the Paris of 1790 her husband was a celebrity. Alexandre's opportunities for oratory were now unlimited. From the rostrum he spoke at length on a number of subjects: religion and the status of Jews; the press; the army; the navy and many, many more. His speeches on filial virtue were particularly admired.

When the Assembly moved to Paris, it was housed in the royal riding school of the Tuileries Palace, hastily remodeled to accommodate it, with green felt-covered benches and plaster casts of illustrious Romans.* Mme de Beauharnais used her celebrated name to obtain seats in its gallery—they were harder to come by than places at the Opéra—and Parisians fought, maneuvered and paid up to fifty livres a day to get one. Germaine de Staël, sitting in the first row, sent the speakers notes of congratulation and invitations to the embassy, while Félicité de Genlis, hedging her bets—opinion was starting to turn against Philippe d'Orléans—was invariably accompanied by her seventeen-year-old charge, Orléans's son, the future King Louis-Philippe.

Political debates raged in the literary societies, smoking clubs and Masonic lodges. The salons were more influential than ever and Rose became a largely unnoticed visitor in many of them. At the Swedish embassy Germaine de Staël's drawing room was still the center of all shades of moderate opinion, and her voice was known to be a determining one in the making of government appointments. Deputies dropped by on their way to the Assembly to rehearse their speeches; each new brochure and pamphlet was examined and discussed with passion.

Rose met all the influential men of the hour there: moderates like the Marquis de Lafayette, whose popularity as commander of the National Guard was still immense; pockmarked Mirabeau, the greatest orator of the Assembly; Abbé Sieyès, author of the most celebrated pamphlet of the Estates-General, and Alexandre's patron, La Rochefoucauld; Charles-Maurice de Talleyrand, immediately recognizable by his limp and the insolence of his expression, was an especially assiduous visitor. Determined to be elected deputy to the States-General he had, the previous year, neglected his official mistress Adèle de Flahaut, to initiate a successful courtship of Mme de Staël. His victorious electoral campaign confirmed his confidence in the political power of women; throughout his life he would believe that "no man could equal a woman in serving the interests of a friend or lover."[1] Adèle had avenged herself by falling into the arms of the American Gouverneur Morris, and Morris, too, was one

---

* The riding school stood on the present site of the rue de Rivoli and the rue de Castiglione.

of those who came daily to the Swedish embassy for the latest news to send back to Washington. But the most cherished man present was the patrician Comte Louis de Narbonne, handsome, brilliant and arrogant, and Germaine's lover, for whom she cherished vast ambitions.

Among those of more "advanced" opinions, Rose became especially friendly with the German Prince Frederick of Salm-Kyrbourg and his sister, enthusiastic admirers of the constitutionalists, and she soon became a regular guest at their house,* where political views were well to the left of Mme de Staël's.

Caught up in all this political and social effervescence, Rose appears to have held no strong political allegiance. "You know," she wrote to Aunt Désirée, "I am too indolent to take sides." Later she would lean toward royalist views and always feel uneasy in her imperial position, but now she inclined toward whatever was the current modish direction. "Her attention," as one of her ladies-in-waiting would remark, "wandered from any discussion of abstract subjects."[2] Certainly she had no interest in the abstractions of political theory. Until the end of her life, to be close to power would be one of Rose's principal aspirations and now she craved to be considered both desirable and influential in Alexandre's world. Increasingly, she found the means and the will to push herself without appearing to do so, to employ her appeal and her celebrated name to make an impression in the more radical groups toward which Alexandre himself was moving. Although described at this time as being "as insignificant a little creature as it was possible to meet."[4] Rose knew how to listen, to exert her own potent brand of charm, and as Talleyrand would acknowledge later, she was intelligent enough to know when to keep silent.

The name of the Citoyenne Beauharnais was the only passport needed for entry into any political gathering, for one of Rose's first discoveries upon arriving in France had been that she had lost her title. It was Thomas Jefferson who had proposed in the heady summer of the fall of the Bastille that the liberal French nobles find some startling way to detach themselves from the aristocracy. Alexandre de Beauharnais had been among the most enthusiastic participants of the celebrated Fourth of

---

* Of the Salm Palace, Thomas Jefferson wrote that he had "fallen in love in Paris,"[3] not with a woman but with a house, and that he watched its construction daily from across the river in the Tuileries Gardens. It is now the Maison de la Légion d'Honneur.

August 1789, the night when the "Americans," followed by dozens of other deputies, had renounced all aristocratic privileges and feudal rights. Amid tears and embraces these were abolished without compensation. A royalist journalist likened the deputies to the Japanese, "who make it a point of honor to cut their own throats in each others' presence."[5]

There were compensations, however, in the title of Citoyenne, or Citizeness, with its fashionable Roman echoes, as well as in all the other new styles. Fortunately, Rose and Hortense had embarked on the *Sensible* without baggage; the pleasure of buying the latest austere fashions had also been an immediate necessity. The Citoyenne Beauharnais wore dresses in "poor" materials, striped patriotically in red, white and blue (red and blue were the colors of the City of Paris, white stood for the royal Bourbons), and linen bonnets *à la Constitution;* these, announced one of the new fashion journals, "give a pretty woman an air of expansive sensibility." Jewelry was made of iron or steel, unless stones from the demolished Bastille were available. (Mme de Genlis's own piece of that fortress was made into a medallion on which *Liberté* was inscribed in diamonds.)

"The Revolution appeared to come to a halt this year," noted Baron de Frénilly.[6] Indeed, in popular opinion it was over. So far it had left little mark on social events. "The spring of 1791 was superb and hot, masses of people showed themselves off in the Champs-Elysées and in the Tuileries Gardens"—Frénilly again recorded—and that "the year promised well," with country parties, balls, the opera and riding in the Bois de Boulogne. Rose's own social life continued to improve. She was seen in the salons, in the Assembly's gallery and at the Academy, where Alexandre's portrait was hung in this year's exhibition. Felicité de Genlis's portrait, painted with her ward Mlle d'Orléans and with her own illegitimate daughter by Orléans, was also exhibited there. The three models, wearing red caps of liberty, visited the exhibition, one long remembered as the year of Jacques-Louis David's *Oath of the Horatii,* a landmark in neoclassical painting. Admiration for ancient Sparta, Rome and Greece, born of the archaeological finds at Herculaneum, was acquiring political connotations. Republican Rome—its heroism, austerity and patriotism—was held as a model, and the subject of the picture, Roman civic virtue, was considered a first essay in republican propaganda.

The Citoyenne Beauharnais was spending recklessly and living on credit, sharing a house in the rue St. Dominique with her friend Désirée Hosten. Besides her children, her own household was composed of Euphémie, who had accompanied her to France, of Hortense's governess Marie Lannoy, a valet and Fortuné, the black-faced pug. Constantly barking, attacking without discrimination, this unpleasant beast was adored by his mistress, though "I never knew a more horrible animal," was Laure d'Abrantès's verdict, and Napoleon would complain that Fortuné bit him in the leg the first time they shared Rose's bed.

Rose was now confronted with some disagreeable realities. Although her relations with Alexandre were cool but friendly—they discussed their children's welfare when they met at the political salons—this did not prevent him from threatening to take her to court for the return of jewelry and furniture she had never owned, nor did it ensure the regular payment of her allowance. Both her father and her sister Manette had died in the course of the year, and the British blockade of the islands prevented Mme de La Pagerie from sending funds from Martinique. Rose's debts grew as the cost of living increased dramatically. There were lines at the bakers' shops as millers withheld grain, already distrusting the assignat, the revolutionary paper money issued now for the first time.

Rose and her children were spending the summer in Fontainebleau on the day Alexandre's name first became known throughout France: the day the Republic became a certainty. His entry into history came on June 21, 1791, when, as president of the Assembly again (a post renewed every two weeks), it was his responsibility to announce first the flight, and then the capture of the King and his family, who had fled the Tuileries Palace in which they had been closely guarded for eighteen months. The news burst on Paris like a thunderbolt.

While Beauharnais, all patriotic energy, dispatched a company to recover the unwieldy coach in which the royal family had been slowly heading for the frontier, he poured out a succession of speeches and decreed that the Assembly should sit in uninterrupted session until the fugitives were arrested. For twenty-six hours Alexandre de Beauharnais represented authority in France.

On June 25, when the huge dusty coach returned to Paris from Varennes bearing the exhausted King and Queen, their two children and a crowd of "patriots" who had ridden in with them, it was Alexandre, president once more of the all-powerful Assembly, whose own doubtful nobility had been insufficient to afford him a place at Versailles, who led the imperious questioning of the fugitives and then gave orders for their imprisonment.

At Fontainebleau, Eugène was pointed out as "the little Dauphin."[7] Alexandre wrote from the Assembly a "Roman" letter full of filial virtue and of vanity to the marquis: "In my present situation, I would reproach myself if the critical circumstances which rendered my presidency more perilous, more painful and more honorable than any previous one, prevented me from offering you the expression of my feelings. I am exhausted, but I find strength in my courage."[8]

After the watershed date of Varennes, there was a dramatic shift in power. As the Revolution moved left, so did Alexandre de Beauharnais. Lafayette and most of the original constitutionalists moved clear across the floor of the National Assembly, from the left of the rostrum to the right, and were daily insulted as "moderates" by the mob in the galleries. The new "left" (a term employed for the first time to denote shades of political opinion) was occupied by the Girondins, deputies mainly from the country around Bordeaux. Alexandre, however, joined the extreme radical faction, the "Mountain," so called because it sat on the benches high up against the wall to the left of the president. The leaders of the Mountain—Jean-Paul Marat, Georges Danton and the icy, intriguing lawyer Maximilien Robespierre—drew their support above all from the political Jacobin Club, a powerful pressure group directing an already efficient propaganda machine. And to his other distinctions, Beauharnais added that of being twice elected president of the Jacobin Club.

By September, however, Alexandre had ceased to be a deputy. With the King's approval of a new constitution, the "Constituent" Assembly declared its work accomplished. Although Gouverneur Morris (himself one of the signers of the American Constitution) informed President Washington that "it is the general and almost universal conviction that the Constitution is inexecutable,"[9] Paris nevertheless believed the Revolution was over, and celebrated with fireworks and illuminations and a tricolor hot air balloon sent sailing above the capital.

The enthusiastic, idealistic tone of the early Revolution was giving way to bitterness, as political and personal vendettas divided both the

Girondins and the Mountain. There was increasing violence in speech and in print, and the tone of political libels became daily more savage. Germaine de Staël was a favorite target of both royalist and radical pamphlets; the Swedish embassy was routinely pictured as the scene of orgies. But still, even on the extreme liberal side, the tone toward the royal family remained deferential. The term "revolution" was unheard of; Rousseau himself, the deputies reminded one another, believed that a republic was possible only in small countries such as the Swiss cantons or in states of classical antiquity. All tomorrow's terrorists—Robespierre, Danton and Saint-Just—were still monarchists. Constitutionalists like Talleyrand agreed with Jefferson that France was not ready for a democracy, and that instead of a parliamentary government the country might well end up with a dictatorship.

As part of the struggle for ascendancy in the Assembly, the Girondins declared war on Austria in April 1792, and a month later on Prussia: a war that was to last for twenty-two years and change the face of much of Europe. The King and Queen were suspected of negotiating with her brother the Austrian Emperor, and the French emigrés in Koblenz, their chief center, were pushing the less-than-eager Germanic princes to rescue the French royal family. In Paris only the King and the Jacobins were against the war; it was Robespierre the Jacobin who correctly foresaw the result of the struggle, though the dictator he visualized was the too-moderate Lafayette rather than Bonaparte. "Are you aware," he asked the Assembly, "that the most dangerous enemy of the liberty of peoples is military despotism? That the fate of revolutions is settled by those who control the armed forces? We are marching with giant strides toward military government."[10]

And finally, Germaine de Staël wanted war. Louis de Narbonne, she believed, was best qualified to lead the nation to victory. She laid siege to everyone of influence and, thanks to endless pressure, succeeded in having her lover named minister of war. Marie Antoinette wrote bitterly to Axel Fersen: "What glory for Mme de Staël, what joy for her to have the army at her disposal!"[11]

When war was declared and the new Assembly decreed that deputies of the Constituent Assembly were ineligible for reelection, Alexandre de Beauharnais proclaimed that he was now ready to "fly to the frontier."[12] Not totally prepared, however, for although he received orders in December 1791 to join the Army of the North as chief of staff with the rank of brigadier general, he remained in Paris until February of the following year. Like his father, Alexandre had acquired his military rank through influence, and he, too, was to fail his country through indecision.

From the northeast frontier, where the republican army under Marshal Rochambeau faced the combined Austrian and Prussian armies, Alexandre started a succession of interminable letters to the new Assembly. And throughout 1792 and into 1793 the speeches and motions of Beauharnais, who had been promoted to the rank of *maréchal de camp* (lieutenant general) and to the command of the Army of the Rhine, were regularly read from the rostrum.

In the beginning the war made little difference in Rose's life. All twenty theaters in Paris were crowded nightly. "We danced," wrote Frénilly, "as on the eve of battle."[13] Gouverneur Morris, now George Washington's representative in France, reported that the city, until August 10, was full of foreign visitors and so calm that he himself had rented an official residence and was completely refurnishing it. He found, however, that life in the political salons had changed. With the dismissal of Narbonne by the King as the minister of war and the appointment of Girondist ministers, Mme de Staël's drawing room was no longer a center of influence or of informed gossip. The court distrusted her, the Assembly laughed at her, and the Girondists, now the right wing of the republicans, ignored her.

They had their own muse, Mme Roland. Members of this radical group of the Assembly met in her austere apartment, where political conversation and sugar water were offered the young lawyers and writers of her party. Thirty-seven-year-old Manon Roland was a pretty, serious-minded woman from the provinces. It was known that she drafted most of the official reports of her elderly husband, the minister of the interior, though she dared not do so openly; the antifeminist position of the Jacobin leaders was too well known. (Manon herself was no more interested than was Mme de Staël in women's newly awakened aspirations of equality.) These occasions were no longer gatherings of members of an intellectual elite, battling for reforms of the political system with brochures and pamphlets. The atmosphere here was very different from that of the early revolutionary salons, whose reputedly superficial tone and lax morality were despised by Mme Roland. Her own upbringing, where chastity and the institution of marriage were unquestioned, prevented her from consummating her passionate, and reciprocated, sentiments for one of the Girondist leaders.

Rose's craving both for masculine admiration and for influence was undiminished. Though not a part of the innermost Girondist circle, she continued to build a network of friendships and alliances within the radical camp, principally by means of letters of introduction and recommendation addressed to the men of the new order. With the old epistolary formulas proscribed (Mme Roland signed her own letters "with antique sincerity") Rose closed hers with *"salut et fraternité"* and other stoic phrases. Following Alexandre's nomination to the Army of the Rhine, and as long as the Beauharnais name was still a password, she would end her letters "Lapagerie Beauharnais, wife of the *Maréchal de Camp*."

While retaining the manners of the old regime so recently mastered, Rose with her native adaptability quickly assimilated the jargon and ideology of the new society. "She was not at all averse to following the requirements of the times and those times required one to flaunt the language and the behavior of the common people," wrote one survivor of the Terror.[14] She was accused of unnecessary alacrity in the adoption of the familiar *tu* and *toi*, even before it became obligatory. This, it was explained in the Assembly was "a Roman fashion, worth more than all our French simperings." Rose had, in fact, adopted *sans culotte* language, a term that originally carried few political overtones, although one memorialist asserted that "long trousers are responsible for the Revolution."[15] In the 1780s, when some "advanced" liberals adopted the British fashion of long trousers instead of the customary *culottes*, or knee breeches, protests had been heard: "What impudence! They are *sans culottes!*" Later the label came to be applied only to militants of the extreme left.

By the end of 1792 all forms of politeness were identified as "superstitions which must go with the wind of liberty and equality. . . . A hat," it was decreed, "should be raised only when a patriot's head is too hot, and no longer upon meeting *Citoyens* and *Citoyennes*." Hand-kissing, too, was out. In bowing the head to kiss a woman's hand "a man loses that proud and masculine posture which should be that of all good patriots."

But in spite of her enthusiasm for every new fashion, ideological or other, it is not recorded that Rose ever wore one sign of political allegiance, the red bonnet, the old Greek symbol of the freed slave. Like Mme Roland, and like Maximilien Robespierre himself, who dressed with exaggerated neatness and elegance, she resisted the Jacobin pressure toward slovenliness. Marat, the radical Swiss terrorist, whose own clothing consisted of the almost obligatory red bonnet, long trousers, loose coat and clogs, once remarked with approval that he did not believe that in twenty years "it would be possible to find in Paris a single worker who will know how to make a hat or a pair of shoes." None, then, could have foreseen that within eight years all the luxury trades would be working harder than ever for the glittering Consular court of Rose's second husband.

The war became a reality for Rose in the summer of 1792. The course of the Revolution was changed after a series of French defeats on the northeast frontier. As the Austrian and Prussian armies marched steadily on Paris, and as volunteers assembled from all over the country in a torrid July, the Duke of Brunswick, in supreme command of the Austro-Prussian and emigré forces, issued a proclamation that exploded into the tense atmosphere. It threatened to destroy Paris and to "treat its citizens with unforgettable vengeance" if harm should come to the royal family and it appeared to confirm French fears of collusion between the French sovereigns and the enemy. It was a sentence of death for Louis XVI.

At a meeting of the Commune—the new revolutionary central government for Paris—the date for an August insurrection was set. Warnings appeared in the press to ferret out the "traitors in our midst." Marat, Danton, Roland, even Stanislas Fréron, a future deputy of the right, issued appeals to do away with all counter-revolutionaries. The signal for the uprising was the arrival of new army recruits, including the Marseilles battalions with a reputation for radicalism, who marched into the capital singing an electrifying new battle hymn henceforth known as the "Marseillaise."

Throughout the night of August 9 the tocsin, the alarm bells of the forty-eight sections or wards of Paris, rang until dawn, calling the city to arms. "No one expected to live more than another day,"[16] remembered Mme de Staël. In the early afternoon of the tenth a mob, reinforced by the newly arrived volunteers, marched in from the eastern part of the city and stormed the Tuileries Palace. The deputies in the neighboring Assembly sat frozen with fear while the Swiss Guards and some of the trapped inhabitants of the Tuileries were massacred and dismembered. The royal family escaped death by making the short dash to the Assembly hall, where the deputies promptly voted the end both of the King's sovereignty and of the experiment in constitutional monarchy.

By the end of August, Paris was a silent and sinister city, its gates closed, its streets deserted. On September 2 posters throughout the city proclaimed "the enemy is at the gates," and on the same day the September Massacres started.

The Commune had spread rumors of a conspiracy of prisoners plotting with the advancing enemy armies. The greater part of the assassins they hired, according to the Commune's registers, was paid twenty-four livres a head. Not all of them were Parisians; many were from the ranks of the radical provincial battalions. "Five hundred madmen," as one deputy remembered them, "most of them drunk, wearing red caps and with their sleeves rolled up, fraternizing in tavern after tavern."[17]

During the five days of the carnage, over twelve hundred defenseless men, women and children were hacked to pieces with sabre cuts, pike thrusts and blows from axes and shovels. Farmers, domestics, lawyers, wine merchants, priests, young children and thirty peasant girls recently brought in from their provincial village were murdered: very few victims of the September Massacres were members of the former nobility. But it was toward the former constitutionalists that the Jacobins directed their full fury. They saw them as their most dangerous political rivals, the only party to which moderates might later turn.

Alexandre's patron, the Duc de La Rochefoucauld, was hacked to pieces; his ninety-three-year-old mother arrested with him had his brains thrown in her face. His nephew, Alexandre's former schoolmate, imprisoned as a "suspect," was beaten to death. Some of the constitutionalists escaped to England. Talleyrand drove Narbonne to the coast, but himself returned to Paris, insisting upon a passport that would not brand him as an emigré. After he had waited for weeks, never removing his traveling clothes, Danton finally issued him one, which read, "Going to London by our orders," and he followed his friends across the Channel. Lafayette, who had tried unsuccessfully to make his troops march on Paris and expel the Jacobins, when informed of his own imminent arrest, attempted to reach the coast and a haven in America. He was intercepted and imprisoned by the Austrians as he crossed the lines.

All of liberal France, most of the intellectual elite of the eighteenth-century Enlightenment, were now exiled or dead.

No man would acknowledge taking any part either in the organization or the perpetration of the slaughter, which, Danton proclaimed, put a "river of blood" between the Revolution and its opponents. Those suspected of complicity in it, like Danton himself and Jean-Lambert Tallien, would be forever branded.

"The deepest grief must reign in your household," King Gustavus III of Sweden, no republican, instructed his ambassador in Paris.[18] But Baron de Staël continued to confer with the revolutionary leaders until, in spite of the famous clause in his marriage contract, he was recalled to Stockholm. Germaine remained in Paris and barely managed to escape with her life. Her former anti-establishment views had been succeeded by equally passionate indignation against the new tyrants. In love with Louis de Narbonne and carrying his child, she first hid her lover in the embassy after August 10 and then obtained a Swedish passport for him for his flight to England. On the day of the September Massacres, the deputy Tallien organized her own escape with some difficulty and, feigning not to see the friends she was sheltering at the embassy, sent her under escort to the frontier.

When the tocsin first rang in August, Rose had requested that Eugène, boarding at a school a few streets away, be permitted to join her and his sister. The three remained together throughout the September butchery, near enough to two of the prisons—the Abbaye de St. Germain and the Carmelite convent—to have heard the screams of the prisoners during those days and nights and to have seen the gutters running with blood and the scrubbing with vinegar of bloodstains on the walls and in the streets. They would have heard nothing of the last massacre of all on the morning of September 7—too distant on the Right Bank—at a prison harboring, besides beggars and common-law criminals, children and adolescents between eight and seventeen. "Those poor children," wrote one eyewitness, "were much more difficult to finish off. . . . At that age it is hard to let go of life."[19]

Even convinced radicals were now ready to leave France, and Rose's friend, the German Prince Frederick of Salm-Kyrbourg, was one of them. He and his sister Princess Amalia decided it was time to emigrate. Rose accepted their offer to take Eugène and Hortense out of Paris with them in preparation for an escape to England. When Hortense wrote sadly from Normandy how much she missed her mother, Rose assured her that she herself would go to England in the spring and bring back both her children. But when Beauharnais, at army headquarters, heard of the plan he sent a special courier to the Salms insisting that Hortense and Eugène be returned to Paris. Two days before the day set for their departure Prince Salm himself turned back to Paris with the children and thereby missed his own last chance of escape (he would be guillotined on the same day as Alexandre). Eugène was sent for, and placed in a school in Strasbourg by his father.

The new Assembly that took over at the end of September 1792 was called the National Convention, a name chosen for its American reverberations. The monarchy was abolished by the new Republic and all history placed in the past by the revolutionary calendar. The first day of the new era was set retroactively on September 21, 1791, "Year I of the Republic One and Indivisible." Months were renamed poetically after the works of nature; weeks were divided into a decimal system of days with the tenth day, Décadi, replacing Sunday.*

One of the Convention's first orders of business was the trial of Louis XVI. When the voting on the King's fate began, Alexandre de Beauharnais, from the northeastern front, hastened to send the Assembly his verdict of "death to the tyrant" rather than the alternative of "exile." The sentence was carried by one ballot. Beauharnais' vote, however, was never considered the determining one; it was popularly credited to the King's own cousin, the former Duc d'Orléans, now Philippe Egalité, who from then until his own death on the scaffold the following year was regarded with equal horror by all parties.

---

* The spring months were: Germinal (month of budding, from March 11 to April 10); summer: Messidor, Thermidor and Fructidor; autumn: Vendémiaire, Brumaire (month of mists) and Frimaire (month of frosts); and winter: Nivôse, Pluviôse and Ventôse (months of snow, rain and wind). This awkward calendar, separating France from the Western world and giving the working man only one day's rest in ten instead of in seven, remained in force until Napoleon abandoned it in the coronation year of 1804.

The winter saw the execution of the King. For this event, the new, merciful and above all speedy machine, the guillotine, was wheeled from its first location (it had been used only half a dozen times) to the more spacious Place de la Révolution. Stalls were set up to dispense food and drink to the spectators on the raised terrace of the Tuileries Gardens overlooking the square; throughout the Revolution, they provided diversion during the long waits for the tumbrils—the cattle carts in which the victims stood, heads shorn, hands bound behind them, as the carts slowly lurched over the cobblestones from the main prisons.

In a single week that winter, fourteen thousand persons fled Paris, bound for emigration. Rose was not one of them. Her life changed little in the perilous winter of 1792, undaunted by rioting in the streets, the many new restrictions and the food rationing, or by the changing face of the capital.

Churches were closing, religious orders abolished, convents and monasteries forcibly emptied of their occupants. In the early days of the Constituent Assembly, Charles-Maurice de Talleyrand, bishop of Autun, had been the first to propose that the country, faced by a continuing financial crisis, sell off the immense properties of the Church. (These were the first estates to be "nationalized," his own euphemism.) Next, he and the many other anticlerical deputies of the Assembly issued decrees that the clergy be required to swear an oath of allegiance to the state and their independence from the papacy; those who refused to take the civic oath, the nonjuring or refractory priests, were outlawed and in danger of a death sentence.

Saints' names had already been superseded in the revolutionary calendar by the names of "nourishing vegetables, agricultural implements and patriots of the past," such as William Tell and Confucius. Place names followed, and Rose's own street became rue Dominique. Although the Jacobins allowed Jesus himself to be "the first *sans culotte*"—undoubtedly crucified by the aristocrats of Judah—the Commune forbade any celebration of Christian religious festivals, and that year the opening ceremony of the Feast of the Goddess Reason took place in Notre Dame, the future scene of Rose's greatest hour of glory. In 1792 an actress played the principal role: wearing the scarlet cap of liberty, she was borne in on a carrying chair—past the statues of the kings of Judah (recently decapitated on the assumption that they were ancestors of the French sovereigns)—and enthroned before the former altar.

Rose's efforts continued to be directed toward the making of useful friendships. Endlessly adaptable and opportunistic and benefiting from the Beauharnais revolutionary credentials, she threaded her way through the complex network of the more radical revolutionaries, international financiers, secret agents of the Bourbon princes and the powerful lobby of the West Indian planters, circulating freely in all these systems of mutual dependencies and shifting loyalties.

Accepted by all parties, she delighted in writing to the new men, drafting petitions, asking for their protection for her friends in danger of arrest, and for other favors. Certainly she was moved by pity, and undoubtedly she enjoyed this power-brokering. Already these intercessions were involving her in some risk, but now the only casualty was her reputation. It was thought that the answers to her appeals did not go unrewarded. Unlike Mme Roland she probably felt no need to "resist the brutal needs of the senses." "She busied herself," wrote a contemporary, "with helping as many people as possible and although her reputation for conduct is questionable, that of her sweetness, her grace, and the gentleness of her manner is not."[20] And another, more forthrightly, recorded: "She was able to help a number of people through her friendship with some of the influential men of the day and the easy morals of Mme de Beauharnais, her love affairs and her native kindness made her popular without any danger to herself, at least for the present."[21]

Undoubtedly Rose traded on her name, so usefully both aristocratic and revolutionary, and on her charm. There were to be many ardent revolutionaries—Jean-Lambert Tallien would be the most celebrated—falling helplessly in love with charming *ci-devants* (the revolutionary term for former aristocrats) in whom, as in Rose, they found the piquant alliance of the exquisite politeness of the *ancien régime* and an enthusiastic adoption of the new manners.

Helen Maria Williams, an English poet and enthusiast for liberal causes, wrote that in revolutionary Paris she admired the fact that the "old-style gallantry in which women sought only to please, and men to flatter, had given way to a mutual esteem, a common interest in the great questions of the day."[22] Although these may have been Mme Roland's own sentiments, she herself, in her austere salon, was one of the principal impediments to that "common interest."

In order to end the murderous struggle for political control between the Girondists (now regarded as the right) and the radicals of the Mountain led by himself and Robespierre, Danton attempted a reconciliation with the moderates. It was Mme Roland herself who rejected his offers, jealous of his power in the Assembly, but primly disgusted too by his uncouth manners, his love of women, food and wine. She correctly suspected this passionate, venal man of accepting substantial bribes, and her open hatred of him was equaled by Robespierre's own, both of Danton and of her. The Jacobins, and Robespierre in particular, were resolved to eliminate women's influence, especially from public service; it was this party which had already persuaded the Convention to close down the revolutionary women's clubs. Manon Roland's authority over her husband did not escape Robespierre, an additional mark against the Girondists. In these personal and political stakes, Robespierre's scorn of Danton was matched only by Danton's own contempt for the prim provincial lawyer in his pastel-colored prerevolutionary clothes, immediately recognizable by his jerky walk, convulsive gestures and pale green eyeglasses.

It was the betrayal on the eastern front, rather than Mme Roland's intransigence, which brought down the Girondists.

In September 1792, after a series of French defeats, the Prussian army, the most splendid of all the professional armies in Europe, crossed the French frontier. General Dumouriez, a Girondist protégé, was given supreme command of the new republican army made up of conscripts, the volunteers of 1791 and the old royal army of the line—troops fired with patriotism and fighting for their homeland. Two thirds of the army's officers had emigrated and been replaced by some of the experienced non-commissioned officers of the old army.

On the first day of the new Republic, the French army under Dumouriez attacked the Prussians at Valmy. The outnumbered Prussian army broke and fled without a fight. It was the first time that a war waged for a principle had been heard of, and at the news of the battle Goethe wrote: "From this place, and from this time, dates a new period in world history." In retrospect, Valmy would be seen as the dawn of all the French victories, Waterloo the sunset.

After Valmy, the French armies took the offensive. Savoy, Nice and parts of the Netherlands and Belgium were annexed and made to pay steep indemnities—levies paid for their "liberation." The Convention announced the exporting of the Revolution, and the war of defense became a crusade to "carry liberty across Europe." France's natural frontiers were declared to be the Pyrenees, the Alps, the Rhine and the Mediterranean, and the nation that at the beginning of the war had renounced all conquests now proclaimed the necessity of "reunion" with some of its neighboring states.

In March 1793, what became known as "the heroic year of the Republic" began when the Girondist General Dumouriez crossed enemy lines. In protest against the Convention's proclamation of a crusade, he first attempted to persuade his army to march on Paris, then went over to the enemy with a handful of officers.

As French troops fell back before the Prussians on the Rhine, the Jacobins in the Convention hurled accusations of Girondist complicity with the traitorous general. "Paris now rests on an enormous volcano," wrote Gouverneur Morris to his president.[23] Military disasters multiplied. Britain entered the war after the execution of the French King. General Custine, an ex-*aristo*, capitulated in the east. With the enemy at every frontier, the country was a besieged fortress. By July, the Austrian and Prussian armies were deep inside French territory and the road to Paris lay open.

A state of national emergency was declared. The black standard was flown from the towers of Notre Dame; cannon on the Pont Neuf, alternating with that of the Arsenal, were fired every hour. The call to arms sounded in all forty-eight sections of the city. The Convention declared a mass levy, and throughout the country volunteers, in a fever of patriotism, registered at trestles set up under tents. Some 500,000 men, conscripts and volunteers, were now under arms, the first of the famous armies of the new Republic. The Convention decreed not only a mass call-up, but all human and material resources were declared subject to use by the government. Within two years, fourteen armies (about one and a half million men) were raised and equipped.

Currency speculation was driving down the assignat. A bad harvest and the requisitioning of food supplies for the armies produced a bread shortage; laundresses rioted, protesting the price of soap. The Convention introduced the Maximum to fix prices on grain and on household items, and to counter the first great inflation of modern times.

The same terrible summer of 1793 saw the start of the savage civil war in Vendée, where the peasants had remained faithful to King and Church. Lyons and Toulon rose against Paris and the Convention.

In April cannon and tocsin signaled the arrest of the Girondists held responsible for the Republic's military disasters. A few of their leaders went into hiding or escaped by ship to Bordeaux. Manon Roland, though her husband and daughter fled to the country, remained defiantly in Paris and was arrested. The greater number of Girondist deputies was immediately guillotined. At least one of them retained some echoes of the early romantic days of the Revolution. Fabre d'Eglantine, the poet-politician and author of the names of the republican calendar, wrote a characteristic farewell from prison: "We were so joyful, so filled with liberty and insouciance. . . . Adieu, adieu, I am full of courage, but also of sensibility."[24]

In June of the same year Mainz, on the northeast frontier, was lost through the ineptitude of Alexandre de Beauharnais, commander in chief of the Army of the Rhine.

In the Paris of the Commune, Beauharnais' effusions throughout 1792 and 1793 had been received with diminishing interest and finally with suspicion. By the summer of 1793 he was still forwarding to the Assembly his proclamations to the troops, along with petitions revealing his patriotism and personal virtues. They reached a capital reeling from the coup d'état against the Girondists, a Paris maddened by fear of invasion and of treachery in the army, and at a time when the entire northeast front was exposed by General Dumouriez' desertion across Austrian lines.

One of the Convention's first emergency measures was to send out "representatives-on-mission," political commissars to the armies, powerful men, always deputies of the Mountain, with full military and civilian authority including that of relieving generals of their command. The arrival of these proconsuls, the "incarnation of power and of terror," was apt to give rise to some anxiety at other army headquarters. Beauharnais, however, welcomed their appearance; they, in turn, reported to the Convention that although they approved of Beauharnais' close ties to the local Jacobin Club, they were less enthusiastic about the public scandal caused by his "spending his days pursuing prostitutes, and his nights in giving balls for them."[25]

When Mainz and its French garrison, under siege by the allies for the past month, requested immediate reinforcements from the Army of the Rhine in June, General Beauharnais with sixty thousand men under his command remained almost stationary, although continuing to report that he was about to advance. And when Mainz fell in July, Alexandre ordered a retreat while, again like his father before Guadeloupe, denouncing "the cowards who had capitulated."[26] Then, as the allies marched toward France's frontier, he abandoned his army and from Strasbourg wrote the Convention that because of ill health he was handing over his command to a subordinate.

He seemed to have no conception of the seriousness of the charge of deserting his post in the face of the enemy and to be unaware of the extreme peril of his position. The Revolution, which demanded victories of all its generals, was pitiless in the case of *ci-devants*. General Custine, commander of the Army of the North and a former noble, had already been recalled that summer and guillotined for allowing his army to be defeated.

When Beauharnais from Strasbourg ordered a further retreat for the Army of the Rhine it was immediately countermanded by the representative-on-mission, who announced: "Whereas General Beauharnais by his own admission has neither the strength nor the moral energy necessary in a General of the Republican army; we order that his resignation be accepted and that he withdraw to a distance of twenty leagues from the frontier within six hours."[27]

One of the representatives added in the margin: "In my opinion, Beauharnais should be arrested."[28]

The "first" Reign of Terror began in 1793 with the dictatorship of the Mountain in a Convention divided by the death struggle between Danton, the idol of Paris and now as sick of blood as was the country itself, and Robespierre, the ideological spokesman of the Mountain. Moderates in the clubs and the Convention rallied around Danton, while Robespierre and his two acolytes, twenty-five-year-old Louis Antoine Saint-Just, the youngest deputy in the Convention, and the paralytic Georges Couthon, watched and waited.

The final step before the start of the Great Terror was the siphoning off of the powers of the Convention into two committees, the Committee of Public Safety and the Committee of Public Security, also known as the Great Committees, and together forming a collective dictatorship with almost independent executive powers. The first Revolutionary Tribunal was set up in which the accused were denied the right of counsel, with death the only sentence. Emigrés were officially declared non-persons, and those caught returning to France were punished by death. The average number of prisoners executed increased tenfold.

Finally it was Saint-Just, known for his severe manner and dark good looks as the Archangel of the Terror, who announced in September that "Terror is the order of the day and the government of France is revolutionary until peace."

In the months following the fall of Mainz, Rose, far more alarmed than Alexandre, had sent off appeals in his favor to members of the radical Commune. No matter how confident she was in her influential friendships, it required courage to defend her husband now; but all her life Rose would be incapable of vindictiveness or of bearing malice or indeed, it would be said, of sustaining any feeling for long. "She was afraid of all painful or prolonged impressions," Mme de Rémusat would note, "and strong feelings were almost foreign to her."[29]

With a generosity that would later be celebrated, Rose was already known to be willing to risk compromising herself in drafting petitions and sometimes even in writing letters of intercession for the lives of people she hardly knew. When one friend, the Marquise de Moulin, begged her to save her nineteen-year-old niece, imprisoned as the relative of an emigré, Rose made the rounds of the authorities and obtained her release.

At a time when all citizens, especially former *aristos*, concentrated on trying to remain unnoticed, neither Alexandre de Beauharnais nor Rose appeared to show the least fear of drawing dangerous attention to themselves. "We dared not even catch the eye of an acquaintance in the street,"

wrote one survivor of the Terror, "so frightened were we of giving ourselves away." Yet Alexandre, unable to believe that a star of the Constituent Assembly and a former commander in chief of the republican army
might be in any danger, harassed the Committee of Public Safety with
memoranda on his services to the Revolution. Rose, meanwhile, equally
confident in the protection of her friends, continued to importune the
men of the Great Committee for favors. Now she went into action for
Alexandre and "spent all day," remembered Hortense "soliciting the same
people as for Mme de Moulin's niece."[30]

It required nothing less than the Law of Suspects to drive Rose out
of Paris. Among the categories of "suspect persons" threatened with death
were "former nobles" and any members of their family "who have not
constantly demonstrated their loyalty to the Revolution," as well as those
making remarks "tending to debase republican institutions and their
elected members." An unsupported denunciation was sufficient; it was
enough to be the child or the spouse of an emigré, or even to have shouted
"To hell with all patriots!" as one boy did when he lost a game of cards
in a café. He was guillotined, as was the exasperated man who muttered,
"Merde à la nation!" in a crowded street.

By September, the new law had started to pack the forty revolutionary prisons, converted from hospitals, seminaries, palaces and barracks. By
October, seven thousand "suspects" were incarcerated, awaiting their brief
appearance before the Revolutionary Tribunal.

It seems unlikely that any of these circumstances, any more than the
lengthening bread lines or the sinister silence that now descended on
the city, would alone have been sufficient inducement for Rose to leave
the capital. However, the Law of Suspects also required a "certificate of
good citizenship based on residence" for every man, woman and child.
These were not easy to obtain in Paris; those who were unable to acquire
one went into hiding. To avoid the dangerous city, some of Rose's friends
camped out in the Bois de Boulogne throughout the winter, queueing* for
potatoes at the public distribution center there and cooking them in the
open on portable stoves.

When her friend Désirée Hosten offered to lend Rose a house at
Croissy, six miles from Paris, she moved there with Hortense, Euphémie

---

* A term now coined for the first time.

and Marie Lannoy; and when Eugène joined them—he had made his own way there from Strasbourg, where his father, in his hurry, had abandoned him—the entire household applied for the coveted certificates. The children were nominally apprenticed on *sans culotte* principles: Eugène to the local carpenter and Hortense to "a dressmaker," in reality to her governess Mlle Lannoy.

In a letter from England that year Talleyrand warned a friend: "Do not stay in Paris or in a château in the country; some quiet suburb is the safest place." Croissy in every respect seemed the ideal refuge. Its inhabitants conformed to revolutionary principles without going to extremes; there had been no "suspects" in the tightly knit community. Mme Hosten, herself a Creole from St. Lucia and an ardent supporter of the Revolution, had decided to leave Paris after some alarming scenes in the street. The West Indies continued to be associated with great wealth and hostile voices had shouted that she should take her "indigo and her sugar-loaves with her and go back where she belonged."

Through Désirée Hosten, Rose now made some useful new acquaintances: the influential radical Bertrand Barère, a former constitutionalist, was one; another was Pierre-François Réal, or "Réal *tête-de-cochon*," the current public prosecutor of the Revolutionary Tribunal. (His nickname was acquired when he urged all patriots to mark the anniversary of the King's execution by eating a pig's head; this appellation was hastily dropped when he became deputy minister of police under Napoleon.) And it was Mme Hosten who introduced Rose to the radical deputy Jean-Lambert Tallien.

Some women in the Assembly's galleries considered the tall blond representative good-looking; there were others who likened him to a ferret, with his pointed nose and retreating forehead, and also because of his reputed advice to the September butchers on how to kill quickly and then get rid of the blood. His role in the massacres was uncertain, though he had undoubtedly been part of the Commune meeting that had organized them. He was known to be vain and lacking in courage. The rapid alternations in his character were unnerving: he had visited Louis XVI in prison, lent him books and then voted for his death in especially violent terms. He had saved the lives of several *ci-devant* ladies, as well as Germaine de Staël's. At the rostrum of the Assembly he was as garrulous as Beauharnais. (Robespierre compared him to "a leaking tap of tepid water.") But the power in the Commune of this ex-printer's apprentice was undeniable.

It was at Croissy that Rose, from her windows, first saw the roof of the Château de Malmaison beyond a loop in the Seine; and here she formed friendships with several key figures in her future: with Mme Campan, formerly a reader* to Marie Antoinette and now in mourning for the recently executed Queen—and with the Vergennes family. Little Claire Vergennes, a few years older than Hortense, was destined to become the Empress Josephine's lady-in-waiting Mme de Rémusat, the source of so many lively and sometimes ill-natured eyewitness accounts of the imperial family. At the age of fourteen, she was already struck by Rose de Beauharnais' charm. "Her figure," she later recalled, "was perfect, her limbs were supple and delicate, all her movements easy and elegant . . . full of grace rather than beautiful and with an expression of indescribable sweetness."[31]

In 1794, the spring of the Terror, Rose and her children returned to Paris, bearing their certificates of good citizenship. A pall of horror seemed to hang about the city. Celebrated heads were falling, including Marie Antoinette's, Philippe Egalité's and Mme Roland's. "From the stupefied expression on people's faces, you would have thought," remembered one survivor, "that it was a city devastated by the plague."

The noisy Paris of the early days of the Revolution had long since vanished. Then, newspaper criers on every street corner shouted the headlines of a dozen journals, brochures and pamphlets, but in the coffeehouses now, men stood in line for the official *Moniteur* and the small number of other licensed sheets allowed to be published, and in silence read the back page listing the next day's executions.

Rose decided to ask, on behalf of Alexandre, for an audience with Guillaume Vadier, the president of the all-powerful Committee of Public Safety. The Great Committee worked in the Tuileries Palace; the outer doors to the apartments were guarded day and night by cannon and lighted matches and by Barère himself, the Great Committee's secretary and Rose's new friend; but when she applied to him for an audience with

* A person engaged to read aloud to the Queen.

Vadier, she was turned away. She then wrote Vadier a sycophantic letter of some adroitness.

"Lapagerie Beauharnais to Vadier, Representative of the People: Greetings, esteem, confidence, fraternity," it begins. "I put myself in your place; you must doubt the patriotism of all *ci-devants*, but Alexandre has always been an ardent friend of liberty and equality. . . . Were he not a republican he would have neither my esteem nor my friendship. . . . I am an *Amériquaine*. My household is a republican one; before the Revolution my children were indistinguishable from *sans culottes*. . . . Like you, I do not believe in patriotism without virtue, like you I am inexorable." The letter ends improbably, "I write you in all frankness as a *sans culotte* of the Mountain."[32]

Within weeks Alexandre was arrested and held for a few days in the prison of the former Luxembourg Palace. Vadier was the first to sign the order, followed by the deputy Jacques-Louis David, who had sketched the agony of some of the victims of the September Massacres and, ten years later, would be commissioned to paint the celebrated scene of Rose's coronation as Empress of the French.

Rose's own arrest may not have been directly due to her efforts on Beauharnais' behalf. There were spies and informers in Croissy too, and an anonymous denunciation from there warned the Committee of Public Safety that all Mme Hosten's group were enemies of the Republic. It ended: "Beware of the *ci-devant* Vicomtesse de Beauharnais who has secret dealings in government offices."[33]

On the evening of April 21, three members of the local revolutionary committee appeared at the house, bearing a phonetically misspelled order "to arrest the woman Beauharnais, wife of the *ci-devant* General, rue Dominique, and the woman Ostenn, same address." Their papers were to be examined and the above-named placed in prison "to be detained as a measure of public safety."

It must be some tribute to Rose's charm that the three men failed to arrest her that night. Instead, they drew up a report asserting that "after the most scrupulous examination of all the papers, we have found nothing against the interest of the Republic, on the contrary a multitude of patriotic letters which can only be to the credit of this Citoyenne."[34]

Sent back the following night for a further search, the men found in the attic a number of Alexandre's personal papers that he had sent for safekeeping. Rose was immediately arrested. "Our mother," wrote Hortense in her *Mémoires,* "did not wake us for she could not bear to see our tears."[35]

The first jails to which Rose was taken that night were too full to receive her. Finally she was admitted to Alexandre's own prison, Les Carmes.

❧ 4 ❧

THERMIDOR

OF ALL THE CROWDED PRISONS IN THE PARIS OF APRIL 1794, LES CARMES was held to be the most sinister, its recent history the most appalling. Only eighteen months earlier, 115 priests imprisoned there had been hacked and clubbed to death during the September Massacres. The cells were still splattered with their blood. The quiet garden where once the barefoot Carmelite monks had cultivated medicinal plants was overgrown. Vermin infested the once spotless cells. The damp was so great that prisoners had to wring the water from their clothes each morning.

Seven hundred souls were packed in there, a whole world in microcosm. The register of Les Carmes gives the occupations of all those imprisoned between 1792 and 1794; button-maker, librarian, domestic, old clothesman, apothecary, mason, musician, ex-member of the revolutionary committee, farmer, water carrier, coachman are some of the trades and professions. The youngest prisoner was a boy of thirteen. Ex-nobles were in a minority, and those few—Prince Salm was one of them—were usually remnants of the liberal aristocracy who had remained in France when others had fled to join Condé's army of emigrés in Koblenz, or to live in exile in England or Switzerland.

Rose found her husband pursuing a passionate love affair with a fellow prisoner, Delphine de Custine, known as the Queen of the Roses for her radiant complexion. She was the blond and heroic daughter-in-law of General Custine, recently beheaded "for betraying the Republic." Her own husband had been guillotined on the day of Alexandre's arrival at Les Carmes, in spite of Delphine's attempts to rescue him. Although she confessed that she had never felt more than "a tender friendship" for

Armand de Custine she was dressed in deepest mourning, a practice unheard of in revolutionary prisons. She made no secret of returning Alexandre's passion.

Rose's own loneliness was soon comforted by the arrival of Lazare Hoche. Although the twenty-six-year-old republican general had been married for only a month and was much in love with his young wife— "angel of my life" he called her in his regular letters from Les Carmes—he nevertheless succumbed to the erotic fever of revolutionary prison life, and to the Citoyenne Beauharnais.

A fellow prisoner, the Englishwoman Grace Elliott, wrote primly that "Hoche was often with the ladies at Les Carmes," and described him as "handsome, of military appearance, good-humored and gallant,"[1] the type of man most admired by Rose. His classical good looks were enhanced, it was said, by the scar of a sabre cut across his forehead. His vitality and his air of authority all gave her confidence; she must have been cheered too by Hoche's optimism and robust enjoyment of life. He had been given the privilege of sending out for his meals, and his notes to the neighboring baker survive: "My health is good. Always gay, joyful and innocent," he wrote in one. "Nothing is as agreeable as a good dinner when one is hungry. *Vive la République!*" And as an afterthought "Send me my wife's picture with my dinner."[2]

A popular hero of the Army of the Republic, commander in chief of the victorious Army of the Moselle and a victim of interarmy jealousy, Hoche was given another special privilege: a cell of his own, next to the dormitory occupied by Rose, Delphine de Custine and twelve other women.*

Les Carmes was as much the scene of a yearning to live the last hours of youth and life to the full as were the other revolutionary jails. Survivors wrote of the "amorous frenzy," of "the sound of kisses after dark," of "the crowning of love's tenderest wishes, thanks to darkness and to loose clothing" and of the "blessed distance between iron bars."[3] At Les Carmes no bars separated the sexes; the chief jailer simply locked the access to the

---

* A smaller cell, up a few steps from a larger one, may still be seen at the seminary of Les Carmes, as may the long dark corridor of the revolutionary prison. The garden where most of the priests were butchered is there too, and the high wall that surrounds it and trapped all but a few who attempted to escape their pursuers.

corridors and to the cells on each floor of the old monastery. (At only one prison had it become impossible for the two sexes to meet at all. They were separated in the former Luxembourg Palace the day after they were summoned to a meeting; elderly, respectable women were startled by the first words of an address by the prison administrator: "This prison is known as the first brothel in Paris," he roared, "and you are all a lot of whores!")

There was a further reason for promiscuity. If a woman declared that she "had had relations with someone in her prison within the last six weeks, and believed herself to be pregnant"[4] her name was temporarily removed from the list of the accused. At worst, this gave her a short reprieve; if she was found to be pregnant she was not returned to prison until the day after the child's birth. The majority of women, however, disdained this ruse. "I have only dirtied my mouth with this lie," wrote the Princesse de Monaco after one night's liberty, "in order to cut off my hair myself; it is the only remembrance I can leave my children. Now I am ready to die."*[5]

When Rose's short idyll was over—Hoche was taken away on May 17 to be judged by the Revolutionary Tribunal (and apparently inevitably to his death)—the remains of her courage deserted her.

She broke down before ten each morning, when the call went up around the prison: "The carts are here!" Two men would stand at the entrance, shouting the names of the men and women they were to remove to the Revolutionary Tribunal, the last step before the scaffold. Those selected had only a few moments for a last look, an embrace, a brief note—and they were gone forever. Then the dead silence that accompanied this scene was immediately replaced by a frenzied gaiety. The remaining prisoners were now safe until the following morning.

For a hundred days after Hoche's departure Rose, the least stoic of women, lived in a nightmare of fear, the only prisoner allowing herself to weep openly. Between bouts of tears she laid out the tarot cards and still found no comfort. In her native island, she told fellow prisoners, an old black soothsayer had predicted that her first husband would die a violent

---

* Intercepted by the People's Courts, this letter was thrown with thousands of others into files now at the National Archives. The hair was delivered to the princess's family by an unknown hand.

death and that she herself would be "even greater than a queen."[6] Now she only wanted to know whether she would survive the carnage.

Rose's fellow prisoners were startled by the openness of her fear. They generally assumed an appearance of good humor, even of high spirits. Some turned their days into theater and played grotesque execution charades. Only in the last letters they left behind—letters seldom delivered to their families and piled high now in France's National Archives—do the tear-stained lines reveal the depths of devotion and despair, of fear and courage, hidden behind so much heroic frivolity.

Yet the other prisoners found Rose touching and graceful, and united in comforting the one panic-stricken figure. "Her lack of courage made her companions in misfortune blush," remembered one of them. "She was excessively fearful, but she was so natural, so engaging; her appearance, her manner and above all her way of speaking had such a special charm."[7]

During their first weeks in prison the Beauharnais had been allowed brief visits by their children and Mlle Lannoy. The children remembered that they always carried Fortuné, the pug dog with them, and hid notes to their mother under his collar. Hortense's father instructed her to transmit his lengthy petitions to the Convention. He should be released without delay, wrote this ancestor of a score of monarchs, "in order to further affirm my hatred of all kings, so deeply engraved in my heart."[8]

Nothing could have been more ill judged than these reminders of his existence. Even the speed with which the accused were now processed through the Revolutionary Tribunal had not sufficiently emptied the overcrowded prisons. But "enemies of the Republic are to be annihilated, not just killed," proclaimed Robespierre's ally Couthon, and in July a new pretext was found in another invented "conspiracy of the prisons," permitting still larger numbers to be sent to the guillotine.

As the summer advanced and the pitiless sun of Thermidor—the republican "month of heat"—shone down, those prisoners sleeping in the corridors were almost overcome by the stench from the open pails used as latrines. The air there was foul enough to extinguish a candle.

On the morning of July 22, Alexandre de Beauharnais, accused of conspiracy with the enemy, went to the guillotine. He bade Delphine an agonized farewell, placed his ring on her finger and left a note for his wife assuring her of his "fraternal attachment."

"Beauharnais was a very pleasant man, but rather conceited," recorded Grace Elliott. "Mme de Beauharnais wept abundantly when her husband was guillotined, but," she added, "she was a Frenchwoman and her tears soon dried. He had not been very attentive to her. The other lady I never saw smile after his death."* Rose did weep for Alexandre, however, and when one of her cellmates asked her how she could mourn a man who had made her suffer so much, she murmured through her tears: "I was attached to my husband."⁹

Only five nights after Beauharnais' execution the prisoners at Les Carmes heard the ringing of the Paris tocsin, the rolling drums of the call to arms, the sound of crowds marching, of cries and proclamations, the preliminaries, they believed, to yet another prison massacre. On the night of July 27 the men barricaded their cell doors with flimsy chairs or broke them up for arms. By morning, crowds of friends and relatives outside signaled to the prisoners the events of the preceding day. The coup of Thermidor, the great watershed of the French Revolution, had ended the Reign of Terror.

A pall of horror hung over the capital during the summer of Rose's imprisonment. The Great Terror had lasted for forty-seven days, from June 10 to July 27, while "a vast and profound silence reigned over the stupefied country."¹⁰ In a season of unprecedented heat the sky was cloudless; vegetables roasted as they grew; even at night the temperature never fell below ninety degrees. These weeks were nightmares of secret activity for a handful of men who knew themselves marked for execution.

In the early part of that year three representatives-on-mission were recalled to Paris: Joseph Fouché from Lyons, a city that had risen in arms against the Convention; Paul Barras from Toulon, which had been preparing to surrender to the English; and Jean-Lambert Tallien from Bordeaux, where he had been sent to put down the incipient rebellion there.

"Father" Fouché, like Talleyrand and Sieyès a defrocked ecclesiastic, had been recalled in disgrace; his atrocities in the rebel city of Lyons were so extreme as to cause even the local Jacobins to complain to headquarters. He had ordered much of the city razed to the ground; the inhabitants, in

---

* Delphine went on to become the heroine of further spectacular romances, but then Grace Elliott's best-selling account of her own prison life is largely apocryphal.

batches of a hundred, were clubbed, bayoneted and shot, their bodies thrown into the Rhône. Much of the ex-Oratorian's fury was concentrated in his blasphemous declarations and on the destruction of Church property. Amoral and violently ambitious, Fouché was nevertheless a tender father, a faithful and devoted husband. All agreed upon his terrifying aspect: only the red rims of his half-closed eyelids relieved the identical color of skin, hair and eyes. This politician of genius who was to serve and betray in turn each regime throughout the Revolution, the Directory, the Consulate, the Empire and even the Restoration, worked always in the dark. Now he was driven to break cover on this one occasion only, by the utmost desperation.

Citizen General Paul Barras, born an aristocrat, was an ex–army officer, embittered against a regime that had forced him to leave the armed services. He found the "new ideas" congenial, and in 1793 he had been among the first of the representatives-on-mission to the armies; in August of that year he had been sent with the deputy Stanislas Fréron to Toulon, the premier military port that had turned itself over to the allies. When the two representatives dismissed the incompetent general in command of the artillery there, Barras replaced him with one Captain Buonaparte, recommended by his fellow Corsican, Saliceti. Buonaparte proved to be an outstanding officer, and it was on Barras's recommendation that he was promoted to temporary brigadier after the lifting of the siege of Toulon. Barras and Fréron then proceeded to "show all the firmness required by the rigor of the times," a current formula for merciless repression; they reported that six hundred executions had taken place within three days, although Fréron was to say later that they had exaggerated by as much as two-thirds.

Tallien had been recalled from Bordeaux, where one of his missions had been to track down the surviving outlawed Girondist deputies from that region, suspected by the Convention of hiding there. After an excellent start—a gratifyingly long list of heads removed was sent regularly to the Committee of Public Safety in Paris, together with reports of denunciations encouraged and of prisons filled—a sharp decline in executions was noted. Robespierre dispatched his own personal agent to Bordeaux, and the two Great Committees assigned three of theirs; all four sent in reports of an especially damaging nature. The unwelcome decline in the death list was, it seemed, directly connected with the representative's infatuation with one Thérésia Cabarrus, an ex-Marquise de Fontenay. Tallien was said to have not only rescued her from prison soon after his arrival in Bordeaux, but could be seen driving with her in an open carriage while the lady, carrying a pike and wearing the red bonnet of militant Revolution, leaned on the shoulder of the representative of the Republic. Her pleas for clemency were known to be heeded, and friends were saved from the guillotine. Money and jewelry were said to have found their way into the hands of the lovers.

By the spring of 1794, Robespierre, with the aid of the Jacobin network, had succeeded in successively eliminating the rival leaders of the Convention. After the sentencing and execution of Danton the Republic of Virtue was at its height, ruled by Robespierre, a man obsessed with cleansing the Republic of corruption, and by a small caste of the Jacobin revolutionary elite: Couthon, Saint-Just and a half dozen more, usually men without any profession other than politics, suspicious of all outsiders and basing their support on what they called *le véritable peuple,* the militants of the party.

Representatives of the Convention were not infrequently accused of malpractices upon their return to Paris. Fouché, Barras and Tallien, however, were unusually vulnerable to final "purification" by Robespierre "the Incorruptible." They had not only violated his tenets of revolutionary purity, but had also personally offended him, a man whose own private life was exemplary: he was incorruptible in the contemporary sense of financial integrity and his views on women were ambivalent. "His abstract dreams," noted a fellow deputy, "his guards and his personal safety [Robespierre was not a courageous man] are all things incompatible with love and leave no room for that passion. He loved neither women nor money."[11]

Like Alexandre de Beauharnais, the returning proconsuls were unaware of the extent to which power had shifted during their absence. The all-powerful Committee of Public Safety was composed of men devoted to Robespierre, and its authority had totally supplanted that of the National Assembly. When Joseph Fouché laid his case before the Convention, the matter was referred to the Great Committee without comment. Fouché, expelled from the Jacobin Club, the equivalent of a death sentence, went underground. Tallien was absolved by the Jacobins, but Robespierre affected not to recognize the proconsul accused of venality, of a liaison with a former aristocrat and of laxness toward the enemies of the Republic. Paul Barras, however, suspected of financial extortion and whose repression at Toulon was considered excessive, decided to lay his case before the Incorruptible himself.

Robespierre's lodgings in the rue Saint-Honoré at the carpenter Duplay's was a center of pilgrimage for the revolutionary elite. He liked it to be known that he lived in austere circumstances and was engaged to the carpenter's daughter. Although he ignored Mme Duplay's hints that the situation might be regularized, he was idolized by the entire family. The house and the carpenter's workshop itself had been transformed into a shrine to the great man. His portraits hung on every wall; the blue and white curtains in his bedroom were made out of an old dress of Mme Duplay's. The family asked no contribution in exchange for the honor of his presence. The best coffee and fruit were ready for him at all hours; reverently they would gather around him as he ate. "He was so good to us," the Duplays would explain. He loved nature and simple pleasures, they said, and in the days before his fears of assassination took over, they would gather wildflowers together in the Champs-Elysées. The carpenter's house was at the very heart of Jacobin Paris, a stone's throw from the Tuileries, the seat of the Assembly; the Jacobin Club itself was on the same street. And the route of the death carts, whose roundabout itinerary was laid out so as to be seen by the greatest number of people, ran through the rue Saint-Honoré.

For this visit, Barras was accompanied by Stanislas Fréron, who had inaccurately described himself as being on good terms with Robespierre. They pushed past the guards helping Mme Duplay prepare salad in the courtyard; unable to stop them, Eléonore, the Duplay daughter, waving a pair of Robespierre's striped stockings that she had been mending, ran upstairs in front of them, calling out, "It's Fréron and a Citizen whose name I don't know." Robespierre, who was dressing, remained totally silent while Barras gave an account of his proconsulship in Toulon; only a "bilious froth oozed from his lips."[12] Brushing his teeth, he spat over his visitors' feet, shook his hair powder over them and never uttered a word, though he appeared displeased by their initial use of the familiar *tu*. After this unpropitious visit, Barras gave up trying to defend himself and, with Fouché and Tallien, set about trying to win over the Plain, the moderate deputies of the Convention.

Those deputies and even some members of the Mountain had started to question the need for a continuance of the Terror. In June, after a defeat of the Austrians and the republican armies' victories on every front, the national peril had ended, yet the war remained the justification for savage repression, and the guillotine worked harder than ever. Protests mounted against "rivulets of blood running through the streets" and the overcrowding of cemeteries, which forced the victims to be buried only a few inches from the surface. Bodies were pushed up by the clay, and the liquid putrefaction under the summer sky was such that the stench from the burial grounds spread across the city. The more militant eastern sections feared "pestiferous diseases" and complained that the guillotine, which had been moved toward the Bastille because the blood would not drain off from the Place de la Révolution, was causing distress. By 8 Thermidor the Commune, which had tried quicklime in the cemeteries, could only suggest burning thyme and sage for the prevention of an epidemic.

The term "Great Terror" is generally applied to the forty-seven days between June 10, the date of the Law of Prairial, and the fall of Robespierre on July 27. That law gave the Great Committees the right to send any "enemies of the people," including members of the Convention, before the Revolutionary Tribunal, which was split into four parts sitting simultaneously for greater speed. Within seven weeks, the rate of executions doubled.*

The deputies' parliamentary immunity had been virtually removed by this law and because most of them feared they were on a rumored list of suspects, more than fifty members of the Assembly gave up sleeping at home. In the Convention hall they preferred to sit at the end of the benches nearest the doors, and whenever Robespierre appeared at the tribune there was a rush for the exits. Any excuse was seized upon to be absent from Paris; to be sent as representative-on-mission to the armies

---

* Norman Hampson estimated that the "reign of Terror, up to the execution of Robespierre, probably accounted for less than thirty thousand deaths, together with another ten thousand who died in prison massacres. . . . The majority of the victims of the terror were obscure men and women."

was the most popular. Indeed, the Committee of Public Safety was finding it impossible to recall a representative for questioning once he had quit Paris.

During the Great Terror Robespierre showed himself rarely at the Jacobin Club, and then only to utter ambiguous threats against "wicked men." He had been accustomed to spending most of his time in the Queen's former rooms in the Tuileries Palace, where the Committee of Public Safety worked around the clock. At a vast table littered with maps of France all the great questions of war, finance and administration were decided, as were the moves of the proconsuls with their mobile guillotines and even the number of heads to be furnished by each province. But by the end of June, Robespierre withdrew his presence from the Great Committee. From his room at the carpenter's he annotated reports and denunciations from his personal agents, signed the lists of those to be guillotined and used this isolation, it was thought, to reinforce his personal power. Only Saint-Just and Couthon were allowed to join him, reputedly drawing up lists of deputies to be purged from the Convention and even from the Committee of Public Safety.

The tension and suspense that pervaded the Assembly spread to the Great Committees. Their meetings during these torrid months became the scene of altercations, fits of weeping and reconciliations. The vast windows looking out on the Tuileries Gardens had to be closed in spite of the excessive heat, for crowds were listening in amazement to the unprecedented uproar.

Robespierre's spies, ordered to shadow the conspirators, were finding it harder to follow them since they seldom slept at home. Fouché's favorite child was dying, but he dared not visit her. Barras, determined to sell his life dearly, transformed his room into an arsenal. Tallien, they reported, was seen to meet the Citoyenne Cabarrus in the Tuileries Gardens. Learning that she had followed her lover to Paris, Robespierre had her arrested, imprisoned and placed in solitary confinement. What appeared to be his unhealthy interest in her and the fact that he instructed that all letters addressed to her were to be shown to him immediately were noted by his colleagues.

At the end of June, the plotters and their allies met at Doyen's eating house in the Champs-Elysées, bringing in recruits from the Convention. Fouché circulated the names of deputies he insisted were to be purged, and at night, in disguise, he would visit them: "You are on Robespierre's next list," he would warn, or "You are in tomorrow's batch."

By July 26 (8 Thermidor in the revolutionary calendar) a coalition was finally cemented between the conspirators, the leading men of the left of the Convention and the uncommitted deputies of the center. And on that day, according to legend, Tallien received a dagger and a letter from his mistress, Thérésia Cabarrus. Contemptuously she wrote that she had made the mistake of believing in her lover's courage, and "I die in despair at having belonged to a coward like you." Whether or not the letter ever existed, this uncourageous man was undoubtedly galvanized into unaccustomed bravery, perhaps by something greater than fear for his own life.

On that day, too, after a six-week absence, Maximilien Robespierre returned to the Convention. Meticulously dressed in a blue silk coat and pale yellow knee breeches, and with carefully powdered hair, he moved straight to the rostrum. In silence he raised his steel-rimmed glasses to his forehead and stared intently at the deputies. After the accustomed self-pitying note ("I am a slave of liberty, a living martyr of the Republic . . .") he launched into a veiled attack on unnamed members of the Assembly and demanded a purge of "wicked men." There was also a menacing allusion to conspirators "working on orders from Mr. Pitt." Finally, he pronounced his own death sentence when he threatened to reveal on the following day only, the list of those to be purged.

"It's for tomorrow," said Tallien, and Joseph Cambon, one of the recently rallied deputies, wrote to his family in the country: "By tomorrow, either Robespierre or I will be dead."

That night the conspirators rallied the panicking deputies. In a room next to the Committee of Public Safety's chambers, Saint-Just was drawing up from Robespierre's secret list the names that he himself was to read out the next morning. At midnight the deputy Jean Collot d'Herbois, one of Robespierre's enemies, burst in. "Are you writing my bill of indictment?" he shouted. "Yes, Collot, I am," answered Saint-Just, and finished his work at dawn, in time to take a quick swim in the Seine.

By seven in the morning on July 27 (9 Thermidor) the corridors of the Convention were filled with tumultuous deputies. Tallien, in a cold frenzy, stood by the entrance, encouraging his colleagues. Outside, the day was already torrid with a storm brewing around Paris.

Robespierre, in a blue coat and striped stock, made a confident entry to a thunder of applause, followed by Saint-Just wearing his familiar white stock and single gold earring. Collot d'Herbois was presiding. Almost as soon as a somber Saint-Just started proceedings he was interrupted by Tallien, demanding to be heard. Other deputies joined in, shouting down Saint-Just and preventing Robespierre from reaching the rostrum. His shrill protests could hardly be heard through the uproar as Collot's bell drowned out his attempts. Tallien, beside himself and waving a dagger, continued to scream, "Down with the tyrant, down with the dictator." As Robespierre appeared to be suffocating, a deputy thundered, "He is choking on Danton's blood!" Saint-Just stood motionless, and Couthon in his wheelchair remained silent.

No one yet had dared name the tyrant until finally, as the heat and the nervous tension became almost unbearable and the Convention hall darkened in the approaching storm, an obscure deputy had the courage to pronounce Robespierre's name and to propose that his arrest be put to a roll call. By five in the afternoon the Assembly had voted unanimously to arrest Robespierre, his brother Augustin, Saint-Just, Couthon and a couple of their followers. Escorted by guards, the men were led away.

Since it was now five-thirty and a full half hour beyond their dinnertime, the deputies proceeded to declare a dangerous two-hour recess; when they returned to the Convention hall it was to find that the Commune, entirely composed of Robespierre's men, had sounded the tocsin, ordered the forty-eight Paris sections to mobilize and forbidden the prisons to receive the outlawed deputies, who were taken to safety at the Hôtel de Ville, the city hall of the capital. There the hours passed while the Commune waited for orders, but none came from a suddenly irresolute Robespierre.

Another night of suspense now began. An armed insurrection of the Paris populace and the deliverance of the deputies were real possibilities. Paul Barras was appointed commander in chief of the Convention's small detachment of troops and instructed to protect the Assembly and to have the outlaws imprisoned.

Scenes in the street were chaotic. The tocsin continued to ring; there was a steady drumbeat throughout the city, calling citizens to arms. Commune men and the Convention's troops under Paul Barras clashed in the dark in the narrow streets.

By nightfall, Barras had deployed his men in a circle around the Hôtel de Ville; the Commune's forces listened as the Convention's decree was read aloud by torchlight. As they heard the terrible words: *"Hors la loi!"* ("Outlaw them!") the thunderstorm so long brewing broke over the city. Under the downpour the leaderless Commune men melted away, at first gradually, then in larger groups.

It was after midnight when Barras and his men broke down the doors of the Hôtel de Ville. They found that Augustin Robespierre had thrown himself from a window, Couthon had rolled from his wheelchair and hidden under a table. Maximilien Robespierre had shot himself in the jaw. Only Saint-Just stood calmly awaiting them.

On 10 Thermidor, the roofs and balconies along the route of the tumbrils were black with people; the faces at some of the windows were greenish white after months or years in hiding. All Paris appeared to have been in the streets since the previous night. For the first time in months, families turned out in their party clothes to follow the carts bearing the outlawed men. The guillotine had been moved back to the Place de la Révolution during the night; the mass of people was so great that it took the tumbrils one and a half hours to drive from the prison of the Conciergerie to the present Place de la Concorde.

The crowd was pitiless, howling abuse at Robespierre, his jaw held together with a bandage, his blue coat bloodstained and his striped stockings hanging over his shoes. In front of his lodgings the convoy stopped for a moment while a boy took a pail of oxblood from the neighboring butcher's and threw it over the carpenter's door.

"From now on," wrote the historian Michelet, "something lofty, inhuman, terrible, had gone out of the Revolution."[13]

✌ 5 ✌

AT THE CHAUMIÈRE

TEN DAYS AFTER THERMIDOR, ROSE DE BEAUHARNAIS WAS ONE OF THE first prisoners to be liberated from Les Carmes. She left with style, falling into a graceful faint when her name was called, then charmingly thanking her friends there before walking out into the Paris sunshine "followed," wrote one of them, "by the wishes and blessings of the whole prison."

It was a short walk home through the jubilant city already transformed from the stupefied Paris of the Terror. Excited crowds around the prison doors awaited the liberation of friends and family; in the streets, passersby no longer hurried along, avoiding one another's eyes. Strangers embraced; noisy groups gathered at street corners to read the gazettes, now again for sale.

Some 100,000 suspects were reappearing from hiding places throughout the city, and by the end of August three thousand prisoners had been released. To begin with they were content, one of them said, "just to walk on the Quais in the sun, to breathe, to look at the sky, to feel my head still on my shoulders."

Still, the release of prisoners was slow. It was commonly assumed that Jean-Lambert Tallien was responsible for Rose's early liberation; certainly he signed the order needed to have the government seals removed from her papers, her linen and "other items of daily use" in her apartment, but the seals remained on the house itself. Désirée Hosten, arrested in Croissy on the day Rose was sent to Les Carmes, would not be liberated for some time.

When Rose moved with her children to a larger apartment shared with her friend Mme de Krény in the neighboring rue de l'Université, she was accompanied, besides her children, by a maid, a manservant, Marie Lannoy and, of course, Fortuné, and she was immediately crippled by debt. The British fleet patrolling the Atlantic stopped all traffic with the Antilles. At last, in November, Rose found "a person traveling to New England" who was willing to take her first letter to Mme de La Pagerie. In it she announced Alexandre's death. "I mourn my husband," she wrote, "my children are now my only consolation." Would her mother, she asked, send letters of credit via Hamburg, or else sugar? She would need fifty thousand livres immediately and then, every three months, whatever her mother could spare. "I confess that I need no less than that to meet my expenses and those of my children, for now we have only you to provide us with our daily bread." She ended "with tender love from your poor Yéyette," and with greetings "to all the negroes on the plantation" and a hug to her wet nurse.[1]

Meanwhile Rose lived on loans and credit. The domestics made a joint offer to forgo their wages for the present, and Mlle Lannoy lent Rose her life's savings. Rose borrowed from friends and her banker Emmery, and drove to Fontainebleau to touch Aunt Renaudin for fifty thousand francs in the unreliable paper money. For this journey Rose needed a passport and, like the carriage and horses she used for this trip, could only have been obtained through influence. On her passport she is described as having "orange" eyes; her age has been reduced by three years.

She borrowed from Lazare Hoche too. Saved by Thermidor and liberated on August 4, he wrote on the same day to his sixteen-year-old wife in Alsace that his love for her "increased daily," and that he was on the point of setting out to join her "on foot, as becomes a republican."[2] Ten days later, still in Paris, the excuses he gave for his delay were contradictory. Adèle was not to try to join him in Paris, he wrote: "The times are too dangerous . . . I live almost hidden. Be patient."[3]

Rose's liaison with the general was not hidden, however. Together they celebrated their joint liberation in the city filled with near-delirious rejoicing. The carnival that would last for five years had started.

No fewer than thirteen theaters reopened that month and already there was a black market in theater and concert tickets. Cafés were as crowded as the theaters, gambling houses were open all night. Although entire buildings already appeared to be made of paper, covered as they were by layers of torn proclamations and decrees of the Convention, they were now rapidly overlaid by posters proclaiming the opening of dance halls; notices of new ones were pasted daily over the revolutionary decrees.

In love with Lazare Hoche and in need of a protector, Rose now attempted to persuade him to divorce his wife—the simplest of formalities in the Year III of the Republic—and although he hesitated, Hoche still found Rose irresistible, lending her money and continuing to forbid Adèle to join him until, on August 21, he was named commander in chief of the Army of the West, raised to subdue the rebels in Vendée and Brittany.

Immediately, he sent Adèle an urgent letter to hurry to Paris, to bring his sword, his pistols and his horse, and after a brief honeymoon with his young wife he hurried off to take up his post in Brittany. With him, besides his wife, went thirteen-year-old Eugène de Beauharnais as aide, a youth fated to serve his mother's admirers in this capacity. He would fulfill the same role with General Bonaparte when Napoleon became his stepfather.

Although in Eugène's and Hortense's *Mémoires* their mother's name is never linked with that of Lazare Hoche, he, undoubtedly, until the day of her reluctant decision to marry General Bonaparte, was of all men the one she would have preferred to marry.

Though Hoche was contrite—Adèle, upon her arrival in Paris, had discovered the truth and bitterly reproached her husband on the liaison that had kept them apart—and enchanted by his wife, his letters to Rose from his headquarters in Cherbourg were both regular and passionate, and she continued to hope throughout the year that the general would decide to leave his wife. They kept up an ardent correspondence at least until the summer, and we can guess how compromising were Rose's own letters by the considerable risks she would take as Mme Bonaparte to recover them.

After Lazare Hoche's departure, Rose's lifelong quest resumed: for influence, for money and for distraction.

Since Thermidor, paper money had fallen to one-third of its price of issue. "Because these mountains of assignats perished if they remained inactive," explained Sébastien Mercier, a former deputy to the Convention, imprisoned until Thermidor, "and because everything went up in price every day, it was necessary to buy literally *anything*, every day; but because the Assignat also lost value daily, although I made a profit on each item, yet still I lost on what I bought the following day." Consequently, since direct exchange had become the only way to eat and to live, and since whatever was in short supply could be bartered, "it is perfectly usual," noted Mercier, "to see well-dressed women selling tobacco, muslin, butter or a pair of saddle-horses. Every age, both sexes and all classes carry samples of coffee or sugar under one arm. Beans are to be found at the hairdresser's and lace at the pharmacy."[4]

Carriages had all but disappeared in the capital—Parisians released from imprisonment or emerging from hiding said that their first great surprise was the eerie silence of the city without the sound of wheels rumbling over cobblestones. But Rose, who did not care to walk, managed to hire one. She paid for it with Marie Lannoy's savings and drove around Paris with her wares for barter.

It was a torn and wrecked city. After five years of bloodshed and pillage, there were chilling reminders of the Terror everywhere. The wooden barrier that had protected the guillotine still stood in the Place de la Révolution. In its center remained the peeling pink cardboard statue of Liberty. The red bonnet attached to a pike staff was still set outside houses and shops. On the Tuileries Palace, pockmarked by gunfire, was daubed in large red letters *dix août* (August 10), the date of the attack.

The noise and bustle on the Right Bank, where life centered around the public dance halls and the restaurants housed in the *ci-devants'* mansions, vanished once the river was crossed. Grass grew in the streets in Rose's own neighborhood, and Mercier described the Left Bank "as the most abandoned quarter of all, the great houses stripped not only of furniture, mirrors, paneling and moldings, but even of the lead from the roofs."[5]

On both banks, however, "the capital of France looked like an immense junk shop."[6] The streets of the city were blocked by carts loaded with mountains of linen, porcelains, tapestries, kitchen equipment and mattresses for sale or barter. Prints, jewelry, paintings, furniture, wine and statues were heaped together in the gutters. Along the quays of the Seine were piled the contents of the university's libraries, precursors of today's bookstalls. Prices were so low that foreigners were starting to send emissaries to pick out some of the priceless collections. From England alone the Prince of Wales's agents acquired for him bronzes and paintings, busts by Coysevox, and furniture from Versailles by Jacob, Riesener and Weisweiler.

Even before the start of the catastrophic winter Mercier noted that "the fear of dying of hunger prompted many citizens to keep a cage of rabbits or an undernourished goat outside their door, in the hope that these might some day prove a precious resource."[7]

The start of this coldest winter in living memory came early. The Channel froze for a full two miles off the northern coastline. All the olive trees were lost as far south as Provence. Neither wood nor coal could be ferried to the capital down the frozen Seine; and not a tree was left to be cut down in the forests around Paris. The Bois de Boulogne and even the Tuileries Gardens were devastated, and "citizens chopped up their beds in the street to cook their food, and to keep themselves from dying of cold."[8]

But there was less and less food to cook. So calamitous had been the harvest of 1794—hail in the spring, rains in the summer, and the harvest itself hampered by mass levies for the armies of the Revolution—that the new government of "Thermidorians" was forced to import grain but, owing to the bitter winter, convoys bearing wheat were unable to unload their cargoes. Posters were placed by the Commune on every house in Paris, fixing the meat ration at one-quarter pound per citizen every ten days. Candles and oil, flour and sugar disappeared from the markets, while farmers hoarded their crops and produce, refusing to be paid in the hated assignat. Families took turns searching the countryside around Paris, bargaining with farmers for some eggs or a handful of white flour that could be paid for only in cash or by barter.

"But it is impossible," wrote a returning emigré that winter, "to die of hunger with more gaiety."[9] He believed that Parisians laughed and sang to numb themselves to the horrors of famine, and noted that they had learned to live without the barest necessities while pursuing the superfluous. The crowds pouring out of the theaters, where tickets cost hundreds of livres, would silently join the bread lines starting in front of the bakers' shops in the freezing dawn. The vast majority of Parisians spent a third of their lives waiting there for the rationed "national loaf," a sticky mixture of bran and beans, as the government struggled to maintain the price of bread at a reasonable level. "I have thrown the national loaf a dozen times against the wall," wrote Frénilly, "and each time it remained glued there. Even my dog refused to eat it."[10] For Parisians, the lack of decent white bread was the worst of all deprivations and the subject of endless conversations. "It was impossible at any dinner table to find a topic amongst the newly liberated," remembered one of them, "other than the white flour one had found or the meal one had nearly eaten."[11]

At the houses where Rose dined, guests wore patched and mended clothes, and owned at most one coat and one pair of shoes—a new pair would have cost a sackful of assignats. Although the Citoyenne Beauharnais managed to acquire several pairs of gray silk stockings "with colored heels," and although even one pair cost seven hundred livres, or the equivalent of an unobtainable piece of beef, it was generally understood that her financial situation was still more precarious than that of her friends. She alone was exempted, in this time of rationing, from the dinner guests' custom of bringing their own candle and loaf of bread. At the Marquise de Moulin's her place at the dinner table was always laid, in gratitude for her role in saving that lady's niece from the guillotine. Another friendship from the time of the Terror would prove still more valuable.

The days of barter and of modest dinners at the houses of friends were over for Rose when she entered the world of the Talliens. Here there was no shortage of bread nor of any luxury that either gratitude or self-interest could provide. Packages of tea and sugar, bottles of wine and oil, piles of firewood, accompanied by letters of adoration and gratitude, were delivered daily to Thérésia Tallien, the heroine of Thermidor.

On the coldest Christmas Eve in living memory a noisy crowd, dressed apparently for a masquerade, shattered the silence of an unlit footpath off the rural Champs-Elysées. On December 24, 1794, all the power and influence of Thermidorian France was on its way to the opening of Thérésia Tallien's "cottage," the Chaumière.

On the night of her marriage to Jean-Lambert Tallien, her savior at Thermidor, twenty-one-year-old Thérésia opened her salon, and for the next thirty years the principal roles in the history of France would be played by some of the cast assembled there that night. Thérésia herself, witty, original and startlingly beautiful, was the heroine of France, promoted by the tale of her contemptuous letter from prison to her lover, Tallien.

Four months pregnant and fashionably draped in an "antique" shawl,

Thérésia greeted her guests in a Greek tunic and sandals, her hair cut short and curled to resemble a Roman bust. Beside her, and similarly attired, stood her friend Rose de Beauharnais.

In the great summer of liberation, Thérésia Cabarrus had become a mythical figure, a symbol of femininity and courage, and of the end of the Terror. Because she was to have paid with her head for saving many lives and because she had galvanized one of the leaders of the coup of July 27, neither Paris nor Thérésia herself doubted that she had "saved the Republic." In the secularized city, where the Catholic saints' names had been erased even from the streets, Thérésia was "Our Lady of Thermidor." From the day she was liberated and carried home on the shoulders of the crowd greeting her at her prison door, she remained the center of Parisian curiosity and adulation. There was delirium whenever she and Tallien appeared together in public. Chancellor Pasquier, a recent prisoner, as starved for news as were all the newly released, and as intensely curious about the couple, recorded their arrival at the Odéon Theater one night. Wildly acclaimed by the crowds outside, the Talliens found upon entering the theater the entire audience standing on chairs and benches, where "the ovation was prolonged into more applause and cries of love."[12]

There was less curiosity about Jean-Lambert Tallien ("rather handsome") than in the staggering beauty at his side, taller than he and, wrote Pasquier, looking like "the caryatid of his glory."[13] Contemporaries are unanimous in recording their shock on first seeing Thérésia. Attempts to describe her physical perfections had been almost incoherent, even before her apotheosis as Mme Tallien. Her dynamism, her riotous originality, her "radiant femininity even more impressive than her beauty," were acclaimed from the day she was married at fifteen to an inadequate Marquis de Fontenay.

When it became known that this heroine had vowed to "end all hatreds and heal all wounds," a bitter and divided France felt that in her lay their hope for French unity. Thérésia's fulfillment of this pledge appeared still more likely when, finding herself pregnant, she married her deliverer on the Christmas after Thermidor.

By the beginning of 1795 the Chaumière had started to symbolize the rightward turn of the "Thermidorians," that alliance of moderates and ex-terrorists, the victors of the coup of July 27, which now controlled an unstable majority in the Convention. At first, deputies who had joined in the plot to bring down Robespierre were amazed to find themselves regarded as heroes. They had expected to take over the Great Committees intact, not to bring them down, and had had every intention of continuing the Revolution. Now they found themselves heading the violent wave of reaction they had let loose.

Public opinion, a voice with which no government had reckoned for some years, was proving impossible to control. From the beginning, the Thermidorians were left in little doubt as to the ferocity of popular reaction. Police reported the first murmurings of revenge from the crowds waiting at the prison doors after Thermidor, and from as many shades of political opinion as were represented by the families of the victims. The country appeared to be intoxicated by the desire for revenge, for a settlement of accounts with the organizers of the executions. At first reluctantly, the former terrorists were forced to get rid of the guillotine and to put on trial the more notorious executioners. One after another the destruction of most of the key institutions of the revolutionary government followed. The reduction in authority of most of the revolutionary committees, the price-fixing, the punishment of some of the more savage terrorists were among the many unplanned measures made under public pressure.

Jean-Lambert Tallien, elected president of the Convention after Thermidor, was perceived as leaning heavily on the side of reaction, as the Thermidorians tried to maintain a balance between Jacobins and the new moderates. In need of support outside the National Assembly, the Thermidorians found it in the newly liberated press, in the theaters, which now assumed a political role—almost the entire personnel of the Comédie-Française had been imprisoned as "suspects"—and, increasingly, in power in the street. There their allies were the Muscadins, or *Jeunesse Dorée*, the "Gilded Youth of the Year III."

These young men, mostly artisans and small tradesmen (they were not joined by former aristocrats, who hardly existed in the France of 1794), were often the sons of guillotined men and women. With the tacit approval of the government they formed almost an irregular militia, organizing noisy demonstrations in the streets and in the Convention's gallery, harassing Jacobins wherever they found them. Their provocative appearance—braided hair and bizarre, dandified dress—underlined their challenge to the *sans culottes*. They maintained their own journal, frequented their own cafés and were united in their worship of Mme Tallien.

Deputies of the extreme left refused to take the path to Thérésia's "cottage," the house of the woman who had triggered the suspension of the Society of Jacobins. Three months after Thermidor, accompanied only by a squad of Muscadins, Thérésia Tallien herself had locked the doors of the Jacobin Club an hour before a session was to take place, and then presented the keys to the Convention. (In England, William Pitt the Younger, upon learning of this action, remarked: "That woman is capable of closing the gates of Hell.") At the National Convention, Jacobin deputies denounced "the new Marie Antoinette." One of them, Joseph Cambon, complained of "public opinion organized in the boudoir of *la Cabarrus*" and, looking directly at Tallien, accused him of being "one of the rascals who have promised our heads to their concubines."

In this decisive year for both Napoleon and Josephine the Chaumière would prove to be the road to success and glory. After the total disruption by the Terror of what was left of any social fabric, the Talliens' house had instantly become the center of the political establishment of the new France.

Here reputations would be made and broken, alliances formed, fortunes started, where the new and the old worlds converged: men of the Convention, republican army officers, financiers, journalists, pretty women, artists, Muscadins, a few returning emigrés and the new race of speculators and army contractors (the acknowledged kings of this new society) met at the Chaumière; the only foreign representative was James Monroe, the U.S. envoy. The deputies regularly seen at the "cottage" were the new moderates: Stanislas Fréron; Paul Barras, one of the organizers of Thermidor; and Joseph Chénier *"le Fratricide,"* accused of not unreservedly resisting the execution of his brother, the poet André; the women were virginal Juliette Récamier; scandalous Fortunée Hamelin, said to have walked the entire length of the Champs-Elysées with her breasts bared; Germaine de Staël, newly returned from her Swiss exile, and, of course, Rose de Beauharnais.

"Incredible luxury, concerts, the theater and the beautiful Citoyenne

Cabarrus, Tallien's wife—these, rather than rationing and the fate of our armies, are the principal preoccupations of most people here!" wrote Espinchal, a royalist spy, to his employers in London.[14] The ideas that were transforming society had been the stuff of talk in the prerevolutionary salons; conversation as it had been understood then was not practiced in Thermidorian Paris—needs were too immediate. At the Chaumière that winter, after the years of intense emotions, there was a common appetite for pleasure and luxury, a universal desire to enjoy, to eat well, to dance, to live. Politics, the arts, the war raging for the last four years on the frontiers and those fourteen armies cited by the royalist agent were equally ignored. Stock exchange tips, barter and high-level contracts were the common obsessions. There was traffic in guns, in food, in gold, in shoes for the army. "Contracts might be for anything," observed one of the Talliens' guests, "from oats to cavalry sabres, and as likely as not carried off by a woman wearing flesh-colored tights and diamonds on her bare toes."[15]

The setting for this heterogeneous group was as new, as fresh and as unexpected as all life appeared now to the men and women mad with joy at having escaped the guillotine. All night long the sound of music from the Chaumière could be heard half a mile away on the Champs-Elysées, a country road still, where wildflowers grew and cows grazed in summer. The house was a stage-set cottage placed in a cabbage patch a few steps from the Seine, on the present avenue Montaigne, and half hidden by elms—a cottage more successfully rustic even than the late Queen's Petit Trianon at Versailles.

The sensibilities of a generation nourished on Rousseau and accustomed to appeals to nature were gratified by the thatch-roofed cottage, painted red to resemble brick ("blood red," suggested Tallien's enemies). The fashion for living in pastoral surroundings had now been reinforced by the yearning of that large number of Parisians who had in the last years seen trees and sky only through prison bars. The interior of the cottage was equally fashionable: severely Roman chairs and stucco pillars in the "Pompeiian" hall; an antique tripod lamp in Mme Tallien's bedroom and a naked statue of Diana, whose features were unmistakably those of the hostess.

The assembly of power under that thatched roof could easily have been mistaken for a fancy dress party. Postrevolutionary society imagined itself to be living in Greece or republican Rome. "In the name of antiquity" Jacques-Louis David, only last year a particularly merciless terrorist, had ordained "that drawing rooms be transformed into atriums, chairs into curules, dresses into tunics and shoes into sandals."[16] Reaction in clothing was as violent as in every other domain. Because David had decreed a neoclassical fashion in dress as well as in decoration (the *"sans chemises,"* it was said, had replaced the *sans culottes*), women threw away corsets and underwear. As so often in times of social upheaval and in postwar periods, both men and women delighted in pushing fashion toward the unexpected; there was an element of self-mockery in their masquerade, a suggestion of sexual license mingled with a Rousseauesque return to the imagined simplicities of nature.

Women's Grecian tunics were split to the thigh and down to the navel, and sometimes made to mold the body by being dipped first in scented oil and so transparent that, wrote one astonished observer, "the twin reservoirs of maternity are seen to palpitate through the gauze." The need to shock was endemic. A visitor from England was astounded by signs of androgynous fashion and wrote home: "This morning I saw a young woman dressed like a man; this is quite common here." And men, too, were involved in the masquerade. "It was something new to see young men disputing the leadership of fashion with women. Some, indeed, wore their hair dressed like women, parted and held up in braids with a tortoiseshell comb," reported Laure d'Abrantès.[17]

Although the Merveilleuses—the name now given to fashionable women—wore only shawls to protect their near-naked bodies against the bitter cold, this garment had other uses too. Mme Tallien was observed to retain hers throughout the evening at the Chaumière. She was not alone in this predicament for, as a German observer solemnly noted: "Owing to the propinquity of recent prison life . . . many women bear the visible signs of approaching maternity. . . . The general permissiveness, the new divorce laws, so many inhibitions overturned, can but have augmented the number of precarious unions which have taken the place of marriage and thus added to the sudden increase in population."[18]

As part of the reaction to the years of "democratic virtue" all Paris had exploded into one vast ballroom. In alleyways, in historical monuments, in churches and cemeteries the frenzy of dancing never ceased. There was even a public dance hall at Les Carmes, where Rose had been imprisoned and where only two years earlier the Carmelite priests had been butchered. There were subscription balls for the new rich where, instead of traditional country dance or stately gavottes, couples now danced polkas and the scandalous waltz. "To embrace each other, to be held close and intertwined—what an attraction for both sexes," wrote an observer in the *Journal de Paris,* who went on to describe the Merveilleuses and their partners "intoxicated by the speed and the voluptuous music, singing together while continuing their wild dance."

The craving for sensationalism and macabre humor that prevailed after the Terror produced the "Bal des Victimes," reserved for families of which at least one close member had been guillotined—a collateral relative would not do—and there was a further distinction between bona fide members and those whose relatives had merely died in prison. At this ball men and women danced with a thread of blood red silk around their necks and their hair cut short as though ready for the executioner; they greeted one another by imitating the motion of the head dropping into the scaffold's basket. Sometimes the men buttoned the collars of their coats above their heads and stuffed their shoulders so that they appeared to be walking torsos.

Though prices soared when the Thermidorians lifted the price-fixing law and the value of paper money fell still further, and though half of Paris was starving, yet on the Décadi, the revolutionary every-tenth-day replacement of Sunday, workmen's eating houses could not find premises large enough for their cash-carrying customers.

Two thousand restaurants opened that year, most of them established by the cooks of the exiled *aristos.* Waiters in the more expensive ones wore "livery" for the first time. And a pretext for a new meal was found. Lunch was discovered. The dinner hour in revolutionary France had been moved to accommodate the National Assembly sessions. Instead of eating at the usual European time of three o'clock, Paris was eating now at five or even later. Consequently, as time stretched out between the morning coffee and the ever-later dinner, a *déjeuner à la fourchette* (a fork lunch), was invented. Oysters, melons, anchovies and cold chicken, however, were available between three and five in the evening in the restaurants thronged with black marketeers and their noisy women, with the men involved in the traffic of national properties and with the purveyors of guns, powder, shoes and food for the army.

"No one wants to be alone," noted one former prisoner, "no one wants to eat, sleep or enjoy alone,"[19] and in Thermidorian Paris there was a universal desire to forget, to enjoy together.

There were some, such as Pauline de Beaumont, whose reaction to the horrors of the Revolution—she had lost her entire family under the Terror—was an extraordinary indifference toward life. Walking with her lover, the poet René de Chateaubriand, on a chilly evening, dressed only in a light muslin gown, she replied, *"Qu' importe?"* ("What does it matter?") when her friends protested that she was killing herself. And indeed she survived for only one year.

But for most, the response was a deliberate flouting of conventions, an explosion of sensuality, a need to live intensely for love. "The Revolution and its horrors," noted a German observer, "seems to have produced a great awakening of the senses and in many liaisons solitude, fear and the long nights without light appear to have disposed the heart to ever more tender effusions."[20]

Of all periods in her life, that year succeeding the Terror was probably the one most in harmony with Rose's own nature. Always adaptable, accustomed to a life of expedients, to adjusting to new customs and to new power, she thrived in this society with needs to match her own, fitting as easily into the period's feverish pursuit of pleasure as she slipped into the Attic poses required by David's decree that women should resemble Greco-Roman statues. Only her search for security set her apart from the crowd at the Chaumière. Dangerously old at thirty-one, permanently in debt, with expensive tastes and two children to support, she needed a protector. She found the Chaumière to be an invaluable base of operations, for tips on the stock exchange and, above all, in her continuing search for supporters and connections. Here passion for meeting the powerful could be fully satisfied; and nothing could be refused to Mme Tallien's closest friend.

Determined to recover some of Alexandre de Beauharnais' confiscated property, still more to identify him as politically closer to the Thermidorian victors than to the now execrated radical Mountain, Rose bombarded the Assembly with copies of his exculpatory letters from prison because, she explained, she wished to clarify their opinion of him. As a result of these pleas the deputies Tallien and Barras arranged for a pair of horses and an elegant town carriage to be assigned to her "to replace those left at the Army of the Rhine by the late General Beauharnais."[21]

Rose continued to arouse pity as an innocent victim of the Revolution, a favorite role after Thermidor. It was still too early, in spite of the tide of popular reaction, to revert entirely to "Vicomtesse", but she introduced herself as "the widow of the unfortunate Beauharnais." Again she started writing letters of recommendation in aid of others, often to men she had met only once, exerting her charm and warmth even on those who had not yet become influential. Her special efforts, however, were reserved for men already in power.

That winter she sent off a graceful little note to Citizen General Paul Barras, easily the most prestigious of the deputies in the Chaumière circle, and Tallien's successor as president of the National Assembly. On the pretext of drawing to his attention a *"sans culotte* volunteer wounded in fighting for the Fatherland," she went on to write that she had not had the pleasure of seeing Barras for a very long time, reproached him gently for "abandoning an old acquaintance" and invited him to visit her in the rue de l'Université.[22]

☙ 6 ☙

A TRANSCENDENTAL REPUBLICAN

IT WAS PAUL BARRAS WHO FIRST BROUGHT THE CORSICAN OFFICER NA-
poleon Buonaparte to the Chaumière in the summer of 1795. The carnival
crowd revolving around Barras and the Talliens ignored this unprepos-
sessing figure, small and emaciated, wearing an expression of sullen disdain, whose uncombed hair and dirty clothes appeared to confirm his
Jacobin reputation. For the next four months he was known simply as
"Barras's little Italian protégé."

Bonaparte himself* was immediately impressed by a phenomenon
new to him: the power and influence of women. In a letter to his brother
Joseph, written shortly after his arrival in Paris, he noted admiringly: "The
women here, who are the most beautiful in the world, are the center of
importance."

Bonaparte, until then, had been solely interested in the acquisition of
money and power. With these words, however, he had already taken a
first step away from his regard only for "those women who bear the most
children," and another toward his union with one of the sophisticated and
pleasure-loving Merveilleuses he described. The ambitious provincial had
recognized that in the new, post–Terror France women were the foun-
tainhead of his twin ambitions.

Few men can have been less prepared for a world where women
represented not only pleasure but also the road to money and success. The
strongest feminine influence hitherto on this misogynist had been a
woman of a very different stamp.

---

* Although Napoleon was to gallicize his family name only after his marriage to Josephine, he
will be referred to from now on as "Bonaparte."

Although his mother was, in Napoleon's own words, "the strong man of the family," Letizia Buonaparte had always deferred to her husband, the frivolous, charming and weak Carlo. Therefore, although in 1767 she had opposed the invasion of Corsica by the French with the courage of a lioness, and had fled with her husband to the mountains while she was carrying Napoleon, when Carlo deserted the Corsican leader Pasquale Paoli and became an enthusiastic collaborator with the French masters, Letizia followed him faithfully. She never commented on the speed with which Carlo progressed from dissident to courtier when the French assumed control of the island. He and Letizia were both of Genoese stock, and in common with most of their neighbors claimed to be of noble descent. Carlo added the aristocratic particle "de" to his name, and as Charles de Buonaparte spent the remainder of his short life—he died at the age of thirty-nine—in the antechambers of Paris and Versailles, soliciting favors and a pension for himself and scholarships at royal schools for his three oldest children. A man noted for a delight in intrigue for its own sake—a trait inherited by most of his children—Charles was seldom thereafter seen in Corsica, and Letizia raised her eight children virtually single-handedly.

A woman of great strength of character she was, like Josephine's mother, more strong-minded than her husband, exceptionally beautiful (as a girl she was known as "Corsica's little marvel"), indulgent toward her husband and strict with her children, beating them unmercifully for any misdemeanor. To her son Napoleon, Letizia remained always a symbol of austerity, of respect for parents and of a sense of family obligations. Napoleon recorded at St. Helena that she instilled in him not only these Corsican virtues, but also the Corsican inclination for carrying on blood feuds of hate and revenge, vendettas that could be "extended to the seventh degree."[1]

The island of Corsica had been in the possession of the Republic of Genoa for two centuries when Pasquale Paoli led a rebellion against its Genoese masters in 1757. He ruled the island for ten years until Genoa sold its right to Corsica to the King of France. The French invaded the island in force; a fierce resistance, again led by Paoli, continued for a year until May 1768, when the Corsican army was annihilated and Paoli exiled to England. On August 15, France concluded the purchase and proclaimed a "reunion" with the island.

With a characteristic sense of the dramatic, Napoleon was born on

August 15, 1769, the day Corsica was celebrating the first anniversary of this "reunion." Signora Buonaparte felt the first labor pains during a thanksgiving Mass in Ajaccio's cathedral and hurried home alone to deliver the child herself. The boy, her second son, was named for an uncle who had recently died fighting the French.

Frugal by nature and by necessity, Letizia practiced the strictest economy. She and her children lived on the ground and first floors of the square stone house in Ajaccio; the second and third floors were inhabited by her half brother, her cousins and remote aunts. The family's olive trees, meager vines and small herd of goats furnished them with most of their food. Letizia's constant concern was the keeping up of outward appearances; this was necessary, she taught Napoleon, for the sake of pride: "Better to have fine clothes and a grand salon, and to eat dry bread in secret," she preached, a lesson not lost on her son when at the age of nine he was sent to the Royal Military School of Brienne in the Champagne region of France, a seminary for children of the nobility destined for the army.

Here the shocks to his self-esteem were incalculable. For the first time he found himself the butt of jokes: for his outlandish names (he dropped the final *e* of Napoleon now), for his appearance—a large head and short, undersized legs—and for his inability to speak any language but the Italian-Corsican dialect. The unaccustomed food and climate increased his sense of isolation. He was never to become used to the cold and fogs of northern France; he is constantly in later scenes pictured standing as near to a fireplace as possible. As Emperor he would complain that he could not share his second wife's bedroom because of her Austrian habit of sleeping with the windows open.

Napoleon's reaction to the blows to his pride was to enclose himself in a shell of silence and resentment. He confessed to his only friend, Louis-Antoine Bourrienne, that he felt his own father "should have followed Paoli and shared his exile," and that he himself would never forgive him for helping to unite Corsica with France. "And," he declared, according to Bourrienne, "I will do all the harm I can to *your* French."[2]

A mediocre student except in mathematics, Bonaparte at fifteen passed next to last in the artillery class examination; nevertheless he was granted a second royal scholarship, this time to the Royal Military School in Paris. In 1784, with the rest of his class, he took the "water coach" to Paris, a two-day journey up the Seine. The little group, in the charge of one of the Brienne Fathers, disembarked at the St. Paul wharf in the old Marais, and for the first time the young provincial saw the capital of his future Empire, a vast, noisy city of 600,000 inhabitants. The boys supped at an eating house on the Left Bank, said a prayer in the church of St. Germain des Prés—Napoleon borrowed a few sous to buy a copy of *Gil Blas* from a quayside stall—and by nightfall reached the nobly classical Royal Military School on the Champ de Mars.

Students at the school saw little of the life of the capital; their days were filled with study—and with "indecent luxury," Napoleon complained. The single but austere bedrooms, excellent food and servants for the future officers were, he thought, unnecessary. It was at the Royal Military School that the richer, titled cadets made Napoleon aware of a sense of social inferiority, one that only emphasized his arrogance and left him with an unending need to wipe out the humiliation. Though he wore the handsome uniform of a king's cadet, this in no way inhibited Bonaparte's savage criticism of everything French and made him as unpopular here as he had been at Brienne. His report upon graduation read: "Reserved and hard working. . . . Silent, capricious, proud and extremely egotistical . . . Much self-esteem . . . Extremely ambitious."

Napoleon's feelings of responsibility toward his family were strong, and when Charles de Buonaparte died in 1785 of the cancer of the stomach that was to kill his second son and several of his other children, Napoleon informed his mother that, in spite of the strict Corsican system of primogeniture, he was now the head of the family. He had seen his older brother, Joseph, in France, and though fond of him, considered him frivolous, indecisive and inadequate for that role.

In September 1785, Bonaparte graduated forty-second of fifty-eight from the Royal Military School (he had, however, completed in one year a course that could take others two or three), was commissioned a second lieutenant and assigned to the artillery regiment of La Fère, garrisoned at Valence in Burgundy.

Fontainebleau was the first relay for the stagecoach traveling to Burgundy, and the group of young officers cut short their supper there to peer through the iron gates of the château, the scene of Emperor Napoleon's abdication thirty years later. By a curious coincidence, September 1785, was also the month when Rose de Beauharnais moved to Fontainebleau and celebrated her own new freedom there.

One of Lieutenant de Bonaparte's fellow officers recorded that at the next relay at Lyons, alone of their group, Napoleon did not celebrate his new liberty with a visit to a local brothel. He did, however, on this journey south, follow in his father's footsteps; he was the only young officer to visit an acquaintance of his family's with a request for letters of introduction to leading citizens in Valence.

In the garrison town, Bonaparte's reading and voluminous note-taking embraced almost every subject except artillery: law, political economy, geography, medicine, sexual mores in Africa. He read the skeptical philosophy of Voltaire and a great deal of history, especially ancient history, with particular emphasis on Alexander the Great; on India, Egypt, Turkey and the more exotic countries of the Middle East—but still about almost nothing to do with his chosen profession. Facts absorbed in his youth, when his memory was faultless, were retained forever. He read the fashionable romantics too, Bernardin de St. Pierre's lachrymose *Paul et Virginie* was his favorite. Above all he read Jean-Jacques Rousseau. At St. Helena he would comment: "Until I was sixteen I would have fought to the death for Rousseau."[3] Thereafter his admiration turned to derision.

At Valence, though, Napoleon was still adopting a neo-Rousseau style for courtship of a kind. In his new uniform—blue coat and breeches, red revers and gold epaulettes—he dined and took tea with some of the local families. Set upon an early and prosperous marriage, he wrote letters in a turgid style to one Adelaïde de St. Germain, and although it was generally understood in the French royal army that only officers with private means could hope to afford marriage before retirement, Second Lieutenant de Bonaparte, aged only seventeen, asked her father for her hand and was courteously refused.

When in 1786 a six-month leave became due, Napoleon returned to his native island. For the first time he met his mother's young half brother Joseph Fesch, and his own younger brothers and sisters born after his departure for Brienne: Luigi was eight years old, Paoletta six, Maria Annunziata four and Girolamo a baby—four future kings, queens and imperial highnesses running barefoot with the family herd of goats.

Although the Buonapartes were the recipients of a good deal of assistance from the French crown, more indeed than any other family on the island, and Giuseppe, Napoleone, Luciano and Anna Maria were all living on French royal scholarships, life at home was of exceptional frugality. Outward appearances, however, were maintained.

Napoleon's notebooks during this stay are filled with the romantic melancholy of a child of the age, nourished on Goethe's *Werther*. In them he sees himself as Rousseau's Virtuous Man—virtue in the Latin sense of the word. Men in Corsica, he wrote, were ruled by love of fatherland, as they had been in Roman and Spartan times, whereas "the French people are entirely absorbed in eroticism." He contrasted the austere life at Casa Buonaparte, the harsh countryside of Corsica, and its poor and frugal society so close to Rousseau's ideals with life in "corrupt, luxury-loving France," and felt that this was indeed his own country, a place where patriotism and a Roman type of civic virtue could flourish. He felt himself to be, like Rousseau, "All alone in the midst of men. . . . What am I to do in this world?" Action was always to be his panacea for melancholy, and he was to discover that action would show him what he was "to do in this world."[4]

At the end of a year in Corsica, Napoleon decided to go to Paris to inquire about a further subsidy for his mother's mulberry bush nursery, a concession granted the Buonapartes by the French crown. We hear no more of the mulberry bush business, nor, in this autumn of 1787, of Lieutenant de Bonaparte's reactions to the mounting tensions in Paris on the eve of the Revolution. He collected his back pay there, however, discovered his lifelong passion for the opera and the theater, and lost his virginity to a young streetwalker plying her trade in the gardens of the Palais Royal.

The arcades of the palace sheltered a variety of shops and eating houses, and were used as a fashionable promenade. The Palais Royal was also then, and throughout the Revolution, the traditional center of prostitution. The more expensive whores had their rooms on the mezzanine of the arcades, from whose half-moon windows they could lean out and call to the passersby, or adopt suggestive poses in the embrasures. The better known ones sent runners circulating in the crowds below to hand out leaflets describing their specialties and prices. Lesser prostitutes lurked in the palace gardens.

Much of young Bonaparte, particularly his thirst for facts and the vital curiosity that would never leave him, is evident in the scene he describes in his private notebooks. As he walked from the theater through the Palais Royal gardens his soul, he wrote, was "agitated by the vigorous sentiments which characterize it, and made me forget the cold."[5] Before taking the girl back to his nearby hotel, he stood talking to her in the gardens, questioning her minutely on the circumstances of the loss of her virginity and the details of her trade.

On one pretext or another, Napoleon had so far taken two years' leave on full pay. When he rejoined the La Fère Regiment in 1788, stationed now at Auxonne in Burgundy, he resumed his studies of history and geography (it was there, in one of his many notebooks of information of all kinds, that he wrote on an otherwise empty page the one poignant line: "St. Helena, a small island"), and he discovered for the first time a passion for the role of artillery and gunnery. For the few months he was to remain with his regiment, Second Lieutenant de Bonaparte studied with a new enthusiasm in the excellent artillery school attached to Auxonne. His superior officers recognized his exceptional talent and encouraged him to write a report on experiments in the use of guns with explosive shells. This was the decade when the role of artillery was being enlarged, as the old tactical principles were being replaced by Comte de Guibert's revolutionary theories stressing the importance of rapidity and of surprise of the enemy—above all of the concentration of numerical superiority on a single target—tactics that would deeply influence Napoleon's own later strategy.

"You should slide over the weak parts," was Napoleon's brisk injunction to one of his biographers at St. Helena.[6] Ambivalent on the subject of all his actions before Vendémiaire, he would remain consistently silent on the years between 1787 and 1793, the six years of which only two were spent in his profession and the rest in gaining invaluable experience in political manipulation—lessons acquired during the leaves he granted himself at the time of France's supreme danger, leaves spent in a manner that neither the future General nor the future Emperor would have tolerated.

In the feverish year of 1789, many of Bonaparte's brother officers saw the abolition of privileges voted on the night of August 4 principally as the opening up to the petty nobility of the higher ranks in the army. But, burdened by no party convictions, still a foreigner in France, Lieutenant de Bonaparte applied for further leave in September of that year and went to Corsica. This time he was to remain there for a year and a half, the beginning of the "lost" years.

With his brothers Joseph and Lucien, Napoleon now entered into the political struggles of his native island. They started by playing the popular and national parties off against each other, first by supporting the national party faithful to Paoli, who had returned from exile in 1790 to scenes of delirious enthusiasm. He was the symbol not only of resistance to the invaders of his island—to the Genoese in the 1720s and to the French in 1768—but the idol of all Europe of the Enlightenment; he had given Corsica a Constituent Assembly and a democratic constitution, and now, at the invitation of the new National Assembly in Paris, returned with a promise of autonomy for the island.

Napoleon's initial letters to Paoli were adulatory, but the leader, who had not forgotten their father's rapid defection, greeted the Bonapartes with some reserve. Thereafter the brothers began to ally themselves with the popular party led by Christophe-Antoine Saliceti, the Corsican representative to the National Assembly in Paris. A sinister-looking man, immensely tall with a long, pockmarked face, he was said to have the subtlest mind in Corsica and his influence on Napoleon's future was to be considerable.

In Corsica, the three older Bonapartes and Representative Saliceti had become involved in some dubious electoral practices that included the kidnapping in March 1792 of a judge believed to be hostile to Joseph Bonaparte's chances of election as deputy to the Assembly in Paris; and in April of that year Napoleon, as a colonel in the local National Guard, had led a Corsican force against French troops at Ajaccio and was in danger not only of being court-martialed but also of being reported absent without leave from his garrison. He had ignored the order from the War Ministry that all officers absent without leave between December 25, 1791 and January 10, 1792, would be discharged, and a further order in February, as the country prepared for war, that all regular officers rejoin their regiments by April 1 at the latest.

When the government declared war on Austria in April 1792, and then on Spain, Austria's ally, French forces were immediately deployed on the northeast frontier and on the Pyrenees. The exiguous Army of the South, to which the La Fère Regiment was attached, was strung out along the south coast. It would be expedient, if he were to be reinstated in the army, for Lieutenant de Bonaparte to plead his case at the Ministry of War.

Arriving in the capital in May 1792, Napoleon found it seething with revolutionary and patriotic agitation. Battalions of volunteers were assembling in Paris from all over the country. That month fifty-four new ones were called up by the Assembly, forty-two more in July. Quickly renouncing the "de" added by Carlo to the family name, but otherwise following in his father's footsteps, he maneuvered his way through government bureaucracy so successfully that he obtained not only back pay—for, in effect, directing a riot against the French regular army in Corsica—but also made sure of the promotion that would have been his had he remained with his regiment.

In the public gallery of the Assembly, Napoleon ran into his old school friend Louis-Antoine Bourrienne, and on June 20 they were seated at a café "near the Palais Royal" when they observed five or six thousand men armed with pikes and muskets "howling the grossest insults," as Napoleon wrote to Joseph, and marching from the Halles section toward the Tuileries Palace. Running ahead of them, the two friends watched the invasion of the palace by the "vilest rabble"—Bonaparte's own term. When the King appeared at one of the palace windows overlooking the gardens, and was seen to agree to the mob's demand to place the red bonnet on his head, Napoleon muttered to Bourrienne, "The fool!"—but the Italian expression was more robust—"he should have turned his cannon on a few hundred of them, and finished them off."[7]

Army enlistments soared in July as, with the Prussian army marching steadily on Paris, Brunswick, the commander in chief of the Prussian and emigré forces, issued his threatening manifesto, and the Assembly declared *"la Patrie en Danger."* Fifteen thousand new volunteers were enrolled in a few days, but the armies were without a commander in chief. Lafayette, who had returned from the front to protest the June invasion of the Tuileries, was now in flight. The new commands went to some of the future generals and marshals of Napoleon's Empire: Davout, Bessières, Bernadotte, Soult. Few were over twenty-four years of age; some had risen from the ranks of the old army of the monarchy; most had been young recruits, the sons of laborers and artisans. The Prussians laughed at the "army of shoemakers and tailors."

These young officers were to remember forever the first time the term "patriotism" was heard in the army. "I still feel its power and its warmth," remembered one of the heroes of the first revolutionary armies, and Stendhal wrote that in the "sublime glow" of 1792 "our only thought was to be useful to our country. Clothes, food, ambition, all were unimportant."[8]

Lieutenant de Bonaparte however, immune to its "power and its warmth," was still in Paris (his business at the Ministry of War not yet finished), when the tocsin rang throughout the night of August 9–10, and he went again to the Tuileries and witnessed the massacre of the Swiss Guards defending the palace and the subsequent mutilation of their bodies. The royal family's flight to safety in the neighboring Assembly marked the end of the monarchy, but "had the King mounted a horse then," Napoleon wrote to Joseph that night, "victory would have been his."[9] And, "how far I was," Napoleon remembered at St. Helena, "as I watched the sack of the Tuileries, from imagining that I would ever live in that palace."[10] The day marked him forever, and his horror of crowds appears to date from this event—a panic that almost lost him the coup of Brumaire, and seized him again in the chaos at the end of his Empire.

The French army's defeats continued in August. After its capitulation at Longwy the road to Paris lay open: the government proclaimed a mass levy and proposed—another first—transferring the Assembly south across the Loire. Although the French army was fleeing before the Austrians, and the La Fère Regiment (now the Fourth Artillery) was serving with the Army of the South, the newly promoted Captain Bonaparte felt greater concern about his brother Joseph's electoral hopes in Corsica. Fortunately, Anna Maria's—now Elisa's—royal school near Versailles was to be shut down, and Napoleon applied for permission to escort his sister "on the dangerous road to Ajaccio," as well as for further leave and for 352 livres "for traveling expenses."

At the end of August 1792, while the Prussian army was advancing upon Paris, Napoleon and his sister journeyed south by easy stages, spending a month in Marseilles and arriving in Corsica at the end of October. Paoli, informed of Bonaparte's arrival, commented that the captain should have immediately rejoined his corps. "Does he not know that France is at war and the Fourth Artillery is fighting with the Army of the South? Where is his duty as an officer?"

When the Convention that month decreed that the "natural frontiers" indispensable to the Republic sanctioned the annexation of Savoy, Belgium and the left bank of the Rhine, it became clear to Paoli that the French revolutionary government would not now grant autonomy to Corsica. In Ajaccio, Saliceti and the Convention's other representatives in Corsica declared war on Paoli when he considered applying to England for help. Napoleon proclaimed his own revolutionary convictions, and in Toulon Lucien, now known as "Brutus" Buonaparte and a pillar of the Jacobin Club there, sent a denunciation of Paoli to the Convention, which, in April 1793, declared the national hero outlawed. A Paolista versus Buonapartista vendetta erupted, and the whole island rose in defense of its leader; with the greatest difficulty Napoleon managed to escape the enraged Paolistas. He was finally rescued by Saliceti on a small coaster bound for Toulon, which then took aboard Letizia and her children, stranded on the coast off Ajaccio. The family house had been sacked, the goat herd and the vines destroyed.

On June 11, 1793, the Corsican Assembly declared the entire Buonaparte family to be "traitors and enemies of the Fatherland, condemned to perpetual execration and infamy."

When the destitute Bonapartes landed at Toulon in June 1793, the situation in France was at its most desperate. In Paris, the Terror had been officially proclaimed in April, and, with the enemy at every frontier, the call to arms sounded in all the sections.

In June, the expulsion of the Girondist deputies from the Convention had been the signal for a revolt of more than half the provinces against the dictatorship of the Jacobin minority in Paris. Royalist Vendée and Brittany were already in rebellion; now the whole of southwestern France was in a state of civil war. Toulon, threatened by the Convention with "execution," had begged for help from the British fleet under Admiral Hood, on condition that the port be taken over in the name of Louis XVII, the imprisoned son of the executed King. The rebellious city of Lyons was being put to fire and the sword by representative-on-mission Joseph Fouché. The guillotine was set up in Bordeaux by the Convention's representative Tallien, and Marseilles was drowned in blood.

These circumstances, together with Lucien's apparently ill-timed denunciation of Paoli, formed the first instance of that luck in which Napoleon already firmly believed. Although he was to say that he "chose" France in the summer of 1793, it was for financial reasons alone that he was now forced to rejoin the army. Far from being considered a deserter or a Corsican separatist, he was reintegrated into the Fourth Artillery now serving with the Army of Italy, with headquarters at Nice. Captain Bonaparte successfully applied again for leave and for three thousand livres in back pay, and was charged with the surveillance of batteries on the coast.

The Corsican network was called into action. In Paris, Saliceti backed Captain Bonaparte's claim to the Convention for compensation for his losses in Corsica, where, in his own words, he had "sacrificed all for his ideals." The Assembly promptly voted 600,000 livres to the family of "Corsican Jacobin patriots." When Saliceti returned to Marseilles as one of the Convention's representatives sent to organize the brutal repression there, he obtained a lucrative post for Lucien in a small town on the coast; for Joseph, service attached to a war commissary in Marseilles; and for Letizia Bonaparte and her four younger children, lodgings in the same city.

Napoleon had left Corsica with the reputation of an extreme radical, which would prove useful for political promotion in the France of 1793. In France he began by playing a double game between the Girondists and the Jacobins—he boasted at St. Helena that he had had an "understanding" with the former. He may have taken some part—his actions during this period are uncertain—in the terrible repression at Marseilles that summer,[11] and been impressed by the superior firepower of the Jacobins. In Corsica he had begun to learn the language to use with those in power, as well as the advantages of self-promotion, and in July, while he was in Avignon organizing a convoy of gunpowder for the Army of Italy, he wrote and published at his own expense a Jacobin propaganda pamphlet, the *Souper de Beaucaire,* so successful that the local representative-on-mission—Saliceti again—had it reprinted at government expense. The pamphlet was an adroit mixture of flattery of the local representatives, criticism of lukewarm patriots ("Marat and Robespierre! These are my saints!") and abuse of Paoli, and although there is still a trace of his earlier declamatory style, Napoleon's own concise and individual prose now emerged for the first time. As First Consul, Bonaparte was to order the police to destroy every copy they could find of the *Souper.*

At St. Helena, while revising his life for posterity, Napoleon dictated to General Bertrand that he was "in Paris when the Committee of Public

Safety chose me to recapture Toulon."[12] The circumstances were somewhat different.

Ordered to return to the Army of Italy headquarters in September 1793, Bonaparte was on his way from Marseilles to Nice when he stopped off to see Saliceti, now a political commissar with the republican army assembling to recover Toulon. Saliceti brought his protégé to the attention of the two principal representatives, Paul Barras and Stanislas Fréron, both major figures in the National Convention. It so happened that the commander of artillery had been seriously wounded the previous week; Barras and Fréron immediately replaced him with Captain Bonaparte. One after the other, the two deputies had already transferred the incompetent commanding generals, Jacobin political appointees to a man. The present one, Carteaux, a former house painter, was not pleased to have this overpowering young officer countermand his instructions. However, as a Jacobin agitator, Corelli Barnett reminds us that "Bonaparte's own political pedigree was unimpeachable."

At Toulon in 1793, for the first time Captain Bonaparte, the student of gunnery, the artillery officer educated for sixteen years at the expense of France, was accomplishing the duty for which he had been trained since 1784, and showing himself to be a formidable artillery officer, a budding tactician and a born strategist. He placed his batteries in position to rake both the port and the British fleet and on a December night of violent winds, thunder and rain, his strategy was put into effect; taking two fortresses by surprise, he turned the British batteries against Toulon and the enemy's own ships. As land and sea were lit by exploding guns, burning ships and lightning, Toulon surrendered on December 18.

Above all, it was Bonaparte's forcefulness and energy that impressed his superiors and had played an all-important part in the recapture of Toulon. His "indefatigable activity" and the fact that he never left his batteries but slept beside them, wrapped in his coat, were mentioned in the representatives' enthusiastic dispatches to the Convention.

His physical courage, too, had been evident. He was to say later that it was at Toulon that he had first known himself to be invulnerable—protected, as he would believe all his life, by his "star." Though given to crossing himself in moments of stress, Napoleon would always find it difficult to accept that a man might be a believer. ("Religion," he said, "is suitable only for weak minds and for women."[13]) He was, nevertheless, deeply superstitious, with a faith in amulets and, though he would deny it, in soothsayers.

At Paul Barras's request, Captain Bonaparte was promoted to the temporary rank of brigadier general after the submission of a written questionnaire. This document, which escaped the wholesale destruction of Napoleon's army files during the Consulate, is understandably filled with misrepresentations, including a denial that he had ever been a student at the Royal Military School.

The fall of Toulon was followed by yet another fearful massacre—bloodshed accompanied by many examples of "revolutionary sensibility." Joseph Fouché, who had hurried south from Lyons to join the pillaging and murder, wrote to one of his colleagues in Paris: "Tonight we will execute 1,213 insurgents. Adieu, tears of joy flow from my eyes and drench my soul."[14]

When Representatives Barras and Fréron moved on to Marseilles in the new year to introduce the Law of Suspects currently terrorizing Paris, Brigadier General Bonaparte, promoted to commander of artillery in the Army of Italy, established his headquarters there too. And there for the first time he made the acquaintance of the Clarys.

The Bonaparte family's position in Marseilles had been materially improved by the friendship and protection of this prosperous merchant family—a protection that had worked both ways. Following its revolt against Jacobin domination the previous summer, Marseilles, like Paris, had become a city of street patrols and denunciations. The guillotine had been set up and a revolutionary tribunal installed. When young Nicolas Clary, who had taken some part in the revolt, was arrested in September, his liberation was due partly to the intervention of Joseph Bonaparte, whose family's impeccably revolutionary background was as useful to Clary as was the Clarys' fortune to the indigent Corsicans.

When Napoleon arrived in Marseilles he found that the Bonaparte women no longer had to make ends meet by taking in laundry and that Joseph was conducting a serious courtship of Nicolas's twenty-two-year-old sister, Julie. Napoleon—his brother informed him that the girls' dowry was 100,000 francs each—soon initiated a flirtation with the younger sister, Désirée.

But in April 1794, Napoleon was back again in Nice. His new position at the Army of Italy's headquarters came as a result of the protection of Saliceti, that friend and patron of all the Bonapartes and now one of the Convention's representatives to the army; of Jean-François Ricord, another representative; and above all of Augustin Robespierre, younger brother of the all-powerful Maximilien and chief delegate of the Convention, with total power over all military and civilian operations in the region. "Bon-Bon" Robespierre wrote to his brother that General Bonaparte was "an ardent republican of transcendental merit, who had resisted the caresses of Paoli."[15] He had placed the General, he reported, in command of the military planning of a proposed campaign against Italy.

This was the beginning of what might be termed one of the two great love affairs of Napoleon's life, the one that preceded his passion for Josephine: the operational plan "to open Piedmont to the armies of the Republic." For the projected attack he drew on all he had read of the wars of ancient history and of the work of the strategists of his own century, principally on Guibert's advocacy of offensive warfare wherever possible, and, above all, of the division of forces in mountainous country.

France was still at war with Austria and Lazare Carnot, the member of the Committee of Public Safety in charge of defense, was in favor of attacking the enemy on the frontier of Spain (Austria's ally). General Bonaparte's plan, however, was to strike at the Austrians on the southern flank of their Empire and he urged Paris to consider that Austria could, after a French victory, be attacked through Lombardy and Tyrol. "The patriotic spirit of the Spaniards," he argued, "would necessitate the use of far larger forces than the Republic can command"—excellent advice that he himself would neglect fifteen years later.

Napoleon's new position and pay in the summer of 1794 enabled him to install his mother and youngest brothers and sisters at Château Sallé, a property outside the small fishing village of Antibes. At the siege of Toulon, he had attached to himself Sergeant Andoche Junot as aide. Junot, sent to escort the family from Marseilles, immediately lost his head over Paoletta, now Pauline, a fourteen-year-old beauty who could barely read or write, and who already showed signs of Napoleon's own egotism and ruthlessness.

These traits were present in most of the young members of the family. All would be seen by their awed contemporaries as vengeful, calculating and supremely possessed of "that calm audacity, that perfect cynicism of all the Buonapartes, fit subject of astonishment for their biographers."[16] Although physically they all resembled their handsome mother, the offspring of Carlo and Letizia appeared to be evenly divided in their inheritance from each parent. While Napoleon, Lucien, Elisa and Caroline were cynical, ambitious and calculating, Joseph, Louis and Jérôme inherited something of their father's easygoing nature. Yet, although as unscrupulous as Napoleon, as pleasure-seeking as her father, narcissistic Pauline alone would show something of her mother's heroism when she joined the dethroned Emperor at Elba while the others scuttled for hiding or bargained to keep what they could of his rewards.

Joseph, now married to Julie Clary, was included in the Antibes household. Lucien was not. To his mother's—and Napoleon's—disgust he had married the local innkeeper's penniless sister. Neither Letizia nor Napoleon would ever stop trying to have him abandon his signally happy marriage for a better match. Lucien, though an opportunist like all his family, would maintain his republican principles all his life. He summed up his doubts about his brother that summer in a letter to Joseph: "I have always," he wrote, "been aware of a completely selfish ambition in Napoleone. He seems to me to have the potentialities of a tyrant, and I believe that he would be one were he a king, and that his name would be held in horror by posterity."[17]

Julie's sister, Désirée, too, stayed at the Château Sallé that summer, but Napoleon did not at that time pursue his never very ardent courtship of her. He was proceeding with another attempt at marriage with a girl with a dowry. Just outside Nice he lodged in a house surrounded by orange groves, the property of Comte de Laurenti, a man of some means. When Napoleon asked for the hand of sixteen-year-old Emilie de Laurenti, her father gently refused it "for the present," pointing out that General Bonaparte might not return from the projected Italian campaign.

The coup of Thermidor and the fall of Robespierre, however, put an end to Napoleon's operational plan as well as, apparently, to his career. The news reached Nice in early August. Augustin Robespierre, in Paris at the time, had been outlawed with his brother and guillotined with him the following day. Napoleon himself was arrested in Nice and suspended from his functions by Saliceti, possibly as a measure to protect a man of his own faction from dispatch to Paris and the guillotine. Bonaparte's imprisonment turned out to be only an agreeable house arrest at the Laurentis's—Emilie's parents had prudently dispatched her to stay with cousins at Grasse—ending with his release on August 24.

Immediately after his arrest Napoleon had written to the Convention denouncing "Robespierre's conspiracy,"[18] and denying his friendship with either brother. "Men," as he would later affirm, "are moved by two motives only: fear and self-interest."[19]

Thermidor had permitted Lazare Carnot, still war minister of the Committee of Public Safety, to halt the projected offensive of the Army of Italy. But Brigadier General Bonaparte was not given back his command. He was simply reintegrated into the army and attached to the planning of an expedition against the British fleet—an expedition that, in spite of some brilliant strategic planning on his part, ended disastrously for the French.

Representatives-on-mission carried more weight than commanders in the field and Bonaparte spent an increasing amount of time in courting the former. Young Representative Turreau had brought his pretty wife to Nice, and when Bonaparte embarked on a brief affair with Louise Turreau he found that her help in promoting his views with her husband was decisive. "This was a great advantage to me,"[20] he remembered. Earlier in the year Napoleon's subordinates, with whom he was not popular, noted with relish his deference to Mme Ricord, the wife of another representative; younger officers described him as "alternately sycophantic and violent," and aped his holding Mme Ricord's fan and her horse's bridle, hat in hand. Bonaparte's commanding officer, General Schérer, who had not been amused to watch the Turreau power play nor, presumably, the small battle that Napoleon later boasted he had organized for Louise Turreau's pleasure,* complained of him to the Committee of Public Safety. Fearful, however, of Bonaparte's political protection, he asked only to be rid of persons he referred to vaguely as "Corsican officers whose patriotism is less certain than is their disposition to enrich themselves."[21]

General Bonaparte's inspection of the coastal batteries continued. Before the Grande Corniche roads linked the towns of the Riviera, these

---

* "It cost the lives of four or five soldiers," Napoleon would tell General Bertrand at St. Helena.

journeys involved two choices: either of sailing from one port to another, keeping close to the shoreline to avoid the British fleet—for Napoleon this method had the added inconvenience of seasickness—or of skirting the sides of the mountains plunging steeply into the sea. For this, his carriage would often require teams of oxen to haul it over the steep dusty paths in summer and out of the muddy ravines in winter.

Napoleon started writing to Désirée Clary throughout that autumn and winter, whenever he was not in Marseilles. He addressed her as Eugénie. Although this was an era of name changes—the Buonapartes themselves had gallicized their first names and in some cases changed them entirely—Napoleon's aim was somewhat different. He considered Eugénie more romantic, more dignified than Désirée. And it had not been associated with any other person. Both the possessive and the romantic considerations would be repeated when he renamed Marie-Joseph-Rose de Beauharnais "Josephine."

Napoleon had decided ideas on all subjects, and his letters to Désirée prefigure many future ones of detailed advice to wives, brothers, mistresses and marshals: on dress, on sex, on protocol, on budgets, on fortifications and army rations. At least until 1806, when the first signs of intellectual and physical deterioration appeared, his powers of concentration were as intense when discussing trivia as they were in the details of warfare or statecraft.

Now he was writing Désirée a stream of letters on what books she should read, on how to improve her piano-playing, her singing, her manners. They are not the letters of a man in love, and when Désirée gently reproached him for his lack of sensibility, Napoleon's answer was a brutal reminder of her own shortcomings.

Désirée, however, was a romantic before her time. Writing in the 1830s, high tide of the literary romantic movement in Paris, Laure d'Abrantès recalled: "When I first knew Désirée, she had a prodigious liking for all that was melancholy and *romantic*. The term then was unknown. Now that we know *what* it is, its resemblance to madness is less obvious."[22] The tart comment is typical of many later ones by contemporaries; perhaps some of the unkind references to the future Swedish Queen's shortness and girth were prompted by jealousy of her astounding elevation, which seemed particularly unfair in view of her lack of beauty.

In 1794 she was a good-natured, affectionate, plump sixteen-year-old with a warm smile and slightly bulging black eyes, whose strong family feeling extended from her adored sister to Joseph, and who easily fell in love with Joseph's forceful young brother.

Although, in a violent reaction to Rousseau's influence, Napoleon had written in his notebook that spring, "Love I believe to be harmful to society and to the individual. . . . Always be master of your soul," the tone of his letters had softened. "You are always in my thoughts, I have never doubted your love, my sweet Eugénie, how can you think I could ever cease to love you?"[23] he wrote. Their most intimate moments when they were together at Marseilles appear to have been confined to long walks and the pressing of hands, in spite of Napoleon's assertion to General Bertrand at St. Helena that: "I made Bernadotte [Désirée's husband] a marshal and then a king only because I had taken Désirée's virginity at Marseilles." The second part of this "revelation" may well be as inaccurate as the first—that he "made Bernadotte King of Sweden"[24]—an elevation he would strongly oppose when he was Emperor.

Bonaparte was in Marseilles on April 16, 1795, when an order came from the Committee of Public Safety to proceed immediately to the Army of the West. The time was ill chosen for Napoleon, for although he and Désirée considered themselves unofficially engaged, the Clary family would not hear of the marriage. Indeed, they had been heard to object that one Bonaparte in the family was quite enough.

Not only was it irritating to leave Marseilles with this matter still unsettled, but there could be no question of obeying orders to proceed to the Army of the West. Vendée was not a field of action that offered either personal glory or fortune. The Great Committee would have to be appealed to directly.

Perhaps out of old habit, however, Napoleon's notion of dispatch was somewhat torpid. By May 8 he was ready to leave Marseilles accompanied by Andoche Junot and Auguste Marmont, both officers removed without permission from the Army of Italy. As his post chaise drove off, Désirée, in tears, went straight to her room to compose the first of the rough drafts of the letters she wrote to him that summer. "You left half an hour ago . . . only the thought of knowing you forever faithful . . . ," she wrote, and across the pages splotched with tears, she trails off into "B . . . Buona . . . *Général à l'Armée.*"[25]

Bonaparte, Junot and Marmont traveled north by slow stages, investigating likely nationalized properties for sale. Joseph had been struck off the list of war commissioners as a result of Thermidor, and his brother was looking for ways of investing the Clary dowry for him. We get a lively picture of Bonaparte's appearance and manner in May 1795 from Victorine de Chastenay, a thoughtful, intelligent young woman of the General's own age, who observed him when they met at the home of Marmont's parents in Burgundy. Excessively pale and thin, his hollow cheeks framed in long greasy hair, he exactly resembled, she said, the Jacques-Louis David sketch made of him later in the year. His manners were brutal. Mme Marmont confided that she was distressed by her guest's "total and steadfast silence," and after Victorine had sung a ballad in Italian and asked the young officer whether her pronunciation was correct, his answer was simply: "No."[26] But Victorine was intrigued by the intensity of the General's expression and by his monosyllabic answers at the dinner table.

The following day when dinner—still at two o'clock in provincial Burgundy—was over, she and Napoleon stood talking, leaning against a marble console, while the rest of the party made bouquets of cornflowers in the garden. Their conversation lasted for four hours. He poured out his literary and political views, his fondness for the fashionable (and spurious) poems of Ossian*; his detestation of happy endings (he would leave the theater, he said, if one appeared imminent), and of Shakespeare ("It's impossible to finish any of his plays, they are pitiful").

As for his political views, it was clear to Victorine that "Bonaparte would just as soon have emigrated if emigration had offered any chance of success." She could not, she recalled, discern "any sign of republican conviction or beliefs"—or of any others. "Toulon," she guessed correctly, "might have had him as its defender, if its defeat had not been an element in his plans ... he was still an adventurer and was never to take an unsuccessful step."[27]

The young men traveled much faster after learning at the next relay of the events in Paris.

Bread rationing had broken down; there had been calls for the return of the Terror "when blood flowed, but there was bread." On May 18 a mob of hungry men and women had broken down the doors of the

---

* This romantic, archaic poetry had been faked by one Macpherson.

Convention hall at the Tuileries Palace, where the Assembly was sitting. A deputy who attempted to argue with them was shot dead and his head presented on a pike to the terrified president, Boissy d'Anglas. By midnight the hall was finally cleared by regular troops.

The Convention had been badly shaken by this apparent resurgence of the left, and the deputies proceeded to guillotine or deport to Guiana the remnants of the more radical Jacobins.

It was clear that the balance of power in Paris had shifted again. Napoleon had pinned his hopes of avoiding the posting in Vendée on the deputies Turreau and Ricord, but they, like other army officers suspected of Jacobinism, like Bonaparte himself, were now being purged.

❧ 7 ❧

I Knew Only Barras

UNAWARE THAT A NOTE IN HIS FILE READ: "BONAPARTE IS THE PERSON-ification of intrigue and deceit . . . somewhat too much ambition and love of manipulation to be promoted," Napoleon proceeded to the Ministry of War the day after his arrival in Paris. He was determined to avoid service in the Army of the West, and went with few doubts of being able to continue his old habit of choosing when and where to serve.

Captain Aubry, the Committee of Public Safety's delegate at the ministry, informed him that since there were already too many artillery generals he, as the last of them to be promoted, could not retain this rank, but as a special favor was to be given an infantry brigade in Vendée. Aware that the Republic, all too rich in generals, might readily accept the resignation of his commission, Bonaparte decided to apply for two Décadis (twenty days in the republican calendar) of sick leave, intending apparently to play for time and to appeal to influential friends.

On no account would he consider going to Vendée. His reasons for not wishing to join his new post were clear, though not precisely those indicated in the *Mémorial* written at St. Helena. In it he asserted that it would have been repugnant to him to take part in a civil war. "A sort of instinct," wrote one nineteenth-century historian, "made the idea of civil war repellent to him."[1] But he had known only civil wars so far, and no such reluctance had been apparent in Ajaccio or Toulon. In Paris two years earlier he had felt nothing but contempt for the King who had failed to order fire on the rioting Parisians; and the true starting point of his own career would come in October of that year, when his famous "whiff of grapeshot" would subdue those same civilians.

Bonaparte was also aware that fighting in Vendée would mean placing himself under the orders of General Lazare Hoche, who had been a commanding general since the age of twenty-three, had led the Army of Moselle before being imprisoned under the Terror and was generally considered the ideal republican officer. Not only did Napoleon's jealous nature rebel at the idea of serving under so prestigious a commander, but he also guessed that Hoche, brought up in the strict traditions of the Army of the Northeast, would have reacted to Bonaparte's customary insubordination exactly as Napoleon himself was to do later. His own series of unauthorized year-long leaves were everything the future Emperor would most deplore, and any officer mixing in militant politics would be excluded from employment under the Empire. About matters of leave, too, he would be adamant. In 1809, General Lasalle, a hero of the Spanish War and on his way to being killed at the Battle of Wagram, dared only, he said, stay in Paris long enough "to order a pair of boots and give my wife a child." And another general who had awarded himself a few days' "unofficial leave" received the following notice: "Unless you rejoin your regiment immediately, you will be shot before midday."

Furthermore, Lazare Hoche, an officer with an irreproachable past whom the Jacobins had almost sent to the guillotine, would probably have suspected that Bonaparte owed his promotion to those same Jacobins. And Napoleon's own promotion had been far from rapid by the standards of the time; he himself would have been surprised to learn that posterity would not notice the unusual fact that in this period of rapid promotions he had remained a lieutenant for seven years, the very years when France needed officers to replace the cadres of emigrés. True, he was a general at twenty-four, but there was nothing unusual in this in the France of 1795. The revolutionary military leaders had almost without exception been very young men. Davout was a general at twenty-three, Augereau and Masséna became "permanent" generals at the same age, Marceau a commanding general at twenty-four; and most of them had risen from the ranks. To his marshals he would always be a "civil war general" who had chosen not to fight by their side in the dangerous days.

The three young men, Napoleon, Marmont and Junot, had little money among them, though Joseph Bonaparte would assert in his *Mémoires* that his brother was never as destitute as he would later claim, and that he retained his full pay of brigadier general. Generals on half pay received eight livres and rations for two persons each month, part of which Napoleon sent to his mother. The Republic also provided each officer with the "national bread" loaves, which they brought to the house of Mme Permon, where they dined regularly until the day that Citizen General Barras, carelessly generous, invited Bonaparte to take all his dinners with him.

Panoria Permon, a striking-looking woman in her forties, was a Corsican friend of the Bonaparte family, whose house had been a haven for Napoleon on his free days at the Royal Military School. Her daughter Laure* had been an infant then; now she was an alert nine-year-old who laughed at General Bonaparte's appearance and, because his reedy legs were engulfed in too large boots, she called him, to his intense irritation, Puss in Boots.

In the gardens of the Palais Egalité the young men ran into Napoleon's old school friend Antoine Bourrienne, and together they visited the theaters, promenades and new eating houses opening up in the city. Junot would later tell his wife that they spent most of their time making plans for the future and thinking up financial projects; but only Bonaparte, Junot would remember, spent his time "calling on anyone with influence, and knocking on every door. He soon became known for this."[2]

In these early, unoccupied days of his "sick leave" Napoleon was free to examine Paris in Floréal, the "month of flowers" of Year III of the Republic. When he had left the capital three years earlier, the guillotine had been at work, the country in danger. Now, five days after the bread riots of May, the chestnut trees were in blossom and the city, only half recovered from the Terror, was money-, dance- and clothes-mad, ignoring the drums still beating the call to arms, the fear of further riots, of famine and of the war at every frontier. As he wrote to his brother Joseph: "The memory of the Terror is no more than a nightmare here. Everyone appears determined to make up for what they have suffered; determined, too, because of the uncertain future, not to miss a single pleasure of the present."[3]

Under the Palais Egalité arcades the young provincials listened to gossip on the two subjects of almost equal interest in Paris—the feverish

---

* As Duchesse d'Abrantès, Laure would become the celebrated memorialist of the imperial court.

fluctuations of the stock market and the latest activities of Mme Tallien, not only the single figure to escape Parisians' criticism, but also regarded by many of them as the reason for their very existence. Thérésia's suppers, the number of her shawls, and above all the domination she exerted through her salon and the men who were a part of it were the staples of conversation. The young officers noted that outside the theaters it was always the violet-colored carriage of the Citoyenne Tallien which was called first, and that when she was driven off to wild applause, a flying wedge of Muscadins accompanied her to the Chaumière.

In the midst of all this revelry it was the insistent presence of women everywhere that appears to have most impressed the chaste young general. At the promenades and in the theaters, Napoleon stared at the provocatively undressed women whose tunics, wrote a caustic Sébastien Mercier, "have no pockets. In order to further reveal their natural contours, the fan is placed in the belt of a fashionable woman, the purse in her bosom, the handkerchief in the pocket of her escort . . . and these are the times which have succeeded Robespierre's!"[4]

At St. Helena, Napoleon admitted that in Paris "I knew no one, only Barras; I attached myself to Barras."[5] And Barras in his own *Mémoires* records that that summer he "took General Bonaparte to the salons of Mme Tallien, Mme de Staël . . . and to several other houses where he dined and was made welcome."[6]

Although Bonaparte's trenchant, perceptive views of the French nation and its destiny would be embodied in letters throughout the summer to Joseph, his earliest ones are full of his astonishment at the leading role of women. "Everywhere in Paris you see beautiful women," Napoleon wrote to his brother. "Here alone of all places on earth they appear to hold the reins of government, and the men make fools of themselves over them, think only of them and live only for them. . . . A woman needs to come to Paris for six months to learn what is her due, and to understand her own power. Here only, they deserve to control so much influence."[7] Predictably, it was the revelation of their power which had most impressed Bonaparte.

"Mme Tallien, Mme de Beauharnais, Mme Récamier and Mme Hamelin, pursuing the current fantasies of Greco-Roman dress and decoration . . . are of more consequence than all five armies on the five fronts," reported Espinchal, one of the great gossips of the century, to his spymasters in London.[8]

Although the military situation of the Republic was of little interest to General Bonaparte that summer, those five armies had been victorious on every front since Thermidor; they liberated the entire territory of France and, owing to the freezing of the rivers and canals of the Low Countries, captured, by a daring cavalry attack across the ice, the entire Dutch fleet.

But it was the women "holding the reins of government" in the political salons who were the subject of General Bonaparte's attention. He observed them with a mixture of admiration and alarm, and not one of their lives would be untouched by him. Rose de Beauharnais would be one of the few not to be disastrously affected by the misfortune of having reigned in that Thermidorian year, when the General was "Barras's little Italian protégé."

As Emperor, Napoleon would do his best to wreck the life of Juliette Récamier. In the frenzy of the Thermidorian drawing rooms, this eighteen-year-old appeared as chastity personified. Dressed always in white, she seemed to be a fragile figure out of a Greuze painting. It was said that her marriage to a rich and elderly banker was unconsummated and that her rebuffs to her admirers came from a physical disability on her part. Their advances were known never to be rewarded, though with "inflexible sweetness" she transformed this sentiment into lasting friendship. Some were provoked by her air of inaccessible divinity and believed that she fled masculine admiration the more surely to attract it. Her narcissism was legendary. Later, on a visit to London, she would astonish the admiring onlookers in Hyde Park by "the ingenuous pride with which she offered her beauty as a spectacle."[9] But there was strength and courage, too, in Juliette Récamier, and later she would dare to become the object of Napoleon's implacable hostility by her refusal either to acknowledge his advances or give up her friendship with Mme de Staël. The Emperor's revenge for these two offenses would be complete.

Fortunée Hamelin, an independent spirit, thought Juliette Récamier a prude and played a cruel trick on her to prove it; it delighted her to announce that she had found Juliette in compromising circumstances with her own lover, Casimir de Montrond. This nineteen-year-old Creole, high-spirited, hardly beautiful (in old age her face was said to resemble a bulldog's), lived a full life, enjoying equally politics, numerous love affairs and solid friendships. Her turn of phrase and sparkling wit were unforgettable. Fortunée was to be a warm and faithful friend at a difficult moment in Josephine's and Napoleon's lives, and her veneration for him would continue throughout her own, uninfluenced by her banishment from the imperial court because of her Thermidorian past.

There was Rose de Beauharnais—remarkable only for being Mme Tallien's closest friend—and wild Aimée de Coigny. A Swiss visitor, Henri Meister, in his study of Paris after Thermidor, noted that "many of the liaisons started in prison or during the days of danger, continued thereafter; sometimes they ended in marriage."[10] Rose de Beauharnais's own liaison continued after prison; Aimée de Coigny's, like Mme Tallien's, had ended in marriage and like her, Aimée had married her own savior immediately after Thermidor.

Nothing could have provided a greater contrast than Aimée's hasty civil marriage to Casimir de Montrond that year and her first one ten years earlier to the Duc de Fleury. Then, the bride and groom were both fifteen, the setting a royal palace, the season spring. This winter the Montronds returned from a freezing village town hall to their nearby cottage; Aimée was in love, Casimir hopeful of obtaining the remains of his wife's once-vast fortune as his debts were considerable. Neither was of the stuff of which durable marriages are made.

The painter Elisabeth Vigée-Lebrun, finishing Aimée's portrait before the Revolution, described her "enchanting face, her burning eyes, the figure of a Venus." Her original mind and her wit caused a sensation in the constitutionalist salon of the Palais Royal, and its unofficial hostess, Mme de Genlis, though admitting Aimée's conquest of the Orléans headquarters, thought her frivolous and scatterbrained, and her "fits of gaiety have something manic, even indecent."

Throughout the dark days Aimée retained this gaiety, as well as a remarkable lack of judgment in all matters. Caring nothing for reputation, fortune or rank she sacrificed them all with style. Her recklessness in love, her indifference to its cost—in every sense—was total. Unlike many of the Merveilleuses, the material aspect of life meant nothing to her, and unlike most of them she could not share her heart.

To avoid arrest during the Revolution, she divorced her husband when he emigrated to Koblenz, a common custom. When she arrived in London she fell in love with dangerous Montrond, "*le beau* Montrond," the adventurer personified, who lived on debts and gambling, making a game of the emigration and no secret of their liaison. Apparently for no better reason than that they were bored with exile, the imprudent pair returned to France on the eve of the Terror. By March 1794 they had been denounced and were sharing a cell at the St. Lazare prison in Paris. Montrond set about organizing a mess; Aimée herself was unaware that this was to be her immortal hour. It is not known whether she ever spoke more than a few words to a fellow prisoner, the unprepossessing-looking Citizen André Chénier. In despair at their nearness to death and ravished by her beauty, Chénier wrote "*La jeune captive*" for her, and as he left for the scaffold he gave her the manuscript of this most famous poem of the Revolution; a tragic, ironic elegy, full of hate against the Jacobins who were destroying his France. Chénier went to the guillotine on July 25 (7 Thermidor). Montrond, by promising one hundred gold louis to the man who made up the daily list of suspects for the Revolutionary Tribunal, managed to have his name and Aimée's removed day by day, so they were still at St. Lazare on 9 Thermidor.

Casimir de Montrond himself was a man so perfectly at ease in the post-Thermidorian world and his self-assurance was so staggering that it was even noted on his passport under "special particularities." After Aimée had sold all her properties to pay for Casimir's unending expenses, the Montronds were divorced. His own sentimental life was to cross that of Fortunée Hamelin, Pauline Bonaparte and a score of others, but his one faithful relationship remained his friendship with Talleyrand. Men of the eighteenth century, they shared the same skepticism and the same taste for women and for gambling. Whereas Casimir, with Talleyrand, followed the fortunes of the Emperor until together they deserted him, Aimée's own opposition to Napoleon started in 1800 when he first exiled Mme de Staël.

It would be Napoleon's contempt for Germaine de Staël's views, his personal dislike of her as an intellectual woman and later as the soul of the resistance against his despotism, which would become the determining influence on her life.

Sent back to France in 1795 to negotiate the official Swedish recognition of the French Republic, Baron de Staël was the first envoy of a foreign government to be received by the Convention, and consequently Germaine de Staël had, at long last, returned to Paris in May from her parents' house in Switzerland. From there she had engineered the escape from France of a number of friends, then, finding that she could not live without either conversation or the presence of her lover Louis de Narbonne, she traveled to England to spend four months in the Surrey countryside where Talleyrand, Narbonne and a number of other constitutionalists had taken refuge. Fanny Burney, the novelist, wrote that before meeting the French circle she had had no idea of what conversation could be. The group felt more comfortable away from London, where the liberal aristocrats were tolerated only by some members of the British opposition and detested by the French ultra-royalist emigrés, who regarded them as truly responsible for the Revolution.

When shortly thereafter the British government invited Charles-Maurice de Talleyrand to leave the country, he decided to emigrate to the United States because, he said, he preferred to go to a country not at war with France. Later it would be Germaine alone who would be responsible both for his return to France and for his subsequent nomination as minister of external relations. That summer her aim at the Swedish embassy in the rue de Bac on the Left Bank—an island now, in the desert of empty houses of the aristocracy—was similar to Mme Tallien's: to reconcile revolutionaries and royalists, the survivors of the Terror with the new men. She was determined to back the Thermidorians, and she believed that her constitutionalist friends must return and rally to the Republic and to public life. Equally disgusted by the Chaumière and the Swedish embassy, the royalist agent Mallet du Pan* described the gatherings as evenings where "the Tallien woman is adored as a queen, and Mme de Staël flaunts her impudence and her immorality."[11]

That summer the men at the political salons were only of secondary interest to General Bonaparte. One of them, however, Gabriel Ouvrard, the banker and speculator, was to be close not only to Thérésia Tallien and Rose de Beauharnais, but was to become the indispensable man in emergencies under both the Consulate and Empire, and the Emperor

---

* An early moderate revolutionary, he was later a secret agent of the court of Vienna.

cordially hated him for this and for other reasons. Twenty-five years old, adored by women, enveloped in an aura of mystery, Ouvrard went so far as to pay journalists not to write about him. Bold, imaginative and generous, he was interested in only the most farsighted ventures. He had made his first millions by the age of twenty-three. That summer his wife and children remained in his native Brittany; later he would be Thérésia's lover and the father of four of her children. To Rose and to everyone or some consequence, or of none at all, he lent money and credit and gave endless hospitality all his life.

There was still a black market in theater tickets in the summer of 1795. Although literature had been all but nonexistent during the Revolution, and the press newly influential, it was the theaters that were the most powerful social and political influence as Bonaparte, a lifelong lover of the stage, would never forget. Every night, Parisians eager to escape from reality crowded to them, and to see the star of the Comédie-Française, the actor Joseph Talma. In spite of the stigma of his recent Jacobinism, Talma was another member of the Chaumière circle and soon became a close friend of Napoleon's, who as Emperor would apply to him for lessons in elocution. The actor had convulsed his audience with laughter when he first appeared in a classical drama dressed as a Roman instead of in the traditional seventeenth-century costume, and he was the first actor to replace pompous declamation with simple diction.

What was left of the world of the other arts, too, collected at the Chaumière. The composers Méhul and Cherubini, friends of the Talliens, would continue to play a part in Napoleon's life; and although Beethoven pronounced Luigi Cherubini to be the composer of opera he admired most among the living, he was to be more celebrated in Paris for having tersely informed the Emperor that a man could be a genius on the battlefield and still know nothing of harmony. The two Duplessis', Louis Boilly, Carle Vernet and Jean-Baptiste Isabey, who had painted all the revolutionary scenes and personalities, were starting to record at the Chaumière the rulers of the future. Isabey's charming sketch of Mme Bonaparte was made that year, and only nine years later he would create the costumes of every last figure at the imperial coronation, and paint the face of the Empress Josephine on that occasion too.

Although throughout the country there was a general indifference to politics, an exhausted apathy, the members of the Convention still reigned at the Chaumière. In the youthful gatherings there, the deputies Paul Barras and Stanislas Fréron, both aged forty, stood out as elderly men. Napoleon had objected to Fréron's projected marriage to his sister Pauline principally on the grounds of his age, and Talleyrand would write to Mme de Genlis without irony and in, to us, the most formal terms: "Only a Revolution and my advanced age permit me to employ expressions which I would never formerly have dared to use."[12] He was forty-one.

The Revolution had been made by men in their twenties. Of all the revolutionary leaders, only Lafayette would live beyond the age of forty. Danton had died at thirty-two, Robespierre at thirty-six, Saint-Just at twenty-five. At the Chaumière, Jean-Lambert Tallien was twenty-seven, the banker Ouvrard twenty-eight. Thérésia Tallien at twenty-one had been twice married, divorced, ruled one city and helped topple a regime.

Nevertheless, the ex-Vicomte de Barras dominated the gatherings at the Chaumière. Since his resourceful actions at Thermidor, his influence had been growing steadily. The only former aristocrat of the deputies, and perhaps the most genuinely republican by conviction, Paul Barras was a tall man with a sarcastic mouth, piercing black eyes and an easy manner. His forebears had fought in the Crusades and acted in the medieval Courts of Love. One ancestress had been canonized. An uncle, Melchior de Barras, had played an important role in the American War, contributing to the victory of Chesapeake and the taking of Yorktown.

Before the Revolution Barras had fought with some distinction against the British in India, where his courage was proverbial and where he was said, on slender evidence, to have acquired "equivocal tastes." Upon his return to France, he was nearly sent to the Bastille for threatening to strike the minister of war, who had refused to listen to his account of the incompetence of some of the officers in the Indian campaign.

Cashiered from the army, he appears to have lived the next ten years on women and gambling. His enemies asserted that he cheated at cards, and it is true that he was never overscrupulous about the source of his funds. He became a friend of some of the champions of the "new ideas," and was among the earliest members of the Jacobin Club. He watched the fall of the Bastille in 1789 with a soldier's surprise that the four regiments close by made no move to defend it. By 1790 he was elected a deputy, and in Paris on August 10, watching Louis XVI abandon his palace, he noted that the success of a revolutionary "day" depended essentially on "order, movement and a man."

His political views were so displeasing to his mother that she prevailed upon him to return to Provence briefly, and in 1791 married him to a neighbor with a useful dowry and strict royalist views. There was no quarrel between the newlyweds, but after a few weeks they parted on friendly terms.

In Paris, Barras resumed his revolutionary career. He voted for the King's death, but, characteristically, he was one of the few regicides who never attempted to excuse himself for that vote. Later he would only say that although he acted at the time according to his convictions, he believed nevertheless he had made a mistake; it would have been better to have kept the King as a hostage. However, he added, "We were no longer the masters, either of events or of men; we had to be bold and *terrible* as the Revolution demanded."[13]

Partly perhaps as a consequence of his bitterness against the regime that had forced him to leave the army, and because of a genuine dislike for injustice, Barras was somewhat more republican than the majority of his colleagues. Though he believed in remaining at the center of power, he also supported the Republic. The same could hardly be said of Tallien or Fréron, or of a number of the other Thermidorians. This ambitious, handsome, adventurous man, cynical and relaxed, was in his element in the world of Thermidor. Certainly he was more devoted to pleasure than many of his fellow deputies; the material advantages of his present position were important to him and, naturally generous, he enjoyed sharing them.

When Paul Barras entered the Chaumière followed by his protégé General Bonaparte, the fate of four people was sealed—Napoleon's, Josephine's, Barras's and Thérésia's. The quartet would remain on the closest terms for the next five years, their destinies interwoven at the most dramatic period of their lives.

❧ 8 ❧

BETTER TIMES WILL COME

"THERE IS ONLY ONE THING TO DO IN THIS WORLD," NAPOLEON WOULD often repeat later, "and that is to keep acquiring money and more money, power and more power. All the rest is meaningless."[1] For families on the way up like the Bonapartes, the years after the Revolution could be prosperous ones.

Napoleon's letters to Joseph throughout the summer revert to financial matters. Confiscated estates were still the best bargains, he pointed out. Ready cash, of course, was needed for these transactions and Joseph had access to this through his wife.

All the newcomers were profiting in this way. Benjamin Constant, Mme de Staël's latest lover, had been in Paris only a few weeks before he wrote to his family in Switzerland that he had just bought an estate for thirty thousand Swiss francs, which would guarantee a yearly income of eight thousand francs because the tenants were forced to pay their rent in produce. Holders of the fast-depreciating paper money were eager to exchange it for property. "If you want an excellent bargain," Napoleon wrote to Joseph, "you should come buy the estate of Monsieur de M. I am sure you can get his place for 80,000 francs cash. Before the Revolution it was worth 250,000."[2]

The acquisition of money, a tip on the value of the assignat and an introduction to a man on the stock exchange were the principal preoccupations of this newborn society. Because of the daily depreciation of the assignat and the dizzy course of the gold louis that rose literally by the minute, the power of the speculators grew. The term *nouveau riche* was invented for them. They formed the government's revolutionary plutocracy, buying up country estates, and furniture and paintings from the royal palaces. Army contracting was the most rewarding venture and a national scandal. There were constant complaints about deficient gun barrels, of shoes made of cardboard. Most of the great financiers of the ensuing years started fortunes as civilian contractors in charge of the armies' supplies, many with no suspicion of venality. Gabriel Ouvrard himself was known to be "absurdly honest"; respected bankers like Récamier and Hottinguer made enormous fortunes out of national defense. Their power was immense; without these men who insisted on being paid only in metallic currency, the Thermidorians were unable to feed or clothe their armies.

Before Barras had transformed his circumstances, unable to fulfill either his desires for money or for advancement at any price, Bonaparte found his first weeks in Paris to be, he was later to say, the low point of his life. "Bold in success, timid and worried in failure,"[3] would be Mme de Rémusat's verdict on him, a judgment borne out by his behavior at the coup of Brumaire, and again after Waterloo.

This was the first time that Napoleon had lost confidence in his "star," his luck. He was driven almost to despair at having so little hope of realizing his pent-up ambition. Prospects of relative wealth, too, were receding with continued Clary opposition. That marriage, in any case, appeared less desirable from the distance of Paris; the stakes were too small.

He had not found time to go to the Poste Restante to retrieve Désirée's letters until nine days after his arrival in Paris. She lived for his letters, she wrote in her tear-stained rough copies. She was afraid to tell him of her dark forebodings, although she admitted that her family was still opposed to the marriage.[4]

The "Désirée business," as Napoleon called it in his letters to Joseph, could still be useful, but his brother's attitude seemed to him equivocal. "Why don't you ever mention Mademoiselle Eugénie?" Napoleon complained. To retain allies in opposing parties was a cardinal revolutionary principle, and perhaps Joseph held the Corsican view that the hand and dowry of his sister-in-law should be retained for a powerful man of another "clan."

As an adolescent Napoleon had shared his generation's identification with Goethe's Werther, who had killed himself because society was against him, and his own suicidal impulses returned to him in Paris that summer.

Despairing and even unbalanced letters were sent both to Joseph and to Désirée. To Joseph he wrote that life held very little meaning for him and he would welcome death; that he would not even step aside if he were about to be run down by a carriage. And he described to Désirée the "condition of his romantic soul." He had, he wrote with some complacency, an imagination of fire, a head of ice, a bizarre heart and melancholy inclinations.[5]

Her own letters to him continued to be written in a romantic vein. She was still trying to be worthy of him. "Knowing your appreciation of the culture of the ladies of Lyon . . . I make a point of being sometimes in their company, believing it would be agreeable to you that I imitate their *ton* and their manner of behaving in society." Then immediately to the subject on her mind, and naturally introduced by the preceding paragraph: "You don't mention Mme T, please send me news of her."[6]

Barras must have taken his Corsican protégé to the Paris salons soon after his arrival from Marseille, for another of Désirée's letters, a mass of misspellings and erasures, runs: "A friend of Joseph's, a deputy, has arrived. He says that everyone enjoys themselves immensely in Paris. I hope that the noisy pleasures there will not allow you to forget the peaceful country ones of Marseilles, and that walks in the Bois de Boulogne with Mme T will not allow you to forget the riverside ones with your *bonne petite* Eugénie."[7] She had read his letters to Joseph about the ravishing Parisians whose elegance and culture he admired; she knew, she wrote, that she was only a shy country girl. It is a transparent picture of a seventeen-year-old's heart; Désirée dared not admit her jealousy, but not for a moment did she try to make Napoleon jealous.

Clearly Napoleon was already boasting of friendship with the legendary Thérésia, and when Désirée wrote again, begging for news of Mme Tallien, Napoleon answered: "I dined last night at Mme T's, she was as amiable as ever, but for some reason her charms have lessened in my eyes. She has aged somewhat. There was a group of about twenty other women there. Only older and uglier women seem to go to her house."[8]

Perhaps this paragraph may have been intended to soften the pain of his last letters; since Thérésia was only twenty-two it could not have been very convincing. But was Rose, who at thirty-two already appeared "faded" to some of her contemporaries, included in this category?

There is a further irony in this observation, since Napoleon was at the same time pursuing another matrimonial venture. According to her daughter Laure d'Abrantès, he proposed marriage late that summer to wealthy Mme Permon, recently widowed. Laure heard her explain to the General that although she would not tell him her age, she was old enough to be his mother; then she heard Mme Permon burst out laughing and close the discussion with: "That's enough. This ridiculous proposal distresses me, coming from you."[9] Napoleon would never forgive Panoria Permon.

Because feminine influence was obviously necessary for advancement in any field, it was a shock to Bonaparte's vanity as well as to his hopes for the future to find that his appearance, manner and accent were all barriers to his success in the salons. "I could never bear not to be first,"[10] Napoleon would dictate at St. Helena. Gabriel Ouvrard recorded that at the Chaumière, Bonaparte was "of all those present, perhaps the least noticeable and the least impressive."[11] His pride suffered from his inability to do more than live on the fringes of the Thermidorian world. When he was noticed at all, it was for his bizarre appearance and graceless French. Foreign accents were apparently admired only in beautiful women: Thérésia's slight Spanish accent and Rose de Beauharnais's Creole inflections were considered additional charms. The smile that later was said to "light up Napoleon's whole countenance" must have been rare at this period. The poet Heinrich Heine would compare the Emperor's face to the "marble heads of the Greeks and Romans," but the cameo profile now was framed in uncombed, unclean hair. Bonaparte had a bad case of scabies,* and the ladies complained that he was unwashed.

With his genius for self-dramatization, he may well have calculated that the pose of shabbiness and simplicity provided a contrast to the elegant Muscadins, the royalists whose black revers symbolized mourning

---

* He had acquired it at Toulon "but in circumstances less heroic than those described in the *Mémorial*."[12]

for the late King, whose speech was filleted of *r*'s to resemble that of the royalist leader in Vendée. Bonaparte was not jealous of them since they held no power, but he noted their success with women. Junot remembered that during their aimless walks about Paris they would sometimes sit at the open-air cafés, where Napoleon would curse the Muscadins under his breath: "And *those* are the men who enjoy all the luck!" he would say, kicking a chair into their legs. Napoleon, Junot would tell his wife, cared no more either for his now powerless former associates, the Jacobins, than for the suffering of the famished men and women searching the streets for some remnants of food.[13]

The Jardin des Plantes was a newly fashionable promenade for Parisians. Since the Revolution it had become a zoo as well as a public garden. All the exotic animals released from the Royal Trianon menagerie during the sack of the palace had been living peacefully and reproducing in the park of Versailles; those that had not been eaten were now recaptured and living behind bars once more at the Jardin des Plantes. Junot would recount that he and Napoleon walked there one night, arm in arm, so intoxicated by the perfume of the flowers that they confessed to each other more secrets than they would otherwise have done.

Andoche Junot confessed that he was "deliriously" in love with Napoleon's sister Pauline and wanted his permission to marry her. This was summarily refused because neither party had any means. "But better times will come," said Napoleon, "even if I have to seek them in another part of the world."[14] "Bonaparte, however," wrote Laure Junot, "who, as we know, would later be totally overwhelmed by one devastating passion, was at this period in love with another woman. His voice trembled with bitterness as he confessed to Junot that he was 'not lucky in love.' "[15]

No one appears to have thought then that the object of his devotion might be Désirée; several of their contemporaries believed it to be Thérésia. As Laure Junot observed: "When Napoleon arrived in Paris, he was in love with all women, and above all, anxious to further his career."[16] It was natural, she concluded, that he should have been in love with Mme Tallien. It would have been this summer that Bonaparte made his celebrated request of her—for some rationed material for a new uniform. "You have your *culottes, mon ami*," Thérésia is supposed to have called out to him one day at the Chaumière. She had been kind, which, their friends thought, led him to believe that he had made a conquest. Was he turned down, though surely not as Barras would assert, "with scorn and ridicule"? More likely, misinterpreting her casual kindness to all, Bonaparte made a proposal, greeted, as Ouvrard would remember, with "an incredulous laugh."[17]

Undoubtedly, Napoleon was haunted by the idea of Thérésia's influence as much as by her celebrated magnetism; and Sophie Gay, a friend of all the parties, wrote later that she was: "Astonished at finding so many qualities united in this pretty woman, Napoleon measured immediately the use her power could make of a situation unique in French history. . . . He built for her a superb future and placed the crown of our Queen's on the head of the woman to whom the French were already bound by love and gratitude."[18] Certainly as long as he lived, Napoleon was unable to forgive the woman who some believed he coveted that summer.

Ambition alone had made Napoleon a Jacobin at the height of Robespierre's power. Now that ambition caused this writer of Jacobin pamphlets to discover an admiration for women of royalist leanings.

A letter that summer to Désirée contained a tactless paragraph on the superior culture, appearance and even patriotism of Parisian women: "Beautiful as in old romances and as learned as scholars . . . all these frivolous women have one thing in common, an astonishing love of bravery and glory. . . . Most of them are also violently royalist, and their labor and their pleasure is to win respectable people over to their cause."[19]

Although Mme Tallien's salon undoubtedly signaled the rightward turn of the Revolution, and although Napoleon might believe that all the influential women were "violently royalist," Thérésia herself, like Germaine de Staël, worked rather for a return to the ideals of the early days of the first National Assembly, and for a constitution to consolidate the gains of the Revolution. The Tallien and de Staël salons remained bases for the "moderate" ex-Jacobin men in the government, under constant attack from both ends of the spectrum. The balance of power, however, was about to change again, as a resurgence of royalist activity created a new threat to the government. In the provinces, especially in the south, the counter-revolution was fast becoming a "white Terror": a scene of random massacres, of settling of old scores.

For the emigré leaders, the "ultra-royalists," it was difficult to grasp that the Revolution was irreversible. Baron Joseph d'André, a royalist agent, had warned the men in London that the effects of the Revolution were now so deeply ingrained in the character of the country that a majority in France would probably like to see the Revolution return to its course of 1789 or even approve a constitutional monarchy to succeed the present government. France might well, he reported, be in for fifty more years of troubles.

The National Assembly had begun to believe that when a new government was formed later in the year a new master, too, must be found: young Orléans—the son of regicide Egalité—or a foreign prince or perhaps a soldier. A soldier, if he could claim to be above politics, might be the best solution, for the army could become a formidable political weapon in his hands. The names of the republican Generals Bernadotte and Hoche were frequently mentioned, Lazare Hoche's the most often. All these hopes were to be shattered by the Proclamation of Verona.

The government's search for a new man intensified in June 1795 as the death of the Dauphin in the Temple Prison was announced. The ten-year-old child, son of Louis XVI and Marie Antoinette, known to royalists as Louis XVII, had been viewed by all the revolutionary leaders as a hostage to be carefully preserved. The Convention had even considered using him as a figurehead monarch on the English model. For the Thermidorians the child had been an insurance against their rivals, still more against the future, and a valuable pawn in foreign policy. So crucial was his survival believed to be that on the night of 9 Thermidor, Barras's first act after asking the troops to renew the oath of fidelity to the Convention had been to proceed to the Temple and, accompanied by five deputies, visit the Dauphin in his prison cell.*

---

* It is not known whether Barras suspected on that night that another child had been substituted for the Dauphin, as now seems likely. (His report after that visit to the Committee of Public Safety differs from the one he made on the subject under the Restoration.) In what appears to be some collective mythmaking, stories would continue to link both Josephine and Barras to the Dauphin. Josephine was rumored, too, to have played a part in the child's escape. The government's agent in charge of the Dauphin immediately after Thermidor was one Laurent, a native of Martinique, a confidant of Josephine's and appointed by Barras.

Both Lucien Bonaparte's daughter and the Empress Eugénie would insist upon Josephine's role in the affair. Tsar Nicholas of Russia would repeat that his brother Alexander told him that at Malmaison Josephine had informed him that she and Barras, with the help of

. . .

It had been expected that at the Dauphin's death the late King's brother, the Comte de Provence, living in exile in Verona, would make some kind of conciliatory statement that would open the way to a coalition of Thermidorians and constitutionalists. On June 24, however, Provence, taking the title of Louis XVIII, issued a proclamation that succeeded in uniting in a bond of fear at least half of the Convention and all the Thermidorian leaders. The Proclamation of Verona threatened "merciless revenge" on all regicides, particularly on the Thermidorian leaders.

The proclamation stipulating that no concessions would be made to holders of confiscated property was still more decisive, cementing the nation and the Revolution. The process of dividing the country's property among all classes had already resulted in a social revolution since fully half of France had benefited from this immense transfer.

All French history from 1795 to 1814 would be influenced by this disastrous proclamation. Hopes of a constitutional monarchy were dashed; a last chance had been missed through the blindness of the "ultras," the ultra-royalists.

Mallet du Pan, the farsighted royalist, reported to Vienna: "The Monarchy will not return until after a usurper has seized power, and perhaps retained it for a very long period." And four years before the coup of Brumaire that would bring him to power, Bonaparte wrote Joseph this month: "The French want peace, order, and an end of debate; it will be through hatred of both the Jacobins and the emigrés that they will eventually surrender to a master."[20] Neither Mallet du Pan nor Napoleon Bonaparte could guess then the identity of that master.

It was time for the Convention to regroup its clients. The delicate balance maintained by the government between Jacobins and moderates had been upset by the proclamation; the Thermidorians were now thoroughly alarmed by the right. The government needed to strengthen the

---

Laurent, had rescued the Dauphin and substituted another child. Hortense confirmed this to a friend, and a former nurse in the royal family swore under oath that Josephine and Barras had showed her Louis XVII. The Dauphin's sister, married to the King's heir, was reported to have confessed on her deathbed: "My brother did not die in the Temple; it has been the nightmare of my life." She was said to have been persuaded by her uncle Louis XVIII that the Dauphin was Fersen's son.

Jacobin party, and the ill-timed royalist landing at Quiberon gave it this opportunity.

The war in Vendée, reminiscent of the maquis fighting in World War II, had temporarily ended with Lazare Hoche's peace treaty earlier in the year. Now it started up again, a guerrilla war of extraordinary savagery with atrocities committed on both sides. The rebel forces were made up largely of peasants, gamekeepers and local nobles, ardently Catholic, obeying no discipline, wearing no uniform and often armed only with scythes and pikes. After each engagement they would melt back into the landscape. Republican troops exacted terrible reprisals against the civilian population of Vendée, and the royalists took ferocious revenge on isolated republican troops.

Two days after the Proclamation of Verona the British fleet landed a force of French emigrés on the coast of Brittany. Before they could join up with the Vendée rebels, and while a storm prevented the British navy from landing reinforcements, the royalist army was annihilated by the republicans under General Hoche.

There had been too many rumors lately on the reported intrigues of the Tallien couple in favor of a constitutional monarchy, and Jean-Lambert Tallien, anxious to reestablish his revolutionary prestige, elected to join the Army of the West in Brittany as a representative-on-mission. Twelve thousand emigrés were captured at Quiberon; Tallien ordered them to appear before a military commission, promised them amnesty and, overriding General Hoche, condemned 748 of them to death.

When Tallien returned to the capital on 9 Thermidor, he appeared before the Convention to celebrate a double triumph: the anniversary of the fall of Robespierre and the victory at Quiberon. The government decided upon an impressive show of republicanism. A ceremonial occasion was held in which foreign ambassadors and Merveilleuses filled the Assembly's galleries, and garlands of flowers hung on its walls. Tallien, resplendent in his old uniform of a representative-on-mission, made an absurd speech and even drew a dagger as a reminder of the previous 9 Thermidor. For the first time the "Marseillaise" was played as the national anthem,* and the press announced that the celebration at the Convention

---

* The artillery captain Claude Rouget de L'Isle, composer of the "Marseillaise," was another friend of the Talliens. Under the Terror, disgusted by so much bloodshed, he had rejected his

was followed by a "frugal banquet" at the Chaumière. Although Tallien hinted that the massacre of unarmed men at Quiberon was not his responsibility alone, his reputation for ruthlessness whenever he felt threatened was too well established. Thérésia herself was heard to say: "Too much blood on the hands of this man."[22] It was the end of Jean-Lambert Tallien's influence, but Napoleon, ever interested in the rise and fall of individual reputations, reported that the power of Mme Tallien's salon continued.

By August, Napoleon's spirits had improved considerably; his world had become the world of Barras and of those salons where the fortunes and reputations in Paris were made. A kinder letter to Désirée described Paris and its pleasures. In an affectionate one to Joseph, he sounded more practical and hopeful. He still showed some ambivalence toward the French people, referring to them as "foreigners," and he noted the importance of fashion in every aspect of French life. "It is very easy," he wrote, "to govern the French through vanity." He reported that discussions on the new constitution had started and that: "It may perhaps determine the destiny of this unchanging people." He speculated upon the differences between France and England and how the characters of the two people were dissimilar "because of climate and diet," and why therefore similar political institutions, notably "the English constitution" [*sic*] would be inapplicable to France. "I am of the opinion that France should have no constitution," he concluded, "she is essentially monarchist."[23]

Paul Barras was one of the principal drafters of the new constitution, and it appeared to Bonaparte more essential than ever not to join the Vendée post but to remain close to power. He calculated that if he applied for two more Décadis of sick leave, the termination of that furlough would correspond with the renewal of the Committee of Public Safety and therefore the replacement of Captain Aubry; something better than the Army of the West might then be offered. He produced a second trumped-up medical report and applied for further sick leave.

On August 17 came the thunderbolt. The Committee of Public

---

anthem and was imprisoned. Under the Consulate and Empire the "Marseillaise" was outlawed by Napoleon because, he said, "It gave men a taste for liberty."[21]

Safety had guessed his stratagem and relieved him of his command "because of this officer's refusal to take up his post." Additionally, it was noted that the doctor who signed the medical certificate was "not qualified to do so."

Deeply shocked by this turn of events, Napoleon appealed to Paul Barras. The health tactic had never caused trouble before and would indeed again be invoked successfully. Barras, informed of his protégé's distress, obtained a post for him in the Topographical Bureau of the Committee of Public Safety—a military operations department most recently headed by General Carnot. It was the ideal post, the very position Napoleon needed to develop and elaborate what he had never ceased to reflect upon: a new strategic plan for the Army of Italy.

To Joseph he made no mention of his dismissal but announced that he was "replacing Carnot" at the bureau; this was an exaggeration, since he worked with three other generals of the same rank. The Republic at the time was at war on all its frontiers except the Pyrenees, and the four men divided the territory among them. General Bonaparte was allotted the plans of the southeast and thereby kept in touch with the two Armies of Italy and of the Alps.

Never was Napoleon's "star" more in evidence than in the apparent bad luck of his removal from the army. Had he not been relieved of his command "for insubordination in time of war," he would not have played a part in the battle of Vendémiaire in October of that year, and the course of his life would have been very different. Not only was his belief in luck justified, but also his often-expressed view that a fatalistic dependence on fortune should nevertheless be based on "dexterity, resolution and perpetual intrigue,"[24] and that timing should then be left to destiny.

But for this demotion, he might also have been preparing his departure for Turkey. On the day he had been relieved of his command he was also informed by the Commission of the Exterior that his proposal to go to Turkey as chief of a military mission to the Sultan had been accepted. (Napoleon had neglected to inform the Committee of Public Safety of this démarche, and the two bureaus were unaware of each other's actions.) He had suggested himself for the Turkish affair just as he was beginning to doubt the wisdom of his decision to opt for France in 1793 because of his setbacks in Corsica. He continued to consider the post in Turkey; to Joseph, weighing the advantages, he wrote that should he decide to go there, it would be with "the flattering title of envoy," and "I would have you named Consul . . . and your two brothers-in-law could be sent there too."

A cheerful letter went out to Désirée. The whole tone had changed. He informed her that as he worked only from midnight until two in the morning, and again for two hours in the afternoon he could, were she in the capital, introduce her into the company of charming Parisian ladies. "If I could be happy far from you, I would be now. I am highly regarded here," he added, "and I have friends, pleasures and parties. Let us hurry, beloved Eugénie, time flies, old age is almost upon us. I kiss you a million times. Your dear friend for life."[25]

Sentiment and style were both invigorated by his improved prospects. At last a field of action had been opened, an outlet for his talents and his nervous energy.

The Désirée relationship must be kept up, though, in case larger Paris calculations went wrong; this was still worth the effort of romantic letters. Marriage to Mme Permon was apparently being considered, at least as late as mid-October. Power demanded money, and that summer had opened a vista of unprecedented spoils.

Bonaparte continued to be haunted by the idea of an early marriage, of an alliance with an acceptable dowry. On September 5, newly confident, he wrote to Joseph that "I might take it into my head to be married," and on the following day: "Don't forget my business [i.e., Désirée], for I have *'la folie'* to own a house,"[26] and the following day he assured his brother that whatever happens "you need have no fear on my behalf: I have all the right people as friends, whatever their party or opinion. . . ." On September 26 he wrote Joseph again that the Turkish business was arranged and would even be acted upon, were it not "for so much unrest here" as Paris filled with troops to oversee the elections on the last day of September.

He would not write to Désirée again until January, when his definitive matrimonial plans had been decided.

9

THE FOLLY AT NO. 6

"AROUND MAY OR JUNE," WROTE A CONTEMPORARY IN 1795, "ROSE DE Beauharnais was admitted into Barras's harem."[1]

That summer Paul Barras was president of the National Convention, a member of the Committee of Public Safety and general in chief of the Army of the Interior. There were rewards as well as pleasure for Rose in this liaison. As Barras's recognized mistress her credit was as good as unlimited; as his hostess at the Palais Egalité—his official residence—and at his country house in rural Chaillot near the Chaumière, she was in touch with every man of influence.

They were temperamentally well suited, both made to appreciate the hedonism of 1795. She was exactly the type of woman Barras favored, for although he had no objection to a little roughness in the men around him, preferred indeed that they had had no connection with the old regime, he demanded of the women in his circle the distinguished manners at least of that world. He took his liaisons lightly, never asking for faithfulness. Cynical and undemanding, he was well known for kindnesses to past and present mistresses, always ready to give advice, to share funds—both state and private—and to arrange useful introductions to the bankers and speculators swarming around the government.

Rose happily resumed one of her favorite occupations, the writing of often disinterested letters of recommendation or of introduction for friends, for acquaintances and for herself. Cultivating new power and making use of influential friends—her passport to survival throughout the Revolution—was more rewarding now that she was known to be under the protection of the most influential man in France.

When Paul Barras wrote in his *Mémoires* that he introduced Bona-parte "into the houses of Mme Tallien, Mme de Staël and others," those others would not have included Mme de Beauharnais, a more or less permanent guest at the Chaumière and not yet in possession of a suitable residence in which to entertain. It was assumed though—and Barras confirmed it—that he paid the rent of the house at Croissy which Rose leased again from Désirée Hosten that summer. Her neighbor there, the future Chancellor Pasquier, finding that the spiral of inflation was less deadly in the country than in the city, had recently moved to Croissy with his family. There they solved some of the food shortage problems by growing their own vegetables, but the banquets sent down to Rose's house from Paris caused some stir among the inhabitants of the little commu-nity, where even a loaf of bread cost the ordinary citizen several hours of standing in line.

"Mme de Beauharnais," wrote Pasquier in his *Mémoires*, "was a neighbor; she came rarely, perhaps once a week, to receive Barras and his large suite. Early in the morning we would see baskets of provisions arriving, then mounted police would start clearing the road from Nanterre to Croissy. Mme de Beauharnais's house, like that of many Creoles, had a certain amount of luxury for show. There was too much of certain things but the essentials were lacking. Fowl, wild game and rare fruits were heaped up in the kitchen—this was at the period of greatest famine—and at the same time she lacked saucepans, glasses and plates which she came to borrow from our modest household."[2]

Rose's perpetual desire for "influence," or the appearance of it, was grat-ified, her debts no longer of urgent concern. But though Barras was never known to abandon the women who had played any role in his life, she could not but be conscious of her precarious hold on him. Her actual position could only be temporary. One nagging anxiety was ever present: the need for a protector who would maintain her in this enviable style.

Rose longed for some kind of security. She had not yet given up hope that Lazare Hoche would divorce his wife, and was so vexed to learn in the spring that Adèle Hoche was pregnant that she insisted on removing young Eugène from his post as aide to the general. But she was not the type of woman to love the absent for long, however. Although their correspondence was passionate for a while, Hoche was soon complaining of a lack of letters from Paris and even accusing her of conducting an affair with the aide who brought her his letters. But he was still besotted by her, and in May he wrote a friend that he had heard that Rose had now become a fashionable Merveilleuse. "Vanity has replaced friendship in her heart," he wrote, and then the customary refrain from the men in Rose's life: "I am in despair at having no answer from the woman I love, the widow whose son I am accustomed to consider my own. There is no happiness on earth for me. I am unable to go to Paris, as you know, to see the woman who is the cause of my grief. Duty, and the war which is about to start up again here, keep me at my post."[3] That post, of course, was the Army of the West which Bonaparte had declined to join.

Probably it was already clear to Rose that Barras would inevitably gravitate toward Thérésia, his feminine counterpart in the firmament of Thermidorian Paris. Certainly this is one of the few recorded instances where she kept her native jealousy under control.

But although all the advantages appeared to be on Thérésia's side, Rose could continue to feel seductive, even in competition with the celebrated younger beauties like Thérésia herself and Juliette Récamier. Her expression was so infinitely sweet, her makeup so artful, her gaiety so contagious that she was as much admired at the Chaumière as the younger women.

And she confirmed the long-held French view of the legendary allure of Creole women. That she was languorous and charming was as it should be—considered inevitable in men and women from the Antilles. "She was still beautiful then," wrote one of the Chaumière circle years later, "with her supple and voluptuous figure as is usual for Creole women, combined with the dignified manner of the old regime. Her voice was so moving, her expression so tender!"[4] And even after the Revolution it was still assumed that Creole women owned large fortunes—vast estates and armies of slaves, especially if, like Fortunée Hamelin, the heiresses came from Santo Domingo. But although Rose did not discourage such speculation and even hinted at funds coming from the colonies, she continued to live on loans and credit.

Rose and Thérésia were soon inseparable, drawn together by their superficial likenesses and almost identical needs. There seems to have been no rivalry between them; competition was really out of the question.

On Thérésia's side was a ten-year advantage in age; her looks, her fortune (her French father was banker to the King of Spain), a historic role in the immediate past and a present one of great influence. Each was endowed with an easy kindness, a readiness to oblige, to go to immense trouble for others; each had extended this kindness under the Terror to the point of risking their lives. And there were other resemblances. Both women, born outside France, had been married at an early age to egotistical men who neglected them, and had been caught in the net of the Revolutionary Tribunal, sending them to prison and to apparently certain death. Now they were united by a need to forget past horrors and a common thirst for admiration and luxury.

Barras's own often-quoted brutal comparison of the two women is believed to have been written by his executor, who had his own reasons to have no love for Mme Bonaparte: "Although Mme Tallien's liaisons were truly enjoyable for her because of the ardor and passion of her nature," he wrote, "Mme de Beauharnais' heart never played a part in these relationships. The men who possessed her may have flattered themselves on her apparently passionate abandon, but the lubricious Creole never for a moment lost sight of business. Her heart played no part in her physical enjoyment.... Mme Tallien," he added, "was then in the full bloom of her beauty; Mme de Beauharnais was starting her decay. This is no exaggeration to those who knew her then, and who were aware that nothing about her was natural, but everything due to an art as subtle and as careful as ever was employed by the courtesans of Greece or Paris in the exercise of their profession."[5]

While the Marquis de Sade, who knew both Rose and Thérésia at this period, recorded: "Mme de Beauharnais was a hundred times more avid for pleasure than Mme Tallien." For Rose this was not a temporary thirst, not solely the release from unbearable tension, but a lifelong dependence. Thérésia, triumphant, sure of her power, could not know the desperation in Rose's frantic need for pleasure, nor in her search for security.

But for the fear of losing a protector the year was proving to be a delightful one for Rose. In this Thermidorian summer she and Thérésia shared everything and dressed alike as often as possible. "Be sure to wear your peach-blossom dress to the ball tomorrow," wrote Rose to Thérésia, "and I will wear mine, with a Creole turban and three curls on my forehead. Our identical costumes will be devastating to our English rivals."[6] Each followed the other in the ever more surreal fashions. When Thérésia abandoned the vogue for blond wigs and exchanged them for blue or violet ones, Rose followed suit. (This custom was condemned in the press; the *Journal de Paris* reminded its readers that wigs were made of the hair of the guillotine's victims, whose heads were cropped just before they entered the death carts.) As it had proved difficult to invent a suitable hat for "antique" costumes, the Merveilleuses solved the problem by wearing over these wigs whatever headgear suited the day's political winds: peasant bonnets, turbans and, as Anglomania returned to Paris, velvet jockey caps of exaggerated size. There was no hesitation in clamping one fashion on top of another; rather the effect was considered enhanced.

Thérésia's labor pains started as she left the theater one night in May. Rose was godmother to the child, who was named Rose and "Thermidor, to commemorate the event to which she doubly owed her life." The second name, so appropriate at the time, was soon dropped; there were changes indeed with each regime. Rose was converted to Josephine when Mme Bonaparte became the first lady of France, and Josephine Tallien turned into Laure when she married into a royalist family. As long as she was permitted to—that is to say, until she was forced to renounce all her former friends—Rose continued to be an affectionate godmother to the child.

In that first summer after the Terror, Mme Tallien, recovered from the birth of Rose Thermidor, and Mme de Beauharnais flung themselves into the newly fashionable outdoor life with special ardor. There was a rage for sports and athletic contests; the craze for Hellenism led to a fashion for exercise of all kinds. "Antique" games were organized. Horse racing on the Champ de Mars was encouraged, a result of the English influence of the returning emigrés. Bowls was played in the Bois de Boulogne, with Mme Tallien as referee; for this role she dressed appropriately. "Like many others," wrote Victor de Broglie, "I saw *la belle* Mme Tallien arrive at Ranelagh clad *à la* Diane, her bosom half naked, sandals on her feet and dressed, if one can use the expression, in a tunic above her knees."[7]

The figures in engravings of the time appear always to be in motion, as though in reaction to the intensity of life under the Terror: dashing away in cockleshell carriages hung with bells, skating, swimming, riding, chariot-racing and, above all, dancing.

Paris was intoxicated by the late good weather, and for the first time social life was taking place out of doors, in the now public gardens of the former aristocracy; the most popular was the grounds of the Elysée, now the residence of the President of the French Republic.

There was dancing, music and tea under the trees; above all "nature," whenever possible, was created in "antique" form: artificial cascades, cardboard rocks and Greek temples made of stucco. Illusionists, trapezists, harpists, tight-rope dancers and ventriloquists performed under the trees, and for those who could find transportation as far out as Chantilly, there were even "licentious *tableaux vivants*." The two friends, eating "divine ices shaped like peaches and apricots," were accompanied to these purely social events by still another new breed of young men. The Incroyables were not, like the Muscadins, political activists but caricatural figures obsessed with fashion, dressed in deliberately oversized coats and exaggerated cravats, partners in every print of the period of the equally preposterous Merveilleuses.

One of the new public ballrooms was so large that "in one window bay alone, thirty black couples were dancing a quadrille." A changing room was set aside for the Muscadins so that the fragile, flesh-colored nankeen breeches could be changed several times in an evening. Rose danced, too, but the feminine star of each ballroom was Fortunée Hamelin. When she appeared very late, preceded by the perfume of a strong essence of roses, all the young men rushed to dance with her. Her waltz was reputed to be the last word in lasciviousness, its sensuality and uninhibitedness already legendary. "Although a marvelous dancer, she is not pretty—very undistinguished-looking" sniffed English Miss Berry, visiting Paris the following year.[8] Fortunée was not, perhaps, a type admired in Gainsborough's England, but her diabolical spirits, her wit and her daring dress were the essence of Thermidorian Paris.

Although Parisians had become accustomed to the contrasts between opulence and destitution, the slowly returning emigrés found these even more shocking than the physical changes in the city. There seemed to be no middle ground between the wealth of the new political and financial worlds and the poverty of those attempting to survive on pensions or fixed incomes; between the unending bread lines of weakened men and women and the indecently lavish windows of the restaurants.

The exiles had been slowly returning since Stanislas Fréron had authorized the return of "some emigrés exercising a manual profession," something that most of these men and women had been engaged in in Brussels, the Rhineland, Switzerland and America. Over the years almost 140,000 would return, roughly one-third of them peasants and artisans, the rest bourgeois, nobility and clergy. Far from the dizzy London life of emigrés like the Montronds, the majority worked all day and met for tea in the evening; many could afford neither food nor a blanket. The poet René de Chateaubriand wrote that in bed he placed a chair over himself to take the place of covers, drank hot water instead of expensive tea and spent much of his time staring into the windows of food shops.

They had all been homesick. Forneron wrote of his fellow exiles in London: "All was distasteful to the French in that country without sun; each of us rebelled against the language we refused to learn, and against the use of pavements, an invention still unknown in our beloved Paris."[9] The greatest happiness, they all agreed, was to hear French spoken in the streets, but they had to become accustomed to an almost new language. Though revolutionary oratory was considered unbearable outside the Convention (Benjamin Constant said that he could no longer hear the words "justice" and "humanity" without nausea), the language had evolved so much in six years, had acquired so many new expressions, that it seemed almost like a foreign tongue. There were semantic traps to be avoided, too. The older exiles who spent their evenings playing whist— like the rest of Paris, they played cards with frenzy—found that the Republic had eliminated royalty. Kings, for instance, had been replaced by "Liberties"; under the Terror, a notary playing cards in a café had incautiously shouted "Three kings!" and was promptly hauled before a revolutionary committee.

The Paris of the new rich filled the returning emigrés with astonishment—the Paris of a ceaseless round of pleasure; of the men at the fashionable restaurants, cravats covering their chins, breeches so tight it took two people to help them into; of Mme Hamelin sitting in a box at the theater, her bare breasts outlined "in a river of diamonds"—was almost as far from their experience or purses as it was from that of the haggard men and women begging in the streets. As disconcerting as the near nudity of feminine fashions were the exaggerated clothes worn by the men and their shocking new habit of "indecently keeping their hands in their breeches' pocket."[10] It was a foreign country to the exiles, and the new ease of manner between the sexes was another source of wonder. "Before the Revolution, a man would not even have placed a hand on the chair on which a lady was sitting," declared one of them.[11]

But the young generation of exiles found the new revolutionary simplicity fresh and delightful. Couples shared the cooking, the standing in line for bread and the housework. Young men escorted girls to the ballroom on foot, sheltering them with umbrellas, and carrying the ladies' dancing slippers, fans and rouge pots, for, although the women's modestly décolleté white muslin dresses showed little more than the ankles, the emigrés, like the Merveilleuses, permitted no pocket to mar the outline of the body.

The future was still hazardous for most of the exiles, however. Once back in France, they lived in fear of denunciation, for they could still be executed without trial if there was proof of illegal entry.

Observing the increasing indigence of Parisians (the bread ration fell again that autumn, while meat and firewood were only obtainable at astronomical prices), the general atmosphere of popular disenchantment and the country's open contempt and distrust of the Convention, the emigrés had some reason to hope for a possible monarchist restoration or at least for a right-wing majority in the coming elections. Tallien himself confessed: "If the country were left to its own aspirations now, the counter-revolution would be constitutionally achieved within the month."

In August 1795, still deeply in debt, Rose signed the lease of a house in the rue Chantereine. It was a high rent for the period, four thousand francs in metal currency (the franc had replaced the livre that year), or ten thousand in assignats, at a time when bread cost twenty-two francs a pound, but it was in "the part of Paris where houses this year are the hardest to get and the most expensive."[12] Because of the difficulty in getting about the city without a carriage, social life was more than ever concentrated within a few sections, and the house in rue Chantereine was in "the favorite quarter now," reported Mercier, "because it is near everything that matters: the Palais Egalité, the Tuileries, the Convention and the main theaters."[13]

The section was fashionable for other reasons too. No. 6 rue Chantereine was surrounded by as much "nature" as was Thérésia's cottage, hidden in the groves off the Champs-Elysées, or Barras's house on the slopes of Chaillot. The concept of a town house in a rural setting was a new one in Paris, instead of the more usual position between a garden and a courtyard.

When the walls of Paris were torn down in the 1780s, celebrated architects like Ledoux and Brogniart built on what had been a girdle of market gardens. Bankers and royal princes had miniature palaces—follies—built here, usually for ladies under their protection. (A "folly" in this context was taken to mean "a pavilion in the midst of foliage," rather than "a financial or amorous imprudence.") The folly at No. 6, which would enter history as the *Maison de Brumaire*, Bonaparte's base for his coup d'état, was a neo-Greek pavilion topped by a Parisian attic and set in a small garden. On either side of the cobbled courtyard were stables and a coach house; like many of the follies built for love, it affected an almost ruined entrance and was reached by a long, narrow unpaved lane lined with high walls and lime trees. Stone steps led up to the house and directly into a semicircular antechamber, followed by the salon; the fireplace here was placed between two french windows opening into the garden; next came a very small study. A narrow staircase led to a bedroom, bathroom, water closet and dressing room. Above this were the attic rooms; below ground, the kitchen.

The setting was elegant, if on a miniature scale. Until quite recently only the most luxurious houses could boast a bathroom; a basin and pitcher behind a screen usually took its place, while the privy was often set on a staircase landing.

Immediately, Rose had the seats of her four mahogany chairs recovered in blue nankeen, tufted in red and yellow. Though the furniture was pitifully meager, it was in the severe Directory style. The lilac and sulphur and pale rose wall colors of its prerevolutionary decoration were swept away in favor of the harsh reds and violets believed to be faithful copies of the hues found in the archaeological digs at Herculaneum. A frieze of black figures on an oxblood ground, reminiscent of a Greek vase, surrounded the bedroom, an "Etruscan" silver urn was displayed downstairs, and a little bust of Socrates remained on the salon mantelpiece until the affluent days. These timid concessions to neoclassical taste would soon be replaced by the very models on which those fashions were based: antique Roman bronzes, mosaics and marbles, all the loot of the Italian campaign.

The folly soon took on the same mixture of apparent luxury and relative poverty as the house at Croissy. Pastiche and trompe l'oeil, deception of any kind, were characteristic of the period and, in Rose's case, necessary. Sharp eyes noted that in the antechamber, sometimes used as a dining room, there were almost no spoons or cups, just three plates displayed in the glass-fronted shelves. But with her sure taste and a ruinous profusion of flowers, Rose could easily deceive her guests with these limited but fashionable possessions.

The stables and the porter's lodge at the entrance to the alleyway required an increase in Rose's staff. She now employed a gatekeeper, a coachman and a gardener, as well as five domestics, including one Citizen Gallyot, a male cook. In the attic she lodged the house servants and her two children, whenever they were in Paris.

It was generally accepted that Paul Barras had provided the large sum for the rent of the folly. Mme de La Pagerie would not be able to send any funds from Martinique until early the next year; the fifty thousand livres lent by Aunt Désirée had long been spent, and it was presumably Barras who paid for the schooling of Rose's children. Eugène, upon his return from General Hoche's army, was placed in the expensive McDermott Academy, the Irish college at St. Germain, and Hortense, who had been living with her grandfather Beauharnais, was entered as a boarder at Mme Campan's neighboring school.

By the end of September, Rose's house was ready but, warned by Barras of coming riots in this month of Vendémiaire, she decided to spend a week with her aunt in Fontainebleau.

❧ 10 ❧

GENERAL VENDÉMIAIRE

IN THE LATE INDIAN SUMMER OF THE FIRST WEEK OF OCTOBER 1795 there were street battles between Jacobins and Muscadins in cafés and at the theater. In the public gardens, men fought in gangs. Anti-republican costumes—green coats with black velvet collars—were seen everywhere. Republicans spread the word that Paris was filled with British spies "disguised as citizens of North America." These were the days of "so much unrest" Napoleon wrote about in his letter to Joseph Bonaparte.

At the Chaumière, and in Mme de Staël's salon, the drafting of the "Constitution of the Year III" had been the subject of endless discussion all summer. Solving the transition to a new legal government was proving difficult. In September rumors had started that the National Assembly was determined to "perpetuate" itself, in spite of the promise of free elections. The government knew that a legal end to the Revolution was the wish of the nation, but its members were unaware of the hate directed at each one of them personally and at the entire Convention. Muscadins and their friends in the galleries shouted insults at the deputies, and journalists joined in the seditious songs and the laughter. The onlookers minutely examined and commented on each vote. Once outside the Assembly hall, deputies in costume were jeered at in the streets, so great was the fear that the same men would remain in office. Tallien's unpopularity increased; the windows of the Chaumière were smashed; on the anniversary of the September Massacres the press made unpleasant references to his role in them. The deputy Joseph Chénier was also pursued in the streets with cries of "Cain, what have you done with your brother?" But generally public opinion made little distinction between the deputies. All were seen as last year's men of blood. The hated Convention was blamed for the ruin of the country, for famine and for poverty.

The text of the new Constitution was finally ready in September and elections were set for the following month. But when the men who had survived the successive purges of the Assembly realized how few of them could hope to be reelected, how likely it was that a right-wing majority, perhaps even an eventual royal restoration would be voted, the largely regicide Assembly decided to protect itself. Their heads once again in danger, the deputies were resolved to stop at nothing to stay in power. To make sure that moderates and royalists would not gain a majority in the impending elections, the outgoing Convention passed an additional decree, the "Law of Two-Thirds," whereby two-thirds of the new legislature must be chosen from the outgoing Convention.

The climate of public opinion was changed when this supplementary decree was made known. Very few of the voters wished to restore the monarchy, most were hostile to the counter-revolution and to the return of the "King of the Emigrés." Even the ultra-royalist d'André reported to London: "If they should decide on a king, he would have to be a child of the Revolution." Virtually all wished to preserve the Republic; simply the idea of a permanent incumbency of the Convention was intolerable to Parisians.

In spite of massive abstentions—by more than four of the five million electors inscribed—the new Constitution was approved. There were violent scenes when the election results were proclaimed and the public realized that only 376 deputies had been elected out of the 500 required by the new decree, and that the government could now make up the number from the present members of the Convention. A revolt became inevitable, and the Great Committee precipitated the crisis by calling the army into the capital—once again illegally. Parisians believed a second Terror was imminent.

On October 2 the more moderate Paris sections declared themselves to be in a state of insurrection and issued a call to arms. They disposed of a formidable force of at least twenty thousand men—National Guardsmen, citizens hostile to the Convention and some genuine royalists (ultraroyalists refused to take any part in this rebellion, believing it not to be in the interest of true monarchists; Napoleon himself at St. Helena referred to the insurrectionists simply as "Parisians")—while the government could count only on the Army of the Interior and the police for its defense.

Throughout Paris on the afternoon of October 4 (12 Vendémiaire) in torrential rain, drums beat the call to arms and the tocsin never ceased ringing. The Convention recognized it was in very real danger. Not only might the government be overturned, but the members' own lives could be at stake. Some of the panicking deputies took refuge with their families in the Tuileries Palace and even discussed leaving the exposed building for the heights of Montmartre. A Committee of Defense sat in permanent session. Supreme command of the armed forces was given to Paul Barras, the man who had taken such energetic command at Thermidor. His orders were to organize the defense of the Tuileries and to break up the rebellion.

Barras added to the forces at the Convention's disposal a mixed collection of between fifty and sixty thousand men, including officers dismissed for Jacobinism, former terrorists recently released from prison—and even, asserted Barras's enemies, some Septembrist butchers. Forty unemployed officers volunteered immediately; Bonaparte was not among them. Barras dispatched a hasty note to Napoleon's lodgings asking him to report immediately and without fail. What then occurred is one of the first examples of the Napoleonic legend in action.

According to Napoleon's later account, he was at the theater when friends informed him of the evening's events. "Out of sheer curiosity" he took a seat in the Convention's spectators' gallery. "Several representatives" proposed sending for him "as the man most capable of serving the Republic." He searched his soul, he recorded, for half an hour and then "consented to save the great truths of the Republic."[1] And, ignoring his and Joseph Bonaparte's many references to Barras during the summer of 1795, at least one historian has depicted the scene when "suddenly" Bonaparte appeared before Barras. They "had not seen each other since Toulon" and Bonaparte "could only hope that Barras might recognize him."[2]

Napoleon himself, however, at St. Helena, would tell General Bertrand that on the night before Vendémiaire he had weighed for and against the two sides, that he had decided to uphold the "monarchist" uprising if it started well, and only changed his mind when Barras gave him the authority to requisition the artillery.[3]

When Napoleon finally reported to Barras at nine that evening he

Josephine by Pierre-Paul Prud'hon. (Musée Marmottan—Tallandier)

Alexandre, Vicomte de Beauharnais—Josephine's first husband—by an anonymous painter. Fatuous and conceited, and both a social and intellectual snob, he could hardly hide his dismay at the appearance of his future wife when she arrived from Martinique. (Musée de la Malmaison—Bulloz)

An execution at the Place de la Révolution (now Concorde). The cardboard statue of Liberty shown on the left. (Musée Carnavalet—Photothèque des Musées de la Ville de Paris)

A corridor in the St. Lazare Prison, 1793. The interior of Les Carmes Seminary looks much like this today. (Musée Carnavalet—Photothèque des Musées de la Ville de Paris)

Pen and ink drawing of
Robespierre made during
the session of 9
Thermidor. (Hennin
Collection, Bibliothèque
Nationale—Hachette)

An engraving of General
Lazare Hoche by
Duplessis-Bertaux. He
was described by a fellow
prisoner as "handsome,
good-humored and
gallant . . . and often
with the ladies."
(Collection Viollet)

A sketch of General Bonaparte by Jacques-Louis David. It was described as the best likeness of him in 1795. (Musée d'Art et d'Histoire, Palais Masséna, Nice—Michel de Lorenzo)

Paul, Vicomte de Barras, wearing the Director's costume designed by Jacques-Louis David. (Bibliothèque Nationale, Paris—Hachette)

Thérésia Tallien by Masquerier. (Hulton Deutsch Collection, Ltd., London)

Thermidorian fashions. (Musée
Carnavalet—Hachette)

An 7.   Costumes Parisiens.
(155)
Bokay.

"Le Bokay" (The Buggy).
(Musée Carnavalet—Hachette)

Josephine's folly, known to history as the *Maison de Brumaire*. (Collection Viollet)

The house from the garden in 1856. (Collection Viollet)

The entrance to the folly. General Bonaparte's couriers from Italy galloped up the narrow unpaved alley leading to the house. The conspirators would gather here on the morning of the military coup of Brumaire. (Collection Viollet)

One of the bronze-painted "Roman" beds in the Bonapartes' tented bedrooms. (Bulloz)

Vendémiaire (October 5, 1795)—General Bonaparte's batteries firing on the rebels at the Church of St. Roch. (Collection Viollet)

General Bonaparte by Guérin in 1797. (Musée Carnavalet—Bulloz)

Josephine by Jean-Baptiste Isabey in 1797. A portrait described as "one of the few which captures her allure." (Tallandier)

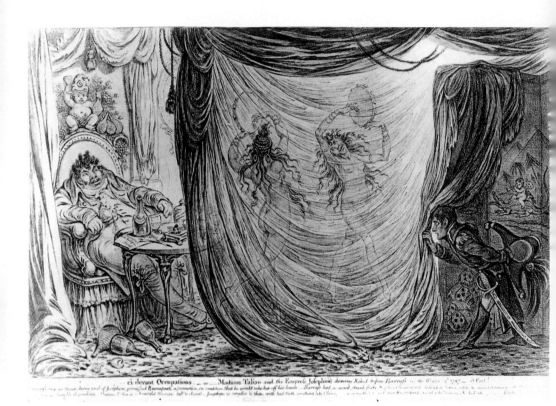

ci-devant Occupations — or — Madame Talian and the Empress Josephine dancing Naked before Barrass in the Winter of 1797 — A Fact!

A savage cartoon by the English caricaturist Gillray published in the coronation year of 1804. It is captioned: *"ci-devant—or—Madame Talian and the Empress Josephine dancing Naked before Barrass in the Winter of 1797—A Fact! Barrass [then in power] being tired of Josephine promised Buonaparte a promotion on condition that he would take her off his hands;—Barrass had, as usual, drank freely, & placed Buonaparte behind a Screen, while he amused himself with these two Ladies, who were then his humble dependents.—Madame Talian is a beautiful Woman, tall & elegant; Josephine is smaller & thin, with bad Teeth, something like Cloves,—it is needless to add that Buonaparte accepted the Promotion and the Lady—now—Empress of France!"* (Bibliothèque Nationale, Paris—Collection Viollet)

Napoleon on the Bridge at Arcola, by Baron Antoine Gros. Josephine persuaded Napoleon to pose for this portrait by sitting him on her knee. (Musée de Versailles—N.D. Roger-Viollet)

The Luxembourg Palace and Gardens. (Musée Carnavalet—Hachette)

The Tuileries Palace seen from the gardens. The Pavillon de Flore is on the right. (Musée Carnavalet—Harlingue-Viollet)

was in fact hesitant. Only the preceding day he had said to Junot: "Ah, if only the Parisians [i.e., the rebels] would name me their chief, I would see to it that the Tuileries would be invaded within two hours, and we would chase those miserable deputies out of there."[4] Planning to wait and choose the winning side, he was therefore much put out when Barras told him he had exactly three minutes in which to decide whether to become one of his seconds-in-command. As soon as he consented, Barras took him to the Committee of Public Safety, sitting in session at the Tuileries, and requested an order be signed reintegrating Bonaparte into the army. Few in the Committee had heard of Napoleon, but the royalist agent Mallet, who knew everyone in Paris, simply described him to his correspondents in Vienna as "a Corsican terrorist named Buonaparte, a professional scoundrel and the right arm of Barras."

Throughout the night of October 4 the drums of the sections continued to beat the call to arms, and a steady downpour never ceased. The situation of the government appeared desperate; during the night twenty thousand insurgents moved silently toward the Tuileries, surrounding it with an ever-tightening circle of bayonets. The rebels, already masters of a large part of Paris, were expected to attack the Tuileries from the rear on the Right Bank of the river; from the Left Bank.

Both sides lacked artillery, the indispensable weapon for street fighting, though forty cannon were known to be stationed at Neuilly, then just outside the city. A call for a cavalry officer unemployed since Thermidor produced Lieutenant Colonel Joachim Murat, a huge man with a big nose, a strong southern accent and three hundred horsemen under his command. Ordered to bring back the guns at all costs, his cavalry galloped straight through the rebels' encampments, harnessed the gun carriages to the horses and through the wet, dark streets hauled them to the Tuileries. The noise of their wheels over the cobblestones sounded like thunder, Murat remembered.

While Murat, the future King of Naples, was taking this first step toward his throne, the future Emperor of the French toured the lines of defense with Barras and with the other unemployed Jacobin generals until nine the next morning. Barras had the government's forces, less than four thousand men, placed in a protective circle guarding the Tuileries. The enemy, however, appeared to hold the Convention in a vise on the Right Bank; all the streets leading to the seat of government were in their hands.

Bonaparte posted batteries to rake the rue St. Honoré, the route the rebels would take in a march on the convention, and in positions directly defending the bridge across the Seine. Although some of the other officers' actions on that day were remembered, none but General Thiébault appear to have noticed Bonaparte's. Seeing him for the first time that morning, he would comment later upon the General's "frail appearance, cameo face and dirty uniform. . . . He seemed to be everywhere at once and his orders were laconic and peremptory to a degree."[5]

Instead of attacking early on the morning of October 5 (13 Vendémiaire), the insurgents waited for the rain to stop, allowing Bonaparte time to place all his batteries. At 11 A.M. Barras appeared before the Convention to give an account of the dispositions taken. Optimistically, he assured the representatives that "the majority of Parisians remain faithful to the Republic and will make a rampart of their bodies before the Convention." While he was speaking, sporadic gunfire could be heard around the Tuileries. A police report of the day noted: "In all Paris there was a fearful noise and the rain, which had been falling since yesterday, increases the disorder; the aspect of the city is sinister." Nevertheless, crowds of Parisians, behaving as though at a picnic, mingled with the troops, chattering about the best position from which to view the battle. The majority appeared to be mostly pro-insurrection, or at least anti-Convention, and certain of victory.

At four in the afternoon, the insurgents were seen to prepare to attack. At 4:45 the advance on the Tuileries started.

For the first time in revolutionary street fighting, the rebels were met by murderous artillery fire. Behind the Tuileries they fell back, then reassembled in the present rue St. Roch, a street leading directly to the palace; the Church of St. Roch was immediately in front of a battery commanded by General Bonaparte. Pushed back onto the church itself by a first barrage, the insurrectionists climbed to the roof, aimed from behind chimneys and shot through the steeple, but when the cannon were moved forward, and the General's famous "whiff of grapeshot"[6] mowed them down, the street was cleared in a few minutes. On the Left Bank the batteries directed across the Seine prevented the rebels from crossing over. By six o'clock they too were defeated, and by nightfall completely dispersed. The dead fell in puddles and in the mud, and the rain continued. Four hundred bodies were piled into St. Roch, about a thousand others left in the rain-soaked streets. That night the theaters were as full as ever.

For Carlyle the historian, Vendémiaire was the moment when "the . . . French Revolution is blown into space and became a thing that was."[7]

On the day after the battle, the Tuileries Palace was said to resemble a fortress under siege, its gardens covered with tents and artillery. The Convention's permanent session was lifted and a military commission set up to judge the perpetrators of the riot. Confident now of the continuance in power of the Thermidorian majority, the government ordered the gates of Paris left open to allow the escape of most of the insurgents.

On the same day, October 6, Paul Barras, now the all-powerful man of the Republic, informed the Great Committee that the victory of the day before was due in large part to the actions of General Bonaparte. He asked that Bonaparte be promoted to major general and given the honors of the day. The committee was reluctant. There was general astonishment at the news that this man had played any role in the battle. No deputy or journalist had heard Napoleon's name mentioned until then. When, a week later, Barras decided to resign his post of commanding general, he requested that his successor be General Bonaparte. Overriding some protests, notably Lazare Carnot's, Barras succeeded in having the Convention name Napoleon commander in chief of the Army of the Interior.

From his vast new official residence on the corner of the Place Vendôme, General Bonaparte sent his brother Joseph an account of the battle (he himself, "with my usual luck," had not been hurt), and of the rain of gold and honors that had been showered upon him since "Vendémiaire." "You know," he wrote, "I live only for the pleasure of what I can do for my family. . . . I have lodgings and a carriage at your disposal here, and I have already sent sixty thousand livres in gold, silver and paper money to the family, so you need have no worries." He would, he added, be able to find a good position for Lucien, probably in charge of supplies in the Army of the Rhine; Louis had been sent for and would be promoted; Jérôme, now twelve years old, was to be escorted from Marseilles and placed in an Irish school near Paris; Uncle Fesch, too, had a post awaiting him; a consulate for Joseph "in a Latin-speaking country" would certainly be found. (Napoleon himself would find still better Latin-speaking positions for Joseph when he made him first King of Naples and then of Spain.) Finally Stanislas Fréron was bringing a letter of introduction to Mme Clary (there was a hint of condescension in this note from Bonaparte to Désirée's mother). The letter to Joseph ends with a postscript: "My respects to Eugénie and Julie."

The years of obscurity were over now. The fortune Napoleon had always dreamed of had become a reality; power, too, was part of his new command. He had reached the summit of the military hierarchy, making up within weeks for the years wasted in political manipulation in Corsica and France. His military rank was equal to that of the most revered republican generals—Hoche and Kellermann, for instance, and Joubert—who had fought the enemy and repelled the invader. His financial situation, however, was incomparably more favorable. The annual pay of a republican commander in chief in 1795 was forty-eight thousand livres, some of it in paper money. In this first installment alone, he had sent his family more than a year's pay.

So rapid an ascension as Bonaparte's had rarely been heard of, even in that period of dizzying changes. Baron Fain, who would become one of Emperor Napoleon's most faithful servants, recalled that at the time "we asked each other, where does he come from, what has he done, for what extraordinary services is he being rewarded?"[8] The answer, for the royalist agents, was obvious. He was still in their reports simply "Barras's man."

Only Napoleon remained unawed. As he would in every succeeding circumstance of his life, he adapted himself instantly to his overnight elevation. He would never, no matter how dazzling his future triumphs, appear to be in the least overwhelmed or even surprised, as though he were prepared for each stage of his destiny. He himself ascribed this to his confidence in his "star." In the future he would attribute even his military victories to it and his faith extended to a belief in its powers of protection. Referring to one of his enemies, he once asked wonderingly: "Doesn't the unfortunate man know that I have my star?"[9] Young Laure Permon recalled the occasion when Captain Bonaparte had told her mother that a mutual acquaintance had tried to harm him. "With an indescribable smile" Napoleon had explained: "But my *star* would not let him."[10]

As governor of Paris too, as well as commander in chief of the Army of the Interior responsible for the security of the capital, General Bonaparte demonstrated his prodigious organizing ability and ceaseless activity. His first care was to take over the police and to employ personally a number of secret agents; soon he had access to private and political details on everyone of note. Playing the part of the "Jacobin General Vendémiaire," he urged harsher measures against the rebels in Vendée and the guillotine for the leaders of the recent rebellion. He offered to supervise public displays of patriotism, and his daily reports to the Directory never failed to mention the number of times the "Marseillaise" was played in the Paris theaters.

Laure Permon remembered how overnight Napoleon became an important person, driving around in a fine carriage. General Vendémiaire—he encouraged the use of that name, partly because of his own unpronounceable Italian one*—commander of this powerful military post, had become the man to know in the Paris world. He gave "luncheon parties for twenty" at his Place Vendôme headquarters "at which ladies were sometimes present,"[12] and invited guests to his private box at the Opéra. A new self-assurance, it was noticed, had changed his expression. He took care now over his appearance. His ill-fitting uniforms were cleaner, he drenched himself in eau de cologne, and he was the most faithful of all the regulars at Paul Barras's receptions.

When, early in November, camp was finally lifted in the Tuileries Gardens, the police noted that the prostitutes had already deserted them in favor of the suddenly fashionable Luxembourg Gardens. On November 3 the five directors elected to head the executive branch of the new parliamentary government bundled into two hackney carriages and arrived at their official residence, the Luxembourg Palace, at nine in the morning. Barras would tell Mme de Staël that when the five entered the Luxembourg, only a concierge was there to open up one small room, lend them his own table with a broken leg, find five chairs and light a few logs of wood. "It was clear," recalled one of the five, "that the situation appeared so desperate that no one believed in the stability of our political existence, and therefore no one was in a hurry to serve us."[13] Domestics refused at

---

* Later he was to regret the name, however, and his "Jacobin" activities on that day. "I would give several years of my life," he told Bourrienne, "to efface that page from my life's story."[11]

first to appear at the Luxembourg, certain that they would not be paid.

On this foggy autumn day it was difficult to see anything in the great gilded, unlit salons; no chandeliers or furniture remained. The palace's last private occupant, the self-proclaimed Louis XVIII, had emigrated in 1790. The palace had then become a somber revolutionary prison; the windows were still barred, walls were marked with the last words of those about to die. Paving stones on the street leading to the palace remained cracked by the weight of the tumbrils driving from the Luxembourg to the guillotine in the previous years.

In an effort both to avoid another dictatorship and another Assembly in which power could be taken over by a minority, the new Constitution of elaborate checks and balances had provided for a legislative consisting, as in the United States, of two houses: the Council of Elders and the Council of Five Hundred. It was this legislature that was to elect an executive of five directors, a separation of powers so total as to make rivalry between the directors and the councils inevitable.

The choice of directors reflected the anti-right reaction following Vendémiaire; all were strongly republican, anti-Christian—and, above all, regicides, bound together by the belief that an "aristocracy of the scaffold" placed them beyond any pardon in the event of a Restoration. (So clearly was this understood to be a prerequisite of office that Talleyrand, to facilitate his nomination as a minister of the Directory, would proclaim himself "a regicide at heart, since I have been associated with all the accountability of the Revolution."[14])

The directors detested and distrusted one another; each had been chosen as a counterweight to the others. Their functions were carefully divided. Barras was given the Ministry of the Interior and Police; Lazare Carnot, War; Jean-François Reubell, foreign policy, or Exterior Relations, the other two, minor positions.

The problems faced by the new government were formidable. They had inherited a desperate situation: an empty Treasury, worthless paper currency, no public revenue and continuing famine; yet the Directory still had the country to feed as well as the fourteen armies in the field.

The directors' lives were as disjoined as their functions were divided, and at the end of their very long working day each returned to his separate apartment in the palace. Without the slightest hesitation Barras installed himself in the best suite of rooms, which included a celebrated gallery painted by Rubens. Though he retained all the revolutionary forms, and preferred to be known as "Citizen General," he nevertheless conserved his prerevolutionary manners. Opinions were divided on his appearance: Victorine de Chastenay, whom we last saw discussing Shakespeare with Bonaparte, described Barras then as: "Tall, dark, proud looking, a lively expression, a distinguished and really imposing air." Thiers the historian, however, would find in his portraits "something dark and sinister in his face."[15] "His face was the very mask of crime," according to one historian, or "the handsomest man of his time,"[16] for another. For Germaine de Staël he was simply "the most imposing figure I have ever known."[17] For the Napoleonic specialists there was never any doubt as to Barras's character. "Barras never knew fear in combat, in riots, nor at the Assembly, but was nevertheless the most vicious, the most venal, the most vile of men—a Talleyrand with courage but with less deceit."[18]

Although Paul Barras's colleagues admired their absurd new Directorial costume designed by David, Barras was disgusted by it and refused to wear the scarlet toga "draped in the antique fashion": knee breeches, lace collar, azure sash, shoes with rosettes and an enormous feathered felt hat. And although it was generally agreed that he was the only director not to appear grotesque in this disguise he always, except at official ceremonies, wore the same long military coat, boots and, according to contemporaries, "a martial air."[19]

The ex-Vicomte de Barras much enjoyed the years of his reign and, like Napoleon, believed that dignified, prestigious ceremonies were healthy in a new regime. The nightly receptions at his rooms at the Luxembourg consisted of conversation, a little dancing, much gambling and children's games, a new rage. Guests appear not to have witnessed what his fellow Director Larevellière described as "filthy orgies" in the course of which, he asserted, "chocolate was served in abundance," a beverage long considered to have aphrodisiac properties. His guests were well behaved, if underdressed; Barras was heard to remind his servants: "Remember to place cushions on the chair seats of the *Citoyenne* guests."[20]

Mme Tallien was Barras's official hostess at the Luxembourg while Mme de Beauharnais continued as official mistress of the director. Her new liaison with General Vendémiaire, however, was quite open.

❦ 11 ❧

To Destiny!

AFTER THE FIRST GLEEFUL REPORTS, JOSEPH BONAPARTE RECEIVED ONLY hurried notes from Napoleon who now, he wrote, had "too many preoccupations." Rose de Beauharnais was one of them.

Although they must have seen each other almost daily at the Chaumière and at Paul Barras's, the liaison of the General and the widow appears to have started only after Vendémiaire.

In Rose's first-known letter to Napoleon written on Thursday of the Republican week and dated "the evening of the 6th," she wrote: "You no longer come to see a friend who is fond of you; you have quite forsaken her. This is a mistake. as she is tenderly attached to you. Come to lunch with me tomorrow, *septidi*. I want to see you and to talk to you about matters of interest to you. Good night, *mon ami, je vous embrasse*," and signed it "Veuve Beauharnais."[1]

She seems to have hesitated after "mistake," placed a full stop there and, perhaps, with the more affectionate ending to the sentence changed the course of her life.

She was probably aware of the reassurance the General needed. The proof came in his hurried reply that same evening: "6 Brumaire: I cannot imagine the reason for the tone of your letter," he wrote. "I beg you to believe that no one desires your friendship as much as I do, no one could be more eager to prove it. Had my duties permitted, I would have come in person to deliver this message. Buonaparte."[2]

We have to guess the sequence of this correspondence, often dated only by the republican day of the week and later deliberately scrambled and mutilated by Eugène and Hortense. If Napoleon's note is indeed an answer to Rose's letter of "the 6th" both would have been written on October 28, only twenty-three days after the street battle of Vendémiaire.

When, after their mother's death, the Beauharnais children published a selection of her correspondence and Napoleon's, they placed this letter much later in the winter, embarrassed by her evident pursuit of the new man in power, by her hint of a position of influence and by the tone of intimacy so soon after the General's sudden rise.

Even before Vendémiaire Rose may well have been the only Merveilleuse in the Chaumière circle to pay any attention to this unpromising protégé of Barras. Her custom of making friends and allies, of assuring herself of even the most unlikely protectors, could have ensured her early interest in a man without any apparent future. At the time, though, she was perhaps for Bonaparte simply one of the "older and uglier women" around Mme T. mentioned in his letter to Désirée.

In her sweetly plaintive letter of "the 6th," Rose had struck the right note for a man whose ambition and whose timidity with women she had guessed: a light reproach, a flattering need for his presence, just a suggestion of useful protection.

Bonaparte may have held back initially either because in October he was still courting Mme Permon or because he needed some encouragement to return to the house of the elegant and desirable creature representing everything he had admired since his arrival in Paris.

"I was not insensible to women's charms," Napoleon dictated in the *Mémorial*, "but I had hardly been spoiled by them; I was shy with them. Mme Bonaparte was the first to give me confidence."[3] Nevertheless, her apparent concern for his ambitions must have seemed as improbable as the likelihood that she might allow herself to be courted; her aristocratic manner could only have added, in the General's eyes, to the impression she gave him of unobtainability; her surrender, however, was perhaps more rapid than he had imagined. The siege appears to have been brief.

At St. Helena, Napoleon dictated in the customary third person he employed there that "When Mme de Beauharnais invited him to visit her he was struck by her extraordinary grace and her irresistibly sweet manner. The acquaintance was shortly to ripen into intimacy."[4]

The date of this "ripening" is unknown, but it must have been the night before Napoleon wrote: "Seven in the morning. I awaken full of you . . . the memory of yesterday's intoxicating evening has left no rest to my senses. . . ." Then, for the first time he uses her new name. Following his procedure with Désirée, he has picked a fresh one for Marie-Joseph-Rose and the letter continues: ". . . Sweet and incomparable Josephine, I draw from your lips, from your heart, a flame which consumes me. . . . A thousand kisses, but do not give me any for they burn my blood."[5]

This, apparently the first of Napoleon's passionate letters, would be dated by the Beauharnais children only after the Bonaparte marriage, for marriage is what the General was insisting upon almost immediately. In one of Napoleon's versions of their earlier meetings, he dictated: "Mme de Beauharnais had always listened with interest to my plans. One day when I was sitting next to her at dinner, she began to pay me all manner of compliments on my military qualities. Her praise intoxicated me. From that moment I confined my conversation to her and never left her side."[6]

Perhaps when he remembered Josephine's characteristic flattery he had forgotten that he would claim "never to have noticed Mme de Beauharnais before."[7] For Eugène and Hortense were to effect several transformations in their accounts of their mother's past. To dispose of the Hoche affair, for instance, they would maintain that it was their father who, presumably in prison, had appealed to Lazare Hoche to take Eugène with him to Vendée—a command to which the General was not named until after Beauharnais's execution. And they successfully created the myth of the first meeting between their mother and the General, one later adopted by Napoleon himself, the "legend of the sword."

Nine days after Vendémiaire, Bonaparte had ordered the disarmament of all private citizens; unauthorized weapons were to be surrendered to the authorities. According to the legend, young Eugène, distressed at the idea of giving up his father's sword, visited General Bonaparte's office to ask for its return. He was accompanied by his mother, a lady unknown to the General. Although weapons from Josephine's Paris section would have been sent to the Arsenal, not to the General's headquarters, out of the thousands of weapons surrendered, this particular sword was found to be at General Bonaparte's headquarters and returned immediately to Eugène, whose grateful mother then invited Napoleon to visit her. This fable, as well as providing the romantic vein required by the times, had the additional advantage of eliminating any reference to Paul Barras's influence on both their lives.

. . .

From the start, General Bonaparte was impressed and intimidated by the air of quiet elegance of Josephine's house. It resembled neither Mme Clary's provincial setting nor the glittering modishness of the Chaumière. At St. Helena, Napoleon would tell General Gourgaud that Josephine's circle was composed of "the most distinguished society in Paris,"[8] evidence of a misunderstanding on several levels. Later, his social sense would become painfully acute, but now he had not enough worldly experience to notice that the exclusively masculine circle composed largely of elderly men, some of them Josephine's admirers from the Fontainebleau days, would not have thought it suitable to bring their wives to the charming small drawing room of Barras's mistress. Not only did they enjoy the company of seductive Mme de Beauharnais, but there were few former aristocrats who were not eager to approach this close to power, if only in the hope of having family names erased from the list of emigrés.

But General Bonaparte, in spite of the close attention he already paid to social matters, could not know that genuine members of the former nobility were more likely, if they were able to recover any of their possessions, to live in circumstances quite different from those of the Director's mistress. No carriage and pair, no army of domestics, no pretense of a salon. Returning exiles like Natalie de Laborde, finding the shell of her family's vandalized house intact, hung the windows and covered some remaining pieces of kitchen furniture in white calico. "No one bearing a famous name wished to receive in 1795," claimed one newly returned exile. But for a member of the new society like Josephine, the necessity as well as the means to maintain influential connections was all-important. Her house must reflect something more contemporary; her decoration and her small amount of furniture were all in the latest neoclassical style.

As Emperor, Napoleon's discriminating judgment for decoration and quality was infallible. Now, his unsophisticated eye failed to note that the apparent luxury of the house was for outward appearance only. He had no more idea that pastiche and illusion reigned in Josephine's house than he had of the fiction of its mistress's claim to familiarity with the court of Versailles. But there was no illusion in what he would describe as Josephine's "calm and dignified bearing of the society of the *ancien régime.*"[9]

"My son-in-law is a great snob," the Emperor of Austria would say, and Napoleon's taste for the French nobility, which would reach ludicrous proportions under the Empire, now found immense satisfaction in his belief that Josephine was closely connected to court circles. He never recovered from his first notion of his singular good fortune in obtaining for himself alone this "authentic Vicomtesse."[10] "Bonaparte imagined that this was an alliance with a very great lady,"[11] wrote Mme de Rémusat, and General Marmont's perceptive comment could well be true, that when Josephine finally agreed to the match, "Napoleon almost certainly believed at the time that he had taken a greater step upward than ever he felt when he married the daughter of the Caesars."[12]

Marmont, though he admitted to some wonder that Bonaparte should be attracted to Mme de Beauharnais, who "had lost all her bloom," decided that "the unbelievable reason" for the General's pride in this union was his attraction to the aristocracy although "his frequent discourses on the subject proved his ignorance of French society before the Revolution."[13]

The General's colleagues speculated upon Josephine's hold over him. Some part of it was thought to be the conviction that he could never be sure of her total surrender. That he saw her as a fortress never fully invested may well have been a powerful aphrodisiac, her apparent unattainability only heightening his urgent need to possess her for himself.

A November letter to Joseph Bonaparte from Napoleon ends with: "My love to your wife and my regards to Désirée" (no longer Eugénie).

Joseph must have regretted his former lack of enthusiasm for the "Désirée business." Resistance in the Bonaparte family was at first discreet, as the brothers watched Napoleon's involvement with Barras's mistress with increasing dismay. The fortunes and futures of all depended on him; a Corsican family's power derived from the strength of its alliances. Joseph's hints to his brother had not yet become open accusations. Out of earshot, Lucien referred to Mme de Beauharnais as a "decaying Creole." Certainly no one could answer less to Mme Letizia Buonaparte's notion of an ideal daughter-in-law.

Atavistically and temperamentally, Napoleon was fated to marry young. He seemed predestined like his parents, married at eighteen and fourteen, and his uxorious brothers Joseph and Lucien, for an early marriage. His proposed union appears still more improbable when the Josephine project is seen as the antithesis of everything to be expected of this exemplary family man, the provider of his family. Even in the case of Mme Permon, the concept of a dowry and of a respectable alliance was uppermost.

Josephine did, however, have attributes considered essential by Napoleon. She remained for him always and to the end *"une vraie femme."*[14] To Lazare Carnot he would describe her as "a woman in the fullest meaning of the term"; and "two things," he would say at St. Helena, "become a woman: rouge and tears."[15] Her preoccupation with dress, her tact and languid grace, her easy and becoming tears, her tender voice, even her debts and her lies appealed to this southern misogynist.

But neither Marmont nor Napoleon's family would ever take into account the intensity of his desire for Josephine. The man who had found his sexual initiation by a prostitute disappointing, who had proclaimed that love was "but a social feeling,"[16] who had observed that the French "are entirely absorbed by eroticism,"[17] and who had written only the previous year that he dreamed of a simple, conjugal attachment, was now helplessly involved in emotions he had not believed existed. In later years he would revert to his initial claim that "'preliminaries' were unnecessary and he would require only that his partner be ready, disrobed, in a room next to the imperial working office at the Tuileries Palace. The Emperor himself often took the time to remove little more than his sword and "the matter," he would inform his subordinates, "was dispatched within three minutes."

Now his erotic turmoil was complete. Forgotten, too, was his observation to Joseph that "women receive too much consideration in France. They should not be regarded as the equals of men; they are, in fact, mere machines for making children."[18]

His physical passion was exacerbated by his view that the manners, the charm and the mystery of the *ancien régime* were incarnated in Josephine. All his senses were stimulated by this voluptuous "great lady" who represented elegance, the unattainable and help for his ambitions.

Josephine's suavity and flatteries, her apparent access to influence as well as his own desire combined irresistibly to have him take one of the few steps of his life made without careful calculation. Some Napoleonic biographers have argued that Napoleon never abandoned these calculations and that ambition was uppermost in his mind that winter. At St.

Helena, Napoleon's cynical comment to Bertrand (who committed it to his ciphered diary) was: "I really loved Josephine, but I had no respect for her. She had the prettiest little c—— in the world, the Trois Ilets of Martinique were there. Actually, I married her only because I thought she had a large fortune. She said she had, but it was not true."[19]

Bonaparte's incandescent love letters alone make this pronouncement unconvincing, though Josephine's hints of large properties in the West Indies may have had some influence. ("She mentioned one or two millions owned by her in Martinique, and property in Santo Domingo.")[20]

There was one confrontation, "the afflicting scene which took place two weeks before our marriage," mentioned by Napoleon in a letter starting, "You thought I did not love you for yourself alone,"[21] which may have been either about her fortune or her influence with the Director. Josephine had discovered that the General had visited her notary to inquire about her properties in the West Indies, and this particular misunderstanding, for which he implored her forgiveness, was to be the source apparently of their most serious premarital quarrel.

The subject could also have been about her relationship with Barras; she may have deluded Napoleon into believing that a physical relationship with the Director did not exist, or else he convinced himself that it did not. It has also been thought that he knew, and accepted the situation; his knowledge of it can hardly be in doubt. Barras, logically this time, argues that since Josephine was well known to be his official mistress and since General Bonaparte was constantly with him throughout that year "he, more than anyone else, was aware of the facts."[22] Other biographers have even believed that it was precisely this relationship that decided Buonaparte to marry Mme de Beauharnais—the conviction that this was the quickest way to achieve his military and political ambitions. (Barras records that that winter, whenever Napoleon had favors to ask he would always come with Josephine or else ask her to plead for him. One of these favors was that Barras put forward Napoleon's name as minister for war. The Directors refused to consider it, and Lazare Carnot, who continued to direct military planning, remained hostile to Bonaparte and to his plan for an Italian campaign.[23])

The violence of Napoleon's passionate letters after his marriage surely proves that neither ambition nor hopes of her fortune were his only or even his principal motive. Even General Marmont wrote that "when

General Bonaparte fell in love with Mme de Beauharnais, it was love in all the power and strength of the term. It was apparently his first passion, and he felt it with all the vigor of his nature."[24]

At St. Helena, Napoleon appeared determined to justify his unlikely union with Josephine. Was it, as one recent biographer has speculated, "to present to posterity a more imposing picture, that Napoleon tried in the *Mémorial* to lessen the importance of love in his life? Did he want to forget—and to make others forget—that he had married an expert, ardent, flighty mistress, not befitting the imperial Majesty beyond the tomb?"[25]

This close-knit group, Thérésia Tallien and Josephine, Barras and Bonaparte, continued to see one another daily; even their children were being educated at the same establishments. The younger of the Bonaparte sisters were enrolled at Mme Campan's, and their education and manners were said to show remarkable improvement. The institution that was to provide the Empire with a host of duchesses, princesses, wives of marshals and even two queens had adopted some of Rousseau's advanced ideas on education. Mme Campan's curriculum included gymnastics, farming and the study of nature, as well as maths, history and modern languages.

Napoleon could now afford to send his sixteen-year-old brother Jérôme to the McDermott Academy, where Eugène was already boarding. The boy's grateful letters to Mme Tallien for opening her house to him on holidays survive today. When Thérésia's Fontenay's son was entered at the Academy, she wrote Mr. McDermott to ask if her Théo might share a room with "Messieurs de Beauharnais and Bonaparte," so that he might be less homesick.[26]

Josephine tried that winter to put off the question of marriage. At first she refused even to contemplate it.

It was incomprehensible to most of their friends why General Buonaparte should wish to marry the expensive widow whose favors had already been granted. Josephine shared this surprise. Entirely happy in her role as Barras's acknowledged mistress at the Luxembourg, a recreation of the Chaumière circle, she saw her life in Paris as now near to her ideal.

All her indolence rebelled against the violence she felt in Bonaparte.

Her "dislike of strong emotions" noted by Mme de Rémusat was overwhelmed by the General's passion. And there were further reasons for her reluctance. Marriage to Bonaparte would not provide that elusive security for which she might be willing to give up other attractions. It was only eighteen months since Alexandre de Beauharnais had been executed; she had little reason to believe in the guaranty of a republican general's future. In a reversal of roles from the days of her Beauharnais marriage, it was Josephine, once the supplicant, who was now so socially aware and sophisticated, and General Bonaparte, the outsider, as awkward in her company as she had been in Alexandre's.

In no way did the General conform to her idea of either a husband or a lover. He did not make her laugh, but in those days, she was to tell Mme de Rémusat, Napoleon, "though silent and awkward with women, was passionate and lively, though altogether strange in all his person."[27] He only, she would say later, became violent and "despotic" after his Egyptian campaign. (She may well, with typical heedlessness, have failed to make the obvious connection, that it was then that he learned of her infidelity.) He had no fortune. Her senses were not engaged. He was not, in her opinion, physically appealing. Her taste had always run to tall, conventionally good-looking men like Beauharnais, Barras and Hoche. She would, of course, have much preferred a banker like Ouvrard, a powerful politician like Barras or, if a man still on the way up, at least one as physically attractive as Lazare Hoche.

Josephine worried too about her hold on Paul Barras. Although she was still his official mistress, Thérésia Tallien was replacing her in all but title. Would he continue, if she were married, to use his influence and his purse in her favor? And she fretted increasingly about her age and her fading looks; Barras was not the only memorialist who mentioned her "early decrepitude."[28]

Josephine's temperamental preference for the line of least resistance held out against the necessity of making a decision, but there was the uncertainty of the future, her appalling debts and what too many friends were suggesting might be her "last chance."

She consulted the old Beauharnais' who advised her to marry the General. Her notary Raguideau indignantly denounced any union with a man who had only his sword. "You should marry a contractor to the armies who could give you all the money you need,"[29] he told her.

She consulted both Paul Barras and Thérésia. The Director records that when Bonaparte too asked his advice, he encouraged him. "Why not, you don't belong anywhere, you are alone; a married man offers a little more surface and resistance to his enemies."[30] "And Barras," said Napoleon at St. Helena, "did me a good turn when he advised me to marry Josephine. He pointed out that she belonged both to the old regime and the new, that the marriage would give me 'consistency,' would make people forget my Corsican name, would make me wholly French."[31]

Marriage was seen by the Directory to be a mark of good citizenship, useful for this insecure outsider. Whereas the Constitution of the Year III decreed that the Five Hundred were required only to be thirty years old and need not be married, the more consequential Elders had to be not only over forty, but either married or widowers.

It was the break with Lazare Hoche that finally decided Josephine. The civil war in Vendée was considered over since the General's defeat of the rebels. The Army of the West was to be disbanded, and Hoche was recalled to Paris in November; on December 26, 1795, he was named commander in chief of the Army of the West Coast in preparation for a projected disembarkation in Ireland.

Although he knew that his wife, eight months pregnant, was expecting him at her home in Lorraine, Hoche lingered in Paris and did not write her immediately of his new appointment. He was still attracted to Josephine. He may have already known that he would find her acting as Barras's hostess both at the Luxembourg and at his suburban house, but he was apparently outraged to find that her new admirer was that same general who had invented repeated excuses of bad health not to serve under him in Vendée. Equally unwelcome was the revelation that this brigadier general, with no claim to a military command, was now his equal in rank and a privileged protégé of Barras.

Ouvrard in his *Mémoires* describes a curious scene at the Chaumière that winter. Bonaparte, "in excellent spirits," was driven, perhaps by jealousy, to uncharacteristically playful behavior; he pretended to be a fortune-teller and "took Mme Tallien's hand, then several others', inventing a thousand follies." When he came to Hoche, "another mood came over him, and in a disagreeable voice he said, 'General, you will die in your bed.' "* Hoche flushed with anger at this "until Mme de Beauharnais changed the subject."[32]

That winter, wrote Barras, "Mme de Beauharnais, to lure Hoche back, told him that she could help him professionally and financially through her influence with the government and with me over whom, she said, she had much influence. But Hoche was too proud to owe his *gloire* to anyone but to himself, and refused any such conversation."[33] Although this statement was undoubtedly written to emphasize the contrast between Hoche's and Bonaparte's reactions to similar claims, it echoes too faithfully Josephine's first known note to Napoleon to be discounted. There is confirmation too in Hoche's own bitter comments on Josephine the following year. When he had reason to detest Bonaparte and all who were close to him Hoche, so Barras claims, said of Josephine: "In prison it is perfectly understandable to take a whore as mistress, but not to make her one's lawful wife."[34] And later Hoche wrote to a friend: "I have asked Mme Bonaparte to return my letters. I do not wish her husband to read my love letters to that woman . . . whom I despise."[35] Nevertheless, Hoche, instead of joining his wife, stayed on in Paris until January 3; their friends thought that he was still uncertain as to whether to break with Mme de Beauharnais. With news of the birth of his daughter he left Paris without mentioning divorce.

After Lazare Hoche's departure events moved fast. In January, Napoleon informed Désirée that unless she could immediately obtain the consent of her family, they must break off relations. He knew, of course, that as a minor she could not marry without her parents' consent. She answered with a piteous letter wishing him happiness; she would never love another, she wrote.

On March 2, 1796, Bonaparte was named commander in chief of the Army of Italy. Although Italy was considered a secondary theater of operations, intended, like the projected disembarkation in Ireland under Hoche, to be diversionary only, Bonaparte's nomination was immediately controversial. There was an explosion of indignation in the press when the first rumors of it leaked out.

The directors were accused of advancing Napoleon Bonaparte beyond his merits because they were afraid of the ambitions of generals with

---

* A prediction fulfilled in 1797.

more glorious military reputations—Hoche, for example, or Moreau, or Marceau or Pichegru. The startling rise of the "calculating adventurer" was seen as a debt of gratitude owed by the government to its own sword, to the political military man who had helped protect the "perpetuals" at Vendémiaire.

Toulon and the street battle of Vendémiaire, it was felt, were hardly sufficient to have Napoleon's apparently transcendental military qualities recognized. He was generally considered a foreigner. His name, his strong Italian accent and the fact that he was unknown to the military hierarchy were all against him. "To be named commander in chief was an enormous post at that period," wrote Lacretelle, "when it was accepted that Generals would enrich themselves by pillage during a campaign."[36]

Although Napoleon at St. Helena would assert that it was Lazare Carnot who had named him to the Italian command, and Carnot himself still critical of Bonaparte and of his proposal of an invasion of Italy, would claim after the victorious campaign that it was he who was responsible for that nomination, Lucien Bonaparte would maintain that "the supreme command of the Army of Italy was Barras's dowry."[37] And Jérôme Gohier, too, later a director and no friend of Barras, concurred and denounced Napoleon's "gross ingratitude"[38] to Barras. There is no doubt that both Napoleon and Josephine regarded him alone as their patron; Napoleon would even find it politic in the following months to write extravagantly flattering letters from Italy to Thérésia as well as to Barras.

Tales of "the dowry" were to continue to haunt Napoleon, and he would blame Josephine for giving them substance. A ferocious British cartoon summed up the more or less general feeling about the Bonaparte promotion; the General is seen peering around a curtain to observe two naked women dancing before Barras, and identified as Josephine and Thérésia Tallien by a lubricious and misspelt caption.

Josephine did not resign herself to the match until February 24, and at least until the fourteenth of that month she was still acting as Barras's official hostess at his house in Chaillot and sending out invitations to dine there *chez elle*. Their physical liaison, too, if Barras's references are to be believed, continued until the marriage in March.

That marriage, Josephine decided, would be no more than a civil contract. There would be no religious service. A civil marriage was hardly binding: divorce was easy; incompatibility could be given as sufficient reason. There would be separate marriage settlements; if the General were killed in Italy, his pension would go to his wife. Naturally, she would retain her own more prestigious name.

The ceremony was set for seven in the evening on March 6 in the mayor's office on the first floor of the former house of an emigré; the gilded paneling can still be seen in the room where Josephine and her witnesses waited three hours for the bridegroom, variously described as working on the plans for the Italian campaign or as forging his birth certificate.

The bride was the picture of republicanism in a white muslin dress and a tricolor sash. Eight years later France's crown jewels would be hers; on that day she wore her only wedding present from the bridegroom, "a simple necklace of chains of hair holding a gold enameled medallion on which was engraved 'To Destiny.' "[39]

Waiting with her were her own witnesses: both Talliens, Barras and her notary Calmelet; and eighteen-year-old Captain Le Marois, witness for the groom.

A hilarious accumulation of illegalities surrounded the event. None of those present could guess that the register was likely to be scrutinized in the future or that it would be used to facilitate an imperial divorce. Josephine, claiming that the British occupation of the Windward Islands barred her from access to her birth certificate, stripped four years from her age by settling for her deceased sister Manette's birth date, 1767, while Napoleon, also claiming to be unable to obtain his own certificate, substituted his brother Joseph's birthday of 1768: thereby not only adding seventeen months to his age but falsifying his birthplace too, inserting Paris instead of Ajaccio. In addition, Le Marois, a minor, could not legally be the General's witness.

Josephine would tell Thermidor Tallien that she would always remember the candle burning low in a tin candlestick while the assistants waited three hours for the bridegroom's arrival. When Napoleon finally erupted into the room he found the assistants half asleep and the mayor departed. His replacement, one Collin, was without legal authority to perform the service. Napoleon shook him briskly by the shoulder, ordered him to "marry us quickly," and within minutes it was over and the newlyweds were driving back to rue Chantereine.

"The young hero," reported the press, "has married Mme Beauharnais, a youthful widow of forty-two, who was not bad looking while she still had a tooth left in her pretty little mouth." And Baron de Frénilly noted later: "Mme de Beauharnais with two children and no money, through hunger and an amorous disposition, had become the *maîtresse en titre* of Barras. The rest is well known. Barras tired of her and got rid of her by giving her the Army of Italy as a dowry. The little General of 13 Vendémiaire took the dowry and the mistress, and made of her an Empress."[40]

❧ 12 ❧

A KIND OF RADIANCE

TWO DAYS AFTER HIS MIDNIGHT MARRIAGE, NAPOLEON BONAPARTE WAS on his way south to take up his command at the headquarters of the Army of Italy in Nice.

By June, he was the established dictator of northern Italy; his army headquarters were in Milan, where the most sumptuous palace of the city was kept in constant readiness for Josephine's arrival.

Between those dates, the forced marches of the French Army of Italy, the lightning descents upon the enemy, the dramatic skirting of the snowbound Alps, the whole immortal series of victories of the Italian campaign were, Napoleon would declare in his letters to Josephine, all undertaken in the hope that they would hasten her arrival.

For 127 days, from March 8 until July 13, General Bonaparte wrote to his wife at least once a day—letters exploding with longing, frustration and explicit sensuality; by turn melancholy, turgid, tender, incoherent, often suicidal—and when she failed to join him, of almost unhinged despair.

One, and often more than one, letter a day was dispatched to the rue Chantereine from general headquarters by the most rapid courier, while a second stream of messengers galloped to Paris with news of fresh victories for the Directory. The dispatch bearers were ordered not to rest at relays. Hoping the messengers would return with letters from Josephine, the General wrote to Barras, Carnot and Joseph Bonaparte: "I beg you to see that my couriers remain less than four hours in Paris."

Before his departure, General Bonaparte had urged the government to permit French armies to "support themselves by making war at the expense of other countries," and one of the means by which he was to establish his ascendancy over his troops was by offering them increased opportunities for loot. He knew that the supply route from Italy back to Nice would mean that the army was to live largely by organized pillage; much of its amazing speed would be due to this strategy.

Like all the French armies of the Revolution, the Army of Italy was made up of the volunteers and conscripts of the great mass levy of 1792 as well as of some former cadres. Although each of the armies felt itself to be the true repository of revolutionary fervor, and suspected the government in Paris of being ready to make peace in Europe—perhaps even with the counter-revolutionaries at home—the Army of Italy was considered to retain even more of the original revolutionary zeal.

It soon became known that these opportunities were greater in Bonaparte's army than in the more prestigious French armies in Germany. In exile at St. Helena, Napoleon would dictate to his biographer the celebrated order of the day delivered, he would say, before the Army of Italy set out on its victorious campaign:

> Soldiers, you are naked and ill-fed; though the government owes you much, it can give you nothing. Your patience and your courage are admirable, but they procure you no glory; no fame shines upon you. I will lead you into the most fertile plains in the world. Rich provinces, great cities will lie in your power; you will find there honor, glory and riches. . . .[1]

The fact that this proclamation appears never to have been made is immaterial, for Bonaparte undoubtedly infected his troops not only with hopes of loot and of glory to match the other armies of the Republic, but with something more. Napoleon's supreme gift, the leadership of men, was already apparent. He knew how to speak to his troops in the field, and the spell of his electrifying addresses never failed him to the end of his empire. This great actor himself acknowledged the power of his near-hypnotic presence. He speculated on how it was achieved—compounded, he believed, of a tone of voice, a certain expression, the alternation of blistering rages and of a rare smile of unusual seduction. To others it would always remain mysterious: "magical" or "demoniacal."

The magnetism of his presence was such as to inspire officers and men with total confidence. Marshal Marmont would remember, long after the Empire had come to a close: "We marched surrounded by a kind of radiance whose warmth I can still feel as I did fifty years ago."[2]

When Bonaparte reached Nice headquarters on March 15 there were three major generals waiting for him—Masséna, Desaix, and Augereau—all veterans of the revolutionary wars risen from the ranks, handsome and reckless, and each one over six feet tall. Their height was exaggerated by the towering tricolor plumes in their hats, which they did not bother to remove when the newly appointed commander in chief of the Army of Italy walked into the room. The story of Mme Bonaparte's dowry was notorious, and they had been exchanging sarcastic comments on "the political general," "the protégé of Barras and the women." Unimpressed by his appearance—"stunted and sickly-looking," Masséna remembered— their low opinion of their new leader was further confirmed when Bonaparte started by handing around for inspection a miniature of his wife.

Their attitude changed, however, as he subjected them to knowledgeable questions about each corps. They were impressed by his firm handling of a near mutiny in the former Army of the Alps and of his disbanding of a battalion that refused to march until it had been paid. Within forty-eight hours he had procured bread, meat, brandy for a week and twelve thousand pairs of shoes. Above all, he assured his troops that once they had broken through to the rich plains of Lombardy the opportunities for loot would be immense.

Bonaparte's army of forty-one thousand citizen soldiers would be facing an Austrian force of approximately thirty-eight thousand men and a Piedmontese army of twenty-five thousand. His artillery was inadequate, his supply line almost nonexistent, and he himself had never fought a pitched battle. Nevertheless, he set out confidently from Nice on April 2, 1796, armed with the offensive tactical plan upon which he had been working for the past two years—and with his ambition.

The French government knew nothing of the personal aspirations of General Bonaparte. The Directory, on the verge of economic collapse, was not interested in conquest; it wished rather for a general European peace now that only Russia, England and the Hapsburg Empire remained in the First Coalition against revolutionary France. The instructions of

Lazare Carnot (no longer minister of war but now the director in charge of the armies) were for the two French Armies of the Rhine to advance upon Austria from the north, while the Army of Italy was to invade Piedmont, Austria's ally, immobilize part of the imperial Austrian army and eventually, by a pincer movement through the Tyrol, join up with the French Rhine Armies of Sambre and Meuse and of the Rhine in Vienna. The operations of the Army of Italy were to be secondary to the Rhine armies under Generals Jourdan and Hoche, who faced greater odds and more prestigious enemy commanders. The ultimate aim of these maneuvers was to obtain a peace treaty with Austria, one above all that would secure for France the sacred "natural frontier" of the Rhine, that major political article of faith since 1791.

Austria was only one of the countries included in the vast Holy Roman Empire, the Hapsburg domain that embraced not only Hungary, the present-day Czech Republic, Slovakia, Romania and part of the former Yugoslavia, but also a large part of Germany. Much of the left bank of the Rhine was therefore included within the empire's boundaries.

In Italy, the Austrian Emperor ruled over Lombardy and Venetia; his principal ally there was the King of Savoy and Piedmont; secondary allies were Rome and the Papal States, the Kingdom of Naples, and a number of small duchies and principalities like Parma and Modena. The first task of the Army of Italy would be to separate the Austrian forces from those of the King of Savoy, master of all the Alpine strongholds in Piedmont and believed by the French government to be ready to abandon his Austrian ally at the first reverse.

To avoid those fortified Alpine passes, Bonaparte started by first making a circuit around the Alps, then, in a campaign that would revolutionize the conduct of war and that remains to this day the wonder of students of military history, he proceeded to disorganize the Austrian defense system by the rapidity of his movements. By pitilessly force-marching his troops, by breaking all eighteenth-century rules of warfare and disregarding almost every principle taught in military schools—above all, by splitting the Piedmontese from the Austrian armies and attacking them separately—General Bonaparte could announce to the Directory on April 14 that he had won six battles, taken two thousand prisoners, killed six thousand men and captured twenty-one flags and forty cannon.

When, at dawn on that April day, the Army of Italy suddenly came upon the promised land, a shout went up from the ranks as they looked down from the heights of Mount Zemolo at the rich plains and cities of Lombardy, gilded by the early spring sun. Far away to the north, the snowcapped Alps they had skirted were just visible.

Nine days later the Piedmontese sued for an armistice. It was clear that the Austrians were definitively split off from their allies, but to the French commander in chief another advantage was equally apparent. His first condition for peace had been that his couriers be permitted to pass through Piedmont. By the treaty that followed the armistice, the King of Sardinia agreed to make a "war contribution" of three million francs, to cede Savoy to France and, most important to General Bonaparte, to allow the French free passage through Piedmont; by avoiding the detour through Nice, a courier's itinerary to Paris was reduced by almost two hundred miles.

Napoleon's earliest letters to Josephine mentioned little of his ambitions or of the campaign. Before leaving for Italy he wrote from Nice that, in the midst of all his preoccupations, "not a day goes by without my loving you; not a night without holding you in my arms. . . . I curse the glory and ambition which keep me from the soul of my life. In the midst of business, at the head of my troops, my adorable Josephine is alone in my heart, absorbs all my thoughts. . . . If I fly from you with the speed of the river Rhône, it is only to see you sooner. When I get up to work in the middle of the night, it is in the hope of advancing by a few hours the arrival of my sweet love." The letter ends with the most impossible of all requests of Josephine: "I ask neither for eternal love, nor faithfulness, only for *truthfulness*, for frankness without limit." And on the next day: "Remember what I once told you, Nature made me strong and determined . . . and made you of gossamer and lace." The postscript contains one of the few references to his preoccupations: "I have had meat, bread and fodder distributed. My cavalry will soon be ready. My soldiers are incredibly confident in me. Only you grieve me; you, the pleasure and the torment of my life!"[3] All this, because he had not heard from Josephine for a few days.

Bonaparte's letters were written in snatched moments: in a tent at the end of a strenuous day's march, at dawn before a battle, during tactical meetings. Half of them, he admitted, went unsent, stuffed into his pockets. Josephine's own brief ones were scribbled between visits to the country, and at ever-lengthening intervals. "I get only one letter from you every four days," the General complained, "whereas if you loved me you would write twice a day. . . . But you have to chat with your callers at ten o'clock in the morning, and then listen to idle talk until an hour past midnight. . . . But I love you more each day. Absence cures small passions but increases great ones."[4]

And then after April, when the letters from her husband became ever more imperious and finally frantic, Josephine's own became rarer still, written distractedly in the intervals of a new love affair.

The armistice with the Piedmontese was signed on April 28; three days earlier Napoleon had sent Colonel Andoche Junot to Paris by the longer route. He carried twenty-two enemy flags for presentation to the Directory, a patriotic proclamation to the government and strict orders not to return without Josephine. The following day Colonel Joachim Murat was also dispatched to Paris by the new, shorter route, bearing orders to all the postmasters of Piedmont to furnish him with horses at every relay.

He sped from Turin, galloped through the Alpine passes and over Mount Cenis, traveling from dawn to dusk and wearing out a dozen post-horses daily. Reaching Paris on the morning of May 6, he presented the General's dispatches to the Directors Carnot and Barras at the Luxembourg Palace and then proceeded to the rue Chantereine with the letter he had been instructed to give Josephine in person. It was an unusually incoherent one. ". . . A kiss on your lips and on your heart. . . . There's no one else, no one but me, is there? . . . And another on your breast. Lucky Murat! . . . little hand! . . ."[5] But his instructions to her to return with Murat were crisp. Her journey was planned to the last detail: maid, carriage, coachman, horses and, at the end of the journey, every luxury.

A few hours later Colonel Junot, too, drove up the narrow alley of the rue Chantereine with the earlier, equally pressing letter from General Bonaparte.

"You must return with Junot, do you hear, my adorable one, he will see you, he will breathe the air of your shrine. Perhaps you will even allow him the unique favor of a kiss on your cheek. . . . You will come, won't you? You will be with me, on my heart, in my arms, on my lips. . . . A kiss on your heart, and then another a little lower, much, *much lower,*[6] the last two words so furiously underlined that the pen stabbed through the paper.

At first Josephine was bewildered by the increasingly peremptory orders to join the man she was unable to think of as a husband, and unequal to the passion contained in them. The idea of a regular correspondence, still less that of joining Bonaparte in the field, had never occurred to her. Leave Paris, friends, parties at the Luxembourg, for a man whose very name she could not even regard as her own! The General shared this doubt. His first letter was addressed "To the Citoyenne Beauharnais," the following ones "To the Citoyenne Bonaparte, care of the Citoyenne Beauharnais in the rue Chantereine."[7] Was he afraid the postman would not be able to find the person with the unknown name? He wrote her that he would like her to use it, but was awaiting her instructions. Only after the first celebrated victories did he address the letters directly to her new married name.

Like most women of her era and her class, Josephine addressed her husband by his family name and for the rest of her life she would call him "Bonaparte." He signed his own letters "B.P." for *Buona Parte*, although for the first time he now adopted the gallicized form.

The writer's Italian accent can be heard through the phonetic and eccentric spelling of the letters; their grammar was deplorable. The violent underscoring of the more erotic passages is scratched almost through the paper headed "l'An IVe de la République Française Une et Indivisible, Bonaparte, Général en Chef de l'Armée d'Italie"; and dated from the small Italian towns whose names, those of his victories, were about to enter history.

Not all of the letters were opened upon arrival; attempting to decipher them took so long, and Josephine was too busy now. It seems more likely that she put many of them aside "to read later," overwhelmed as she was by parties, celebrations of all kinds and the daily visits of her dressmaker.

She was gratified, though, by the adoration she had aroused in her husband and would complacently read aloud to visitors some of the violently passionate lines. Her friend, the poet and playwright Antoine Arnault, visited her on the day Murat delivered his general's letter. "I remember her," he wrote, "reading out a passage in which her husband seemed to repel the doubts which tormented him. 'If it were true, fear Othello's dagger!' he had written. I can still see her smiling as she said in her creole accent: "*Qu'il est drôle,* Bonaparte!" ("Bonaparte is so amusing!")[8]

Her semicircular boudoir was once again open to visitors—the General's unsmiling presence had tended to keep them away in recent months—but conversation was constantly interrupted by couriers galloping up the narrow alley bearing further illegible bursts of disconcerting idolatry.

The torrent of incandescent passion must have appeared slightly ridiculous to Josephine. This, after all, had been a marriage of convenience, entered into with barely hidden reluctance on her part. The woman who "was afraid of all strong emotions" could only be further offended by so much turgid passion; her lighthearted sensuality was unable to respond to its violence. Yet in these spring months she was living as intensely in her own way as Bonaparte himself.

After each new victory in Italy she was recognized and applauded; the entire theater stood and clapped as she entered her box at the Feydeau. No one could have accepted more naturally the adulation that began to surround the Citoyenne Générale. To those who congratulated her on her husband's military successes, she answered simply: "Why yes, I believe Bonaparte to be a very good fellow." It is possible that she remembered that only three years earlier Alexandre de Beauharnais, too, had sent his proclamations to the army, and had his patriotic effusions read aloud to enthusiastic applause in the Assembly.

One immediately tangible result of her husband's victories was the gratifying amount of tradesmen's credit now extended to Mme Bonaparte; another was that the General's increasing personal power gave her a preeminent place at the Luxembourg Palace, at the Chaumière, at all the subscription balls. She was almost as much a queen now at the Luxembourg as Thérésia. Paul Barras surrounded Josephine with something like a court; he never failed to send her the first news of her husband's victories. She was certain that closeness to Barras was where real power lay.

Barras himself was becoming less certain, however. The directors were beginning to wonder just how much part personal ambition played in the General's sure command of public relations.

When Bonaparte had set out in the previous month, his name was known only to a handful of people, few of whom could even pronounce it. Yet not one of the other republican generals, his contemporaries, some with great victories to their names, had achieved instant celebrity.

The government was uneasy about the art with which the General ensured that the electrifying proclamations to his army should explode in Paris with maximum effect, and about the stage management of the relays of his officers galloping back to Paris, bearing the torn and bloodstained enemy standards. Already the General's system of agents and his propaganda bureau in Paris, orchestrated by his brother Joseph, had succeeded in presenting him not only as a heroic young revolutionary general facing overwhelming odds (odds it often magnified), but more formidably, also as the only man capable of bringing peace to the country.

The Directory was aware that the armies of the Republic had remained ardently republican, and were known to feel more loyalty to their chiefs than to the government. And the government had not forgotten that it had been saved by the army one year earlier.

General Bonaparte's letters to Paul Barras—and to Mme Tallien—remained obsequious for the present. He paid little attention to the other directors, but all of them, in view of his popularity, made a great show of their admiration for him. Carnot, for one, was taking no chances; Joseph Bonaparte records that after a dinner at the Luxembourg Lazare Carnot unbuttoned his waistcoat to reveal to Napoleon's brother a miniature of General Bonaparte "pinned over his heart."[9]

Since Josephine refused to accompany either Murat or Junot to Italy, both officers stayed on in Paris, awaiting further instructions. Joachim Murat, a dashing giant with long black corkscrew curls, remained only a few days, recovering from his epic ride and enjoying the adulation of Parisian ladies. But as a result of this stay in Paris, Murat lost his commanding general's confidence and never regained it, either as marshal, as King of Naples or as brother-in-law. Soon after his return to Italy, Laure Junot d'Abrantès's husband later told her, Bonaparte heard that Murat had bragged to his fellow officers during a champagne breakfast in his tent that "a charming Creole" in Paris had taught him to make a certain West Indian punch, and "a good many other things too. . . . Details barely decent and fit only for a supper of Hussar officers" were given, "as well as the particulars of a breakfast, a dinner, and a supper, all on the same day, in the country [the Champs Elysées], and all with the most beautiful woman in Paris, and with the prettiest."[10] These were taken to be Mme Tallien and Mme Bonaparte.

Although Murat's friends believed that in his Gascon exuberance he had simply exaggerated his Paris successes, it is certain that within twenty-four hours his commanding general had heard gossip of the champagne breakfast. And, ever a prey to superstition, Napoleon would not have forgotten that on the very day of Murat's arrival in Paris, according to Auguste Marmont, the glass broke on Josephine's miniature, always carried on his person. "He paled alarmingly, and said: 'Marmont, either my wife is very ill or she is unfaithful.' "[11]

It is, in fact, highly unlikely that Josephine would have taken an excessive interest in Murat as in that week in early May she had begun what was to be the most passionate love affair of her life.

Only a few days earlier, Colonel Leclerc of the Army of Italy had brought his aide, Lieutenant Hippolyte Charles, to the rue Chantereine. While his name and hints of his place in Josephine's life had surfaced occasionally in contemporary memoirs, Hippolyte Charles's very existence has been confirmed only in recent years by the historian Louis Hastier. The more reverent Napoleonic biographers had often dismissed even the presumption of his identity.

From the start Josephine was enthralled by Hippolyte Charles's looks and by his irresistible humor. Nine years younger than she, five feet two inches—her own height and Napoleon's*—and far from handsome, he was nevertheless charming-looking by the standards of the day. With merry blue eyes, a dimpled chin and silky black hair, he cut a valorous figure in his hussar's sky blue uniform, worn with a fox-trimmed pelisse thrown over the left shoulder. These were the hussars described by a contemporary as "a reckless and hard-swearing lot, clad in heavily-braided dolmans . . . the showiest uniforms in the army, wearing long pigtails and seeming particularly to embody much of the panache associated with the French cavalry as a whole, which had changed but little from pre-Revolutionary times."[12]

---

* Historians have long been divided on the question of Napoleon's exact height.

Hippolyte Charles loved life, loved women, loved his army career and was above all forever good-humored and full of jokes. Napoleon would be described by Talleyrand as *"inamusable,"* whereas Lieutenant Charles had Josephine "laughing till she cried, though she was careful to hold a handkerchief in front of her mouth so as to hide her teeth."[13] To Talleyrand, newly returned to France from his American exile, Josephine wrote immediately: "You will be mad about him. Madame Récamier, Madame Tallien and Madame Hamelin have quite lost their heads over him. His own is so beautiful! I think that no one before him has ever known how to tie a cravat."[14]

Lieutenant Charles had a good deal more to recommend him than this description of a military dandy would suggest. At the age of nineteen he had enlisted as a National Guardsman and had fought at the revolutionary battle of Valmy. "I have never," said one contemporary, "known a better comrade, or a better-humored one."[15] "In his youth," wrote another, "he was witty and full of charm; as an old man, little, thin, ugly and very amusing."[16] "The gayest, most even disposition, and a delightful companion,"[17] wrote Arnault, and Laure d'Abrantès described him as "a good father, a good friend, and with the warmest heart."[18]

He was a man of honor too. On his deathbed in 1837—he had lived alone and in poverty for some years—he asked his niece to burn before his eyes all his love letters from the former Empress of the French, letters that no amount of bullying, tenderness, recrimination or sarcasm had been able to extract from Josephine by either of her husbands.*

Napoleon's biographers—those who would admit to Hippolyte's existence—have had some difficulty in believing in Josephine's long preference for the lieutenant, but, as one historian has noted, "There is a vast difference between an academician's views of Napoleon's merits, and those of a pretty woman in love."[19] It is hard to believe that at this time Josephine felt the least physical attraction for her husband. His appearance, before the days of glory, was considered not far from comical, with

---

* Captain Charles's dossier in the War Ministry had been lost or removed, but references to him in cavalry officers' registries led Hastier to important letters in the possession of Charles's descendants. By chance, these had escaped the wholesale destruction Charles ordered on his deathbed. When Hortense, therefore, inquired later whether any of her mother's papers had been found, the Charles family denied it in good faith.

his ill-proportioned big head and short, skinny legs, and his skin still disfigured by scabies. Devoid of small talk or any form of diversion ("his forced laughter made others uncomfortable") and very possibly as expeditious a lover then as he would later prove to be with other women, it is not difficult to see why a frivolous and sensual woman might prefer Hippolyte Charles.

In spite of Barras's assertion that Josephine, "even when she appeared to have surrendered totally, never loved but out of self-interest,"[20] there is every reason to believe that, on the contrary, she enjoyed all her life the physical side of love for its own sake. And her liaison with Charles proved that when she was passionately involved she could behave with perfect rashness too. Even while she lived in the full glare of public attention, as virtual sovereign of Italy and wife of a national hero, she remained ardently and indiscreetly in love with Hippolyte Charles, who, though probably an attentive and considerate lover, was still a man with no funds and little future.

Josephine asked Colonel Murat to write a letter to her husband advising him that she was pregnant and too ill to write to him herself, and that the doctors did not advise the long journey at this time. Junot remained in Paris, waiting to escort her across the Alps. Colonel Leclerc rejoined the Army of Italy, but at Mme Bonaparte's request left his aide Hippolyte Charles to accompany her and Junot on the journey to Italy.

Murat's letter to his general was written on May 9. Barras and Joseph Bonaparte must have assumed that Josephine's personal triumph on that day, mentioned in every Paris journal, was too public not to have been reported to her husband by his spies and correspondents in Paris.

On May 9 Junot officially presented the Directory with the first battle trophies won by the Army of Italy. The ceremony took place with great pomp at the Luxembourg Palace. Josephine, Thérésia Tallien and Juliette Récamier shared a dais near the directors. "On one of the loveliest days in May," as Arnault remembered it, "each of the three wore the costume best calculated to set off her particular type of beauty. All three wore garlands of flowers in their hair; they looked like the three months of spring, gathered together to fete our victory."[21]

Laure Permon's description is less lyrical. Mme Tallien, "in the full bloom of her admirable beauty," she describes as Josephine's closest friend; she was there, Laure dryly adds, "representing some part of Directorial royalty—a role with which Josephine herself, both as Mme Beauharnais and perhaps also a little as Mme Bonaparte, had been equally invested, so to speak. Mme Bonaparte," she continues, "was still charming-looking in those days; her teeth were already horribly decayed, but with her mouth closed, and from a short distance, she gave the illusion of being a young and pretty woman."[22]

Junot, Laure's future husband, was very proud, she writes, of giving an arm to two of these ladies at the end of the ceremony. "He was twenty-five years old, extremely good-looking and wearing the uniform of a Colonel of Hussars." Outside, an immense crowd waited to see the celebrities leave. "Long live *la* Citoyenne Bonaparte, she's good to the poor people!" they heard as they went by. Then one of the fishwives from the Halles district shouted: "She's Our Lady of Victories!" "Yes," answered another, "and the lady on the officer's other arm, that's Our Lady of September."[23] Thérésia could no longer be forgiven for marrying one of the reputed authors of the September Massacres.

The victory of Lodi on May 10 was not only a decisive event in the Italian campaign—by outflanking the Austrian army at this point, Lombardy's capital, Milan (the seat of the Austrian government), was now opened to the French armies—but also, Napoleon was to say at St. Helena, some sort of personal watershed. It was then that he first felt set apart from others, a man of destiny, called to influence the fate of a people. "Already," he remembered, "I felt the earth flee beneath me, as though I were being carried to the sky."[24]

But still the burden of his thoughts and energies was directed to rue Chantereine. Murat's letter announcing Josephine's pregnancy reached him at Lodi immediately before the French army's entry into Milan. He wrote her at once, totally preoccupied by "your illness, that is all I think of, night and day. Without appetite, without sleep, without interest in friendship or glory or country. . . . A magnetic fluid flows between persons who love each other. . . . A thousand kisses upon your eyes, your lips, your tongue, everywhere. . . . Things are going well here," is his only reference to military operations before he goes on to bewail the fact that he cannot see "the little belly which must give you a wonderfully majestic and respectable air."[25]

Three days after the victory at Lodi, General Bonaparte, riding his white horse Bijou, entered the cheering, delirious city of Milan to the sound of the "Marseillaise." The Milanese, pressing forward to stare at the French general who had liberated them from Austrian rule, were unprepared for the sight of the small, emaciated figure, half eclipsed by a large hat decorated with an immense tricolor plume. After the planting of a ceremonial Tree of Liberty, the General rapped out a rousing republican proclamation in Italian. The French army, he declared, "comes to break your chains . . . our only quarrel is with the tyrants who have enslaved you." Freedom and France's eternal friendship were to be theirs. To the intellectuals and the liberals of Milan it appeared that the day of the Enlightenment had dawned.

Bonaparte, who had left Milan almost immediately to harry the Austrians to the north, was forced to return two days later to put down revolts throughout Lombardy and the outskirts of Milan. These uprisings, the result of the French army's policy of requisitioning at the point of bayonets and taking, and usually shooting, hostages, were crushed with some ferocity. When he reentered the city, the menacing tone of General Bonaparte's proclamation differed greatly from that of two weeks earlier. He threatened that his army would be "terrible as the fire of heaven toward rebels and the villages which harbor them." The Italian republicans would never recover their illusions.

These setbacks, however, did nothing to diminish the General's belief in his lucky star. "For luck is a woman," he told his aide Auguste Marmont, "and the more she does for me, the more I ill ask of her."[26] Only in one domain was that lady deficient.

At the time of his triumphant entry into Milan, "thin and hollow-chested with a look of fire, consumed by success, victories and glory, in love with one woman and already caught up in an incredible fairy tale," not one of the General's officers guessed that he was bleeding internally, racked by barely admitted misgivings about Josephine. In Paris, only Carnot and Barras knew of his agonizing doubts. His dispatches to both of them were accompanied by frantic appeals. To Carnot he wrote charmingly and incongruously of his wife: "I commend her to you; she is sincere and patriotic and I love her to distraction."[27]

Every time Bonaparte returned to his headquarters in the Serbelloni Palace, the most magnificent residence in the capital, he expected to find Josephine there. After signing an armistice with the Kingdom of Naples in June he had dashed back to Milan to find her "scrap of a letter" saying that she was ill, with three doctors in attendance. "My emotions are never moderate," he wrote, "since the moment I read that message, I have been in an indescribable state . . . the ardent love which fills me has perhaps unbalanced my mind."[28] By the same courier, he sent a letter to his brother Joseph and another to Barras. "I am in despair," he wrote his brother, "reassure me about my wife's health. You know that Josephine is the first woman I have ever adored. . . . I love her to distraction and I cannot remain any longer without her."[29] And to Barras, together with an official dispatch on an armistice with the Papal States, he added: "I hate all women. I am in despair. My wife won't come. She must have a lover keeping her in Paris."[30] In another letter to Josephine he tried a new tack: "As though a pretty woman could be expected to desert her friends, her Madame Tallien, dinner at Barras's, a new play or Fortuné—yes, Fortuné! You love everyone more than your husband."[31]

He attempted to arouse her jealousy: "Five or six hundred of the prettiest women in Milan have tried to please me, but I could see only you, think only of you." No sooner was the letter sent than he regretted it and pleaded with her to write him that she was quite certain that he loved her "more than can be imagined," that she knew that it had never occurred to him to think of any other woman.

Even his jealousy was held in abeyance. He had written Josephine that rather than that she be melancholy he was himself ready to send her a lover. Now, panic-stricken, he retracted: "You know very well that I could never bear your taking a lover—much less seriously suggest one to you. To see him and to tear out his heart would be one and the same thing. . . . A thousand kisses upon your eyes, your lips, your tongue, your c——."[32] (After reading some of these letters, the novelist Prosper Mérimée commented to Josephine's grandson Emperor Napoleon III: "He can talk of nothing but kisses, kisses everywhere, and upon portions of the anatomy not to be found in any dictionary of the Académie Française."[33])

Never again, after the early years of his obsession with Josephine, would Napoleon allow himself to care deeply for anyone with all the concentrated force of his nature, certainly not to the extent of subordinating his own well-being—and even his luck—to another. Now he was ready to give up the most precious thing in his life: his star, his guardian spirit, his destiny. He wrote that he would gladly forfeit his own luck and "deliver himself to the fates" if that would protect her. She should be "as free from sadness as your beautiful body from sickness; may my guardian spirit, which has always shielded me in the midst of danger, surround and envelop you and leave me unprotected."[34]

Laure d'Abrantès would claim that Napoleon was born without a heart, that "although open to family feeling,"[35] he was always incapable of affection, whereas Mme de Rémusat believed that he "might have been a better man had he been more loved."[36] It seems more likely that his passion for Josephine was an aberration, and that he would, in any case, have reverted to his native cynicism and misogyny. "Egotism in a soul of fire," was Lacretelle's description of him[37]—an egotism that grew with power until it knew no bounds.

Still, now, his first thought was always of Josephine. "If one of us has to be ill, could it not be me, so much stronger, so much more able to bear it. Destiny is cruel, she strikes me through you." Life without her would be impossible, though "there is some consolation in the thought that, though fate may have the power to make you ill, no power can force me to live on without you."[38]

By the end of June, after a month of near silence from Josephine, Bonaparte's letters are increasingly filled with thoughts of suicide. "My premonitions are so dire that I limit my hopes to seeing you just once more, to holding you in my arms for just two hours—and then dying together." It is difficult to imagine Josephine taking the time between parties to decipher the desperate pages of this letter. "If you die, I shall die immediately, a death of despair." And then, the first mention of a threat:

> . . . All my thoughts are concentrated upon your bed, upon your heart. Your illness, that is all I can think of, day and night. . . . Without appetite, without sleep, you alone, and the rest of the world has no more reality for me than if it had been annihilated. . . . I value victory only because it gives you pleasure. . . .
>
> Should you be in danger, I warn you, I shall leave at once for

Paris. My presence will conquer the disease. . . . I have always been able to impose my will on destiny.[39]

The next letter is the one that spread consternation, perhaps in Josephine, certainly in the government. "If your illness continues," he wrote, "you must obtain leave for me to come and see you for one hour. In five days I can be in Paris, and on the twelfth, back with my army. Without you, I can be of no value here . . . when my beloved is in pain, I cannot coolly calculate victory. . . . Remember that there has never been a love like mine, it will last as long as my life."[40]

It now appeared likely that if Josephine refused to join her husband, the commander in chief would desert his army.

When he first entered Milan, Bonaparte had informed the Directory that Italy was now in French hands, but the Austrians were known to be regathering their forces that month and preparing for a major counter-offensive. The Italian situation could not be allowed to collapse because Mme Bonaparte refused to join her husband. Lazare Carnot, probably at Barras's direction, signed a preposterous letter to the General, amounting to a kind of certificate of good conduct for Josephine, claiming that the Directory, "which had opposed the departure of the Citoyenne Bonaparte for fear that the care her husband would lavish on her might divert him from those efforts which the safety and the glory of his country require of him," had agreed that she should leave only when Milan was taken. "Now you are there; we have no further objections."[41] It had been six weeks since Milan was first occupied by French troops.

So seriously was the threat of Bonaparte's return to Paris taken that, within three days, Barras literally dispatched Mme Bonaparte across the Alps. After a last supper at the Luxembourg, Josephine was bundled, sobbing, into the first carriage in a convoy of six. "She wept," said a fellow guest, "as though she were going to a torture chamber, instead of to Italy to reign as a sovereign."[42]

In the first carriage sat Fortuné, wearing a new leather collar with two silver bells and a narrow label inscribed "I belong to Madame Bonaparte"; Joseph Bonaparte, Andoche Junot and Hippolyte Charles were waiting with the dog. In five more coaches, each drawn by six horses, were seated Prince Serbelloni, the proprietor of the palace in Milan; Nicolas Clary—brother of Désirée—Mlle Louise, Josephine's maid; two menservants and a vast amount of luggage.

At the Fontainebleau relay, where Josephine stopped long enough to embrace Aunt Désirée and the octogenarian marquis—now at last united in marriage—their caravan was joined by the financier Antoine Hamelin in a hired post chaise. The entire convoy was escorted by a detachment of cavalry. Bonaparte's special courier, Moustache, rode ahead to make sure of horses at each relay, as well as to dispatch a daily report to the General.

As they drove south from the mild Parisian July into the blaze of an Italian summer Josephine, with Fortuné on her lap, complained of the heat, of a fever and of a headache. Hamelin recorded that Junot's and Mlle Louise's bedrooms at the inns were always found to be adjoining, as were Josephine's and Hippolyte's. Joseph Bonaparte, incapacitated as a result of a recent liaison in Paris, spent the nights alone, working on a novel.

They traveled by slow stages; Josephine was in no hurry to reach their destination. They lingered in Turin where, on Bonaparte's instructions to the King of Piedmont, she was treated like royalty in his capital.

Eighteen days after their departure from Paris, a rapturous commander in chief, accompanied by an immense crowd, escorted his wife from the gates of Milan to the Serbelloni Palace, which he had filled with flowering shrubs for her arrival. Lieutenant Charles left immediately for general headquarters in Brescia, and the Bonapartes spent the third night of their married life together. Forty-eight hours later General Bonaparte returned to the field.

ℬ 13 ℬ

GRANDEUR, HOPE AND JOY

IN THE GREAT CLASSICAL PALACE OF THE SERBELLONI FAMILY IN MILAN, the headquarters of the Army of Italy resembled a royal court. The marble and porphyry rooms opening on to the terraces and vast gardens were crowded day and night with General Bonaparte's young officers, French war commissioners and their wives and mistresses, representatives of all the principalities of Italy, of the Hapsburg Archduke of Tuscany, of the Kingdom of Naples, of the Papal States, of the Republic of Venice and of the King of Piedmont, and with the most beautiful women in Milan and Paris.

Josephine had summoned some of her friends, and Fortunée was the first to arrive. It was her husband, Antoine Hamelin, who had joined Mme Bonaparte's military escort from Paris. ("If there is anybody you want taken care of," Napoleon had written Josephine—he had not yet learned of her passion for this form of intercession—"send him to me and I will place him"[1]), and when she met Hamelin during a game of blind-man's buff in Paris she suggested that he apply for a post in Milan as army commissioner. Immediately thereafter she borrowed a hundred gold louis from him and asked him to buy her some lace and a few other necessities before her departure. Some of the sour references to Mme Bonaparte in Hamelin's *Mémoires* are perhaps partly due to the fact that she would never repay any of these sums.

Initially, Josephine's friends were a shock to Milan. Journals complained of their "immodest behavior; arms, bosom, shoulders, all are uncovered. The arrangement of their hair is a scandal—sown with flowers and feathers, and the whole crowned with little military helmets from which locks of untidy hair escape. They even have the effrontery to dress in tunics revealing legs and thighs barely hidden by flesh-colored tights. Their manners match their clothes: arrogant talk, provocative looks, and meat eaten on Fridays."

Milan became so rapidly gallicized, however, that it was said to be the only place outside Paris where respectable French bread could be found. Soon the Milanese ladies were outdoing the French in daring fashions and although some Italians refused to collaborate with the occupiers of their city, the majority of society women could not resist Josephine's balls and receptions—nor the gallant French officers.

During her husband's absence in the field, Mme Bonaparte presided over popular fetes and received delegations alone with grace and dignity, and appeared to be acquiring some taste for the enthusiasm and deference surrounding both Bonapartes. Few of those who came to the Serbelloni Palace to pay homage appeared empty-handed; jewelry, mosaics, marbles and bronzes poured in. The rulers of Italy hoped that Mme Bonaparte's influence on her husband might spare them some of the looting and the colossal indemnities already imposed on them. The Duke of Modena had vainly offered thirty million francs to keep just one Correggio painting; the King of Naples sent a necklace of perfect pearls. The Pope presented his Daughter in God (he did not know that she was living in sin, her marriage unblessed by the Church) with a collection of antique cameos.

As soon as he had left Milan, Napoleon's passionate daily letters from the field continued. "I adore you more than ever. . . . I keep remembering your kisses, your tears, your charming jealousy. [Josephine had pretended to resent the Italian ladies' flirtatious advances to the supreme commander; her own days of genuine jealousy were yet to come.] Your charms burn my heart and my senses. . . . When I am with you, I want it always to be night. . . . I had thought that I loved you, but now that I have seen you again, I love you a thousand times more. . . ." As an occasion to endorse conjugal fidelity, he reported each time one of his officers had caught a venereal infection in Milan. "Good God, what women! What morals! Tell my bother Joseph to be faithful to his Julie."[2]

His letters abound in references that underline how little he understands his wife. "You know the pleasure your letters give me, and I am certain that you love writing them, too."[3] He fails to comprehend that she is no Désirée-Eugénie, in love with Rousseauesque romance. When he camps near Virgil's village by moonlight, he writes that she would have shared his pleasure.

"I am sure your health is better now. As soon as you are well, come and join me."[4] There is so much talk about Josephine's health—though none of her presumably fictitious pregnancy—that we are left with the impression that during their brief hours in Milan she must have pleaded various indispositions in order to restrain some of her husband's ardor. The dramatic premonitions recur: "Come and join me as soon as you are well," he pleads, "so that at least before we die we can say we were happy for a few days."[5]

Nevertheless, Josephine's first letter to Thérésia Tallien starts: "I am dying of boredom here. In the midst of the marvelous fetes given for me, I never cease to miss my friends of Chaillot [the Talliens], and the one at the Luxembourg [Barras]. My husband doesn't only love me, he worships me. I think he will go mad. I have seen him for a moment only, he is very occupied with the siege of Mantua."[6]

The ending, however, sends a coded signal to Thérésia: "Tomorrow night I am going to Brescia. That will bring me closer to general head-quarters." And, of course, to Lieutenant Charles.

The month of Josephine's arrival in Milan had marked the end of Bo-naparte's triumphant advance; by July the Army of Italy was on the defensive. After the defection of the Piedmontese, the Austrians were regrouping to the north, poised to come down through the Alps. To the south, the French army was threatened by a major enemy force in the walled city of Mantua.

Nevertheless, nine days after his wife's arrival the General sum-moned her to meet him in Brescia where "the tenderest of lovers awaits you." She went immediately. Lieutenant Charles, too, would surely be at the headquarters of the Army of Italy. Antoine Hamelin was to accom-pany her, an introduction which should smooth the way to the assignment of army contracts.

As the Bonapartes sat drinking coffee with Hamelin on a terrace in Verona, Josephine was the first to see in the distance the white flecks of Austrian uniforms on the foothills of the Alps. Bonaparte at once suspected that the imperial army had outflanked the French by taking the road leading down from the Brenner Pass. His first care was to send off Josephine with Hamelin under the escort of Junot and thirty dragoons, before she could be cut off from Milan by an Austrian column.

Skirting Lake Garda, their coach was fired on by an Austrian gunboat; an outrider and a horse were killed. Junot pushed the two passengers out of the carriage on the offside; crawling along a ditch, they managed to rejoin the carriage on a sheltered road. Once again, as on the day of her flight from Martinique, Josephine experienced the terror of an escape under gunfire, across open land without cover.

There were further reminders of the past. Later, Hamelin remembered, Josephine recognized the face of the colonel in charge of their escort of dragoons. He had been one of the representatives-on-mission to the Army of the Rhine, "and he is the one," she whispered, "who denounced my husband."[7]

Junot left them to return to the army, and for ten days Josephine and Hamelin traveled throughout Tuscany, escorted by Bonaparte's dragoons. In Lucca, Leghorn and Florence, the Italians, uncertain how the battle was going, viewed Josephine's arrival with some suspicion. In Florence, she stayed with its governor, the Austrian archduke with whom Napoleon had signed a treaty. One night Italians broke into his residence in order to verify the rumor that Josephine was traveling with her defeated husband's body in a coffin. Finally, after the great battle of Castiglione on August 5, under an escort of thirty hussars sent by her victorious husband, Josephine and Antoine Hamelin departed once more for the rendezvous at Brescia. Once they arrived, they found instructions to follow the General to his new headquarters twenty-five miles away. Hamelin was for obeying; Josephine objected that she was too tired. He could join her, she said, in the General's former rooms for supper at a table beside her bed. When he went to her room, he found the table laid for three; Charles was there, returning from a mission. As the two men left after supper, "a languishing voice" called Charles back. "Finding that I had left my hat and my pistols in the antechamber outside the bedroom," Hamelin recalled, "I returned to get them. A grenadier posted outside the door forbade me to enter."[8]

Josephine had indeed met "the tenderest of lovers," but not the one intended by her husband.

. . .

With Mantua still under siege, General Bonaparte waited until September to find three weeks for a visit to Milan. Then, wrote Hamelin, he would abandon maps and conferences to fly to Josephine's private apartments, playing with her like a child, teasing her and making her cry. "Even in my presence, he would stride ever to Madame Bonaparte, caressing her so passionately and so coarsely that I considered it best to walk to the window and pretend to be observing the weather."[9]

Though Josephine now lived in splendor more regal than Thérésia's, she was not consoled—not for the loss of Paris, nor for her place of "influence" near Paul Barras, nor for the continued absence of Hippolyte. In a letter to Aunt Désirée she informed her that she was "feted in Italy wherever I go. All the Princes of Italy give me parties, even the Grand Duke of Tuscany, brother of the Emperor of Austria. Well, I would rather be a private citizen in France. . . . I am bored . . . my husband remains all day in adoration before me as though I were a divinity; it would be impossible to have a better husband."[10]

She missed her children too. To Hortense, Josephine wrote: "I adore you both; kisses to my dear Eugène and to Jérôme [Bonaparte]. . . . Your letters and your brother's are some consolation for my being so far from my dear children."[11]

She sent "a length of crepe" to Thérésia and "some Florentine straw hats, some sausages and cheese for your husband's breakfast and some coral for little Thermidor," her goddaughter. And she asked for news of Paul Barras. "Oh, I do love him; I am devoted to him. I have his letter and will answer it by the first courier. I was so touched by this proof of his friendship."[12]

Most of her letters from Milan were to Barras. Her overriding wish was to continue to be the link between him and her husband. This, she was beginning to believe, was her major claim to influence. Her letters to him always end with: "Bonaparte sends you many messages; he still adores me."[13]

Barras continued to support his protégé in Italy, though Carnot, the minister of war, was enraged by the insubordinate general. For some months now, Bonaparte's fame and popularity had prevented the government from giving him any direct orders. "This is not an order given you by the Executive Directory," begins one wary communication, "but rather its *wish*."

In November, after a series of military reverses, it suddenly appeared likely that the French might be pushed out of Italy. Josephine in Milan, fearful for the safety both of her husband and of Hippolyte Charles, heard of the French army retreat from Verona followed by a defeat at Vicenza. So certain were the Milanese that this was to be the end of what was now thought of as the French occupation that she was awakened several times a night in the Serbelloni Palace by citizens "coming for news," in reality to see whether she had fled, and to prepare for the insurrection that was planned to follow.

At last a report reached Milan of two great victories. Marching all night by moonlight, Bonaparte had outflanked and defeated a superior Austrian force, first at Rivoli and then again the next day at Arcola. Rivoli was the more decisive battle, but it was the storming of the bridge at Arcola which would be the subject of the vivid engravings to be imprinted forever on the imagination of Bonaparte's generation: of an eagle-faced general charging across the bridge under fire, in one hand the flag of the Republic, the other urging his troops forward.

The French had now won back northern Italy, and Mantua was sure to fall. Only the preceding week Bonaparte had written to the Directory: "We are on the verge of losing Italy." He had even contemplated a general retreat. His relief now was so great that for once his letter to Josephine from his tent that night was simply a triumphant account of the action. Two days later he reverted to his erotic fantasies. "I am going to bed with my heart full of your adorable image. . . . I cannot wait to give you proofs of my ardent love. . . . How happy I would be if I could assist at your undressing, the little firm white breast, the adorable face, the hair tied up in a scarf *à la créole*. You know that I never forget the little visits, you know, the little black forest. . . . I kiss it a thousand times and wait impatiently for the moment I will be in it. To live within Josephine is to live in the Elysian fields. Kisses on your mouth, your eyes, your breast, everywhere, everywhere."[14]

This letter of November 21 would be the last to mention the little black forest,* the last to list kisses in thousands. On November 27, back in

---

* Hortense, in her publication of some of these letters, would regularly excise these allusions.

Milan, General Bonaparte tore up the staircase of the Serbelloni Palace to their empty bedroom. Josephine was in Genoa, almost certainly with Lieutenant Charles.

So great was the shock that Napoleon all but fainted. In the nine days he waited in Milan for Josephine's return, he wrote her three raging, pitiful, disillusioned letters. "I left everything to see you, to hold you in my arms. . . . The pain I feel is incalculable. I don't want you to change any plans for parties, or to be interested in the happiness of a man who lives only for you. . . . I am not worth it. . . . When I beg you to equal a love like mine, I am wrong. . . . Why should I expect lace to weigh as much as gold. . . . May the fates concentrate in me all sorrows and all grief, but give Josephine only happy days. When I am sure that she can no longer love me, I will be silent and content only to be useful to her." After closing the last letter, he reopened it to send her a kiss and to add: "O Josephine, Josephine!"[15]

He would never recover from this blow. His letters to her would continue: affectionate, teasing, imperious, even passionate in turn—often only accounts of his health, his battles, his plans. The total surrender of mind and senses was finished.

Not until February 1797 and the fall of Mantua after an eight-month siege was General Bonaparte in a position to follow the Directory's standing instructions to invade Austria from the south in order to meet up with Generals Hoche and Jourdan and the French Armies of the Rhine. Although the directors had learned to address Bonaparte with infinite caution, their new instructions reemphasized the need for the armies to join forces.

By the end of March, Bonaparte was only ninety miles from Vienna. There the whole court was packing enormous trunks into carriages, preparing to flee before the French advance—days of fear never to be forgotten by the Emperor's daughter, the infant Marie Louise. But on March 26, Bonaparte suddenly offered an armistice to the apparently hard-pressed Austrians. He knew that two French armies under Hoche were advancing along the Danube and likely to reach Vienna at the same time as the Army of Italy; he was determined not to share any glory with Hoche, although a peace treaty more advantageous to France would almost certainly have then been concluded. He needed terms that would highlight his personal success and cause him, he said, to be "seen in France as the man of peace."

Without consulting the Directory, Bonaparte sent General Leclerc to the French generals on the Rhine, urging them to halt their offensive, and in April, again without referring its terms to Paris, he signed a preliminary treaty with the enemy at Leoben. Austria was to give up two provinces, Belgium and Lombardy, which were already in French hands. In a secret clause, directly contrary to the French policy of renunciation of conquest and of the violation of natural frontiers, France was to "concede" to Austria the still neutral and independent Republic of Venice.* Most importantly, the main aim of Directory policy was ignored—control over the left bank of the Rhine. The old Roman concept of Gaul extended to its "natural frontiers" was still an article of faith in republican France; the oath to the Constitution included it, Bonaparte had accepted it.

The government in Paris was further outraged when it learned that General Bonaparte, after engineering some anti-French riots in Venice, had deposed the Doge, ruler of that ancient republic, removed all the treasures of the Arsenal, the Lion of Venice and the four bronze horses of St. Mark's, and dispatched the lot to Paris.

When they learned of the rape of Venice, the furious deputies of the council inquired of the Directory why Bonaparte had been allowed to destroy a fellow republic, the oldest government in Europe. They demanded an explanation of the plundering by the Army of Italy, "whose generals are known to send home entire wagonloads of paintings, jewelry and other treasures," and whose commander in chief was described as "an unscrupulous demagogue forever posturing on the stage."

Even before the Directory heard of the destruction of the Republic of Venice, the government was convinced that Bonaparte had sacrificed the interests of France in order to gain power in Italy, and that his jealousy of Hoche had caused him to rush the Treaty of Leoben. They were aware that Bonaparte had had the rumors printed and circulated in Paris of a possible peace. His active machine there presented a picture of the young

---

* For some, Pieter Geyl has noted, there seemed to be two men, Bonaparte and Napoleon. For Stendhal, there were even two Bonapartes, and he believed that in 1797 "the truly poetic and perfectly noble part of Bonaparte's life comes to an end with the occupation of Venice."

republican general dictating terms to the reactionary Austrian Emperor—terms that would finish the endless war with Europe.* Except in Italy, he was seen as a man who cared only for the Republic and for peace.

Lazare Carnot was not deceived by the garbled excuses Bonaparte sent; he and the Directory would have been ready for a peace treaty, but this was now almost impossible.

When reports of protests in the council chamber first reached him in Milan, General Bonaparte wrote a violent letter to the Directory, and in one of those calculated rages so often to be repeated, he requested that his successor be appointed immediately. There were no further protests from the government. General Pichegru, when he heard of this exchange, sent a private message to Paul Barras. "The Directors," he wrote from his headquarters in Germany, "believe that in Napoleon Bonaparte they have their own creature. One day he will eat them up without any warning."[16]

Barras commented only: "Pichegru is right. We will all perish by the generals."[17]

After nearly a year in Italy, Josephine had managed only one rendezvous alone with Hippolyte Charles. With little further prospect of seeing him, she announced in April that her health required her to return to Paris.

After the preliminary peace of Leoben, however, and before the final treaty set for October, there was a pause in military operations, and in May of 1797 General Bonaparte moved his headquarters and his family to the vast baroque palace of Mombello in the countryside outside Milan. Lieutenant Charles would be on duty there throughout the summer.

Josephine no longer insisted upon a return to Paris. She would be able to see Hippolyte daily, though never alone, under Napoleon's jealous eye and the hostile ones of the entire Bonaparte clan. The General had sent for both his brother Jérôme and Eugène de Beauharnais from the McDermott School. Of the family only Lucien had not been invited; he

---

* Even the legend of Bonaparte exacting peace from a vanquished Austria was, as a recent historian has shown, far from accurate. After a temporary panic the Austrians "came to understand" that the French general was in haste and that, even before the Treaty of Leoben, "his terms showed the price he was prepared to pay to reach an agreement. . . . The Austrians could hardly believe their luck."

was in disgrace for having married for love and "beneath him," and without requesting either Napoleon's or their mother's permission.

This was the first meeting of Josephine and the Bonaparte women. On his way to command the Army of Italy, Napoleon had spent a full three days in Marseilles, attempting to soften the shock of the news of a marriage he had been too prudent to announce to any member of his family. Mme Letizia had been stunned. Although her son had brought her a courteous letter from Josephine, it took her some time to have a coldly formal answer drafted by Joseph Bonaparte in correct French. Her permission had not been sought, and like all the family, she feared that Josephine would take for herself and her children all the personal benefits won by the General which the clan felt were legitimately theirs.

Josephine might have been redeemed in her eyes had she borne her husband a child each year, but Letizia noted that *Madame la Générale*'s clinging dresses betrayed no immediate possibilities in that direction. Her extravagance was too obvious to be overlooked. Although to her mother-in-law she always showed deference and sweetness, as Napoleon admitted at St. Helena, there was never the smallest chance that his mother would accept the entrance into the clan of this fashionable older woman of questionable reputation. (Joseph, of course, had given the family an outline of Mme de Beauharnais' recent past.)

The General's mother observed with displeasure that he joined in the card-playing and dancing at night and, with still more distaste, his behavior toward his wife. The officers at Mombello, as well as the Italian visitors, were surprised to see the General kiss Mme Bonaparte on the mouth and caress her breasts in public. "He takes conjugal liberties which embarrass us all," wrote one of Napoleon's aides to his family.

Josephine was never able to overcome the jealousy of the Bonaparte family. Her celebrated charm was powerless against their naked animosity; she herself had never been able to feel hate and was unable to understand their aggressiveness. The sisters were initially intimidated by so much natural ease, certain that their sister-in-law would laugh at their lack of education, their Corsican accents and their provincial manners; even at their new, expensive clothes, which made them appear overdressed compared with her simple elegance.

Caroline was still too young to take any position, but no amount of kindness would ever neutralize the insolence of beautiful, spiteful Pauline.

The seventeen-year-old took an instant dislike to her sister-in-law. As soon as Josephine's back was turned, she would put out her tongue at her and call her *"la vieille."* One of the objects of her more than flirtatious approaches was Lieutenant Charles, but she appears to have soon suspected that his heart was otherwise engaged. "Pauline was the prettiest and also the worst-behaved person imaginable," wrote Antoine Arnault, now an officer in Bonaparte's entourage, "chattering without pause, and nudging me with her knee when I did not pay her enough attention."[18] Her brother saw that it was time Pauline was settled, and when he found her in compromising circumstances behind a screen with his aide Victor Leclerc, he insisted upon an immediate marriage.

Elisa, however, plain and pretentious, needed Josephine as an ally. She was the only ill-favored one of the sisters and Mme de Rémusat wrote: "Those things we call arms and legs looked as though they had been haphazardly stuck onto her body . . . a most disagreeable ensemble."[19] Now twenty-three, she had had trouble finding a husband, and six weeks earlier, against Napoleon's wishes, had married an insignificant Corsican, Captain Felix Bacchiocchi. At Josephine's pleading, the General consented to a blessing of the Bacchiocchi civil union at the same time as the Leclerc marriage. It was she who organized the magnificent joint religious service in the Mombello oratory and the ball that followed, and even the stately honeymoon—no fewer than thirty persons accompanied Pauline and her husband to Lake Como. The General's presents to his family were sumptuous: immense dowries for both brides; a promotion for Leclerc, a promotion for Bacchiocchi too, and a post for him in Ajaccio.

As for Joseph, Napoleon, never a judge of character where his family was concerned, had sent Josephine a letter of introduction to his brother, who was in Paris badgering Barras for some important diplomatic post, buying up national property and enjoying a number of liaisons. "I am writing to Barras to have Joseph appointed Consul in one of the Italian ports," he had written. "He wishes to live with his little wife, far removed from the tumult of great events. I recommend him to you."[20]

Fortunately, Barras knew that Joseph was not in the least interested in either of these propositions, and sent him as the Directory's envoy to Madrid. As for this "little wife," the former Julie Clary, she was the only member of the Bonaparte family who appeared to appreciate Josephine's thoughtfulness to them all. Yet only fourteen months earlier she had helped her sister Désirée write the heartbroken pages with which she greeted the news of Napoleon's marriage. "All that is left to me now is to wish for death,"[21] Désirée had written.

It was observed that Bonaparte's household was now virtually that of a sovereign. Eighteen months earlier the General had been an obscure officer on half pay; with the greatest naturalness, he now reigned over his court. Austria had accredited two ambassadors to the headquarters at Mombello, as had every principality and kingdom in Italy. The residence and the park surrounding the palace were filled with French officers in splendid uniforms, their spurs clanking on the marble floors; with men of letters and scientists; with pretty women from Milan and with Josephine's friends from Paris.

Mme Letizia, majestically knitting a stocking in the great salon, was tacitly acknowledged as hostess. Officers bowed to her first, then to the General's wife. Not only were low bows required before each member of the family, but Bonaparte's officers and aides no longer ate at his table. Like a Bourbon king at Versailles, the General now often dined alone in a tent in the garden while crowds of respectful visitors were permitted to file slowly past. Even on picnics and excursions Bonaparte insisted upon being surrounded by rigorous etiquette.

General Bonaparte's own self-confidence had grown further since his role as statesman at Leoben, dealing with politicians, and in effect changing the map of Europe. There, the Austrian and Piedmontese officers had been struck with incredulity at the sight of the small, unsmiling young general who had soundly beaten both their armies. This was succeeded by awe as he barked out his terms for a treaty in his strongly accented French, and "armed," remarked one of them, "with a look that went straight through you."

The change in Bonaparte's manner had occurred at the very start of his command. Admiral Denis Decrès, who had known him well in Paris, would relate that before the start of the Italian campaign he had visited the General in Nice in order to congratulate him. "When the door opened," he remembered, "I was on the point of hurrying toward him when something in his attitude, his expression, the tone of his voice, was enough to stop me. There was nothing insulting, but it was enough. From that day on, I never attempted to bridge the distance he had imposed." And a shaken General Augereau, an illiterate giant of a man, left Bonaparte's presence at headquarters muttering: "I don't know why, but the little bugger scares me."

At Mombello they all felt the "unique spell" of that summer. It had, remembered Auguste Marmont, "a character of its own which no later circumstances could re-create. There was grandeur, hope and joy. We were all very young, from the supreme commander down to the most junior officers; all bright with strength and health and consumed by love of glory . . . we felt unlimited confidence in our destinies."[22]

Though Josephine could not evade the vigilance of the Bonapartes, it was enough to know that Hippolyte was part of all their gatherings. That summer, to his delight, he was promoted to captain in the First Hussars and mentioned for gallantry in dispatches. And secretly, though almost everyone except the General was aware of it, he gave Josephine a puppy to replace her beloved pug. Fortuné, on an early morning round of the gardens, had been killed by the cook's dog. Josephine was in despair. Her husband was not. A few days later, spotting the cook hiding in the shrubbery, he inquired the reason. The man explained he was overcome by remorse, but assured the General that his own dog was no longer allowed to enter the park. "Bring him back," ordered Bonaparte, "perhaps he will rid me of the new dog too."[23]

At Mombello that summer Josephine was able for the first time to gratify her love of gardens and animals. Napoleon had ordered greenhouses built for her and birdcages, and she filled the vast park with flowers and the lake with aquatic birds. This was the year she chose the swan as her emblem, henceforth to be represented in the furnishings of all the Consular and Imperial residences.

At three every afternoon after a siesta, the whole company, including Bonaparte's aides and officers, the foreign envoys and the guests from Milan, would assemble for dinner to the sound of martial music ("deafening," according to Arnault). After dinner Josephine, always dressed in white muslin, "a wreath of ivy in her hair, not yet adorned with the crown diamonds,"[24] would take the whole company out onto the cool of the shaded terraces to drink coffee, eat ices and watch the fireflies. The French officers had never seen these before, "like so many sequins hovering just above the ground," one of them marveled.

The Milanese ladies had been curious to see the creature who had so bewitched the supreme commander that, in her absence, he had paid not the slightest attention to their advances. They were forced to concede that, although older-looking and less beautiful than they had expected, Josephine was compellingly charming. One French visitor that summer saw her as infinitely seductive: "An angelic face . . . an unusually perfect body. . . . There was a suppleness, an incredible lightness in all her movements." He raved about her walk—"both aerial and majestic"—her dazzling skin, ravishing voice and, above all, her eyes: "dark blue, always half closed under long lids, fringed by the longest eyelashes in the world" and their irresistible expression of sweetness.[25]

Josephine's royal ease of manner, her instinctively right words and actions, made her the perfect consort in this summer rehearsal of her future role. At least one observer later speculated that at Mombello she may well have believed that the fortune-teller's prophecy was already accomplished: "Adored by a man universally admired, surrounded by everything which can intoxicate a woman, and without yet having to feel the weight of a crown."[26]

The General's family dispersed. Captain Charles returned to Brescia. The Bonapartes now presented the picture of a devoted couple. We do not know how much of an element of playacting this may have represented on Josephine's part. It would become evident, though, in the future, after the break with Charles, that a quiet family life was a fundamental need of Josephine's nature. Her present facade—if such it was—of domestic bliss would grow with time into reality; the happiest moments of her life would be those hours spent at Malmaison with her family and her garden, before the imperial days.

She would always prefer easy, intimate gatherings to the etiquette and parade that Napoleon would increasingly demand. What she missed in Italy was not the official life in the great salons of the Luxembourg Palace, but the small company, always the same, assembling in Barras's private apartments for supper and conversation, and the lazy mornings in her own house, surrounded by friends.

Meanwhile, affectionate and kind by nature, she appeared content to conform to her husband's ideas of a wife's duties. As for Napoleon, he was now not far from possessing the helpmate he had hoped for. Together they received delegations or watched from a balcony of the Serbelloni Palace yet another planting of a Liberty Tree; she joined him at forward army camps without complaining. Visitors to Milan commented on their apparent mutual affection.

None who witnessed the painting of Gros's celebrated portrait of Bonaparte would ever forget the circumstances. Baron Gros, a pupil of David, wished to commemorate the famous occasion of the storming of the bridge at Arcola. Bonaparte found it impossible to remain immobile for a pose that required him to stand with arm upraised, so every day after dinner Josephine would take him on her knee and keep her arms around him until the painting was finished.

Visitors to Mombello were struck by the extent of the help Josephine gave in the double role now increasingly being played by Bonaparte. There was a piquant contrast between the violently revolutionary tone of the General's dispatches to the Directory and of his exhortations to his army—befitting the "transcendental patriot," protégé of the Robespierre brothers—and the elegance of Josephine's salon. Its tone, with Napoleon's complicity, was set by her own *ancien régime* manners; her tact and courtesy reconciled to him many who would otherwise have been offended by his violently expressed republican sentiments. In private he "spoke with disdain of republican demagoguery,"[27] but his diatribes against the "counter-revolutionaries, the blasphemers who have insulted liberty and glory"[28] evoked an enthusiastic echo in his army, outraged by news of criticism by the deputies in Paris of the rape of Venice and of the pillaging by the Army of Italy. There was probably not a single man in that army who did not assume that his commander in chief was an ardent republican, nor one who would have believed his confidence to two men that summer.

The mask slipped when Comte François Miot de Mélito, the French Republic's envoy to Turin, paid a visit to the General at Mombello. While they walked together in the garden, Miot listened for two hours without interruption. What he learned would have shocked both the Directory and the Army of Italy.

Miot was, he wrote, totally unprepared for "a man shorter than the average, his powdered hair cut square and worn in an unusual manner below his ears. His coat was buttoned to the chin and ornamented with very narrow gold embroidery. . . . His brusque and animated gestures revealed both passionate feeling and profound thought. His speech was brief, and in those days very incorrect."[29]

Bonaparte soon disposed of Miot's speculations on an ideal republic. "What an absurd idea! Impossible with our customs and our vices. The French are obsessed with the idea of a Republic, but it will pass." He would not himself, he said, be willing to leave Italy until he could be sure of playing as important a role in France as the one he was starring in here. "As for me, my dear Miot, I have tasted authority and I will not give it up. I have decided that if I cannot be the master I will leave France. But it's too early now, the fruit is not yet ripe." And when Miot hazarded a question about the Directory's desire for peace, he was left in no doubt as to the General's cynical views on the subject. "Peace," Bonaparte confided, "would not be in *my* interest now. . . . I would have to give up all this power. If I leave the signing of peace treaties to another man, he would be placed higher in public opinion than I am by my victories."[30]

Miot was not the only man to whom Bonaparte confided his plans that summer. At Mombello he received his first letter from the new minister of exterior relations, Charles-Maurice de Talleyrand. It was the beginning of a courtship of incalculable consequences.

✥ 14 ✥

FAREWELL, GENERAL AND PEACEMAKER!

WHEN CHARLES-MAURICE DE TALLEYRAND RETURNED IN 1796 FROM HIS two-year exile in America, he found a world as new and uncharted as the American wilderness itself. Paris, he wrote to a French friend in New York, was unrecognizable. People lived differently—they dressed, ate, made money and used power in a totally new fashion.

He felt immediately at home in the intoxicating atmosphere of political and financial intrigue. The frantic need for material pleasures, the infinite possibilities for making a rapid fortune, the fluid political scene, the familiar, pervasive atmosphere of feminine influence of which he had been deprived in exile, were all equally congenial.

In the absence of Germaine de Staël—herself now in exile—Talleyrand set out to realize his two ambitions: to make a fortune and to attain high government office. He deliberately assumed a course of conduct that, a year later, he would recommend to General Bonaparte upon his return from Italy: first, to profess a total lack of interest in playing any political role; and second, to emphasize, in suitable company, his passionate republican convictions. He adopted, too, the role of a "delegate from the New World," and his lectures at the Institut de France caused a stir. Their subject—the proper conduct for a country that has just been through a revolution—he claimed to have learned in America.

In order to build a network of friends and supporters, Talleyrand turned, as he had always done, to his women friends. In his prerevolutionary clothes, knee breeches, buckled shoes and powdered hair, he presented a disconcerting picture as he glided into the new salons with the peculiar half-skating walk he had adopted to disguise his lameness.

Although his supercilious smile and what Mme de Rémusat termed his "gracefully insolent manner" offended orthodox Jacobins, he had no trouble fascinating the women, nor enlisting them in the service of his ambitions. When he was asked why he spent so much time in these salons instead of discussing politics, he would answer, "But women *are* politics."

Talleyrand's first visit was to Mme Tallien. Next only to Mme de Staël's, it was her influence which had obtained the erasure of his name from the list of emigrés. (Thérésia, he reported to a friend in New York, was "as expensively undressed as it is possible to be.") Daily he returned to the Chaumière and its unrivaled opportunities for making contacts with bankers, deputies and the newly powerful world of generals of the republican army. Daily, too, he attended the receptions or intimate gatherings at the houses of new friends and old. And he became a regular guest at the influential salons of some ladies he had barely noticed before the Revolution: Fortunée Hamelin was one, Juliette Récamier another, and before her departure for Italy, Mme Bonaparte, whose husband's defiance of the government, no less than his Italian victories, appeared to be changing the political balance in Paris. All of these houses, including Josephine's, were devoted to Paul Barras's interests, and the Director was one of the two men Talleyrand had decided were the keys both to high position and to the destiny of France. The second man was, in his opinion, Mme Bonaparte's husband.

Josephine's friend (and his, from the days of the Orléans salon), the ravishing Aimée de Coigny, was another woman whose fate would continue to be intertwined with Talleyrand's and the Bonapartes'. Her own political allegiances still depended on the men in her life. Her husband, Casimir de Montrond, would, from this time to the end of his days, be Talleyrand's closest associate. Their house was a source of well-informed financial gossip, and with Montrond's help Talleyrand started to lay the groundwork for making a fortune. Still, it was clear that to amass serious wealth and attain high government office he would have to await Germaine de Staël's return in order to have feminine influence deployed at its most powerful.

In his letters to her from Philadelphia and New York, he had recounted his disappointments—the severest of these being George Washington's refusal to receive him. Though Talleyrand insisted that the action was prompted by the Committee of Public Safety's representative in Philadelphia, rumors of his private life had also reached the President: tales of the former bishop limping down the main street, his black mistress on his arm, had scandalized the Quaker capital. Among his triumphs was the making of a small fortune in real estate—he even tried to persuade Germaine to buy property in the Bronx.*

Of all the remarkable men he had met, Talleyrand wrote Mme de Staël, Alexander Hamilton was the most admirable. Thirty years later he would write: "I consider Napoleon, Fox and Hamilton the three greatest men of our age, and of these I would unhesitatingly place Hamilton first. He foresaw Europe."[1] In each letter he reminded Germaine that he was no common emigré, and that prudent enough to leave France only with Danton's own certificate of "government business to be done in London for the Convention," he had chosen, when the British government ordered him to leave, to go "only to a country not at war with France."[2]

When Mme de Staël had first returned to Paris after Thermidor, intent upon the reconciliation of republicans and constitutional royalists, and had set about pleading for the return of scores of her emigré friends, the return of "the Bishop," as she continued to call him, was especially close to her heart. She enlisted Thérésia Tallien, Rose de Beauharnais, the deputy Joseph Chénier and half the Convention in this cause. Chénier was instructed to argue that Talleyrand had gone to America in order to "observe the spectacle of a free people from the very heart of a Republic."[3]

When at last the news of Chénier's successful plea to the Convention reached Talleyrand in New York, he sent Germaine a letter of obsequious gratitude. "No matter where you are, I want the rest of my life to be spent near you,"[4] he wrote. Might he hope for a continuation of "our little world," and perhaps a room in the Swedish embassy? Would Baron de Staël permit this?

Meanwhile, as Talleyrand awaited the end of the winter storms on the Atlantic (and the answers to some prudent soundings on the political temperature in France), Mme de Staël had been exiled once again, this

---

* Mme de Staël refused Talleyrand's offer. Her father, however, had already purchased for her, through Gouverneur Morris, property in New York State; and when Dupont de Nemours (saved from the guillotine by Thermidor) emigrated to the United States, he acquired further acreage for Germaine in Kentucky.

time as a result of her intrigues at the time of Vendémiaire. While the mortified Swedish ambassador listened from the galleries of the Convention, one of the Jacobin deputies thundered threats against Germaine, denouncing her as the protector of emigrés and "a corrupter of all those deputies she invites to dinner"; then, referring to her well-known liaison with Benjamin Constant, for cuckolding her husband. Only weeks before the installation of the Directory, that new, democratic regime she had awaited so eagerly, Germaine had been forced into a second exile.

From her father's house in Switzerland she fired off a succession of pamphlets supporting the French government, alternating with passionate appeals to Barras for permission to return to France. Three simultaneous love affairs retained the rest of her attention, though she maintained that living a solitary life in exile was not favorable even in that domain, for "to be alone with anyone is a terrible test for any sentiment. One needs people around one to be witty, to be in love, to be anything. . . ."[5]

At last, in May 1797, Germaine was permitted to return. Baron de Staël was stunned when he heard she was en route and contemplated having her turned back at the frontier. But his behavior, once she arrived, was impeccable even when, one week later, she gave birth to a daughter, presumed to be Constant's. "Though making no great show of feeling," Germaine reported "he was full of attentions and concern."[6]

Even then her salon never closed; there were seldom fewer than a dozen people in her bedroom. Immediately she addressed herself to the needs of "the Bishop," lending him money and her own horses and carriage, and finally organizing an introduction to Paul Barras. She was at the Luxembourg morning and night, pleading Talleyrand's cause with mounting hysteria. His affection and respect for Barras, she assured the Director, were such that "he regards you as superhuman. He idolizes you."[7] Barras would never, she assured him, find anyone more totally devoted, more ready to be his slave, than the Bishop.

Little wonder that Paul Barras felt that he had, at least, a loyal collaborator. When, at the end of his life, he wrote, "Sometimes I remind myself with some pride that it was I who created Talleyrand and Bonaparte and so many others," he added, "but then I wonder whether those were really my finest achievements."[8] Yet, although in the future Talleyrand had no wish to acknowledge his debt of gratitude either to Germaine or to Paul Barras, when Napoleon as Emperor asked him whether it was true that Mme de Staël was an intriguer, he admitted: "To such an extent, Sire, that but for her intrigues I would not be here today."*

In Talleyrand's view the present vulnerable government would soon be succeeded by a strong regime supported by the army and very likely headed by one of its revolutionary generals. Although he maintained a correspondence with all those commanders in the field who appeared to have a political future, it was in General Bonaparte that he began to divine the likelier "sword," a soldier to form a rampart against a restoration of the monarchy and work toward peace with the enemy.

His first letter to the General was one of such graceful flattery that he received an immediate reply. In his answer Bonaparte showed an immediate understanding of the minister's position as a former emigré. The Executive Directory, he wrote, had shown discernment in recognizing Talleyrand's "purified good citizenship" and his distance from the "aberrations which dishonored the Revolution"—two code expressions in revolutionary vocabulary signifying that the minister was untainted by either royalism or terrorism.

It was not Bonaparte's custom to answer all the flattering messages he received in Italy; some, indeed, like Mme de Staël's, threw him into a rage. No copies of these exist, but Bourrienne recalled that Germaine, in her one-sided correspondence, assured the General that she felt that her soul of fire was predestined to adore him, and that he was surely meant to set aside his mistaken union with an insignificant beauty. "How dare she compare herself with Josephine!"[10] was Bonaparte's angry comment.

But each one of Talleyrand's letters would receive careful answers. The General was flattered by their tone and by the minister's assumption that they shared the same views. Bonaparte's own ideas on peace he kept to himself. His faith in this correspondent's judgment was reinforced by Josephine; her letter to Talleyrand on the elegance of Captain Charles's

---

* A disillusioned Germaine had already noted in a psychological study published in 1796 that "if a man were given evidence of devotion by another man, he would feel dishonored were he ever to forget it. If, however, that same evidence were given him by a woman, he would feel absolved of any need for gratitude by simply attributing it to love. It is as if this further offering diminished the value of the other."[9]

cravat was evidence at least of her supreme confidence in his taste, and she continued to sing his praises at every opportunity.

That summer the Bonapartes invited Miot de Mélito to join them on an expedition to Lake Maggiore. He and General Berthier* made up a foursome in the Bonapartes' carriage, and although, Miot wrote, he and Berthier were embarrassed by some of the General's conjugal liberties, "yet his bold ways were so full of ardent affection for that kind and charming lady that he could easily be forgiven. Nevertheless," he continued, "our conversation was occasionally serious too," and when Napoleon brought up Talleyrand's name, Miot noted that Josephine warmly supported her husband's appreciation of the minister's ability and judgment.[11]

Talleyrand's nomination in July to the Ministry of External Relations was, in fact, a purely political choice. Barras was looking for a supporter in this key post after the major cabinet reshuffle that followed the disastrous elections of 1797.

Throughout the country that year, the voting had been overwhelmingly anti-Jacobin. Signs of reaction were visible everywhere: revolutionary forms were being discarded; the title of Citizen was "now used only ironically"; women hid the tricolor cockade under their hats, and in the streets young men wore the rebels' gray coats with eighteen brass buttons for the Pretender Louis XVIII. Churches were reopening, and although Sébastien Mercier believed that "people go to Mass because they imagine it annoys the Republic" the fiercely anticlerical government feared a massive return to faith.

With their fragile political equilibrium in tatters, the three radical directors—Barras, Reubell and Larevellière—prepared to mount a republican coup. When Barras, determined in the cabinet reshuffle to have his own men in the key positions, pushed through his own choices to head the Departments of War, Police and the Interior, he had some trouble with foreign affairs. Mme de Staël had worn down his resistance to Talleyrand, but the Bishop's execrable reputation caused furious opposition within the government—more especially with Reubell, the director

---

* General Alexandre Berthier, Napoleon's invaluable chief of staff until the end of the Empire.

in charge of foreign policy. An orthodox revolutionary, Reubell wanted a continuation of the wars against monarchist Europe and suspected that Barras and his client were ready for peace with Austria.

But the specter of a restoration of the monarchy, the one solution that Charles-Maurice de Talleyrand believed would remove him definitively from political life, was of as lively a concern to him as it was to the Directory, and from the date of his appointment as minister of exterior relations he collaborated with the three radical directors in the preparation of a coup d'état to annul the recent elections.

By early July 1797 it became obvious that the anti-revolutionary tide could only be stemmed by appealing to the intensely republican army. One of the announced objectives of the new moderate legislature was to work for peace with the enemy, an aim calculated to alienate all four armies in the field, as well as their commanders.

The choice lay between three "swords," current jargon for a military man willing to back a politician's coup d'état: Bonaparte, Hoche and Bernadotte. Of these, Hoche and Bonaparte were the more prestigious, their personal and professional rivalry well known.

The three leftist directors decided to start by sounding out General Bonaparte. "Napoleon," recorded his secretary Bourrienne, "was in no doubt as to where his own interests lay."*[12] The newly elected deputies, whose declared aim was to work for peace, might, he feared, form a stable government before he himself could achieve his own political ambitions. As he had defined it to Miot: "I am willing to weaken the Republican party some day, but only for my own profit," and the Directory should be defended now "as a power whose only justification is to hold the place open for my return."[13]

A republican posture suited him now. The Jacobin journals continued to refer to him as "the shield of the Republic" and emphasized his lack of ambition, whereas much of the criticism of the Venetian affair was circulated by right-wing deputies and journalists. And monarchists had not forgotten his role at Vendémiaire.

Bonaparte sent back a message informing the directors that he would guarantee for their coup the support of the Army of Italy under the command of one of his officers, General Pierre Augereau. He had thus

---

* Bourrienne, his school friend and now secretary and confidant.

blocked the possible appointment of any other charismatic general, yet would not be seen once again to use armed force against the Parisians.

In Paris, in late August 1797, it was felt certain that a coup d'état was being prepared. The heat and the feverish atmosphere recalled the days preceding Thermidor.

Talleyrand had so alarmed Germaine de Staël with fears of a monarchist restoration that she became his willing collaborator in circulating rumors of counter-revolutionary plots by the new deputies. Much of the organization of the coup took place either at Talleyrand's house or at the neighboring Swedish embassy. It was remarked that at both residences visiting officers from the Army of Italy, as well as any friends or relations of Bonaparte's, were accorded special consideration. After dinner, guests at Talleyrand's official residence were led into a room where the only ornament was a portrait of the General. On one occasion, it was said that Germaine made herself ridiculous by refusing to walk first through a door before one of the General's aides.

By early September, she was warning her friends to burn any imprudent letters she might have sent them. Barras was advising Thérésia Tallien to leave Paris for a few days. General Augereau, the most Jacobin of Bonaparte's generals, wearing an exotic uniform of his own design, was seen blustering around the capital with his men, loudly proclaiming his contempt for the deputies.

At nightfall on September 3 (17 Fructidor) the streets of Paris were deserted as citizens remained indoors. The silence was broken only by the rumble of gun carriages on the cobblestones as cannon were placed in position around the Tuileries Palace where the Assemblies sat. At three in the morning of the fourth, Parisians were wakened by the firing of cannon. At this signal Augereau, with two thousand men behind him, forced his way into the council rooms at the Tuileries and arrested all the recently elected deputies as they entered, hastily summoned for an emergency session. Augereau's troops then moved on to the Luxembourg to arrest the two "dissenting" directors. One of them, Lazare Carnot, escaped through the garden in his nightshirt; the other, Barthélemy, was arrested in his bed.

Overnight the city walls had been hung with posters announcing the discovery of a royalist conspiracy and the government's "escape from a new peril." There was little public reaction. Unlike at Vendémiaire, there had been no popular curiosity, but, just as after Vendémiaire, the theaters were filled that night, outdoor balls opened at the usual time and "pretty women, all the goddesses of the hour, continued to sweep the streets of the capital with their trailing, transparent dresses."[14]

One hundred sixty-three citizens of varied politics were deported in iron cages to Guiana, known as the "dry guillotine" because few ever returned from that penal colony. The purged council annulled the results of the recent elections, thirty newspapers were closed down, and new ferocious laws decreed the firing squad for illegally returning emigrés and for anyone guilty of wishing to restore the monarchy or the Constitution of 1793.

It would be some time before Mme de Staël realized that she had helped destroy the first French democratic parliamentary government. Later, she would consider that the only time a republic had existed in France had been under the Directory, and then only until 18 Fructidor; it had been, she would declare, the expression of a liberal government such as the men of the Enlightenment had dreamed of. As for Charles-Maurice de Talleyrand, who had remained at home playing whist with friends all through the day of the coup, he wrote to Bonaparte the following day: "Paris is calm, Augereau's conduct was impeccable," adding with a courtier's bow: "It is clear that he has been to the right school."[15]

The coup known as Fructidor had relieved the Directory of its fears of a royalist revival. But there was another consequence. The generals of the Republic noted that for the third time the government had been saved by the army, with all the long-term effects on foreign and domestic policy that this implied. For General Bonaparte, Fructidor meant that not only had the propeace deputies been eliminated, but also his own support of the coup had put the Directory in his debt, and, more immediately, that he now had a free hand to dictate the terms of the treaty with Austria.

When he left Milan on August 22 to hammer out the final draft of a peace treaty with the Austrian representative, General Bonaparte was not accompanied by his wife. Army records show that Captain Charles left Milan on August 31 for leave in France, and on the following day Mme

Bonaparte left to join her husband at Passeriano, the summer retreat of the Venetian Doges outside Venice.

She found the General in a towering rage. The Franco-Austrian negotiations were dragging on and he was frantic with alarm lest the Directory take them over and deprive him of the glory of "his" peace. He was aware that although Barras wanted peace, preferably with the frontiers defined by the Constitution, and Talleyrand wished for a treaty that would reconcile Europe with revolutionary France, Talleyrand's nominal chief, Reubell, would certainly insist on the war's continuation until the orthodox revolutionary aim of achieving France's "natural frontiers" was achieved. Furthermore, Reubell would want the left bank of the Rhine exchanged for Bonaparte's Italian conquests, all of which the French government regarded as so many bargaining chips. Finally, every communiqué from the Directory had stressed that the abandonment of the independent Republic of Venice was not to be considered.

Although Bonaparte himself, like most of his fellow commanders, was prepared to continue the war indefinitely, he was in a hurry now. Winter would soon be closing the passes into Austria; after that he would no longer be able to threaten the Austrian delegation with instant invasion if a treaty on his terms was not concluded.

Meanwhile the Directory's foreign minister, Talleyrand, still confident that his aims of peace and a moderate policy were identical with Bonaparte's, was secretly assuring the Citizen General that although the government was opposed to abandoning the Venetian Republic, it wished to send him "directions only, not orders."

Unfortunately for Bonaparte, the Austrians had decided to play for time, aware that the French policy of acquiring the left bank of the Rhine had so far been sacrificed to the General's personal policy on Italy. They could not guess that his role in the forthcoming coup in Paris would give him a free hand to write his own treaty.

Until the news of the successful Fructidor coup reached him Bonaparte's frustration was such that he not only threatened the Austrians with an immediate invasion but twice attempted to blackmail his own government with the menace of instant retirement. The Directory could send a new negotiator, he wrote. He would make no further sacrifices for his country; his health was impaired; his virtue was unassailable, but "his soul needed to be nourished by contact with the great mass of citizens."

"The government believes in the virtue of General Bonaparte," read the full text of the Directory's reply. Mme Bonaparte's arrival coincided with this latest conciliatory message from the government.

Josephine was immediately aware that her husband and Paul Barras disagreed over the treaty. Sure of her role, of the importance of her link between the two men, she continued to underline this tie in every letter to the Director. "Bonaparte sends you *mille amitiés*. He still adores me,"[16] she ended her first message to him for Passeriano. In another letter to Barras—was it inspired by her husband or simply an expression of her longing for Paris?—she wrote, "I can hardly wait to tell you myself of my affection for you. It depends entirely on you to make it happen. Write to Bonaparte to sign the treaty, and then I will soon be with my friends again. Goodbye, *je vous embrasse* and love you with all my heart."[17]

Working sessions, sometimes lasting until three in the morning, took place on alternate days at either the Austrian or French headquarters, and the official dinners also alternated between the two. Bonaparte found that Josephine's presence made the Austrians less rigid and that the tone of the meetings benefited. At his request she set out to flatter them, entertaining the heads of their delegation, their staff officers and her husband's aides; she gave dinner parties and receptions, and organized picnics for them in the Venetian countryside.

The Austrians had sent as their top negotiator Count Ludwig von Cobenzl, a small, ugly man of immense sophistication who had served his country in all the important embassies. Josephine concentrated her charm on him and listened attentively to his anecdotes of the courts of Europe. Cobenzl noted that Bonaparte was gratified to be able to show that he had married an aristocrat, a woman of the same world as the Austrian's, but he was surprised to find the General eager to impress him by his own claims to Corsican nobility. And finally, he noted that Bonaparte was still in awe of his wife.

The Austrian—and even the French—delegations were astonished when in the course of a large official dinner Bonaparte, seated at the other end of the table from Josephine, took to pelting her with pieces of bread. Shaken by her look of reproof, he continued for a few minutes, but with less confidence, and finally "hung his head and stopped."[18]

When at last news reached Bonaparte of the successful coup of Fructidor it came accompanied by a secret letter from Talleyrand assuring him that the coup had given the General total freedom to negotiate and warning him that he must move fast. The new Directory would certainly stress that the abandonment of the Republic of Venice was not to be considered.

Negotiations became feverish. Bonaparte took to biting his nails and, unusually, to drinking large quantities of punch. At Austrian headquarters one night, as Cobenzl insisted that his emperor could not act alone on the question of the Rhine frontier but must submit it to a general congress of the empire, Napoleon shouted: "Your Empire is nothing but an old maid servant accustomed to being raped by everyone!" Next, stamping, ranting and threatening to set his grenadiers on the Austrian delegation, he picked up an enormous porcelain tea service, a treasured gift to Cobenzl from the Russian Empress Catherine, and dashed it to the floor, shouting: "This is what will happen to your Monarchy!" Then, ramming his hat on his head he stormed out, bumping into the furniture and roaring from the doorway: "Now you can have your war!" "He behaved like a madman," reported a shaken Cobenzl to his government.

The Austrians gave in once the results of Fructidor became known. General Bonaparte, it was clear, would have a free hand. Late on the evening of October 16 the ratification of the terms of the treaty arrived from Vienna. They were exactly those that General Bonaparte had wanted. Belgium was ceded to France and Venice, under the secret articles of the peace terms, handed over to Austria. Cobenzl, too, was content; he had obtained very favorable terms for a beaten country. Both men were seen to be in excellent humor as the Peace of Campo Formio was signed by the light of candles that night. An hour later the text was on its way to Paris.

With Napoleonic luck a stern warning arrived from the Directory the following morning only. Too late, the government cautioned its representative once more that the French Republic should not be dishonored by the surrender of Venice, a free republic, to an imperial state.

The treaty was, of course, a personal triumph for General Bonaparte, although its inherent weaknesses were immediately clear to the French government and to the councils. Only Paul Barras, the General's patron who was blamed by the other directors for their representative's insubordination, urged its ratification. Even Emmanuel Sieyès, the only major figure of the Revolution to have survived it, and a supporter of Bonaparte, declared to the Five Hundred that he had "believed that the Directory was to dictate the conditions of peace to Austria, but I see now that it is rather Austria which has imposed them on France. This peace is not a peace, it is a call for a new war." And Talleyrand, aware of many of the disastrous aspects of the treaty, particularly the granting of so much power to the Austrian Empire, foresaw that Campo Formio could be no more than a truce.

After four hours of furious deliberation, the Directory reluctantly, and out of fear of public opinion, signed the ratification of the treaty. As the news of peace spread, there were scenes of wild enthusiasm in Paris that night; streets were illuminated and the General's health drunk in every café. Nevertheless, opposition continued within the Directory and there was a storm of protest from the councils when Barras proposed the following day that General Bonaparte be appointed the government's representative to the ratification of the treaty in Austria, and subsequently be given command of the French forces along the Channel, now preparing for a proposed invasion of Britain.

While these tumultuous discussions continued in the government throughout October, the Bonapartes, or Napoleon at least, were debating their return to Paris.

Josephine herself suffered no doubts at all, no regrets for the loss of their viceregal court in Italy, for the adulation, the deference, the gifts, the solemn receptions and the acclamations everywhere. All these were outweighed by the happy prospect of a return to her world: to the Luxembourg, center of influence and of pleasure, and to the beloved house in the rue Chantereine.

Although she had learned much at Passeriano of her value to her husband in charming his opponents and in limiting the effect of his rages, the time there had not been happy. For her, the summer palace of the Doges would be remembered as six weeks of boredom and sadness. She wept when a rumor reached her from Milan of Hippolyte Charles's love affair there with an Italian, even though the lady was said to be so like her in appearance as to be almost her double. And she wept again when news reached Passeriano of the death of General Hoche.

Two weeks after Fructidor, at the age of twenty-nine and after two further spectacular victories on the Rhine, Lazare Hoche had died in his bed (of pneumonia, it was said), just as Bonaparte had predicted at their first meeting. He had shared Napoleon's gift for electrifying his troops, and at his funeral the sobbing of his grenadiers could be heard above the muffled drums and the thunder of cannon. The funeral cortege was headed by a company of maidens bearing a banner proclaiming: "He would have been the Bonaparte of the Rhine"—exactly what Napoleon had feared.

In his lifetime Hoche was always seen as the personification of the ideal citizen-soldier of the Republic, of the "bold and blameless warrior,"[19] a reputation that was to survive him. Fifty years after Bonaparte's seizure of power, Hoche's monument in Versailles was pointedly inscribed: "He died too soon for France. Had he lived, his glory would never have cost his country her liberty." Lazare Carnot's own view was that "Hoche, had he lived, might have had his own Brumaire"—that is, he, too, might have overthrown the Republic to his own advantage.

Though Hoche was considered incapable of trickery, Napoleon's unforgiving evaluation of his rival was that he was "only an intriguer," and writing of himself in the third person, "Hoche had esteem, even admiration for Napoleon, but his own morals were scandalous."[20]

General Hoche's death resulted in a number of unforeseen repercussions. Ever since Josephine's marriage he had written to her insisting, without any reply, on the return of his passionate love letters. Now it was Josephine who, terrified lest her own to him might fall into the hands of the Bonaparte clan, enlisted Hippolyte's help. It was Hippolyte Charles's Polish friend Brigadier Sulkowski who finally succeeded in the delicate mission of retrieving them from Rousselin de St. Albin, the guardian of young Mme Hoche, a nineteen-year-old minor.

Rousselin, however, expected adequate compensation and, one year after the imperial divorce, he wrote a sycophantic letter to Napoleon, hinting at the great services he had rendered Mme Bonaparte. The Empress Josephine, he wrote, had always promised him honors and an impressive reward; he had yet to see them. The Emperor's only answer was to send Rousselin off to a distant and insalubrious post.*

---

* Rousselin was to have his own revenge. As Barras's executor, it became his duty to finish and to edit the Director's posthumous *Mémoires*. He took this opportunity to add his own, often vindictive notes. Those on Hoche and on Josephine, among others, are usually attributed to him.

After Hoche's death there remained little doubt in Talleyrand's mind as to which general should be the "sword" in a future coup. Bonaparte appeared to offer the best hope of ending the five-year-old war, and Talleyrand, who at first characterized the rape of Venice as "a disgraceful act for the young Republic," wrote one last, obsequious letter to Napoleon in Italy. "Now there is peace, peace *à la* Bonaparte," he wrote. "The Directory is pleased, the public overjoyed. The Italians may do some squealing, but that does not matter. Farewell, General and Peacemaker! My regards, admiration, respect, gratitude—words fail me, the list could go on forever."[21]

In November the Serbelloni Palace was in an uproar. After weeks of indecision Napoleon was finally prepared to leave Milan. He had sent out feelers in Paris to inquire whether the law requiring a director to be at least forty might be repealed in his case "for the Great Pacificator"; the answer was not encouraging. This was not the time, came back the report, to ask the councils, still scandalized by the text of Campo Formio, to violate the Constitution. Still unsure as to what form his ambition should take, Bonaparte was certain only that he should show himself in Paris without delay while he could capitalize on the picture of the Man of Peace. But first the Treaty of Campo Formio had to be ratified.

Josephine's effects were being packed. Both her magnificent presents from the rulers of Italy and her own acquisitions—bronzes, paintings, statuary and cases of liqueurs—were being directed to the rue Chantereine. But her jewel case never left her side during her journey home. Every municipality spared by the General had contributed to it: a diamond and sapphire parure acquired as a bribe through Antoine Hamelin and several sets of antique cameos were only part of the collection.

Josephine had written from Passeriano to the celebrated cabinetmakers, the Jacob Brothers, to order new decoration for the Paris house. The latest furniture in Roman military style was ordered and 120,000 francs dispatched for the initial cost. "I wish it," she wrote, "to be supremely elegant."

But now, unaccountably, and in spite of these delightful prospects, Josephine informed Bonaparte that she wanted to visit Rome before their joint departure from Italy. The General so informed his brother Joseph, now the Directory's ambassador to the Holy See, and asked that every preparation be made for her reception there. After a short visit, he wrote, she was to rejoin him in Paris.

On November 16, Bonaparte himself set off on a carefully orchestrated journey to Rastadt in Austria, modestly dressed, but preceded at each relay by splendidly uniformed staff officers. In Turin, he held one last confidential talk with Miot de Mélito, still France's representative there. If he "found that he could not be master in France," he confided, "he would leave that country."[22]

Her husband had no sooner left than Josephine changed her plans. At the very moment when Napoleon was sealing the fate of Venice she decided that she would go there rather than to Rome.

Since May the Venetian Republic had been occupied by a French garrison. In spite of this, and although General Bonaparte had already sent the great lion representing their patron saint to Paris together with other treasures, the Venetians still had hopes of preserving their independence. They had not started on that "Italian squealing" dismissed by Talleyrand, since they had not yet learned their fate, but the better, they hoped, to plead their cause with the conqueror's wife, they put on four days of such dazzling festivities that Josephine would remember them to the end of her days.

Some 150,000 people crowded the roofs and windows along the length of the Grand Canal to witness her arrival. So tightly packed were the gondolas that they "looked like a whole city in movement."[23] By night, the light reflected from the fireworks and illuminations appeared to turn the canals into so many rivers of fire. At the opera, at the ball in the Doge's palace, in all this revelry Mme Bonaparte was the central figure, accompanied by her husband's aide General Marmont, and by another young French officer, unnamed, but almost certainly Captain Charles.

At Rastadt, General Bonaparte appears to have heard some unpleasant gossip. Laure d'Abrantès's husband would tell her later that at headquarters in Milan that month "a rumor suddenly went the rounds to the effect that the commander in chief had ordered the arrest of Captain Charles and that his execution by a firing squad was shortly to follow."[24]

In fact, Bonaparte's orders, signed by General Berthier and taken by him to Milan, read: "10 Frimaire Year VI of the French Republic One and Indivisible, Bonaparte, Commander in Chief of the Army of Italy: Citizen Charles, aide-de-camp, is to leave Milan immediately for Paris, there to await further instructions."

By chance, Josephine's carriage and Berthier's arrived at the same time at a relay in the Alps, she on her way to Paris, he returning to Milan to replace Bonaparte as commander of the Army of Italy. Berthier owed Josephine many kindnesses—she was his confidante in the matter of his passionate, lifelong affair with the Italian Mme Visconti—and she must have persuaded him to alter the tone and substance of the order he carried. A new one was issued, granting Charles permission to return to Paris on a three-month leave "for family business."

This second order was signed on December 22; by this time Josephine had reached Lyons on an itinerary that was nothing less than a royal progress. But, as she lingered interminably at each provincial relay, it was a singularly dilatory journey for one who had, for the last year and a half, dreamed of her return to Paris.

Torches lit the approaches to each country town; every village was illuminated. At Lyons, where she spent two nights, a proclamation informed citizens that "the city walls enclosed all that the conqueror and pacificator Bonaparte holds most dear: his wife, as celebrated for her qualities and her virtues as for the luster of her name." Speeches continued until the early hours of the morning. It took her three days to reach the next relay at Moulins, only one hundred miles away. There, cannon announced her arrival; the National Guard, the police and an army detachment accompanied her to her inn, where she was welcomed as "the virtuous spouse of the greatest of heroes, one who, by her virtues and her literary accomplishments, shares all his glory."

Josephine's own answer to these speeches was characteristically tactful. "If my husband has been so successful," she declared, "it is because he has had the good fortune to command an army in which every soldier is a hero." She drove out of Moulins through triumphal arches inscribed: "We wish to retain her longer, but she burns with desire to join her husband."

Whatever the object of her burning desire, Hippolyte Charles, by leaving Milan on December 22, and by riding hell-for-leather, could have caught up with Josephine on the twenty-eighth at her next stage outside Nevers. Together they must have celebrated New Year's Eve, for the journey on to Paris, a mere 145 miles, would not otherwise have stretched to another five days.

At last, on January 2, Josephine arrived home in Paris.

·❧ 15 ·❧

SON AND HERO OF THE REVOLUTION

ON DECEMBER 5, 1797, GENERAL BONAPARTE RETURNED TO THE HOUSE IN the rue Chantereine. He had spent only the first two days of his married life there, and two disagreeable surprises awaited him. The bill for "improvements" to the house had arrived; Josephine, expected in Paris the previous week, had not.

Paul Barras visited the General that evening, and they talked late into the night. Early the following morning Bonaparte sent a message to the minister of exterior relations: he would wait upon him at eleven o'clock. The moment when Talleyrand met Napoleon at the door of the ministry and escorted him to his own rooms overlooking the garden marked the start of what in the early days was close to a love affair between the two men which would have far-reaching consequences for the history of Europe.

Of the two, it would be the experienced politician whose misunderstanding of the nature of his ally would be the greater, he who was the more dazzled by the personality of the other. Talleyrand was unprepared for the effect the physical presence of Bonaparte produced upon him. Unlike many of his contemporaries, who sometimes found the little General initially unimpressive, Talleyrand in his *Mémoires* remembered "his pallor, his fine expression and his air of apparent exhaustion. Twenty victories are so becoming to youth."[1]

This first meeting was marred only by the presence of Germaine de Staël, who, with her usual impetuosity and lack of judgment, had insisted upon being present. Admiral Bougainville, too, the illustrious explorer and one of the heroes of Bonaparte's youth, had been invited to wait in the salon behind Talleyrand's study, and the General made a point of talking only to him and to the minister and of ignoring Germaine, whom he already both feared and despised and whose letters belittling Josephine he had not forgotten.

Paris was now caught up in a fever of hero worship as Bonaparte proceeded to take up his role of ideal citizen-soldier. The image of the victorious general was to be replaced in the public eye by that of a modern-day Cincinnatus, a French George Washington. Bonaparte proclaimed his determination to be above all political parties, going so far as to refuse to receive a deputation of the *dames de la Halle,* those harridans so warmly received by every revolutionary leader since Lafayette. The more the General hid, the more intense was the curiosity he aroused. Paris journals wrote of little else but his activities. His orders to the porter's lodge at the end of the alley were to admit to no one. Crowds gathered in the rue Chantereine, peered through the new gate designed by Jacob and reported that they believed they could see the General "walking alone in his modest garden." One journal, which had certainly not been privileged to enter his house, described it as "small, simple, and without any luxury."

Although the Emperor Napoleon was to own no fewer than forty-four palaces, each one entirely refurnished at state expense with millions of francs' worth of new decoration, twenty years later he would still remember with exasperation at St. Helena that Jacob's furniture for the salon alone ("all of it made to order") had cost 130,000 francs.[2]

Josephine, when she ordered the redecoration of the Paris house, must have been confident that Georges Jacob, the last of the great pre-revolutionary decorators and cabinetmakers, was still the most fashionable. In the days of her early married life he was known as the Queen's principal decorator; beds and chaises longues, fire screens and ottomans issued from Jacob's workrooms for all the royal palaces.

But in his search for "the noble serenity of republican Rome," Jacob created, both for the Committee of Public Safety and for the hall of the National Convention, settings very different from the pastoral ones designed for Marie Antoinette at Trianon. By the time Josephine could view them from the galleries of the Convention, the symbols of watering cans and lyres, of gardening rakes and rose wreaths had long been replaced by severely draped curtains, and curule chairs copied from antique vases and designed to evoke "the virtuous austerity of Rome and of Sparta."

Although Marmont wrote that for Bonaparte the house was still the *temple de l'amour*,[3] little remained of the charming and inexpensive decoration of that temple, crammed now with fine if sober mahogany furniture. The dining room was paved in mosaic; some of the fine bronzes sent from Italy had been placed there by Jacob and his brother. Napoleon worked in the third small room, called in the Jacobs' accounts "General Bonaparte's study"; and even here, with his maps of the Channel coast laid out along the floor, he was disturbed by the arrival of additional furniture from the cabinetmakers' workshop. But it was in the conjugal bedroom that Jacob, in his determination to create a setting worthy of the nation's hero, had created a unique "military-Directory" style, somewhat heavy, not always successful but evocative, even moving.

Josephine's bedroom had been stripped of its mirrors and tented in blue and white striped canvas. The twin beds, "in the antique Roman style," were painted to resemble bronze, and, by a device presumably unknown to the Roman Republic, could be drawn together or separated by a spring. Somehow space was found in the little room for six stools in the form of drums.

Did Bonaparte, as he slept alone in this miniature martial splendor, resent the vast changes in decoration, or was he restlessly calculating its price, or else tormented by the lack of any news of Josephine?

Hortense, when she came a few days later with Aunt Désirée and the marquis, could not get over the changes in the house, both inside and out. Even the street had a new name—the rue de la Victoire. A directive announced that the government "considered it its duty both to eliminate any signs of royalty which could still be found in the name of the street, and desired to consecrate the triumphs of the French army by one of those monuments which recall the simplicity of the customs of antiquity." The directors, no etymologists, had taken offense at the syllable *reine* ("queen"), unaware that it was only the rustic term for the frogs that once sang in the former swamp.

When the three Beauharnais had pushed their way through the crowds and been admitted through the alley gate, they found a new entrance to the house itself: a striped canvas vestibule now screened the front door, so that visitors no longer walked immediately into the antechamber. "How many changes in our little house, once so quiet!" Hortense recalled in her *Mémoires*. "The sentries had trouble keeping back both the common people and persons of fashion, all impatient to see the conqueror of Italy. Finally, in spite of the crowds, we managed to get through to the General, who was breakfasting, surrounded by his general staff. He greeted me with all the tenderness of a father."[4]

To the visitors' questions as to Josephine's whereabouts, there could be no answer. Presumably they all assumed that she would be back for the scene of the General's triumph, the solemn ceremony at which the Directory was to honor him.

General Bonaparte continued to restrict his public appearances and to maintain the element of surprise as brilliantly as though conducting a military operation. Consequently, on December 10, when the streets between the General's home and the Luxembourg Palace were filled with crowds, certain at last of observing their hero driving there in state, he made a point of disappointing them by taking a roundabout route to the palace and sitting well back in a "very simple carriage" in which he could barely be glimpsed.

At the Luxembourg, the great courtyard of the palace was hung with the flags of each of the armies of the Republic. On a dais in front of an altar to the fatherland sat the five directors in their scarlet togas, surrounded by members of the diplomatic corps and the cabinet ministers. Everyone of any consequence in Paris was seated on either side in a semicircle. The entire courtyard and every window and even the roof of the palace were filled with an eager crowd.

Suddenly the silence was broken by an explosion of shouts of *"Vive la République! Vive Bonaparte!"* from the street outside. Guns boomed, music struck up, and the frail figure of the General appeared, dressed in a plain gray coat, "looking calm and modest."

"Although every beautiful woman in Paris was in the great courtyard of the Luxembourg that day," wrote Paul Thiébault, "and in spite of the luxury, the elegance of the women's clothes and the sumptuous costume of the Directors, every eye was fixed on the spare, sallow, sickly-looking man in a simple coat, who appeared to fill all the space around him."[5]

There was total silence as Talleyrand introduced Napoleon as "the son and hero of the Revolution," as the citizen and the peace negotiator, rather than as the General. Bonaparte could only be gratified by Talleyrand's perfect perception of how he would wish to be presented. Without a smile, the Bishop wound up his introduction with the words: "When I reflect upon all he has done for us that we might forgive him his glory; on his profound contempt for pomp, for luxury and for display, those pitiful ambitions of vulgar souls! . . . Ah! Far from fearing what some might call his ambition, I feel that one day we may have to implore him to tear himself from the calm of his studious retreat."

The General's reply, in a strong Italian accent, was short, vigorous and noncommittal, after which he was engulfed in a tide of ostrich plumes and swirling togas as each director enfolded him in an embrace. Barras, president of the Directory that year, concluded the ceremony by exhorting General Bonaparte to march on to the banks of the Thames "to purge the universe of the monsters which oppress and dishonor it. May St. James's Palace crumble! Your country wishes it, humanity requires it, revenge demands it!

The agent of the Bourbon princes in London, Mallet du Pan, reported the ceremony thus: "Either because his profound dissimulation urged him to one more effort, or because he had the wisdom to judge both the theater and the actors, Bonaparte suppressed his pride. The Jacobins and the terrorists observe every step, every visit, every word spoken by this man who has become the object of their distrust and will soon be that of their hatred."[6]

Perhaps only one other person in all of Paris had a thirst equal to the General's for self-promotion, but one for its own sake as it were, with no ulterior motive. Behind the directors, the cabinet and the foreign ambassadors, on the benches reserved for distinguished guests, were seated Juliette Récamier and her mother. Just as Bonaparte finished his short speech Juliette stood up to see the General more clearly. "As she did so," wrote her niece, "and her whole form could be seen, the eyes of the crowd turned toward her and greeted her with a long murmur of admiration." The General heard it and looked around "to see who could have diverted the crowd's attention from him. He saw a young woman dressed in white and threw her a look of intolerable harshness. She quickly sat down."[7]

After this ceremony General Bonaparte measured his appearances still more carefully. When it became known that he would welcome an invitation to become a member of the French Academy of Sciences, predecessor of the Institut de France, it was immediately forthcoming.

According to newspaper reports on the day he was received into that body: "Bonaparte, judging by his modest demeanor, appeared not to be aware that he was the center of the attention,"[8] and he let it be known that henceforth he did not care to admit to his company any but his fellow academicians.

There was, however, one social event that, because of its circumstance, Bonaparte felt at liberty to attend. Talleyrand, whose instinct for timing seldom failed him, guessed that Paris was ready now for a display of luxury, dignity and patriotism worthy of the national idol. To ensure its nonpolitical aspect, and in a gesture certain to please Bonaparte, he determined to give a ball—nominally in honor of the hero's wife. The date was set for 5 Nivôse (December 25).

It was soon known in Paris that the five hundred invitations sent out by the minister of exterior relations were intended for an evening reminiscent of the *ancien régime;* Talleyrand, it was said, wished to eliminate the coarser elements of Directory society.

Although those invitations were accompanied by a slip of a patriotic nature reading "You will, I feel sure, find it appropriate to abstain from wearing fabric manufactured in England," the very rumors of the unrepublican nature of the evening caused two of the directors to refuse their invitations outright. The others, Reubell, Larevellière and Barras, decided to mark their displeasure by attending in plain cloth coats and riding boots.

It was known, too, that Bellanger, the architect of Bagatelle and of other royal follies, was to be responsible for the decorations for the ball and that the interior of the noble Hôtel Gallifet had been regilded under his orders for the occasion. This great house in the rue de Grenelle (now the Italian embassy), set between the Doric columns of the entrance to the two courtyards on the street side and a vast garden on the other, had been finished just before the Revolution; its owners had emigrated and the government had designated it as the official residence and offices of the Ministry of External Relations. There were few houses in the capital that could match its salons or the perfection of its double oval staircase.

By December 24, Mme Bonaparte still had not returned from Italy. The ball was hurriedly canceled and new invitations were sent out by messenger for December 28. Still no Josephine. Once again the minister postponed the elaborate arrangements and the date was reset for 14 Nivôse

(January 3). Five hundred guests had been twice reinvited, 930 trees and shrubs removed and brought in again, wine and food canceled and reordered for the second time.

On the night of January 3, in a light snow, the crush of carriages stretched from the rue de Grenelle all the way to the Seine. At the entrance to the first courtyard a bivouac scene was set up, complete with smoke, lights, campfire and martial music—perhaps the first *son-et-lumière*. In the second courtyard, in equally obvious homage to General Bonaparte, a small temple had been constructed to house a bronze bust of Brutus—principal hero in the selective body of Jacobin divinities—and "liberated" from the Roman Capitol by the Army of Italy.

Within the house were hung reproductions of most of the great paintings looted by that army—Titians, Correggios, Raphaels and Leonardos. There was further allusion to the General's triumphs in the myrtle garlanding the double staircase, at the top of which stood the host leaning on an ebony cane, welcoming each guest with carefully measured affability according to rank—a warm handshake to some, two fingers to another. A cloud of the minister's favorite amber perfume greeted arrivals, mixed with the fragrance of jasmine from the flowering shrubs, as well as an unusual quantity of warmth and light generated by a prerevolutionary profusion of candles in the wall sconces and chandeliers.

At half past ten the music stopped and the chattering crowd fell silent.

A hush more impressive than any ovation marked the entrance of the Bonapartes. Paris was unprepared for the frail, upright figure of the General in his now customary civilian coat buttoned to the chin, or for the intensity of his cold gaze. Josephine, as usual, had found the exact note. She had not made the mistake of wearing any of the splendid jewels pressed upon her by the Italian rulers, but was crowned with a small gold cloth cap and a simple diadem of antique cameos, the gift of the General.

The pair looked and acted the role of sovereigns, and Talleyrand made it clear that in his house, and on this evening, they did indeed reign. As they advanced, the crowd in deadly silence parted for them as for royalty. The General was, perhaps for the only time on record, taken aback, almost embarrassed, by the ardor of the veneration directed at him. To give himself countenance he took Arnault's arm, telling him to continue to talk to him for a while so as to prevent other guests from approaching him. But he seemed incapable of leaving his wife's side for long, "making no secret of the fact that he was insanely jealous, head over heels in love."[9]

Talleyrand would never forgive Germaine de Staël for providing the only contretemps in this harmonious evening. In spite of the entreaties of her friends, she literally cornered the General at the foot of the great staircase. A crowd immediately gathered. Dominating him by a head, she fired a succession of questions at him, the answer to each one of which she hoped would be: "You, Madame." He refused to reply until she asked: "General, which woman could you love the most?" "My wife." "Of course, but which woman, alive or dead, do you most admire?" Icily, he replied: "The one who makes the most children," and pushed his way past her. Germaine, said a witness, stood as though petrified with astonishment.[10]

At eleven, supper was announced and, as once at Versailles, only the ladies were seated. Each one was personally served by one of the male guests standing behind her chair. With exquisite politeness, Talleyrand himself served Josephine throughout the evening and never left her side. Paris noted this; Paris had not seen an evening to match it for more than a decade.

Dancing at the ministry continued until dawn, but by midnight the Bonapartes had left.

The bills presented to Talleyrand the following day were formidable, and Bellanger "begged the Minister to observe that the various delays caused by the late arrival of Madame Bonaparte occasioned a very large extra expense for rented items twice replaced like the 930 trees,"[11] as well as additional payments for the painters, carpenters, masons, gardeners, candlestick makers and engravers, and that these did not include the additional bills for musicians and the buffet. Nevertheless, Talleyrand must have felt that the evening had been a sound investment. Only four years after the Terror was entering its bloodiest stage, when half the guests present had been in prison or under sentence of death, and the other half were themselves terrorists, Talleyrand had proved that it was possible to unite the worlds of the *ancien régime* and of the Directory. He guessed, moreover, that Bonaparte had understood the ball's every implication and had missed none of the flattery directed at him through his wife.

At St. Helena, Napoleon still remembered that evening. From it, he wrote, he learned how much the French appreciated protocol, grace and dignity.[12]

"Patriotism was in the air, as well as pleasure," announced the Paris journals the following day; the republican nature of the evening at the Ministry of External Relations was emphasized. The dresses of the Citoyennes were applauded. They had wisely confined themselves, reported one newspaper, to the more naked Greek styles, so much more flattering to those with fine figures, but whose faces might lack beauty. As for the men, one Incroyable "buried to above his chin in an enormous cravat" was so struck by the simplicity of the General's attire that he urged his friends to join him in giving up monstrous neckcloths forever.

It was Bonaparte—whose avian profile was still considered "bizarre"—who had been, the newspapers pointed out, the center of attention rather than Josephine. She was "remarkable only for the charm of her person and the good taste of her dress," and still more for the unceasing attention paid to her by the hero, who "appeared to take pleasure only in the consideration directed toward her rather than to himself."

Could this have been the reason for Josephine's dissatisfaction? It was generally noticed that she appeared distracted at the Talleyrand ball— even as close to ill-humored as it was possible for her to be. Some thought it was because she was conscious of not looking her best. The choice of the gold cloth cap was not universally admired, and she may have overheard sarcastic references to the "Doge's bonnet." The same Girardin who had noted Napoleon's jealous care of her had also estimated her age at "nearly 40," recorded that she looked fully that, and that she was "no longer beautiful, although her bearing was elegant and her kind heart would certainly never grow old." Girardin also described Bonaparte on the same evening as: "Not more than five feet tall, his face is pale, his cheeks hollow, his eyes small and lackluster. His expression is one of profound dissimulation."[13]

It is unlikely that there had been any acrimonious discussions between the Bonapartes over her late arrival. Josephine had only to point to the newspapers, which had kept the capital informed of "Mme Bonaparte's triumphant progress occasioned by the celebrations which embellished her journey," and to claim that it was the fault of his victories.

Surely only the pain of being parted from Hippolyte could account for her lack of appreciation of this near-royal fete given in her honor alone, upon her first return to Paris.

Newspapers continued to marvel at the General's lack of ambition and at his retired life, reporting that he "avoids anything which might draw attention to himself. His wife too has adopted a way of life as retiring as his own." At home, guests remarked on the air of domesticity and the apparent harmony between the couple. Bonaparte's social life remained that of a man who wished to take no part in public affairs; political figures, with few exceptions, were excluded, as was Josephine's retinue of Merveilleuses.

The company that would gather for dinner at six-thirty in the rue de la Victoire was now as changed as the rooms in which they sat. Joseph Chénier, Antoine Arnault, Paul Barras and the Talliens remained from the past, but now the salon was full of twenty-year-old generals, of savants like Monge and Berthollet; the actor Talma and Jacques-Louis David, who had painted a neoclassical frieze around the room in which they dined. Barras and Talleyrand were usually seated on either side of Josephine; after dinner Méhul would sing and Arnault read his poems aloud. When Josephine tapped her husband on the shoulder to suggest that they move to the drawing room for coffee, "Bonaparte would playfully ask those present to note that his wife beats him."[14] "She alone has that privilege," was the not unexpected response from the company.

Thérésia and occasionally Germaine de Staël were the only women present besides Josephine. When Napoleon was told after the Talleyrand ball that Germaine had gamely pretended to admire his answers to her questions, he commented: "Josephine, however, reproached me. She said that people in Paris would accuse me of behaving like a celibate monk."[15]

He quoted this with admiration and as proof of her generosity, for Germaine's courtship of him continued. She wrote almost daily letters addressed, however, to Mme Bonaparte, who would hand them with a smile to her husband, saying only: "I believe these are intended for you!" She knew, of course, that she had no cause for jealousy; that in spite of Mme de Staël's romantic idealization of Napoleon, her admiration for his "firm republicanism" and what she believed to be his lack of ambition, he saw in her only an intemperate, unfeminine—worse, intellectual—woman. He was irritated by her brilliant conversation, and when he compared the two women it was always to his wife's advantage. The difference between the two women he would sum up as: "Josephine is a woman from the soles of her feet to the crown of her head, whereas the other one was not even . . ."[16] and he repeated an obscene observation of Benjamin Constant's.

Although, as a worldly woman of the eighteenth century, Josephine may have felt Napoleon's reply to Germaine to be distressingly boorish, she probably deplored another aspect of the Bonaparte/Staël exchange. She was increasingly sensitive to any reference to childbearing, although she felt as certain as did her husband that her Beauharnais children absolved her from any responsibility in the matter.

Barras was vitally important to Napoleon now. The surest path to power, he had decided, was to be appointed a director himself, and Paul Barras, as the most likely to satisfy his ambitions, remained the principal object of his attentions.

Josephine as a link to Barras was proving ever more useful. The Bonapartes' manservant, Blondin, flew back and forth to the Luxembourg bearing a flood of affectionate notes, asking for interviews or inviting the Director for dinner. But Napoleon would have been ignorant of one of Josephine's requests to see Barras alone, for when, on February 10 the General returned unexpectedly from a visit to the Channel ports, she sent an urgent note to her friend, Barras's secretary: "Bonaparte returned last night; I beg you, my dear Botot, to tell Barras how much I regret not to be able to dine with him tonight. Tell him not to forget me! You, my dear Botot, know my delicate position better than anyone."[17]

Ostensibly Bonaparte's twin tasks were to work with the Directory on instructions to the French representatives at Rastadt and on the projected attack on England. All his iron will, his energy, his gifts for diplomacy and intrigue, and his powers of seduction were now bent toward one aim: that of being named a director. Working separately with each of the directors at the Luxembourg at the daily sessions that continued until dinnertime, he gradually succeeded in acquiring considerable ascendancy over them although each one, except Barras, was initially distrustful of him, for "Bonaparte," as the King of Prussia's ambassador reminded his master, "has the talent of attracting and captivating men."

After January 27, Bonaparte ceased to attend the daily meetings of the Directory. On that day he had suggested to Barras that if he, the conqueror of Italy, the peacemaker, be made eligible as director at the age of twenty-eight, he and Barras could thereafter mount a coup d'état "in their own interests."[18] When Barras refused, the General stormed out of the Luxembourg.

Three problems now remained for him: to find a pretext to remain in Paris without losing prestige, to extricate himself from the English expedition and to eliminate his army rivals. Lazare Carnot, from his exile in Switzerland, had heard enough from Paris and was sufficiently familiar with the tactics of the general so recently under his orders, to guess that "Bonaparte probably believes that a hero loses some of his prestige on a vast stage, especially when he is the object of prolonged observation. . . . Already he has rid himself of Masséna, Joubert and Augereau, men whom the Jacobins had raised as rivals to himself. If he has a plan, he will stay in Paris only long enough to keep up enthusiasm on his behalf."[19]

Bonaparte had no trouble in contriving to have Augereau (too much admired by the Directory since Fructidor) removed from the command of the Army of the Rhine and sent to the less important one of the Pyrenees. Jean Bernadotte, however, was a more formidable competitor: another political general, as jealous of rivals as Bonaparte himself, six feet tall, and so arresting-looking that it was "impossible to be unaware of his presence in a room." Napoleon, under whom Bernadotte had served in Italy, knew him to be both an experienced soldier and administrator. "He's a devil of a man and he doesn't like me,"[20] Bonaparte confided to a friend. When he learned that Bernadotte had been appointed commander in chief of the Army of Italy, Napoleon objected that Bernadotte was too able a diplomat not to be used in that capacity, and had sent him as the Republic's representative to Vienna.

General Bonaparte continued to appear to be absorbed in conferences with the Navy Ministry and with bankers, to work feverishly on the English expedition and to make short visits of inspection to the Channel ports. It was after returning from one of these, Napoleon would relate to General Bertrand at St. Helena, that Louise Compoint came to see him. Louise was the maid who had accompanied Josephine to Italy and had shared the viceregal life in Milan. She had been dismissed, she said, "because Mme Bonaparte did not like her sleeping with Andoche Junot," and she proceeded, said Napoleon, to tell him that Captain Charles had ridden in her carriage on the way to Italy and spent the night at the same inns.*[21]

When Napoleon questioned Josephine on this, he said, he tried to make her confess by urging her to tell the truth. "After all, a man and a woman can sleep in the same inns without there being any harm in it," but she dissolved into floods of tears and could only repeat "No! No!"[22] And "she was basically a liar," was Mme de la Tour du Pin's verdict. "Even when the truth would have been more interesting and more amusing than the falsehood, she still preferred to lie."[23]

That was in January. The "day of the catastrophe," as Josephine would call it, occurred in the third week in March.

Two of Josephine's letters to Hippolyte Charles escaped the holocaust ordered by the captain on his deathbed. Probably because of their mixture of passion and financial considerations they had been filed with his business papers in his family home in the country. Found there in the 1950s by the historian Louis Hastier, they comprise the main testimony of Josephine's passionate involvement with Hippolyte—the only written proof we have.

This is what she wrote to Hippolyte Charles on March 19:

Joseph had a long talk yesterday with Bonaparte and afterwards he asked me whether I knew Citizen Bodin, whether I had procured for him the purveyor's contract with the Army of Italy, and whether it was true that Charles was living at Citizen Bodin's house at 100 Faubourg St. Honoré, and that I went there every day. I answered that I knew nothing of anything he was talking about; that if he wanted a divorce he need only say so, that he had no need to resort to tactics such as these, and that I was the most unfortunate of women and the unhappiest.

Yes, my Hippolyte, they have all my hatred. You alone have my tenderness, my love. . . . They must see the despair that I am in at being deprived of seeing you as often as I wish. Hippolyte, I will kill myself! I prefer to end a life which would be a burden if it cannot be devoted to you. Alas, what have I done to these monsters? . . .

---

* Josephine may not have known who had betrayed her, but characteristically, when Louise came to her for help later, she was treated generously.

Please tell Bodin to say that he does not know me, that it was not through me that he obtained the Army of Italy contract . . . Oh, no matter how much they torment me, they shall never separate me from my Hippolyte!

I will do everything possible to see you during the day. . . . I will send Blondin to tell you what time I can get away to meet you in the Parc Monceau. Goodbye my Hippolyte, a thousand kisses as passionate as my heart, and as loving. . . . They also said on the day of the catastrophe that you had been to the War Ministry to hand in your resignation.

There is a second distracted note on her efforts for the Bodin Company and her letters to the Minister of War and to Barras on the subject. Then:

I am going to the country, my dear Hippolyte. I will be back at 5 o'clock and will come at 5:30 or 6:00 to Bodin's to see you. Yes, my Hippolyte, my life is a constant torment! Only you can restore me to happiness. Tell me that you love me, that you love only me!

Send me 50,000 livres by Blondin out of the funds on hand. Collot is asking me for the money.

Adieu, I send you a thousand tender kisses—and I am yours, all yours.[24]

Ever since Thermidor the government had been forced to take out contracts for army provisioning only with those suppliers who operated on a large scale—large enough to be willing to accept deferred payment. At the Chaumière, Josephine, in common with many others, had dealt with the companies that held a near monopoly of supplying the army with clothes, food and fodder, often at inflated prices. Even in Milan she may have had an understanding with several of the civilian army contractors and received a cut from at least one company, probably through Antoine Hamelin. It was impossible to refuse Mme Bonaparte any favor and now she set about harrying everyone, including the Minister of War Schérer and Barras, to obtain a contract for the Bodin Company to supply the Army of Italy. This was probably the "delicate position" that she mentioned to Botot.

Once she had obtained the contract, Josephine succeeded in having the Bodins employ Hippolyte Charles, who, in mid-March, had surrendered his commission. He must have guessed that his beloved army career was now finished and that he would be forced to resign. Officially affiliated with the Bodins, Josephine apparently arranged for Charles to lodge at No. 100 faubourg St. Honoré, the Bodin headquarters.

Even had Joseph not hurried to his brother to pour out the story, the wonder is that Josephine could ever have imagined that General Bonaparte would not come to hear of her connection with the Bodins and of theirs with the Army of Italy. Here was *inconséquence,* as he called it, of a really major nature.

The "they," the "monsters" who had all Josephine's hatred, who were making her life "a constant torment," were, of course, the clan. The entire family was now converging on Paris. First Joseph Bonaparte, his wife, Julie, and sister-in-law Désirée Clary returned from the embassy in Rome after an anti-French riot there, partly provoked by his actions. Joseph's own account of the insurrection was not accepted by the Directory, but passed over because of his relationship with the powerful General. The rumor current in Paris was that Joseph had shipped from Rome a vast quantity of treasure—gossip that took on new life when he acquired a superb house near the rue de la Victoire, built by the architect of the Place de la Concorde, Ange Gabriel.

The circumstances of the indigent Bonaparte family had changed considerably since the beginning of the Italian campaign. Only Joseph, with the Clary dowry at his disposal, could for a while point to his wife's fortune as the origin of his funds, as he acquired successively not only the Paris house, but soon afterwards the Château de Mortefontaine, whose hundreds of acres, lakes and forests were only a four-hour carriage drive from Paris.

Napoleon himself, the man who three years earlier had arrived in Paris dreaming of fame and of "making a fortune in speculation," had neglected neither himself nor his family. Although he would always maintain that he had returned from Italy with nothing but his general's pay, he sent enough funds to his mother that year to enable her to rebuild and refurnish the ruined family home in Ajaccio, to buy for himself Josephine's rented house in the rue de la Victoire, and in the same month, a large property in Belgium, as well as to pay for the education of Caroline and Jérôme at expensive schools. In Italy, of course, he had lived magnificently, as well as provided his sisters Elisa and Pauline with large dowries.

Except at the sessions of the Councils at the time of the rape of Venice, there had been little criticism of any of this expenditure, although the government suspected General Bonaparte of retaining the entire sum raised in Italy for the financing of the coup of Fructidor. Indeed, recent historians reckon that of the fifty million pillaged by Napoleon in Italy, less then ten million were sent to the Directory "and that at least three of those millions" are believed to have been kept by the General himself.[25] It was not, at that period, considered unreasonable that the Bonaparte family, although regarded as particularly rapacious even for the times, should share in the spoils of the Army of Italy. With the exception of Hoche, all the generals and their commanders in chief were expected to take some part in their armies' plunder.

Either because he did not want to believe his brother or because he was totally preoccupied with the disquieting state of his ambitions, Bonaparte appears to have dismissed Joseph's accusations against Josephine. Bourrienne puts this down to "his love for his wife, his inspection tours of the coast, and his preoccupation with plans for the Egyptian campaign."[26]

The proposed attack on Egypt—Talleyrand's suggestion—appeared to solve all of General Bonaparte's problems. It came just in time, for the negative result of the Barras démarche and the fear that the command of the Army of England would do nothing to increase his prestige had plunged Bonaparte into the same profound depression from which he had suffered in the summer of 1795, and which was to recur throughout his career whenever his ambitions appeared to be thwarted. It showed itself this time in a paranoid fear for his life.

The press reported that General Bonaparte believed that the Jacobins wished to assassinate him. Their newspapers, as Mallet du Pan had predicted, were attacking him with greater violence daily and, without naming names, alluding to "a person who wishes to be dictator of France." Arnault wrote that a saddled horse was always in readiness in the stable of the rue de la Victoire, and that during the four months he spent in Paris the General, although dressed in civilian clothes, never removed his spurs.

From now on, Bonaparte brought his own servant to any public engagement to serve him alone and pour his wine. He took his own glasses, plate and silver and seldom touched anything but a boiled egg, on one occasion deeply offending his host, Paul Barras. Bonaparte told Director Reubell that month that he was afraid of being arrested, that he dreamed every night that he was a prisoner in the Temple, and that if the Egyptian expedition were called off, he "would travel and then retire to Prussia."[27]

Bonaparte had already considered striking at British sea power and commercial traffic in the east; now he put forward the idea of the invasion of Egypt as a means of cutting British communications with India; a further justification would be that French commercial interests were being threatened there by the Mamelukes, the warrior caste which had governed that country even before it became a province of the Ottoman Empire.

In the future, all those involved would disclaim any responsibility for the disastrous expedition, Talleyrand in his *Mémoires*, the directors in theirs. And even before he set sail for Egypt, Napoleon started the rumor that the government wished to send him into exile.

The members of the Directory, however, were united in believing that the timing was not propitious. They felt that risking war with Turkey, France's oldest ally, could lead to a conflict with Russia. Without mastery of the seas, maintaining communications with Egypt would be difficult, and the chances of avoiding Nelson's British navy in the Mediterranean, either on the way out or on the return, were slim. And although the Treaty of Rastadt was still not signed, the government believed it saw evidence of the formation of a new coalition; the European situation was such that France could ill afford to spare, as the General was requesting, the flower of France's officers and men at a time when troops should be concentrated at home. Only Paul Barras supported him— reluctantly. The Director's own fighting days in India had given him little confidence in the prospect of attacking the British there.

Bonaparte, however, was unprepared for the reaction of one of the other directors. After one more visit to the coast, he presented the government with a report which concluded that the French navy was inadequate for an invasion of Britain and that he would, in any case, be unable to obtain the necessary funds. Informed that further ships and supplies could be placed at his disposal, and that the vast sums he demanded were accepted, he pounded on the directors' table and threatened to resign his command. Reubell, especially hostile to the Egyptian project, coolly handed him a pen. "General," he said, "the Directory awaits your letter."[28]

Bonaparte did not sign his resignation, and the government dared not hold out against him, although the project was clearly unreasonable and egotistical. On March 5, 1798, the directors gave in.

In the two months before the General sailed for Egypt, the near-bankrupt Republic was required to furnish between eight and nine million francs to subsidize the undertaking. He requested, furthermore, that General Joubert be sent to Holland—now the "Batavian Republic"—to raise more funds; then that General Berthier travel to Rome on the same mission and finally that General Brune be ordered to invade the neutral puppet Helvetian Republic—Switzerland—for the confiscation of the Treasury of Berne. Although the expedition was supposedly secret, a cartoon in April depicted the directors announcing "Swiss GOLD WILL BUY US EGYPT!" Years later gold coins stamped with the Bear of Berne could still be found in the Egyptian desert.

The secrecy of the expedition's destination was all-important. Most of Admiral Nelson's fleet was still protecting the English coast against the expected invasion by the French fleet being outfitted in Toulon. In England, militia units of volunteers were being trained, a telegraph station was installed on one of the towers of Westminster Abbey, and the government recommended that in the event of an invasion barricades be set up in the squares and streets of London.

In France, few of the participants in the Egyptian expedition had any idea of their port of disembarkation. One of the scientists enlisted wrote to his family: "None of us yet knows our destination. Some believe it to be America, some Africa, others Asia."[29] This was the more remarkable since the civilian group numbered a large number of Orientalists, for it was General Bonaparte's imaginative decision that the expedition should include a Commission of Arts and Sciences composed not only of technical personnel, but also of physicists, geologists, paleontologists, astronomers and cartographers.

In spite of the General's minute and detailed planning, however, the date of embarkation remained uncertain. In a renewed bout of depression and irresolution, he kept finding new obstacles to the expedition. He could not even decide whether his wife should accompany him, although this time she begged to do so and assured him that the climate of Martinique had prepared her for the rigors of Egypt.

Fouché believed that while "the elite of our scientists and artists, his old Italian troops and all the treasury of the country" awaited him at Toulon, Napoleon still continued to hope for some event that would enable him to achieve supreme power without obliging him to undertake the expedition to the Orient. He ignored the Directory's request that he return to Rastadt to sign the treaty.

First the departure was set for April 28. Bonaparte paid his official farewell visit to the Directory, then abruptly canceled the sailing date. Before resetting it he took Josephine to look at country properties for sale; one of these was the Château de Malmaison. The General was tempted by it but found the price too high, a consideration that had certainly never yet occurred to Josephine. From there they went to say goodbye to Caroline Bonaparte and to Hortense at Mme Campan's school. They found Caroline still mortified at being sent there by her brother. He had told her that she should model herself upon Hortense—a member of the detested family and she was further outraged at being deprived of Paris and the society of General Murat, with whom she declared herself to be in love.

When the last obstacles to the Egyptian expedition were removed, Bonaparte finally recognized, he said, that his political ambitions were premature: "The fruit is not yet ripe," he confided to Bourrienne. Four months was the time he calculated it would take for a new coalition of powers to be formed in Europe, and he hoped that within that time he might return, after a short campaign and new victories. "I've tried everything but they don't want me. I should overthrow them and be crowned king, but it's not time to think of that yet."[30] And to Arnault the General admitted: "If I mounted by horse now, no one would follow me. We leave tomorrow."

It is hardly surprising that, in view of Josephine's habitual lies and of her conduct during the Italian campaign, many of her biographers are inclined to believe that she never intended to accompany her husband to Egypt; that the close-lipped smile and apparent compliance with his wishes concealed a firm determination to remain in Paris.

Yet there does now appear to be a change in her feelings for her husband, either because of her fundamentally affectionate nature and some degree of gratitude, or of a dawning recognition of the extraordinary stature of the man she had so nonchalantly married. Progressively, too, she was becoming accustomed to being the first everywhere, in France as well as in Italy, and although divorce had not apparently been mentioned since the "day of the catastrophe," some realization must have set in of the prospect of a very different life as Mme Charles.

There was a further change in Josephine. For the first time she was showing signs of that amiable readiness to go anywhere with her husband, often at a moment's notice, which would mark her life as Empress, the more admirable since "no words can describe the terror felt by Josephine in a carriage."[31]

Bonaparte was "so passionately in love with his fascinating wife that he took her with him to Toulon to put off the cruel parting until the last possible moment."[32] Without complaint now she accepted that she was not to know until the day of embarkation whether she was to sail, nor for how long she might be leaving Hortense.

Still Bonaparte had made no final decision on this when, after dinner with Barras and an evening at the theater to see Talma play Macbeth, they left Paris together at four on the morning of May 5, too early for English spies to observe their departure.

As their traveling carriage rolled into Toulon, the Bonapartes beheld a magnificent sight. The vast harbor was covered for miles with ships "whose masts resembled a huge forest"; the armada itself spread to almost three square miles on the open sea. On board were thirty-seven thousand land troops (many of them units that had served under the General in Italy), sailors and marines, one thousand civilians and seven hundred horses.

On that first morning, as he set foot on the admiral's barge taking him to review the fleet, as every gun on every vessel and in the port's fortresses fired a salute, and every ship broke out its flags, perhaps Napoleon remembered his arrival in Toulon five years earlier, in flight from Ajaccio with his destitute family.

During the six-day wait for the dispersal of the storm that had blown up, Josephine toured her husband's flagship, the *Orient,* formerly the *Sans Culotte,* 120 guns. Bonaparte's own quarters were "astonishingly luxurious." Arnault had been asked to assemble for him a superb library aboard: history principally, and philosophy and poetry. The legs of the General's bed were provided with casters in the hope of alleviating the seasickness that tormented him (as it did Nelson). Eight hundred bottles of the best burgundy and a city carriage for use in Egypt were also on board.

In spite of so many comforts, however, Napoleon decided it would be more prudent for Josephine to wait in France until she received word that the expedition had passed Sicily and successfully eluded the British fleet. But she continued to press him to take her with him. When General Alexandre Dumas, a black giant from Santo Domingo (and father of the author of *The Three Musketeers*), presented himself early one morning at the commanding general's quarters in the Marine Intendancy, he found the Bonapartes still in bed. Josephine, naked, Dumas noticed, under the bedclothes, was in tears because, so Napoleon told him, he could not decide whether to allow her to accompany him on the expedition.

Later, fully dressed and leaning affectionately on her husband's shoulder, Mme Bonaparte is described as welcoming some of the company about to sail. There were no fewer than thirty-two generals from the Italian campaign, including the faithful Chief of Staff Alexandre Berthier and Andoche Junot; Louis Bonaparte and Eugène de Beauharnais were accompanying the General too. Vivant Denon, the artist who would bring the glories of Egyptian art and architecture to the West, was to sail with the Commission of Arts and Sciences, and Gaspard Monge, too, who, as part of the Directory's commission had shipped at least eight hundred great paintings from Italy to Paris, including the *Mona Lisa.*

On May 18 some vessels believed at first to be English were sighted. It was a false alarm. The British Admiralty, fearing that the "English expedition" might be only a diversion, had at last dispatched Nelson and a squadron to the Mediterranean, but the same storm that held the French in Toulon nearly wrecked Nelson's ships and prevented them from reaching Toulon until a week after Bonaparte's departure.

On May 19, the General gave his final sailing orders. The Bonapartes' farewells to each other were said to be deeply affecting. From the highest balcony of the Marine Intendancy Josephine watched the fleet's departure.

It was a majestic and, at one moment, an alarming spectacle, as the overloaded vessels listed dangerously and the flagship itself was grounded temporarily. (After the fleet's destruction at the Battle of the Nile, the superstitious navy would not fail to say that this had been an omen.) Finally the *Orient* righted itself and the fleet proceeded out to sea to the thunder of cannon and the sound of the regimental bands aboard. Josephine remained standing until they were out of sight, her handkerchief fluttering a farewell in the strong wind.

⚜ 16 ⚜

There Is Nothing Left for Me

"I WROTE YOU THE DAY BEFORE YESTERDAY, MY DEAR BARRAS, BUT I AM afraid my letter may not have reached you as I did not understand how to stamp it. In it, I begged you to give me your news and to send me Bonaparte's as soon as you have any. I need it. I am so distressed at being separated from him that I cannot overcome my sadness. Besides, his brother, to whom he writes so often, has behaved so abominably to me that I am always uneasy when I am away from Bonaparte."[1]

Josephine's letter was written from the watering resort of Plombières in Lorraine. She had waited at Toulon for two weeks, as Napoleon had instructed her to do, for news to reach her that the *Orient* had safely passed the coast of Sicily. It had been decided that she would first take the waters at Plombières, famous since Roman times for their action against sterility, and there she was to wait for him to send for her when the Mediterranean was proved safe from Nelson's fleet.

The little resort was made up of two-storied houses, all appearing to be linked together by communicating balconies running the length of the second floors. Josephine's quiet life in a pension consisted only of daily visits to the steaming spring and of sending letter after letter by courier to Paris.

Writing to Bonaparte, once so tedious, was now a need, indeed a pleasure, and "I enclose a letter for Bonaparte," she wrote to Barras, "which I beg you to forward to him immediately. I shall send all my letters to him through you and I urge you to be sure to see that they are dispatched to Egypt as speedily as possible. You know him and you understand how much he would resent not getting news from me regu-

238

larly. The last letter I received from him is very tender. . . . He says that I am to rejoin him as soon as possible and so I am hurrying to finish the cure so as to rejoin Bonaparte very quickly. I am very fond of him in spite of his little faults."[2]

Josephine must have been the only human being to see his "little faults." To his adoring generals, to his idolizing public and to his bitter enemies, everything was on a giant scale.

Only four days out of Toulon, Bonaparte had indeed decided, in spite of the risks involved, to send the frigate *Pomone* to pick up his wife at Naples. She had had every intention of leaving for Egypt as soon as it could be arranged. But by the time the *Pomone* arrived in Naples (it was the same vessel that had escorted young Rose Tascher de La Pagerie's ship on her first voyage to France), Josephine was seriously ill at Plombières.

On the afternoon of June 20, as she sat with two visitors hemming a madras kerchief of the kind ladies tied over their heads to take the baths, one of them called her from the balcony to look at a little dog passing in the street below. Josephine and her companions ran to join her and the wooden balcony collapsed. All three were injured, but Josephine was the most seriously hurt, partly paralyzed and with suspected internal injuries.

The reports of the local physician, Dr. Martinet, on "our good and interesting patient" were sent daily by courier to Director Barras, to be forwarded to the headquarters of the Army of the Orient. Leeches were administered and compresses of camphor, brandy and boiled potatoes applied; hot baths were ordered, while "the stomach is kept open by frequent enemas." Doctors were called in from all over Lorraine. Hortense was sent for.

In agony for weeks, and depressed at not being able to set sail for Egypt, Josephine wrote Barras that she had had "a charming letter from Bonaparte. He says he cannot live without me and that I should embark at Naples. I very much wish that my health would allow me to leave immediately, but I cannot remain standing or sitting for ten minutes without terrible pains in my kidneys and lower back. All I do is cry. . . . My dear Barras, you have no idea how much I am suffering!"[3]

But even her sufferings could not stop Josephine from sending Barras the usual stream of letters of recommendation: for Dr. Martinet, of course, for his son, for his newborn daughter (she and Barras were to be godparents to the child), for the chief of police and for half a dozen others.

She had learned how to answer speeches and receive delegations with dignity and grace—as effectively, apparently, as she had mastered those other lessons of deportment received at Penthémont—and on her way back to Paris through Nancy, Josephine even managed a gentle rebuke when she was presented with a sword sent by the Directory and destined for General Bonaparte. "Perhaps," she said, "this tribute might have been given to him with more ceremony, but certainly not received with more pleasure than by one who is conscious of the duty of silencing her heart and of seeing only the glory and the well-being of *la Patrie.*" [4]

When Josephine reached Paris with Hortense on August 16, the city was starting to celebrate what had only been learned that very day, a great victory in Egypt, the Battle of the Pyramids. Paris went wild with enthusiasm at the news. Gigantic portraits of General Bonaparte against a background of palm trees and pyramids were hoisted onto buildings. But although Josephine returned to the rue de la Victoire on the tide of this euphoria, she had already heard the catastrophic news that followed it. "I arrived during the night, my dear Barras," she wrote off immediately, "and my first thought was to send a messenger to inquire after you. . . . I am so disturbed by the news which has just come in via Malta that I must ask to see you alone tonight at nine. Please give orders that no one else be admitted." [5]

The victory bulletins, Josephine learned, had been followed immediately by a brief message from General Bonaparte by courier to Malta. The entire French fleet, except for four ships, had been attacked and sunk by the British on August 1.

The General's message was cool and gave no hint of the disasters that would result from what the French called the Battle of Aboukir and the British the Battle of the Nile. Although Bonaparte's report of the destruction of the fleet conveyed the impression that Admiral Brueys's defeat was unimportant, and not to be compared with his own victory, the government was under no illusion. The Army of the Orient was now cut off from France. But though Nelson left a small cruising squadron off the Egyptian coast, the blockade was only partially effective. Bonaparte's transports remained untouched at Alexandria, and most of his optimistic reports would eventually reach Paris in the following year. One vessel, however, carrying letters from the troops to France, was captured by the English, and it was therefore some months before Josephine learned of the scene that would affect her life and her own immediate behavior.

. . .

Aboard the *Orient*, Bonaparte remained in his cabin during most of the six-week crossing, although less incommoded by the rough, choppy seas than he had feared. In his own quarters he had Bourrienne read to him for hours, largely on history, often on Islam. But "Josephine almost always formed the subject of our intimate conversations," remembered Bourrienne. "Passionately as he loved glory—both France's and his own—still Josephine engrossed much of the thought of a soul dedicated to vast designs. His attachment to her bordered on idolatry."[6]

By night, lamps could not be lit for fear of the pursuing British. By day, in the library next door to Napoleon's cabin, most of his general staff sprawled on the divan that lined it, talking, reading and playing cards. When Napoleon found Eugène and General Berthier reading novels— *Paul et Virginie* and Goethe's *Werther*, which had been such influences on his own romantic youth—he was disgusted. "Reading fit for chambermaids! Men should read only history!"[7] he scolded them.

Living conditions on the other ships were deplorable. Even before reaching and occupying Malta on June 18, the sailors and the seasick troops had been eating only wormy biscuits and drinking fetid water; at Malta they had been unable to take on much food and water, and beyond it conditions were a great deal worse.

Although Bonaparte remained supremely confident in his "star," his officers were far less sanguine, aware of how slender the French fleet's chances would be in a battle with decks encumbered by the stores and arms of almost forty thousand troops.

Both the French and British fleets were unaware that they had passed within miles of each other during the night of June 23. Nelson had arrived at Malta one day after Bonaparte's departure, continued on to Aboukir (the port of Alexandria), reaching it before the slow, unwieldy French fleet and, in this prolonged game of hide-and-seek, had left the port again only two days before Bonaparte's own landing there.

When the French fleet finally arrived at Aboukir Bay, and Bonaparte, fearing Nelson's return, insisted on disembarking his troops by night and in rough seas, his luck still held. Only a few men were lost, and the seasick, hungry and thirsty troops were ordered to march on to Alexandria within hours. It was only the prospect of finding drinking water, they would say, which drove them forward. Alexandria surrendered almost immediately, and on the following day the French troops started their march to Cairo.

In the blazing heat, the men carried the same heavy equipment as in the Italian campaign, but the need for water flasks had been forgotten. The commander of one advance division reported that when his troops at last halted in the desert beside two wells "more than thirty soldiers died, trampled to death in the rush for water; some of them, finding the water exhausted, committed suicide."[8]

The troops had not yet met the enemy; they found the Mamelukes awaiting them on a small eminence, ten miles outside Cairo. The French army knew little about this highly trained military caste that, with the beys, ruled the Turkish provinces of Egypt as local lords. What they saw, drawn up before them, was a medieval array of turbaned horsemen bristling with javelins, swords and pistols and accompanied by a large body of untrained Egyptian infantry.

At sunrise, Bonaparte ordered the playing of the "Marseillaise." Brandishing swords, the screaming Mamelukes swept down on the French divisions formed into squares six ranks deep; their first wild charge was broken by a hail of bullets. For two more hours their cavalry continued to be smashed against the guns and solid squares of the French. When they broke and fled they left behind, beside their dead, the kind of booty the troops had dreamed of: pearl-encrusted saddles, gilded helmets and jeweled harnesses. The Mamelukes' water flasks could be dispensed with since the French forces entered Cairo the following day.

Because the pyramids could be faintly discerned in the distance, Bonaparte named the victory the Battle of the Pyramids, a name of oriental resonance forever associated in French imagination with Bonaparte and the Egyptian campaign. All Europe would be electrified by the legendary romance of the scene and by the General's own report of his celebrated proclamation to his troops that day. "Soldiers!" it began. "From these Pyramids forty centuries of history look down upon you!"

Napoleon's victory bulletin reached Paris on the same day as his terse message that followed it. On August 1, Nelson had returned once more to Aboukir Bay, found the French fleet at anchor there, and after an all-night battle sank or set on fire all but four ships of the line, killed or wounded over three thousand sailors and lost not a single British vessel.

The carnage was the most fearful ever seen in a naval battle. Flames lit the sky for miles, and when the flagship *Orient* was hit and went down with Captain Casabianca and his son—the "Boy on the Burning Deck" of Felician Hemans's poem—the explosion rocked Alexandria twenty-five miles away.

In his report to the Directory, General Bonaparte blamed the catastrophe on Admiral Brueys—unfairly, as can best be judged (as Emperor, Napoleon would have all the dossiers on the Egyptian campaign destroyed), since the admiral appears to have remained at anchor on Bonaparte's orders, rather than followed those of the Directory to wait in safer waters. Badly wounded, Brueys had continued to command from the bridge until he was almost cut in half by an English cannonball.

Two days before the Battle of the Pyramids, General Junot, walking at a desert oasis with his commander in chief, had revealed to him Josephine's affair with Hippolyte Charles. His reasons for doing this are unknown, although his own close ties with all the Bonaparte family were thought to have been a possible motive.

Bourrienne, standing nearby, had observed the scene and General Bonaparte's increasing agitation, his "pale face becoming even paler." He saw him call on General Berthier to join them, as though appealing for confirmation, then, striking his forehead with his fist, he came toward Bourrienne. "If you had cared for me you would have told me all that I have just heard from Junot," he cried. "*He* is a true friend . . . Josephine! And I am six hundred leagues from her. Divorce—yes, divorce—I want a public and sensational divorce! I don't want to be the laughing stock of Paris. I shall write Joseph and have the divorce pronounced."

When Bourrienne tried to calm him and suggested that he should think of his future and his glory, "My glory!" Bonaparte exclaimed: "I love that woman so much I would give anything if only what Junot had told me were not true."[9]

Two days later from Cairo, Napoleon wrote his brother Joseph that he hoped to be back in France in two months, and then: "The veil is torn. . . . It is sad when one and the same heart is torn by such conflicting feelings for one person. . . . Make arrangements for a country place to be ready for my return, either near Paris or in Burgundy. I expect to shut myself away there for the winter. I need to be alone. I am tired of grandeur; all my feelings have dried up. I no longer care about my glory. At twenty-nine I have exhausted everything. There is nothing now left for me but to become completely selfish. . . . I intend to keep my house in Paris, I will never let anyone else have it."[10]

Five days later Bonaparte's letter was intercepted in the Mediterranean by British cruisers, which also captured Eugène's letter to his mother, a tactful warning written two days later. "Bonaparte has been very melancholy as the result of a talk with Junot and Berthier," he wrote. "All I have heard amounts to this, that Captain Charles traveled in your carriage until you were within three posting stages of Paris, that you have seen him in Paris, that you have been to the theater with him, that he gave you your little dog, and that he is with you now. . . . I am sure that all this gossip has been invented by your enemies. Bonaparte loves you as much as ever and is just as anxious to embrace you. I hope that when you come here all this will be forgotten."[11] In his *Mémoires*, Eugène remembered that every night in his tent after the fatal interview, General Bonaparte would talk to him of his mother's betrayal.

In Cairo, even after the news of the loss of the fleet became known there, General Bonaparte appeared as calm and confident as his reports to the Directory indicated. He admitted later that he was relieved at being even freer of constraint than he had been in Italy, where he had still been forced to maintain some connection with the directors and with Carnot, the minister of war,[12] and he was buoyed up by his confidence that he could return to France as soon as the bad news he anticipated would strike there.

Meanwhile, installed in a magnificent palace in Cairo, a Thousand-and-One-Nights dream of marble and of alabaster fountains, he applied himself to the administrative and religious problems of Egypt. Civilians in the expedition were put to work setting up hospitals and irrigation projects and starting newspapers. (Jean-Lambert Tallien, a member of the expedition, was directed to edit the weekly *Décade Egyptienne*.) On the General's order, the piercing of the Isthmus of Suez was considered, although this vision would take until the middle of the next century to achieve.

In his first proclamation in Egypt, Bonaparte had maintained that the French were there only as liberators and, in a bid for the loyalty of the fellahin—the Egyptian peasants—"as allies of his Majesty the Sultan, and to punish the Mameluke tyrants." Above all, he declared that their religion was to be protected: "God is Prophet and the Koran will be respected."[13] Napoleon would admit to what he himself called the charlatanism of these appeals. "The only way to succeed is by charlatanism," he maintained at St. Helena, "but it was charlatanism of the highest kind."[14]

In Cairo, Bonaparte announced that he and his army were about to embrace Islam. To celebrate the feast of Mohammed's birthday, he put on a turban and caftan, but removed them after one day when his general staff burst out laughing, and even Tallien told him that he looked ridiculous.

No one was taken in by this charade, neither the ruling beys, to whom Bonaparte continued to pretend that he was in Egypt with the Sultan's approval, nor the fellahin, who saw only that the infidel was living off the land and still further reducing their livelihood. There were street revolts when some of the Cairo mosques were made into cafés for the French troops, and Bonaparte ordered reprisals. Every night at least thirty heads were cut off as examples. A deliberate policy of desecration of the mosques followed, and his troops profaned the Great Mosque, urinating, looting, and destroying the sacred books.

Bonaparte ruled only a small area around Cairo, but his proclamations to the army and his heroic bulletins made it appear otherwise. Although most of his own messages eventually reached France, he knew that letters from his demoralized officers and men did not. "All goes well here. . . ," he reported to the Directory. "France will, in the long run, be mistress of India; the Cabinet in London is perfectly aware of it."[15] "Imagination governs the world" was another of his maxims, and he never, in his calculated effects, forgot the image he wished to present to France, an awareness that underlay many of his actions in Egypt.

He knew that, thanks to his foresight in planning the civilian side of the French expedition, the glories of ancient Egypt would eventually be revealed to Europeans. The only artefacts of that ancient civilization known to Europe were objects such as the obelisks and statues brought home by the Romans. The science of Egyptology itself was invented when Vivant Denon accompanied a French army corps into Upper Egypt as far south as Aswan, sketching every monument, often from the saddle. When he returned to France he would describe the scene of awe and enthusiasm of the French troops at the site of the Temple of Karnak at Thebes where, without any orders being given, "the Division of four thousand men formed ranks, struck up the band and presented arms."

Although the Rosetta stone was discovered that year, the unlocking of the secrets of the Egyptian hieroglyphics would take another thirty years. Using two of the three different scripts, the Greek and the Demotic, on that black basalt slab, Jean-François Champollion was then finally able to translate their meaning.

By November Bonaparte had heard of the publication in the British newspapers of his letter to Joseph about his domestic drama. On his orders, his general staff organized an evening of Egyptian dancers for the commander in chief; none of the women appealed to him. His ideal remained Josephine's slender form, and he complained that they were all too fat and that he did not care for their perfume. But as soon as he saw pretty twenty-year-old Pauline Fourès he knew how to take a very public revenge on Josephine. Pauline, a blond and rosy milliner's apprentice, was still dressed in the uniform—blue coat and tight white breeches—of her husband's regiment, which she had worn in order to embark for Egypt with him. Bonaparte issued orders for Lieutenant Fourès to take urgent dispatches to Paris. Only a day out from Alexandria, Fourès's ship was captured. The English captain, familiar with Cairo gossip, made a point of returning the French lieutenant to Alexandria on parole and as rapidly as possible; there Fourès was enraged to find his Pauline installed in the commander in chief's palace and presiding over his dinner parties. He protested, but the General had a rapid divorce pronounced and was said to have promised Pauline to marry her if she could produce a child. Until he formally requested to be spared this humiliation, Eugène de Beauharnais, as his stepfather's aide, was forced to escort him and Pauline as they drove around Cairo in the General's carriage. Bonaparte left her in Cairo, however, with the injunction to "make a son," when he set off for Syria in January 1799.

Although Bonaparte had feigned to ignore it, the news of Turkey's declaration of war on France had been known in Cairo since October. His insistence on the Egyptian expedition had led to precisely the results foreseen by the Directory; when Sultan Selim III* of Turkey declared war on France, he was immediately joined by his ally the Tsar of Russia.

As a consequence of Napoleon's insubordination in the matter of Rastadt, Austria had remained in a state of war with France, and it now joined the British and Russians to form the Second Coalition against the Republic. The coalition's first aim was to drive the French, deprived of their ranking armies, out of Italy and Germany. To add to the French government's problems, news of the loss of the French fleet led to a flare-up of hostilities in Vendée and to the diversion of the still-standing Army of England to put down the rebellion.

This setting in motion of a European war may have been temporarily fatal to France's military posture, but hardly to the General's ambitions, as he had already foreseen. In January, Bonaparte decided on a bold counteroffensive against the Turks and their British allies: to strike the Ottoman forces assembling in the north he would march across the Sinai Desert to Syria through Palestine—modern Israel—Syria, Lebanon and Jordan.

As the force of thirteen thousand men started out the troops noted how happy the commander in chief always appeared in the desert. He was known to set store on the legend that the name Napoleone signified "desert lion," and the desert always had a powerful hold over his imagination.[16] As he rode, his head full of oriental fantasies, his imagination was afire with the names of the Holy Land, the Crusaders and Alexander. "I saw myself," he would say later, "on the way to Asia, riding an elephant, wearing a turban, attacking the English in India. . . ."[17]

For his troops, for those who were able to return to France, the memories would be different. In the pitiless desert they were already overcome by heat, flies, dysentery and endemic thirst. The commander in chief's savagery, first against the enemy and then against their own comrades, had not yet started. Although his cruelty, first revealed during this march, has often been attributed to his anguish over Josephine, it seems more than likely that the ruthless cynic, the man whom General Jean-Baptiste Kléber accused of "needing an income of ten thousand men a

---

* The Sultan's favorite concubine was the Sultana Valideh, born Aimée du Buc de Rivery, that distant cousin of Josephine's captured on the treacherous Atlantic crossing and sold by Algerian pirates to the Sultan.

day,"[23] who was to sacrifice millions of lives without compunction, had always existed; the ferocity, however, was usually due to pragmatic reasons. Whether or not the transformation in him was hastened by Junot's revelations, Bonaparte undoubtedly returned from Egypt a changed man. His literary views were affected too by his Egyptian experiences. "I am disgusted with Rousseau since I have seen the East. Primitive man is a dog," he declared.[18]

When the fortress of Jaffa in Palestine (now a suburb of Tel Aviv) surrendered after a short siege, it was sacked and looted and its garrison, including women and children, massacred. The army would never forget the shame of what came afterwards—the murder of three thousand Turks who had capitulated after a promise that their lives would be spared—nor the full horror of the circumstances. Three days after they had surrendered, General Bonaparte ordered them to be drowned or bayoneted in order to save gunpowder. He could not, he said, feed both them and his army. French troops were forced to wade in after those who attempted to swim out to sea, sometimes with their children still clinging to them. One officer wrote to his wife on March 11: "Sooner or later the blood of those three thousand victims will destroy us."[19] And, on the following day, bubonic plague struck the Army of the Orient, but only, General Bonaparte maintained, those who were afraid of it. To prove his point, to raise morale—and incidentally to provide subject matter for one of the most powerful scenes of the expeditionary campaign—at the military hospital at Jaffa he helped carry out the corpse of one of the victims of the plague.

In April the French forces had reached Acre on the Syrian coast. There they were unable to breach the walls of the castle built by the Crusaders, once besieged by Saint Louis and by Richard the Lionheart, and now defended by a Turkish garrison, and a base, too, for the English fleet. Just as at the siege of Mantua, Napoleon was half-demented with impatience. To add to his fury the fortress was commanded by Sir Sidney Smith, one of his opponents at Toulon, and by Edmond de Phélippeaux, a classmate he had particularly resented at the military school in Paris.* To

---

* Phélippeaux was destined to be a scourge to Napoleon. At the military school, where they shared a desk, he invariably won higher marks. After emigrating at the beginning of the Revolution he returned to Paris during the Terror in order, by a Scarlet Pimpernel-like ruse, to free this same Sir Sidney Smith from prison.

Napoleon's relief there was soon a call to action elsewhere. General Klé-ber, who was guarding the French right flank, had been attacked by the Pasha of Damascus on the plain beneath Mount Tabor, and had sent an urgent message. On April 15, Bonaparte dashed to the rescue; upon seeing the French reinforcements arrive, the enemy fled. A bulletin to the Directory which did not arrive in Paris until seven months later, but in time for his own return, announced a great victory and "the total destruction of the Turkish army."

Bonaparte was back at Acre within the week. "I've not been lucky at Acre; Cairo calls me," he told his officers soon after his return. The standoff at Acre was to be presented to the Directory as another decisive victory. The fortress, he reported, had been successfully razed and was no longer worth actually taking. Two thousand wounded and plague victims lay in tents outside Acre, but the General refused the offer of the commander of the British squadron offshore to take the French wounded aboard, since he did not wish to be beholden to the English. "The heart of the army was pierced by our leaving our plague-stricken men behind. They pleaded with us not to abandon them. . . . Their heads were cut off by the enemy as soon as we left," wrote an officer in a letter intercepted by the British.[20]

The decimated and thirsty columns struggling to return to Cairo endured marvels of fortitude. For the troops, the most harrowing part of the long march from Jaffa to Cairo was the spectacle of their badly wounded comrades and suspected plague carriers left by the side of the road. They would never forget the men they had left behind tearing off their bandages to prove that they were only wounded and not carriers of the plague.[21]

Throughout the nightmare retreat, the commander in chief's attention was concentrated on what resembled a modern publicity campaign. In his dispatches to the Directory, military disasters, retreats and massacres continued to be transformed into triumphs over superior forces for the French army and its commander. Neither the lack of food and water nor even the plague was mentioned. "We want for nothing here," he wrote, "we are bursting with strength, good health and high spirits." A civilian's bitter letter to his family which was captured by the British read: "The report of the commander in chief which I enclose will prove to you how much a man must lie to be in politics,"[22] and he provided his own description of the retreat from Syria to Cairo.

Victory bulletins preceded the remnants of the Army of the Orient as it reentered Egypt. Bonaparte said that he wished his return to Cairo "to resemble that of a victor of antiquity." He was obeyed. Turkish prisoners of war and captured Turkish flags were sent on ahead to Cairo, and the army entered the city with bands playing, palm fronds woven into their caps and helmets. The commander in chief was met at the gates by the French garrison of Cairo, by the muftis of the Mosque, and by gifts of black and white slaves, arms, rugs and incense. Sheik El Bekir, descendant of the Prophet, presented General Bonaparte with an Arab horse saddled with cloth of gold and pearls; a young slave, Roustam, held its bridle.

It was no good. Cairo knew the truth. The army knew, too, but it would be twenty-four more months before the men reached France, by that time living the glorious days of the Consulate.

One week after his return to Cairo, General Bonaparte had a genuine victory to report. A large force of the Turkish army that he had informed the Directory had been destroyed at Acre disembarked at Aboukir from English and Turkish vessels. Bonaparte and a force of ten thousand men met them at the port. The Turks were defeated easily; many of them were drowned swimming out toward their ships, and Bonaparte would remember "thousands of turbans floating on the water." Doubling the enemy's number in his report to the directors, he was able to announce an important victory, another report that would arrive in France in time to herald his own return.

Bonaparte instantly noted that his luck had been restored. Not, however, in one quarter. He had gone immediately to see Pauline Fourès, "but the silly woman has not been able to give me a son," he told General Berthier. Pauline only laughed and answered, "But it is not *my* fault." He had no reason to doubt her.

Further "good news" followed immediately after the victory. The English officers aboard the transports were only too happy to send General Bonaparte the British newspapers, certain that he would be demoralized to read of a succession of French military disasters. Although the information was several months old, he learned that the French had been driven out of Germany by the Austrians, while in Italy they were being defeated by a combined force of Russians and Austrians. And a political crisis appeared to be brewing in France.

Although he already knew much of this news, the officers who brought him the journals reported that Bonaparte "affected great surprise and indignation."

The fruit was now undeniably ripe and the General's only fear was that he might not get back in time to take advantage of it.

❧ 17 ❧

THERE'S YOUR MAN

WITH HER HUSBAND NOW A NEGLIGIBLE FACTOR IN POWER POLITICS, Josephine found herself no longer the focus of attention in the capital. The Luxembourg, Barras's own domain, was the only place in which she did not feel relegated to the periphery of Paris life and where, although she did not yet know of Junot's revelations to Bonaparte, the Director's protection seemed the best insurance against the uncertain future.

The somber palace had been restored to some of its former pomp; very few recollections of the revolutionary prison remained. The five red velvet thronelike armchairs in the great public salons downstairs stood against regilded paneling and a blaze of tricolor flags. Barras's visitors advanced up a monumental staircase and through the Rubens gallery before reaching his apartments. There the host, towering over most of the men present, could be found greeting with equal courtesy the usual crowd of bankers, artists, generals of the republican army, remnants of the aristocracy and the civilian contractors supplying the armies.

Since the beginning of the Second Directory, as the period after Fructidor was known, the government had become increasingly the prisoner of these contractors who kept the Directory afloat. Although France was economically and financially in better order than at any time since 1789, with a metallic currency at last beginning to replace the eternally depreciated paper money, the country had still not recovered from the inflation of 1793–96. All the Directory's attempts to better the economy finally foundered on its dependence on feeding the war machine.

The government, therefore, remained more than ever perpetually in debt to corrupt men like the Belgian Michel Simon, supplier to the French navy; Pierre Collot, bound up with Napoleon and the Army of

Italy; Hainguerlot—Talleyrand and Fouché were both said to be in his pay—and Hamelin, who had traveled to Italy in Josephine's train and was presumably still involved in her traffic with the Bodin Company and in her connection with several other army contractors.

The Directory was a prisoner of the army, too. Just as the army officers and the war commissioners needed the looting and requisitioning to line their own pockets, the government itself needed the "generals' war" to fill the state coffers and to pay off its creditors, the bankers and the army contractors. Even in foreign policy the Directory remained hostage to the generals.

The newspapers had resumed their ferocious invective against all the directors. Their pages were filled with accusations of corruption and venality in the government departments and in the financial world, of crime in the streets and of the terrible state of France's roads, gone to ruin in the ten years since the beginning of the Revolution.

While his fellow directors were eternally preoccupied with the attacks made on them by the press, Barras continued apparently unruffled. He was under no illusion as to his personal unpopularity, aware that the general public simply enveloped the entire Directorial team in contempt, but that it was he himself, as the most visible and long-lasting of the Directors, who was seen as the personification of the government, responsible both for the country's financial recovery and for all that was wrong with the post-Fructidorian Directory. His hunting parties at Grosbois, his staghounds, his instantly recognizable carriage and silver-harnessed bays, his Luxembourg receptions and his mistresses were the subject of general gossip. His extravagance was held to be monumental. Undoubtedly, like many of the men in public life of the period—and with as few financial scruples—he benefited from tips on the stock market and from his friendship with the army contractors.

Outwardly imperturbable, Barras took his turn with the other directors, continuing to give morning audiences. But it was noted that his working habits had changed. Accustomed to putting in the longest day's work of any of the five, he now appeared distracted at sessions of the councils and started to spend more time at Grosbois and less in Paris, seeming to observe with detached fatalism both the downward spiral of the "Second Directory" and the military reverses of the French armies in the spring of 1799.

Paul Barras's private life remained unchanged. At its core was his warm friendship and protectiveness toward Thérésia and Josephine. His liaisons with other women continued and none held him for long; when their possessiveness went too far, they were politely dropped. Witty, pretty Clothilde de Forbin and the Duchesse de Montmorency, later a lady-of-honor at Napoleon's court, were both thought to have hoped for permanent ties. Clothilde's love letters to Paul Barras started with *"J'ai faim de vous voir . . ."* ("I am hungry for the sight of you"), and she left Paris in despair when he ordered his door closed to her.

As for Barras's rumored homosexual tastes, it is worth recalling that Talleyrand, the author of many of these stories, believed that Bonaparte and Bourrienne were lovers; and that Napoleon himself—so obsessed with the subject that in his St. Helena diary he accused General Gourgaud of attempted attacks upon his own person—went only so far as to say that he "would not be surprised" if Barras were homosexual.

One argument, however, to support the likelihood of this disposition is that Paul Barras seldom carried on a liaison in which jealousy or recriminations formed a part. Hoche, though jealous of Bonaparte, seems not to have objected to Josephine's notorious relationship with Barras; both Bonaparte and Tallien constantly commended their wives to Barras's care. Either for that reason or, it has been suggested, because of the very number of his feminine partners, other men seemed to be immune from normal jealousy in his case.

Thérésia's and Barras's own relationship continued to be full of affectionate understanding; her notes to him usually ended with "I love you and will love you all my life, with a devotion nothing can touch."[1] She meant it, and would prove it.

The Talliens were now officially separated, yet Jean-Lambert could write from Egypt that it was only the hope of returning to the Chaumière which gave him comfort. In a letter intercepted by the British fleet he wrote that "we lack everything here. . . . I have not slept for five nights, devoured by fleas, flies and ants . . . but I am sustained by memories of your goodness, of our love, and by the hope of finding you as amiable and as faithful as ever."[2]

But "faithful" Thérésia had left the Chaumière even before Tallien's departure to live in the house given her by her lover Gabriel Ouvrard, and was within months of presenting him with the first of the four children she would produce at yearly intervals.

• • •

The government, and Napoleon's own family, took a realistic view of his chances of returning to France, and Josephine's anxiety turned to panic when she realized to what an extent she had to reckon with the malignant hostility of the Bonapartes.

The brothers were now powerful enough to be serious enemies. Both Joseph and Lucien had political ambitions, possessed vast fortunes and were using their brother's name to advance their own political futures. Joseph, who had converted the millions his brother had brought back from Italy into a common family fund, would only grudgingly pay Josephine part of her monthly allowance; soon he stopped altogether. Lazier, more easygoing than Lucien, had resigned his seat in the Five Hundred, preferring to work on his investments and to add ornamental lakes, a theater, an orangery and a grotto to his country property. The Château de Mortefontaine had become a center for political and social entertaining; its courtyard was always full of carriages, and Joseph's great receptions there and in Paris were already a feature of Parisian life.

Self-satisfied, tall and gangling, eyeglasses on the tip of his nose, Lucien, too, was Josephine's declared enemy. He held court in an immense country domain near Joseph's, and like him, frequented every important political salon in Paris. The brothers could always be seen at Barras's receptions, at Germaine de Staël's and at Talleyrand's.

By a fraudulent election (he was twenty-six years old instead of the required thirty), Lucien had become a member of the Five Hundred and, believing that power lay in the center, was moving from an extreme Jacobin position toward the anti-Jacobin right. Even more relentlessly than Joseph, he kept a careful account of his sister-in-law's blunders and extravagances and dispatched the lists to Egypt. These reports did not reach their destination, but the intercepted letters were read with some enjoyment in England.

Mme Letizia, Napoleon's mother, though she might call Josephine *"la putana"*—the whore—in private, was the only member of the family to maintain decent, if hardly cordial relations with her daughter-in-law. Forced by ill health to abandon Corsica, she had now moved in with Joseph and Julie in Paris, although she loudly regretted having to leave the rebuilt and redecorated family home in Ajaccio. Thanks to fruitful investments made through the Army of Italy, she had been able to afford elaborate furnishings for it; most of them, notably some daffodil-colored damask, were dispatched to Corsica from Marseilles by Mme Clary.

Mme Letizia's daughters, however, felt no need to display unnecessary courtesy to Josephine. Elisa loudly proclaimed her contempt for her sister-in-law. Caroline was happy to join in the fray; she hoped to no longer be forced to stay at Mme Campan's school, nor to have Hortense forever held up to her as a model.

But Josephine had no more tenacious enemy than Napoleon's sister Pauline Leclerc, reported her friend Laure d'Abrantès. Pauline could not forget the traumatic weeks at Mombello, nor the shock of being made to feel provincial, outclassed by this "old woman" who had captivated both her brother and Hippolyte Charles. She badgered Victor Leclerc, attached to the Army of Italy, with demands for more money, more plunder; he owed it, she said, to General Bonaparte's sister. Leclerc concurred so enthusiastically and was so greedy in the accumulation of spoils that the army's commander in chief was obliged to request him to change commands. Leclerc did not return to Paris empty-handed, however. Even before being sent on to the still-standing Army of England, he and Pauline were able to move into a palatial house in Paris and acquire a country château not far from Joseph's and Lucien's.

Once Leclerc had left for the Channel coast, and little Dermide put out to nurse (Napoleon, before his departure for Egypt, had decreed that the Leclerc baby should be named for one of Ossian's melancholy heroes), Pauline was free to concentrate on the serious business of rivalry with her sister-in-law, spending many hours with Josephine's dressmakers and jewelers and, so she alleged, with Josephine's lovers, "seeking the secret of her success in that field." "I am as good as she is," Pauline told Laure d'Abrantès, "she is only more experienced than I am."

The Bonaparte family's definitive triumph would come at the end of the year. By November 1798, Josephine and most of France knew that Napoleon had learned of her liaison with Captain Charles. The contents of the mailbag of the Army of the Orient, intercepted by the British fleet, were published in full in the London newspapers both in English and in French. Although Barras persuaded the Paris journals that reproduced them to eliminate Bonaparte's letter to Joseph and Eugène's to his mother, their contents were soon known in government circles, and a reprinted comment from a London paper made it easy for the general public in France to guess the contents of both communications.

The bad news seemed to be confirmed for Josephine when Louis Bonaparte returned from Egypt. Napoleon, worried by Louis's ill health, had arranged his brother's risky journey back to France. Though his ship had been chased by British frigates, he had landed safely and delivered a letter to Joseph only, which ended: "Show some courtesy to my wife, go and see her sometimes. I am asking Louis to give her some good advice."[3] This hint of forgiveness was never communicated to Josephine, and when Louis, who had hitherto been her only friend in the clan besides Jérôme, refused to visit her, she seems to have reached a new desperation.

Paul Barras was also Josephine's chief bastion against the Bonaparte brothers, on the best of terms with the all-important Director. But whether wearied by her constant letters of intercession, or because he did not wish to have his name connected with a new Bodin scandal, Barras was evidently responding with less alacrity than usual. One of her letters asking for help in keeping Louis Bodin out of prison begins: "I hate to distract you for a minute from your important occupations, but I count on your friendship to such an extent, my dear Barras, that I know I often impose on you"[4]; this was followed by another apologetic note protesting that she would "die of grief if I had compromised you even for one minute."[5] But compromise him she did, and as the Bodin scandal grew— the already venal company was said to have requisitioned horses for the Army of Italy without paying for them—Josephine wrote letter after letter to everyone in the government. On the day that Louis Bodin himself was to be arrested, a revealing letter of hers to the minister of the navy shows that she was aware, at last, of the dangers of her recommendations. "The more you oblige me, Citizen Minister, the more I fear to compromise you," she warns him, and adds that if he goes further in the matter of that obligation, "it might look as though it were I who had made the request."[6]

After the autumn's revelations Josephine found Paris ever more intolerable. She felt increasingly unprotected there, hunted and almost hysterical, and she could not forget a scene at a dinner at the Luxembourg. When Talleyrand, seated between her and Mme Tallien, made a point of turning his back on her and of talking exclusively to Thérésia, Josephine felt sure that he knew of some new drama—Napoleon's death perhaps, or her own disgrace. Obviously a man like the Bishop would never have ignored Bonaparte's wife were there any chance that the General could still protect her. Shaken and in tears, she left the table before the end of the meal.

She was lonely, frightened "and so deeply in debt," remembered Claire de Rémusat, "that she could not pay the smallest bills. Despairing of her husband's return, she used her influence with the powerful of the day . . . on worse terms than ever with her brothers-in-law, and furnishing them steadily with all too much concrete evidence to support their accusations against her."*[7]

She knew now that even her house might be taken from her. Napoleon, in his letter published in the London papers, had underlined his intention of keeping it for himself. Her longing for a garden and a house of her own, for birds and flowers and animals, was finally fulfilled in April when she acquired the Château de Malmaison, which Napoleon had found too expensive when they visited the house before he left for Egypt. All winter she had been bargaining with its owner, the banker Lecoulteux du Moley.

Part of the group of *philosophes*, the Moleys had "prided themselves before the Revolution on running Malmaison like an English country house."[8] Their house parties, sometimes lasting as long as ten days, had been made up of the liberal elite, whose conversation was mainly about the overthrow of the government. Elisabeth Vigée-Lebrun, the portrait painter—a fervent monarchist—remembered a pre-Revolution dinner there in June 1789 when M. du Moley "was vociferating against the nobility," leading one of the guests, the Abbé Sieyès, to murmur: "I sometimes wonder whether we will not go too far." In spite of his advanced views, M. du Moley was imprisoned under the Terror and saved by Thermidor, but was so much in debt that he was forced to sell the property.

Malmaison was a working farm, only six miles from Paris and not in any way to be compared to the princely establishments of the Bonaparte brothers. The house itself, more of a countrified manor house than a

---

* Claire de Vergennes, Hortense's friend at Croissy during the Terror, recently married to Charles de Rémusat. In her comments on Josephine, there would always be an element of condescension in Mme de Rémusat's *Mémoires*, written for a royal Restoration public.

château, was directly attached to the farm buildings. The du Moleys pointed out that the wheat fields and stables, the twelve cows, the pigs, the 150 wool-bearing sheep, the poultry, turkeys and pigeons meant that the farm tenants had no need to buy any outside produce, and that the property's principal glory, and its most productive, was the light, slightly acid white wine that sold at a very respectable price.

Mme Bonaparte, of course, had nothing with which to pay the sum of 325,000 francs finally agreed upon. She may have sold some jewelry to make a down payment on the house, and it is thought that Ouvrard and perhaps Barras came to her aid, but more probably she simply took on one further debt. Since the sum included all the house's furniture—old-fashioned and unpretentious—she was able to move in immediately.

Malmaison's three hundred acres of woodland, fields and vineyards ran down to the poplar-fringed Seine on the east, and on the west were separated from the St. Germain road only by a deep ditch. From there the house and some of the grounds could be clearly seen by passersby. Malicious Paris tongues were soon repeating an innocent neighbor's comment that "poor Mme Bonaparte can be seen at dusk walking in her garden, leaning on the arm of a young man, probably her son. Poor woman! Perhaps she is thinking of her first husband, killed in the Revolution, or of her present husband, lost in the Egyptian desert!"[9]

Josephine now proceeded to lose her head entirely. In her hopelessness she appeared incapable of putting an end to the downward slide to disaster. Although aware that the Bonapartes were keeping careful notes of her every move, every extravagance and error, she started to see Hippolyte Charles again, at first secretly and finally almost openly.

He had returned in the spring from Italy, where he had been working for the Bodin Company, and when Josephine moved into Malmaison he was at first invited for the day, then to spend entire weeks there, always vanishing when visitors appeared. They had rows—one of Josephine's cold, hurt letters survives—and then made it up.

"Because of the closeness of the Seine," wrote Mme de Rémusat, who visited the house that summer, "nothing could be fresher or greener than the fields and park of Malmaison."[10] In this green paradise Josephine spent the last summer of the century in a state of desperation.

Her letters during this sinister period of her life are almost unbalanced in their self-pity. To an offer about some business affair from Rousselin de St. Albin, that emissary who had helped her retrieve her love letters to Hoche, her answer ends: "Your letter, kind Citizen, touched me because of the interest you take in my miserable situation . . . and the idea of your being my guardian angel has given me hope of being less unhappy."[11]

But the main role of guardian angel was, of course, reserved for Barras. Her notes to him contain an increasing element of panic, and for the first time she starts to appeal to him in Bonaparte's name: "I need to talk to you, my dear Barras, I must see you alone. For friendship's sake please sacrifice a quarter of an hour's time and either come to me or tell me when I can find you absolutely alone. I hope, my dear Barras, that you will not refuse this kindness to the wife of your friend. . . ."[12]

For Josephine there had been few summers in the last fourteen years when protection of one kind or another—sometimes for life itself—had not depended on charming the influential. She had written elegant notes, flirted—and perhaps more—first with the older men close to the court at Fontainebleau, counting on them to obtain privileges that mattered to her; during the Revolution and up to the threshold of the guillotine, she had been a "patriotic *Amériquaine*" in resolute and desperate letters. In the hopeless summer of her imprisonment she had continued writing to her friends, the bloodiest of the terrorists. The next summer she had seen the success of her appealing letter to Barras, and, that year, she had not discouraged little General Vendémiaire.

Josephine was, of course, unaware of the power play in the summer of 1799, of the revival of the Jacobin movement and of the shift of power in the government. The Second Directory no longer existed; the yearly election of members of the Assembly in the spring had resulted in what amounted to a parliamentary revolution and virtually a new Directory.

The war that Napoleon had heard of with so much satisfaction in Egypt had broken out at the end of 1798, when England, Austria and the newly alarmed Ottoman Empire and Russia attacked the French armies in the annexed territories of Italy, Switzerland, the Rhineland and Holland. That summer was a time of military reverses for France, and the neo-Jacobins thundered against the "traitors in government responsible for our defeats."

A new Jacobin Club demanded a return of the guillotine and pitchforks for the defense of citizens, and urged the Five Hundred to proclaim "the Fatherland in danger." Moderate French men and women were convinced that the worst days of the Terror would soon be back. There were even rumors of the return of the Great Committees.

But ten years after the start of the Revolution, France had had enough turmoil. An end to the Revolution and the certainty of holding on to property were the wishes of the increasingly conservative country. Only the truly poor—pensioners and members of the liberal professions—had not been able to afford to buy up nationalized property, but peasants, merchants and the profiteers would have everything to lose in the event of a Bourbon restoration.

Disgust with the present regime and with the eight-year-old war was such that, according to Benjamin Constant, "nine-tenths of the French people are now counter-revolutionaries."[13] Indeed, France, in the opinion of many, was ripe for a dictatorship. Foreigners who expected to see a ruined and ravaged country found that although social polarities were profound, inflation barely curbed and highway men operating only a few miles outside Paris, dominating all was the traditional legacy of revolutions: a universal desire to live for the present.

New restaurants and gaming houses opened almost daily; once again, as in prerevolutionary days, a parade of carriages drove up the Champs-Elysées every afternoon. Spectators sat on crowded rows of chairs, four deep, the entire length of the avenue, watching the actresses, the kept women and the new rich drive by.

More avidly viewed that summer even than Mme Tallien's was the carriage of Mlle Lange of the "brown velvet eyes." The actress's succession of lovers, said to include both Barras and Talleyrand, was notorious, but it was her portrait by Louis Girodet that was the year's scandalous success at the Louvre exhibition. Lange's new husband, the millionaire Michel Simon, contractor to the French navy, had neglected to pay for her portrait, and the artist's revenge was to paint an easily recognizable naked Lange portrayed as Danaë receiving the shower of gold.

Although exhibitions, theaters and the circus had never been more popular, one foreigner returning to Paris after a year's absence noted that though crowds were as great as they had ever been since Thermidor, "gaiety and insouciance" were now notably absent.

Political apathy was so complete that Parisians admitted that they barely noticed the recent Jacobin violence, were interested only in food, gossip and moneymaking, and that "France would belong to the man who would provide order, victory and peace."[14] The country was awaiting anyone to "finish the Revolution"; patriotic pride was stirred only by anything related to General Bonaparte, whose hold on popular imagination far exceeded that of any other general.

Although the Jacobins, Barras's own constituency, were now a powerful minority in the Five Hundred, it was the unfrocked ex–Abbé Sieyès, one of the four new directors (the other three were Jérôme Gohier, Roger Ducos and an obscure General Moulin), who was starting to assume a larger part of Barras's power.

Elegantly phrased invitations to lunch with Mme Bonaparte evoked little response from the former abbé, but the carriages of Jérôme Gohier, the new president of the Directory, and of Joseph Fouché, the incoming minister of police, were soon rattling over the half-paved road to Malmaison; these were associations, Josephine was certain which provided her with an air of respectability, one more barrier against the clan and the uncertainty of the future.

Napoleon would say at St. Helena that "Gohier had been courting my wife," and that Josephine's role in "neutralizing" the last head of government of the Directory had been crucial at Brumaire.[15] That summer Gohier visited her daily at four o'clock whenever she was in Paris, and sometimes again in the evening. With Mme Gohier, formerly the Director's cook, Josephine maintained a semblance of friendship.

Jérôme Gohier, who had been minister of justice under the Terror, was a tall, dignified man of fifty-four whose ponderous exterior hid the proclivities of a Don Juan and who kept a secret list of his sexual conquests. Undoubtedly he hoped that his platonic visits to Mme Bonaparte would result in a closer relationship, and when she asked his advice on her sentimental life he recalls in his *Mémoires* that he advised her, not perhaps with total ingenuousness, to break off her liaison with Charles. Although Josephine assured him that she and Hippolyte felt only friendship for each other, "yet," he warned, "it compromises you in the eyes of the world."[16] She could only, he cautioned her, resolve this ambiguous situation by divorcing Bonaparte and then, if she wished, marrying Charles. Probably he hoped that such an outcome might lead to a less temperate relationship between himself and Mme Bonaparte.

But the idea of divorce was a suggestion that Josephine seems not even to have considered; this was a time when her association with Charles may have become tenuous, and her whole being was concentrated on matters essential to her security. Perhaps the emotion she showed before Napoleon's departure for Egypt—solely self-interest, or budding attachment?—may have played a part.

As for the new minister of police, Josephine had known Joseph Fouché since the days of Thermidor. He had remained Barras's protégé since the days of their alliance, quietly making a fortune in army commissions—one which he had hoped to increase by asking his patron for a lucrative diplomatic post. He was first sent as minister of the French Republic to Milan. Two months later Talleyrand, recently appointed minister of external relations, requested his immediate return. He knew, the Bishop said, the trouble caused by former members of the Convention in diplomatic posts, and still more by their wives. Fouché, nevertheless, had insisted on a full year's pay, and returned to Paris, accompanied by the *Citoyenne Ambassadrice* in the mission's own government carriages—piled with all the furniture of the official residence.

In 1799 he had no sooner taken up his duties at the embassy in Holland—another post owed to Barras—than he was recalled to be named minister of police. Sieyès, Barras and Talleyrand had decided that in this period of a revived Jacobin challenge, only another Jacobin could deal with the threat from the extreme left.

Like his three patrons, Fouché was searching for a safeguard against that counter-revolution dreaded by all the regicides, and believed that Bonaparte, were he ever to return from Egypt, would take over the government and provide that barrier. Intent upon learning through Mme Bonaparte any news she might receive from her husband, he drove to the rue de la Victoire almost as regularly as Jérôme Gohier. If Fouché is to be believed, this is also when he started to provide Josephine with a regular income from police funds, one which he claimed to have continued throughout the Consulate and Empire. And during this summer of maneuvers and intrigue, keeping a foot in each camp, he continued to frequent the crowded salons of the Bonaparte brothers as well as that of his patron, Barras.

And, almost immediately, Joseph Fouché began plotting with Sieyès.

. . .

Emmanuel Sieyès, once described by Robespierre as "the mole of the Revolution," was again secretly burrowing under the established government. A political philosopher and a "man of 1789," one of the inspirers of the Estates-General, a member of the Convention and part author of the Declaration of the Rights of Man, this sententious former Jesuit priest enjoyed immense prestige and a reputation as a begetter of constitutions. This was the man who had successively betrayed first Danton and then Robespierre; and it was he who had made the celebrated reply when asked to describe his activities during the days of the Terror: "I survived."

The former abbé was in his element in the atmosphere of plot and counterplot, accustomed to leaving no trace of his mole's passage. In this excessively polarized France of 1799, he was becoming the focus for moderate republicans. In common with the majority of regicides, he wanted a strong government that would consolidate the gains of the Revolution and prevent a monarchist restoration, but though he spoke often and at length of a revised constitution that would strengthen the executive branch, he refused to reveal his further intentions. He was cautiously preparing a coup d'état of his own. His initial idea was to unseat three of the other directors, to keep Barras temporarily and to find an accommodating "sword" to command the forces of the interior who would not be retained very long after the coup.

His principal allies in the present plotting were Talleyrand, Fouché and Lucien Bonaparte. His relations with Barras were uneasy; he despised his fellow director but needed him for the present. Barras himself had only contempt for the plump and cowardly former priest (in fear of assassination, Sieyès slept each night in a locked closet off his bedroom at the Luxembourg). Furthermore the ex-Vicomte Barras had not forgotten that it was Sieyès who, after Fructidor, had proposed that former nobles be considered foreigners and excluded from political life. Although a clause was added to the effect that some exceptions be made in favor of directors and generals who had rendered signal service to the Revolution, Barras nevertheless felt threatened.

Almost single-handedly, Sieyès proceeded to fill the key cabinet posts, although it was Barras who named General Bernadotte minister of war. As for the foreign ministry, the Jacobins, joined by the Bonaparte brothers, had started to circulate the fiction that Talleyrand, as well as Barras, had "sent General Bonaparte and the cream of our troops and savants into the deserts of Araby." The theme of the Citizen General betrayed by the politicians was a popular one. However, after Barras privately brought up the subject of Lucien's illegal election to the Five Hundred, the brothers confined their accusations to Talleyrand alone.

The Bishop responded by blaming the Egyptian expedition on Charles Delacroix, his predecessor in the foreign ministry, but Delacroix, stung by this additional insult, had no difficulty in proving Talleyrand's major role in that affair.* The Bishop's other paternity remained undisputed.

But Talleyrand, it was felt, was too difficult to maintain as minister of exterior relations; his corruption was too notorious, his financial transactions too well known. Happy to abandon a government now losing the remnants of its credibility, Charles-Maurice appointed a faceless collaborator as his successor and resigned. His move from the ministry to a small house shared with his current mistress, Mme Grand, and the dog, Jonquille, was thought to aid, rather than impede, the plotting for the coup; this house, to Sieyès's profound relief, immediately became the principal center for the conspirators.

By August, the final touches for the coup d'état were in place. Everything was settled but the general needed as a temporary instrument. Sieyès knew that the choice was vital; it was clear that the army could become the arbiter of the coup's success.

In 1799 all the generals were in a state of political ferment, almost all strongly republican; each one owed his career and his fortune to the Republic; each was full of political ambition and remembered that at Vendémiaire, and again at Fructidor, it was the army that had been called in to crush the counter-revolution and so advance the career of the political General Bonaparte.

It was not easy to find the sword for Sieyès's purpose. The country was still obsessed only with Bonaparte. General Jean Bernadotte, but for

---

* Talleyrand not only had Delacroix dismissed from the ministry, but was generally believed to have fathered the painter Eugène Delacroix, born in 1798.

his openly expressed leftist sympathies, was the obvious choice, and Lucien Bonaparte, who guessed that his own messages urging Napoleon to return immediately had not reached Egypt, was pushing for the appointment of this new member of the clan.

The influence of the Bonaparte family had been further enhanced that year by Bernadotte's appointment to the War Ministry. This strikingly tall Gascon with an eagle's beak was as energetic and ambitious as General Bonaparte, Désirée Clary's former suitor, and she would say later in life that only when she was told that Bernadotte's career might equal Bonaparte's did she accept his proposal of marriage.

Although her recollections on this point must remain open to doubt (Désirée, in her old age, was subject to flights of fancy), as must be the question of whether *Mort aux Rois* was tattooed on the chest of the future King of Sweden and Norway, as it was rumored to be, there was no doubt whatever of Bernadotte's deeply held Jacobin sentiments in 1799.

The Bonapartes were forced to recognize that Bernadotte was not only too openly republican, but also far too independent to be counted on for the projected coup. To begin with, he had refused Désirée's and Julie's pleas that the two families share a house. And what was to be made of a man unprepared to enrich himself during a campaign? Said to be the only general returning from the Army of Italy without a fortune, he had had to borrow fifty thousand francs from Gabriel Ouvrard—scrupulously repaid—in order to acquire a small house in the suburbs.

As minister of war, Bernadotte found that the Bonaparte brothers kept him under close surveillance. At three-thirty every morning the general left for the ministry, and every evening that summer he returned around seven o'clock accompanied by his aides, always to find one or other of the clan in his house. Either Lucien or Joseph and Julie would be there on the pretext that Désirée was still recovering from the birth of her son, Oscar.*

Within a few weeks in September, the fear of invasion was ended and neo-Jacobin power effectively broken. First came the news of General Guillaume Brune's victory over the English and Russian forces in Hol-

---

* Yet another character out of "Ossian"; the child's godfather, Joseph Bonaparte, was as warm an admirer of the mythical bard as was Napoleon.

land, followed by a greater one over the Austrians and Russians in Zurich. When the Senate heard of the extent of the Russian losses—all their cavalry and artillery, baggage-train and flags captured, and twelve thousand dead or prisoners—the deputies cheered and tossed their red toques in the air. In the following weeks the Austrians, Russians and British were beaten again and again on France's frontiers. Then on September 13 a two-month-old message from General Bonaparte arrived by one of the transports that had escaped the British fleet. The announcement of his defeat of eighteen thousand Turks at Aboukir was followed by news of yet more victories in Europe—General Brune's again over the Anglo-Russians, and General Ney's on the Rhine—each one of which was announced in Paris by the thunder of cannon.

Sieyès's preparations accelerated. On the night of the news of General Brune's second victory, he insisted as a security measure on the verbal resignation of the Jacobin Bernadotte. The general at least had the satisfaction of giving the press his own letter to Sieyès, thanking the director "for accepting a resignation I had not offered."

Throughout the rainy summer of 1799, Josephine remained at Malmaison, struggling to maintain some outward decorum.

The Bonapartes and most of Paris knew of Hippolyte's presence there, yet, with Gohier's warning ringing in her ears, aware of the gathering power of the clan and of its brooding hatred of her, Josephine seemed incapable of changing her course. She became increasingly reclusive. Sometimes she got as far as Paris and then turned back her carriage. In a distracted letter to Barras after one such occasion, she fell back again on invoking her husband's name: "I came to Paris, my dear Barras, meaning to see you, but I was told when I got there that you had a large party today," she wrote upon her return to Malmaison. She asked him to let her know what morning she could come for breakfast, but it must be alone. "Since I have started living in the country, I have become so shy that I am afraid of the great world. In any case, I am so unhappy that I don't wish to be an object of pity to others. You, my dear Barras, love your friends even when they are in trouble. I need to talk to you, to ask your advice. You owe this to Bonaparte's wife, and to his friendship for you."[17]

But her sure haven was still the Luxembourg, Barras and Thérésia

Tallien her steady friends, and the Director the ultimate source of power. There is a vignette of her at the palace at this time: "An extremely elegant woman of medium height walked by, leaning on Gohier's arm: it was Mme Bonaparte—Josephine—who would later be Queen of France! She bowed deeply to Mme de Staël as she passed her. As soon as she entered Barras's salon he got up, went to meet her and taking her by the hand led her to an armchair. . . . Mme Tallien came and sat beside her. They were very close friends then, and there was nothing to indicate that only a few months later she would be a sovereign in the very salons where Mme Tallien now reigned."[18]

At the beginning of October 1799, Josephine and Hortense were told they could send one letter each by the Directorial mailbag to Egypt. Josephine's to Bonaparte is missing, but Hortense's to her brother carefully describes their blameless life in Paris and in the country, the many visits to Director Gohier and his wife. "*Maman* has bought Malmaison, near St. Germain," she wrote. "She lives a very retired life there, seeing only Mme Campan and me. She has only given two big dinner parties since you both left. The Directors and all the Buonaparte family were invited, but the latter always refuse to come. Even Louis refused to stay with us and never comes to see us. . . . *Maman* is, I assure you, very distressed that the family won't live on friendly terms with her, which must vex her husband whom she loves very much. I am certain that if *Maman* could have been sure of reaching him she would have gone, but you know how impossible that would be now. . . ."[19]

In her own hand Josephine attached a postscript, telling Eugène how much she longed for his and his stepfather's return, "especially if I find Bonaparte as he was when he left me, and as he should always have been toward me; then I will be able to forget all I have suffered as a result of your absence and his."[20]

Was this a case of massive self-deception, or of what Napoleon would surely have labeled Josephine's "*inconséquence,*" her heedlessness, or simply a plea for amnesty?

Neither he nor Eugène was to receive this letter. On October 4, the day it was written, they were already in Corsica.

By the beginning of October everything was settled for Sieyès's coup d'état, except for the general. He had decided earlier on General Joubert, whose party politics were considered sound, and after Joubert was killed on the Italian front, on General Macdonald, who refused the invitation to take part in the plot. The cabal's next candidate was the victor of the Battle of Hohenlinden, General Jean Moreau, who was hesitant.

On October 14, Sieyès sat in his office at the Luxembourg, awaiting Moreau's visit. The general had returned from Italy only that morning, and Sieyès hoped to overcome his unwillingness. Just as Moreau arrived, a messenger rode up with the news that Bonaparte had disembarked on the south coast on the ninth and was even then on his way to Paris.

"There's your man. He will make a better job of your coup d'état than I would," said Moreau as he walked out.

⚜ 18 ⚜

THE FRUIT IS RIPE

IN CAIRO THAT AUGUST OF 1799, GENERAL BONAPARTE DECIDED THAT the risk was worth taking. It was essential to capitalize on the recent Egyptian victory before the truth about the expedition could reach France, and to choose a time when the coast was temporarily clear of British ships.

At the end of August a handful of officers were warned to be prepared. Childless Fourès was to follow on an early transport. "My ship may be taken by the English," Bonaparte told her. "You should think of my reputation; what would they say if they found a woman on board?"[1]

General Kléber was to be tricked into taking over command. First he was dispatched on a nonexistent mission, then on his return to Cairo he was handed a message from Bonaparte informing him that he was now in command of the army—an army at half its original combat strength. Bonaparte's letter assured Kléber that immediate reinforcements would be sent to Egypt. "I will regard as wasted," he ended his letter "every day of my life in which I do nothing for the army I am leaving you." Not until the following June, however, was a small amount of aid dispatched. As First Consul, Bonaparte would assert that five-sixths of the army had returned to France. Although no one at the time disputed this, in fact, one-half of the expeditionary force had perished, and several thousand more were blinded or crippled. Kléber himself would be assassinated in Egypt in 1801.

By the time Kléber returned to Cairo, Bonaparte had already set sail secretly from Alexandria. On a moonless night on August 22, the General left, consumed with fear that the "fruit might be overripe." On board two small frigates were Bonaparte's cook, his secretary Bourrienne, the nineteen-year-old Mameluke Roustam, four aides including Eugène and those generals he knew to be devoted to him—the future Marshals Murat, Berthier, Duroc, Lannes and Marmont. Junot was left in Egypt. Under the Empire it would be noted that he alone of all the officers close to Napoleon would never be promoted to marshal, punishment perhaps for the revelations about Josephine.

On board his ship, the *Muiron*, Bonaparte returned again and again to the subject of luck. He was, he asserted, a fatalist, "but all great events hang by a hair and I believe in luck; however, the wise man neglects nothing which helps his destiny."[2] He would indeed need luck to avoid quarantine on landing in France, coming as he did from a country ravaged by the plague, and greater luck still to avoid being tried for desertion. Still, "neglecting nothing," he picked out the books to take with him in case he were interned.

As the two frigates skirted the African coast, the men on board twice saw British sails in the distance. Bonaparte told his companions that if they appeared to be about to be taken by a British vessel, he and two or three of them would disembark and make for a port on foot.

Miraculously the two vessels reached Corsica and cast anchor at Ajaccio. Napoleon spent the next few nights in his childhood home, the house only recently rebuilt after its destruction in the anti-Bonaparte riots. Nothing could overcome his impatience, not the visit of his wet nurse, nor the dinner for forty friends and relatives, nor the sight of the vineyards again yielding wine. During eight windless days he stormed back and forth to the port, raging against the total calm. The only newspapers available were too old for him to be sure he had not missed his chance in Paris. "I will be there too late," he was heard to mutter as he read the latest news from Paris.

The gamble paid off. When they landed at Fréjus preceded by reports of Bonaparte's latest victory over the Turks, he knew he was unlikely to be tried and shot for desertion; the enthusiasm that greeted the General settled this, as well as the question of quarantine. Flags, music and cheering crowds greeted him at each relay. Even the early, unseasonable cold and fog could not keep townspeople and villagers from massing along the route as the news of his landing spread. Cavalrymen carrying flares preceded his carriage at night. The acclamations grew as he approached the capital. On October 12 he entered Paris with Eugène, and with Lucien and Joseph, who had joined him at Lyons. The city was illuminated in his honor and the frenzy of enthusiasm was reminiscent of the early days of the Revolution. Total strangers shouted to each other, "Bonaparte is back!" Martial music was played in the theaters. "In their emotion, certain citizens were taken ill," reported the press. The triumphant drive through France was the decisive signal Bonaparte had been waiting for.

When the General's carriage finally drew up in front of his house before dawn and he found that Josephine was not there, his anger was terrible. Under the tented portico the women of the clan were waiting, shrilly assuring him that she had fled, no doubt with Captain Charles. Napoleon appears to have returned with every intention of forgiving Josephine: it was the idea of her flight, he was to say at St. Helena, that tortured him. He would never forget the deep impression made by the empty house. There was plenty of time in the silent rooms and in the melancholy, leafless garden to fuel his rage.

Bonaparte's first visit that evening was to Paul Barras. He stayed at the Luxembourg until two in the morning, sounding out the Director as to his own political future and repeating his determination to divorce Josephine. And he went back again the next day, obsessively returning to the subject of her unfaithfulness. Barras urged the General to be philosophical, but his brothers, Napoleon said, had filled him in with additional details on the drive from Lyons, and he had promised them to divorce her without listening to her pleas.

Later that day Jean-Pierre Collot, the banker who had had some financial dealings with Bonaparte in Italy, visited the rue de la Victoire. He found the General piling logs onto the fire, more than ever sensitive to the cold after the Egyptian climate. When Napoleon burst out that he would never allow Josephine to set foot in the house again, that he would send her to live at Malmaison, Collot replied that when she returned and made her excuses she would be forgiven and Napoleon would be the happier for it. "Never!" Napoleon shouted, brandishing a poker. "I will never forgive her! How little you know me. If I were not sure of myself, I would tear my heart out and throw it into that fire." "All France is watching you," argued Collot, "you are its idol. Your grandeur would disappear if you were seen to be embroiled in domestic disputes. Later on, if you are not satisfied with your wife you can get rid of her."[3]

Bonaparte's state of unaccustomed indecision was obvious in the number of persons whose advice he sought. That night he visited Fortunée Hamelin. To his surprise—the incurable misogynist was always incapable of believing that one woman would stand by another without an ulterior motive—she defended Josephine. He was impressed by her arguments; she reminded him that a noisy separation now would be enough to kill his reputation with ridicule. Nevertheless, afraid perhaps of weakening when he saw Josephine, Napoleon emptied her closets of all her clothes and sent them down to the porter's lodge. That is where she found them the following morning when, after an agonizing forty-eight-hour journey, she and Hortense finally drew up at the rue de la Victoire in a thick fog.

Josephine had been dining with the Gohiers when a message from Eugène arrived by the newly installed telegraphic post: he and the General had arrived at Fréjus and were on their way to Paris. Turning deathly pale, Josephine left the table murmuring, "I must reach him before his brothers can talk to him."[4] As she and Hortense drove south through the night, they saw the triumphal arches at each relay; but whey they reached Lyons they were told that the General had passed through there earlier, taking the alternative route to Paris.

When, forty-eight hours later, the exhausted women reached the entrance at the end of the alley, the porter told Josephine that his orders were not to let her in. With Hortense she left the carriage and raced up the alley into the silent house. Napoleon, a terrified maid told them, was barricaded in his dressing room. He refused to open his door. Josephine wept; she protested in her irresistible voice that she could explain all. Huddled for hours on the last spiral of the narrow staircase, she continued her appeals, finally calling upon Eugène and Hortense in their attic rooms to come down and add their pleas and tears through the door before subsiding into an exhausted faint. After the General's door was at last thrown open, the ensuing stormy scene in the bedroom could be heard by the Beauharnais children and the quaking servants. And when Lucien appeared early the following morning, bursting with schemes for his brother's political maneuvers and further details of his sister-in-law's offenses, he was received by both of them in the conjugal bed.

What was said or promised that night is unknown. The relationship between the Bonapartes, however, was now reversed. The dialogue was no longer between a condescending and influential woman and a dazzled provincial who owed his marriage and promotion to a powerful Director. Some part of Napoleon was stifled forever—the poet and the dreamer awakened by Josephine, although her influence over his heart and his senses would remain paramount for years. Childless and guilty, she knew herself to be on trial each day; the hours of agony spent crouched on the stairs outside the closed door would never be forgotten by the woman who, except in this one instance, was never known to dwell on the past.

The call to power was uppermost in Bonaparte's mind the following morning. The fervor of the spontaneous acclaim that had greeted him had settled his mind as to his destiny. Only the means to achieve that power were still unclear.

It was a nervous moment for him when he appeared before the council the following day. When his landing was announced there, it had been greeted with muted enthusiasm. Only one deputy proposed he be court-martialed on the spot. Bernadotte, however, at the news of his arrival, had sent a message to the Directors warning them that there was not an instant to lose before court-martialing the General for abandoning his post.

In painful circumlocutions Bonaparte announced that he had been recalled by his own notion of duty. His reception was cool, his speech frequently interrupted by members of the Assembly standing and shouting abuse. His new appearance was observed with curiosity; his short unpowdered hair, sunburned skin and generally exotic appearance were emphasized by theatrical clothes and a Turkish scimitar worn in his sash. No action was taken against him.

Though he had not yet decided how to cut his way through the thickets of intrigue, Bonaparte was certain that only a man seen to be above all parties, neither a Jacobin nor a reactionary, could bring down the government; once again he started to play the role so successfully assumed two years ago: that of the intellectual civilian of moderate political views, without ambition and above factional strife. Delegations, particularly military ones, were turned away. He declined any public engagement except for two carefully chosen visits to the Invalides, where he was seen to embrace veterans of the Italian campaign. And Josephine seconded him—innocently, it must be said—in the hectic twenty days leading up to the coup of Brumaire. The picture Bonaparte wished to present of the family man, the Citizen General, was completed when politicians visiting the rue de la Victoire found the General and his wife alone in front of the fire, playing backgammon.

After only a week in France, however, Napoleon learned that he had to move fast. Although the misleading bulletins from Acre were still coming in, and the failure of the Syrian campaign not yet known, his public appearances were already attracting less interest. Victorious generals like Ney, Masséna and Brune were the new heroes, and the military situation was disappointingly stable. Napoleon began to be attacked by some of the press, especially by the leftist journals. One of them even suggested that he had "only left Egypt so suddenly and so secretly to escape a mutiny of his entire army."

Lucien Bonaparte and Talleyrand were urging him to ally himself with Emmanuel Sieyès and his party of liberals and moderates. But in spite of that group's ready-made plans for a coup and a revised constitution, Bonaparte could not bring himself to like or trust "that priest." He found him, he said, repulsive looking and cadaverous; and he had nothing but his usual contempt for him as an ideologue and for his reputation as a thinker and philosopher.

A full week was wasted, partly because of absurd personal sticking points. Two days after Josephine's return Gohier, as president of the Directory, gave a dinner for the General. Throughout the meal Bonaparte refused to speak or even look at Sieyès, vexed that when he had paid an official visit to the director earlier in the day he had not been accorded full military honors. And not only had he been kept waiting, but the doors of the council chamber had not been opened fully, as they had once been for Princes of the Blood and still were for distinguished persons.

Sieyès was enraged by Bonaparte's open contempt and left immediately after dinner, but first he whispered in Gohier's ear: "Have you noted the behavior of that insolent little man toward me? We should have had him shot."[5] Bonaparte was pleased rather than otherwise by this reaction and told Josephine after dinner that he had clearly seen the offense that his obvious disdain had caused Sieyès.

The General was almost equally irritated by Gohier, although the president attempted to support him when he was commanded to appear before the five directors. After much hesitation they had decided to reprimand the General for deserting his army. Bonaparte took the offensive by denying the rumors of the fortune that he had brought back from Italy. Gohier defended him. "General," he said, "the Directory is certain that your laurels were the most valuable treasure you brought back from Italy. However," he continued, "we know you do not wish to remain inactive while the armies of the Republic are victoriously fighting on every front. The Directory wishes you to choose which of those armies you prefer to command."[6] Thoroughly exasperated by what he interpreted as an attempt to dislodge him from Paris, Bonaparte answered only that his health required further rest. From this session he concluded that he must lose no time in making a choice between what now appeared to be the two parties, either of Sieyès or of Barras.

Talleyrand was finding it difficult to effect a meeting between the two protocol-conscious men who he believed so obviously needed each other. He assured his fellow ex-priest that only Bonaparte could help him found the ideal republic to be built on Sieyès's projected constitution. But Emmanuel Sieyès, too, had to be persuaded. He would have preferred to carry out his project of modifying the Constitution without the aid of this ambitious general.

Bonaparte took to his bed, blaming the weather; his passionate desire for power and the uncertain state of his ambitions made him ill. As he confided to General Bertrand, before a major decision he was always as nervous as on the eve of battle. "I exaggerate all the dangers possible. . . . I am painfully agitated though I may appear totally serene. Once I have made up my mind, I screen out everything except what will make it succeed."[7]

Finally, his decision was made. At St. Helena, Napoleon would confide that he might have preferred to work with Paul Barras had not the Director insulted him when they dined together on October 30. After they had agreed that a republic on American lines "but without the Federalism" would be the best solution for France, Barras suggested the name of some nonentity to head the French Republic; Bonaparte, he said, would doubtless wish to return to the field to command the Army of Italy.

Napoleon was beside himself as he recounted the interview later. It was clear, he said, that Barras had only summoned up some ridiculous personage's name to disguise the fact that he himself wished to be president; Barras was apparently incapable of imagining his former protégé in any such role. Bonaparte never wished to hear Barras's name again; in any case, the man was finished politically, finished in public opinion. The General did not add that he went straight downstairs from Barras's dinner table at the Luxembourg Palace to Sieyès's apartment and announced that the abbé could now definitely count on him.

He did, however, keep his options open with regard to Barras until almost the last day, always reassuring the Director that whatever happened would be within the law and would not be undertaken without his knowledge. When asked about Barras's role in the plot, he invariably answered, "Barras is with us." And while the Bonapartes continued to dine with the Director almost nightly, Josephine, like so many others, including Barras himself, continued to believe that her husband would undertake nothing without their protector.

Immediately after his decision to play the Sieyès card, Bonaparte started to sound out men in all parties, disclaiming any wish for a role for himself. He wanted only, he said, a Republic founded on democratic principles. He made no promises, asked for no guarantees, adopting one tone with the army officers—Paris was full of them on unearned leave, and the government dared not protest—and another with the politicians. To the army he charged that all civilian administrators were corrupt and should be replaced. To the right, the General would refer to Barras as "a dangerous democrat who would revolutionize France." To one of the Jacobin generals, Jean-Baptiste Jourdan, he said "Do not worry, all will be done in the interests of the Republic." The bankers were easily won over, relieved to learn that they were working with anti-Jacobins.

But Bonaparte had no wish to shed his republican aureole. Wishing to make sure of the intellectual society that governed opinion in France, he needed the support of the members of the Institut, the surviving Encyclopedists. With them he spoke of the maintenance of the Republic, of the importance of observing the Constitution. Forthcoming events would reestablish the principles of 1789 he assured them, and once the Directory was overthrown, he would await their decision as to how best he might serve his country.

"He allowed himself," wrote one historian, "to be carried to power by an enormous misunderstanding coupled with his universal prestige."[8]

In the last days of the conspiracy, Napoleon had a specific request to make of his wife. He particularly did not wish for a break with the leftist military men; he had managed to neutralize most of the rival generals, but he needed her help in charming General Bernadotte, the most refractory of them all. Désirée Bernadotte and Napoleon had not seen each other since 1795 in Marseilles; now the two couples met almost daily in one or other of the Bonaparte family's houses. The two men's hostility was undisguised; Bernadotte was clearly becoming what Napoleon termed "the obstacle man." He knew that from the time of his return Bernadotte had taken every opportunity to make his opinion of him evident. Bernadotte, when asked to subscribe to an official dinner for Bonaparte, had replied that he thought the dinner should be put off until Bonaparte had explained in a "satisfactory manner his reasons for abandoning his army." And, he added, "that man has not been through quarantine and may very well have brought back the plague, and I have no intention of dining with a plague-stricken general."[9]

Bourrienne was working one day in the little study on the rue de la Victoire when Jean Bernadotte was announced. After his departure Bonaparte came bursting in. "Bourrienne," he shouted, "Bernadotte has come here with his ridiculously exaggerated accounts of brilliant French victories, of the Russians beaten, of victorious armies everywhere. . . . He even had the nerve to tell me that he looked upon the army in Egypt as lost. Josephine was there. You know her grace and her tact, she changed the conversation. . . . Well, now I will leave you to work and I will go back to Josephine."[10]

There was a piquant scene before Brumaire when the Bonapartes and Bernadottes shared a carriage on the four-hour drive to Mortefontaine, Joseph's estate. Bonaparte had instructed his wife to exercise her charm on the other couple. It cannot have been a success. As soon as they arrived at their destination, Désirée, who had not seen her former fiancé since he left Marseilles, hurried to sister Julie to mimic what she described as Josephine's languishing flirtatiousness and caressing manner during the journey.

The two days the Bonapartes spent at Mortefontaine were full of crosscurrents. Désirée was still jealous of Josephine, and Napoleon's attempts at conversation with Jean Bernadotte were unsuccessful; it was obvious that the most he could hope for from the other general was some sort of neutrality on the day of the coup.

General Bonaparte, confident now of having the country behind him, informed Sieyès that the coup would take place on November 9 (18 Brumaire). The next week was taken up by increasingly feverish discussions. Because all five directors lived at the Luxembourg Palace and spied on one another, plotting became ever more complicated. Talks were held at Sieyès's apartment there, and at Joseph Bonaparte's house. Talleyrand's became another center of maneuvering, but No. 6 rue de la Victoire was the principal center in those last days for rapid meetings and for bargaining. These were never interrupted by the police; Joseph Fouché, who knew the house so well, saw to that.

In the best tradition of political intrigue, very few were aware of the whole plot; most knew only their own small role in it. Many of the conspirators sincerely believed that they were saving the Republic by changing its outward form only.

Josephine's regular afternoon and evening "at homes" were not only the perfect cover, but a useful way of filling the house with those who must be misled and those Napoleon had still not won over. Serene and gracious, pouring tea, Mme Bonaparte conversed reassuringly about agreeable nothings. "The talk in this house appeared to be all about fashion and horses,"[11] but the crowded drawing room and the antechamber were simply a passageway to Napoleon's little study in the back of the house where he received some of the guests privately one at a time, sounding out the generals, bankers and deputies, to find out how each one would stand on the day. All the principal actors in the coup were at these parties, as well as bit players: young officers in uniform and pretty girls such as Pauline Leclerc and Hortense. Roustam, the Mameluke slave now serving as bodyguard and valet to Napoleon, dressed in his exotic clothes, carried in the tea tray.

Napoleon had instructed Josephine to make sure that Gohier continued his four o'clock visits and to elicit his views on a future government. It was all the easier for her to follow these instructions since she still had little idea as to what was afoot. She was not alone in her innocence. Her old friend Antoine Arnault came in one day to find the usual company. Josephine was on the sofa, drinking tea and sitting between Gohier and Joseph Fouché, who had just arrived from a secret meeting at Talleyrand's. When Gohier asked Fouché whether there was any news, Fouché answered, "None at all, Citizen Director, still the same old talk of a conspiracy." "A conspiracy?" asked Josephine, in a flutter. "Yes, that's the rumor," answered Fouché. "But if there were any truth in it there would be evidence by now on the Place de la Révolution," meaning that they would all have been guillotined. Fouché burst into laughter, but Josephine was, or appeared to be, shocked. "For shame, Citizen Fouché," she said. "How can you laugh about such matters?" Ponderously Gohier broke in, "Do not be alarmed, Citoyenne. When the Minister speaks of such things in the presence of ladies it is proof that the rumors are without foundation. Follow the example of the government, Madame, do not be worried by rumors, and sleep peacefully tonight." Throughout this scene Bonaparte was leaning on the mantelpiece, smiling.[12]

Collot was right. Napoleon *was* "all the happier for it"—all the happier for being once again in Josephine's soothing ambience. He described to Talleyrand "the infinite delight"[13] of living with his wife, and in the midst of all this feverish activity Napoleon apparently still found time to show Josephine more than just appreciation for her help. Two days before the coup she wrote to her lawyer that she was very happy. Bonaparte, she assured him, was "more affectionate than ever." Philippe de Ségur, one of those who believed apparently that Josephine was aware of all the intricacies of the plot, wrote that "her discretion, her grace, her gentle manner, her cool composure, her ready ingenuity and wit were of great service. She justified Bonaparte's renewed confidence in her."[14]

Within the week all was ready. The plan was to move the two legislative bodies to St. Cloud outside Paris. It was thought that there they would be persuaded more easily to vote for a "constitutional revision," when surrounded by troops under Bonaparte's command and separated from the capital.

First, a threatened public danger would have to be invented. Lucien and some friendly deputies of the Five Hundred were to spread rumors of a terrorist Jacobin plot to assassinate the moderate directors and guillotine the more liberal deputies in the two councils. This would be the pretext for the Elders to give General Bonaparte the command of the Paris troops.

For the Directory to be brought down legally at least three of the directors had to be persuaded to resign. Sieyès and his acolyte Ducos were, of course, secure; perhaps Moulin too. It was essential to trick Barras and Gohier. Barras had to continue to believe that nothing would be done without him; Gohier into believing that nothing was afoot. Sieyès would have been astonished to learn the greater part of this plan, since his aim was not to overthrow the government but rather to consolidate it, above all to change the Constitution by a vote in the two assemblies. Bonaparte, who preferred to retain some democratic semblance, was careful not to fill in too many details.

He was aware of how uncertain and risky were some of the military dispositions he was now taking; the weak point of the plan, he knew, was the attitude of the army. His fellow generals were jealous of him; the Jacobin officers would not be likely to wish to overthrow the government. Although he could be sure of the troops now in Paris—most of them had served under him in Italy—the Grenadiers of the Directorial Guard were an uncertain element; "undisciplined and ultra-democratic," their allegiance could go either way. Bonaparte knew, however, that he could have total confidence in two men: his own brother-in-law General Leclerc and Joachim Murat, who would undertake anything in the hope of obtaining the hand of Caroline Bonaparte.

Napoleon was still more certain that he could not count on the Jacobin generals after he returned from the last—and most farcical—ceremony of the Directory.

On the afternoon of November 6, 1799, in the Temple of Victory, formerly the Church of St. Sulpice, took place what was possibly the least successful of any of the revolutionary fetes; "glacial" and "sinister" were some of the adjectives applied to it.

The subscription dinner was given by the two councils in honor of Generals Moreau and Bonaparte. The church itself was icy. Fog seeped in; outside, a fine rain changed to hail. A statue of the Goddess of Reason still stood on the former altar. Napoleon made it clear that he was present only reluctantly; with a face of thunder, he sat silent. The guests included the directors and all the most important political men of the day. The atmosphere of tension, the belief that a coup was in the making, the uncertainty as to who was part of it and who not, ensured that hardly a word was spoken throughout the meal. Two hundred fifty places were set; General Bonaparte, making it clear that he feared poison, had brought his own bread, a bottle of wine and a pear. As soon as the toasts were over he left. Outside, as upon his arrival, there were both cheers and protests. He blamed the crowd's hostility on ultra-republicans since the Jacobin Generals Jourdan, Augereau and Bernadotte had all refused to attend the event.

On November 7 Sieyès took the last of a series of "secret" riding lessons in the Luxembourg Gardens while Barras watched him from his window and laughed.[15] It was the abbé's intention to cut an impressive figure at the head of the Directorial Guard as he rode from the Luxembourg to the Tuileries the following morning. He knew nothing either of the tracts and proclamations organized by Bonaparte, or of the military dispositions taken since, purposely or not, he had been inadequately briefed by the General's aides.

Once every detail was secured, Bonaparte was again confident and in excellent spirits. He spent that morning singing tunelessly, correcting the posters and pamphlets to be printed later in the day. To reassure Jérôme Gohier, he invited himself and Josephine to dinner with the director for the following evening, November 9. Then, in order to take by surprise those officers whose attitude was not clear, he had each senior officer sent a message asking him to present himself at the General's house at six-thirty the following morning. No reason was given; each believed himself to be summoned alone. That night, in a room at the Tuileries with the shutters closed, letters were written to certain Elders convening them to an important meeting again at seven the next morning; not every deputy was invited, only those believed to be sympathetic to the cause. At 5 A.M. the letters were carried around Paris.

At eight o'clock on the foggy night of November 8, Josephine sat at her desk. At her husband's direction she wrote: "Do come, you and your wife, my dear Gohier, to breakfast with me at eight tomorrow morning. Do not fail me. I must talk to you about matters of the utmost importance." Eugène, on his way out to a dance, was instructed to deliver the note by midnight.

Then Napoleon sent for Bourrienne. "Barras is expecting me at eleven tonight," he told him. "Take my carriage and tell him I cannot come, that I have a bad headache and have gone to bed, but that he need not fear. Try not to let him question you, return as soon as you can and come up to my room. Tomorrow our business will be done. I don't want to see him tonight."[16]

When Bourrienne returned he reported that Barras had heard him out. Looking him directly in the eye he said, "I see Bonaparte has tricked me. He will not come back. It is finished. And yet he owes me everything."[17]

♠ 19 ♠

INTO THE HANDS OF VULTURES

IT WAS NOT YET LIGHT ENOUGH AT SIX-THIRTY ON THE MORNING OF November 9 (18 Brumaire) for the officers in dress uniform to recognize one another as they rode up to the Bonapartes' house. The men, each one of whom had expected a private audience, found that in the dark they had trouble controlling their mounts, jostling one another in the narrow alley.

Soon the courtyard and the garden—white with the first frost of the season—and finally the house itself were filled with dismounted officers and the sound of the rattle of sabres and the clink of spurs.

While Josephine welcomed the men indoors, Bonaparte "serene as on the morning of battle," took some of the more obviously reluctant ones into his study and reasoned with them there. Occasionally he went out into the courtyard and pulled an officer in by the arm. Bernadotte, in civilian clothes, arrived with Joseph Bonaparte. Bernadotte was seen to look angrily about him and expostulate with his brother-in-law; a shouting match in Napoleon's study followed. "You are not in uniform, Bernadotte." "I am dressed as I always am when I am not on duty." "You will be, shortly." "I will not take part in a rebellion." Napoleon tried flattery and threats, insisting that his only ambition, "after saving the Republic," was to retire to Malmaison with a few friends, but all he could extract from Bernadotte was a promise to remain neutral during the coming events. Joseph was ordered to follow his brother-in-law, take him home to breakfast and not lose sight of him.

The two men on whom much of the day depended were yet to come. Bonaparte was determined that Gohier, the president of the Directory, should be part of his new government. Equally important was the adherence of General Lefebvre.

François Lefebvre, the military governor of Paris, was a bluff, emotional soldier and staunch republican, with a soldier's frankness of speech, as uninhibited as his wife's.* When Bonaparte, at his most seductive, took him back into the little study and presented him with the sword "which I wore at the Battle of the Pyramids" and called on him to assist in saving the Republic, Lefebvre asked one question only: "And Barras?" "Barras is with us." General Lefebvre burst out of the room into the courtyard, weeping and swearing: "Let's throw those buggers of lawyers into the river!"[1] With Bonaparte's command of all the Paris troops thus ensured, only the support of the Guard of the Directory remained uncertain.

The next maneuver was less fortunate. Jérôme Gohier, starting to suspect something and suspicious of the extraordinary hour of Mme Bonaparte's invitation—ten o'clock was the more usual hour for breakfast—sent his wife alone. She, of course, already suspected any invitation from that house, and when Bonaparte asked her angrily why the president had not accompanied her and sat her down at Josephine's desk insisting that she write her husband to join her immediately, she scribbled a warning of the trap and then attempted to return to the Luxembourg.

In vain Josephine assured her that her own carriage would take the letter and that the director's presence was all-important. Mme Gohier should have understood, said Josephine, that when she sent her son with the breakfast invitation, the message was indeed urgent. However, she added, she was authorized to transmit the following request: it was her husband's wish that the president resign voluntarily in order to become a member of the new government about to be established by the General.

Eight o'clock, and General Bonaparte had already sent three messengers to the Tuileries for news. The Elders had been in session for an hour, but

---

* The general's wife, Catherine Lefebvre, the former laundress and future Maréchale Duchesse de Danzig, was the celebrated "Madame Sans Gêne" of comedy.

the decree appointing him commander in chief of the armed forces in the capital had not arrived, and he could not indefinitely retain all the army chiefs, some of whom were still hesitant. The officers had no idea that they were effectively his prisoners; a detachment of dragoons was now stationed at the end of the alley with instructions to prevent anyone from leaving the house.

Finally, at eight-thirty a messenger from the Elders arrived with the decree. The two councils, it read, in danger of intimidation, would move to the Palace of St. Cloud. General Bonaparte, responsible for their protection, was hereby appointed commander of all the troops in the Paris region.

Bonaparte first took the decree to his study and altered it so as to also retain the Guard of the Directory under his own command. When he appeared at the top of the front door steps, General Lefebvre, still "visibly moved," was beside him as he read aloud the Elders' decree. This appearance of legality helped resolve the last doubts of the generals of the Army of the Republic. The call was answered by cheering and the waving of swords. Napoleon went inside for a moment and called out to Bourrienne: "Gohier didn't come, so much the worse for him,"[2] and mounted his black charger.

As he and his general staff clattered off toward the Tuileries in a sea of tossing tricolor plumes, a pale November sun came out, glinting on the epaulettes and on the gold embroidery of the uniforms. Only Bonaparte, riding a few paces ahead of the sixty or so other officers, was an easily recognizable figure in his plainest uniform and the too-large hat, made familiar by a thousand prints.

Another revolution appeared to be in the making. Passersby waved, seemed well disposed; there was no wild enthusiasm. Ten years of revolution had taken their toll.

General Sébastiani's troops were already in place around the Place de la Révolution, in the Tuileries Gardens and around the palace, seat of the Council of Elders. When Bonaparte entered the Assembly, followed by a dozen generals of his escort, he found the Elders in some disarray. Alarmed by the display of armed force around the Tuileries and by the absence of so many of their colleagues, they had finally realized that the summons for the early session had been signed by none of the directors. The president of the Commission of Inspectors had opened the session at

7 A.M. by hinting at unnamed perils, at foreign plots and "conspiracies," a term to evoke bloody memories. "The skeleton of the Republic," he warned, throwing metaphor to the winds, "will fall into the *hands* of vultures!" and he urged the Elders to place all military power in the hands of General Bonaparte, "that illustrious man . . . who burns to crown his noble labors by this act of devotion to the Republic."[3]

Although there was distinct unease at the mention of the military aspect of the proceeding, and there was no answer to questions concerning the extreme danger, the decree was hastily adopted and the Assembly agreed to meet the following day at St. Cloud for unspecified reasons.

Meanwhile, the five directors were in various stages of uncertainty. As soon as he was informed that the General had received the decree of the Elders, Emmanuel Sieyès sent an order to the Guard of the Directory to escort him to the Tuileries, but he found that there would be no magnificent cavalcade through the city after all, since Bonaparte himself had taken over the Guard. And later in the morning, after his wife had returned—she had had some difficulty in eluding the guards at the rue de la Victoire—Gohier discovered that his fellow Directors Sieyès and Roger Ducos had left the Luxembourg. Gohier and Jean Moulin therefore decided to go to the Tuileries Palace, where they found General Bonaparte setting up his headquarters. He had finished the ceremony of swearing to protect the Constitution he was about to overthrow, but now he was faced with the difficulty of keeping up the appearance of legality.

To become law, he was told, the Elders' decree giving him command of the armed forces of Paris had to be signed by the president of the Directory and sealed with the Great Seal of the Republic. Bonaparte was already in a towering rage at this holdup when Gohier appeared. No sooner had the president signed the Elders' illegal decree than Bonaparte brutally informed him that the Directory no longer existed. "No more Directory?" he inquired. "You are quite wrong, General. And you know that you are dining with its president today." Exasperated, Bonaparte warned him that as Paul Barras had resigned (Barras's position was in fact unknown), Gohier and Moulin, now in the minority, should tender their own resignations without further delay. "And I am not dining *anywhere* today!"[4]

Gohier either would not or could not understand Josephine's message relayed through Mme Gohier and both he and Moulin refused to resign. As the two directors were now a possible rallying point for the councils, Bonaparte, under the pretext of a possible terrorist uprising, dispatched an armed guard to surround the Luxembourg. Their orders were to allow no one in or out. By nightfall, sentries were posted at their doors; one, complained Gohier, even spent the night in the director's conjugal bedroom.

Barras, inaccurately informed of the resignation of the four other directors, remained in his apartments expecting a summons from the General. Like the majority of the government and Josephine herself, he had never ceased to believe that he would play an essential role in the coup. That one would be attempted without the man of Thermidor, Vendémiaire and Fructidor was unthinkable. To the last, Talleyrand, Sieyès, Napoleon and Lucien Bonaparte had repeatedly assured him of this.

Barras closed his door to visitors. The only one admitted that morning was Thérésia Tallien, too far advanced in pregnancy to move freely around Paris. Gabriel Ouvrard, too, came in for a moment. In the last few weeks both he and Thérésia had tried to warn Barras about Bonaparte's maneuvering, but without any success.

At eleven o'clock, the Director was about to sit down alone at the dining room table, set as usual for thirty places, when Talleyrand and Admiral Eustache Bruix entered. There were no other eyewitnesses to the scene that followed, and each actor reported it with wide differences. Bruix (another Barras protégé) and Talleyrand informed Barras—again incorrectly—that the four other directors had abdicated and that the Republic was in grave danger; for no other reason would General Bonaparte have flown to its aid. To prevent disorder and bloodshed, the General must ask Barras to sign his own resignation. The text of this was then presented to him; it was full of praise for Bonaparte "for whom I had the happiness of opening the road to glory." Barras signed without comment. Since it had not been necessary to offer Collot's two million francs with which Talleyrand was to buy him off, the money remained in the Bishop's pocket. Talleyrand kissed Barras's hand, assured him he was "the foremost of French patriots," and the Director left the Luxembourg immediately for Grosbois. The following year he would be ordered to leave that property within twenty-four hours; he would not be allowed to reenter Paris until the fall of Napoleon's Empire.

Several explanations were put forward to account for Paul Barras's uncharacteristic lethargy. Bourrienne believed that his own visit on the preceding night had been an effective warning to the normally optimistic Barras of what was to come. Undoubtedly, given Barras's views on friendship, the shock of betrayal by Bonaparte, Talleyrand and apparently Josephine must have been considerable.

At the Tuileries, the high command of the coup remained in session until late into the night. The General's forces were disposed at strategic points around Paris and on the road to St. Cloud, and at the Luxembourg troops guarding the directors remained armed and booted.

Most of the conspirators were optimistic about events the next day. There was some merriment about Gohier and his dinner. But when the meeting broke up, two major questions remained unanswered. First, how, legally and constitutionally, might the two councils at St. Cloud be induced to vote for the abolition of the Directory, and second, how would the ultra-republican army react to the next day's events?

When Bonaparte returned late at night to the rue de la Victoire he found Josephine anxiously waiting for news. Earlier that morning after the cavalcade had departed and the street regained its calm, she and Bourrienne had sat down to talk. She was fearful of the outcome of the day, and Bourrienne, though he had his own doubts about what seemed to him an ill-prepared venture, pretended to be confident that all would go well. Josephine was tormented, too, by the subject of Jérôme Gohier's fate. She was distressed, she told Bourrienne, that she had not been able to tell him herself that he must not hold out, that if he would resign "Bonaparte told me he would then do everything for him." (Napoleon's own comment later was: "Had Gohier come to breakfast that day, I would have forced him to ride with me."[5])

Bourrienne remained at the rue de la Victoire until Bonaparte returned. At nightfall Fouché had come to see Josephine and assure her that all was going well. The other Bonaparte ladies had been kept in ignorance of the day's activities until the evening; Fouché had seen to that, remembered Laure d'Abrantès. The sisters Julie Bonaparte and Désirée Bernadotte were in a position to know more than the others, but their concern never stretched beyond a wish for harmonious relationships between their husbands. Mme Letizia declared that Josephine's house was the last one to which she would apply for news. Pauline, however, sent messengers there every hour to inquire. Germaine de Staël's came as frequently. Returning from her Swiss exile, she heard of the day's events as she drove through the Paris barriers.

Napoleon bade goodnight to Bourrienne before going upstairs: "Today went well. We shall see about tomorrow," he said, and placed two loaded pistols beside his pillow. The danger to the whole Bonaparte family was very real that night. Had the directors been less closely guarded, the councils might well have had all the conspirators arrested.

Early on the damp, cool morning of November 10, a stream of carriages and chattering crowds on foot and on horseback left Paris in the direction of St. Cloud. But for the presence of the troops the atmosphere was that of a picnic, reminiscent of the "Day" of Vendémiaire in 1795. Some observers brought their own provisions; more relied on the local cafés and inns, so there was not a seat to be had in them after eleven o'clock. But it was not too cold to set the baskets of food and wine on benches under the rusting trees and observe the arrival of conveyances from Paris. Deputies of the two councils arrived early; Lucien Bonaparte, president of the Five Hundred, and his brother Joseph shared a carriage. Benjamin Constant, who had instructions to send reports every hour to the Swedish embassy, came alone. Sieyès and Roger Ducos shared a post chaise that was instructed to remain close to the château, ready to flee if matters became dangerous.

Together, Talleyrand, Montrond and Fortunée Hamelin had repaired to Mlle Lange's house nearby, where they were already enjoying a meal ordered in advance. A six-horse traveling coach was waiting at the door—there was no telling how events would end that day.

That morning Bourrienne, driving past the spot on the Place de la Révolution where the guillotine had stood, turned to a friend and said:

"Tomorrow we will either sleep at the Luxembourg or we will end here."[6]

Fouché, too, was taking no chances. As Napoleon was later to learn, he had made sure that the General and his accomplices would be arrested if the coup failed. He had closed the gates of Paris and intended to keep them shut until the identity of the day's victor was certain. And General Bonaparte's own carriage and horses were ready at the barriers too.

At St. Cloud, the deputies of the upper and lower chambers were in a hostile mood. The palace, uninhabited since the summer of 1790 when Louis XVI and his family had spent their last days of semi-liberty there, was not yet ready for the midday session. Decorators had not finished their work, carpets and tapestries were still being hammered over broken windowpanes. The Elders were to sit, they found, in the Gallery of Apollo, a vast hall with a ceiling painted for Louis XIV by Mignard, while the Five Hundred were to occupy the Orangerie, unattached to the main building; some benches were being placed there, and a chair for the president perched on a platform. Conveniently for the plotters, communication between the two rooms would be difficult.

Unable to take their seats, the deputies of both bodies were soon engaged in heated discussions on the terrace outside—the very situation that the coup leaders had hoped to prevent by keeping the councils apart. During the long wait the members of the lower house hurled questions about the terrible peril that had brought them there, questions that the shaken Elders were unable to answer.

Furthermore, the deputies were dismayed to find themselves surrounded by troops. Six thousand men under Joachim Murat's command could be seen lining the approaches to the palace; General Sébastiani's dragoons surrounded it and the Grenadiers of the Guard of the Directory—blue coats, red revers and bearskin bonnets—were massed in the courtyard of the château itself. It was felt unlikely that so much protection was needed this far from Paris and the "anarchists' plot."

At the rue de la Victoire, the house had filled since early morning with the military and civilian leaders of the coup. General Bonaparte appeared less sanguine than on the previous day. Just as he was about to leave Josephine sent a message asking him to come upstairs to see her again. "Still more in love than he wished to admit," the General appeared pleased. "I will go up," he said, "but this is not to be a day for women. This business is far too serious."[7]

When he arrived at St. Cloud at midday, General Bonaparte was outraged to find the château still unready and the deputies arguing in angry groups outside. As he and his general staff went to inspect the Orangerie there were sullen stares and murmurs of "scoundrel" and "ruffian" from some members of the Five Hundred huddled around the stove there.

In an attempt to remain out of sight in what the General privately called "this parliamentary comedy," he joined Sieyès and Roger Ducos in a room next to the Gallery of Apollo to await the result of the sessions. Nervous, restless and cold (there were too few logs in the fireplace to keep him warm), he marched up and down for two hours after the meetings had started. The session of the upper chamber had begun on a hostile note. Receiving no proof of the "terrible peril" that had brought them to St. Cloud, and upon being falsely informed that all five members of the Directory had resigned (Gohier and Moulin were still holding out at the Luxembourg), the Elders simply passed a resolution calling for the election of a new Directory.

The General, advised of this resolution, could barely contain his fury. The scene was not going according to plan. White with rage, he stormed into the Gallery of Apollo followed by a few officers and Bourrienne. His presence was in itself illegal; that, and his threatening manner, caused a sensation. A wave of protesting red togas greeted him. Forgetting that his role was supposed to be only that of defender of the Constitution, and that the council was expecting to hear details of the plot that had brought them there, the General began a confused harangue delivered in a hoarse voice. "As soon as these dangers are passed," he declaimed, "I will abdicate all power. I wish only to be the right arm of whatever government you are about to elect." "Name the conspirators!" "Names, names!" from the Elders. As the uproar became ever more violent, the General, unused to interruptions, pointed to the armed guards at the door and shouted that should there be any attempt on his life, those brave men "whom he had so often led to victory and to the humiliation of kings" would protect their general. As the howls of protest grew louder, Bonaparte, apparently beside himself, screamed: "Remember that I walk accompanied by the god of war and the god of luck!" He had used this line with some effect in Egypt. Bourrienne pulled him by the sleeve and whispered: "Leave, General, you don't know what you are saying."

When he first emerged from the gallery Bonaparte appeared not to realize the disaster his appearance there had been, but messengers from Talleyrand and Fouché were awaiting him. Both warned that no time was to be lost, that the two councils' hostile reaction to him was already known in Paris and that the Jacobin Generals Jourdan and Augereau, who had refused to come officially to St. Cloud, were now at the château talking to the troops outside, urging them to resist the Bonapartist coup and to remain faithful to the constitution and to the Republic. On the reaction of these soldiers, they reminded him, the result of the day would depend.

First Bonaparte sent off a messenger to Paris to inform Josephine that all was going well, then at four o'clock he entered the Orangerie flanked by two of his towering grenadiers. Not only was he in uniform and present illegally, but troops with bayonets at the ready could be seen through the open door. The enraged deputies climbed over benches, overturned chairs and rushed at the trio, shouting, "Get out," "Kill, kill," and finally the dreaded, *"Hors la loi!"* ("Outlaw!"). Some started to pummel the grenadiers; one took Napoleon by the collar and attempted to shake him like a rat.

Generals Murat and Lefebvre, fists flying, pushed their way through the crowd, followed by more troops. Step by step, walking backwards, four grenadiers surrounded and half carried General Bonaparte, nearly fainting, overcome by his old horror of crowds. Throughout the château the terrible *"Hors la loi!"* could be heard as far as the Orangerie, its echoes no less ominous five years after Thermidor.

When he rejoined his aides and Sieyès, Bonaparte was at first speechless, then became incoherent. He had scratched open some of the boils on his face; the blood, he told Sieyès, was the result of an attempted assassination.* The abbé, who knew that the deputies were unarmed, was not

---

* One of the grenadiers, whose sleeve was torn in the fracas, was easily convinced that he had saved Bonaparte's life. He was granted a pension, and Josephine, in tears, presented him publicly with a large diamond. This greatly helped the legend of the attempted assassination.

sorry to see the imperious Bonaparte half paralyzed with shock. "They appear to think that this is 1794," he said coolly. "Well, General, throw them out of the Orangerie."

This was clearly the end of any hope of a purely parliamentary coup. Everything now depended on whether or not the Guard would take up the cry of "outlaw him!" It was Lucien Bonaparte who saved the day. Abandoning the stormy session of the Five Hundred and still wearing his red toga, he bounded onto a horse, rallied the troops in the courtyard and ordered the Guard to arrest the deputies, "scoundrels probably in the pay of England."[8]

For a moment the Guard hesitated. Some deputies still hung out of the Orangerie windows screaming, "Down with the dictator! Outlaw him!"

Then the call to charge rang out, a drumbeat heard throughout the palace and in the Orangerie, where in the gathering dark, step by step, bayonets at the ready, the Guard pushed back the protesting parliamentarians. General Leclerc called upon the citizen representatives to withdraw. When they refused General Murat roared to his troops: "Throw these people out of here!" Now it was five o'clock and almost dark. The drums never ceased beating the call to charge. The Guard continued forward, serenely unconscious of the fact that they were attacking the very Assembly they were sworn to protect.

Soon the hall was empty. Hampered by their skirts, the deputies scrambled out into the garden through the tall Orangerie windows and disappeared into the fog; the next day their red togas were found strewn on the ground or hanging from the almost bare branches of the trees.

It was Lucien again who, in search of some semblance of legality, sent out to find stragglers from the Five Hundred in order to recompose something of the lower chamber. The grenadiers rounded up approximately fifty wet and shivering deputies from hiding places in the park and in the neighboring wine shops. At 2 A.M. in the Orangerie, by the light of some guttering candles, before the overturned benches, these fifty, together with the remaining Elders, recognized the end of the Directory and swore an oath of loyalty to a triumvirate of provisional consuls: Napoleon Bonaparte, Emmanuel Sieyès and Roger Ducos.

• • •

Talleyrand went off to dine. Murat hurried to send word of the coup to Caroline Bonaparte at Mme Campan's, and Benjamin Constant delivered the last of his hourly reports of the day to Germaine de Staël at the Swedish embassy.

A messenger had already informed Josephine, terrified by rumors of Bonaparte's assassination, that "the General has saved the threatened Republic, and the spirit of the Republic has saved the General."[9] Fouché himself went briefly to the rue de la Victoire to confirm this; however, he preferred to keep the other Bonaparte women in the dark. Mme Letizia, Pauline Leclerc and Laure Permon were at the theater when an actor announced from the stage that "General Bonaparte has escaped assassination by traitors to our country."[10] Pauline screamed while Mme Letizia, deathly pale, hurried her outside. At the rue de la Victoire, they found the alley, the courtyard and the street outside it filled with the horses and carriages of supporters waiting for news. An anti-Bonapartist friend of Laure's pulled down the carriage window and whispered to her, "Your friend Lucien has just made his brother a king!"[11]

But the street was deserted by dawn the next morning when General Bonaparte and Bourrienne returned to Paris. Bourrienne complained in his journal that he was kept so busy all day at St. Cloud that he had no time to eat until one in the morning, when Bonaparte went off to be sworn in as Consul. Immediately before that the General had called him in to dictate a proclamation in which the chaotic scene of fisticuffs in the Orangerie was invested with some dignity; "twenty armed assassins," he insisted, "fell upon me, seeking my heart with their daggers."[12]

The two men started back to Paris together at 3 A.M. Bonaparte uttered not a word until they reached the rue de la Victoire. Then he asked: "Bourrienne, did I talk a lot of nonsense?" "Quite a lot, General." After Napoleon had calmed his wife and described some of the day, she inquired about Jérôme Gohier. "My dear," he answered, "the man's a fool; he understands nothing. Perhaps I should have him deported." But he was more interested in "the obstacle man," and wanted to know whether Bourrienne believed that Bernadotte had kept his word, or had been at St. Cloud with the other Jacobin generals. "But," and he echoed Bernadotte's thought, "if so, revenge is out of the question because Joseph loves him and Joseph's sister-in-law, Bernadotte's wife, has some influence over him. And I myself. . . .* They would all be against me. Oh, how foolish it is to have to consider family ties.† Good-night, Bourrienne, and by the way, tomorrow, we sleep at the Luxembourg."

---

* If Napoleon, indeed, so expressed himself, he must have believed that Désirée, and through her Bernadotte, might still be affected by him.

† Generals Augereau and Jourdan had attempted that afternoon to convince Bernadotte to lead a revolt against Bonaparte. Bernadotte refused, but later, in the year the Empire was proclaimed, he confessed the true reason for this abstention. In a letter to Lucien Bonaparte—himself in flight for a violation of republican principles—he reproached himself for failing in patriotism "because of Joseph's pleas." "And why?" he wrote, "because Joseph is the husband of Julie, the sister of my wife, Désirée! On such trifles do the destinies of a great Empire depend. . . . You know that there were arms and men who would have served under me . . . but frailty triumphed, thanks to you at the Orangerie and to me, who allowed myself to be cajoled by fine speeches when I could have prevented everything."

❧ 20 ❧

"A Republican Simplicity"

AT TEN IN THE MORNING OF THE DAY AFTER BRUMAIRE, THE BO-
napartes left the house on the rue de la Victoire forever. Josephine's pretty
folly, her mirror-lined dressing room painted with birds and butterflies
and her elegant modern furniture were exchanged for the Gohiers' somber
apartment at the Luxembourg.

Not a minute was wasted on that first day. At noon the three provisional consuls met at the palace. Several ministers were sworn in: Fouché
at Police, Talleyrand at Exterior Relations. When Bonaparte appointed a
new man, Martin Gaudin, to the Treasury he ordered him to take over
there within two hours and to report to him personally that same evening.

For the next five weeks, a commission met daily in Bonaparte's
office. Its task was to replace the provisional government and prepare a
new constitution. Consul Bonaparte could barely remain seated through
the frustrating hours of Sieyès's views on the proposed constitution; he
would bite his nails, cut the arms of his chair to shreds with a penknife
and then escape for a few minutes to Josephine's apartment upstairs.
Finally, in December, Bonaparte summoned the members of the commission to read to them the articles of a "new constitution." It was, as he
once said all the constitutions should be, "short and obscure," and owed
little to Abbé Sieyès's original document. Though they resented the procedure, or rather lack of any—for eleven successive days the meetings had
lasted late into the night—the exhausted men under Napoleon's eye dared
not ask for a vote. Once the "Constitution of the Year VIII" was agreed
upon, Bonaparte proposed that a vote should be taken to name a First
Consul who would be granted full executive powers. He then outmaneu-

vered Sieyès, who had himself hoped for the title, and nominated himself First Consul with a renewable ten-year term and the right to name a Second and a Third Consul whose roles would be consultative only. The essential feature of the new regime was the concentration of authority in the hands of one man, although the First Consul's dictatorial power would be veiled for a time by the creation of a Senate, a Tribunate, a Legislative Body and a Council of State. Bonaparte chose as his two fellow consuls Régis Cambacérès, once a member of the Committee of Public Safety, representing the left, and, to placate the right, Charles Lebrun, a man of the Voltairian Enlightenment but believed to have monarchist leanings.

The Constitution itself and the Consul's powers were to be voted on by the nation in a plebiscite in February. Bonaparte, however, knew that he was already strong enough to mark the first year of the new century as his own. And without waiting for the outcome of the referendum he announced on the last Christmas Eve of the old century that the new Constitution was already in force: "Citizens," he proclaimed, "the Revolution is now established on the principles on which it was founded. The Revolution is finished."

Every morning Bonaparte would leave Josephine's bedroom at eight o'clock. Happier than he had ever been, whistling and humming as he dressed, he could hardly wait to get to his office on the floor below to attack the mountain of work. He would remain there for eighteen or twenty hours at a stretch, breaking off only to run up the communicating staircase several times a day to talk to Josephine.

He was faced by nothing less than the titanic task of reorganizing the whole of central and local government. All his political genius, his organizational powers and his relentless memory were bent to the effort of transforming a ruined country into an essentially modern state. Confronted with a continuing war, a country torn to pieces with murderous hatreds, the rebels in Vendée in arms again and an empty Treasury, he had no trouble in holding his prodigious concentration on the subject at hand. "I never saw him distracted from one affair by another," wrote a colleague, "either from the one under discussion in order to think about the one we had just debated, or the one on which he was about to work. . . . Never was a man more absorbed in whatever was immediate."[1] Napoleon himself would comment on how watertight were the compartments of his mind. Those he worked with during this period agreed that his attention could be centered equally on each of the urgent decisions to be made, whether it was the desperate situation of the unpaid armies, the bad news from Egypt (General Kléber, still unaware of the military coup, continued to forward his despairing reports to the Directory),* a ruined industry, unemployment or the foreign situation.

France was still at war with most of Europe and even with the United States; men were deserting from the armies, the fleet was almost nonexistent since the Battle of the Nile, there were robber bands on the highways and in the cities. Since almost the beginning of the Revolution beggars and the homeless in the streets of Paris had been lining up daily at the free soup kitchens. From the start Bonaparte's minute attention embraced every aspect of the necessary renewal, from the replanting of trees throughout the country to the importing of heifers and bulls from Switzerland to restock the empty cowsheds.

Each minister was instructed to submit nightly reports to the First Consul on the state of the armed forces, civil affairs, law and order, public opinion and the Treasury.

The problem was to raise funds in the First Consul's first months in office. The results of the plebiscite were not yet in. He understood that he would have to wait for the financiers' full confidence in his government before he could be granted the loans that would enable him to put order in the Treasury. Cautiously, some private bankers granted Bonaparte a

---

* The Egyptian situation was one more example of Napoleon's extraordinary luck. General Kléber's indignant dispatches informing the government that his mutinous army was reduced to half its combat strength, that there was a deficit of twelve million francs and that an attack by a Turkish army was imminent were received not by the Directory, but by the First Consul himself.

Further proof of Bonaparte's luck could be seen in the assassination of General Kléber in Egypt before he or his deserted army could return to France.

Additionally, Pauline Fourès, assisted no doubt by Kléber, was hurried onto the U.S. ship *America* soon after Bonaparte's departure. Her arrival in Paris at this early date would have created some embarrassment for the First Consul. However, she was removed from the American vessel and put on a British ship, returned to Egypt and would not reach Paris until late in the following year.

temporary loan in the hope that he would balance the budget and, above all, end the war.

Popular enthusiasm after the coup was only moderate; few believed that the new regime would be long-lived. In Paris there was some optimism and cries of "Down with the Jacobins" and "Peace!" "But peace through Bonaparte," wrote a historian in 1902, "an association of ideas that stupefies us today, was imprinted on everyone's mind. . . . There was not a poster, not a proclamation, not a brochure printed in support of the coup d'état which did not emphasize this end, and the return of the Bourbons in 1814 would be greeted with the same call for 'Peace.' "[2]

Although they might not believe in the permanence of Bonaparte's government, Parisians had heard the words they were waiting for: "the Revolution is finished." The reaction was immediate. Almost overnight the last tricolor cockades vanished from hats. In this first winter of the new century the official almanacs began to give the corresponding dates of the old Gregorian calendar opposite the republican ones, the saint's day printed alongside a vegetable or agricultural implement. 5 Frimaire, "Pig," was now also November 26 (Sainte Geneviève) and 8 Nivôse, "Manure" was printed facing December 29 (St. Thomas). Parisians, however, were grateful for the return of Sunday and a seven-day week; soon only civil servants were required to observe the Décadi. On New Year's Day 1800 a long line of hackney cabs—up to 157 were reported by the police—waited outside the confectioners of the Palais Egalité as citizens resumed the old custom of exchanging sugared almonds and *marrons glacés.*

There was immense curiosity about the First Consul's appearance. Very few Parisians had ever seen him. Avoiding ostentatious or elegant events, he was observed visiting either the Institut or the disabled servicemen at the Invalides—always alone. His "simple Republican dignity" impressed the public, though few were prepared for his appearance.

Baron Guillaume Hyde de Neuville, the head of the royalist spy agency directed from London, was granted an interview at the end of December. While he waited in an anteroom at the Luxembourg Palace "a small man came in, head lowered and shabbily dressed," whom he first mistook for a servant. But as soon as the General stood by the fireplace and raised his head, "he suddenly appeared taller, and the blaze of the look he flashed at me revealed him to be Bonaparte."[3]

To charm those he wished to work with, the First Consul counted as usual on what was described as his "almost feminine seductiveness," and "his original ideas, couched in speech unusually direct for the period, and his dynamism,"[4] were nearly always irresistible. Even Hyde de Neuville, the fervent royalist, was impressed when Napoleon said to him, "Come to me; my government will be a government of spirit and of youth."

Josephine's ascent was not immediate. She was never seen with her husband at any public event. The First Consul still wished to be perceived as the Son of the Revolution, and it was important to him in the beginning to show that the Citoyenne Générale, sometimes referred to as "the Citoyenne Spouse of the First Consul," in no way shared her husband's rank.

But her life changed as radically as her surroundings. In the palace where until a few weeks earlier she had reigned jointly with Thérésia Tallien, she was now forbidden by Napoleon to see any woman of less than perfect reputation, and thus was deprived of every one of her old friends. Her only visitors were those provided with an oval ticket signed by Bourrienne on the First Consul's orders. The type of entertainment was prescribed with equal rigor: by day, charitable events, accompanied by Hortense; and after dinner at five o'clock, usually a game of cards with the two other consuls.

How often did Josephine with her easy forgetfulness think of her admirer Jérôme Gohier in those Luxembourg apartments? Or, more unlikely still, did she ever recall that the palace had been Alexandre de Beauharnais' first prison under the Terror? Les Carmes itself was only half a mile down the street she now inhabited. The acceleration of events in people's lives during this period was so great that even those more thoughtful than Josephine experienced similar lapses of memory. But her forgetfulness would never include the terrible scene after Bonaparte's return from Egypt; the chill of that night never left her. It was noted that now she continually sought his eye, seemed ever to be watching his reactions. "She trembled like a leaf when he appeared," recorded Victorine de Chastenay.

The First Consul declared his wish not only to unite the French nation but also to return to old-fashioned family values and even to decency in dressing. When someone mentioned the recent reign at the Luxembourg, he exploded: *"I* will not be governed by whores," taken as a reference to Josephine's dearest friend. She dared not protest either Thérésia Tallien's exclusion from the Luxembourg or the First Consul's proscription of "voluptuous transparencies." He was sending a message to his wife when he ordered newspapers to print: "Women are wearing silk again, not because of the cold but because both decency and fashion demand it." And he had the already censored press report that at the Luxembourg the First Consul had demanded that in the evening all the fireplaces be lit "as the night is cold and these ladies are practically naked."[5]

One journal noted that when Mme (no longer Citoyenne) Bonaparte was seen at the theater with her husband; she wore white satin and fashionable antique cameos but "no diamonds," it was emphasized. The days when Josephine's friend Fortunée could sit in a box at the theater, naked to the waist and covered in diamonds, were indeed gone forever.

Hortense wrote that her stepfather wished to encourage the silks and velvets of the Lyons manufactures as well as "to free us from the tribute paid to England. [Sheer muslin, woven in India, was imported from Britain.] When my mother and I were dressed, his first question was always, 'Are you wearing muslin?' Sometimes our smiles betrayed us, and then he would rip our dresses in two."[6]

When Talleyrand told the First Consul that there was gossip in Paris about his wife's debts, Napoleon ordered Bourrienne to extract the full sum from Josephine and to show him all the bills. "I can't do it, Bourrienne," she protested, "I know how violent he is and I couldn't face his rage."[7] The sum was so large, she said, that she could only confess the amount of 600,000 francs rather than the 1.2 million that she owed. In vain Bourrienne pointed out that as Napoleon could not conceive of even the phenomenal 600,000, his anger would not be much worse for double the amount; however, he took the halved sum and the bills to his master. Together they examined them. How, they asked each other, could Josephine have ordered thirty-eight hats in one summer month in retirement at Malmaison, while Napoleon was in Egypt? Bourrienne was ordered to pay exactly half the total of the merchants' bills, and Bonaparte imagined the matter to be finished.

• • •

The first two years of the new century, supremely optimistic ones for France, would be remembered by both Napoleon and Josephine as the happiest of their lives. The atmosphere of new beginnings was symbolized above all at the Malmaison court. Its "Republican simplicity," its fresh and pastoral atmosphere, proved to be an ideal setting for the First Consul.

The five-mile drive down from Paris in one of the new light and rapid carriages took under an hour (far less time than by car two centuries later), and the Bonapartes spent as much time there as possible. Ministers of state drove to Malmaison twice a week. Dinner was out of doors in fine weather, and afterwards the First Consul, the ministers and their wives and the young people of Malmaison would play children's games until dark. Bonaparte seemed to have found a childhood he had never known, throwing himself into games of blindman's buff and prisoner's base, and shamelessly cheating at both.

In those early days of Bonaparte's glory, all the principal roles were played by the young. At Malmaison, girls dressed in white were escorted by generals in their twenties. Hortense and the Bonaparte sisters invited their schoolmates from Mme Campan's establishment; many of them were to become part of the imperial court as the consorts of future marshals. Ney, Macdonald, Larines and Bessières all met their wives there. Another boarder, Eliza Monroe, daughter of the American special envoy to France (and future President of the United States), joined the big Wednesday night dinners and the picnics on the lawn, the games and the amateur theatricals beloved by the First Consul, and invariably after dinner, Hortense remembered, Bonaparte would take his wife's arm and lead her off for a walk alone under the trees.

The First Consul, who was determined to create an official family, urged the girls to "marry young, and start a salon." Laure Permon was the first to do this. She married General Andoche Junot when he returned that summer from Egypt; he, of course, was the young man who had accompanied Bonaparte for meals at her family's house when the two officers first shared lodgings in Paris. Laure had been an eleven-year-old at the time Napoleon had proposed marriage to Mme Permon. Neither Bonaparte nor Laure's mother had forgotten the past, and neither was pleased to hear of the engagement. Panoria Permon had hoped for Laure's alliance with one of the great names of France; as for Bonaparte, he warned Junot of his future mother-in-law's "impossible character"[8]; Junot respectfully reminded him that it was the daughter he was marrying.

Laure d'Abrantès never forgot that the Permons had befriended the indigent young Captain Bonaparte, nor that her mother was piqued by his marriage to Josephine so soon after she—Mme Permon—had turned him down. Though Laure might be half in love with charming Eugène and would come to detest her later rival Caroline Bonaparte, there was solidarity between the two Corsican families and resentment of the Beauharnais intruders, enough to account for an occasional undercurrent of malice in her views on Josephine.

Bonaparte insisted that he should decide all the marriages in his entourage. When romantic Hortense fell in love with young General Christophe Duroc, her stepfather's favorite aide, she was forbidden to mention the subject. A more splendid match would be arranged for the First Consul's stepdaughter. Hortense wept, but did not rebel. She was the most popular girl at Mme Campan's school; never beautiful (her portraits, ironically, show her likeness to Alexandre de Beauharnais, who at her birth had disputed his paternity), but "slender as a palm tree,"[9] with her blond coloring and Josephine's charm and kindness, she was everyone's favorite. Napoleon was even a little in awe of her. He did not, it was noted, "use indecent expressions in her presence."[10]

Her brother, handsome and sweet-tempered Eugène, appeared to be the only man present devoid of ambition—other than in his military profession. His stepfather had just promoted him to captain in the newly named Consular Guard, which the First Consul intended to become an elite corps; he himself as its colonel would wear most often the dark green coat with red cuffs and facings, the undress uniform of the cavalry squadrons of the Guard. All his life Eugène would remember the luminous days at Malmaison of the early Consulate.

Bonaparte's pleasure in the property equaled Josephine's own. He bought up to five thousand acres of surrounding land—woods, fields and vineyards. Stables were built. They owned horses, cows, sheep, pigs and chickens, and were proud of their celebrated wine. The house itself had to be enlarged. First, as in the rue de la Victoire, the entrance was closed in with a metal awning painted to resemble striped canvas, to provide some room for the First Consul's aides. As the château was plainly visible from the road and attempts on Bonaparte's life had not ceased, barracks six times larger than the residence itself were built for the Consular Guard at Fouché's insistence.

Soon fashionable decorators would be called in to rearrange the priceless paintings and marbles acquired by the Bonapartes in Italy, and Bonaparte commissioned Louis Girodet to paint a series of murals based on the poems of his beloved Ossian. But for the present, the house was simply made livable, although already in the First Consul's dressing room hung a Leonardo and a Perugino "liberated" during the Italian campaign.

But it was still an unpretentious country house and Laure d'Abrantès complained of the discomfort of the bedrooms on the second floor and the cold of the bare, red tiles underfoot. Three small rooms on the ground floor were converted into a council chamber used for cabinet meetings. They were decorated like a campaign tent and hung with emblems of war, "an ideal model of grandeur on a domestic scale, breathing the same air of elegance and simplicity as the whole Château."[11] There the First Consul worked at a table on which he kept a model of the *Muiron,* the ship in which he had escaped from Egypt the preceding year. He liked to work out of doors, and in summer a little tent containing a desk and a chair was put up on a bridge. In the open air, he said, his ideas were "loftier and larger." Gazelles roamed the park and Bonaparte watched them from his study and sometimes went to the window to feed them all the tobacco in his snuffbox. Josephine was stricken one day when she found him at his bedroom window aiming at her swans on the lake. "Don't, Bonaparte, don't!" she begged, and finally persuaded him to put down the gun.

As Bonaparte was known to prefer women to be dressed in white, this was considered a uniform by all the women there. Perhaps at Malmaison he suspended his habitual question, for Josephine seldom wore anything there other than muslin, "so fine," said Laure d'Abrantès, "that in India it is woven under water so that the threads do not break. It was exorbitantly expensive."

The First Consul knew perfectly well how often Josephine had broken another rule by asking that English seeds and plants be brought to her from captured enemy ships. Her gardens had more than their informal "romantic" design to entitle them to be called *jardins à l'anglaise.* The greenhouses themselves were largely inspired by those Pierre Redouté had visited at Kew Gardens outside London. His first paintings of roses and camellias hung in her bedroom, though his most famous series, *Les Roses,* would be published only after her death.

In her new greenhouses, Josephine had started to grow every known species of plant. She had already introduced several unknown in France: camellia and phlox and the Martinique jasmine. Enormous sums were spent on her favorite carnations and on tulip bulbs from Holland. Roses, though now associated with Malmaison, were not yet popular; they were small, simple flowers that bloomed for a short time only. Josephine liked to point out that three of her plants recalled her husband's conquests: the lily of the Nile, Parma violets and Damietta roses.

By the following winter, a rotunda had been built in the cool greenhouse; the company often took their meals there amid the flowering shrubs. After dinner, in the house there were charades, amateur theatricals and billiards and there were evenings when Napoleon retired to the salon and the candles, remembered Claire de Rémusat, would be "covered with a piece of gauze and he would enjoin complete silence . . . then he would listen to slow and soft pieces of music. We would see him fall into a reverie. On coming out of this condition he was usually more serene and communicative, and liked to describe the sensations he had undergone. . . . The geometrical turn of his mind always led him to analyze even his emotions. No man ever meditated as much as Bonaparte did on the 'why' that governs human actions."[12]

He did not, however, attempt to analyze "the romantic, almost mystical element in his character," which Claire de Rémusat was sure he believed linked him to Josephine, though she could not have known of Napoleon's letter to his wife describing the "magnetic fluid" he imagined flowing between "people who love each other,"[13] a fluid he apparently envisaged as some form of electricity.

It was Laure d'Abrantès who noted that Napoleon's reveries were always associated with visions of women in white dresses walking under the trees at dusk, a dream naturally associated in his mind with Josephine.[14]

Those radiant days of the early Consulate would remain an ineffaceable memory for both the Bonapartes, and Josephine herself reached perfect satisfaction in the joy of Malmaison then, her interests now limited to her family and her flowers, her greenhouses, her animals and her collection of exotic birds; above all, to pleasing her husband.

"Josephine possessed an exact knowledge of all the intricacies of my character," Napoleon once explained.[15] She studied his moods and learned to adjust to them, ever ready to satisfy his caprices, transformed since his return from Egypt into that tender, submissive and helpful wife he had dreamed of. These two years were indeed the zenith of her life, before grandeur and protocol, before the tormenting question of the succession, before her jealousy and Bonaparte's infidelities, and before the threats of divorce.

҉ 21 ҉

HE IS A COMET

"THERE IS NO FEMININE OF THE FUNCTION OF CONSUL," SAID BONAPARTE, and neither Josephine nor any other woman appeared on official occasions. All this was changed when, after one hundred days spent at the Luxembourg Palace, Bonaparte decided to move to the Tuileries, the palace of the Bourbon kings, uninhabited since the August massacre eight years earlier.

In March 1800, after the endorsement of the new Constitution, Parisians guessed that Bonaparte was to leave the Luxembourg when they read in the press that "the First Consul has ordered Citizen David to place in the Tuileries Gallery* the bust of Junius Brutus"—the very one liberated from the Capitol in Rome which Talleyrand had borrowed for his ball for Josephine.

The Committee of Public Safety had met in the Queen's apartments overlooking the garden and had had Liberty Trees planted near the palace windows. Bonaparte had them cut down and, pointing at the red bonnets and revolutionary emblems painted on the palace facade, ordered: "Get this filth out of here!"[1] To disarm the republican party, however, the inscription on the main gate remained: "On 10 August 1792 royalty was abolished in France and will never return."

Early on February 19, Josephine left the Luxembourg; a little later the three consuls drove off too, followed by the Council of State in a procession of hired hackney cabs. There were not enough carriages to be found in Paris, and the cabs' hackney numbers were pasted over for the

---

* This gallery, in a wing of the Tuileries Palace, was to be the nucleus of the Louvre Museum.

occasion. The Consular carriage, escorted by a cavalry guard, stopped in front of the riverside entrance to the palace, the Pavillon de Flore. Less than four years earlier Captain Buonaparte, in his ragged coat and shabby boots, had entered the same door each day to climb to the offices of the Topographical Bureau of the Committee of Public Safety, the post secured for him by Citizen Barras.

The First Consul alighted and, before mounting "or rather *leaping* onto" his horse, looked up and waved to Josephine, standing at a window with Hortense and a number of other ladies. From there they watched as Bonaparte inaugurated the first of the celebrated military reviews in the Louvre courtyard.

Bourrienne has described the crowds' cheers as the troops marched past, with drums beating and bugles sounding and with their torn and blackened standards, and in the following years, all contemporary travelers would write unending descriptions of these reviews. One English visitor that year described the First Consul taking the salute of the different regiments, including his own Consular Guard in their green-faced dolmans and red plumes: "Every man at least six foot and in bearskin bonnets," and the dragoons "wearing a helmet from which is suspended a large braid of hair . . . General Bonaparte removed his hat and bowed as three brigades went by, their colors in shreds and full of bullet holes." Then came the cavalry "approaching at full gallop and stopping with marvelous neatness." Dazzled as this onlooker was by the scene and the martial music, he was still more impressed by Bonaparte's own appearance: "His complexion uncommonly sallow, his countenance expressive, but stern . . . his whole person, like the mind it contains, singular and remarkable."[2]

When this first review was over the Bonapartes returned to the palace and inspected their new apartments. The First Consul was realistic about the chances of the permanence of his occupancy. "It's not enough to be here," he said to Bourrienne, "the problem will be to stay," and leaning out of a window, he pointed at Bourrienne's brother's house: "I watched the siege of the Tuileries from there and the capture of that good Louis XVI, but *I* will remain here."[3]

There were still patches of dried blood in the corridors and on the stairs of the palace, shed by the King's defending noblemen and by the Swiss guards in August 1792, before the royal family was sent to the prison of the Temple. Napoleon took over Louis XVI's rooms on the first floor, but although he had a state bed set up there he slept in Josephine's bedroom. Her own apartments on the ground floor, formerly Marie Antoinette's, were even darker than those at the Luxembourg because the windows looking out on the gardens were above eye level. "I was never made for so much grandeur," Josephine confessed to Hortense. "I will never be happy here. I can feel the Queen's ghost asking what I am doing in her bed."[4]

Napoleon's view was more robust. On their first night at the Tuileries, he picked up his wife and carried her into their bedroom saying, "Come on, little Creole, get into the bed of your masters."[5]

Opposition to Bonaparte had not dissolved. The results of the plebiscite, though trumpeted as overwhelmingly favorable, confirmed a general absence of enthusiasm for the Brumaire coup. There were four million abstentions, but few negative votes. Balloting was not secret, and citizens feared reprisals in the event of a further change of regime. The army, which did not vote, was nevertheless counted as unanimously in favor of the Constitution.

Moderate Parisians had appeared at first to be no more than relieved that the man who stood for peace was now in charge of the country. The masses always thought of him as a protector of the Republic, within and without; they had never imagined him as a head of state,"[6] and much of the current pro-Bonaparte feeling appeared—except in the case of the *philosophes* and the intellectual elite—to be based on an exhausted reaction to the years of Revolution rather than to any feeling that Bonaparte might be a permanent ruler.

The nation as a whole and the newspapers—and the majority of these were rightist in 1800—continued to expect that Bonaparte's pseudo-republic was merely an interim arrangement before the advent of a constitutional monarch: the Pretender (the future Louis XVIII) or perhaps one of the Duc d'Orléans's sons.

The First Consul recognized the fragility of his power; he knew that his government would dissolve were he to suffer a military defeat and Jacobins and monarchists were waiting in the wings. "My power depends on my glory, and my glory on my victories," he reminded Bourrienne.

Although the French armies had defeated the Second Coalition immediately before Bonaparte's return from Egypt, France was still at war with Austria, Russia and England, and the United States; on the Rhine and the Danube, on the Atlantic and in the annexed lands in Holland, Italy and Switzerland. Bonaparte decided on a spectacular plan to relieve the French besieged in Genoa by the Austrian army. It would, he knew, be necessary to leave Paris secretly in order to lessen the period of plotting which would inevitably succeed the news of his departure and when he slipped away before dawn one May morning, dressed in civilian clothes, he warned Josephine to tell no one his true destination.

Inevitably, when his absence became known Paris, as Bonaparte had foreseen, gave way to panic. The Tuileries became a hotbed of defeatism and intrigue as to who should succeed Bonaparte if he were beaten or killed in battle. There was plotting by Jacobins, by former Thermidorians, by royalists, by Sieyès ready with a new constitution, by Fouché and by most of the "Brumairians." Each faction drew up its own list of a new government and a new First Consul. Lafayette was mentioned, as were Carnot, Bernadotte and the Duc d'Orléans. Josephine was ignored by all of them, not least by Lucien Bonaparte, who refused to set foot in the Tuileries because as heir presumptive he claimed it was beneath him to see her.

The scenario of four years earlier resumed. Bonaparte's letters, no longer a passionate flood, but tender notes, were sent to Josephine by every courier, and she, in spite of her fears, was still too indolent to answer, as he constantly complained. He continued to need her near him, however. On May 15, he wrote to her from Switzerland: "I've had no letters from you . . . a thousand tender thoughts, my sweet little one."[7] In his next letter he wrote that in twelve days she could come and join him. On the same date he ordered the women who followed the troops to return to France; rejecting their petition to stay he wrote across it: "Here is an example to be followed: Citoyenne Bonaparte has remained in Paris."[8] He still had not heard from her the following week, but wrote that he "hoped in 10 days' time to be in the arms of my Josephine."[9]

From Milan he sent her a brief account of his daring logistical maneuver. Like Hannibal two thousand years earlier he had transported his army across the great St. Bernard Pass, still covered in snow in May. The Austrians were taken by surprise when Bonaparte came down behind enemy lines; nevertheless they attacked at Marengo on June 14 with superior men and firepower. By two in the afternoon the French army was defeated. Suddenly, General Desaix appeared with reinforcements and by five Marengo had been turned into a French victory. Bonaparte had gambled his future on that battle and almost lost it; had Desaix not arrived in time his career would have ended then.

On June 20, just as she was to hold a reception for the diplomatic corps and members of the government, Josephine was informed of a rumor that the French army was defeated and Bonaparte killed. All those present had heard the same news and watched her carefully. She kept her head, and the reception was just breaking up when a messenger burst in. As he laid two bullet-ridden Austrian flags at her feet, the government and the foreign envoys learned that General Desaix had saved the day and turned the defeat into a brilliant victory.

In Paris the explosion of popular joy and relief was so great that it was, remembered Cambacérès, "the first *spontaneous* public rejoicing in nine years." It was to be almost the last. The nation was certain that peace had come in their time. The entire population of Paris appeared to spill into the streets at the news that an armistice had been signed on the same day as the victory. Cannon roared, every window was lit at night, fireworks exploded over the Seine and Napoleon returned to be greeted, he told Bourrienne, by "acclamations as sweet to my ears as the sound of Josephine's voice."[10]

After Marengo Bonaparte's true reign would start. The First Consul's popularity was so immense that even the royalist Mathieu Molé would write: "Never, except for Washington in America, has the chief magistrate of a Republic been so universally popular."[11]

Already, by the purposely vague Constitution of the Year VIII, the First Consul held more power than either the President of the United States or the King of England, and with his additional mandate of power, Bonaparte set about forging a new France for the nineteenth century. Most of his great institutions were built in the interval between Marengo and the end of the Treaty of Amiens, while the country still believed that the end of the ten-year war had been achieved.

In those two years, the "ardent years of the Consulate," he laid the foundations of all of the administrative and fiscal achievements that were to be his real monuments, created the tightly centralized administration that survives in France, much modified, to this day, restructured the judicial and public educational systems, and created the Bank of France.

Napoleon's longest-lasting civil accomplishment was the Civil Code, better known as the Code Napoléon. His own imprint is most visible in the emphasis on the rights of property, in his view of the family as the basic unit of society, in the civil status of women and in the clear, instantly recognizable language, devoid of legal jargon. In Europe it was exported by the revolutionary armies to the satellite republics and to the conquered and occupied countries, and its basis remains in the civil law of many modern states today.

Under the Civil Code women lost even the freedom and the property rights that had been theirs under the old regime and the Revolution. "A wife must promise obedience and fidelity in marriage" is inscribed in one of the articles of the Code. Josephine herself and the Chaumière circle must have affirmed both Napoleon's doubts of conjugal faithfulness and his distaste for the domination of society by women. Undoubtedly his wife was not far from his mind when he commented during his revision of the code: "We need the notion of obedience, in Paris especially, where women think they have the right to do as they like."

There was only one exception in the Code's attempt to restore family values: divorce laws remained flexible. France noted this, and Josephine's barrenness, and believed that the First Consul had his own reasons for making this exception.

Economic progress was not immediate. After Marengo there was a rebirth of financial confidence as peace appeared certain, but as long as the wars lasted—throughout the First Consul's, and then the Emperor's, reigns—his position would be considered precarious by the financiers. The stock market would lose several points at the beginning of each new military campaign and rise again at each new announcement of peace.

Nevertheless, in the first two years of the Consulate the country's recovery was spectacular, even taking into account the inevitable exaggeration by Bonapartist historians of the state of disruption under the Directory. And "another aspect of this miraculous monument," Madelin has pointed out, is "the singular duration of a work built under conditions of what one deputy described as 'a furious whirlwind.' "[12] At St. Helena the

Emperor himself would recognize that "my greatest victory was my civil government."

Although after Marengo there was a general rallying to the regime, but the Civil Code was bitterly fought by the Institut and by the intellectual elite of the Tribunate. After Brumaire liberals and intellectuals still opposed "the Constitution written in blood" and remained offended by the military aspect of the coup. They believed that in the Code Napoleon much of the democratic promise of the Revolution was betrayed and they could not agree with the First Consul that the Code "gave permanence to the essential accomplishments of the Revolution."

Fouché, who was under instruction to crush all organized opposition, be it royalist, Jacobin or intellectual, attempted with little success to convince the First Consul that it would be politic to permit some token opposition. Talleyrand, too, who knew how much Bonaparte feared the extent to which liberals like Mme de Staël might determine public opinion in Europe, persuaded Bonaparte that a visit to the widow of the *philosophe* Helvétius might go far to reconcile some of the influential ex-constitutionalists.

Mme Helvétius's house at Auteuil, then just outside Paris, was still a meeting place of the "ideologues." The First Consul went there only once; the visit confirmed his view that the salons of the returning aristocracy were a more hopeful terrain, and resulted in his urging both Josephine and Talleyrand to interest ladies of the *ancien régime* in opening salons that would encourage pro-Bonapartism.

The first steps of open opposition between the First Consul and the Revolution, however, came with the announcement of a pact between Bonaparte and the Pope. The First Consul was resolved to reestablish religion "not for *your* benefit," as he announced to the representatives of Catholic Vendée, "but in my own interest." An agreement, the Concordat, was signed, recognizing Roman Catholicism as the official religion of the majority of the French people. However, the clergy was not to be an independent body; it would be paid by the government and be virtually independent of the papacy.

The restoration of the Catholic religion was undoubtedly a shrewd political move, if only, for many, because resting on the seventh day was preferable to waiting for the tenth. Not only was a great part of royalist disaffection neutralized by the Concordat, but the pact, as the First Consul was well aware, was also very much in the new spirit of religious toleration in the country. Some of this religious revival, at least in Paris and among the middle classes, was almost a matter of fashion. The first seeds of faith, as well as of the romantic movement, had been sown by the poet René de Chateaubriand in his newly published *Génie du Christianisme*, whose vogue owed something to the glamour of the author's personal legend. Not a seat was vacant in the fashionable Church of St. Roch when it became known one Sunday that Mme Récamier, a beauty most often in the public eye, was to pass the plate at Mass.

The red bonnet was removed from steeples, in the countryside church bells rang again and on Easter Day 1801 the bells of Paris rang out for the first time in ten years for a *Te Deum* to celebrate the new alliance between France and the Holy See. Though many in the city had been melted down for cannon, the famously deep voice of "Emmanuel," the church bell of Notre Dame, was instantly recognizable. By seven in the morning the First Consul's carriage left the Tuileries Palace to attend Mass at the cathedral, escorted by mounted dragoons, hussars, grenadiers, Mamelukes, and his general staff. Coachmen and lackeys wore the new green Consular livery with silver facings. Mme Bonaparte rode in an unescorted carriage and sat in the cathedral with the First and Second Consuls.

At that famous first Mass only the two defrocked priests, the former Bishop Talleyrand and the ex-Oratorian priest Fouché, could correctly time their genuflections. Most of the rest of the congregation was obliged to take its signals from them. At the solemn elevation of the host, the congregation was astonished to see the troops present arms; Generals Lannes and Augereau were heard to laugh loudly during the service.

Bonaparte was determined to ignore the violent resistance in the army to this betrayal of the Revolution. When General Augereau asked permission to dispense his troops from attending, since the service would be "a denial of the Revolution," the First Consul told him to obey orders; and when Bonaparte asked another general of the revolutionary army what he thought of the service, he replied: "The only thing missing was the one hundred thousand men killed for trying to destroy what you have just reestablished."

As for the private beliefs of the Consular pair, it was assumed that

Mme Bonaparte's attitude would be that of a lady of the *ancien régime*, one of outward observance, at least. The First Consul's own views were hardly ambiguous: "It is not we nobles who need religion," he explained, "but it is necessary for the masses, and I shall reestablish it."[13]

At the Tuileries as much as at Malmaison, Josephine was an essential part of Bonaparte's eighteen-hour day. In their home life she provided the serenity and smiling blandness he needed to calm his relentless tension and impatience. As soon as he left their bedroom at eight he went upstairs to his own apartment, drank a cup of tea or orange-flower water, and had a bath immediately while Bourrienne read him telegrams and newspapers. Sometimes he joined Josephine again for a twenty-minute lunch and again for dinner, which could be as late as midnight. But between meetings, dictation and military reviews he would go to find her, charging down the narrow stairs that linked their apartments at the Tuileries for a few minutes of relaxation. "If he had as much as a few free moments, he came to spend them with Josephine," Claire de Rémusat noted. When he sat quietly reflecting next to the fireplace in her blue and white tented boudoir, Josephine would remain silent. If she was at her dressing table— her makeup was a work of art that took an increasing amount of time—he would mess up her pots and bottles and rumple her hair and deal out some of his painful pinches. "Do stop, Bonaparte," she would sigh.

She was aware that her physical appeal for him remained strong. He continued to spend every night in her bed, but although she knew he needed her Josephine was afraid of him now, of his sudden rages, of the ever-recurrent dread of confessing her debts, and, most of all, of the threat of divorce.

Her fears of Bonaparte's infidelity had been calmed when she learned that Pauline Fourès had returned from Egypt—still childless—the previous winter, and that Bonaparte, although he sent her money and arranged a marriage for her, had refused to see the "Cleopatra of the Nile." Her alarms revived, however, when she heard that General Berthier had found the First Consul and Giuseppina Grassini, the celebrated singer, in bed together in Milan, on the way back from Marengo. Grassini had attempted to seduce Bonaparte during his earlier stay in Milan, before Josephine's arrival there, when his thoughts were only of his wife. Grassini reminded the First Consul that then, when all Italy had been at her feet and she was "in all the splendor of my beauty and my talent, inflaming all hearts, only you remained cold," but now that she was "no longer worthy of him"[14]—she meant no longer young enough at twenty-seven—he had condescended to look at her.

Voices would always have a strong effect on Bonaparte—Josephine's above all—and this time *la* Grassini's soprano and her voluptuous charms prevailed. She was installed in Paris in a little house not far from the folly of the rue de la Victoire, was promptly unfaithful to the First Consul and was soon forgotten by him.

As soon as Josephine discovered Grassini's presence in Paris, she turned to her old friend Mme de Krény: "I am so unhappy, dearest," she wrote, "every day there are scenes with Bonaparte, and for no reason . . . I tried to guess the explanation and learned that *la* Grassini has been in Paris for the last week. Apparently she is the cause of all my troubles. . . . Please try to find out where that woman is living, and whether he goes to her or she come to him here."[15]

Josephine had exchanged the comparative liberty of her life at the rue de la Victoire for one of careful protocol at the Tuileries Palace. In spite of the danger, however, she could not resist once again trafficking in army supplies. At least twice, when the deals fell through or the firms went bankrupt, she abandoned the friends who had negotiated for her and who loyally refused to make use of her name. Napoleon apparently knew from Bourrienne of some of her involvement in these messy affairs.[16]

She wrote an apparently unsuccessful letter of recommendation for a friend of Hippolyte Charles, again on a matter of army contracts, and a letter to Hippolyte himself in which she reproached him for not having called upon her sooner. "I regret all the more not having succeeded," she wrote, "since I would have been happy to prove to you that nothing will change my feelings of the tenderest and most enduring friendship for you."[17]

But she did not see him again. Or did she? Her mysterious letter about a certain gardener has aroused the curiosity of her biographers.

Only one woman had been allowed to escape the universal proscription of Josephine's friends. Mme de Krény, the fellow Creole with whom she had shared an apartment immediately after Thermidor, and to whom she wrote about *la* Grassini, was reluctantly allowed into the Consular circle. Bonaparte had no particular liking for her, but he wished to please her lover Vivant Denon, his companion on the Egyptian expedition and now in charge of setting up the Louvre Museum.

It was to Mme de Krény that Josephine wrote the following enigmatic—and undated—letter:

> Bonaparte decided at seven o'clock yesterday evening that we would sleep at Malmaison; we left immediately, so here I am, dearest, confined to the country for I don't know how long. It makes me deathly sad, Malmaison which once held so many attractions for me is only a forsaken and tedious place for me this year. I left in such a hurry yesterday that I had no time to leave a message for the gardener. As I am absolutely determined to write to him, please tell me what I should say. I do not know what you had arranged with him. Above all I want to express my disappointment to him because, dearest, it is very real.[18]

Mme Bonaparte's days in those first months at the Tuileries were monotonous. She and Hortense went to the theater on most evenings, then upon their return she played whist or a hand of piquet with the Second Consul.

Her former friends were not permitted to appear at the Tuileries. The First Consul, however, had no qualms about borrowing millions from Gabriel Ouvrard whenever none of the other bankers would lend him large sums—and then refusing to repay him. At the beginning of the Consulate, Josephine sent a warning to Ouvrard that he was about to be imprisoned for declining to lend the new government any funds; he was not at home, but staying with Thérésia, who was about to give birth to their child. Imprisoned on some specious excuse, he was freed on condition he finance the Marengo campaign. It could not, Bonaparte admitted, have taken place without his eleventh-hour aid, doubly unwelcome as Bonaparte undoubtedly knew of the banker's loans to Josephine in the past.

There could be no question in the new moral climate of Thérésia's return to their circle, nor of Fortunée Hamelin's, another reminder of the days after Thermidor. And although Germaine de Staël's letters to her father—which she was well aware were all opened by the police—continued to praise the First Consul, she complained that she too was never invited to the Tuileries.

It was made clear that Bonaparte did not wish to hear of anyone visiting Paul Barras in his exile at Grosbois. Very few were willing to risk the First Consul's displeasure. Mme de Staël was one of them. She reproached Barras for his "inertia," but he argued that there was nothing to be done for France: "The country is fascinated by prestige and military glory," he said, "and must submit to despotism before the need for liberty is revived."[19]

Barras's letters to Josephine and to the First Consul remained unanswered. He reminded Bonaparte that "when you were buried in Italy and your enemies attacked your republican glory, I defended you . . . and when your brothers were threatened, they came to me for help. How often have I protected you and your brothers in difficult times? Is this the reward for what you called my great services and for which you vowed eternal gratitude?"[20]

There was no answer from either Bonaparte. A year after Brumaire, Napoleon's police informed Barras that he must leave Grosbois. Threatened with prison, he was forced to depart within twenty-four hours. Immediately, the police removed all his papers, including three large cartons of his correspondence with the Bonaparte family. Paul Barras's long exile had begun.

From the start Bonaparte had made clear that he wanted the adherence of monarchists above all. Immediately after Brumaire he abolished the Law of Hostages, which had made the illegal return of emigrés punishable by death, and by 1802 he had proclaimed a general amnesty for virtually all categories of proscribed exiles. He started by using a selective general pardon: men who had fought against France in foreign armies were not to be granted immunity, and neither could emigrés claim their former possessions if these had already been acquired as national property. In the first year of the Consulate alone, over forty thousand families were permitted to return.

Fouché well knew to what degree the rallying of the former nobility continued to preoccupy Bonaparte, both out of his preference for the manners and language of the aristocrats over those of the men of the

Revolution and of admiration for their tradition of service. Searching for additional means to draw the returning exiles to him and to neutralize the royalist party, Bonaparte decided to have them come to him through Josephine.

Besides her habit of trading in illegal deals, Josephine would continue, to the end of her days, her other old custom of soliciting favors for others from men in power. She was now to be given an opportunity to employ these appeals with official sanction.

"It suited the First Consul to appear to give way to his wife's influence on this matter," noted Pasquier.[21] Although not openly expressing the wish, Bonaparte encouraged Josephine to receive the former aristocrats and to herself apply to have their names struck off the list of "enemies of the Republic." He signified to the ministers involved that they should deal lightly with his wife's protégés. Josephine's kind heart delighted in reuniting members of families parted sometimes for the last ten years, and she was flattered to have some of the great names of France imploring her help. In her celebrated Yellow Salon, they invoked blessings from heaven on this "angel of goodness." Some of the more ungrateful were said to whisper that although her manner and speech were nearly indistinguishable from those of the court of Versailles, her almost too great eagerness, her somewhat deferential wish to be of service, marked her as not one of them.

Josephine flooded ministers and civil servants with applications for forfeited property and civil rights of the returning exiles. She would be infinitely obliged, she wrote over and over, if the Citizen Minister would kindly accelerate the case of Count X and Mme Y. The records of hundreds of returning exiles contain petitions written by Mme Bonaparte, who was never, apparently, tired of listening to their tales of distress. Her successes are attested to by the many files containing her letters confirming that she has "the honor to convey her compliments to Citizen Z and to inform him that he has been struck off the lists." With her customary grateful recognition of the past, any relative, however distant, of hers or of Alexandre's was given special attention. She even secured the return of her brother-in-law François de Beauharnais, although he had joined the Army of the Princes at Koblenz. The First Consul not only had the matter covered up, but also gave Beauharnais an ambassadorial post.

Napoleon believed that he owed Josephine a great deal for the success of what he called his "policy of fusion." "The circumstances of my marriage to Mme de Beauharnais," he dictated at St. Helena, "allowed me some contact with a whole party necessary for my system of fusion, one of the principal and most important points of my administration. . . . Without my wife, I would not have had a natural rapport with that party."[22]

At the same time Josephine was useful to Bonaparte by further splitting the already divided monarchist parties. The Pretender, Louis XVIII, in his faraway exile in Poland, knew that, in his followers' haste to return to France, he was losing all but the most irreducible of them. The Concordat, too, was detaching Catholics from the royal cause and rallying them to the Usurper.

Inadequately informed both as to the state of mind in France and the ambitions of the First Consul, the Pretender sent Bonaparte a letter suggesting that his sword should be used to return the Bourbons to the throne. To Josephine, who was generally assumed to be a royalist by taste and inclination, he wrote assuring her that her views were well known to him and that he had confidence in her influence. Bonaparte's answer to Louis was that Brumaire had been "made in my own interest" and not in anyone else's. Furthermore, to return to the throne, he wrote, the Pretender would have to march in over 100,000 corpses.

Republicans were reassured by the First Consul's response—he had had it leaked to the press even before it was sent to the Pretender—but Josephine was dismayed by it. Her lack of confidence in the revolutionary title of Consul, her need for security and her dread of another Revolution were all part of these fears. And she was certain that Bonaparte himself aspired to the throne and that a king would want an heir.

When she and Hortense begged him to reconsider the royal proposals, Bonaparte only laughed and confided to Bourrienne, "Those damned women are mad. They've had their heads turned by the faubourg Saint Germain [the old aristocratic quarter of Paris]. They should get back to their knitting and leave me alone. But I don't hold it against them."[23]

Although Bonaparte was aware that both royalists and Jacobins had been frustrated in their plans to assassinate him, he was convinced that leftist opposition was the greater danger to his regime. He also suspected Joseph Fouché of protecting the former members of the Convention and wished to get rid of him. After an attempted assassination on Christmas Eve 1800, it was clear that the dismissal would have to wait.

It was a shawl, and Bonaparte's interest in his wife's dress, which saved both their lives. Cashmere shawls had first become fashionable when Bonaparte's officers brought them back from Egypt, "stuffs woven from the down of Kurghize goats, softer than silk, warmer than wool, and so supple that they could be drawn through a ring."[24] They were a supreme luxury, worn only by the wives and mistresses of financiers, women like Mme Récamier and Mme Tallien, until they were finally copied by a Scot who wove them in Paisley. Hortense described them as the "only garment not made in France which survived Bonaparte's proscription, in spite of his frequent threats of burning them." For Josephine, it was the heaven-sent means to veil gracefully, but not entirely, the clinging dresses she continued to wear.

On Christmas Eve, Josephine, Hortense and Caroline, recently married to General Murat, had finished dressing to attend the opening of Haydn's *Creation* at the Opéra. Newspapers had announced that the First Consul was to accompany them. Just as all four were prepared to leave, Bonaparte, who always examined every detail of his wife's clothing, objected that her cashmere shawl did not match her dress. He went ahead in his carriage; she changed her shawl, and almost immediately followed with Hortense and Caroline. Moments later the women were thrown to the ground by an explosion just ahead that destroyed their carriage and one of the horses. There was blood on Hortense's dress. Josephine fainted. Caroline, eight months pregnant, remained calm. They continued to the Opéra, where they found the First Consul safe and already in their box. He said nothing as they entered, but coolly sent for a program. The bomb had gone off in the rue St. Nicaise precisely between the passage of their two carriages, killing and wounding fifty-two bystanders and part of his escort. They were all wildly cheered at the Opéra, but upon their return Fouché was sent for and Bonaparte shouted that the Jacobins responsible for this attack must be shot and France purged of this poison. The minister of police coldly replied that the assassination attempt was the work of royalists and he could prove it. Fouché was right; two Chouans—the royalist guerrillas in the

West—were guillotined and a third escaped to America. Nevertheless, the First Consul ignored the proof and insisted on having almost one hundred former Jacobins deported.

As part of his plan for his own increased power, the First Consul was resolved that his wife's role, too, be seen to be ever more important. She began to appear at official dinners, and when she set off for Plombières again and its fertility-giving waters, accompanied this time by Hortense and Mme Letizia Bonaparte, he ordered that their carriage be escorted by a detachment of cavalry, while some of his aides followed in two more carriages.

Bonaparte directed the ladies to give balls and receptions while they drank the waters and took the mineral baths. On one of these occasions they watched Hortense dance with Astolphe de Custine, son of Delphine, with whom her father had been so passionately in love at Les Carmes, while Josephine and Delphine exchanged reminiscences of prison days.

Tender letters arrived from Bonaparte, whom his wife rightly suspected of carrying on an affair with an actress during her absence. Nevertheless, he wrote, "I love you as I did on the first day because you are so sweet and lovable," and "I haven't had any news from you yet . . . I am sad all alone. A passionate kiss, endless love."[25]

It is impossible to know whether Josephine or her doctor continued to have faith in the Plombières waters. Napoleon at least was still confident in 1801. After Josephine's return from the spa he burst into his study one day and announced to Bourrienne: "My wife's menses have started again!" Even in 1807, the Emperor was writing her that he hoped the Plombières waters might grant her "a little red sea." But Mme de Rémusat recalls a brutal scene this year. When her sister-in-law Elisa brought up the subject of her sterility, Josephine pointed out that Eugène and Hortense were, after all, her children. Sourly, Elisa Bacchiocchi replied, "But sister, you were younger then." The First Consul came in just as Josephine burst into tears. "There are some truths better left unsaid" was his only comment.[26]

• • •

Although Josephine had a mission—the implementation of Bonaparte's policy of fusion—and could feel she had influence and a role, her insecurities increased as her husband's ambitions became ever clearer. She knew that the Bonapartes were constantly pushing him to take another wife, and although they shared Napoleon's own doubts of his capability of fathering a child, the family believed that they would recover their influence once they were rid of her and her children, and that the chance of their own sons' inheritance would be the stronger.

Josephine's attempt to secure at least one ally in the Bonaparte family had been unsuccessful. When Caroline Bonaparte declared her intention of marrying Joachim Murat—handsome, vulgar, sometimes ridiculous, but an insanely brave officer—her brother at first refused his consent and Josephine took up her cause. Napoleon, she knew, was never able to forget the gossip about the famous rum punch supposedly made by her for Murat during the Italian campaign, and that he could not bring himself to like the general in spite of his famously mad courage. At first he refused to hear of the marriage. "Murat is only the son of an innkeeper," he objected, "and in my position, I do not wish to mingle my blood with his." However, Josephine won the day, if not Caroline's support.

For these high stakes Josephine was willing to sacrifice devoted Hortense. Perhaps the least creditable action of her existence was her unspoken appeal to her daughter to preserve her mother's marriage and the Bonaparte succession, too, by marrying Louis Bonaparte. Napoleon immediately fell in with this suggestion; he had long hoped that Louis might be his successor, apparently ignoring the fact that this once charming boy, whose guardian he had effectively become, was now a man suffering from delusions of persecution and from an "undiagnosed" physical disease, believed to be gonorrhea.

Romantic Hortense was the darling of the court, with her mass of blond hair, her perfect and willowy figure, and an expression that matched her genuinely sweet nature. She believed that in this new era she might be allowed to marry for love, although Eugène warned her that Napoleon's ascent would make this increasingly unlikely. She had refused a number of suitors and had recently been deprived of the husband she wanted. Bonaparte was much attached to General Christophe Duroc, his most trusted aide-de-camp, but Bourrienne records the following scene. One evening the First Consul asked Bourrienne, "Where is Duroc?" "He has gone to the Opéra." "As soon as he returns tell him he can have Hortense. The wedding must take place within the next forty-eight hours. I will give him 500,000 francs and the command of a division at Toulon. They are to go there the day after the wedding. I want no sons-in-law around me and I wish to know this very night whether that suits him." Bourrienne was hardly surprised that when a deeply offended Duroc returned and was given Bonaparte's conditions, he stormed out shouting, "In that case he can keep his daughter, and I am off to the whorehouse."

Both Bonapartes lectured Hortense on Louis's merits. It was usual, of course, at the time for a girl to have her marriage arranged by her parents. Though Hortense cared nothing for Louis, nor he for her, her mother's welfare would always be one of her first concerns.

The announcement of the marriage brought a flood of venom from the Bonapartes. Caroline Murat, the most ruthlessly ambitious of the sisters, was especially incensed, foreseeing that a son of Hortense and Louis would now have a better chance of succeeding Napoleon than the child of any of his other siblings. As for Lucien, he informed the perpetually suspicious Louis that Hortense was certainly already pregnant by Napoleon.

The glacial marriage scene took place at the rue de la Victoire. In the house itself—a wedding present from the First Consul—the salon had been transformed into a chapel.* Hortense was whiter than her wedding dress, her eyes swollen by a night of weeping; Louis was sullen. After a nuptial mass—the Concordat had just been signed—Caroline and Joachim Murat, too, knelt for a blessing. In spite of Josephine's efforts, Napoleon refused to have their own civil marriage similarly blessed. She could only conclude that he was keeping open the road to divorce.

On their first night together, Hortense would relate in her *Mémoires,* Louis proceeded to list her mother's alleged former lovers and warned her that under no circumstances would he ever permit her to spend the night under the same roof as Josephine. He ended with the threat that should she give birth to a child even one day ahead of the prescribed term, "I shall never see you again as long as I live."

---

* The *Maison de Brumaire* would be torn down in the mid-nineteenth century, after serving for a few years as the U.S. Legation.

. . .

Although in Cambacérès's eyes, "no word of Bonaparte's ever betrayed a wish to go beyond his present situation, to be anything more than the head of an orderly republic,"[27] those closest to the First Consul were under no such illusion, for his ultimate aims were becoming more apparent daily. Fouché had been instructed to exploit the St. Nicaise assassination attempt and to play up the First Consul's courage on that night.

Even the pretender, who realized perfectly that the recent assassination attempt had strengthened Bonaparte's position, was better informed than Cambacérès. Early in 1802 his agents in Paris reported rumors of the First Consul's desire for a more permanent title, that his taste for pomp was increasing and that he was even said to be contemplating naming some ladies-in-waiting for Mme Bonaparte. The betting in Paris, his agents informed him, was that the Josephine-Fouché coalition would win out against the Bonaparte family, all in favor of a law of succession and the dissolution of Napoleon's marriage.

This outline was accurate. A titanic struggle for power began between Talleyrand and Fouché, who took opposite sides on the question of Bonaparte's now obvious monarchical ambitions. Talleyrand believed these aspirations to be a bulwark against the return of the Bourbons; Fouché, like most of the former Jacobins, was hostile to the idea, but neither did he wish to lose his client Josephine. She, of course, dreaded the issue of heredity.

Bonaparte's popularity in the country was unbounded. Already he was the author of the Civil Code, the man who had "preserved all the benefits of the Revolution," balanced the budget (the new franc would remain stable until 1914) and given France growing prosperity. Pictures of the First Consul before the pyramids, at the Jaffa pesthouse, on a rearing horse crossing the Alps hung in every house.

Only Britain now remained in arms against France, and in 1802 Bonaparte granted the nation's greatest wish when he signed a peace treaty at Amiens between the two countries.

The First Consul recognized that this was the moment to obtain supreme power. The Senate at his instigation was urged to "give him the century which began with him . . . a gift worthy of his devotion,"[28] the Consulate for Life.

For Napoleon there was now only one step short of the crown; it was the beginning of Josephine's torments. The dangers of her own position were inherent in the General's new title and in the principle of heredity that had been added to the Constitution.

Fireworks and illuminations in Paris celebrated the First Consul's new title, and his own star, thirty feet high, blazed above Notre Dame. But "Josephine's melancholy presented a striking contrast to the prevailing gaiety," noted Bourrienne. "She had to receive a host of dignitaries and officials on that evening and did it with her customary grace, despite the profound depression that weighed down her spirits. She believed that every step toward the throne was one step away from her."

The First Consul decided this year to move to a residence more fitting than Malmaison for a court ushering in the beginnings of supreme power. At first he considered Versailles, but rejected it as being ugly, old-fashioned, even "monstrous," and chose the palace of St. Cloud, only a quarter of an hour's drive from the Tuileries. Millions were spent on its redecoration and furnishing. Aware that the Tuileries was considered to be "neither a court nor a military headquarters, but something in between the two," the First Consul was resolved to initiate the first steps toward the pageantry of a glittering court.

Although initially he had rejected David's idea of uniforms for the consuls and members of the government, in this autumn of 1802 he himself wore for the first time a red velvet coat embroidered in gold and a sword hilt set with some of the crown jewels including the historic "Régent" diamond. Smart carriages, liveries for the Consular footmen and a uniform for court officials were the next step. "I have only to gild the court dress of my virtuous Republicans for them to belong to me,"[29] said Bonaparte when he learned that not one former Jacobin had protested against the new court uniform of heavily embroidered red velvet, worn with a blue sash and knee breeches.

He insisted that Josephine's role be seen to be ever more important. Increasingly she appeared at official dinners, at daily receptions and audiences, and at Mass on Sunday at St. Cloud, where for the first time she was placed next to him, above the Second and Third Consuls. In the chapel's royal box Napoleon stood in a military posture, arms crossed, while Josephine was seen to sink gracefully to her knees.

The atmosphere of youth and hope disappeared as the court's center shifted from Malmaison. One observer surmised that it would have been more intelligent of Napoleon had he retained some of the "apparent austerity" of the early Consular days and its "republican simplicity."[30] And after the move from idyllic Malmaison to the cold grandeur of St. Cloud, as dark and sumptuous as the Tuileries, Hortense commented sadly, "My stepfather is a comet of which we are but the tail; we must follow him without knowing where he carries us—for our happiness or for our grief."[31]

⚜ 22 ⚜

A Comfortable Woman

For the first time in ten years all Europe was at peace and foreigners, avid for a first sight of the revolutionary capital, started to pour into the country even before the Treaty of Amiens was signed. Few of them could believe that this dirty and animated city, full of amusements and pageantry, of excellent food and theater, with many of its old customs revived, was the one described by the emigrés a few years earlier.

For the returning exiles it was a city of unrecognizable customs, and yet of a familiar landscape—one in which they almost daily passed the spot where members of their families had been executed. But for the foreigners, overwhelmed by the seductiveness of the new Paris, the shock of the new city was altogether captivating.

Besides the Germans, Russians and Austrians there were ten thousand British visitors alone in 1802 and 1803. Lively descriptions of the restaurants, the museums and libraries, the parks, the shocking fashions and the gossip about the Bonapartes were sent home by the grand milords who had come over in their own traveling coaches and by the comfortable families on their first European outing.

The city itself was still dilapidated. The First Consul was known to be planning majestic streets, and already near the Tuileries Palace the foundations of the arcades of the rue de Rivoli were being prepared in the dust and debris between the Tuileries Gardens and the rue St. Honoré, where the Convention had once sat.

Streets had been renumbered and some of the grotesque revolutionary street names changed. Under the influence of emigrés returning from London, pavements were attempted on some streets, but as these were interrupted in front of each carriage entrance they were discontinued until

329

later in the century. Still, on rainy days Parisians and visitors alike were obliged to wait for planks to be thrown as bridges across the central stream rushing down the middle of each street. Contemporary prints and paintings by Boilly and Duplessis show many scenes of women holding white dresses high in the back, stepping across the boards in their flat sandals.

In the public gardens of the Tuileries, the foreign tourists were alarmed by the "disquieting sexual differences" all too plainly visible on the colossal statues, but they could feel secure in the Summer Gardens almost as popular now as immediately after Thermidor. Where Thérésia and Josephine once reigned, couples still ate ices in the shady groves, but a sign of the new morality was evident in the reassuring note added by the management to a poster announcing a ball: "The extreme decency which reigns in so large an assembly permits the mothers of families to bring their young ladies to a place where they can find amusement without damage to their morals."

English visitors were surprised to find that the new waltz could be danced with any propriety. "I was astonished," wrote one of them, "to observe that even men dancing with the handsomest women in the room, have sufficient command of themselves not to shock either their partner or the company by being guilty of the slightest impropriety."[1] And they found that the Palais Egalité was as much the center of entertainment as before the Revolution. Even the boutique devoted exclusively to hot waffles had survived. All the best restaurants were there, as were the gaming houses, print sellers and bookshops. There was no sign of the "new morality." However, some of the books displayed under the arcades were "such that Sodom and Gomorrah themselves would have prevented their being printed," noted one English visitor. He had hardly set foot in the Palais Egalité before a voice whispered: "Would Monsieur care to buy the 'Licentious Life of Madame Bonaparte'?"[2] It remained the center of prostitution of Consular and imperial Paris much as it had been in 1787 at the time of Captain Bonaparte's initiation there. In the low windows of the mezzanine floors the girls could be seen all day long, singing, playing cards and hailing passersby. Visitors commented that they obviously wore not a stitch under their clinging dresses—garments that were always held "tightly at the back against their thighs, so that," wrote the German Kotzebue, "nothing of their shape would be lost"[3]—and appeared able to survive rain and sleet in the winter streets, clad only in these exiguous garments.

In spite of the First Consul's commands, French styles could still alarm and disgust foreigners. Those who had never witnessed the exaggeration of fashion immediately after the Terror could not guess how radical was the change from the days of Thermidor. For the British tourist the "gross display of bosom" was deplored, "inspiring sensations of disgust and disrespect rather than admiration,"[4] and the recently arrived British author Fanny Burney was warned by her Paris dressmaker that she would be stared at in the street if she continued to wear her six petticoats and her old-fashioned corset.

Parisian men, too, were pronounced by the English to be "remarkable by their total lack of elegance," yet it was Beau Brummell's cross-Channel influence of black or dark blue coats and immaculate white linen which had taken hold and would evolve into the masculine costume of the nineteenth and twentieth centuries. The effect was disconcerting to some. The portrait painter Elisabeth Vigée-Lebrun, who had returned to France from exile in St. Petersburg and was unaccustomed to seeing men only in dark colors, could never, she said, resist the impression she was at a funeral. The cut of men's hair in Paris was still modeled on Roman busts; one Englishman submitting to a French hairdresser on his first night in France found his powdered queue cut off, his hair cut short and curled, and a pair of sideburns glued to his cheeks before he could protest.[5]

Food, the restaurants and the new mealtimes and customs of postrevolutionary Paris were all subjects of intense curiosity, and of most of the letters written home by the visitors. They soon became used to the "abominable habit of dining sometimes as late as seven in the evening." At old-fashioned wealthy houses the dinner table would still be laid with up to eighteen dishes, but at more up-to-date ones the new custom of passing the courses separately had started. The French innovation of place cards laid on the napkins of guests was viewed with alarm. In one German's opinion this was an unpleasant custom "since it sometimes places guests next to persons they would not have chosen."[6] Some private houses even featured a menu, and visitors noted with surprise that "in certain restaurants the price of refreshments is indicated on a long piece of paper called a *carte*."[7]

As soon as dinner was over there was a mass movement toward the theater; the revolutionary dependence on it remained. "The French need to go out for distraction," observed one English visitor. "The Parisian will first buy a theater ticket and then, if there is money left over, go and drink some coffee and nibble a biscuit. In London, a steak and a pint of sherry is more important than the theater."[8] One Englishwoman recorded her wonder that whenever dinner was not succeeded by the theater "whatever occupies us in the evening is shared in common, as ladies and gentlemen never think of separating or finding amusement out of one another's society." Germaine de Staël's decision not to choose political grandeur in London appears to have been based on sound information.

It was clear that an era of conspicuous consumption had returned with the First Consul's insistence on the importance of luxury industries. "Goldsmiths and jewelers are obliged to work night and day to keep up with orders," reported the now ubiquitous police. Carriage-makers and dressmakers worked around the clock, and that winter more than one million yards of satin and tulle were sold for dresses to be worn at what was calculated as eight thousand balls and five thousand dinner parties.

"Jacob's Fine Furniture warehouse is making various things for Bonaparte," wrote one visitor.[9] No one who could afford it would continue to own a Louis XVI or, worse, a Louis XV rococo piece. Cabinetmakers were creating fine mahogany furniture in the Consular style for the bankers and financiers, as well as for all the Bonaparte family members. Military themes were more popular than ever, and the little tented room and the bronze-painted beds of the rue de la Victoire were much copied, on a grander scale, in all the fashionable houses.

Still, the ultimate aim of every foreigner, after sampling the pleasures of the Summer Gardens, the restaurants and the military parades at noon, was to be invited to a reception at the Tuileries. Such was the aura of the First Consul's personal legend that it was not unheard of for English visitors to arrive in Paris in the morning, watch the parade, see their hero across the Tuileries courtyard and leave for Britain the same evening.

To be received at the palace required a request for presentation from the foreigners' ambassador, and as the First Consul was becoming increasingly difficult about whom he would receive, the visitors, while awaiting the magical summons, crowded through the Tuileries and Malmaison.

There was enormous interest in the interior decoration of the private apartments of the palace. The dark, high-ceilinged rooms, hung with tapestries and painted in the seventeenth century, had been "lifted" by gilding and by mirrors everywhere; these were not framed, but draped in material. At the request of the First Consul, sconces and chandeliers, too, were swathed in gauze. He could not stand bright lights—as little, he said, as highly colored dresses on women. Tables, chairs, candelabra and Sèvres porcelain ornaments were all decorated in the contemporary taste with sphinx heads, winged lions and Roman helmets.

Miss Berry wrote back to England that gold-fringed, blue-and-white-striped curtains hung in the First Consul's and Mme Bonaparte's bedchamber, "the one where they actually both sleep in one bed"—still a subject for marveling by the pre-Victorian upper classes—and that Mme Bonaparte's dressing room was "very elegant with a low ceiling and curtains embroidered in muslin. Between it and Hortense's red bedroom were several little negro servants."[10]

Bonaparte was known to be unable to abide any sarcasm from the foreign visitors about his court or his dwellings. Reports of their disdainful references to Malmaison infuriated him.

Bertie Greatheed, a Shropshire squire, recorded in his journal that Malmaison was "a poor old affair, washed yellow and backed by a good square patch of wood and planted without the least taste. . . . But there are swans and Cape geese, etc., and a pheasantry and the whole looks snug, and gives the idea that the mistress is a comfortable woman." He noted that in Josephine's room, books on botany were the only ones to be seen. "The bed, very handsome against the wall with mirrours as usual. Bonaparte always sleeps with his wife."[11]

The First Consul's reaction to these sneers was a resolve to make his court the most imposing in Europe. The Swedish Count Armfelt, who had known the court of Versailles, was amazed by the "grandiose public splendor, far greater than what you see in our time in most courts." The Prussian minister whose own king, like the Swedish and the English monarchs, followed the late eighteenth-century fashion for simplicity, wrote that the etiquette of Versailles was enforced at the Tuileries and that the opulence of liveries and of equipages was unimaginable. Bonaparte, wishing, he said, to revive the "tone" of the *ancien régime,* ordered that the Versailles curtsy be taught to the young women of his court. They learned to plunge into it as Bonaparte and Josephine, following a few steps behind her husband, entered a salon for the reception of distinguished visitors. To the undisguised rage of the Bonaparte sisters, women stood up when the First Consul's wife entered the room and rose again as she left.

Mme Bonaparte's own new eminence was generally considered to show the extent of the changes accomplished by the First Consul. Ambassadors were invited to bring with them notable persons of their own countries, and when they were presented to Josephine the same etiquette was reserved for her as formerly for the Queen of France. Although she herself remained seated during those introductions she had found a tactful way of half rising from her chair at each presentation, murmuring a few suitable words.

At these receptions, always held in Josephine's apartments, once the visitors were assembled, she usually came in before her husband, her left hand placed on the back of Talleyrand's right hand, as he presented her to each of the guests. The First Consul would then erupt a few minutes later from Josephine's private rooms.

Visitors invited to the still more prestigious weekly dinners advanced up the Tuileries stairs between a line of grenadiers, then through several antechambers filled with military music, until they reached Josephine's Yellow Salon. In the room selected for dining, where the First Consul and Mme Bonaparte in a blaze of diamonds were seated on a dais, the perfume of orange blossoms and roses planted in moss down the full length of each table was said to be intoxicating.

"People were unanimous on the subject of Josephine's perfect grace and her skill, both natural and cultivated, in the salons of the Consulate," wrote Napoleon's valet Constant, but there was never any doubt as to which Bonaparte was the center of the visitors' attention.

J. F. Reichardt, the German composer, described his visit to St. Cloud. Millions had been spent on the palace; fountains, cascades and frescoed galleries had been restored by Bonaparte's favorite architects, Percier and Fontaine. Arriving visitors found the soldiers of the Consular Guard drawn up in the courtyard. Over the great marble staircase hung David's *Bonaparte Crossing the Alps* and a portrait of Josephine by Gérard. In the audience chamber where palace prefects and ladies-in-waiting marshaled the visitors, they waited with a hundred or so other guests. This time Bonaparte came in first, a palace prefect "shorter than he" on either side of him. He asked a few questions and hurried on, usually without waiting for an answer. Josephine followed a few paces behind, similarly introduced by the prefects, taking her time and showing lively interest. Mme Bonaparte appeared to Reichardt "older and thinner than I had thought; her manners are those of the former court though showing perhaps more graciousness and amiability than her position required. She spoke to the Russian and Polish ladies for some time, but it was amusing to note that the most dazzling smiles, the most seductive glances were aimed at the First Consul; the Polish ladies especially, with their languorous airs and their expressive eyes fixed on their hero, were charming. Their manners toward his wife, though proper, were quite different. They looked at her diadem and that was all."[12]

Each visitor recorded his or her impressions of Bonaparte at the age of thirty-four. Many were struck by "the magical power of his expression." "He looks like no one else in the world. . . . The most seductive smile ever seen."[13] Redhead Yorke, too, was struck by his "strikingly fascinating smile. . . . His expression becomes terrible when angry; his manner is that of a man who nourishes vast projects. His features seem to betray a violent and murderous ambition; something in them reveals somber and turbulent passions."[14]

They were all a great deal less interested in Mme Bonaparte's appearance. Miss Berry was another who found Josephine older-looking than her portraits and wrote that she compounded this by hanging the too-flattering portrait by Gérard in one of the reception rooms. She granted, however, that Mme Bonaparte "is very distinguished looking," while another visitor, who saw but did not speak to Josephine, was surprised to find that there was nothing immediately striking about her. "If chance had not placed her on such a pinnacle, she would escape minute observation."

There was general agreement, however, that the two principal actors, at least, appeared to have lived all their lives in this royal stateliness. Josephine had taken quite naturally to the position of first lady of France and "her knowledge of the world," wrote Méneval "her exquisite politeness, her sense of the right word and the right action and her irresistible attraction convinced us all that she might have been born for the role good luck had given her." There had never been any doubt in the First Consul's mind that *he* had been born for that role.

For the visiting foreigners, almost as interesting as the rigid presentations at the Tuileries were the glimpses of the unfamiliar social life resulting from the Revolution, the emigration and the new caste. "The fusion," as Miss Berry noted, "was far from complete."

The foreign visitors flocked to Talleyrand's "days," to Laure Junot's, to all the Bonapartes' and to the salons of the dissidents—above all, to Mme Récamier's Thursdays, viewed in much the same light as a visit to the theater.

As indispensable to have been seen as any national monument, Juliette Récamier's house itself exemplified the latest in fashionable *nouveau riche* taste. The interior decoration, furniture and marble mantelpieces were a riot of reproductions of the antique: of lion's muzzles and paws, of rams' feet and sphinxes, above all the Egyptian motifs, popular for the last twenty years in all neoclassical forms and doubly so now, since they could be labeled *"Retour d'Egypte."* Members of the government and of the Bonaparte family, foreign visitors, court officials and a sprinkling of returning emigrés crowded into the Récamier rooms. The hostess greeted each guest with "Would you like to see my bedroom?" before leading them in to exclaim over the bed, placed on a dais and enveloped in a cloud of white muslin, its head, unusually, set against the wall.

Juliette ended each evening reception by dancing for her guests, or rather by melting into a succession of "attitudes" said to resemble those on ancient Greek vases. Foreign visitors had no hesitation in standing on the Jacob chairs for a better view, and M. Récamier himself, a thrifty man, would place napkins under their feet to protect the seats of violet nankeen.

Miss Mary Berry was struck by the ingenuous pride with which Juliette offered her beauty as a spectacle. "She seems to think only of herself and never to be interested in others," she noted. Some of the new customs were startling to the foreigners. During a ball at her house that winter, Mme Récamier retired to bed beneath "muslin sheets trimmed with lace, her beautiful white shoulders exposed, perfectly uncovered to view, in short completely undressed and in bed. The room was full of men."[15]

If Mme Récamier could not yet be included in the rank of dissidents, the First Consul's animosity toward Thérésia Tallien Cabarrus was well known.

I have it on good authority that Bparte was refused by Madme Cabarrus, Talien's wife before he married Madme B——, who was at that moment Talien's Mistress. That an hour after he did marry her he set off for Italy, and an hour after that she was in bed with Talien. Now Talien is abandoned, deserted by all the world. The good-hearted Cabarrus is cut by the Ladies for being Unchaste, while the wife of the

First Consul sees all France at her feet, and the representatives of all the Sovereigns of Europe bending before her!!! . . .[16]

The information of the "good authority" was somewhat confused, but Thérésia Cabarrus, although "cut by the First Consul," continued to open her doors to any lady not afraid of him. Returning emigrés were grateful to her for her role at Thermidor; over and over they asked to recount the tale of her days in the prison cell and of Robespierre's particular spite toward her.

Foreign visitors were "absolutely transfixed by her air and appearance." One of them wrote "even before I knew that it was she, I was caught by the most enchanting smile I ever saw . . . the sweetest expression and mildness. . . . I cannot describe my astonishment at hearing it was the ill-renowned Mme Tallien who I had pictured as daring, intrepid and dazzling. . . . But no Frenchwoman is dashing, nor none attempts to take your admiration by storm."

All Thérésia's correspondence was opened by the police, her every move watched. Fouché never failed to call to Bonaparte's attention any item that might ridicule or discredit her. No word reached Thérésia from the Tuileries. Accounts of some of the First Consul's sallies to the women at court were repeated to her. Although the Merveilleuse connection was outlawed at the Consular court, Aimée de Coigny was still seen occasionally at the Tuileries. At a court function in front of a packed assembly, Bonaparte was said to have appeared shaken by her cool answer to his crude question, "Do you still like men as much as ever, Madame?" "Yes, Sire," she replied, "when they are polite."

Perhaps Thérésia was fortunate not to have to leave herself open to so much brutality. She did not think so. It was painful, after the years of sovereignty in Paris, to be denied any part of the new order or of the society of her old friends.

It was noted that Gabriel Ouvrard himself never appeared at Mme Cabarrus's receptions—out of delicacy, it was assumed. He, too, along with most of the other financiers, bankers and former members of the Chaumière circle, was never invited to the Tuileries court. The First Consul's hostility to bankers and financiers was well known but there were additional, and personal, reasons for his special detestation of Gabriel Ouvrard. A man of legendary generosity and countless friends, he was known to have often "lent" large sums to Josephine as to so many others. There may have been some residual jealousy too of his success with Thérésia; and, finally, Ouvrard had had the courage to visit Barras after Brumaire.

Bonaparte's contempt for intellectual and independent women had always found its ideal mark in Mme de Staël. Now he could detest in her the "ideologue" who still believed in the original liberal aims of the Revolution and who was beginning to criticize openly the Life Consulate. She had been tireless in her praise of the General immediately after Brumaire, violently disagreeing with her father when he wrote from Switzerland a warning that although there "would now be the appearance of a Republic, yet all authority will be in the hands of the General."

Germaine, however, remained fascinated by Bonaparte. Knowing that all her correspondence was opened, in every letter to her father she applauded Marengo and praised the government. No invitation to the Tuileries arrived and an ungrateful Talleyrand ignored her. Bonaparte complained loudly and in crude detail that "*la* Staël" was too masculine and furthermore that she was continually throwing herself at him. He knew that although her husband was no longer his country's ambassador, Germaine's salon remained crowded; that it assembled every shade of opinion, all the Napoleonic elite, the ministers and officials, as well as the Bonaparte family, Talleyrand himself and Fouché.

When Germaine learned that she at last would meet Bonaparte again at a soirée given by General Berthier, she prepared herself with a number of profound ideas and opinions. Once again she was routed. It was her custom to wear particularly low-cut dresses revealing her generous bosom. Napoleon, passing by and noting an unusually vast display of flesh, almost involuntarily shot out, "You must have nursed all your children yourself, Madame?"[17] Shocked and unprepared, Germaine froze and could not answer.*

As she watched the increasing authoritarianism of the regime Mme de Staël's disillusion grew, and with the announcement of the Life Consulate her salon became a rallying point of opposition to the regime as she attempted to mobilize the intellectual elite of the country against the Life

---

* So well attended was this reception of General Berthier's that no one was surprised when some guests who had left their residences at nine that evening arrived only at five the next morning. Police had calculated that twelve hundred carriages, each with its horses taking up a space of thirteen feet and allowing its passengers one minute to dismount, could make the drive as long as twenty hours.

Consulate. Bonaparte was aware that at least two of his generals, Moreau and Bernadotte, formed part of the de Staël dissident circle; both were regarded as leaders of the republican faction and as rivals for his power.

But Germaine continued to hope to win over the First Consul by her writing. Her novel *Delphine* came out in the winter of 1802. The first reviews were ecstatic. In Paris it was noted that the streets in the center of the capital appeared emptier than usual. The English recorded in their diaries that they stayed in their hotel rooms without going out until each member of the family had rushed through the novel. "We are all in floods of tears," wrote Lady Bessborough, ". . . not a soul in the streets."[18]

Paris gossip recognized most of the thinly disguised protagonists in the novel. Many of Germaine's former lovers played roles in the book; two of them, models of the unfaithfulness and insensitivity of men, were clearly based on Benjamin Constant and Louis de Narbonne. Talleyrand was cast as an evil old woman. As the heroine Delphine, Germaine depicted herself as brilliantly witty as well as sensitive and desirable, and also (she had, she admitted to Juliette Récamier, always longed above all for her friend's beauty) ravishingly fragile.

Talleyrand's own verdict on *Delphine* was the most devastating. "Mme de Staël," he pronounced, "has succeeded in disguising us *both* as women."

The First Consul, intensely irritated by the book's success, read a digest of *Delphine*. He found its themes obnoxious and immoral. He was outraged at the notion of love being above social rules, its heroine disdainful of the world's opinion, in love with love and with liberty and a victim of society. His reaction was brutal. He ordered the official *Moniteur* to write a withering review; then he gave orders that Mme de Staël not be allowed within forty leagues of Paris. She had been visiting her father in Switzerland and had been on her way to Paris, hoping to be there when the novel was published. When she came to within ten leagues of the capital, she was driven back by the First Consul's police.

Foreign visitors congregated in the salon of Joseph Bonaparte, too, almost openly criticizing the extreme physical deficiencies of his wife. "Madame Julie is a perfectly vulgar little woman—very thin and very ugly," was one visitor's description of Désirée's sister.[19] The house of the other Clary sister, married to General Bernadotte, was not on the visitors' circuit, but the General himself could be seen at Mme de Staël's salon and at some of the other dissidents'.

Jean-Lambert Tallien was another one of the Chaumière circle who had vanished from the scene, too obscure now to qualify as a dissident. Upon his return to France from Egypt he was unaware at first of the changes in Consular France, or that Bonaparte had read his last letter from Cairo. Writing to Director Barras, Tallien had described the situation of the French army "abandoned by a general given the command of an expedition instigated by himself." He then compounded this offense by going to visit Paul Barras at Grosbois the day after his return to France, just weeks before Barras was ordered by the Consular police to leave the property. Without money or friends or a roof over his head (Thérésia had sent a message informing him that the Chaumière was rented), he found that the First Consul's ministers had orders not to allow him to hold any office.

The Lafayettes were a family rapidly qualifying as an opposition household. The First Consul remained preeminently jealous of all the liberal establishment figures, of the ex-constitutionalists and of the remains of the "American School," who refused to admire or support him. Although it had suited him at one time to copy George Washington's model of a modern Cincinnatus—a bust of the American President was always present on his dressing room mantelpiece—he was jealous of him, too. When Washington died in 1799, a few days after the coup of Brumaire, Talleyrand had proposed that a statue of the President be erected in Paris. The suggestion was brusquely rejected and Bonaparte was equally displeased by Talleyrand's funeral praise of the President and of "the people who will one day be a great nation, and who are already the wisest and happiest on earth."

Intensely irritated by the enthusiasm that had greeted Lafayette upon his recent unauthorized return to Paris from prison, the First Consul sent word that he wished him to show himself as little as possible. The final break came in 1802 when Lafayette refused to vote for the Life Consulate on the grounds that he could not do so "until public liberty was sufficiently guaranteed." Bonaparte's vengeance was immediate and embraced the entire Lafayette family. The name of his son, George Washington Lafayette, was removed from the army promotions list; his son-in-law, too, was forced out of the army.

Charles James Fox and his wife paid a visit to the Lafayettes. Fox, briefly minister of foreign affairs in England, was the exemplification of liberal, pro-French opinion in London. The legend of a warm friendship between Fox and Bonaparte was formed before the two had even met, but

Fox's reception by the First Consul proved disappointing to both men, and they parted "displeased with each other." Afterwards Fox confided to his secretary, Trotter, that he had had a long conversation with Mme Bonaparte on gardens: "Whatever her past errors," he commented, "she has now redeemed them by the many good actions she has performed." "Alas," Trotter added in his journal, "she has to depend on a great display of rouge because of the great differences of age between herself and her husband."[20]

While Fox and Trotter were still in Paris the London papers had apparently published some ungallant reference to Josephine. In February 1803, Trotter noted: "Bonaparte is extremely out of humour with the articles in the *Morning Post* and *Chronicle*; it seems to me very blaggard and illiberal to attack a woman for faults which every woman would willingly get rid of if she could—viz. being neither young nor handsome. I think it worse in this instance because she is already oppressed enough and yet generally beloved for her extreme goodness and humility."

Trotter's own final verdict on the First Consul was: "Never was there any character that united such contrast of greatness and littleness, never one that roused admiration and contempt, compassion and indignation, so much as in this man."

In spite of the seductiveness of the new Paris, visitors were becoming increasingly conscious of the climate of constraint. They found themselves under the strictest surveillance from the moment they arrived in France.

The power of the police was obvious; French citizens, too, were considered suspect. When, after Brumaire, Bonaparte invited Fouché to reorganize the police, "Spy on everyone except me" had been his instruction.

"Unlike the English," wrote Bourrienne, "Bonaparte could never bring himself to despise newspaper libels and he would always revenge himself. He was, at all times, the declared enemy of the liberty of the press. There was always a quarrel between the First Consul and the English newspapers." Bonaparte, he said, had asked the English Chancellor of the Exchequer for legislative measures against the licentious writings he complained of, but "the Chancellor advised him to treat the libels with profound contempt.... I believe," added Bourrienne, "that this nervous susceptibility to the libels of the English papers contributed as much as, and perhaps more, than the consideration of great political interests, to the renewal of hostilities."[21]

23

SAINT NAPOLEON

EUROPE'S HOPES FOR PEACE VANISHED ON MARCH 13, 1804, WHEN BO-naparte insulted the British ambassador at an official levee at the Tuileries, a scene that led, as he had apparently intended, to the abrogation of the Treaty of Amiens.

The ambassador had already spent some unpleasant months in Paris. Requests for meetings with government officials were met with hostility and proved increasingly expensive. Joseph Bonaparte, the principal negotiator of the treaty, had demanded large sums of money for an audience; Talleyrand's own price was astronomical. Unlike his American counterpart, Lord Whitworth paid without question.*

Both countries had been violating the terms of the peace. France, London claimed, was continuing its policy of annexation and occupation (Holland, Switzerland and Piedmont were still occupied) whereas Britain had not withdrawn its forces from Malta, the key to the command of the Mediterranean, nor returned the island, as had been agreed at Amiens, to the Knights of Malta.

The subject of Malta was not the British ambassador's only claim to unpopularity at the Tuileries. Bonaparte particularly disliked tall men. Lord Whitworth stood over six feet so the First Consul was compelled to

---

* Livingston, the U.S. minister to Paris, had been astounded when Citizen Minister Talleyrand told him frankly that the commercial treaty between the two countries could not be concluded for less than two million francs.

  Livingston should perhaps have been forewarned when he was greeted by the First Consul at a diplomatic reception with the words, "You come to us from a free and virtuous republic into a world of corruption."[1]

stand on tiptoe as he hurled insults at him in language so coarse that the ambassador refused to quote them precisely in his diplomatic dispatch. For the next two months discussions dragged on between the two countries. Neither Bonaparte nor the British cabinet would yield. Lord Whitworth and most of his countrymen left for England, and on May 18, 1803, King George III declared war on France.

In spite of the opening of hostilities, France continued to believe the successful government propaganda that presented the First Consul as a man of peace, pushed into war against his will.

Once again Bonaparte proceeded to build an army for the invasion of England. By June he was already on the Channel coast setting up camps for sea and land forces, examining new types of invasion craft capable of conveying an army, horses and armaments across the Channel. He had apparently forgotten his doubts about the French navy, made in his report to the Directory before that planned invasion of England, and before the destruction of one entire squadron of the French fleet at the Battle of the Nile. Far more optimistic than any of his officers, the First Consul believed that "in three days, granted favorable circumstances and foggy weather, I could be master of London, the Parliament, and the Bank. . . . "[2]

From one of his tours of inspection along the coast, Bonaparte must have written Josephine a letter that filled her with such happiness and gratitude that it jolted her into writing her own poignant answer. It is almost the only surviving letter we have of hers to him:

> All my sadness vanished, as I read your touching letter and the expression of your feelings for me. How grateful I am to you for taking the time to write at such length to your Josephine. You cannot think how much joy you have given to the woman you love. . . . I will always keep your letter which I press to my heart. It will console me for your absence, and guide me when I am near you, for I want to be always in your eyes as you want me to be, your sweet and tender Josephine, my life devoted only to your happiness.
>
> When you are happy or for a moment sad, may it be upon the bosom of your devoted wife that you pour out your joy or your grief; may you have no feelings that I do not share. All my desires amount only to pleasing you and making you happy. . . . Adieu, Bonaparte. I

will never forget the last sentence of your letter. I have locked it in my heart. How deeply it is engraved there and with what ecstasy my own has answered it! Yes, oh yes, that is my wish too—to please you and to love you—or rather to adore you. . . .[3]

But the idyllic years were over for France and for Josephine too. Never had her fears of Napoleon's monarchical and dynastic ambitions been more justified. Within a few months of the end of the Amiens Treaty the pace of his grand despotism increased.

On August 15, 1803, a date celebrated for centuries in every Catholic country as the Feast of the Assumption of the Virgin, the First Consul's birthday was formally celebrated and Saint Napoleon's Day proclaimed a public holiday. This may well have been the first time the nation had been aware of its ruler's bizarre and unpronounceable first name. Hitherto, he had always been referred to either by his title or as Bonaparte. Within a few months the country would recognize it, however, when, while still maintaining the fiction of a republican regime, gold coins were first inscribed "Napoleon Bonaparte, Premier Consul."

Each manifestation of increasing hubris was encouraged by Talleyrand, who now devised a new precedent to bolster the First Consul's arrogance.

It was announced in the spring of 1804 that court mourning was to be worn for ten days by the First Consul and his family, by ministers, palace and government officials, and by the diplomatic corps to mark the death of General Victor Leclerc. The ambassadors accredited to the Tuileries were stunned when they learned that they, the representatives of the Holy Roman Emperor, of the Tsar of All the Russias and of all the other European monarchs, were to express their sovereign's condolences on the death of a general risen from the ranks of the *sans culotte* army.

General Leclerc was, of course, the First Consul's brother-in-law, sent by him to reconquer France's richest colony, Santo Domingo (modern Haiti). At St. Helena, Napoleon would describe the expedition as "one of my greatest errors. . . . I believe that Josephine, being born in Martinique, had some influence on that expedition—not directly, but a woman who sleeps with her husband always exerts some influence over him."[4] (On another occasion, however, he declared: "It would be enough for my wife to wish one thing, for me to do the contrary.")

Slavery had been abolished in the island in 1789 and it was now ruled by the remarkable Toussaint l'Ouverture, who had proclaimed its independence in the previous year. "Remember, brave Negroes," Napoleon had announced immediately after Brumaire in a proclamation to the people of Santo Domingo, "that France alone recognizes your liberty and your equal rights," a message conveyed "From the First of the Whites to the First of the Blacks."

General Leclerc arrived in the island with an expeditionary force of thirty thousand men and with the First Consul's decree maintaining slavery in all the islands of the French West Indies including Martinique, where it had not yet been abolished—and "limiting" their emancipation in Santo Domingo, where there had been total disenfranchisement since 1789. The decree also authorized the further importation of black slaves to all the islands.

Although General Henri Christophe—later King of Haiti—put up a valiant resistance, he was finally defeated by Leclerc's troops. Toussaint l'Ouverture was captured by a trick and imprisoned in an icy fortress in France, where he died within a few months. One year after their victory, the French garrison surrendered to the British navy; by then almost twenty-five thousand men, including General Leclerc himself, had died of yellow fever.

Bonaparte, who could rarely bring himself to reprove his siblings for their scandalous conduct, had insisted that Pauline accompany her husband on the expedition to Santo Domingo. Fouché had just informed him of what was known to all Paris, that his sister had recently spent three days and nights locked in her bedroom with General Macdonald. Though Napoleon promised to send her regular shipments of Paris dresses, she was heartbroken at the idea of leaving Paris and her lovers, one of whom wrote later: "Before she left for Santo Domingo, there were no fewer than five of us in the same house sharing Pauline's favors. She was the greatest tramp imaginable and the most desirable."[5]

Power was emphasizing the First Consul's arrogance. Increasingly intolerant of any opposition, he expelled from the Tribunate fifteen members whose views he considered too liberal, and took to referring to that body as "an unnecessary democratic appendage." Some of those around him believed they now discerned the first signs of mounting Napoleonic megalomania. One of its manifestations was a desire to follow in the traces of previous monarchs.

The Prussian minister, in his dispatches to Berlin, observed: "Now the First Consul has started to enjoy the hunt, and the forests where once only the kings of France and the princes of the blood rode are to be reserved for him and for the officers of his suite."[6] At the Tuileries it was believed that Bonaparte, a mediocre rider, enjoyed the pleasure of following in the royal footsteps rather than the hunt itself.

But there were other royal distractions, also once common to princes of the blood, which now appeared to torment Josephine, obsessed by the hereditary question, by the knowledge that should Bonaparte really fall in love with one of his occasional mistresses—above all, if one of them should become pregnant—a divorce would become inevitable. Although Hortense had produced a son, Napoleon Charles, mercifully a few days beyond the term imposed by Louis, and though the First Consul seemed to consider the child as his heir, a legal separation was still a possibility.

At St. Cloud, for the first time, Napoleon now chose to sleep in a separate room. At St. Helena he expressed an unexpected view of a wife's rights: "We [Josephine and I] were a very bourgeois couple, tender and united, sharing a bedroom and a bed. This is important to a married couple, ensuring both the wife's influence and the husband's dependency, maintaining intimacy and morality. . . . As long as this habit lasted, no thought, no action of mine escaped Josephine. She guessed, she knew everything, which was sometimes inconvenient for me. All this ended after one of her jealous scenes. I resolved not to return to my subjugation."[7] And later, in his second marriage, he feared that Marie Louise would insist on sharing his bed, "for I would have given in. It's the true prerogative, the true right of a woman."[8]

On some nights, in his dressing gown, a handkerchief knotted over his head against the cold, Napoleon would cross the corridors that separated their bedrooms at St. Cloud, Constant lighting the way with a candle. After he had left her at the usual eight in the morning, Josephine would call her ladies and make a point of informing them where her husband had spent the night, adding a languishing, "That's why I am getting up late today."[9]

Bonaparte no longer made serious attempts to hide from his wife his brief affairs with actresses. When Bourrienne was dismissed that year, guilty of shady financial dealings, Bonaparte asked for the keys to his secretary's room next to his own study. From this time it was reserved for his rendezvous and furnished with fresh flowers daily by the same Mme Bernard who decorated Josephine's apartments.

Through her spies in the court entourage, Josephine knew that her husband's recent affair with Mlle Duchesnois, an actress of the Comédie-Française, had lasted only a short time. When Duchesnois was shown into the room next to the First Consul's study, he answered when Constant knocked on his door: "Tell her to wait." An hour later his answer to another knock was: "Tell her to get undressed." Duchesnois shivered and waited undressed for another hour or so. When Constant knocked again, Bonaparte shouted: "Tell her to go home."[10]

But Josephine was aware that Bonaparte's affair with the great dramatic actress Mlle George was not to be treated so lightly. "Georgina" (her name was Marguerite Josephine, but Bonaparte immediately renamed her) was not only beautiful but also quick-witted, intelligent and high-spirited. Ironically, a couple of years earlier Mlle George had been taken to visit the Consular couple at St. Cloud. Too frightened to wait for the requested audience with the First Consul, she had, she wrote in her *Mémoires,* found herself, "strangely attracted to Josephine, magnetized, aware of a mysterious influence, a charm infinitely suave which emanated from her."

Bonaparte now often stayed late into the night with Mlle George in Bourrienne's old apartment overlooking the Seine. One evening Josephine and Claire de Rémusat were waiting for him in the Yellow Salon. Suddenly, at one in the morning, Josephine stood up and said: "I cannot stand it any longer; Mlle George must be up there. I am going to surprise them," and she insisted on Claire accompanying her up the narrow staircase between the two apartments. Halfway up they believed they heard Roustam, who habitually guarded the First Consul's door. "He'll cut us to ribbons," shrieked Josephine, dropping her candle, and they came running down again in the dark, shaking with fear.

That affair came to an end on the night Georgina's screams could be heard throughout the palace. Bonaparte had been taken ill by one of his convulsive seizures resembling epilepsy, and the man who dreaded ridicule above all else came to, to find valets and Josephine herself beside his bed and a hastily departing and unclothed Mlle George.

Bonaparte was perfectly aware of Josephine's constant spying, and was exasperated by it. He despised her jealousy, he told her, and it was time she understood that he would do as he pleased: "I am not like other men and the ordinary rules of morality and propriety do not apply to me." He asked at least one of her ladies-in-waiting to persuade her of this. "Josephine," he told Mme de Rémusat, "worries more than is necessary. She is always afraid that I will fall seriously in love. . . . What is love? A passion which sets all the universe on one scale and the loved one in another. It is certainly not in my nature to surrender to any such overwhelming feeling. Why does she worry about these fancies in which my affections are not engaged?"

"As soon as he acquired a new mistress," wrote Mme Rémusat, "Bonaparte became hard, violent, pitiless toward his wife. He did not hesitate to tell her about the affair, nor to show an almost savage astonishment that she should disapprove of any distractions which he could prove were both permitted and necessary to him. . . . When Mme Bonaparte wept or complained at such declarations, he turned on her with a violence which I do not choose to record."

There was one terrible scene at Malmaison that both she and Laure d'Abrantès remembered all their lives. Josephine was suffering from one of her agonizing migraines, a consequence of her time in prison, but dared not refuse the First Consul's command to accompany him immediately to a property he had acquired nearby.

Terrified as she always was in a carriage, she nevertheless obediently drove off with Laure and two other ladies, while Bonaparte and Bourrienne rode ahead. When they reached a ditch between high banks, which the riders had taken in their stride, Josephine begged to be allowed to leave the carriage while it attempted to cross. "Please, Bonaparte, let me get out," she pleaded, but he called her childish and ridiculous and hit the postillion with his riding crop, ordering him to take the slope very fast. The horses managed to leap across, but the shock to the carriage was so violent that it broke nearly in two and Napoleon shouted at his now convulsively sobbing wife that tears made her ugly—a judgment he would contradict at St. Helena. Yet after their quarrels, Claire de Rémusat noted, "they would return to terms of an ardour and an intimacy more pronounced than ever."

Perhaps Josephine feared that some of the widespread rumors about her married life would reach her mother in Martinique. In a letter to her, Josephine wrote that she was sure that her mother had some "occasional concerns about me," but assured her that they were unnecessary. After listing the splendid presents that accompanied the letter and again begging her mother to come to France, a request in which, she wrote, her husband joined her, she wrote another of her startling appraisals of her husband: "You will like Bonaparte very much, he is making your daughter very happy. He is kind, pleasant, in every way a charming man, and he truly loves your Yéyette."[11]

But there were consolations. The part Josephine played in official voyages and ceremonials was shared by no other woman and added to the First Consul's popularity. She accompanied him on what was nothing less than a royal progress through northeastern France, Belgium (now a French *département*) and Holland, the "Batavian Republic," and a French protectorate. This month-long tour was a triumph for Josephine. Wherever the pair traveled the cheers, ovations, speeches, galas and banquets appeared to be directed as much to her as to him. Her genuine warmth and interest in everyone she spoke to, her memory for names, were remembered for a long time. "When I visited those regions fifteen years later, I discovered that the memory of her graciousness and kindness was still fresh in men's minds," wrote Mme de Rémusat. One child remembered fifty years later the warmth with which Bonaparte kissed Josephine on both cheeks—and the sight of Roustam sleeping on a mat outside the First Consul's bedroom door.

Bonaparte had given Josephine the French crown jewels to wear on this journey. His interest in her attire was as permanent as his feeling that luxury was a political statement. Had Josephine felt the slightest need to justify her extravagance in clothes, she had Napoleon's orders to appear splendidly dressed on all public occasions. Claire de Rémusat once heard Bonaparte tell his wife to appear at "her dazzling best in jewelry and costume." When she failed to reply he asked her: "Did you hear me,

Josephine?" " 'Yes,' Mme Bonaparte replied, 'but then you will reproach me or even go into a tantrum and refuse to pay for my purchases.' She pouted, but prettily, like a little girl and with the utmost good humor. She looked at him so sweetly, approached him with such grace, the desire to please him shining so unmistakably bright in her eyes that he would have had a heart of stone to resist her."

Even by Tuileries standards, Josephine was fabulously dressed. Some of her more exotic inspirations lasted just one day. A celebrated pink crepe gown entirely covered in hundreds of thousands of real rose petals (a garment in which the wearer was unable to sit) was one of these; for a visit to the "Josephs" at Mortefontaine there was another memorable dress made of toucan feathers, each one tipped with a pearl.

But even Mme Bonaparte's greatest admirers often felt that the youthful clothes she ordered in such quantity were sometimes a mistake. Rose-colored tulle, for instance, sown with silver stars, vivid, almost theatrical makeup and hair crowned with dozens of diamond wheatears, her ladies believed to be unsuitable for the midday presentation in 1804 of the first Legions of Honor by Bonaparte. Yet after the impossible test of the open-air ceremony "the elegance of her bearing, the charm of her smile and the sweetness of her expression made such an impression," wrote Claire de Rémusat, "that on that occasion she was given an ovation, as the entire procession and escort of the First Consul was forced to slow down to match Mme Bonaparte's own unhurried step."

Josephine was aware that her ascendancy over her husband went beyond her usefulness in rallying monarchists or her incomparable grace as his consort or her role in setting the pace and style of the new court; it went even beyond the physical spell she still cast. It rested too, she knew, on the conviction that she was his talisman, the essential element of his star.

The English visitors in Paris noted this, one of them wrote: "Bonaparte's superstition about his wife is very extraordinary. When he came from St. Cloud though quite ill, she came with him to satisfy his feelings, and went to bed as soon as she arrived at the Tuileries."[12]

In spite of Bonaparte's continuing appeals to revolutionary principles and to "the sovereignty of the people," many of those around him now believed him to be more than ready to replace the Republic with himself at its head.

Josephine, who guessed that much of his autocracy and continual irritation stemmed from his determination to achieve total power, attempted to plead with him. She came into his office one day as Napoleon was dictating to his secretary. "Approaching him in her gentle and beguiling way," wrote Bourrienne, "and setting herself on his knee, she caressed him and brushed her fingertips softly across his cheek and through his hair. Her words came in a tender rush. 'Bonaparte, I implore you, don't go making yourself a king. It's that horrid Lucien who puts you up to such schemes. Please, oh please, don't listen to him.'" Bourrienne reported that Bonaparte simply smiled and replied, "You must be out of your mind, Josephine, you could only have heard such wild tales in the Faubourg St. Germain."

Talleyrand, Josephine well knew, even more than Lucien, was her adversary in this matter as well as in the argument for a divorce. She could not know, however, that among the many disastrous consequences of the breakdown of the Amiens Treaty, the defection of Charles-Maurice de Talleyrand was not the least. From that day Bonaparte's minister of external relations became his most dangerous enemy. The country as a whole might continue to have confidence in Bonaparte as a man of peace, but Talleyrand's own illusions were broken. He saw that the cynical opportunism of the First Consul's foreign policy and the senseless destruction of the peace with England meant that Bonaparte believed that the only way to retain power depended on a never-ending succession of military victories.

Like Josephine, Talleyrand perfectly understood that Bonaparte was waiting only for a suitable pretext to have the crown pressed upon him. What better excuse could there be than to prove the uselessness of assassinating the First Consul by establishing a throne and a hereditary succession? That pretext now presented itself.

That year Bonaparte was again threatened simultaneously by both royalist and Jacobin conspiracies. When a Vendéan rebel leader was arrested in Paris in 1804 and confessed that he and his accomplices had planned to assassinate the First Consul and were "waiting only for the arrival of a prince of the blood royal" to lead them, Bonaparte—and Talleyrand—decided that that justification had been found. Although

Talleyrand always denied any responsibility for the kidnapping and murder of the Duc d'Enghien, and although he burned every compromising paper in his possession at the time of the allied entry into Paris in 1814, one letter was found eighty years later in the back of a desk drawer that had belonged to him. It proved what had been suspected even in 1804, that he had been deeply implicated in the murder of an innocent man.

The Duc d'Enghien, thirty-two years old and a nephew of Louis XVI, lived just across the Rhine in the neutral Duchy of Baden; might he not well be the awaited prince?

On the night of March 14, 1804, Enghien, accompanied by his dog, set out to pay a visit to his fiancée in a neighboring village, still in the duchy. On Napoleon's orders he was kidnapped in a raid across the border by a small French detachment, hurried across the Rhine and driven to the dungeon of Vincennes just outside Paris. As the first news of the still-secret kidnapping became known, a pall of horror descended on the Tuileries. Royalist courtiers, notably Josephine's lady-in-waiting Claire de Rémusat, implored her to save the duke. When, according to Mme de Rémusat, Josephine knelt before Bonaparte in tears and begged him to spare the young man, he snapped, "Women shouldn't meddle in affairs of state." Later in the day, when she returned to the subject, he said, "Go away, you are only a child; you understand nothing about politics," and forbade her to mention the subject again.*

Mme de Rémusat described the First Consul's apparent serenity that evening, playing chess and seating little Napoleon Charles on the dining room table. When Bonaparte pointedly asked Claire why she looked so pale, and she answered that she had forgotten her rouge, he laughed. "That could not happen to my Josephine! She knows that there's nothing more becoming to a woman than rouge—and tears." Then, wrote Claire de Rémusat, he began to caress his wife "with more freedom than decorum," and as usual when he needed calm and relaxation, he spent the night in Josephine's bedroom.

Later that night Enghien arrived at Vincennes, still ignorant of the

---

* Was Mme de Rémusat writing to please her royalist readers, or was Napoleon correct when he told General Bertrand at St. Helena: "Like everyone else Josephine wept and said she had spoken to me on the subject, whereas in fact she never mentioned the matter to me"?[13]

charges against him. His grave was already dug in the dungeon's enclosure. Bonaparte had ordered that the duke be sentenced to death and executed immediately; there was to be no legal counsel, no hearing. At two-thirty in the morning, in the dark of the fortress courtyard, his dog still beside him, Enghien was commanded to hold a lantern near his heart to direct the musket fire. The men of the firing squad were so struck by his grace and courage that they refused to take what was theirs by rights— the duke's clothes, his watch and his money.

Three days later the First Consul, who had not forgotten the successful public relations effect of the evening that had marked his return from Italy, commanded Talleyrand to give another ball. The atmosphere was said to have been "tense and constrained." The entire diplomatic corps was in a state of shock. In monarchist Europe the violation of frontiers, the lack of any trial and the shedding of royal blood were never to be forgiven.

The censored press account of the duke's guilt was readily believed in France. To test public opinion in Paris, Bonaparte went to the theater the following week. The occasion was one of the few times he was known, since Brumaire, to have shown even a shadow of irresolution. Usually he went straight to his box without waiting for Josephine's following carriage. On this day, "very pale," he delayed his entrance so that they could enter together; apparently he trusted her certain popularity to carry them both through. Then "as though facing enemy fire" he marched in, followed by Josephine, resolutely smiling her closed-lip smile.

He need not have feared. As usual, the house erupted into wild applause. The First Consul's popularity with his public was undiminished.

Talleyrand, as Barras put it, had wished to "put a river of blood between Napoleon and the Bourbons." The regicides were relieved; now Bonaparte was one of them. He too had shed royal blood; there would be no restoration of the House of Bourbon. They no longer feared any designs of Bonaparte's upon the throne of France.

Joseph Fouché, equally averse to the divorce and to the restoration of any monarchy, was not displeased by this definitive severing of any link with the Bourbons. Talleyrand, he knew, was deeply involved in the matter, so Fouché was not sorry to refer to the execution of the duke as "worse than a crime: a blunder"—a quotation usually credited to Talleyrand.

In retrospect, Bonaparte was to feel that it may have been a mistake. At the time he made very little pretense of believing in Enghien's guilt but insisted: "I have forever silenced both royalists and Jacobins." By establishing a hereditary successor he would, he declared, put an end to their assassination plots. Three weeks after the Enghien execution, at Bonaparte's instigation, the Senate voted that the Life Consul be declared Emperor.

❧ 24 ❧

CITIZEN EMPEROR

THE CANNON IN PARIS WERE STILL ROARING OUT A TWENTY-ONE-GUN salute when the senators arrived at St. Cloud on May 18, 1804, the day the Empire was proclaimed. Napoleon "received them calmly and as though he had had a right to the title all his life." He seemed the least embarrassed of all those present, the only one not to share the senators' very visible unease as they got caught up in their "Citizen Consul," "Citizen Emperor" and "Monsieur Sire." Josephine was said to be the only other person equally at ease, though she trembled when first addressed as "Your Imperial Majesty." Perhaps at that moment she remembered the words of the Martinique soothsayer "that she would be greater than a queen."*

At a family dinner that night, all the jealousies and recriminations of the Bonaparte family came flooding out. The two angriest were Napoleon's sisters Elisa and, especially, Caroline. The Emperor teased his family by addressing each one by his or her new title. Only those members of the imperial family who were in the line of succession were to have the title of Prince or Princess. Joseph and Louis Bonaparte were immediately given the title of Prince, and Caroline burst into tears when Napoleon addressed Hortense as Princess Louis, while she and Elisa remained Mme Murat and Mme Bacchiocchi.

The following day Elisa and Caroline returned to the attack and accused their brother of "condemning them to obscurity and contempt while foreigners are covered with honors and dignities." Napoleon started by impatiently reminding them that "anyone would think I had robbed

---

* This story had already been reported in *Le Thé*, a royalist newspaper, in 1797.

my family of the inheritance of the late king, our father," but when Caroline fell on the floor in a faint of frustration and rage, he was unable to resist her despair. Ten days later he gave both sisters the title of Imperial Highness while their husbands remained commoners. Pauline, too, became an Imperial Highness, although she was married now to the Roman Prince Borghese and therefore, she pointed out, "a *real* princess." This was only the first of the colossal rows before the coronation; the most serious ones would all be on the subject either about the succession or about Josephine's superior rank.

The Senate had stipulated that if the Emperor had no legitimate heir the succession should go first to Joseph and any male descendant of his, and secondly to Louis and his male descendants, but only after Napoleon had exercised the right of "adoptive succession." (Lucien and Jérôme were ruled out by Napoleon himself because of their unsuitable marriages.)

After the final break Lucien had taken his family to Rome, swearing he would not return to France during Napoleon's lifetime. The unforgiving brothers were not to meet again until the last days of the Empire. Their mother, already angry at being left out of the shower of titles, followed her favorite son into exile. She was not to stay there, however; she returned, but only after the coronation, in order to be spared the sight of "that woman's" triumph. Jérôme, the youngest Bonaparte, was not in France. He had no place in the line of succession since he had married without consultation and without Napoleon's permission.

There was one subject on which the divided Bonaparte family could agree: Josephine must not be allowed to be crowned and anointed; after that it would be impossible to dislodge "*la* Beauharnais." Their brother, as each one pointed out to him, would certainly have to divorce her eventually.

Napoleon was surprised, but unmoved, by the vigor of reaction to the proclamation of the Empire. The army and most of its generals were disconcerted. Andoche Junot, a fervent republican, wept on hearing the news. There was bitter disappointment in the liberal establishment and among ex-constitutionalists, many of whom had believed that they had found in Bonaparte the heir of the Enlightenment and of the Revolution. Germaine de Staël was indignant: "For a man who had risen above every throne, to come down willingly and take his place amongst the kings!" The animosity between Napoleon and Lafayette deepened when the Emperor was informed that Lafayette's distaste for the Empire was so profound that he termed it "the least honorable of political misfortunes." Joseph Fouché, however, once so ardently against the Life Consulate, was now in favor of the Empire; since Enghien's murder he felt certain that no return of the Bourbons was possible.

But even in the government there was a lack of confidence in the new title. Second Consul Cambacérès confided to Third Consul Lebrun that he foresaw that "what we are building now will not last. We made war with all Europe to give her republics, daughters of the French Republic, and now we will go to war again to give her new monarchs, the sons or brothers of our own."[1]

Throughout Europe, reaction to the news was violent. In Germany, Beethoven tore up the dedication to Bonaparte of his *Eroica* Symphony. In England, Lord Byron lamented his disenchantment in "Champion of Liberty."

Napoleon had hesitated some time over a suitable title. "Emperor" would eliminate any reminders of Bourbon kings, the resonance being rather of Rome. The ambiguities of his position were already numberless. He was Emperor "by the grace of God and of the Constitution of the Republic," he was "Emperor of the French," (coins were inscribed "Napoléon Empereur" on one side and "République Française" on the other), and he had sworn to "maintain the integrity of the Republic's territory." The Legislative Body and the Senate remained; the Tribunate would last another three years before being dismissed.

By proclaiming himself a descendant of Charlemagne—the founder of a European empire, the successor of Roman emperors and for the past ten centuries one of France's heroes—Napoleon could present himself as his spiritual son. (In private, Talleyrand was vastly amused. "The combination of Charlemagne and the Roman empire has quite turned his head,"[2] he confided to Mme de Rémusat.)

Charlemagne had traveled to Rome to be crowned, but there would be no question of who would be traveling this time. A reluctant Pope Pius VII, elderly and in bad health, would be commanded to come to Paris for the ceremony.

The Emperor knew just how difficult it would be to persuade his largely anticlerical legislative bodies that an anointment as well as a coronation would be necessary. There was already some difficulty in convincing them that the coronation should take place in a church. The majority of the Council of State was made up of former presidents of revolutionary clubs, of fanatical anticlericals who had sent cartloads of priests to the guillotine. They were particularly scandalized by the prospect of an anointment by the Pope, in spite of the Emperor's arguments that he must dazzle French opinion, impress Europe's sovereigns and make himself their equal.

Napoleon made it clear that the coronation was not to be a popular event. Only distinguished persons and army officers were to be invited to the ceremony. "Not," he announced, "twenty thousand fishwives, nor any other members of the corrupt population of great cities." His fear of the mob had not diminished and he was particularly truculent in his views on Paris, going so far as to threaten that the coronation might take place in some other city. "If," he said, "I were to marry the Madonna, I still could not astonish Parisians."[3]

The born showman Napoleon oversaw every detail of the ceremony, set first for November 8, the anniversary of Brumaire, and then put off until December 2. Many hours of intense concentration were needed to decide on the emblems and symbols of his reign. After much hesitation and some consideration of the rooster, a traditional Gallic emblem, he decided upon the eagle of the Caesars and the star of his destiny. And the bee. There had been some doubt over this image of the fifth-century Merovingian dynasty. The queen bee, although known since the Revolution as the president bee, had been a stumbling block, but the insects were nevertheless reckoned to be "members of an organized republic," and they were to swarm over imperial carpets, court dress and even the borders of banners.

Notre Dame was to be the setting for the coronation, though its interior had been vandalized at the time of the Goddess of Reason saturnalia. Jacques-Louis David and the Percier and Fontaine team* were instructed to hide the "barbarous Gothic" aspects of the cathedral (the Gothic style would not be fashionable for another thirty years) and to change the ravaged "Temple of Reason" into a pseudo-Roman temple. The exterior was to be boxed in with cardboard, and the space around the

---

* It was Josephine who had first employed the two young men at Malmaison. Napoleon admired them and felt that their taste for "Roman" style matched his own.

cathedral, unsuitable for the deployment of a procession, cleared by the demolition of a number of houses, although their inhabitants, reported the police, were "reticent."

Inside, the cathedral was to be transformed into pure theater. Two side altars were removed and tiers of seats installed on either side of the nave. Painted cardboard simulated a "Greco-Egyptian" style; a dozen chandeliers were hung, candelabra attached to every pillar and any bare stone covered with tapestries, flags and velvet hangings.

Ever mindful of the gaze of posterity, Napoleon commissioned Jacques-Louis David to record the ceremony and to be present at its rehearsal as well as on the great day itself. Both David and Jean-Baptiste Isabey were ordered to design the clothes to be worn at the ceremony. They settled on the style of the Renaissance reign of Francis I of France, an unfortunate choice since it clothed the men—marshals, civil and military dignitaries and Napoleon himself—in puffed pantaloons, ruffs and highheeled shoes with rosettes. Only Fouché was excused from this obligation.

At the Tuileries, several hundred paper dolls were placed on a mock-up of the cathedral, with their assigned places during the service indicated. Each figure bore its name on its back, and the Emperor himself was colored purple. Only the Josephine doll's position was uncertain; her courtesy title of Empress gave her no official standing.

Still Napoleon remained ominously silent on Josephine's role in the forthcoming celebrations, and that summer, while her destiny hung in the balance, she came very close to catastrophe. In July, she decided to take the spa waters once again, this time at Aix-la-Chapelle, the site of Charlemagne's tomb. The Emperor left for the Channel coast for another inspection of the military and naval bases for the invasion of England, and from there he organized Josephine's first imperial progress. A minute twenty-four-page directive was sent to Paris; every detail, the presents to be given, the entourage to accompany the Empress, were all laid out. "She is a good, easygoing woman," Napoleon explained to his minister of the interior: "Her progress and her conduct will have to be dictated to her."[4]

The imperial trappings were to be splendid. Josephine was to take four of her fourteen ladies, two chamberlains, two women-of-the-bedchamber, the first equerry, a master of the horse, a comptroller, two ushers, ten footmen, kitchen staff and coachmen. At least fifty persons would be requiring seventy horses and twenty-four postillions at each relay.

Into every illuminated town on the route the Empress was escorted by drums and gun salutes. The Emperor was sent reports of all that was said around her and how she was received. He was delighted to learn of Josephine's resourcefulness on those occasions not foreseen in his directions. When, upon visiting Charlemagne's tomb, she was presented with a bone said to be from his arm, instead of recoiling she refused it, saying only "she had for her own support an arm as strong as Charlemagne's."

The Emperor's letters were especially affectionate. "You are still essential to my happiness. . . ." "I cover you with kisses." And then the inevitable, "I have not heard from you for several days, but I would have liked to have your news."⁵

It was often remarked that Napoleon chose his mistresses from among Josephine's ladies. All her life she preferred to be surrounded by attractive women, with no apparent fear of possible competition, and that year the prettiest of them was Elisabeth de Vaudey. At Aix the Empress, with her usual lack of discretion, chose to confide in Mme de Vaudey some of the stories of Napoleon's unfaithfulness, the consequence of what he himself referred to as his "rutting season" and his harshness to her at those times. ("Love is a singular passion, turning men into beasts," he once said. "I come into season like a dog."⁶)

Vaudey's own appraisal of Josephine was written later: "I fear that the Empress's need to open her heart, to repeat all that happens between herself and the Emperor, takes away much of Napoleon's confidence in her. . . . Josephine is like a ten-year-old child in her generosity, her frivolity and her rapid emotions, she can weep and be comforted all within minutes. . . . As ignorant as most Creoles, she has learned almost entirely by listening; but having spent much of her life in the best circles, she has acquired graceful manners and that jargon which, in fashionable society, often takes the place of wit. . . . But what I find charming about her is that diffidence, that lack of self-confidence so remarkable in her position. . . . Her character is perfectly gentle and equable; it is impossible not to love her."⁷

When Napoleon suddenly announced that he would meet Josephine and her retinue at Aix and accompany them on an official visit down the

Rhine, Josephine burst into tears of joy. His letter ended with, "I cannot wait to see you and to cover you with kisses. A bachelor's life is a horrid life and I miss my good, tender and beautiful wife."[8]

And, as it turned out, he also missed his mistress. It took Josephine some days, as the imperial party slowly sailed down the Rhine in two ships, to realize that Elisabeth de Vaudey was the real reason for Napoleon's change of plan, for the first sign of the liaison was, as usual, a new form of persecution in his treatment of his wife. When one night Josephine declared she felt too ill to go to a ball at Mainz, the Emperor literally pulled her out of bed by one arm and insisted she dress immediately.

Vaudey, accused of petty larceny, was dismissed by Napoleon when the party returned to Paris, but one further trial awaited Josephine—one that was nearly her undoing.

The Murats introduced to the court one Adèle Duchâtel, a twenty-year-old divorcée eager to follow Caroline's instructions to become pregnant by the Emperor. One evening at St. Cloud, Mme Duchâtel was seen by Josephine to leave the drawing room where the imperial household was gathered before dinner. The Emperor had also disappeared. Whispering to Claire de Rémusat that she was going to confirm her suspicions, Josephine left the room. Half an hour later she came back very pale and in tears, took Claire up to her bedroom and confessed that she had gone up the private staircase behind Bonaparte's study, heard his voice and Adèle's inside the locked room next to it and insisted on the door being opened. She found the couple in a state of undress and fled before the Emperor's rage. Mme de Rémusat warned her that Napoleon would be in an even greater fury if he guessed that Josephine had told anyone of the scene, and she hurriedly returned to the room where the rest of the imperial household was still gathered, including the anxious Duchâtel, who had quickly rejoined the company. Soon shouts were heard from the Empress's apartment. Mme Duchâtel called for her horses and left for Paris. Josephine, sobbing, described to Claire the horrific scene of Napoleon kicking and smashing furniture and ordering her to leave St. Cloud immediately, storming that he was tired of her spying, that he wanted to marry a woman capable of giving him children.

Josephine implored Claire to go to Hortense and beg her to intervene, but Hortense only answered, "I cannot; Louis has forbidden it. My mother will only lose a crown and," she added sadly, "there are women more to be pitied than she. Besides, her only hope lies in the influence she exercises over Napoleon by means of her sweet and gentle nature and her tears."[9] Eugène, too, refused to interfere. Napoleon sent for him the same evening, and when the Emperor told him that he was to divorce Josephine but would compensate Eugène for any loss of rank, he replied that he required no favors, that his duty would be to accompany his mother wherever she wished to go, even to Martinique.

A few days later there was another scene when Napoleon asked Josephine "whether, if he found that in the national interest she should go, would she be the one to withdraw and save him the pain of forcing the issue?" She was wise enough to answer that she would await his direct orders to leave the throne upon which he had placed her. By "her adroit and tender sweetness, her complete submissiveness and her attitude of unresisting victim," wrote Claire de Rémusat, Josephine had succeeded in reducing Napoleon to a state of "agitation and uncertainty."

Still Napoleon hesitated on whether Josephine should be crowned. The contrast between the behavior of his own family and that of the Beauharnais children and of Josephine herself had made a deep impression on him. When Pierre-Louis Roederer pressed him on the subject of divorce, he answered that his own family was jealous of Josephine, Eugène and Hortense, and that he loved his stepchildren, who never asked for anything. As for Josephine, "I have never loved her blindly. . . . It is only fair that she should be an Empress. If I had been thrown into prison instead of ascending a throne, I know she would have shared my misfortune. . . . My existence would be unbearable without some happiness and relaxation in my private life. . . . It is right that she should share in my grandeur. . . . Yes, she will be crowned, even if it should cost me two hundred thousand men!" was his curious conclusion.[10]

While over the next months Napoleon continued to hesitate over the question and to endure a ceaseless barrage on the subject from his family, Josephine continued to maintain her outward composure. Mme de Rémusat noted, however, that her nonchalant movements had become more hurried and that she lost weight. Her sweetness never faltered. She asked for nothing either for herself or for her children.

Flushed by their victory—the apparently terminal scene at St. Cloud had been witnessed, or at least heard, by most of the court—the clan behaved with noisy arrogance. It was their behaviour that decided Napoleon. Finally, wrote Claire de Rémusat, one night in November, "pushed and harassed too far by his scheming family and resentful of their premature air of triumph ... Napoleon suddenly went to Josephine's room, took her in his arms and stroked her as he would a child ... 'The Pope will be here at the end of the month,' he said. 'He will crown us both. Start to prepare for the ceremony.' "[11]

The news that Josephine was to be crowned and anointed set off a new wave of recriminations in the Bonaparte family. Not even Marie Antoinette had been crowned, they pointed out. The last Queen of France to be crowned and anointed was Marie de Médicis, and then only because it seemed probable that she would become the regent for her young son, Louis XIII. And, Joseph Bonaparte reminded Napoleon, "*she* was a mother," and, he added, "a distant relation carried *her* train, not the King's own sister!"

But the family's mortification was not yet over. Caroline was the ringleader in the strike staged by the sisters when they learned that Napoleon expected them and Julie and Hortense to carry Josephine's train at the coronation, twenty-five yards of crimson velvet sown with golden bees, and entirely lined and bordered in Russian ermine. "Madame Joseph," pronounced her husband, "could not, as a virtuous woman, be expected to bear the train."

"For six days," Napoleon confided, "I've lost sleep over this. Only my family can exercise so great an influence over me."[12] Worn out, he decreed that the Bonaparte women would only have to make the gesture of "supporting the mantle" during the ceremony, and each one of them, moreover, would have her own train carried by a chamberlain.

Ever since his arrival from Rome, the Pope's apartments in the Tuileries had been filled throughout the day with persons begging for an audience. Parisians were impressed by the Pope's obvious humility and simplicity and by the nobility of his emaciated features. For the saintly man, it made no difference whether the figure kneeling before him was an ardent Catholic or a revolutionary formerly in favor of "de-Christianization." Informed before leaving Rome that the French had remained profoundly irreligious, he had brought with him only a small number of rosaries and medallions. These were soon exhausted (by revolutionary decree no rosaries had been made for years), and now he was required to bless watches, scissors, inkpots, eyeglasses and other objects brought in not only by pious Catholics, but also by republican generals, former terrorists, Encyclopedists, Jacobins and high dignitaries of the imperial court—even Dr. Guillotin and the atheist Jacques-Louis David waited outside his apartments. Daily he was called to his balcony to bless the crowds kneeling in the Tuileries Gardens.

Ex-Merveilleuses, too, knelt before him and kissed his ring. Among them were Fortunée Hamelin and Thérésia Cabarrus, whose need for his blessing and possibly for an annulment was especially urgent. She was about to marry Joseph de Caraman-Chimay, whose mother had been one of Marie Antoinette's most faithful ladies-in-waiting. Joseph's father, who had emigrated and served with the Army of Condé, had already vowed that he would never again speak to his son, even if Thérésia succeeded in having both her marriages annulled.

The Empress's claim was still more pressing. On December 1, the day before the coronation, Josephine asked for a private audience with the Pope. In tears she confided that, due entirely to the disturbances of the Revolution, her second marriage had been a civil one only. There could be no question, Pius VII replied, of his consecrating and anointing with holy oil a couple living in sin. As the Emperor's concubine, Josephine could not be crowned. On this one point Pius VII, who had already submitted to so many humiliations, refused to give in. He had accepted the many changes in the ritual of consecration insisted on by the Tuileries; he had agreed to the elimination of a large part of the ancient ritual, he was willing to walk into the cathedral instead of being borne in on the usual carrying litter. (The Tuileries excuse here had been that the Goddess Reason had been carried into the cathedral in a chair on the backs of *sans culottes*.)

When his uncle Cardinal Fesch informed Napoleon of the papal decision, Napoleon decided instantly that the highly publicized events of the next day could not be canceled; he would not be the laughingstock of all Europe. The scandal and the sarcastic comments of the opposition he could well imagine. This point of canonical law he knew to be irrefutable. Uncle Fesch, the Grand Almoner, was told to organize a secret marriage service that night. At midnight, before an altar erected in the Emperor's study, Napoleon and Josephine were married in a brief service, without either witnesses or the presence of their parish priest and because of those two circumstances, this service was almost as irregular as the earlier civil one. Before leaving, the Empress asked Cardinal Fesch to give her a copy of the marriage certificate, her supreme insurance against divorce.

Napoleon seems never to have reproached Josephine for this piece of trickery. Perhaps he was aware of the illegality of the service, or else his explanation at St. Helena was correct: when he decided that Josephine should be crowned, he said, he had already resolved to divorce her "when it suited me. The coronation had nothing to do with the matter."[13]

⁂ 25 ⁂

PROOF OF MY AFFECTION

IT HAD SNOWED ON THE NIGHT BEFORE DECEMBER 2 AND THEN RAINED in the early morning. It was the coldest day of the year. By dawn Parisians had taken up their positions in the icy streets. Although hemmed in by three rows of troops guarding the route between the Tuileries and Notre Dame, they were still splattered by the slush thrown up by the carriages and the horses' hooves.

Punctually at nine, the Pope drove out of the Tuileries, escorted by four squadrons of dragoons. A frail white hand could be seen raised, blessing the onlookers along the route. Though many remained hatted and standing, a surprising number of Parisians found themselves dropping to their knees. The Pope was followed by six carriages of cardinals, bishops and priests; the last time so many clergy had been seen along this route had been ten years earlier, bundled into tumbrils.

As the bells rang out and the cannon thundered at irregular intervals, the state coaches followed, each drawn by six horses at breakneck speed through the narrow streets, and each preceded and followed by detachments of chasseurs, cuirassiers and Mamelukes. The carriages appeared to be filled with tossing plumes and gold glittered everywhere: on grand cordons of the Legion of Honor and on embroidered uniforms; even the horses' reins and harnesses were gold-embossed.

Murat as governor of Paris came first, then heralds at arms in violet-colored velvet, followed by the coaches bearing ministers, the grand chamberlain, the diplomatic corps, all the Bonaparte princesses and their maids of honor. The Grenadiers of the Guard came last.

The spectators, whose enthusiasm was "more muted than had been hoped" were at least able to recognize the faces of some of the former members of the Convention, in spite of their velvet toques and ruffs, and of the more famous marshals and generals, though they too wore Isabey's fancy dress. It was harder to identify the politicians and administrators.

At the Tuileries, candles were lit long before dawn. Many of the ladies had slept upright in their chairs, their hair dressed since the evening before. At six, Isabey arrived with his brushes to help the Empress paint her face and to take a last look at the costumes he had helped devise.

Napoleon was late; he had dressed in the highest spirits, humming tunelessly. He wore so much jewelry, with the great "Régent" diamond now removed from his sword's scabbard and stuck into his velvet toque, that he was said to "resemble a walking mirror."[1] Punctual as usual, Josephine was waiting in her white dress veiled in gold tulle scattered with golden bees, and blazing with diamonds.

At last, almost two hours late and announced by a salute of guns, the imperial state coach drove out of the palace. The carriage, newly built after a design by Fontaine, was covered with the emblems of the new Empire—stars, bees and laurel leaves in relief—surmounted by eagles and topped by a copy of Charlemagne's crown. Caesar the coachman, twelve feet up on the box, drove the eight bay horses, a groom rode one of the leaders and a footman walked at each of the horse's heads. Through the eight large windows Napoleon and Josephine could be clearly seen, Joseph and Louis Bonaparte facing them. All four were dressed in white satin and diamonds, but the spectators' eyes were on Josephine. The Paris crowd knew her age; they had not expected to see "a radiant girl of twenty-five."[2] Much of their cheering appeared to be directed at her. There was some speculation as to Napoleon's thoughts as he drove to his coronation. Apparently one subject was an evaluation of the temper of the crowd. Police reports the next day flatteringly referred to the warmth of the acclamations, but the more realistic Emperor wrote Joseph afterwards: "I noticed that there was no real enthusiasm anywhere, but then nothing untoward happened either."

Disaffected monarchists were predictably savage. One ultraroyalist was particularly affronted by the sight of "the three imperial sisters who had left their laundry behind and now appeared in all their finery and diamonds to carry the train of Barras's former mistress."[3]

Just as the state coach reached Notre Dame, the sun broke through at the same date and the same hour, as Napoleon would later point out, as the "Sun of Austerlitz" was to do one year later. To the roar of cannon and the peal of bells, the imperial pair stepped out and the crowd near the cathedral had an unimpeded view. Midway now between the lean and hawk-eyed Captain Bonaparte and the later paunchy and balding Napoleon, the Emperor, with his increased weight and short legs, was not flattered by the abbreviated, flared velvet coat over puffed pantaloons. At least one spectator decided that Napoleon's costume became him less than his uniform. "Perhaps successful on the drawing board," wrote Mme de Boigne, "it looked terrible on the Emperor who is short, fat and awkward. . . . He looked like the King of Diamonds."[4] But the crowd caught its breath at the sight of the Empress, of her expression of bliss, of her graceful majesty and simplicity.[5]

Meanwhile, most of the assembly had already sat for five or six hours in the freezing church. Fortunately, the long wait had been relieved for some by the surreptitious sale of rolls and hot sausage. Without this sustenance or any form of heating, the Pope sat, bowed over on his throne, silently praying.

But the imperial cortege was not yet ready. The Emperor and Empress proceeded to a robing room next to the cathedral, where they were to disrobe and then dress again. Over Napoleon's long satin garment, his imperial purple velvet mantle sown with bees and lined in ermine was attached at the waist and over the right shoulder. In his right hand he held a scepter. Crowned with "an antique wreath of gold laurel leaves, he exactly resembled," it was remarked, "a Caesar on a Roman coin."[6] He appeared dignified, very pale and much moved. An hour later they emerged. Josephine came first, still smiling, still perfectly at ease, wearing a diadem and her own imperial mantle. As she advanced, slowly pacing under a canopy, the great weight of her mantle was sustained by the five Bonaparte princesses whose own trains, as finally agreed to, were carried by their chamberlains. In front of the Empress walked the heralds at arms, the pages, the grand master of ceremonies, three marshals and the Empress's chamberlains and equerries, each one ten paces apart. General Murat carried her crown on a cushion, another marshal bore her ring.

The Emperor's cortege followed. His crown and his regalia, the sword, the necklace and the globe, were carried before him by his mar-shals and by Cardinal Fesch, his purple mantle held up by his two broth-ers and by the former First and Second Consuls. Under his canopy the Emperor appeared as much at ease as the Empress, so much so that, as the cortege in his opinion was walking too slowly, he unself-consciously tried to hurry it by prodding Uncle Fesch between the shoulders with the imperial scepter.

As the two processions entered Notre Dame, the four orchestras broke into a triumphal march and the congregation, forgetting where they were, burst into prolonged applause that lasted as long as the imperial couple's slow advance to the two thrones set before the altar. After each had knelt for what was described as an exceedingly brief prayer, there followed the service which the Emperor had organized so that all of the ceremony carried out near the altar could be seen by very few members of the congregation. Even so, the Emperor, dreading the reaction of his marshals and generals, had informed the Pope at the last minute that he and the Empress would not be taking the customary coronation Com-munion. Neither would they follow another custom of the kings of France who invariably lay full length, faces to the ground, for the most solemn moment of the service. Napoleon knew better than to provide the spectacle of his body and Josephine's lying side by side before the high altar; the Emperor and Empress would merely kneel on cushions to receive the Pope's triple unction of the holy oil on their heads and both hands.* Laure d'Abrantès, standing only a few feet from Napoleon, was certain that his thoughts at this moment were centered on how to wipe off the oil.

When the Pope had finished High Mass, Napoleon and Josephine, once more followed by their entire retinue, their trains spread out and carried, returned to their thrones while the Pope first blessed and then placed on the altar the two crowns. Then, in deep silence, Napoleon strode up the steps to the altar, and, before the Pope could do so, seized

---

* Ironically, the kings of France, starting with Clovis in 496, had all been anointed with oil from a certain holy flask; Josephine might have been anointed with oil from this relic had it not been destroyed after Alexandre de Beauharnais, in one of his furious diatribes at the Convention, proposed that "these baubles of tyranny and superstition be burned on the altar of the Fatherland."

the larger crown with both hands, turned to face the congregation, lifted it high and then slowly placed it on his head.

"At this moment," wrote Laure d'Abrantès, "he was truly handsome and his countenance was illuminated by an expression almost impossible to describe." Then he picked up Josephine's smaller crown and deliberately stepped down. Mme de Rémusat wrote:

> She was so unaffected, so graceful as she advanced toward the altar, she knelt down with such simple elegance that all eyes were delighted with the picture which she presented—the personification of elegance and majesty. In Napoleon's countenance, I could read all I have just said. He looked with an air of complacency at the Empress as she advanced toward him and when she knelt down, when the tears which she could not repress fell upon her clasped hands as they were raised to heaven, or rather to Napoleon, both appeared to enjoy one of those fleeting moments of shared felicity which are unique in a lifetime. The Emperor performed with peculiar grace every action required of him during the ceremony, but his manner of crowning Josephine was most remarkable. After picking up her small crown, he first put it on his own head and then transferred it to hers. When the moment arrived for [placing] the crown on the head of the woman whom popular superstition regarded as his good angel, his manner was almost playful. He took great pains to arrange this little crown, which was set over Josephine's diadem; he put it on, then took it off, and finally put it on again as if to promise her that she should wear it gracefully and lightly.[7]

Now that the sacred (and to most of the congregation invisible) part of the service was over, the secular portion could be observed by all those present. The seating of the congregation made this intention clear. The least eminent persons were closer to the altar, and the most important were clustered around the base of two larger thrones placed high over the cathedral's great entrance door, closed off today for the ceremony.

First the Empress and then the Emperor began the dangerous ascent. This was the moment for the revenge of the Bonaparte sisters. As Josephine started up the twenty-four steep steps, they dropped—or failed to "sustain"—the heavy mantle. Josephine was seen to nearly lose her balance as its full weight pulled her backwards. A sharp word from the watching Napoleon brought his sisters to attention.*

After blessing the sovereign and proclaiming: "Vivat Imperator in aeternum!" the Pope and his suite returned to the east end of the vast cathedral, finished Mass at the altar there, then retired to the sacristy, unwilling to appear to countenance all the tenets of the Emperor's constitutional oath, administered to him by the presiding officers of the legislative bodies. In a firm voice that could be heard throughout the cathedral, Napoleon solemnly swore to "maintain the integrity of the territories of the Republic, to respect political, civil and religious liberties, and the irrevocability of the sale of national property." He was destined to perjure himself on each count except the last.

Cannon once again thundered and the great bell of Notre Dame boomed as the crowned pair slowly descended the steps and, preceded once more by pages, heralds, masters of ceremonies, chamberlains and marshals, their mantles upheld by the princes and princesses of the family, they emerged from the cathedral.

It was now three o'clock and would soon be dark. The return to the Tuileries had been routed along a wider itinerary so that the largest number of Parisians might acclaim their newly crowned sovereigns. The crowds were greater, and in the more proletarian sections, enthusiasm and cheers were warmer than they had been that morning. Five hundred torches carried by pages and footmen, both mounted and on foot, lit the same sumptuous procession.

Vast Ns surrounded by laurel wreaths were on every building and on the still unfinished Madeleine. In the Place de la Concorde a huge star was placed on the exact spot where Louis XVI's scaffold had stood. Chandeliers hung between the columns of the Gabriel buildings of the Place, and finally, as the coaches rolled in through the Tuileries gates, the garden and the palace itself sparkled with a thousand lights.

The newly anointed Emperor decreed that he and his Empress

---

* An alert Austrian, Prince Clary, seated in the cathedral that day, watched the Bonaparte sisters with some amusement. "Nothing was more comical than the manner in which they acquitted themselves of their duty. Hortense and Mme Joseph were perfectly dignified, but one sister sulked, another held smelling salts under her nose and a third let the mantle drop; and this made things worse because then it had to be picked up."[8]

should end this interminable day by dining alone together. He asked her to wear her crown during this tête-à-tête "because it was so becoming, because she looked so pretty," and because "no one could wear a crown with more grace."[9]

Louis David continued to work on his painting of the coronation for another four years. Some changes were made. The Bonaparte sisters are no longer depicted "sustaining" Josephine's mantle; they are standing to the left with Hortense and little Napoleon Charles, and the Empress's ladies-in-waiting are holding her train. The absent Madame Mère and her own chamberlains and maids of honor are painted in (it was noted that Mme Letizia appeared to be wearing an improbably wide smile), and David has added his own presence in the same tribune overlooking the high altar.

The central moment of the painting portrays the coronation of Josephine by the Emperor. This decision appears to have arisen from David's difficulty in linking harmoniously the three principal personages—the Pope, the Emperor and the Empress. After six months and innumerable sketches of Napoleon's gesture of crowning himself, one of David's apprentices suggested the scene as it was finally painted; and it was the Emperor's proposal that for the sake of unity, the Pope's gesture of blessing be added.[10]

At St. Helena, however, Napoleon would tell General Bertrand that the composition of the celebrated painting was the result of "one of Josephine's little intrigues."[11] If this conversation took place, did either the Empress or the artist recall that his signature was one of those on Alexandre de Beauharnais's order of arrest? Certainly not David. Two years earlier, when a man who had managed to escape the guillotine asked the artist whether he could remember once signing the order for his arrest, David replied "No, it would have been impossible to remember all the orders of arrest I signed when I was a member of the Committee of Public Safety. Every day I was brought hundreds of them to sign and in the heat of the moment, I did not even read everything I signed."[12]

When, in 1808, Napoleon and Josephine visited David's studio to inspect the finished painting, the Emperor spent over an hour examining every detail of the grandiose composition. He was predictably delighted by the picture's realism and by all the recognizable portraits. And "I am grateful to you, David," he pronounced, "for recording for posterity the proof of the affection I wished to give to the woman who shares with me the burden of office."

‎26‎

The Sun of Austerlitz

WHILE DECEMBER 2, 1804, MAY WELL HAVE BEEN THE HAPPIEST DAY OF Josephine's life, Napoleon's own was still to come. It was, he would say, the moment when the sun broke out exactly a year later, on the first anniversary of the coronation.

The newly imperial couple were fully occupied for the next months following the list of festivities prescribed, in minute detail, by the Emperor: the "Distribution of the Eagles," out of doors on the Champ de Mars—it rained so violently and relentlessly on this occasion that Josephine and her ladies were forced to flee halfway through the ceremony, hair and makeup streaming, court dresses and trains soaked—the reception at the Tuileries for foreign princes, a dinner for the great dignitaries of the Empire, balls given by the ministers of war and navy, the opening session of the Legislative Body and the presentation to the Empress of each of the Bonaparte princely households.

Napoleon, already president of the Republic of Lombardy, which he himself had created, decided in the spring of 1805 that he should be its king, too, and the puppet deputies of that state were instructed to offer him the iron crown once owned by Charlemagne. On their way to Milan for the coronation, the Emperor and Empress together visited some of the battlefields of the first and second Italian campaigns, while he explained each maneuver in detail; it is not difficult to imagine Josephine's resistance to any such attempt in the early days of her marriage. He had been in high good humor since the coronation, and her feeling of security was now so strong that there were few recriminations when it became apparent that Napoleon was pursuing an affair with her pretty new "reader." Serenity was restored when he did not resist the rapid return of Mlle Lacoste to France.

The Italian coronation was modeled on the ceremony at Notre Dame, except that this time the Empress was an uncrowned spectator. Now "Her Majesty the Queen of Italy," she was, also, as predicted by the soothsayer in Martinique, "even greater than a queen," both Empress *and* Queen. Napoleon's spirits were so high that night that when they returned to their apartments he began by mimicking the day's ceremony (he had during the service once again placed the crown on his own head and had even shocked the congregation by negligently carrying it into the cathedral under his arm, as though it were a hat), then started playing children's games with Josephine, chasing her around the room, tickling and pinching her until she pleaded: "Stop it, Bonaparte!"

Napoleon's brothers and sisters had been ordered to attend this coronation, too. In silent outrage they viewed "*la* Beauharnais," Queen of Italy, seated on a second throne at the ceremonial levées, but when in Milan they heard that Eugène was to be appointed Viceroy of Italy and adopted by Napoleon as a "son of France," Caroline Murat pleaded a sudden indisposition preventing her from attending any functions, and Marshal Murat in a fury broke his sword across his knee.

From Milan the Emperor went directly to the Channel coast to inspect the army for the invasion of the British Isles, and from there continued to send affectionate, even flirtatious letters to Josephine. "I have a fine army here and a fine fleet, everything I need to pass the time agreeably; only my sweet Josephine is missing . . . but women are better kept in suspense, uncertain of their power. A thousand affectionate kisses everywhere. . . . "

Josephine may have sensed a guilty note in that letter—she probably already knew that Napoleon had sent for an Italian girl "to pass the time agreeably"—but she was determined to remain silent. Her children had always urged her to overlook the Emperor's liaisons, and she wrote to Eugène that month: "No more jealous scenes now, my dear Eugène, I can truthfully say, and so we are both much happier."[1]

Napoleon, in fact, was by no means passing the time agreeably, but was in an unending violent rage. His invasion troops were ready to embark, and he informed his minister of the navy that if the French fleet could control the Channel for just twenty-four hours he would be able to land his army of ten thousand men at Dover. Admiral Villeneuve was directed to sail up the Channel and secure that control. Napoleon, ignorant of the importance of wind and tides, sent him hourly insulting messages, as Villeneuve remained trapped by the British fleet in the Spanish port of Cadiz, and the Channel was still under English command.

The Emperor was therefore on the Channel coast in the summer of 1805 when Talleyrand sent him proof that Austria was now definitely preparing for war. Napoleon's assumption of the crown of Italy and his reign over most of the former Austrian possessions there had proved the ultimate offense, and the Emperor of Austria was now prepared to join the Third Coalition with Britain and Russia; the King of Prussia, however, still hesitated to risk an alliance with them, and Napoleon immediately decided on the audacious plan of force-marching his army straight to the heart of Europe and of beating the Austrians and Russians before they could be joined by Prussia. His plan was then to return to the Channel coast and annihilate England.

Josephine implored Napoleon to take her with him, at least as far as Strasbourg. She would, she pleaded, be closer to him to receive his couriers and his letters, and nearer to be sent for—arguments certainly unheard of during the Italian campaign after their marriage—and at four in the morning of September 24 they drove together out of the Tuileries in the Emperor's sleeping coach, traveling for fifty-eight hours without a stop. Buckets of water had to be thrown over the steaming coach wheels at each relay, while the eight exhausted horses were changed for fresh ones.[2] At the former Episcopal palace in Strasbourg, the imperial apartments had been redecorated for their arrival, and silver, linen, furniture, table and kitchenware had been dispatched from Paris by the invaluable Pierre Fontaine.

After one long session in a steaming bath the Emperor departed, heading one prong of the Grand Army fanning out "in five torrents" across the face of Europe. The elite corps of the Imperial Guard formed his bodyguard and his escort on the march, a troop of its cavalry surrounded his carriage and its commander rode at his carriage door. The

Guard surrounded him whenever he left his sleeping coach to relieve himself; while the entire caravan halted, four of its chasseurs presented arms and formed a square, their backs turned to him. In the field, two officers of the Guard slept in the imperial tent. Once the numbered components were taken out of their leather tubes, the tent could be put together in half an hour; the steel bed and its green silk curtains and the folding desk took even less time to assemble. As soon as the Emperor left his carriage the Guards escort dismounted to guard his "palace" (in Guards' terminology, this meant any residence of His Majesty's, whether St. Cloud, the Tuileries or the campaign tent itself), and the units of the elite corps selected for guard duty would change into the impeccable "palace" uniform stowed in their knapsacks.

General Berthier, the chief of staff, usually accompanied the Emperor in the famous campaign carriage, and Roustam the Mameluke was responsible for keeping it furnished with medical supplies, a telescope, Napoleon's coat, handkerchief and gloves, some brandy, pens and ink, sealing wax and a compass. There were compartments for maps and papers so that the Emperor's dictated material might be sent back at the next relay, and a small travel library of specially printed, small-format books. Out of the coach's windows would come flying—and sometimes hitting the escorting officers—dismembered books, maps found to be inadequate and torn-up dispatches. These last would have been presented through the opened window by an officer galloping beside the carriage, holding in one hand his gloves and his mount's reins, in the other, on his folded hat, the dispatch itself.

The following carriages contained kitchen utensils, a portable stove and the Chambertin wine. When the Emperor on campaign decided that it was time for a meal, Roustam and the footmen removed the silver-gilt plates from their leather covers and served the imperial version of fast food from already prepared dishes. Half an hour later everything was packed away into the fifty-two carriages that followed the Emperor, a departure always made, said his valet Constant, "with the speed of light."

Everything in this campaign was dependent on speed. Napoleon was determined to catch the Austrians while their Russian allies were several days' march away and the Prussians still undecided. Much of the French army's legendary mobility depended on their traveling light. Their supply trains were unable to keep up with the troops who, though they carried a week's rations in their packs, sometimes were down "to just one hard biscuit tied by a string around the soldier's neck."[3] But while they were still in Germany they lived off the land; one Austrian officer thought the men looked like "walking larders, hung about with long sides of bacon, and pieces of meat hanging from their belts."[4]

The headlong drive across Europe was so swift that as soon as the Grand Army crossed the Danube it fell upon part of the Austrian army waiting to be joined by the Russians. Their general had believed Napoleon was still on the Channel coast. The Austrians were encircled and routed, and their entire army capitulated at Ulm. "I have fulfilled my destiny. I have destroyed the Austrian army. . . . I have lost only fifteen hundred men. . . . This will be the shortest, the most successful and the most brilliant of the campaigns I have fought. . . . Adieu my Josephine, a thousand sweet kisses everywhere,"[5] exulted Napoleon, announcing this victory.

He was writing to her faithfully every few days, while she followed his directives at Strasbourg: presiding over dinners, giving audiences, receptions and suppers and visiting hospitals as the wounded French were brought in. For two months Strasbourg was the staging post for all who had any business with the Emperor or with France. And at Strasbourg, Josephine heard news that Napoleon still ignored: that on the day of the victory of Ulm—October 21—the French fleet had been destroyed by Nelson at Trafalgar. By the time Napoleon learned of this end to his hopes of invading Britain he was issuing the triumphant army bulletin of the victory of Austerlitz, and immediately ordered the French press to make only a passing reference to the defeat at Trafalgar.

The need for a total victory on the continent was now doubly necessary. Anything less would cause Prussia to join the coalition. (Napoleon, in common with the rest of Europe, believed the Prussian army still to be the powerful instrument of the Great Frederick's day). His next letter warned Josephine that there might be a five- or six-day interval before she heard from him again, but "I am in good health and I love you"; there was soaking rain, his feet were cold and: "I am about to march against the Russians; they are as good as beaten."[6]

In November the pace of the Grand Army slowed in the unending sleet and icy rain, as it wheeled east to pursue that part of the Austrian army which had joined up with the Tsar's. The horses plowed through mud up to their bellies. Until at least 1807, Napoleon's endurance was extraordinary; on campaign he could ride for ten hours at a stretch, oblivious to rain or snow, sitting hunched, his mind elsewhere and his reins held loosely or not at all.* The Emperor also abandoned his coach and his portable bed and slept in shelters or in the open, on his rolled-up coat. His gray coat was soaked, his cocked hat a formless mass. No wonder his notes to Josephine from this campaign usually started with: "I have a slight cold."

By the time the army reached Moravia in the present-day Czech Republic, it was snowing steadily. Napoleon knew that the Austro-Russian armies were not far distant. He knew too that they were as aware as he that he was far from his base, his supply line overextended as usual, his baggage train long outdistanced, his men exhausted. The allies, he was sure, were bound to attack soon in an attempt to sever the French lines of communication. Once again it was imperative to take terrible chances.

Napoleon decided to await the inevitable attack on ground of his own choosing and to trick the overconfident allies into believing that he was about to withdraw. His confidence in the coming battle was absolute: his own superior tactical skills would compensate for the enemy's superiority in troops and guns. It was his capacity to read the mind of his opponents that was to win him what has been called the first great battle of modern history, and, by his own estimate, his most brilliant tactically.

On December 1, Napoleon awaited the allied forces near the village of Austerlitz. In the silent foggy night of the eve of this first anniversary of the coronation, only the sounds of spurs and the jingle of harnesses from the enemy encampments could be heard; the Emperor knew that this meant that the Russian and Austrian armies had fallen into his trap and were taking up the positions he had assigned them. The battle, Napoleon knew, would depend on the enemy reacting to his plan and to the sun rising, as it had for the past week, promptly at eight o'clock and dispersing the heavy ground mist at exactly that hour.

---

* His falls were numerous but the imperial escort was always provided with several extra mounts for him. These had been especially trained to be prepared for sounds of battle and slack reins; hens and even sheep were thrown at their legs, horns blared in their ears.

On the morning of December 2, the entire landscape was enveloped in a milk-white mist, hiding the French battle positions and Marshal Soult's concentration of troops in a valley.

At exactly eight o'clock, a great red sun, the celebrated "sun of Austerlitz," broke through, just as it had on the morning of the coronation—the sun immortalized in Tolstoy's account of the battle in *War and Peace*. The enemy had been certain that the French army had started a strategic retreat and was unprepared for an early morning attack. As the sun rose, at a signal from Napoleon his troops charged the Russian lines at what he had foreseen would be their most vulnerable point.

Within three hours the Austro-Russian forces were cut in two. Though the giants of the Russian Imperial Guard were thrown in at noon, their bayonet charges were smashed by the French Imperial Guard and by the scimitars of the Mamelukes. It was almost dark when several thousand Russians retreated with their cavalry and artillery over a thinly iced-over lake, and when Napoleon ordered his cannon to fire red hot balls on to the ice, twenty thousand men, he would claim, were drowned.

The Emperor himself had remained on his hilltop, not through any want of courage—his star, he believed, made him invulnerable—but because there had been little need to change any of his tactical plan. In his letter to Josephine he described the battle as "the most beautiful of all those I have fought . . . more than 30,000 dead, a horrible sight!" The surrounding fields and villages were filled with the dead and dying. As he wrapped himself in his coat and lay down on some straw that night, Napoleon said to Méneval*: "This is the happiest day of my life."

The victory at Austerlitz was total; the Austrians asked for terms and the Russians retreated east. Napoleon went on to Vienna, staying in the imperial palace of Schönbrunn while he prepared for the peace treaty with Austria. The Hapsburg family was once again in flight and the Austrian Emperor's daughter, fourteen-year-old Marie Louise, burst into tears at the news of her country's defeat and the harsh terms of that treaty. She wrote in her diary that the French ogre was said to be the Beast of the Apocalypse, that his death that year was predicted, and "how happy I

---

* Baron de Méneval, Bourrienne's successor as Napoleon's secretary.

would be if this were true."[7] In Vienna, when one of Napoleon's generals suggested that he should divorce his barren wife and marry one of the nubile Austrian archduchesses, the Emperor replied that that solution was out of the question. "The Austrian Archduchesses have always been disastrous for France," he replied, "and the memory of Marie Antoinette is too recent."[8]

In Talleyrand's opinion, a moderate treaty now would have made an ally of Austria, a bulwark against Russia, and ensured a balance of power in Europe; Napoleon, however, insisted upon the savage dismemberment of Austria and the abolition of the Holy Roman Empire. Some portions of it—Bavaria and Württemberg, for instance—forced to join Napoleon's newly formed Confederation of the Rhine, were to be promoted into kingdoms, the better to provide the extended Bonaparte family with brilliant alliances.

The first member to benefit from this policy was Eugène de Beauharnais. He was, his stepfather informed him, to be married within days; the announcement had already been published in the French newspapers. His bride, the daughter of the Elector of Bavaria, was pretty, he wrote, "better looking than her portrait painted on the cup I am sending you."[9]

Correspondence with Josephine was as unsatisfactory as ever. In Vienna, Napoleon, who had received no answer to his two letters on the victory at Austerlitz, wrote her a heavy-handedly playful reproach: "Mighty Empress . . . I have not had a single line from you . . . not very nice, or very loving. Deign from the height of your splendor to take a little notice of your slave. . . ."[10] And he informed her of his plans for Eugène, and told her that she should leave Strasbourg and join him in Munich for her son's wedding.

There followed succinct instructions on every detail of her first imperial progress alone. Her own carriage, shared by two ladies-in-waiting, was to be preceded by one carrying two chamberlains of her household and followed by her maid with her luggage and the imperial jewel cases and, last in the convoy, a carriage bearing two masters of the horse and her personal physician. Her arrival in any town, escorted by a guard of honor, was to be heralded by the sound of church bells, cannon, drums and trumpets. All the rulers of the German courts she was to visit on her way were already, or were shortly to become, the Emperor's vassals; therefore, "Be civil to all of them," Napoleon wrote, "but accept their homage as your due." However, "treat the daughter of the King of England [married to the Elector of Württemberg] with courtesy, but nothing more. A thousand kisses."[11]

The days were past when the First Consul had felt it necessary to dictate the "spontaneous thanks" Josephine was to memorize. Already as professional in her public role as Napoleon was in his, she left a trail of goodwill in the new Confederation of the Rhine, as confident, as informally regal as her hosts the electors, princes and dukes of the German states who vied in welcoming the conqueror's wife. Handing out snuffboxes and miniatures, dazzlingly dressed, seemingly tireless at dawn or late at night, she never appeared less than grateful for the honor arches at each arrival or too tired to listen to the obligatory harangues addressed to "Enthroned Virtue" or to "The French Minerva." Napoleon was gratified but hardly surprised when told of her success. "I win battles," he said, "but Josephine wins hearts."[12]

When Napoleon himself arrived in Munich, the Bavarian capital, he came up against an impressive list of objections to the projected marriage. First, Princess Augusta, the sovereign's daughter, was already engaged to the Crown Prince of Baden and intended to marry him; her father objected too that Eugène was not even the Emperor's son but "merely a French gentleman." Then the Elector made it clear that he would prefer Napoleon himself to marry Augusta after a quick divorce from Josephine; and lastly, Princess Augusta's young stepmother was not only the Prince of Baden's sister, but had herself hoped to marry the murdered Duc d'Enghien and execrated Napoleon.

The Emperor sliced through the whole embroilment, sent for Eugène to come immediately, decreed that the Prince of Baden should marry a Beauharnais niece of Josephine's, and sealed it all by promoting the Elector King of Bavaria, and Eugène Viceroy of Italy, Imperial Highness and officially adopted son.

Eugène galloped from Italy—four days from Padua to Munich, his fiancée's portrait on a cup in his saddlebags—and was married off within three days of his arrival. Hortense wrote in despair that Louis Bonaparte forbade her to assist at her brother's wedding. Josephine, at first in tears at the thought of Eugène leaving Paris, regained her spirits as she realized she could now feel doubly secure. Eugène, as Napoleon's adopted son, might well be named his heir to the throne, and the Emperor had already proposed adopting Napoleon Charles, her grandson, as his successor.

The marriage proved to be a love match, and it would be Eugène's eldest daughter, Josephine, who, married to Désirée and Jean Bernadotte's son, would make of Alexandre and Josephine de Beauharnais the ancestors of virtually every royal house in Europe.

By a clause in the peace treaty, Francis I of Austria assented to the abolition of the Holy Roman Empire, whose head for centuries had been the Emperor of Austria. Napoleon, when he "accepted" the title of Protector of the Confederation of the Rhine, started immediately to impose the members of his own family and of Josephine's onto the dismembered principalities and duchies that had composed the late empire. By making the states of the Confederation into family fiefdoms he hoped to create a glacis surrounding France and within the year two German princelings, the Prince of Baden and the Duc d'Arenberg, were drawn into the imperial alliance by marriages to two of Josephine's young relatives.

As soon as the sovereigns of the joint throne of Naples and Sicily—allies of the British—had been thrown out by French troops, Joseph Bonaparte was allotted that crown. Holland was transformed from the vassal "Batavian Republic" into a kingdom, and that throne was given to Louis Bonaparte. Although Joseph's shy wife was permitted to remain in Paris, the Emperor insisted that Hortense accompany her husband to The Hague. She hated to leave her mother, cared nothing for the trappings of royalty and dreaded virtual banishment from Paris. As Louis Bonaparte's physical condition worsened, he tried ever more bizarre and repulsive treatments for it, and now she was required to sleep in the same bed, though he wore at night the rags off the back of a beggar.

The Murats, to their disgust, were given not a kingdom but the newly minted duchy of Berg in Germany, with Düsseldorf as its capital. The new grand duchess objected that both her sisters-in-law, Hortense and Mme Joseph, were to be queens; how could her brother be so cruel? Even Mme Letizia sulked because the only title given her was Madame Mère. Elisa was granted the Grand Duchy of Tuscany, where she organized a court at which her husband was required to walk several steps behind her. Only Pauline had other ambitions. Still almost endearingly determined to outshine every other woman always, everywhere, she could be heard chattering unself-consciously to her mother about their indigent days in Marseilles.

There was nothing to be done that year about Jérôme, since the Pope had so far objected to annulling the valid church marriage of this youngest Bonaparte brother. While France and England were at war, Jérôme had deserted the ship he commanded in the West Indies and sailed off alone to visit the United States. There he had met and married "the belle of Baltimore," Betsy Patterson. When he and his pregnant wife attempted to land in Holland on their way to France, a furious Napoleon had Talleyrand inform the authorities in that vassal state that "a woman named Patterson who has followed Mr. Jérôme Bonaparte to Europe"[13] was not to be permitted into the territory of the Empire. Once in France, Jérôme, upon the promise of a kingdom, agreed to the annulment of his marriage by the "Officiality of Paris," an invention of the Concordat. Betsy took refuge in England, where she gave birth to a son and was feted as a victim of Napoleonic tyranny.

Lucien, with more character than Jérôme, refused to leave his Alexandrine, though he was offered a crown on condition that he declare his wife a concubine and his children illegitimate. There was a heated confrontation between the brothers, and when Napoleon shouted that Lucien had "married a whore," the response was prompt. "At least *my* whore is young and pretty!"[14]

None of these promotions, however, could settle the burning questions of the inheritance of the imperial crown of France. Although Eugène, Napoleon's loyal viceroy in Italy, was not ruled out of the succession, and although Joseph and Lucien had fathered only daughters, Louis refused to have his son Napoleon Charles named the Emperor's heir. He accused his brother of "disinheriting" him, of being outranked by his own son, and before being given the Dutch throne, he threatened to leave France and to take Napoleon Charles with him.

There were endless jealous squabbles within the clan, with Madame Mère siding alternately with one or the other member. But the entire family was united in one determination—to be rid of "that woman"—although they tended to agree with Napoleon that his "genius" was concentrated in his head, rather than in any other place that might provide him with a natural successor.

Caroline Murat had almost given up hope of her brother's divorce from "*la* Beauharnais" unless it could be proved that he could father a child. That winter she introduced him to another former pupil of Mme Campan's school, Eléonore Denuelle, eighteen years old, slender, black-eyed and ambitious. It was decided in the interest of a controlled experiment that Eléonore should be virtually quarantined in a wing of the Murats' house outside Paris, where the Emperor could visit her regularly. Paris soon knew that in this loveless arrangement, "boudoir conscription" it was called, Eléonore was so bored by Napoleon's visits that she made it a practice to put the clock in her bedroom a half hour forward each time.

ᴁ 27 ᴥ

One of the Rays of His Star

WHEN THE EMPEROR RETURNED AFTER THE VICTORY AT AUSTERLITZ IN
the winter of 1805, he would remain in Paris for eight months, until the
next campaign. Rejoicing over that victory was tempered in France by the
knowledge that everything had once again hung upon the outcome of one
battle. Fouché, who had been reinstated as minister of police (like Talleyrand, he believed that there was "no power without office"), informed
Napoleon that owing to the lack of public confidence in the Emperor's
victories, the financial situation was critical, and that citizens lining up in
front of banks to remove their savings were being savagely attacked by
police. There had been several bankruptcies and there was mounting
opposition to the Empire. Fouché had, however, succeeded in keeping the
terrible news of the defeat at Trafalgar from the public.

Fouché noted that the Emperor, though irritated by this lack of fiscal
confidence, dismissed the information as unimportant. He was in a hurry
to change certain observances at the Tuileries. Deeply impressed by his
first view of the royal households of the Austrian and Bavarian courts and
struck by the regulations of Munich, he resolved to echo them at his own
court, but there was to be more pomp and more rigid etiquette. Minute
rules of precedence were drawn up for the Tuileries. Napoleon did not feel
secure enough to live the domestic life of King Maximilian of Bavaria or
King George of England, accustomed to walking around the streets of
their capitals like simple citizens. At those courts there was a simplicity,
a certain familiarity with the world outside.

Still as unable as he had been in youth to tolerate any sense of social
inferiority, Napoleon resolved, from the pinnacle of success and power he
had reached, that his court should outshine any in Europe. His civilian

and military households were to be even more numerous, more glittering than at Versailles before the Revolution. Like the Bourbon kings he now had a grand almoner (Uncle Fesch), a grand marshal, a grand equerry, a grand huntsman (his chief of staff Marshal Berthier) and a grand master of ceremonies.

Josephine's household was an echo of his, with the difference that none of the male members of her household, almoner, chamberlain, equerry, chief equerry in charge of the stables, lords-in-waiting, ushers, footmen or pages might enter her private apartments. There was an oriental air, a whiff of the harem in some of the Emperor's rules, such as: "The Empress never receives any man in her interior apartments unless he is in her service." If the chamberlain of the day "has to traverse the outer apartments of Her Majesty in order to take orders, he must scratch lightly* on the door of the bedroom, where one of the Ladies of Her Majesty must be always in attendance, and seek permission to be introduced into her presence."

The observant Emperor, to whom social prestige still meant a great deal, was gratified to find Josephine giving an example of ease and simplicity to the insecure ladies married to his generals and court dignitaries, who felt that an unaffected manner could not be in good taste and who cultivated a carefully studied voice and stiffness—small nuances all noticed by the Emperor. Aimée de Coigny noted that the members of the new court were "self-conscious and snobbish and didn't know how to laugh, while Germaine de Staël observed that "a woman's political opinions were made clear by the way she entered a room," and that to underline this difference the ladies who had known Versailles made a point of exaggerating their effortless manner of talking and laughing.

One day, wrote Claire de Rémusat, the Emperor, when he first returned from the Bavarian court, decreed with his usual precipitation that there should be an immediate dress rehearsal of a court presentation. The imperial pair sat on their gilt armchairs surrounded by the Bonaparte princes and princesses on stools. High officials, ladies-in-waiting, marshals and ministers and their wives slowly advanced, bowing or curtsying. For the women who were to be presented, there was a first curtsy at the door, a second one a few steps further, then a third, after which the person presented had to back out, making three more curtsies. (Neither one of

---

* It had been the custom at Versailles to scratch rather than knock on a door.

the imperial couple had, of course, themselves been "presented"—that source of so much grief to Alexandre de Beauharnais.) Claire de Rémusat soon saw that Napoleon was becoming impatient at this lengthy ceremonial. To begin with, he had been fascinated by the etiquette; in the end, he could barely remain on his throne and had to be persuaded to stay to the end of the dress rehearsal he had ordered.[1]

The court was undeniably splendid, brash and even vulgar, but it was precisely this, said foreign visitors, which gave such an overwhelming impression of power. Though etiquette might be more rigid and a terrified silence the general rule, Napoleon's Tuileries had one advantage: the wives of generals and marshals in their twenties and thirties tended to be young and pretty.

Napoleon's sense of propaganda and eye for style and grandeur were visible everywhere: in his army's fantastic uniforms—he even brought back the helmet with trailing horsehair of Louis XIV's armies—in his campaign tent lined in *toile de Jouy* and carpeted in a mock tiger rug; in the decor of state occasions; in "the pomp and splendor of the imperial court and army, with their glittering helmets and swords and eagles, their clattering of cavalcades, their mixture of feminine grace and military dash . . . providing a spectacle and creating a mystique that intoxicated a generation and set the style for a century."[2] However, the Emperor's thoroughly modern understanding of the use of the visual image ensured that he never, in all this sumptuousness, abandoned his own carefully constructed silhouette, familiar in a thousand prints, of the cocked hat, the simple uniform and the long gray coat.

In the eight months he was to spend in Paris, he was to see that everything in the city, as well as all that surrounded the Emperor, should proclaim the majesty and might of the Empire; architecture, decoration and commemorative monuments were to express political power.

Napoleon, who had an innate sense of proportion and a love of noble perspective as well as of self-propaganda, made few mistakes during this period, though he came within an ace of pulling down the whole palace of Versailles—but then, it was always Rome, whether republican or imperial, that ruled his taste. In this still triumphant year, he set himself—and Percier and Fontaine—the task of constructing monuments, august and splendid, to commemorate himself, though he warned his architects that he did not wish them to be too obviously destined for self-glorification. "What I want above all is grandeur," he said, "whatever is grand is always beautiful." A monument to tower over the straight avenue of the Champs-Elysées, leading down to the Tuileries, was immediately important. At first, an elephant sixty feet high was proposed, to be inscribed with the names of the Emperor's victories. Not only were the blueprints for an arch there changed almost yearly, but the builders objected to working so far out of town, and the Arc de Triomphe that finally replaced the elephant was not finished until long after Napoleon's reign.

Napoleon himself lived to see only one commemorative monument: the bronze column to the Grand Army in the Place Vendôme, on which was placed a statue of the Emperor. The column itself was made of melted-down Austrian cannon captured at Wagram, and the spiral of scenes from that battle showed Roman-looking warriors, naked but for helmet and shield, but often wearing the mustaches and sideburns of the Grenadiers of the Guard. Marshals and generals quarreled over their respective positions on the column. The monument was not ready for inauguration until 1810, but the ceremony had to be postponed when it was found to coincide with the Emperor's Austrian marriage; he did not consider it diplomatic on that occasion to celebrate a victory over his new father-in-law.

Napoleon was not always certain of his taste, and hundreds of architectural drawings from the drawing boards of Fontaine and Percier were discarded, but there was no hesitation when a question of classic mythology was in doubt. Upon being presented with a project for a fountain featuring mermaids spouting water from their breasts, he wrote in the margin, "Remove those nursing mothers! The Naiads were virgins."[3]

The spoils of war were installed around the center of Paris and moved, then moved again. The lion from the column in St. Mark's Square in Venice was dislodged three times from one plinth to another; the quadriga of bronze horses pulled off the facade of St. Mark's traveled around Paris and ended up, separated, on four columns in the Tuileries Gardens.

New bridges and avenues were planned. The Palladian arcades of the rue de Rivoli were finally going up on the foundations of the old riding school, sacred to the memory of the Convention; the street should, the Emperor decided, represent luxury only, butchers and bakers were to be banished, and a new street, which the Emperor resolved should be the most splendid in Europe leading out of the rue de Rivoli into the Place

Vendôme, was to be the rue Napoléon. At the Restoration, it was re-named the rue de la Paix, and the only street in Paris that now bears his name is the rue Bonaparte on the Left Bank.

The interior setting, too, for the pageantry of his court was minutely ordered by Napoleon. Charles Percier and Pierre Fontaine, the team of architect and decorator who had invented the idea of designing an entire interior and had transformed Malmaison and St. Cloud, were called in to create a banqueting room, a gallery and a grand new central staircase for the Tuileries, "more of an indoor parade ground," groaned the courtiers. Napoleon, who had originally stipulated that the decoration of the Tuileries be "simple and inexpensive," soon found the interior of the palace "too bare and simple." Now he insisted that the rooms in all his palaces be of unparalleled magnificence. The Lyons manufacturers were ordered to make elaborate silk brocades for upholstery and for wall hangings for each of the imperial palaces. "Out of sheer ostentation," sneered Mme de Genlis, "the damasks on the walls were pleated instead of stretched," while the rooms were filled with new furniture by the Jacob Brothers in the imposing, even heavy Empire style, replacing the more austere Consular fashion. Josephine herself put a brake on some of this pomp and imposed some of her own taste in her apartments at the Tuileries; at Malmaison, especially, she managed to successfully combine the domestic scale and intimacy that characterized the courts of European monarchs with the latest in updated forms of the Roman antique.

When Napoleon and Josephine were alone—neither one interested in food or wine—they dined in a few minutes. But even official banquets must reflect what Napoleon called the "social mirror," and he demanded for these occasions the complicated dishes promoted by the imperial chefs (gastronomy had become an art form since the Revolution); all the courses except for the dessert were still placed on the table together in a minutely ordered pattern. The *service à la Russe* (our custom of serving courses successively) would seldom be seen until later in the century. The serving dishes themselves, most often of Sèvres porcelain portraying imperial victories, were set between the massive silver gilt services, the candelabra and the four-foot-high soup tureens, all stamped or painted with the imperial arms.

. . .

Those around the Emperor had noted that since his return from Auster-litz and the Bavarian court "his despotism increased daily"[4] as did his passion for power. The weakened Tribunate, the Senate and the Legis-lative Body were allowed to remain in order to maintain the fiction that the Emperor ruled a republic. Napoleon drew up an imperial catechism this year in which he was practically sanctified. To the question: "What should one think of those who fail in their duties to our Emperor?" the French child's answer was to be: "According to the Apostle St. Paul, they would be resisting the order established by God Himself and would deserve eternal damnation."

Napoleon was far less accessible than in the past, or interested in the exchange of ideas or the acquiring of knowledge. His prodigious memory, however, remained unchanged, particularly in connection with the army. Caulaincourt maintained that there was never a time when the Emperor was unaware of the exact location of each regiment, of the names of its officers (even of some of the individuals who composed it) and of the state of its equipment.

But there were changes now in his daily routine. His increasing despotism was shown even in small ways: his rages and impatience em-braced every aspect of his life. "In the morning," wrote his valet Constant, "the Emperor had himself dressed by others from head to foot, allowing himself to be dressed like a child"—even to his socks embroidered with the imperial crown. Constant rubbed him down with eau de cologne (only eau de cologne or lavender water could be worn in his presence; casual mistresses were warned never to wear perfume). When he was completely dressed, the valet handed him his handkerchief, his snuffbox and a little tortoiseshell box full of licorice cut very fine.

None of this assistance was totally without hazard as the Emperor exhibited the same uncontrolled violence, hitting his servants when they irritated him, pushing them, throwing the nail scissors about. He had al-ways torn off any garment that constricted him in any way; now he would throw it in the fire, hitting the person who had tried to put it on him. At night, reported Constant, he would hurl his hat, coat, shoes and decora-tions all over the room, on the floor, on the bed and slap the nearest person to him. It was up to his valets to reorder whatever was necessary—

boots, most often; it was his habit while talking to kick the blazing logs burning in his rooms, summer and winter.

At nine each morning the Emperor entered his office to set about governing France and Europe. Sitting or standing near the fireplace, he dictated very fast and without hesitation to Claude de Méneval. Méneval had invented his own form of shorthand, but sometimes he had to be joined by a second secretary to keep track of the flow. Then, walking up and down, Napoleon would continue to dictate for at least six hours, ending with some articles for the French press. (When Méneval read him the morning newspapers, Napoleon would say: "No, not the *Moniteur*, I already know what's in it."[5]) The Emperor's interest embraced domestic details, too. Regularly he went through the palace accounts with Duroc, insisting that such items as bed linen be changed only once a month in the courtiers' apartments and towels once a week. Usually he lunched alone; sometimes with Josephine. He would decide in the morning in which rooms they would take their meals that day. Although in some private homes the returning emigrés had started the English custom of dining rooms, there would not be one at the Tuileries until the middle of the century.

For Napoleon's lunch, the cloth would be laid on any handy table and the meal served by the maître d'hôtel, while the palace prefect of the day stood nearby. He ate in haste, often with his fingers, sometimes the two or three courses in reverse order. Ten minutes later he had finished and was ready to give audiences or assist at meetings of the Council of State.

"Napoleon's habit of eating very fast often caused him terrible stomach pains, usually ending in vomiting," wrote Constant. The valet remembered a scene, apparently one of many, in which he found Napoleon lying full length in his bedroom, "on the carpet, which he often did when he felt ill. Josephine was seated at his side and Napoleon's head rested in her lap."[6]

After five he usually went down to watch Josephine dress, but just as often he then returned to his bureau and did not think of dinner, ordered for six o'clock, until nine or even later, sometimes not until midnight. This made no difference to the food, for at any time of the day or night in the Tuileries kitchens, chickens were turning on the spit and the Emperor never had to wait more than a few minutes for his evening meal, which was carried upstairs from the kitchens in closed baskets. One thing never changed—after dinner, only the Empress would pour his coffee, add sugar and taste it for him with one of the two silver gilt spoons always laid on the tray. If the meal had been at a reasonable hour, Napoleon and Josephine were joined in the Yellow Salon after dinner by some of the chamberlains and the generals of the Imperial Guard and their wives. Sometimes Napoleon talked for a short time or played chess or billiards; Josephine could always beat him, or anyone else, at billiards. Everyone in the Yellow Salon appeared to be stiff and worried, but when he left conversation resumed. At around nine or ten the Emperor retired either to bed or for further work at his desk and then often called for Josephine to talk or read to him. Sometimes he got up at night, sent for Méneval and from a steaming bath dictated for a couple of hours.

The Empress's own day never varied from the moment she was woken or the Emperor left her bedroom. Her door was opened to her dogs (no longer allowed to sleep in her room), and her four maids were called in. She bathed, painted her face and dressed in a negligé while her hairdresser arranged her hair for the day. A senior colleague arranged it more sumptuously in the evening, adding, when necessary, some dye "of a vigorous chestnut color."[7] While the hairdresser was at work, the ladies of the wardrobe carried in hampers of dresses, shawls, hats and shoes to be chosen for that morning; there would be two more entire changes of dress and underwear during the day. Dressed at last, Josephine reviewed the merchants waiting in an outer room—booksellers, portrait painters, jewelers, dressmakers, cabinetmakers—gave audiences; wrote at length to her children in Holland and Italy, and, of course, the inevitable letters of recommendation, tirelessly applying for posts and pensions for friends. The letters themselves were as elegant, as warm, and even more accomplished than they had been in the past.

She kept up a large correspondence on the subjects of her seed and plant collections and of the animals at Malmaison. (Nowhere in any European zoo were animals found in semi-liberty as in the Malmaison grounds.) When an expedition returned from Australia that year, Josephine asked to be given some of the animals they had brought back. Soon there were kangaroos, a gnu, a zebra, a female orangutan, llamas from Peru and a couple of emus at Malmaison. The Empress loved to feed the peacocks and the silver and gold pheasants in the gardens, but her greatest pride was the black Australian swans, never before seen in that hemisphere.

In spite of the war and the Continental Blockade, and though she continued to buy from French horticulturalists and rose growers, Josephine bought huge quantities of plants for Malmaison from a London nurseryman and even obtained a passport for him so that in time of war he could still travel back and forth between the two countries.

In her years as Empress, Josephine grew, for the first time in France at least, two hundred new plants, flowers and trees. Tree peonies, dahlias, pelargonium and a dozen more varieties of flowers were introduced. She was generous with all of these, sending duplicates to friends (Chateaubriand remembered a gift of "a purple-flowered magnolia, unique in France then"). She hoped to create botanical gardens in each section of France. "I wish," she wrote to one prefect, "that Malmaison may soon become the source of riches for all the *départements*. . . . For this reason, I have planted a large number of trees and shrubs from Australia and North America. In ten years' time I would like each *département* to own a collection of rare plants from my nurseries."[8]

Josephine gave countless gifts and was generous to her charities in Paris and St. Cloud, and many of her letters concerned the innumerable relatives and friends she supported. Her mother still refused to leave Martinique, but Uncle Robert Tascher and five of his nine children accepted her offer. She put them all up provisionally in the house on the rue de la Victoire, paid her uncle's debts, and obtained posts and embassies for his children. Her maternal cousins, the Vergers de Sannois, came over, too. Hortense's governess Mlle Lannoy, Euphémie Lefèvre (who had accompanied Josephine to France) and Josephine Tallien, her goddaughter (very much in secret), were all generously provided for, as were Alexandre de Beauharnais's wet nurse, his illegitimate daughter and his mistress Laure de la Touche, who had done her so much harm.

At exactly a quarter to ten—Josephine was so punctual that Laure d'Abrantès claimed she had "never once seen the Empress enter the salon either at 9:43 or 9:47—she received a few friends for lunch in the Yellow Salon if she was not invited to share Napoleon's meal. Dinner was always alone with the Emperor except on state occasions or on Sundays, when the Bonaparte family was expected to attend. Dressed and bejeweled, she would wait patiently for him to finish the work in his office in the evening.

Once the buying and correspondence were disposed of, she never, according to Mme de Rémusat, appeared to *do* anything; she did not read;

she might hold some needlework and ask some ladies or visitors to help her; if occasionally at Malmaison she played the harp, "it was always the same air,"[9] Méneval noted unkindly. After dinner she played cards or backgammon.

Josephine's spending was already legendary. "Not all the revenues of all the provinces of France," the Marquis de Sade had remarked of Josephine de Beauharnais in the days of the Directory, "could have satisfied her extravagance." She bought almost any merchandise brought to her, seldom asked the price and made not the slightest attempt to stay within her allowance.*

No queen ever owned a jewel collection like Josephine's—her own could not fit even into Marie Antoinette's jewel cabinet—for as well as her own personal collection, she owned the crown jewels of France. Yet something still remained of the sixteen-year-old bride who kept the three pieces of jewelry given her by her husband in her pocket, so that she could play with them. Josephine would summon Mlle Avrillon, who was in charge of the imperial jewelry, and have her open the cases containing some of the treasure the Empress had accumulated. Beside fabulous pearls, there were sets (a set comprised a diadem, a necklace, earrings, bracelets and pins) of rubies and diamonds, turquoises and diamonds, opals and diamonds, emeralds and diamonds, of agate, malachite, amber and an infinite number of pieces made of coral, steel and, especially prized, of classical cameos.

There were still colossal rows about her debts and violent scenes over her extravagance and reckless granting of pensions, but though the Emperor swore and shouted, he appeared to view with a certain satisfaction what he saw as these manifestations of her femininity.[10]

He liked Josephine to be heavily made up and correspondingly underdressed. She continued to wear the deepest décolletés and if he thought her shawl concealed too much of her person, he would tear it off her and throw it in the fire. She never protested, but calmly sent for another one, since she owned hundreds; cashmere shawls draped her boudoir in one

---

*Josephine's annual personal expenditure on clothes, jewelery, charities and gifts was "in the region of one million francs, which by a rough conversion equals almost one million United States dollars."

palace and were converted into bedspreads and dresses, and even cushions for her dogs.

Napoleon continued to be fascinated by everything connected with Josephine's clothes. When he irrupted into her dressing room as she was changing for dinner, he would rummage through her jewels and gowns and make her change several times until he was satisfied with the effect. Once, to make sure he would not again see a certain pink and silver lamé gown, he threw a bottle of ink over it when Josephine was already dressed for an evening reception.

Napoleon had always seen dress as propaganda. All luxury at his court was, in his estimation, a sign of power and glory. If every woman in the court at the Tuileries was dressed extravagantly it was not because she was copying the Empress, but rather because of the Emperor's insistence that women never appear at court in the same dress twice. "Madame," he said to Laure d'Abrantès, "you have worn that dress several times. It is pretty, but we have seen it before."[11] In those imperial years women's clothes glittered—embroidered, embossed and reembroidered in gold and silver on top of metallic lamé—in gowns less unforgiving than the "Greek" models decreed by David. To further help the Lyons manufacturers, velvet court trains were imposed on all the ladies of the Tuileries; Josephine's silent protest against the banishment of gauze and the imposition of brocades and heavy satin was to have her own trains made of tulle and swansdown.

Consecrated, anointed, crowned and married according to the rites of the Church, she was now apparently invulnerable. She continued to lead a life of stupefying sameness entirely regulated by the Emperor, waiting for his orders and bent only on pleasing him. Never heard to utter a complaint, she appeared not to know the meaning of boredom. Serene, smiling and composed, she was always ready to talk, to drive, to read to him aloud. Her gentle submissiveness suited him and perhaps her, too. Her existence was more that of a mistress or favorite sultana, not unlike, wrote one biographer, that of her cousin Aimée du Buc de Rivery, taken by pirates on her way back to Martinique and now the Sultana Valideh, mother of Selim III of Turkey. "Only a pipe and rose-petal sherbets were missing."[12]

Napoleon's affection for Josephine at this period appeared to be as strong as it had ever been since his return from Egypt. He admired her indulgent serenity before his family's attacks; his affection was based, too, he said, on the fact that she never lent herself to intrigue, never agitated him and was not vindictive. "If ever," Mme de Rémusat was forced to admit, "Napoleon were really stirred by any emotion, it was by her and for her."

After the nights Napoleon spent with her, Constant would go to the Empress's apartments "in the morning between 7 and 8 o'clock. I hardly ever found the couple asleep. When the Emperor asked me for tea or for an infusion of orange flowers and started to get up, the Empress would say to him smilingly, "Must you get up already? Stay a little longer." His Majesty would answer, "You mean you are not asleep?" and he would roll her up in her blanket, giving her little taps on her cheek and on her shoulders, laughing and kissing her."[13]

But when Constant, her faithful admirer, would answer the door of the room next to the Emperor's office with, "I have orders to let no one in, not even Her Majesty the Empress," Josephine knew that another of Napoleon's liaisons had started. Ladies about the court and actresses were increasingly brought to the room behind his office, or occasionally set up briefly in private houses in Paris. "Napoleon would comment on the physical imperfections and anatomical peculiarities and the performance of the ladies"[14] to the men at court and to Josephine herself, information immediately sent by diplomatic courier to all the cabinets of Europe.

"The price of Josephine's determination to remain as consort was her willingness to ignore her husband's liaisons," noted Mme de Rémusat, "and he would give her an account of his current affair with the most indecent openness," telling her more than she wanted to know, and he added to her pain by informing her of other ladies of the court who had granted him their favors, but of whom even Josephine's spies had been ignorant.

The scenes of tearful jealousy on her part and of brutal rejoinders on his would start again. There would be constant arguments, too, on the subject of whether he could father a child. Whenever she would point to the Beauharnais offspring, he would quote her doctor: "But your menses have stopped." There was proof, however, that Napoleon could also feel jealousy. "Napoleon never uttered Monsieur Charles's name," wrote Laure d'Abrantès, "never allowed it to be uttered in his presence. He hated

Charles, and I learned of something that astonished me because I had not believed Napoleon capable of such profound emotion. . . . One day while he was out walking with General Duroc, Duroc felt a pressure on his arm . . . the Emperor's face had paled beyond even its normal pallor. Duroc was about to summon help when the Emperor silenced him. 'There's nothing wrong with me, be quiet!' A carriage had sped past and the passenger in the carriage had been Monsieur Charles and Napoleon had caught sight of him for the first time since the Italian campaign."

But in Napoleon's increasing isolation, Josephine was the only person left who could *tutoyer* him, use the informal second person singular, and call him Bonaparte. She was aware that no romantic notions were attached to his liaisons with other women; she knew this because Napoleon, counting on her lack of vindictiveness, would ask her to help him disengage himself from women he no longer cared to see.

Her own place was still firm in the poetic element that continued to exist in Napoleon's imagination, the romantic surviving in the man who admired moonlight and ruins, ghost stories, melancholy music and, always, women—or rather one woman—in white drifting through a sylvan landscape. Josephine's appearance in one of those white dresses could still arouse him and move him. Laure d'Abrantès saw Josephine at St. Cloud enter a room in a misty white muslin, a gold and black medallion of a lion's head at each shoulder. "It was clear that the Emperor was as struck as I by her charming ensemble," she wrote, "for he went to her, kissed her on the shoulder and on the brow, led her to a mirror so that he might see her from all sides at the same time. 'Now, Josephine, I think I should be jealous; you must have some conquest in mind. Why are you so beautiful today?' Josephine answered, 'I know that you love to see me in white and so I put on a white gown, that's all.' 'Very well then, if it was to please me, then you have indeed succeeded.' Whereupon he kissed her again."

His sentimentality about Josephine was relative, however. When Fouché and his own family urged Napoleon to divorce her that year, Napoleon answered: "There's no hurry. When she dies, I'll remarry and have children."[15]

He did not add that secretly he continued to feel that she was the talisman of his destiny. Josephine told her friend Sophie Gay that she believed she was Napoleon's "superstition rather than his love . . . he considers me one of the rays of his star."[16]

Charles-Maurice, Prince de Talleyrand, at the age of eighty. (Bibliothèque
Nationale, Paris—Collection Viollet)

An anonymous engraving of Joseph Fouché, Duc d'Otrante. (Bibliothèque
Nationale, Paris—Collection Viollet)

The Consular entrance to Malmaison, painted to resemble striped canvas. (Musée de la Malmaison—Cap-Viollet)

Malmaison from the garden. Napoleon is pictured on the left. (Musée de la Malmaison—Collection Viollet)

This portrait of Josephine by Gérard was described in 1803 as "too young looking" and "too flattering." (Musée de la Malmaison—Bulloz)

Napoleon Bonaparte wearing the red velvet coat of the Consular uniform designed by David and a sword hilt set with some of the crown jewels. His hand rests on a scroll bearing a list of his peace treaties including Amiens and "18 Brumaire." (Musée de la Legion d'Honneur—Tallandier)

The Tuileries Palace (burned down in 1870) seen from the Left Bank. The Pavillon de Flore (right) and the wing along the quay are still standing. The windmills of Montmartre are visible on the horizon. (Musée Carnavalet—Bulloz)

Hortense de Beauharnais, wife of Louis Bonaparte, King of Holland. (Collection of Prince Napoleon— Collection Viollet)

Eugène de Beauharnais, Arch Chancellor of State and Viceroy of Italy, aged twenty-five. (Bibliothèque Nationale, Paris—Collection Viollet)

Lucien Bonaparte, Prince of Canino. (Musée de la Malmaison—Collection Viollet)

Pauline Bonaparte, Princess Borghese. (Musée de Versailles— ND-Viollet)

Caroline Bonaparte, Queen of Naples and the Two Sicilies. (Collection of Prince Napoleon—Collection Viollet)

The Coronation. When the painting was ready four years later, several changes had been made. The Bonaparte princesses were no longer "sustaining" Josephine's mantle, but were standing to the left; the absent Madame Mère had been painted in. (Musée du Louvre—Collection Viollet)

1. The Emperor
2. The Empress
3. The Pope
4. Marshal Berthier
5. Charles-Maurice de Talleyrand

6. Eugène de Beauharnais
7. Marshal Bernadotte
8. Cardinal Fesch
9. Prince Joseph Bonaparte
10. Madame Mère
11. Marshal Murat

The Shower by Louis Boilly. A Paris family in 1807 waiting for a plank to be thrown across the street's central stream. (Musée du Louvre—Bulloz)

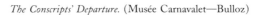

The Conscripts' Departure. (Musée Carnavalet—Bulloz)

Josephine in her coronation
robes. The sculptor has
restored the "plump little
cheeks" of her youth.
(Musée de la Malmaison—
SPADEM)

Josephine at Malmaison by
Prud'hon. (Musée du Louvre—
L. L. Roger-Viollet)

The Empress Josephine. (Musée de Versailles—Roger-Viollet)

Napoleon I by Horace Vernet. (Tate Gallery, London—Collection Viollet)

Marie Louise and the King of Rome by Franque. (Musée de Versailles—Photo R.M.N)

"The *Arch* Dutchess Maria Louisa going to take her *Nap*." An English caricature full of double entendres. "My dear Nap your bed accomodations are very indifferent! Too short by a Yard. I wonder how Josephine put up with *such things* even as long as she did!!!"

"Indeed Maria I do not well understand you. The Empress Josephine who knew *things* better than I hope you do, never grumbled—Le Diable! I see I never will be able to get what I want after all!!!" (Bibliothèque Nationale—Phototèque des Musées de la Ville de Paris)

Josephine is shown gazing at a bust of her son, Eugène. Her left hand rests on a table bearing a vase of hydrangeas (hortensias), a reminder of her daughter, Hortense. (Musée d'Art et d'Histoire, Palais Masséna, Nice)

Apotheosis. By the mid-nineteenth century and the height of the Napoleonic legend, Josephine had replaced Marie Louise. She is pictured here between Napoleon and the King of Rome. (Private Collection—Philip Charles)

❧ 28 ❧

I Saw Only You

IN THE SUMMER OF 1806, KING FREDERICK WILLIAM III OF PRUSSIA signed a treaty of alliance with his close friend the Tsar of Russia. Prussia, already alarmed by the creation of the Confederation of the Rhine, believed itself threatened by the French Grand Army, an arrogant occupying force still quartered in the vassal states of Southern Germany. The two powers declared themselves ready to join with England in another coalition unless French troops were withdrawn from beyond the Rhine.

By August, Frederick William decided to mobilize, although Tsar Alexander could not possibly come to his assistance for several weeks. At St. Cloud, Napoleon was informed that the Prussian troops were already approaching the advance posts of the Grand Army. He decided to strike immediately, before Russia could join its ally, but this time he appeared reluctant to start on a new campaign. Claire de Rémusat believed that he "had no wish to return to camp life and was enjoying the luxury around him"[1]; the Emperor, it is true, had spread this report, preferring the foreign envoys in Paris to include in their dispatches the rumor that Napoleon was going to war against his will, "taking up arms to defend myself," as he phrased it to the King of Prussia.

When the Empress learned on September 24 that Napoleon had ordered his campaign coach for four in the morning, she flew down the stairs and into the Emperor's arms just as he was about to get into his carriage, and off they drove at breakneck speed to the Rhineland. The Empress's own suite, her ladies and her maids, did not catch up with her until Mainz, bringing with them the trunkloads of clothes and Mlle Avrillon with the jewel cases, all packed into six coaches.

Both Napoleon and Josephine arrived in Mainz in a state of deep depression—he, still reluctant to start on this campaign; she, filled with deep sadness and premonitory fears, as though she were expecting the longest-ever separation to come and the consequent fatal changes in their relationship. M. de Rémusat witnessed their emotional parting. Holding Josephine in his arms and with one hand in Talleyrand's, Napoleon murmured—implausibly—"It is painful to leave the two people I love the most." "The Emperor held his wife for the longest time in his arms," continued M. de Rémusat, "as if unwilling to release her. . . . He gave way to tears, then to a nervous spasm and convulsions which brought on severe vomiting"[2]—a scene recalling, among others, the one that had ended his affair with Mlle George.

The Emperor left on October 1 and Josephine continued to obey his instructions on maintaining imperial pomp in the vassal city. Dispiritedly she opened balls, went to the opera, received delegations, visited the wounded, presented vast amounts of watches and snuffboxes set with her cipher in diamonds and gave receptions for the German princes and monarchs. As soon as she returned to her apartments in the archbishop's former palace, she would go back to her tarot cards, telling her fortune over and over again. She was constantly in tears, either because of what the cards foretold or because she knew that Eléonore Denuelle, promoted by the Murats as a potential mother of Napoleon's child, was now six months pregnant.

In October, reviewing his troops in southern Germany, Napoleon found them less enthusiastic than formerly, but he knew how to galvanize and to flatter them with a special kind of familiarity. He wrote to Josephine that everything was going even better than he had expected, but "With God's aid, events will become even more terrible, I fear, for the poor King of Prussia, whom I personally like. The Queen is with him. If she wants to see a battle, she will have that cruel pleasure."[3]

The Grand Army began its march north, and before Russia could join its ally, Napoleon had cut off the Prussian army's road to Berlin and beaten it at Jena. Josephine's confidence in her cards only increased when one night in mid-October she called out to her ladies that the tarot foretold "a great victory," and then, minutes later, the Emperor's page burst in with a letter announcing the victory. "The Prussian army no longer exists," he wrote.

Napoleon's letters reached Josephine regularly, letters that were no longer stuffed into drawers for later perusal, nor considered too difficult to decipher. They were dictated, with a beginning and an end and no longer thrown haphazardly onto the pages. "I love and embrace you," they ended, and "I love and desire you." Sometimes there were notes twice a day, and even the possibility of a two-day gap would be signaled in advance.

Josephine knew that Napoleon had always believed that "his powers would decline" and that he would grow fat at forty. He was thirty-seven now, but already fretting, and he wrote several times that he had already put on weight since his departure "although I ride twenty or twenty-five leagues a day on horseback."[4]

But although his letters became increasingly tender, Josephine was filled with somber premonitions. "Everything in this world must come to an end," he wrote from Prussia, "wit, sentiment, the sun itself, but that which has no end is the happiness I have found with you—in the unending goodness and sweetness of my Josephine."[5]

After a night at Sans Souci in Potsdam, the palace of his idol Frederick the Great, Napoleon entered Berlin in state, riding under the Brandenburg Gate surrounded by his marshals and the Horse Grenadiers of the Imperial Guard. The Prussian King and his Queen Louise had taken refuge in their easternmost provinces; and it was believed that much of the brutality of the treaty he now imposed on Prussia was owing to his special spite toward the beautiful Queen. She was known to have decided the hesitant King to mobilize his army against France, and the Emperor's previous references to her in his army bulletins had been invariably contemptuous. When she dared to remonstrate now on the treaty's terms, Napoleon added to an official bulletin: "How unhappy are those princes who permit their wives to interfere in affairs of state."[6] Josephine had apparently reproached him for insulting the Queen, and he wrote back: "You seem displeased by my speaking ill of women. It is true that I detest scheming women. I am accustomed to ones who are gentle, sweet and captivating. It is your fault—it is you who have spoiled me for the others."[7]

On November 21, 1806, in Berlin, Napoleon signed a treaty that included the closing of Prussian ports to British trade, and, in an attempt to conquer the enemy he could no longer reach by sea, this "Berlin Decree" would be expanded to become the famous Continental Blockade, by which the prohibition was applied to all France's allies and vassals. The Emperor believed that the blockade would ruin Britain; instead of invading that country, he would starve it into submission. The blockade would, of course, also deprive the continental countries of their biggest trading partner, as well as of all colonial produce. For so vast a project, Napoleon must be master of the entire continent of Europe and impose on it all the privations implicit in the decree, and from then on he would have to make war to apply that blockade; it would be the principal cause of the desperate wars with Spain and Russia.

To support their ally Prussia, a Russian army was advancing west through Poland, a country still partitioned among Prussia, Austria and Russia. Napoleon decided to undertake a risky winter campaign (no greatcoats had been issued in September to the troops and the campaign would mean taking on a long-distance march through Poland with an unenthusiastic and exhausted army), smash the Russian army and settle for a magnanimous peace with the Tsar. First Napoleon held out a promise for Poland's independence, then he threatened that unless the Poles joined his Grand Army for the invasion of Russia, they could forget their hopes of freedom.

He seemed unusually reluctant to travel farther from Josephine, and she was increasingly filled with a sense of doom. "Talleyrand [the French foreign minister as well as the other ministers of state had been summoned to Berlin and had come by way of Mainz] tells me that you are always in tears," Napoleon wrote her. "You must be brave and remember that you are an Empress."[8] The most welcome letter of all for Josephine came as Napoleon started his advance east. "I am sorry to hear you are not happy in Mainz. You could perhaps join me here, for the enemy is on the other side of the Vistula. I will wait and see what you think of this."[9]

Napoleon wrote her twice on December 3, ending with a piece of his customary philosophy: "I see that you have lost your little Creole head. I wrote you that you could come as soon as our winter quarters were decided. . . . The greater one's position, the less one's choices and the more one must depend on events and circumstances. I myself am chained; my master has no pity, and that master is the nature of things."[10]

Now their roles were reversed. It was Josephine's turn to write imploring letters, pleading for leave to join her husband. When later in the day he received a letter from her saying that she had dreamed that he had found a woman he could love, he replied: "You say that your dream does not make you jealous. . . . I think therefore that you *are* jealous, and I am delighted. In any case you are wrong. In these frozen Polish wastes one is not likely to think of beautiful women. . . . There is only one woman for me. Do you know her? I could paint her portrait for you but it would make you conceited. . . . The winter nights are long, all alone."[11]

For another month he kept assuring her that he would send for her. She wrote again, begging him to let her join him when he reached Warsaw, again alluding jealously to "Polish ladies." On New Year's Eve 1806: "Your letter made me laugh," he answered. "You overestimate the fascination of the Polish ladies."[12]

On that same New Year's Eve a courier brought him a note from Caroline Murat. Eléonore Denuelle had given birth to a son, registered "of unknown father." Napoleon was only cautiously elated. He guessed that the priapic Joachim Murat had had access to the pavilion in Neuilly and, as Eléonore would later admit, to her bed too.*

And, again on that same New Year's Eve, at the last post relay before Warsaw, an enthusiastic crowd surrounded the carriage of the man who had proclaimed that he would liberate Poland. In the falling snow a girl in what appeared to be peasant's clothes, her blond hair curling under her fur cap, timidly came forward and asked General Duroc to present her to the Emperor. When Napoleon lowered his window he was struck by her beauty, by the fact that the "peasant" spoke French, by her obvious shyness and her expression of childlike adoration, as she whispered her joy at seeing the man who had defeated Austria, Russia and Prussia, the three countries that had dismembered Poland. He thrust through the window one of the bouquets that had been thrown into his carriage and then the six-horse coach rumbled off to Warsaw. Once there, the Emperor ordered Durac to find "the peasant of the post relay before Warsaw."

By January 3 the tone of Napoleon's letters had changed. On that day he wrote Josephine: "I am inclined to think you should go to Paris where you are needed."[13] And four days later: "The roads are bad and not at all safe; I cannot expose you to so many fatigues and dangers. Go back to Paris for the winter. Lead the same life at the Tuileries as when I am

---

* Photographs of the future Comte Léon in middle age, however, show undeniable Bonaparte features; so much so that Napoleon in his will would recognize him as his son.

there. It is my wish; believe me that it costs me more than it does you."[14] And on January 8: "Paris claims you. It is my wish. I would have liked to share the long winter nights with you here."[15]

But by the eighth he was no longer spending the long winter nights alone. January 3 was the day Duroc informed Napoleon that "the charming peasant" had been found. She was, he told him, Countess Marie Walewska, the eighteen-year-old wife of an ardent patriot and the mother of a small son. Napoleon threatened not to attend a ball to be given in his honor unless Countess Walewska could be induced to attend. The Polish magnates had not expected any resistance, but a delegation of dignitaries had had to plead with seventy-year-old Count Walewski to force Marie to accept the invitation. They had made quite clear what this acceptance would entail. She refused to listen to the pleas—"threats" she would say later—of the men, first from outside her bedroom door, then ushered in by her husband. The members of the Polish provisional government and Count Walewski himself insisted she accept in view of the supreme importance of her presence for the whole nation. Esther, they pointed out, had given herself to Ahasuerus, had had the honor of sacrificing herself for the sake of her country.

Finally, indignant and ashamed, she entered the ballroom with her husband. She wore not a single jewel and an ostentatiously covered-up ball dress. Napoleon went up to her and murmured, "White on white is no way to dress, Madame." Contemporaries appear to have taken this as an attempt to convey his understanding of Marie's motive for covering herself entirely in a cocoon of white tulle, rather than as an airing of one of his customary pronouncements on women's fashions.

To Marie's mortification Napoleon's whispered words occasioned an immediate rush of men and women toward her, the new power. She refused to dance with anyone, but Napoleon's jealousy was already aroused. Two of his officers observed attempting to flirt with her were ordered to leave that night to report to distant army headquarters.

After the ball Marie received the first of the Emperor's letters. "I saw only you, I admired only you, I desired only you. A prompt answer to calm the impatient ardor of N." "There is no answer," she told the waiting messenger.

The unedifying, crude procedure continued. Marie Walewska continued to refuse to dine alone with the Emperor. He wrote daily passionate letters, or rather dictated and signed them, accompanying one with a red leather jewel box that Marie threw on the floor without opening it. "He must take me for a prostitute,"[16] she protested.

For Napoleon, here was another citadel to be assaulted, the first since the brief siege of Josephine de Beauharnais. Letter followed letter. "Oh, do not deny a measure of joy to a poor heart ready to adore you." And then, blackmail: "Come to me; all your hopes will be fulfilled. Your country will be dearer to me when you take pity on my poor heart. . . . Whenever I have thought a thing impossible or difficult to obtain, I have desired it all the more. Nothing discourages me. . . . I am accustomed to seeing my wishes met. Your resistance subjugates me. I want to force you, yes, *force* you to love me. Marie, I have brought back to life your country's name. I will do much more!"[17]

It took the pleading and the threats of the Polish patriots and of her own husband to make Marie Walewska decide to go to Napoleon's official residence one night. When she started to resist him, he shouted: "Remember, if you push me too far the very name of Poland, and all your hopes, will be smashed like this watch,"[18] as he flung his on the floor and ground his heel on it. In her *Memoires,* written for posterity, or at any rate for her son, Marie wrote that she fainted dead away with fear and that when she awoke she "found she had been abused by the Emperor."[19]

"She did not struggle overmuch," was Napoleon's own version at St. Helena, and then, as though referring to a prostitute, "It was Talleyrand who procured Mme Walewska for me."[20]

Marie Walewska records that when she recovered from her faint the Emperor wiped away her tears and assured her: "You may be certain, Marie, that I will fulfill the promise I made you."[21] But although the Polish nobles had convinced Countess Walewska that through her they could get Napoleon to guarantee their independence, and although Napoleon told them that it was his mission "to save the Poles from Russia," at least one patriot was not deceived. "He will not reconstitute Poland; he thinks only of himself and he is a despot. His only aim is personal ambition," noted the Polish patriot Kościuszko.[22]

While Napoleon marched into East Prussia, hoping to crush the Russian army there, Marie Walewska left her husband and young son and retired to her mother's estate, ready to join the Emperor whenever he should summon her. She herself was in love now, though she knew, she would admit later, that "his passions were transitory."[23] He did respect her, however, admired her both for the qualities that were Josephine's and those that were not. Virtuous, truthful and ardently patriotic, she was also, like Josephine, pliant, gentle and undemanding. For a while Napoleon, too, was in love, inflamed by Marie's unexpected resistance. From every camp he wrote her tender letters, encouraging her to believe he would get a guarantee of Polish freedom from the Tsar. Just as in his letters to Josephine from the Italian campaign, Napoleon's Italian accent can be heard through his phonetic spelling, and the same endearments: "*Mio dolce amore.*"

Napoleon's love affair with Walewska did not mean that fewer couriers galloped into Paris with his letters for Josephine. On the contrary (perhaps it was the uneasy conscience of the Corsican family man), he had never, since the honeymoon days, written to her more often than during the Polish idyll. "Believe me," he wrote to Josephine from Warsaw, "that it is harder on me than on you, to put off the happiness of our meeting. . . . I am sometimes bored with these long nights. . . . Say to yourself: 'It is proof of how precious I am to him.' . . . Go back to Paris now, it is my wish. Adieu, be gay and show the character and the bearing of an Empress."[24]

The following day he wrote again about the impossible roads between Mainz and Warsaw, adding once more—and this was the last time he dared to do so—that he would have liked to share the long winter nights with her. "But circumstances must be obeyed. . . . I see very few people here." And he continued to urge her to return to Paris; it was her duty to show the capital a little life. "Be worthy of me, show more strength of character, I don't like cowards." And then in a transparently erotic code: "An Empress must have heart—everywhere—even on the little cousins. I kiss them, they must be very low since you are always sad."[25] Josephine had evidently shown some pessimism about the Polish campaign because he wrote that he was humiliated to think that his wife could be uncertain of his destiny. Then he tried an unexpected tack: "Your letter is too sad, that's the trouble with your not being religious! If I listened to my heart we would be together,"[26] he wrote as he left Warsaw for winter quarters in East Prussia.

Josephine had delayed leaving for Paris, always hoping Napoleon would change his mind and allow her to join him. She knew how much his affection for her depended on her presence, and nothing could wipe from her imagination the vision of a Polish rival.

It was more painful than ever to travel with the pomp insisted upon by the Emperor, but she knew that the news of any disobedience would travel across Europe. She came back to a somber Paris. Napoleon was right when he suggested that her return would help to raise morale.

The army, some of the cabinet and everyone in Napoleon's entourage had been away from Paris for six months. Ministers were hoping to hear that peace would soon be signed. The capital was full of rumors about the terrible sufferings of the French army during the winter campaign, of reports of mud so deep that whole gun carriages sank into it, of the infantry, "sinking in up to our knees . . . we would take hold of one leg and pull it out as you would a carrot, carrying it forward, and then go back for the other"[27]—even of suicides. The winter in Paris was made more dismal still by the Continental Blockade, which meant that almost no rum, coffee, chocolate or sugar were coming in from the West Indies. When court dignitaries went home they, like other Parisians, were reduced to hanging a piece of sugar on a string from the ceiling; each member of the family was allowed to dip it in his or her cup of coffee for a few, very few, carefully controlled seconds.

In spite of the Emperor's ten-month absence and her own isolation, Josephine never sought out her closest friends of the days after Thermidor. Even after the divorce she would never contemplate disobeying his commands on this subject.

"Morality," or the lack of it, was the excuse used by the Emperor when Josephine asked to be permitted to receive the newly wedded Princesse de Chimay, ex–Mme Tallien. He issued a savage warning from Prussia: "You are not to see her. Some wretch has married her with her litter of eight bastards; I find her more despicable than ever. She was a nice enough trollop; she has become a horrible, infamous woman."[28] Preoccupied as he was by the hereditary question, there may have been some envy of Thérésia's fertility, compounding the resentments of the past. She had now added four Chimay children to the four illegitimate ones by Gabriel Ouvrard, and to her Fontenay son and her Tallien daughter.

That winter Josephine learned of "the Polish wife." Hiding her depression, she held a series of state receptions for the Senate, the Legislature and the Chapter of Notre Dame, and attended state dinners, galas at the Opéra and receptions for ambassadors. Each occasion had to comply in every particular with Napoleon's detailed quarto volume, "Etiquette du Palais Impérial." When she was allowed to go to Malmaison (the Emperor decreed from Prussia which days she might be there, which at St. Cloud), she spent most of her time conferring with her English head gardener and planning the new "great greenhouse."

She could not get used to being without either of her children or of her two grandsons. She wrote to Eugène in Italy and Hortense in Holland that her heart was "very sad at the long absence of the Emperor, in spite of his frequent letters."

Word was reaching the Emperor of disaffection in Paris; of dismay at the news of a new call-up of recruits; that after the near catastrophe of the Battle of Eylau in February 1807, the stock market had dropped sharply, reported by Fouché to have been caused by the universal fear that "each time, the destinies of France appeared to depend on a single bullet." Napoleon angrily assured his minister of police: "Never has France been in better position . . . as for Eylau, I repeat that the Bulletin exaggerates the losses . . . what after all are twenty thousand dead for a great battle?"[29] But while he waited in East Prussia for the weather to improve, he was aware that if he allowed the Austrians to join up with the Tsar's army, it would be the end of the Empire. His victory over the Russians must be total.

It was not. On February 11 Napoleon had barely defeated the Tsar at Eylau, but it was an inconclusive battle with the worst butchery so far in modern history, and not decisive enough for him to pursue the enemy. Though the full extent of French losses was not disclosed in the victory bulletin, for the first time rumors were instantly alive in Paris of casualties higher than the enemy's, possibly up to twenty-five thousand men—of the wounded lying all night on the frozen battlefield.

Napoleon warned Josephine not to listen to any foolish gossip about the victory; his bulletin, he said, listed more, rather than less, than the number of French losses. The bad weather, he added, meant that he would be taking up winter headquarters, "but soon the happiness of seeing you will make me forget my weariness. Thousands and thousands of kisses."[30]

There was one further warm letter, excusing himself for not having written for two or three days: "I reproach myself, knowing how much you worry," but from then on there is no more talk of lonely nights, but rather, sharp orders on how to conduct herself in Paris, and one letter giving a characteristic view of his vision of himself and of his destiny: "I am just as anxious to see you as you are to see me, and yes, I do know how to do other things besides make war, but duty comes first. All my life I have sacrificed everything—tranquillity, pleasure and happiness—to my destiny."[31]

It was necessary to wait for the late northern European spring before returning to the offensive, and Napoleon moved his headquarters into the luxurious Schloss Finkenstein in East Prussia, sent for Marie Walewska to join him there and wrote Josephine an innocent-sounding report: "This castle has enormous fireplaces which is very pleasant since I get up so often in the night. I love to see a fire."[32]

Her doleful complaints continued and he answered one of them: "I am sorry to see by your letter that you have been sick, but it's the sickness you get every month. [Did he really believe that his wife's menses had not stopped?] It would be wonderful if the spa waters could cure you with a little red sea. Never doubt my love. N"[33]

But Josephine must have suspected Countess Walewska's presence at Schloss Finkenstein: "I don't know what you mean," he wrote in May, "about ladies with whom you say I am connected. I love only my little Josephine, good, sulky and capricious, who knows how to quarrel gracefully as in everything she does; for she is always sweet except when she is jealous—then she becomes a demon. . . . But to return to those ladies, I hope the ones you have in mind have pretty rosebud nipples!"[34]

Napoleon's domestic life at Finkenstein was as serene as though Josephine herself had been there. His valet Constant, much as he admired the Empress, had to admit that "the Polish wife" was the perfect companion, waiting for Napoleon as patiently as his real wife. He did note some differences, however. Marie Walewska when she was alone spent her time reading—and she refused any presents offered by the Emperor. When the Sultan of Turkey sent Napoleon thirty perfect cashmere shawls she would accept only one—for a friend in Poland.

Meanwhile from Prussia, Napoleon continued to govern his subjects, now numbering close to seven million. From Paris to the shores of the Baltic and back, the stream of couriers galloped, carrying orders of every kind: on education, on health, on theater gossip, on the Empress's conduct. Junot, governor of Paris, must organize a parade daily at noon on the Place Vendôme. Fouché should see to it that "that mad Madame de Staël" did not leave Geneva. A snuffbox must be presented to the director of the Opéra. His brother Jérôme should use leeches for his hemorrhoids. The female students of the new school of the Legion of Honor must be religious and not argue, learn some geography and history, but no Latin nor any foreign language; above all, for three-quarters of the day, they must sew, learn all kinds of feminine skills and some cooking. "I do not think we need to trouble ourselves with any plan of instruction for young females," he wrote.

The Emperor reminded his mother of the Sunday night custom of family dinners at the Tuileries. The Empress would replace him as head of the family in his absence, he wrote, and it was Madme Mère's duty to be present. Joseph, King of Naples, was sent a tart reminder of the duties of a vassal state. And he wrote General Murat that his own "amorous drive had never been more vigorous."

Over and above all this, the Emperor prepared for his second campaign against Russia. He organized army equipment and billeting, studied maps, sent out reconnaissance parties, analyzed reports on enemy advance guards and requested further reinforcements. He ordered the 1808 class of conscripts to be called up in France eighteen months ahead of schedule and required the German satellite states to contribute over 100,000 men—immediately. Once again, total and decisive victory was necessary. If the Austrian army were united with the Russian, a catastrophic defeat would be certain.

At last, in June, came the long-awaited engagement near Friedland in East Prussia, and this time, after fighting for two days in a snowstorm, it was a decisive victory for Napoleon. In all, thirty thousand men on both sides were killed or taken prisoner in that battle. The Emperor sent his favorite courier, Moustache, to Josephine at St. Cloud; he rode so hard that his horse fell dead as he dismounted in the palace courtyard.

That victory had wiped from the Emperor's mind the shocking news he had received in mid-May: Hortense's adored four-year-old, Napoleon Charles, had died suddenly of the croup in The Hague. Napoleon had loved him too; a great part of his affection, though, had been based on the idea that the boy would be his heir. Now that this was no longer possible—and with the news of the birth of Denuelle's child, his own hopes of fathering a son revived—he became impatient with Josephine's mourning. (She, of course, had reasons besides her grief to agonize over its implications.) "I wish that you would be reasonable," Napoleon wrote. "Would you wish to increase my own sorrow? Grief has its limits; be more moderate in yours."[35] He was impatient, too, with the account of Hortense's prostration: paralyzed for hours and then living in a stupor, unable to weep or speak or eat. Josephine's fear of the Emperor was such that she had not even dared to fly to Holland to comfort Hortense until permission arrived by courier from imperial headquarters. Napoleon wrote Josephine that his stepdaughter should have more courage, and then, outrageously: "Hortense is not being reasonable, she does not deserve our love since she only loved her child. Try to be calm, and don't add to my distress."[36]

Talleyrand told Claire de Rémusat that when he warned the Emperor to display more concern as he was about to receive a delegation bringing condolences on his loss, Napoleon answered that "he hadn't the time to waste on feelings and on grieving, like other men."[37]

He was still irritated with Hortense. "I am very displeased with Hortense, who has not written me so much as a line,"[38] he complained to Josephine, and he wrote his stepdaughter: "I wish you were more courageous. . . . Your mother and I had hoped to take up more place in your heart. I won a great victory on June 14."[39]

The Emperor found it hard to believe that the two women were still mourning the little boy while the victory of Friedland had changed the map of Europe. The Tsar of All the Russias had requested an armistice, and in view of the reported disaffection in Paris, the horror there at the loss of men sustained at Eylau and Friedland and at the news of the new call-up, Napoleon decided that this was the time for a peace treaty with Tsar Alexander.

On his way to the rendezvous of Tilsit in Prussia, Napoleon wrote his wife: "I have received your letter of June 25 and I am hurt to see that you are thoroughly egotistical and that you appear to be uninterested in my military successes. I, too, am eager for our reunion, but that must depend on the will of destiny."[40]

. . .

On a tented raft moored in the middle of the Niemen River, the two emperors set out to charm each other. Each was a little dazzled by the other's reputation—Alexander by Napoleon's sheer power, Napoleon ready to be impressed. He already knew that the Tsar was celebrated for his fascination, his superb looks and his attempts to end serfdom in Russia; he knew nothing of his unstable character, a mixture of idealism and vanity.

While their aides on the riverbanks entertained each other at gargantuan feasts, the emperors talked late into the night in their canvas pavilion, garlanded in green. In an atmosphere of competing grandeur; they attempted to outdo each other in sumptuous gifts (Alexander's present of a sable-lined coat would be worn by Napoleon on all his subsequent winter campaigns).

Napoleon had already determined that the Tsar must join the Continental Blockade, a harsh imposition in view of Russian dependence on British goods of all kinds, while for Alexander an assurance from Napoleon that he would not create a Polish state was all-important. Not only did Napoleon agree to give up the idea of a free Polish state; he offered Alexander all of Prussian Poland too. The Tsar, however, refused to take any part of his ally's possessions and insisted that a reluctant Napoleon invite the Prussian sovereigns to join them at Tilsit.

Although Napoleon had decided on a magnanimous peace with the Tsar (he insisted only on his adherence to the Continental Blockade), his separate treaty with Prussia was brutal and dangerous for the future. There were those at the meeting who had the distinct impression that the Prussian Queen's presence had some bearing on this. That she was popular, courageous, a friend of the Tsar and known to have influence over her husband were so many marks against her. When she heard of the extraordinarily cruel peace terms accorded her country—the loss of one-half of its territories, an indefinite occupation and a vast indemnity—she literally threw herself at Napoleon's feet, begging for even the smallest concession. He refused to change so much as a line of its text, and showed what he thought of her assuming any political role by asking her at this traumatic moment whether "her dress was made of crepe or Italian gauze."[41]

Napoleon left Tilsit certain that he had seduced the Tsar, whereas Alexander, initially overwhelmed at meeting a man he secretly admired, believed, nevertheless, as he explained to his mother, that Napoleon's terms were due to "the vanity of a Monsieur Bonaparte" treating the Tsar as an equal. Alexander did not dare to mention to her that "the Ogre" had hinted that he would welcome an alliance with the Russian Emperor's sister.

Although by his treatment of Prussia, Napoleon had started to ignite a national spirit in Germany which would eventually open the way to the unification of all the small principalities, these ominous signs were ignored at the time, and Tilsit was considered the pinnacle of his reign. His empire stretched from the Hanseatic ports to southern Italy and from Brittany east to Russia. The entire continent of Europe was now composed of his allies or vassals; only the Iberian Peninsula and Russia itself were not parties to the economic blockade against England, the one remaining enemy.

⚬ 29 ⚬

Our Extraordinary Destiny

NAPOLEON RETURNED TO PARIS A CHANGED MAN. EVERYONE WAS AWARE of it. Even the sound of his voice was different.[1] His new sense of limitless power since Tilsit seemed to those around him to have intoxicated him. Talleyrand saw immediately that the Emperor was "fascinated by himself." He made even less effort than usual to hide his contempt for all around him; the few signs of affection, and these quite unreliable, were reserved only for Josephine and Hortense.

The 8 A.M. audiences started twenty-four hours after the Emperor's return. He entered into a towering rage before Fouché had completed his first report. Rumors in Paris of the terrible sufferings inflicted on the troops during the campaign by the cold, and the indecisive outcome of the battles, had led to several kinds of disaffection, reported the minister of police.

Fouché felt that the Emperor was no longer able to take in unwelcome facts, such as the state of mind in Paris, that he appeared hardly aware of the new social and economic problems as war became France's almost sole industry, or that the country's apathy grew out of its gradual realization of the cost in blood of so much military glory. In spite of the adroit propaganda of the splendid bulletins, the French had guessed the narrow margin by which the recent victories had been won.

Now Napoleon appeared to care only for universal domination as he started to repress political institutions, dismissing protests with the remark that it was "vanity, not the desire for liberty, which had made the Revolution." The few remaining facades of constitutionalism dating from the Consulate were weakened or done away with. The Legislative Body's sessions were reduced to a few weeks a year. The Council of State was now said to be occupied by one long monologue of the Emperor's on whatever subject he pleased.

He appeared no longer interested in any of the great institutions he had founded during the Consulate: Police spies were everywhere; academicians, merchants, women around the court, politicians were all recruited and ordered to send in reports; "suspects" were immediately arrested and imprisoned. Censorship extended to all intellectuals alike, even to Napoleon's once-beloved Institut, as well as to books and plays. The press was forbidden any allusion to politics, and Parisians, who had formed a taste for lively gazettes during the early days of the Revolution, found that all but four journals were suppressed. Napoleon even complained to Fouché that he saw no need for more than one newspaper, the official *Moniteur*, with the possible addition of—and this was only half in jest, since he regarded fashion as a mirror of the economic and political conditions of the Empire—the *Journal des Modes.*

His meeting with the Tsar had only confirmed Napoleon in his desire for a royal connection. Time spent in the imperial circle had made him more than ever conscious of a certain freemasonry from which he felt excluded. Only a semi-royal son of his, he told his brother Joseph, would be a suitable successor, and a sister of the Tsar of All the Russias, for instance, would be a fitting mother for his son. At St. Helena he would say that when he returned to Paris after Tilsit he was "so certain of his destiny" that he knew that his divorce and remarriage were inevitable.

But he dared not press that issue yet. Marie Walewska, who at seventeen had borne her husband a son, was not pregnant. To divorce Josephine in order to marry a Russian grand duchess and then be unable to beget an heir would make him the laughingstock of Europe. British lampoons were forever mocking his apparent inability to father a child. Even Denuelle's pregnancy, by her own admission, could well have been by Murat.

The generals, and statesmen like Fouché and Talleyrand, foreseeing the end of this military dictatorship, were putting increasing pressure on Napoleon to beget an heir. Both men were working toward the divorce. Of the two, Fouché was in the greater hurry because, he said, if there were to be a divorce and Napoleon were to insist upon an alliance with an imperial family, then let it be with the Tsar's. The Austrian alternative, marriage to a niece of Marie Antoinette, he would not contemplate and so Josephine's old ally now decided to abandon her.

"It is much to be hoped that the Empress will die," Fouché informed Bourrienne. "It would remove many difficulties. . . . Napoleon's brothers are disgustingly incompetent and we must prevent the return of the Bourbons." But when he broached the subject to the Emperor, Napoleon replied that he still clung to Josephine both by habit and "by a sort of superstition," and that what he dreaded most was telling her of his decision to divorce her.

At Fontainebleau, after Mass one Sunday, Joseph Fouché drew the Empress aside and told her that it was she who should initiate the "inevitable sacrifice" of a divorce, since only a son of Napoleon could assure the continuation of the dynasty.

The Empress, according to him, turned first red and then deathly white. Stammering, she asked Fouché, "Did the Emperor direct you to tell me this?" When the minister denied having received any such orders, she replied, "I owe you no answer. I see my link with the Emperor as one written in the record of the highest destinies. I will never discuss the matter with anyone but him, and I will never do anything without his orders."[2] She then went directly to Napoleon to ask whether Fouché had spoken with his knowledge. He denied it. "But Fouché was being overzealous and should not be blamed," he said. "We need only be determined to ignore his advice. You know very well I could not live without you."[3] Then, since Josephine appeared to be calm, he asked her, she told Claire de Rémusat, what she herself thought of Fouché's proposal, and whether she might "take the initiative to help him make the sacrifice" if he found it necessary. She repeated that she could never be the first to suggest anything that would separate her from him. "Our joint destiny has been too extraordinary not to have been decided by Providence. Only you must decide my fate." And then, astutely: "I am too afraid of bringing us both bad luck if, of my own accord, I should separate my life from yours." In tears they clung to each other desperately, and for a while Napoleon returned to her bed every night, "always vowing eternal devotion."[4]

However, Count Metternich, the new Austrian ambassador, reported to Vienna that nothing would convince the court that Fouché would have dared go so far without the Emperor's permission, and the minister himself noted: "I understood then that the Emperor had already secretly decided on the divorce as otherwise he would have sacrificed me, instead of simply disavowing my démarche."[5]

In private life Napoleon was, as before, both hard and sentimental, and always careless of the feelings of those closest to him. Upon his return from Tilsit, he was exasperated to find that both Josephine and Hortense were still mourning their beloved Napoleon Charles. Hortense was a wraith, thin and nervous. When she greeted him upon his return, with tears in her eyes, he burst out, "Come, come, stop this childishness. You have wept enough over your son. It is becoming ridiculous. . . . Be gay, enjoy the pleasures of your age and don't let me see any more tears."[6]

It was clear that he had no intention of making Hortense and Louis's younger son, Napoleon Louis, his heir apparent, and Hortense was stunned when he, with unconscious brutality, told her the reason. Napoleon himself was truly astonished by her reaction when he explained that, because half of Europe had believed that Napoleon Charles was his son, it was useless to adopt her surviving boy. Puzzled, he asked why Hortense should make a scene when she learned this. Her own reputation was secure, "and it was lucky that everyone *did* believe it, and that is why I look upon his death as a great misfortune," he concluded.

The Emperor's relationship with Josephine underwent its usual changes. From Prussia he had preceded his return to Paris with another of those painfully playful warnings, once so full of passionate jealousy, now only a cliché. "One of these fine nights I shall arrive at St. Cloud like a jealous husband, so beware . . ."[7]

Count Clement Metternich reported to Vienna that "the Emperor, since his return from the campaign, has behaved toward his wife in a cold and often embarrassed manner. . . . They do not share a bedroom. Many of his daily habits have changed."

Whenever Napoleon and Josephine were apart he found it easy to resolve on a divorce and to listen to his family. Now, again, he fell under her spell. His very irresolution about the divorce was a near miracle, a lack of decision accorded to nothing else in his life at this time, a testimony to his unique feeling for her. Josephine, however, when asked after the divorce how she could have borne the hesitations of the last two terrible years of her marriage, replied: "I understood my Bonaparte better than anyone. I knew very well that in the end he would get his way."[8]

Claire de Rémusat noted that soon after Napoleon's return from Tilsit "he again felt for Josephine the kind of affection she genuinely inspired in him and which often made him uncomfortable, leading as it did to a feeling of embarrassment when he had particularly upset her." He felt no particular embarrassment, however, in pursuing, though in dilatory fashion, two simultaneous liaisons, because when he came to Josephine's room almost nightly now, he felt free to give her not only the ladies' names but the physical details of the encounters too. These had nothing to do with love, he assured her. As to "particularly upsetting" her, there was one name never mentioned between them: Marie Walewska.

Josephine knew that in his eyes she could still eclipse the insultingly young beauties at the court, that her unequaled grace remained his ideal, and that he preferred the vivid crimson and white of her makeup to the unpainted faces of the younger women. "Go and rouge your face," he shouted at one courtier's wife, "you look like a corpse." "Josephine was invariably, unfailingly sweet with the Emperor" wrote Mlle Avrillon, "adapting herself to his every mood, every whim with a complaisance such as I have never seen in anyone else in the world. By studying the slightest change in his expression or tone she offered him the only things he now required of her." It is possible that Josephine's gifts as a matchless consort were as important in his eyes as any of her other attributes. Although nothing in her past or her upbringing had prepared this commoner for her role, she, more than many royal wives, had adapted herself to the discipline required of court life. Her naturalness, her faculty of instant recognition, her appearance of constant interest and attentiveness, and her readiness with the right word were truly regal. He admired all this and her smiling endurance in their official progresses around his immense territory. Undoubtedly, too, the man who appreciated theater in all its aspects recognized showmanship comparable to his own.

But although the Emperor felt that Josephine's presence provided the aura of an authentic court, he remained unsatisfied, shocked by the contrast between the Tuileries and the royal and imperial entourages he had so recently observed. In spite of his "natural impetuosity," he became still more fascinated by ceremony. The subjects that occupied him now were too often protocol, and the regulation of court ceremonial. Napoleon spent hours with the survivors of Versailles for details on the subject. More than ever he insisted upon being surrounded by members of the former aristocracy, as efficient servants of the early Consular days were being gradually replaced. "I will not deny," wrote Méneval," that the Emperor's penchant for the old *noblesse* had an effect on his mind which he strove to conceal."

Napoleon now determined to create a hereditary imperial court. The "son of the Revolution" who, in 1791, in the full flush of his Rousseauist principles, had written an eloquent condemnation of feudality, now proceeded "with a single stroke of the pen, to wipe out the resolutions of the night of August 4th, 1789," the night the French aristocracy gave up all rights to titles and feudal privileges.

In the coronation year of 1804, he had promoted fourteen of his generals to Marshals of the Empire, six of them representing the great days of the republican armies, and another six from the Army of Italy. He also gave them the titles of his armies' victories in a dozen countries, and created several hundred more princes, dukes, counts and barons of the Empire.

Laure d'Abrantès described the comical and touching scenes at the Tuileries when she and thirteen others learned that they had become the wives of dukes and princes. She ran from one to the other to find out by which glorious victory or siege their husbands were to be known, for Napoleon had given them titles and property only outside France. Laure's own husband acquired the title of Duc d'Abrantès (he would, she learned, have been offered the dukedom of Nazareth—a battle in the Egyptian campaign—had Napoleon not feared that the marshal would be known as Junot of Nazareth).

The great dignitaries of the Empire were also given titles too: Talleyrand became His Serene Highness the Prince de Bénévent and Vice Grand Elector, giving Fouché, now Duc d'Otrante, the opportunity to point out that "this is a new vice for Talleyrand."

With the prestigious titles of glorious battles like Magenta and Montebello went enormous fortunes and huge domains. The Emperor decreed that the beneficiaries must acquire houses in Paris and live in state—with his customary passion for order he even laid down the wording of the inscription over the main entrances of these future houses. Public opinion, though shocked, was relieved to learn that no feudal privileges went with these titles, and amused that there was a rush by the marshals to be granted armorial bearings.

During the ten months Napoleon and his army had been campaigning, the Tuileries had been a melancholy place with husbands, sons and lovers absent. Napoleon was not prepared to tolerate the low spirits of his court. From his Prussian headquarters he had ordered the total redecoration of Fontainebleau, that magnificent château built by Francis I and inhabited by each of his royal successors. Furniture, regilding, silk wall coverings and a new throne room were finished in record time by Percier and Fontaine, and his court and cabinet ministers, the Emperor decided, were to spend the autumn months of 1808 there, as the Bourbon kings had done. Over twelve hundred persons lived in the palace and its dependencies that dreary autumn. The Ministry of Foreign Affairs came from Paris, the entire court and all the Bonapartes lodged there with their own attendant ladies-in-waiting and chamberlains. The Emperor decreed that every night, after he had dined alone with Josephine, they would both attend a ball to be held in the apartments of one of the princely households staying in the palace, and that the court revels be conducted exactly as they had been in the past.

He was determined to orchestrate every detail of the "rejoicings" celebrating his victories, but social life of the court as envisaged, or rather commanded by, the Emperor proved to be a disappointment even to him. He was forced to admit its failure. He could not understand, he told Talleyrand, why, with all its entertainment minutely organized by him personally, the court "refused to be amused, and sat around looking tired and sad, with long faces."[9]

"Boredom and fear," wrote Mme de Rémusat, "were the principal sentiments of the court whose ceremonial was now such that no one could reach the Emperor except Josephine." He became more conscious than ever of the climate she created around her, one of harmony and gaiety; but in spite of her usual lightening influence, the court that year remained stiff, uneasy and somber. Laure d'Abrantès described the panic that overtook the rows of men and women, ministers and foreign ambassadors "covered with jewels and decorations, when the little man, simply dressed in the uniform of a colonel of Chasseurs, entered the room." Napoleon, of course, was serenely aware of the state of nervous apprehension around him. "Uneasiness stimulates zeal," was one of his theories.

The terrible evenings at Fontainebleau started after dinner while the court sat in a circle, silent. Josephine would enter with a word for all and then take her place; she too awaited in silence Napoleon's arrival. As soon as he appeared, they all stood with one accord and waited for him to sit next to his wife and then, "with a forbidding expression," watch the company dance.

Above all, Napoleon loved the stag hunts for their color and as reminders of royal Fontainebleau. He insisted on the hunt taking place, rain or shine, three times a week. Each of his brothers and sisters with their households wore riding coats in their own hunting colors. His own were green velvet embroidered in silver, Josephine's and her suite's purple, Caroline's rose-color. Hortense was ordered to shed her mourning and wear her blue and silver velvet. The ladies, with their tricorne hats and white plumes, followed the hunt in open barouches and joined the men for the hunt breakfast under a tent in the forest.

Etiquette was even more rigid in 1808 than at the court of Louis XVI; it seems unlikely that a charming, though "unpresented" woman like the young Mme de Beauharnais would now be invited to follow the hunt at a distance. Certainly, twenty-three years earlier there had been more pleasure for Rose "returning soaked and exhausted" to her aunt's house, than the Empress now experienced, heading the line of open carriages and presiding over the hunt breakfast.

Josephine then had barely noticed the cruelty of the hunt, too exhilarated by the honor and intoxication of following it from afar, an indulgence extracted by months of cultivating—and, by her own account to Napoleon, of having affairs with—the courtiers accompanying the King on the royal Fontainebleau stag hunts. And she had never been close enough to see the kill; now it was torture for her to witness it. One day a hunted stag took refuge under her carriage, just ahead of the hounds; she pleaded for its life and was given a silver collar for the animal's neck, "for its protection next time," said the Emperor.

Laure d'Abrantès wrote that nothing could describe "the magnificence, the magical luxury that now surrounded the imperial couple," or the contrast between it and their sad faces. Fontainebleau that autumn of

1807, she said, was alive with court intrigues and wild gossip: on the Emperor's newest mistresses, on his often abstracted expression, on the Empress's efforts to appear happy, on her nevertheless obvious melancholy—above all, or on the rumors about the divorce.

Josephine felt, correctly, that the death of Napoleon Charles and the birth of Eléonore Denuelle's boy within six months of each other were bound to have an effect on her future. Moreover, the Bonaparte family, and soon the whole court, were whispering about the "Polish wife" and her discreet presence in Paris. Napoleon had sent for Marie Walewska a few months after his return and visited her regularly, always disguised, as Fouché made it his business to know, as a portly and easily recognizable civilian. By the following spring, when Napoleon himself left Paris, the docile Marie was told to return to Poland.

When news finally arrived of the death in June of Josephine's mother, Napoleon decreed that it should not be made public. A month of court mourning would have put an end to the "rejoicings." To the last, Rose-Claire de La Pagerie had maintained her dignity and her prejudices—against men, probably, against the Revolution, certainly. Royalist to the end, she could not bring herself to refer to her son-in-law as the Emperor. Pressed to come to France to have her own court and given all the honors due to the mother of the Empress, she refused every suggestion. She lived in near poverty; a month before her death Napoleon had granted her a generous annuity. It came too late to benefit Mme de La Pagerie and she would have resented it, as well as the imperial pomp of her state funeral.

The court hoped for an end to the tedium of Fontainebleau when the Emperor announced that the King of Westphalia's marriage was to be solemnized in Paris with all the pomp expected of a Bonaparte alliance. Napoleon's youngest brother, Jérôme, was now the monarch of a recently created kingdom; to provide one for him Napoleon had patched together an artificial country from pieces of Prussia, Brunswick and Hesse. A grand alliance had also been arranged for him. Although the Pope still refused to annul Jérôme's American marriage ("I hope, nevertheless," Pius ended his letter to the Emperor, "that your Imperial Majesty will see this as proof of my personal affection"), an irritated Napoleon had had to make do with an imperial edict to the Officiality of Paris.

The bride, Princess Catherine of Württemberg, commanded to leave Stuttgart at four in the morning for a nonstop drive to Paris, was learning to live at the Napoleonic tempo. Her father, one of Napoleon's vassal kings, wrote her that he could not understand the reason for this kind of haste, "but I hope you will usually be spared this custom."

All the vassal princes of the Confederation of the Rhine arrived in Paris in the spring of 1808 for the splendid celebrations. Princess Catherine, fat and shy, was immediately taken under Josephine's wing. Dazzled by Jérôme, she blushed violently when first presented to her fiancé, and would remain in love with him throughout a marriage filled with his infidelities.

One of Napoleon's greatest satisfactions during the three months of festivities was to see that his court maintained the rigid rules he had set for it after observing those of Bavaria and Vienna, and the royal couple left Paris with a book expressly written for them by the Emperor himself, entitled "Etiquette at the Royal Court of Westphalia."

⚜ 30 ⚜

SIMPLY PERFECT TO ME

JOSEPHINE'S FEELING OF IMPENDING DOOM WAS NOW SO STRONG THAT when Napoleon left for Italy in November 1807 she failed to protest when he did not invite her to accompany him to Milan for a visit to Eugène. Although she did not know that the Emperor was traveling with a list of all the eligible princesses in Europe, she seems to have guessed that one of the reasons for his visit was to inspect Princess Charlotte of Bavaria, Eugène's sister-in-law, as a prospective bride. The princess, however, failed to please.

So little was left of the former Merveilleuse or of the giddy Mme Bonaparte that she could write Eugène that spring: "For me the Emperor's *heart* is all that matters. If I must lose that, I care little for all the rest. . . . My own defense is to live a blameless life. I no longer go out, I have no pleasures. People are astonished that I can endure such a life, accustomed as I have been to a greater independence."[1]

While Napoleon was still in Italy, Josephine was too frightened even to be flattered by the obvious admiration of Crown Prince Frederick Louis of Mecklenburg-Strelitz, a handsome young widower in his twenties who had come to Paris for Jérôme's wedding. Her manner with him was "restrained," wrote Claire de Rémusat, and she trembled when Napoleon teased her about this conquest. Although Napoleon himself had started a new liaison, and Josephine knew all about it, she repeated to Eugène that there were now "no more jealousy and no more scenes. . . . My ambitions are limited to one only, the possession of his heart."[2]

The Emperor's attention, as usual when abroad, was never deflected from Paris. Upon hearing that Josephine had been to the theater with some of the German princes including Frederick Louis, he blasted off a furious letter to her, likening her "scandalous behavior" to Marie Antoinette's, and ordered Talleyrand to have the prince out of Paris within two days.

In spite of his resolutions Napoleon still dreaded any change in his domestic life. Who, besides Josephine, he asked Talleyrand could fill it so serenely, knowing his tastes and habits so perfectly? "I would be giving up all the charm she has brought to my private life. . . . She adjusts her habits to mine and understands me perfectly. . . . I would be showing ingratitude for all she has done for me . . ."[3]

Yet on one spring morning in 1808, Talleyrand told the Rémusats that the Emperor had finally decided upon a divorce. A grand reception was to take place at the Tuileries that night and the Rémusats were hardly surprised when, after a long wait, word was given out that "the Emperor had a slight indisposition," and that Their Majesties would not appear. At the end of the evening M. de Rémusat went to the Emperor's apartments to inquire and was told that at eight o'clock Napoleon had retired to bed with his wife. Later they learned that Josephine, waiting in her apartments in a ball dress and wearing the crown jewels, had been ready to enter the Yellow Salon with Napoleon when word reached her that he was ill. She found him fully dressed on his bed and in tears, complaining of severe stomach spasms and in a pitiful state of nerves. He pulled her down onto his bed, put his arms around her and between convulsive sobs murmured: "My poor Josephine, I can't possibly leave you." Nothing could calm him, he said, but that she should get into bed with him. "It was a night of love, interspersed with intervals of restless sleep," Josephine reported to Claire.[4]

"Why can't the devil of a man make up his mind?"[4] stormed Talleyrand when the scene was reported to him. But he, unlike Fouché, was in no hurry. Opposed to the Russian alliance, the minister could wait until that proposal collapsed, as he knew it inevitably would.

It was the Spanish crisis that once again put off Napoleon's decision on the divorce. His obsession with tightening the blockade of Britain now led him to the Iberian Peninsula and what he would call "the running sore which brought down my Empire."[5] The previous year, when Portugal, Britain's longstanding ally, had refused to apply the blockade, Napoleon had sent a small army commanded by Junot to take over Lisbon. To march into Portugal, Napoleon had first signed a treaty with King Charles IV of Spain, allowing the French army to invade his country. When in March 1808 the Spanish King was thrown out by a popular riot and his son Ferdinand proclaimed King, Charles IV appealed to the Emperor to "advise" him. Napoleon immediately sent French troops under Marshal Murat to Madrid and summoned the royal family—the King, the crown prince, Queen Maria Luisa and her lover (and the King's favorite) the Spanish Prime Minister, Manuel Godoy—to Bayonne on the French side of the Pyrenees. His intention was to keep them virtual prisoners in order to depose the King and give the Spanish throne to one of the Bonaparte brothers. Meanwhile he wished to dupe the Spanish sovereigns into believing he would return them to their throne.

As Napoleon left for the Spanish frontier to meet the royal family he was determined on the divorce, once away from Josephine's influence. But in Bayonne he sent for her immediately, needing her support in his wooing of the Spaniards.

This was to be almost the last time Josephine had any real confidence in the future of her marriage. She was his usual effective hostess, helping the impossible conversation after the stormy negotiations, and she felt pity for the grotesque Queen, as hideous and raddled as in the pitiless Goya portraits. She lent Queen Maria Luisa, dirty and half mad, her own clothes and her jewels, even her hairdresser.

While the Spanish royal family was still in Bayonne, the riot of May 2 erupted in Madrid—the famous *Dos de Mayo*. Brutally suppressed by Marshal Murat, the rebellion was used by Napoleon as a threat to Charles IV, who then and there abdicated in favor of the Emperor of the French. This was the first spontaneous national uprising against a French occupation, and it was put down with the utmost savagery.

Once the royal family had been dispatched to a gilded prison in France, Josephine and Napoleon behaved like a couple of children. They were inseparable, romping and running barefoot on the beach along the Atlantic; Napoleon threw her shoes into the ocean, pushed her over in the sand. When he bathed in the Atlantic, it was under considerable guard.

Out of fear of a British landing in Portugal, an entire detachment kept watch to prevent any English attack, "the cavalry advancing into the water as far as possible."

In July, when Napoleon and Josephine left Bayonne, the heat was so intense that the journey back to St. Cloud was made by night stages only. Their entry into any town the following morning involved an immediate acceptance and handing out of gifts, listening to welcoming speeches and presiding at banquets, all the invaluable formalities at which Josephine shone, forever apparently grateful and radiant, only to collapse again into the rattle of the nightly journeys.

At St. Cloud only bad news awaited the Emperor. Mass revolts in Spain had continued. In Portugal, Junot had capitulated before the insurgents, who were now supported by a British expeditionary force. Joseph Bonaparte had been installed as King of Spain, but even before being crowned he had fled from Madrid and taken refuge near the frontier, upon news of the defeat of French troops at Bailén in Spain. The report of that defeat electrified Europe, and Napoleon knew that this blow to his prestige was certain to encourage Austria to seek revenge. He felt a need to be sure of the soundness of his alliance with the Tsar; only then, his rear protected, could he march on Spain to command his army there. Alexander agreed immediately to a meeting in September at Erfurt in Germany.

Before leaving Paris the Emperor, accompanied by Josephine, visited the newly constructed arcades of the rue de Rivoli, and just before his departure he "and the Empress and some of their friends," wrote Constant, "played a game of prisoner's base for the last time. It was at night. Two footmen carried torches and followed the players. The Emperor fell once, running after the Empress, and when he had had enough he went off with her in spite of the protests of the other players. This was the last time I ever saw the Emperor play."[6]

Josephine, after these happy weeks, wrote to Eugène: "You know what stress I have been under. I have paid for it with excruciating headaches, but the Emperor showed his attachment by so much concern, sometimes getting up as often as four times a night to come and see how I was feeling. For the last six months he has been simply perfect to me, so when I saw him leave this morning it was with sadness at the parting, but with no disquiet about our relations."[7]

Napoleon had left for Erfurt that day, resolved to ask for the hand of the Tsar's sister.

The need to protect his rear in Spain was perhaps secondary to Napoleon's determination to wrest from Alexander his consent to a marriage with one of his sisters. Ostensibly, of course, his object was to get Alexander to recognize the implied agreement at Tilsit: to come to his assistance in the event of an attack by Austria. But it was perhaps rather for the second end that Talleyrand was commanded in the regal third person to "arrive two or three days before us, in order to get close to my friend the Tsar"[8]; and possibly also the principal reason for Napoleon's explaining further: "Before we begin, I wish the Emperor Alexander to be dazzled by the spectacle of my power." Aware of the Tsar's mystical tendencies he added: "Use the language he understands. Tell him that the grand designs of Providence are evident in the benefits our alliance will have for mankind. . . . We are both young, there's no hurry. You should emphasize that point."[9]

The vassal kings of Bavaria, Saxony and Württemberg and all the dukes and princes of the Confederation of the Rhine were ordered to join the Emperor at Erfurt—explicit proof that all Europe, except only for Sweden, Britain and Spain, was either under his rule or allied with him. Magnificent lodgings were provided for the Russian suite, each furnished with paintings, bronzes and tapestries sent from Paris. French chefs were in charge of the banquets. The Comédie-Française and its star, Talma himself, were summoned from Paris to play before this company of princes. There were daily parties and receptions; several shoots were laid on, and one day a slaughter of hares and partridges was organized on the very battlefield of Jena, the burial ground of thirty thousand men.

Although soon after his return to Paris from Tilsit Talleyrand had resigned from the Ministry of Foreign Affairs, the Emperor still called upon him for delicate negotiations. His intention of betraying Napoleon had been made after the end of the Peace of Amiens, when he had first foreseen unending wars of territorial conquest. The harsh terms for Prussia, and above all the savage dismemberment of the Austrian Empire had shocked him; Austria, Talleyrand maintained, should form the southern barrier against Russian aggression, for "defeat," he believed, "would come to Europe from the East." France's return to the frontiers of 1792 was, in Talleyrand's view, the only hope for peace. His final decision was made, and his serious subversive plotting started, when the war with Spain became certain and that one last "natural frontier," the Pyrenees, disregarded. It is not certain whether he was already in Austria's pay.

Talleyrand had personal reasons, too, for resentment against the Emperor. As First Consul, Napoleon had forced the foreign minister to marry Catherine Grand, his blond, beautiful and silly mistress, within twenty-four hours, on the slender grounds that the diplomatic corps in Paris objected to the irregular liaison. "To have once loved Madame de Staël," Talleyrand would explain later, "is all that is needed to understand the satisfaction of loving an idiot";[10] Napoleon's own version at St. Helena was: "In spite of all I could say, and to the scandal of all Europe, Talleyrand married his shameful mistress."[11]

Mme Grand was reputedly stupid, but this is hard to credit. When she visited the Tuileries soon after her marriage, Bonaparte favored her with a brutal lecture. Like most of his scenes, this one was made in front of a large gathering. She was to try, shouted the First Consul, to have her past immoral conduct forgotten by behaving in a more dignified fashion. "In this respect, as in all others, I cannot do better than to model myself on Mme Bonaparte," is said to have been the answer of the new Mme de Talleyrand.

Outwardly obsequious, Talleyrand, as grand chamberlain, spent many hours at Erfurt with the Emperor, regulating the all-important questions of protocol. Urged by Napoleon to see the Tsar privately, he met him daily at the tea table of a member of Alexander's retinue, Princess Thurn and Taxis, the sister of the Queen of Prussia. He was quite decided upon treason, and he consistently advised the Tsar to resist Napoleon's demands. That cause, he emphasized, was no longer the cause of France alone, and for the good of Europe as well as of France, Napoleon must be stopped and forced to make peace; only an alliance between Russia and Austria could achieve this and restore the balance of power in Europe.

Alexander's own enthusiasm for the French alliance had cooled since his return to St. Petersburg. He had found his family and his generals unanimously hostile to his pact with the Ogre, indignant at Napoleon's savagery toward Prussia and disquieted by the Emperor's insistence that the Tsar expel from his territories any French citizen who had taken refuge there since 1801. When Alexander learned that a silent party of opposition existed in France, his resolution to hold out against Napoleon's demands was stiffened. Each time Napoleon complained that he was unable to get the Tsar to agree to a formal treaty, Talleyrand would assure him that Alexander was as charmed by him as ever. He would then report the conversation at the princess's tea table and help draft the Tsar's agenda for the following day.

Napoleon's former foreign minister soon understood the principal reason he had been called out of retirement. One night Napoleon insisted on Talleyrand staying up late with him. "His agitation was remarkable; he asked questions without waiting for the answers; he was trying to tell me something," Talleyrand wrote in his *Mémoires*. Clearly embarrassed and evidently unsure of himself, Napoleon almost timidly asked Talleyrand to press the Tsar on the matter of the alliance with his sister. "Tell him I will agree with him on any of his plans for the partition of Turkey. . . . Use any arguments you want. I know you favor the divorce, Josephine knows it too." To Louis de Caulaincourt, his ambassador in St. Petersburg and a friend and admirer of Josephine's, he used another argument: "It will be proof of whether Alexander is truly a friend of mine and cares about the fortunes of France, for it would be a real sacrifice for me. I love Josephine; I will never be happier with anyone else, but my family and Talleyrand and Fouché and all the politicians insist upon it in the name of France."[12]

Alexander sent an evasive message through Talleyrand. If it were up to him, he said, he would gladly give his consent, "but there is another's to be obtained."[13] He was not, of course, referring to his sister's; Russian grand duchesses and Austrian archduchesses were expendable, accustomed to being used as pawns. Talleyrand was relieved, and hardly surprised, when only a month later the engagement of the Duke of Oldenburg and the Grand Duchess Catherine (the more suitably aged of the Tsar's sisters) was announced. The Dowager Empress had lost no time in protecting her older daughter.

By the end of the conference, Napoleon would still not acknowledge that the Tsar had no intention either of committing himself to containing Austria or of giving him his favorite sister in marriage.

Alexander had achieved his own objectives. France agreed to give him a free hand in a takeover of Finland and of the provinces on the Turkish frontier, but Russia would undertake to come to Napoleon's assistance only in the event of a declaration of war by Austria. To save face, a vague convention was signed and on secondary issues only. Yet the Emperor wrote to Josephine, "I am satisfied with Alexander and he should be satisfied with me. If he were a woman I think I would make him my mistress.* I will soon be with you. Stay well, and may I find you plump and rosy."[15]

After Erfurt, Napoleon spent only ten days in Paris on his way to direct military operations in Spain, a war he found already unpopular. The country was aware that this was the first time that conscription could not be justified by the excuse of a European coalition united against revolutionary France. And public opinion was further antagonized when the Emperor announced that he proposed to return to Spain to command his armies and then to crown his brother as King Joseph I: thousands of Frenchmen, it appeared, were to be sacrificed to dynastic considerations that had little to do with the interests of the nation. And when it was learned that the Murat couple was to be moved up to the Kingdom of Naples vacated by Joseph—Caroline at last a queen—Paris laughed at Chateaubriand's description of the Bonaparte family game of musical chairs, one in which the Emperor "rammed those crowns on to the two new kings' heads, and off they went like a couple of conscripts who had exchanged caps by order of their commander."

If Napoleon was unaware of the extent of his own and his family's new unpopularity, they themselves were not. Pauline, upon learning that he was about to command the army in Spain, wailed that all the Bonapartes would be massacred if the Emperor were killed.

It was noted upon his return from Erfurt that Napoleon appeared embarrassed in Josephine's presence. He did not know how much she had

---

* If Napoleon's comment appears surprising, another one of his at St. Helena was still more astonishing. He noted that his friendship with handsome men usually began with physical attraction "in the loins and in another place which I leave nameless."[14]

learned of his proposal to the Tsar; she did not dare to question him, and this unusual restraint made him still more uneasy. "To her sorrow, the Empress was not asked to accompany him"[16] but Napoleon, as he left the Tuileries for Spain, went to Josephine for his usual good luck kiss. "Will you never stop making war?" she pleaded. To which he answered in words he so often used to justify his actions, "It is not I who direct the course of events, I only obey them."[17]

Within the week Josephine had written Napoleon to tell him she was alarmed by talk of Austria rearming, but he would have none of it. "You are in a black mood of depression," he answered. "Austria will not make war on me . . . nor will Russia desert us. People in Paris are mad! Things are going splendidly here."[18]

But in Spain in the fall of 1808 the morale of the Grand Army was very low; there was no question here of one of Napoleon's customary lightning wars but, rather, of forced marches in mountainous country and the men's fears of being massacred by guerrillas if they were left behind. During one snowstorm the army had refused to advance, and throughout Europe the news of this insubordination created a sensation. By December Napoleon had fought his way to Madrid, but instead of continuing on, to meet a British expeditionary force advancing into Spain from Portugal, he left upon receiving, on January 3, 1809, a packet of dispatches from Paris. The minor piece of news was that there was further proof of Austrian rearmament.

Far more disconcerting was the report of a spectacular rapprochement between the two old rivals Talleyrand and Fouché. There could be no doubt about it: every courier confirmed it; Even Madame Mère had painfully taken up her pen to warn her son. The two men had made a point of being seen walking arm-in-arm in whispered conversation through the salons of the Tuileries. The astonishing thing about it, it was agreed, "was the publicity the two persons obviously wished to give it." They must, it was felt, have been very sure of the imminent end of the Empire. Napoleon knew that all Europe would have been advised of this thunderbolt by diplomatic courier and that Austria would have come to the same conclusion. Within hours he had left Spain and his army, never to return.

General Thiébault, riding in a carriage in the same direction, was overtaken by the Emperor and his escort galloping north on the road to

Paris. He never forgot the sight of Napoleon digging his spurs into his own mount while whipping the rump of his aide's horse next to him, and followed at a furious pace by Marshal Duroc and Roustam.[19]

Although Napoleon learned that Talleyrand and Fouché had been planning a provisional government and had even sent a message to King Joachim Murat in Naples asking him to be ready to return to Paris at a moment's notice if Napoleon were killed, he still dared not attack Fouché directly. Of the two, it was the minister of police whom he feared the most, the only man left from the days of the Terror who knew how to tear down a regime, who had both delayed the Life Consulate and helped establish the Empire.

The minister's ambition, he knew, matched his own, as did his contempt for all men. ("That comes," said Talleyrand, "from the fact that Fouché has studied himself closely.") And Fouché, Napoleon knew, would not hesitate to use the Police Ministry's files as arms against him. Once, when the Emperor had attempted to frighten him with a public reminder of his regicide vote, Fouché had answered with his accustomed imperturbability, "Yes Sire, and that was the first of the many services I have had the honor to render your Majesty."[20]

Talleyrand was summoned, however, and a celebrated scene was enacted before a large number of witnesses. This time Napoleon's rage was genuine. Talleyrand, supporting himself and his crippled foot against a table, listened, expressionless, for three hours as the Emperor stormed that he had heaped Talleyrand with benefits, and that he had been betrayed. Then, though the name of Enghien was not pronounced: "And who urged me to strike at that unfortunate young man? Who told me where he was living?" he shouted. The scene ended with Napoleon's famous insult: "You are nothing but shit in a silk stocking!"[21]

Impassively Talleyrand stood to the end, then went straight to the Austrian embassy. "The time has come," he said to the new young ambassador, Clement Metternich. He asked, and was immediately given, one million francs for services to be rendered.

Count Metternich had every reason to know more about the Talleyrand-Fouché plot than almost anyone else, even that the purpose of their alliance may have been to overthrow Napoleon. He had been one of the first to recognize the sinister implications of that rapprochement because of his own excellent sources of intelligence. First he had become the lover of Laure d'Abrantès, who gave him a good deal of confidential information; then he found a better mole in Caroline Murat.

For some time Caroline had been plotting her own and her husband's succession to Napoleon's throne and, mixing business with pleasure, was conducting simultaneous liaisons with both the Austrian ambassador, whose country she planned to interest in an alliance, and with Andoche Junot, Duc d'Abrantès, governor of Paris and the indispensable man in a takeover, guaranteeing for her coup the military forces of Paris. A doubly bitter Laure, whose own liaison with Metternich had been ended by this superior source of information, now entertained an interested Paris by some spirited skirmishes with Caroline.

Napoleon learned of this family betrayal only gradually, for Fouché, who knew that the Emperor preferred to be told nothing of the sexual exploits of his siblings, and was—unexpectedly—more lenient on the subject of his sisters' dissolute lives than his brothers', also enjoyed "revealing and concealing as he pleased."

The Minister of Police, however, had no intention of concealing the deteriorating state of public opinion at the end of 1808. The economy was only partially responsible. Until then it had flourished; the huge expenses of war (as well as the major outlay needed to maintain the family, Josephine herself and even the constant redecoration of the Emperor's palaces) were all paid for by the occupied countries of Europe. But now French ports, as well as the textile industry, had started to complain that they were being ruined by the Continental Blockade.

More serious was public reaction to the riots occurring in Paris and in the provinces each time conscripts drew lots. One-tenth of new recruits were deserting, others hid from the authorities or mutilated themselves, rather than risk the draft. It had been customary for some years to read army bulletins and victory proclamations aloud at the theaters. Talma now stopped this practice; too many in the audience fainted as the names of officers killed were read out.

When Napoleon informed his minister of police that he was about to call up another half million recruits, Fouché warned him that with one million Frenchmen under arms, and 200,000 dying yearly in Spain alone, victory celebrations could no longer count on public enthusiasm. Although "spontaneous" acclamations were often subsidized by the police, the Ministry of Foreign Affairs was forced to ask the prefect of the Seine what he could do to "facilitate an explosion of enthusiasm" in Parisians.

But the Emperor had faced at least one reality. He acknowledged to Fouché: "This year is an inopportune time to shock public opinion by repudiating the popular Empress. Already I am not loved. She is a link between me and many people, and she is responsible for attaching a part of Paris society to me which would then leave me."[22]

❧ 31 ❧

L'Enfant de Wagram

JOSEPHINE APPEARED TO KNOW THAT THIS WAS ONLY A RESPITE; SHE could not now bear to have the Emperor go anywhere without her. When he learned in April 1809 that the Austrians had already invaded Bavaria, France's ally, Napoleon decided to leave immediately.

According to Constant, on April 13 he tried to leave at one in the morning "without telling the Empress who wanted to go everywhere with him . . . but she heard the sounds of departure and sprang out of bed and down the steps into the courtyard in her bedroom slippers and without stockings. Crying like a child, she threw herself into his carriage, she was so lightly dressed that His Majesty threw his fur-lined coat over her shoulders and then issued orders for her luggage to be sent on to her."

This would be the last journey they would make together.

Once Josephine had been installed in the Rohan Palace in Strasbourg, Napoleon set out to pursue the Austrians and she stayed on through a few unhappy weeks. There was little good news from the army and the Emperor's letters were brief, even chilly. Jérôme had joined his brother's army, but his wife, Catherine, had had to flee his kingdom after a revolt of the Westphalians, and she took refuge with Josephine in Strasbourg, without any baggage or any of her court.

Hortense, too, joined her mother and brought her two boys. A brief reconciliation with Louis after Napoleon Charles's death had resulted in the birth of a son, born eighteen days before term as Louis had doubtless noted. For the first time he might have had some reasonable grounds for suspicion; Hortense in her misery had been courted by several would-be consolers. The child was named Louis Napoleon and would become

Napoleon III, Emperor of the French—perhaps Napoleon I's nephew, and certainly Josephine's grandson.

The Emperor had set out this time without the veterans of the Grand Army, still pinned down in Spain. The Confederation of the Rhine provided forty percent of the troops: Saxons, Bavarians and Württembergers as well as Polish volunteers, the companies of Mamelukes and the French conscripts of 1810, boys who had not yet been under fire and were inadequately trained. But while only half of this army were native Frenchmen the enemy was led by Archduke Charles, Austria's ablest soldier, who commanded men eager to face the hated invader. The Emperor's presence alone, however, on a field of battle, was worth forty thousand men, according to Wellington.

After one indecisive battle the Austrians retreated toward Bohemia; Napoleon forged ahead to Vienna, sending the imperial family there once more into flight. And, once again, he took up headquarters in the Hapsburg palace of Schönbrunn outside Vienna.

A few weeks later the two armies faced each other just outside the capital. The Battle of Essling was at best an indecisive victory for the French, a stalemate that the Austrians called the victory of Aspern. It was known throughout Europe that the French army had retreated and come close to being routed, and that each side had lost over twenty thousand killed, wounded and missing. Still the Tsar had not come to Napoleon's aid.

In Paris the stock market fell dramatically. The country was well aware that once more the fate of the Empire depended on a single battle "more so than at any time since Marengo." It was known, too, that from the Tyrol to the Baltic there was a new spirit of resistance in the vassal countries and that Austria was in a state of patriotic ferment.

From Schönbrunn the Emperor sent to France and Italy for reinforcements and six weeks later he won the difficult Battle of Wagram. The fighting continued for over two days during violent and unceasing thunderstorms. It was to be the last great victory and the greatest butchery of all; fifty thousand men were left dead or dying on that field.

All that summer of 1809, between the Battle of Wagram and the signing of the Treaty of Vienna, Napoleon continued to govern France and his Empire from Schönbrunn in the romantic Viennese countryside. A string of couriers galloped from Paris carrying leather portfolios labeled *Dépêches de l'Empereur*. These messengers rode without interruption, hoisted half asleep from one horse to another at each post relay. In his impatience to read the contents (the portfolios were brought to him even on the battlefield), the Emperor sometimes tore the entire leather case apart. Once a week the ministers of the Council of State forwarded their own dispatches to him, while Napoleon's couriers carried his own orders to Paris, to the vassal states and to the countries governed by members of his family. Louis, King of Holland, was the recipient of particularly imperious instructions: "A King commands and seeks no one's counsel. . . . In your domestic life you should display the paternal and effeminate character you show toward your government, and toward the government the severity you show your wife."[1]

Every afternoon that summer, Constant was ordered to drive to one of the villas in the Schönbrunn Park and return with Countess Walewska. She had written the Emperor to ask to join him in Vienna. His reply was affectionate, but hardly passionate—a good deal more formal than the letters that had helped him gain his objective in Warsaw.

"Marie: I have read your letter with the pleasure your memory always inspires in me," he replied. "Yes, come to Vienna. I would like to give you further proof of the tender friendship I feel for you . . . ,"[2] and in September, in these final days of his popularity and the first of his military setbacks, Napoleon learned that Marie, his first "controlled" mistress, was pregnant. Josephine's fate was sealed.

His last hesitations were removed. He was sure now that he could have everything—found a dynasty, marry a "belly" from a legitimate royal house and keep Walewska, all without losing Josephine. As he told his brother Lucien: "Naturally I would prefer to have my mistress crowned, but I must be allied with sovereigns."[3]

After the news of the near disaster at Essling, Josephine decided to return to France, profoundly depressed by the first of the Emperor's reverses; she knew that it had created an even greater resonance in Europe than had the surrender of the French corps to the Spanish insurgents at Bailén. Letters from Napoleon were becoming more rare. That year Napoleon sent her no reminders that she was to be seen at the Opera or to give receptions at the Tuileries. After a visit to Plombières, this time without the usual object, Josephine went directly to Malmaison.

Even before the news of Marie Walewska's presence in Vienna reached her, she never once suggested to the Emperor that she join him during his long stay at Schönbrunn; she appeared frozen into a despairing lethargy, though the final blow of the Walewska pregnancy was withheld for a few weeks.

But there was further bad news. The British had reconquered Martinique and, more chilling to Josephine's superstitious nature than any spiritual qualms, she learned that the Emperor had been excommunicated by the Pope. From Vienna, Napoleon had ordered Pius VII arrested for his refusal to join the Continental Blockade or to close the ports of the Papal States to British ships. In Rome, the old man was roughly thrown into a carriage; even his breviary was taken from him. When he at last reached his prison or "restricted residence," in northern Italy, it was "with regret" that he pronounced the excommunication of "my son Napoleon."

Josephine found little peace that year in the garden and the summer roses, or in the aviaries full of tropical birds. She was so despondent that she was physically chilled too. Even in the Malmaison hothouses she was pulling her shawl around her as she confessed to Laure d'Abrantès, whose little girl had accompanied her, "I, who have never known envy, have truly suffered when one of you brought one of your children to me. I know I will be shamefully dismissed from the bed of the man who crowned me, but God is my witness that I love him more than my life, and much more than the throne."

At last, in mid-October, the Treaty of Vienna was signed. It was an unusually savage one. Francis I lost three million people, several provinces, part of Poland and the entire Adriatic coast. Young Archduchess Marie Louise, informed that Napoleon might visit the imperial family in their refuge, wrote in her diary: "To see the man would be the worst form of torture." Her marriage to him was only six months distant.

On the eve of his departure from Vienna and of his adieus to Marie Walewska, Napoleon's thoughts were centered on his divorce and speedy remarriage. His ambassador in St. Petersburg was instructed to find out immediately whether the Tsar's younger sister, the Grand Duchess Anne, nearly sixteen, was ready to bear children. With Marie still with him at Schönbrunn and assuming that Alexander would insist on a free hand in Poland as a condition of his sister's marriage, Napoleon sent him an urgent message. He was in entire agreement with the Tsar, he wrote, that the very words "Poland" and "Polish" should be "obliterated not only from any transaction, but from history itself."[4]

Did Walewska know that her sacrifice had been in vain? Only she no longer viewed it as a sacrifice, for she was in love. She asked to return to Paris and give birth to her child there, but Napoleon instructed her to rejoin her divorced husband. Valiant Count Walewski, too, urged her to return to his roof. The child, wrote the Count, should be born there and take his name.*

When asked about the future of the expected child (characteristically, Napoleon had no doubt as to its gender), he replied that it was secure. *"L'enfant de Wagram* will one day be King of Poland,"[5] he answered.

But now that there could be no doubt that it was Josephine who was sterile and not he, Napoleon still dreaded the thought of divorce. He repeated his familiar plaint: "All my life I have sacrificed everything, all tranquility, all happiness, to my destiny," and now it seemed that "that destiny demand he sacrifice" his love for Josephine too.[6]

Josephine, who by now had heard the fatal news of Walewska's pregnancy, was hardly cheered by an unusually affectionate letter from Napoleon: "I am impatient to be with you again," and by the usual heavily playful "watch out . . . one of these nights. . . ."[7] This was followed by a summons to meet him at Fontainebleau "on the 26th or 27th of October."[8] She left immediately but with no joy. That short note had been sent just as Napoleon was leaving Munich. He must have wanted to put Josephine in the wrong from the start, knowing that she could not possibly reach Fontainebleau on the very day of his courier's dismounting at Malmaison. He arrived at the palace in the early morning of the twenty-

---

* Marie's son Count Alexandre Walewski would become foreign minister in Paris to his cousin Emperor Napoleon III.

sixth; she did not get there until it was already dark. For the first time the Emperor did not come to greet her. He was writing in his study and hardly lifted his head from his work when she came in, saying only, "Ah, here at last?"

When Josephine went to her newly redecorated rooms she saw immediately that the door between her apartment and Napoleon's had been sealed. The order, she was told, had come from him in Vienna. She dressed hurriedly, but he barely greeted her when she came in; they had only sat down at the table for a moment before he left, without eating, to confer with his ministers.

The next three weeks at Fontainebleau were the most painful of Josephine's life. Napoleon had thought that he had been separated from her long enough to feel sure of himself, but even now he could not trust himself to be alone with her.

All their meals, for the first time, were shared with one or another of the Bonapartes. At night, alone in bed, she could see the lights across the courtyard in Pauline's apartments. Every evening Princess Borghese gave a party for her brother to which Josephine was not invited; a group of pretty women, including a blond Italian she had invited for him, was always there.

Sometimes the Emperor went galloping through the forest alone, for hours at a stretch. He seemed bent on venting his frustration on a savage slaughter of game. The ladies covered their eyes on the day that over eighty wild boar were massacred in an enclosure built for the purpose. Josephine forced herself to follow these sickening events, to smile, to hold back her tears, to talk to members of the court as usual, to behave as though nothing was altered and pretend not to notice the change in attitude of some of those around her. Not only members of the triumphant Bonaparte family, but others too, turned their heads away as she approached. Some ladies were even seen to sit in her presence—a breach of protocol never before tolerated by Napoleon. Nevertheless, the Empress treated each one as graciously as ever, remaining regal and smiling, "her manner both dignified and charming."[9]

Instead of facing Josephine with his decision, Napoleon either remained silent or flew into a rage whenever he saw her; perhaps this anger helped suppress his Corsican family man's guilty conscience. The valet Constant noted "unwonted coldness in the Emperor . . . storms provoked on the slightest pretext which troubled this usually peaceable couple." And Hortense remembered "There was no more tenderness, no more consideration for my mother. . . . He became unjust, he tormented her."

Josephine continued in this agony of suspense while the Emperor still put off breaking his decision directly to her. He asked Hortense to do so but she refused. Then Cambacérès, then Eugène. They all refused. When the court moved back to Paris on November 27, Napoleon sent Eugène a semaphore telegram to come immediately.

Still the Emperor had not spoken. The couple exchanged hardly a word during their meals, now alone together again; these now tended to last only fifteen minutes instead of the usual twenty. There was no sound except for the removal of plates and the clink of glasses. Josephine's eyes were always swollen, and their attendants saw Napoleon observing her covertly. He would ask the prefect of the palace about the weather and then relapse into silence.

Then came November 30. At dinner, Josephine appeared to be holding back tears with difficulty and looked "the image of sadness and despair. The most profound silence reigned during dinner. "Except for the sake of appearances,"[10] wrote Comte de Bausset, the palace prefect in attendance, "they barely touched the dishes offered them. The only words spoken were when Napoleon asked me, "What time is it?" Without listening to the answer he got up from the table. Josephine followed slowly, her handkerchief to her mouth as if to check her sobs. Coffee was brought in and, as usual, the tray offered to the Empress so that she should pour it for the Emperor. But he took it himself, poured the coffee into his cup and let the sugar dissolve, gazing all the time at the Empress, who stood as if stupefied. He drank it and gave everything back to the page. Then he made a sign that he wished to be left alone and shut the drawing room door behind him."

Bausset, from the next room, heard piercing cries from Josephine. The Emperor came to the door and asked him to come in and shut it behind him. Josephine was stretched out on the carpet, weeping and moaning.

Between them, Napoleon carrying a candle, Bausset stumbling backwards, tripping over his ceremonial sword, they carried Josephine down

the narrow staircase that led to her apartments. During the whole operation, "in an extraordinary state of agitation and with tears in his eyes . . .
panting with exertion and emotion," Napoleon "enlightened" Bausset, a
man in whom he would not normally have confided anything, a well-
known gossip and eavesdropper. "National welfare . . . ," he heard, and
"violence to my heart . . . political necessity . . . took me by surprise . . .
her daughter was to have prepared her. . . ."

Once Josephine was deposited in her bedroom, the Emperor gave
some violent pulls to the bell rope and left. Bausset himself was somewhat
reassured as to the Empress's health because she had whispered to him on
the way down, "You are holding me too tightly."

Napoleon sent Hortense to Josephine. "We will go with you,"
Hortense soothed her mother. "I know my brother will feel as I do. For
the first time in our lives, far from the world and the court, we will lead
a real family life and know our first real happiness."[11]

When Napoleon first sent for Hortense he had started by saying
sharply, "Nothing will make me go back on it, neither tears nor entreaties." Hortense, with her mother's tact and dignity, calmly answered, "You
are the master, Sire. No one will oppose you. If your happiness requires
it, that is enough. . . . Do not be surprised at my mother's tears. It would
surely be more surprising if after a union of thirteen years she did not shed
them. She will submit, and we will all go away taking the memory of your
kindnesses with us." At this Napoleon paled, and "in a voice broken with
sobs, cried, 'What! You are all going to leave me? You are going to desert
me? Then you don't care for me any more?' " It was as though for the first
time he faced the fact of losing Josephine and her children too. Hortense
answered that she owed herself to her mother. "We cannot live near you
any more. It is a sacrifice that has to be made and we will make it."[12]

Napoleon took up the subject immediately after Eugène's arrival. He
could not bear the idea of all three of them leaving him. He began to
question whether Josephine should entirely separate herself from him and
even talked of putting a stop to the divorce. Eugène and Hortense said
that it was too late, that "what was in his mind being known to us, the
Empress could not live happily with him."[13] The Emperor offered Eugène the sovereignty of the Kingdom of Italy, but he refused it, saying he
could not accept anything that appeared to be a reward for his mother's
unhappiness.[14]

Josephine should now have felt some relief. Since the night of Napoleon's return from Egypt she had spent her days dreading the divorce, with only a few months of respite. Anything must have been better than the petty scenes and the suspense of the last five weeks; but now that it was no longer dangerous, Napoleon again became affectionate—and full of self-pity. Once more he saw himself as "a captive of circumstance," certainly not as a man deliberately parting from his wife.

During those days, he could hardly find generous enough provision for her. Josephine was, he announced, to retain the rank and title of Queen and Empress, to keep Malmaison, to be given the Elysée Palace as a Paris residence, an allowance of three million francs a year and have her current debts paid. But there was a storm of tears when the Emperor offered her a principality in Italy, with Rome as its capital. To be forced to live outside France, to lose Paris, would be almost as tragic for her as losing her husband.

With all the iron discipline of which she was capable, Josephine now set about perfecting the image she wished to leave. No public announcement had yet been made of the divorce, and that month every German king and princely vassal of the Emperor was due to arrive in Paris to celebrate the victories of the Austrian campaign. Every day and night was filled with receptions, military reviews, and suppers for five hundred. By day she was all welcoming smiles; by night all tears and migraines.

But now the Emperor decided to revert to his earlier tactics. In order, he said, to prepare public opinion for the divorce—and to sound out that opinion—he gave orders that the Empress should not be met or accompanied at any official function. He himself ignored her in public. When the fifth anniversary of the coronation was celebrated at Notre Dame in December, the Empress wore her imperial crown, but was not permitted to be seated with the Emperor either in his coach or at the cathedral. At the banquet given by the City of Paris that night, Napoleon was accompanied by his sister Caroline. Josephine was not met at the entrance and made her way alone to the dais. "Seating herself quickly," wrote Laure d'Abrantès, "her legs almost giving way beneath her, she must have wanted to sink through the floor, yet somehow she managed a smile."[15]

December 14 was to be Josephine's last public appearance. At the Grand Circle and supper at the Tuileries, either pride or discipline or perhaps defiance came to her aid. It was as though she was determined to be remembered always as the most charming, the most captivating of all. Pasquier, the future chancellor, and her neighbor in the indigent days at Croissy, wrote that he could never forget how nobly she played her role of Empress during these last fetes, when every eye was upon her. On the night before the divorce was to be pronounced she gave her especially gracious little bow to those who came up to her, though she and they too knew it was for the last time. "I doubt," he wrote, "whether any other woman could have acted with such perfect grace and tact. Napoleon's own bearing was less successful than his victim's."[16]

Invitations for the ceremony of the divorce had been sent out as for a social occasion, and indeed as many candles lit up the Throne Room as for a state ball. The whole court was present, wearing diamonds and decorations. "The Bonapartes gloated," wrote Hortense. "Try as they might not to show it, they betrayed their joy by their air of satisfaction and triumph." Josephine entered in a simple white dress, pale and calm, leaning on Hortense's arm. Eugène stood, arms crossed, trembling violently.

First the Emperor spoke. He announced the divorce, then pushing his notes aside, started: "God alone knows what this resolve has cost my heart. I have found courage for it only in the conviction that it serves the best interests of France. . . . I have only gratitude to express for the devotion and tenderness of my well-beloved wife. She has adorned thirteen years of my life; the memory thereof will remain forever engraved upon my heart."[17] Then he sat down with tears running down his cheeks.

Josephine started bravely: "With the permission of my dear and august husband, I proudly offer him the greatest proof of attachment and devotion ever given a husband on this earth. . . ."[18] She tried to go on; there was a full minute's silence; then she handed the text of the rest of her speech to an aide, who finished it for her. She had not meant to break down before the silent victory of the clan.

After the Emperor, the Empress and members of the family had signed the official record of the proceedings, Napoleon kissed Josephine, took her by the hand and led her to her apartments, "like a wounded soldier carried from the field of battle."[19] Eugène fainted with emotion as soon as he left the Throne Room.

❧ 32 ❧

An Elegant Equality

THAT NIGHT JOSEPHINE, "HER HAIR IN DISARRAY AND HER FACE CON-
torted," wrote Constant, "came to the Emperor's bedroom. . . . She fell
onto the bed, put her arms around His Majesty's neck and lavished upon
him the most touching caresses. . . . The Emperor too began to weep, he
raised himself to a sitting position and pressed Josephine to him saying,
'*Allons*, my dear Josephine, be brave, I will always be your friend.' Suffo-
cated by her sobs, the Empress could not answer. There followed a silence
lasting several minutes, while their tears and their sobs mingled. . . ."

Napoleon made sure that he would not be left alone with Josephine
on the morning of her departure. Accompanied by Méneval, he came
down the private staircase, embraced her and left to review the guard. A
weeping crowd of retainers gathered in the courtyard as Josephine set off
in driving rain for Malmaison, followed by a caravan of carriages containing her ladies, chamberlains, luggage, all her dogs and a parrot in a
cage. The Empress, Hortense beside her, never looked back at the palace
she was not to see again.

An hour later Napoleon left for Versailles. He shut himself up in the
Grand Trianon. There were no memories of Josephine there. At midnight
he woke the curator to tell him that he wanted all the chair covers and the
wall hangings in the palace changed and insisted on rehanging every
painting that night.

The next day he drove to Malmaison. He and Josephine walked hand
in hand in the rain, lost in conversation, always within sight of watchful
eyes at the windows. For a week there were daily meetings; Napoleon never
entered the house, they never embraced. The rain never let up.

At Versailles Napoleon was irritable, rude to his sisters and to his current Italian mistress, brought along by Pauline. Only Josephine knew him well enough to have lightened his black mood. Unbelievably, for three whole days the Emperor neither gave audiences nor asked for news. He seemed plunged in depression and could think only of Josephine.

There were daily exchanges of feverish letters. Napoleon urged Josephine to be strong for his sake; he still felt that the "sacrifice" he was making to maintain his dynasty was as hard on him as on her. She answered each of his with passionate letters of her own. But when his tender messages reached her at bedtime, she was unable to sleep. Worse still, when the Emperor returned to Paris and wrote that he felt lonely in the great palace ("I am going to dine all alone"), she was filled with despair, as Mme de Rémusat told her husband, asking him to implore Napoleon to "moderate his expressions of regret."

Napoleon sent Josephine some extra funds to "plant whatever you want at Malmaison," and in a further access of guilt, ordered an entire dinner service for her from the Sèvres porcelain factory, and he spent infinite time on Josephine's dowry and Civil List. With his usual attention he examined the fourteen pages of copperplate handwriting composing "the inventory of the clothes of Her Majesty the Empress" made in December 1809, opening with ten pages devoted to "court dresses" and ending with one page listing 280 pairs of shoes, and one page for underwear only. Besides the lace-trimmed chemises and camisoles there were just two pairs of flesh-colored pantaloons "for riding" (Restoration prudery would bring these back under the next reign, but the Austrian archduchess packed thirty-five pairs in her wedding trousseau).

Napoleon was still envisioning a life that would include Josephine. They both considered the idea of sleeping under the same roof in the country house of one of the marshals, and it was Josephine herself who warned against it. The Emperor agreed that it might be considered improper "during the first year."

Proof that he still had hopes of a triumvirate with two empresses can be seen in his instruction to archivists to search royal records for Josephine's future rank at court. There were, of course, no precedents for a divorced consort. Should Josephine, he asked, as Empress Dowager, have the higher position as in Russia? Finally, he decided that she should be placed on the right of the throne and the new Empress on the left, where

Josephine used to sit. He still seemed to think of Josephine as his wife and the other as a dynastic political necessity.

However, by February, the Emperor's letters were becoming less frequent. Whenever Josephine heard that he was to hunt near Malmaison, she would go up to a second-floor window hoping to see his carriage go by. Napoleon, during his earlier visits, had noted several defections from Josephine's household and few visitors; in Paris he asked his courtiers: "Have you visited the Empress?" and the question changed all that. "In spite of the rain," wrote Claire de Rémusat, "the road from Paris to Malmaison became one unending procession of carriages of persons paying their respects." Visitors remarked that though her tears were never far off, Josephine uttered no word of recrimination or of anything other than affection for the Emperor. Claire noted that she was "truly as gentle and affectionate as an angel."

Unlike some of the courtiers, the Austrian ambassador's wife had not needed any hint from Napoleon that he would appreciate a visit to Malmaison. What she had not expected was that Josephine would confide in her in early February of 1810 that she hoped that a marriage, arranged by herself, between Napoleon and a daughter of the Austrian Emperor would "prove that the sacrifice that she had just made had been worthwhile." Whatever Josephine's motives, whether because she wanted once again to be at the center of events, or to secure the future Empress's friendship and gratitude, or to have an assured place at the court or perhaps simply a return to the habits of a lifetime, the ambassador's wife was thunderstruck and could hardly wait to return to Paris to give the news to her husband.

Any perceived advantage to Josephine was lost, however, since Napoleon had already taken the matter into his own hands. On February 5, he received dispatches from his ambassador in St. Petersburg describing the Tsar's hesitations and excuses over granting him the hand of his fifteen-year-old sister. Suddenly, the Emperor realized that Alexander would never authorize this marriage. Instantly, he put a battle plan into action while there was still time to appear to be able to choose. He sent Eugène (apparently to prove that Josephine was not exactly *divorced*, "repudiated" was a term much used by him) to the Austrian embassy. In his stepfather's name, Eugène relayed a demand for the hand of the Emperor of Austria's daughter; the proposal, however, must be accepted immediately and the contract signed by the next day, with no time to refer the offer to Vienna. The ambassador, recalled in haste from a shoot, sweated, attempted excuses, but was forced to accept. Napoleon, Eugène reported, when he heard the news, "was filled with mad, impetuous joy," and that very evening the announcement was made to the nation. In Austria, nothing was yet known of the forthcoming alliance.

The rest of Napoleon's triumphant plan was then put into effect. He dictated two dispatches: the first one informed the Tsar that Napoleon had decided to renounce the projected marriage with the too-young grand duchess; the second went off the next day to St. Petersburg, announcing his forthcoming marriage to an Austrian archduchess. Both French couriers crossed the Tsar's own, announcing his definite refusal to give his sister to Napoleon.*

The Austrian foreign minister, now "Prince" Metternich, commended his ambassador in Paris for his decision given under duress. The marriage, he declared, would give their country breathing space. "From now on," he announced, we must continue to maneuver, to avoid all military action and to flatter . . . until the day of deliverance."

In Vienna, the nineteen-year-old Archduchess Marie Louise was in despair, and terrified at the idea of marriage to a divorced and excommunicated man old enough to be her father, the enemy of her country and the sovereign of a people who had beheaded her own great-aunt. A childhood of discipline and awe of her strict father, however, overcame her fear and repulsion. She was ready, she wrote a friend, for this "painful sacrifice" for the good of the state.

In Vienna, her dowry of clothes and jewelry was being prepared and the invitations to balls and receptions had already been sent out, when the Archbishop of Vienna raised the question of the French Emperor's marriage and excommunication. The Austrian Emperor was appalled to hear that the forthcoming marriage would be nothing in the Church's eyes but the blessing of an adultery, or of bigamy. Even by current French law,

---

* There was gossip—and Napoleon was to return to it at St. Helena—that Josephine herself was partly responsible for the Russian refusal. She was said to have told her admirer the Prince of Mecklenburg that Napoleon was impotent, and he in turn had informed the Russian Empress Dowager, his former mother-in-law. As a result, Metternich was alleged to have sent an official to Malmaison when the Austrian marriage was decided to question her crudely on the subject. Josephine was reported to have been "shocked."

only the Pope was capable of annulling a royal marriage. A repudiation had been pronounced in Paris, but how could it be valid unless blessed by the Pope, now under house arrest by order of that same emperor?

Uncle Fesch argued that the basis for the annulment was that no priest of the parish had been present at the hasty ceremony and that there had been no witnesses; furthermore, His Majesty had assured Fesch that he had acted under duress and at Josephine's insistence and had not given his free consent to the marriage.* The Austrians laughed at the idea of a violated Napoleon, as that loophole was more often used for virgins forced into matrimony against their will.

For five weeks Napoleon had been immersed in his past and in Josephine; now he turned his full attention to his matrimonial plans. Marshal Berthier had already been dispatched to Vienna (he had been reminded not to make use of his title of Prince of Wagram) to stand in for Napoleon at the proxy marriage. And in February, Josephine decided to return to Paris. Her haste was understandable, her timing deplorable. She found it even lonelier than Malmaison.

Napoleon, who had encouraged her to stay at the Elysée Palace at the end of January, where he "could see her more often . . . and you know how much I love you," found that he was too busy to visit her regularly. With the Austrian marriage set for April, Paris was celebrating with a round of festivities, all attended by the Emperor. Josephine heard from Hortense of dinners, balls and receptions at court, at the marshal's houses and the Bonapartes'. She herself was, of course, included in none of them, and her household, she felt, looked at her reproachfully. They, too, would have preferred to be caught up in the excitement at the Tuileries, where Napoleon was taking waltzing lessons and having new clothes made.

Josephine heard that the Emperor had forbidden the press to mention her. No wonder, she said, that she "felt as though she had died."[1] "I told you to arrange that the journals do not speak of the Empress Jose-

---

* When the "illegalities" of the Bonaparte service before the coronation were presented to the Officiality of Paris (a body established by Napoleon at the time of the Concordat), its members pronounced the annulment of the imperial marriage as rapidly as they had that of Jérôme Bonaparte to Betsy Patterson.

phine," Napoleon had written to Fouché, "but they do little else. See to it that they do not repeat this new publicity."[2]

Napoleon himself was so immersed in every detail of his forthcoming marriage that he seemed to be neglecting his government and his army. Determined that his own marriage should follow in every detail that of Louis XVI and Marie Antoinette, he spent hours in endless discussions with the master of ceremonies and studying the 1770 files of the earlier wedding. Decorations were handed out, prison sentences commuted, popular rejoicings and charitable donations organized. The Emperor ordered a total redecoration of the Château de Compiègne where, again following Louis XVI's marriage arrangements, he expected to meet his bride. Much of the Tuileries, too, was redecorated, including Josephine's own apartments.

Caroline Bonaparte was nominally in charge of the bride's trousseau, but in the end (and Josephine cannot have been surprised to learn this) Napoleon made all the final decisions and (and this *could* have been a surprise) finally raised the sum he planned to spend on it by one-third. At the Tuileries he had all the wedding presents for his future wife, and all the gowns and underwear ordered for her, unpacked in front of him. Paris dressmakers had been given the archduchess's measurements and in any case would never be allowed to fit clothes directly on her. Josephine's favorite dressmaker had been forbidden to work for anyone but the new Empress before the end of March. It took Napoleon many hours to inspect the court dresses, ball dresses, riding habits, underwear, cashmere shawls, shoes trimmed with mink and swansdown, fans—their spokes set in diamonds—and the wedding dress itself of satin and ermine. He went several times to Compiègne to survey Marie Louise's redecorated apartments; only the bathroom remained draped in Josephine's cashmere shawls.

Hortense, designated as one of the new Empress's ladies-in-waiting, described all this to Josephine as well as the especially bitter news that Napoleon had summoned her mother's favorite hairdresser (Duplan was made use of only for evenings and great occasions), doubled his salary and ordered him to work from then on only for the new wife.

Marie Louise was to be married by proxy in Vienna on March 11 and arrive at Compiègne on the twenty-seventh. Suddenly Napoleon realized that Josephine must leave Paris before the Austrian's arrival in France. On

March 12 he informed her that he had granted her the Château de Navarre in Normandy. "You may leave here on March 25th and spend the month of April there,"[3] he wrote, seeming to expect her to return to Malmaison or Paris immediately thereafter. Josephine, however, delayed her departure so long that the very night she left Paris was the one on which Napoleon himself was traveling to Compiègne to meet the archduchess on April 2.

Eugène and his wife had been summoned from Italy for the marriage, and between him and Hortense there were no details left unrecounted to Josephine when they visited her in her new damp and ugly mansion immediately afterwards. Napoleon, they reported, had been in his usual state of wild impatience at Compiègne, counting the number of days it would take for the long procession of coaches and carriages to drive from Vienna. He spent his time alternately going over every detail of the etiquette required for the bride's reception, "as minutely as on the night before a battle," and gazing at the miniature of the young, blond princess, entranced above all by the historic Hapsburg lip, unaltered for generations and a reminder of the last consort, Marie Antoinette. He had dispatched one hundred persons to the French border, headed by Caroline because he believed that his sister being a queen, Marie Louise would feel she was talking to an equal. This was regarded as a strange choice, however, since Caroline occupied the throne from which the French had ousted Marie Louise's own great-aunt, Queen Marie Caroline of Naples.

The unhappy archduchess, lonely and miserable, with a heavy cold, surrounded by her unknown French suite, was being bullied by Caroline, who had forbidden her to keep any of her Austrian ladies or even her little dog, and sent them all back to Vienna; but Marie Louise had the unexpected pleasure of being met at every relay by pressing love letters from her "fiancé." "You will find a husband who wants your happiness before all else. . . ," he wrote, and in the next letter, "Nothing now interests me but you." (This was not strictly true since his unsatisfactory Italian mistress had remained installed in the palace until the previous day.)

At Compiègne the Emperor, described as "intoxicated with happiness and impatience," decided that in pouring rain he would drive off and intercept the coach bearing Marie Louise and Caroline. At a signal from his own coachman, the incoming carriage stopped, the steps were pulled down by footmen, and the chamberlain accompanying the two women exclaimed: "The Emperor!" His gray coat soaked, Napoleon jumped in and embraced Marie Louise. It was dark when the carriage arrived at the Compiègne palace, Hortense related in her *Mémoires*. The Emperor brushed aside the kings and queens, the children with their bouquets, the courtiers waiting to be presented, hurried Marie Louise upstairs, ordered dinner for three in her room (Caroline was still with them) and sent for Uncle Fesch. Was he now married? he asked the cardinal. Civilly, yes, was the answer; religiously, no. Napoleon informed Marie Louise that he would join her in bed immediately. At St. Helena he concluded his account of that night with the celebrated quotation: "She asked me to do it again."[4] It was hardly surprising that the next morning Hortense found the new Empress's expression "sweet, but a little embarrassed." Metternich, in Paris for the event, smoothed over any questions of protocol, assuring everyone that the Emperor had thereby spared his young wife "all the formalities of etiquette."[5]

Parisians' first chance to see their new Empress came a week later on the day of both the civil and religious marriages. The Beauharnais felt sorry for the bride, alone among unfamiliar faces, as she drove into Paris with her husband, followed by thirty-two carriagefuls of their households and escorted by aides and pages down the Champs-Elysées, and on through the Place de la Concorde, where seventeen years earlier her aunt, hands tied behind her back, had climbed the steps of the guillotine. It was not easy to recognize the Emperor in frills and feathered toque. "Who is the respectable lady accompanying the bride?" one spectator was heard to ask her neighbor, peering at Napoleon through the coach windows. "Probably the Archduchess's duenna," came the answer. The crowd appeared not to be overenthusiastic in spite of the open-air buffets and the fountains running with wine.

Once again Hortense, with the Bonaparte sisters, carried Marie Louise's imperial mantle at the religious ceremony in the Tuileries. Eugène was one of the attendant kings, viceroys and courtiers; countless former members of the Convention and of the Committee of Public Safety, now members of the Tribunate, were present, regicides almost to a man. The court, Hortense told her mother, was less admiring of the bride than was the triumphant Emperor. Critical and pitiless, they pronounced her ungainly, her complexion red-faced rather than rosy, her bosom too large, her blue eyes expressionless, her walk heavy and graceless. Her very robustness, however, noted a police report, seemed a happy omen for the hopes of the nation, and Metternich noted in his diary that although her face was ugly rather than beautiful, "once she is properly dressed and 'arranged' she will be perfectly all right."[6]

Undoubtedly, some of the criticism came from the fact that, as Fouché reported, Napoleon's divorce was unpopular. Josephine had been a reminder of the Emperor's revolutionary past, and instinctively the French felt that a link between the Empire and some of the great days of the country's history was broken. What remained of the revolutionary entourage of the Emperor—the marshals, the generals and some of the ministers—felt a certain solidarity with the Empress, who had risen along with them and known the same turmoil and the same prisons. Furthermore, a baseless rumor had started that a secret clause in the marriage contract would oblige all who had voted for the death of Louis XVI to be exiled.

At the huge, dilapidated Château de Navarre, rain and a freezing wind blew through the insecure windows; the fireplaces smoked, and Josephine's household was sulking. Her evenings were spent playing backgammon with the local bishop. Some of her ladies- and gentlemen-in-waiting were leaving and had the insolence to ask her to propose their services to the new Empress, which she invariably did, adding a warm letter of recommendation.

Now it was the rumor of exile from France that replaced all Josephine's other fears. She heard that it was reported in Paris that Marie Louise had said that the Dowager Empress lived too near; then that Malmaison was to be taken from her; that the Emperor did not wish her to return to Paris and, indeed, when she asked for permission to go back to Malmaison, Napoleon dictated a cool letter of reluctant permission. Josephine's reply, both pathetic and deferential, started "Sire," and was written in the third person. Halfway through it reverted to "Bonaparte." "Bonaparte! You promised never to abandon me! I need your advice, you are my only friend. . . . I feared I had been entirely banished from Your Majesty's memory. . . . While I am at Malmaison, Your Majesty may be sure I will live as though I were a thousand miles from Paris and Your Majesty will not be troubled in his great happiness by any expression of my own regrets. . . . Confident in the sentiments which Your Majesty once held for me, I will ask for no further proof but I will expect justice from his heart."[7]

Napoleon answered with an affectionate letter, but a few months later Mme de Rémusat, clearly under orders, wrote from Paris that Marie Louise was pregnant and that the Emperor would prefer Josephine not to live at Malmaison just now. "Marie Louise's jealous disposition. . . . At this time of great rejoicings . . . you might feel yourself forgotten by an entire nation. . . . The Emperor will be caring for his young wife although still moved by his sentiments toward you . . . asks of you one more sacrifice. . . . Will you write the Emperor that the winter will be spent in Italy?"[8]

Napoleon admitted to Hortense that he had hoped that his two wives might meet, but that "the Empress Marie Louise is alarmed by what she has heard of your mother's attractions and of the hold she is known to have over me."[9] (A politer version of Marie Louise's indignant: "How can he want to see that old lady? And a woman of low birth!") And indeed Marie Louise had wept silently one day when, driving near Malmaison while Josephine was absent, Napoleon had proposed visiting the château. So when Josephine herself asked to meet the new Empress Napoleon answered: "No, she thinks you are very old. If she sees you and your charms she would be worried; she would ask me to send you away and I would have to do it." A bittersweet compliment.

Josephine's principal reason for wishing to make a friend of Marie Louise was her belief that as long as the new wife was jealous of her, she must always fear exile; it was the dread of living away from Paris which had made her refuse, a few weeks after the divorce, the offer of marriage by her admirer young Prince Frederick Louis of Mecklenburg-Strelitz.

After a year of travel in Switzerland and Savoy, Josephine was allowed back at Malmaison, and a new correspondence started between Napoleon and Josephine, affectionate and protective on his side, tender and devoted on hers. He continued to oversee her every word and action, reproved her for her failure to maintain imperial etiquette—she was not to go out driving without a full ceremonial escort—and for her continued extravagance and too-generous charitable gifts, which he compared with the modest sums spent by Marie Louise. He had the secretary of the Treasury lecture her on her new debts at Malmaison, pointing out that

Marie Louise kept strict accounts and was never in debt. But when he heard that Josephine was in tears at the receipt of this message, he reproved his minister: "You should not have made her cry,"[10] and he wrote to comfort her.

Still, Josephine at Malmaison was wrapped in her cult of the Emperor; nothing was allowed to be moved in his rooms, which she was said to dust herself. No member of her family or household ever heard a word of criticism of him. The entire Merveilleuse connection remained severed; she never communicated with either Paul Barras or Hippolyte Charles. Her interests were centered on her family and on her swans, her chamois and ostriches, her sheep and her celebrated greenhouses.

For some time after his marriage, Napoleon's life remained a contrast to his previous one. His extended honeymoon lasted for almost a year, in which he spent time at balls, hunts and the opera, was late for council meetings and kept postponing his departure for Spain, where he was expected to take command of his army. Metternich, who thought it politic to remain in Paris for several months after the marriage, wrote to his king: "The Emperor is much taken with his wife . . . and if the Empress continues to dominate him, she could render very great services to herself and to all of Europe. He is so evidently in love with her that all his habits are subordinated to her wishes." Marie Louise was extremely fond of Napoleon and as dependent on him as she had formerly been on her father. The Emperor appeared to remain somewhat in awe of her, and she told Metternich: "I am not afraid of Napoleon, but I am beginning to think he is afraid of me."[11]

It began to appear as though Napoleon was as uxorious as his brothers; instead of caring for his immense Empire, he continued his superficial life. Ministers and marshals were amazed to see him eating, or at least sitting through, huge banquets with his new bride. His custom of spare meals forgotten, to please her, he insisted on a choice of fourteen desserts at every dinner.

The Emperor became supremely conscious of the difference between his two wives when he took Marie Louise on an imperial progress through Belgium, Holland and the provinces of the Rhine, each one of them former possessions of Austria. Unlike the simplicity of Austrian imperial journeys, Napoleon and Marie Louise were accompanied by thirty-five carriages carrying assorted kings, queens and viceroys and their attendants. The Empress herself was followed by her ladies, her trunks of clothes and household linen, and expensive presents to be handed out. Napoleon found to his astonishment that his Hapsburg wife was inadequate on public occasions—shy, cold and haughty, incapable of small talk and smiles, rebelling at the series of receptions, audiences and processions, complaining about the weather, her wet shoes and her headaches.

In her own frank diary Marie Louise listed the horrors of the journey. "Nearly two o'clock and the Emperor would not allow me to eat in the carriage! He says a woman should never have to eat. I was so angry and so hungry that it gave me a fearful migraine and so much bad humor that the Emperor was furious. I didn't care. If I return in another world, I would certainly not remarry."[12]

Napoleon was irritated by his wife's lack of success; possibly his sense of political theater was outraged too. Josephine had always provided him with this in both their private and their political lives. At St. Helena Napoleon accounted for it with: "Marie Louise was shy and always frightened in the midst of the French people who had murdered her aunt."[13]

When Marie Louise's pregnancy became certain, Napoleon, convinced that he would have a boy, was instantly absorbed in the details of his son's household. In spite of his superstitious nature, every detail of the birth and christening was to be copied from the preparations for the last Dauphin. The child's apartments were prepared at the Tuileries, the furniture and the silver gilt services designed and the infant's library was already in place. Fontaine was instructed to draw up the plan for an immense "Palace of the King of Rome."* It was announced that a son's title would be "King of Rome"; a daughter's, the "Princess of Venice."

Both Eugène and Hortense were summoned to be present at the birth of the Emperor's son and they went to Navarre immediately afterwards to describe the scene to their mother. With the Empress's first labor pains, they reported, the bedroom was filled with courtiers, doctors and the Bonaparte family, all dressed in formal court clothes. Napoleon was distressed by Marie Louise's suffering and cries; he left her for only a moment during the long labor, and almost immediately the obstetrician

---

* It was to be on the hill of Chaillot where the Trocadéro now stands.

followed him to warn: "It is a breech presentation and there is some danger for mother and child." "Save the mother," Napoleon answered without hesitation, "it's her right. We will have another child."[14] Eugène acted out the scene in the room next to the Empress's immediately after the birth was announced; at the unwelcome news depriving them of their own hopes of succession, both Caroline and Elisa gave way to hysteria. Cannon were to herald the birth of the child, twenty-one rounds for a girl, one hundred for a boy. At the twenty-second report there was dancing in the streets, excitement and enthusiasm; there was also despair for the royalists. "The twenty-second salute was a death blow for us," wrote Frénilly.[15]

Napoleon sent a page to Josephine to announce the birth. "My son is plump and well. . . . I hope he will fulfill his destiny,"[16] and she replied with a selfless letter full of joy. For two years she would beg to be allowed to see the King of Rome "who had cost her so many tears," and Napoleon arranged a stratagem whereby she could meet the little boy and his governess as though by chance. She spent an hour with him and could hardly bear to part. Marie Louise, of course, heard of this and extracted a promise from the Emperor that neither he nor their child would ever visit Malmaison.

Josephine adored all her grandchildren. Staying in Milan that year, she met all four of Eugène and Augusta's boys and girls, but her favorite was Hortense's youngest son, Louis Napoleon, future Emperor of the French. He would remember that, characteristically, when he stayed with her at Malmaison she would "flatter his pride by repeating his *bons mots.*"[17] She spoiled him outrageously and taught him to chew the sugarcane in her greenhouse as she had once done as a child in Martinique.

Visitors recalled a good deal of pomp and ceremony at Navarre and at Malmaison—thirty footmen standing around the main hall, and on drives through the forest, an equerry at each door and fourteen mounted cuirassiers following the carriage. Josephine was, of course, obeying the Emperor's directives, but still tried to do away with much of the etiquette prescribed by him. At Malmaison, when she returned there, it became fashionable to dine on the exotic fruit forced in her greenhouses, to admire the rarest flowers and taste the ice cream-and-biscuit invention of her Italian chef, the milk and cream from her herd of Swiss cows, and even what she wrote of as *mouphines,* or muffins, made by the English wife of her concierge. An orderly life and regular meals had not only banished Josephine's migraines, but also caused her to put on weight. "One special feature of her figure assumed truly incredible proportions," reported Laure d'Abrantès, "and she agreed with the utmost reluctance to wear boned corsets like the other ladies."[18]

Her entertainments became known, too, for their liveliness. Josephine's small talk is often described as bland, so it is a surprise to read sharp-witted Victorine de Chastenay's description of the conversation at Malmaison dinners. "That distinguished woman," she wrote, "had the gift of making it both general and animated."[19]

Paris did not believe that the Empress Dowager was entirely disconsolate. The relationship between Josephine and her only unmarried chamberlain was the subject of gossip in her own household, too. Théodore Lancelot de Turpin Crissé was twenty-seven years old when he entered her service after the divorce; it was said that the Dowager Empress did not appear to be indifferent to his obvious admiration. When she went to Aix in the summer of 1810, she traveled incognito with only two men, Lancelot and one equerry, and Claire de Rémusat and another woman friend. Mme de Rémusat, her eyes too sharp to be trusted, soon returned to Paris, and the foursome proceeded on an extended trip through Savoy and Switzerland. Turpin, an accomplished draftsman, made daily sketches of the little group, of Josephine riding a mule, picnicking, viewing waterfalls and glaciers under a parasol.*

In Savoy they were visited by Hortense. Her husband had been forced to abdicate the throne of Holland and Napoleon had finally allowed the couple to live separately. The party was joined by Charles de Flahaut, the son of that celebrated quasi-marriage of Adèle de Flahaut and Talleyrand, once the subject of Gouverneur Morris's jealousy in the early days of the Revolution.† And it was here that he and Hortense embarked on the beginning of their long and passionate liaison.

. . .

---

* His sketchbooks can now be seen at Malmaison.

† Hortense and Charles's son, the Duc de Morny, would be a prominent figure at the court of his half brother, Napoleon III.

After his son's birth in March 1811, Napoleon returned to some of his old habits. He lunched alone again, was in his office longer, but still refused to command his army in Spain. He was working more slowly and capriciously, and was spending more time on trivialities such as court etiquette and dress. He started a number of transient liaisons. Marie Walewska and her son were set up in a house in Paris. There was no more talk of the "sacrifices" made for the sake of his dynasty for Napoleon had come to believe that his own was as ancient and as legitimate as the Hapsburgs', and took to referring to his predecessor on the throne as "my poor Uncle Louis XVI." When Marshal Bernadotte was elected to the Swedish throne, he even objected that "that places a commoner on a throne, an injustice to crowned heads."

The war in Spain was an unending hemorrhage, and the price of bread had gone up by one hundred percent, a warning that in earlier days Napoleon would not have neglected. There were serious financial crises in 1810 and 1811, and the first seditious placards went up in Paris after another demand for further conscription; this time the cannon fodder was to be men between the ages of twenty and sixty.

After Josephine, there was no one to temper the Emperor's inhumanity. Constant wrote that the court missed her unfailing gaiety,[20] and a memorialist visiting Paris after three years' absence recorded the totally changed atmosphere in the capital. Not only was there unemployment and the Emperor's new unpopularity, he wrote, but there was also the stiffness of the new court, for "as long as Josephine shared Napoleon's throne, her presence retained a memory of the past—an elegant equality."[21]

"Napoleon will open his new campaign," Prince Metternich informed his Emperor, "in the spring of 1812. This year therefore must be employed by Austria in raising an army for the campaign of 1812."

Franco-Russian relations had deteriorated to such an extent that it was obvious that Napoleon was ready for a showdown with Russia. Because the Continental Blockade was ruinous to Russian commerce, by the end of 1810 the Tsar had opened his ports to neutral shipping, and this gap in the Continental System made it impossible to bring Britain to its knees. The Tsar himself was ready for war with France, a country that continued to hamper Russia economically, and that now, after annexing the Hanseatic ports, controlled the Baltic too.

Though Talleyrand warned against a second campaign while the army was still in Spain, Napoleon proceeded to mobilize the greatest army in history—over 675,000 men, including the contingents the Confederation of the Rhine was forced to furnish. All of vassal Europe—Switzerland, Poland, Italy, Belgium, Holland and Germany—were represented in it; even Austria was forced to provide thirty thousand troops.

Before the start of the campaign, Josephine sent for Constant and begged him to look after the Emperor's health and security; the valet was struck by how much she "cared for the man who had abandoned her, as much as though she was still the most-beloved wife." Napoleon himself visited her at Malmaison before leaving and sat for two hours, always carefully in full view of those windows, talking to her on a circular bench under a tulip tree.

Although he had not declared war on the Tsar, by May Napoleon and his army were ready to leave for the Russian campaign. He needed first, however, to make sure of Austrian neutrality. Marie Louise accompanied him as far as Dresden, where he had convened a meeting of his vassals and allies and of the Austrian imperial family—to impress the latter, it was supposed, by a show of power.

The French entourage both dazzled and offended the assembled monarchs and one shocked Austrian commented: "Marie Louise has one hundred and fifty lackeys, pages and footmen; the Emperor of Austria has just two." The Empress of the French showed off her fabulous jewels to her family and wrote to her mistress of the wardrobe in Paris that even her oldest dresses looked superb in comparison with theirs.

On his march north Napoleon wrote Marie Louise almost daily, gently repeating his instructions on whom to see and how to behave. He was careful never to mention his increasing doubts as to Austrian neutrality; and when he wrote Josephine his letters were as cheerful as those to Marie Louise.

As he progressed east the Emperor lost thousands of men a day from desertions, hunger and forced marches. In Russia, for only the second time, Napoleon was confronted by a patriotic, fanatically religious people in arms against the invader. As they advanced through the Russian wasteland—the Tsar had ordered that "nothing be left for the enemy"—some of the Old Guard, veterans of Italy and Egypt, were heard to murmur that *la vieille* had brought them more luck than had the Austrian and that "he shouldn't have left his old lady."

On September 14 the exhausted French army reached Moscow only to find that the Russians had set fire to their capital as the French entered the deserted city. In mid-October, dangerously close to the winter snows, the Emperor gave the order to retreat. He could have spent the winter in Moscow—there was sufficient food—but a courier took two weeks to ride from Paris to Moscow and he was afraid of being cut off for too long from his Empire.

In the murderous retreat, the army had no fire, no light, and their boots had been worn out on the march north. Partisans attacked and massacred them; if they fell asleep they froze to death, "artillerymen would place their hands near the nostrils of their horses to feel the heat of the animal's breath, . . ."[22] but then the horses died in the thousands and the army lived off the horseflesh. The troops perished even faster from hunger and cold after the snow started falling on November 5. By now the Grand Army had lost 540,000 men dead, prisoners or deserters.

On December 5, Napoleon decided to abandon his army and drove off for Paris in a horse-drawn sleigh, accompanied only by Caulaincourt. "The next day at dawn the army knew everything," wrote an officer to his family, "the impression left by the news cannot be imagined, many of the soldiers blaspheming and reproaching the Emperor for abandoning them. There was a general malediction."[23]

On their drive across Europe, the Emperor's monologue, as reported by Caulaincourt, showed a man whose sense of reality had deserted him. He seemed unaware of the loss of his superb army, of all his artillery and his calvary; only a few garrisons now remained in occupied Europe. His conversation was full of self-delusion and self-justification,[24] of unrealistic plans for the future. He blamed himself for nothing except for having lingered too long in Moscow. He had attacked Russia, he claimed, solely to protect the continent from British supremacy and thereby protecting European industry. He loved above all to give pleasure but too many people had tried to take advantage of him. Josephine had often trapped him into giving her what he ought to have refused her "by an ambush of tears."[25] "Our disasters" he confided to Caulaincourt, "will create a sensation, but my return will counterbalance the unfortunate effects."

In Paris on December 16, the Twenty-Ninth Army Bulletin announced "the destruction of the Grand Army" to an unprepared Paris, still ignorant of the magnitude of the disaster. The dispatch ended with: "His Majesty's health has never been better." There had been stupefaction at Malmaison upon learning from Eugène about the horrors of the retreat from Moscow. "We were all the more terrified," wrote Mlle Avrillon, "because for twenty years so many uninterrupted successes made us think reverses impossible. The effect produced by the army bulletin is impossible to describe."

Josephine had been in tears for weeks, terrified for the Emperor's safety and for Eugène. She knew that the command of the army after Napoleon's departure had been left to Murat, who had deserted, claiming to have jaundice, and that his assignment had been turned over to Eugène.

On December 19 she learned that the Emperor had arrived in Paris the previous night, accompanied only by Caulaincourt. He had entered the Tuileries secretly by a back door, unshaved and unrecognizable, wrapped in sables. By midnight he had sent off a courier to Malmaison and soon drove out there to visit Josephine. General Berthier's dispatch reached him the following day: "Sire, your army exists no more."

The day after Marshal Berthier's bulletin reached him, Napoleon appeared at court in a costume of satin and lace. Constant found the Emperor "exactly as he was before the Russian campaign"—the same serenity. It was as though the past was no longer anything to him and that he was already living in the future. Aware of their propaganda value, he ordered that balls, receptions and galas take place immediately at the Tuileries.

"In the short time I spent in Paris that winter," wrote one officer, "I found my family, and my friends in general terror-stricken. The famous 29th Bulletin had informed France abruptly that the Grand Army had been destroyed. The Emperor was invincible no longer. The campaign of 1813 was about to open . . . The stories told by officers who had survived the retreat were such that the diversions of the carnival stopped. In the midst of this general consternation people were shocked to see the Emperor entertaining at the Tuileries. It was an insult to public grief and revealed a cruel insensitivity to the victims. I shall always remember one of those dismal balls, at which I felt as if I were dancing on graves."[26]

∽ 33 ∾

THE BEGINNING OF THE END

NAPOLEON WAS RIGHT. HIS SUDDEN APPEARANCE IN DECEMBER, TWO days after the shock of the Twenty-Ninth Bulletin, helped to minimize the horror of its impact, but day by day Paris became gloomier as news of so many deaths poured in. Constant noted that the city, for the first time, appeared to be full of people in mourning.

The Emperor, it was clear, did not understand how much the legend of his invincibility had been weakened by the Russian campaign. His defeat encouraged resistance in all of subject Europe, and by the end of the year the King of Prussia had concluded a secret alliance with the Tsar and declared war on France.

When Napoleon left in April 1813 on a new campaign to defeat the allies, he was in an optimistic mood. His army was stronger than those of his combined enemies. He was certain that his marriage would prevent the Emperor of Austria from making war on him, and he had no idea of the strength of the hate aroused in Europe by the imperial armies of occupation. It was the burning and pillaging by the French garrisons in Prussia, the ruin and desolation throughout the countryside, as well as the taxes and requisitions there, which were lighting the fuse of a national movement in that country.

Although Metternich in his diplomatic dispatches always alluded to the links of blood between the two countries, as an additional safeguard Napoleon had Marie Louise named regent during his absence. He had even attempted to have her crowned, but his prisoner the Pope refused to crown and anoint this new "concubine." From campaign headquarters the Emperor wrote Marie Louise daily tender letters containing the customary instructions on how to conduct her daily life and diffident suggestions as to how she should write to her father, sending her only favorable news on the campaign to be passed on to him. Napoleon warned ministers to show Marie Louise "nothing which would worry her" or which might interfere with the optimism she should show in her letters to the Austrian Emperor.

When, after several costly and inconclusive battles, Napoleon asked the Tsar for an armistice, he still believed that his matrimonial links would be stronger than any European coalition. Austria, it was agreed, would be the mediator, and in the course of an interminable nine-hour conference with Metternich Napoleon confessed: "I committed an unpardonable mistake in marrying an Austrian Archduchess and I regret it now." According to Metternich, he talked wildly during those hours, declaring that if "fortune turned against him, he would willingly drag down the whole of society in his fall." And when the conversation turned to the Russian campaign, Napoleon observed that "a man such as I does not concern himself much about the lives of a million men," adding undiplomatically that to spare the French in the Grand Army he had "sacrificed the Poles and the Germans—only thirty thousand French out of the three hundred thousand were lost," at which Metternich was obliged to remind him that he himself was German."[1]

When Napoleon rejected the coalition's peace terms, which would have returned France to its natural frontiers, the frontiers of General Bonaparte in 1797, he sealed the fate of his Empire. In August Austria declared war and Bernadotte, now the elected Prince Royal of Sweden, who had signed a treaty of nonbelligerence with Russia, joined the coalition. The Emperor was unaware of one irony. The Tsar's need of the Swedish alliance was so strong that he even offered the former Marshal Bernadotte his own sister Catherine in marriage—the sister whose hand he had denied Napoleon—on condition, naturally, that he repudiate his wife, Désirée, General Bonaparte's "little fiancée."

Napoleon sent orders that Marie Louise not be told yet that Austria had joined the allies. When he returned to Paris it was to call up the 1814 conscripts, named *les Marie-Louise* (as regent, she had signed the decree for the levy) and, at this inopportune moment, to ask for further taxes. He found his marshals appalled by the continuation of war. Macdonald, Duc de Tarente, Augereau, Duc de Castiglione, and Davout, Prince of Eckmühl, agreed that the Emperor had now completely lost his head and that he was more apt to listen to his entourage of chamberlains, equerries and aides than to them. They complained that he no longer visited battlefields, that his orders were few and disjointed, that the best military commands went to former nobles, that he paid little attention to the lack of discipline of his troops and to their scandalous pillaging "which makes us the object of hatred and dishonor in other nations." It was for his reputation that he was fighting, they claimed, rather than for France.

As soon as he returned to Paris, Napoleon sent Méneval to Malmaison to reassure Josephine. From the start of what would be known as "the sinister year of 1813," she had lived in a state of permanent anxiety both for the Emperor himself and for Eugène, who had replaced Murat as the Emperor's lieutenant on the eastern front.

"No one," Josephine assured her ladies, "knows the Emperor's character as thoroughly as I do. He believes himself to be a predestined being and will bear the blows of fortune with the same composure he shows on the battlefield."[2] Nevertheless she felt that what she described as her lifelong forebodings of disaster were now justified. Her migraines had returned. Avrillon believed that it was her deep unhappiness and sleeplessness that broke her spirit now and would contribute to her death the following year.

Hortense's two boys spent most of the summer with her, and Walewska and her little Alexandre came to Malmaison for frequent visits; any connection with the Emperor was balm for Josephine. Together the two women read the army bulletins forwarded by Hortense and any news of Napoleon she learned from Marie Louise.

When she learned that, after a succession of inconclusive engagements, the Grand Army had been defeated at Leipzig in October of 1813, Josephine wrote a noble and loving letter to the Emperor: "Sire, although I may no longer share in your joys, your grief will always be mine too. . . . I can no more resist the need to tell you this than I could cease to love you with all my heart." Mme de Rémusat could hardly feel now that Josephine was incapable of "sustained emotion."

As the Grand Army retreated across a Germany risen against the occupier, the Emperor set off in his traveling coach and drove back to

Paris to raise more men, money and supplies. In the last fifteen months he had lost two armies and close to a million men. Marmont recorded that for the first time Napoleon felt that "luck was no longer with him."[3]

Now all the vassal princes of the Confederation of the Rhine prepared to abandon Napoleon. The King of Württemberg was first. Next came the family. Elisa, Grand Duchess of Tuscany, bargained with the enemy, hoping to retain her territory. None, however, behaved with quite the impudence of the Murats. Supported by Caroline, Murat signed a treaty with Metternich guaranteeing the throne of Naples for himself. (When Napoleon heard of this he commented: "Caroline! Mine is a family of tramps!") Without waiting for the allies to liberate them, Holland, followed by Belgium, threw out the occupying French troops.

Josephine was infinitely relieved when she received news of Eugène's loyalty, after the first of the defections that followed Austria's abandonment of neutrality. She knew that when King Maximilian of Bavaria joined the coalition he had offered Eugène the crown of Italy if he too would join it; his daughter, however, approved her husband's refusal and Eugène wrote to his mother: "The Emperor's star pales, but that is a further reason to remain faithful to him."

In Paris, in the spring of 1814, although the allies were already on the Rhine, Marie Louise, like so many others accustomed to Napoleon's miracles, had little idea of the imminence of the invasion. Hortense sent a messenger to Malmaison to warn her mother that a Regency Council had been summoned for March 28; that Parisians could hear the sound of distant artillery fire as the enemy approached, that the imperial archives were being burned at the Tuileries, and that Josephine should be ready to leave for Navarre immediately.

No one was prepared, however, for the scene at the Tuileries described by Hortense, where the Regency Council, composed of Joseph, Marie Louise, Talleyrand and Cambacérès, all agreed that the Empress and the King of Rome should remain in Paris. Their departure, the council decided, would be interpreted as proof that the government considered resistance hopeless. Joseph alone disagreed and he produced his bombshell: two letters from Napoleon dated early in February, recommending that "if the battle is lost" the Empress and the King of Rome should go to Rambouillet accompanied by the ministers, the grand dignitaries, the Senate, the Council of State and the Treasury; and adding that "if I die, my son and the Empress must not let themselves be taken. . . . I would rather see my son's throat cut than see him brought up as an Austrian prince in Vienna." Although it was argued that the letters had been written for different circumstances, and that Marie Louise would certainly now obtain better conditions for the capital from her father, they were all terrified of disobeying the Emperor's orders.

The Empress immediately wrote to Napoleon: "I would have been quite brave enough to stay and I am very angry that they wouldn't let me, especially when Parisians are showing such eagerness to defend themselves. I am sure you won't like it."*[4] And in the next letter she revealed that Joseph had begged her to throw herself on the mercy of her father, certain, he said, that the Austrian Emperor would arrange a suitable life for all the Bonapartes.

It took some courage for Marie Louise to be prepared to remain in a Paris full of the same citizens who, less than twenty-one years earlier, had massacred the inhabitants of the Tuileries when the enemy was a great deal farther from Paris. And she continued to protest, writing Napoleon once again: "I believe that in a few days' time you will agree that I should have remained, but I have no choice. Joseph has shown me your letters."[5]

At ten the next morning the households of Marie Louise and the King of Rome set off toward the Loire followed by the Bonapartes, the equerries, some of the ladies of the palace and carriages packed with furniture, silver, clothes and all the Treasury. Even the coronation coach was piled with cases and trunks. As they lumbered south, the roads were already clogged by refugees with their household belongings, their sheep and their cows.

Hortense defied her husband's orders to accompany the family and drove off for the Château de Navarre with their two sons. Josephine was already on her way there from Malmaison, her petticoats sewn by Mlle Avrillon with her diamonds and pearls and in deadly fear of attack by

---

* The correspondence between Marie Louise and Napoleon was turned over to Joseph Bonaparte by Napoleon before the Battle of Waterloo. It was found in the papers of Désirée Bernadotte, Queen of Sweden, and is now in the Royal Swedish Archives in Stockholm.

Cossacks. Before leaving Malmaison she had written Hortense that she "had never lacked the courage to meet the many dangerous situations in which I have found myself during my life,"[6] but that now her heart was broken by the ingratitude of those who owed Napoleon everything. She was hardly surprised, even before her departure from Malmaison, to find most of her ladies and chamberlains returning to Paris. Mme de Rémusat was already wearing a white cockade, the color of the Bourbons, and Lancelot de Turpin was agitating for a post with the museums under the new regime. When Josephine arrived at Navarre on April 3, one of the marshals sent a courier to tell her of the occupation of Paris. Napoleon, he informed her, unable to reach the capital, was at Fontainebleau awaiting the allies' decision as to his fate.

Josephine may not have been aware of how large a part Claire de Rémusat had been taking in Talleyrand's intrigues. Certainly Claire knew every detail of the plotting at Talleyrand's house, all centering on the return of the Bourbons. At the news of Napoleon's return from the Russian campaign, Talleyrand had announced, slowly and gravely: "It is the beginning of the end." He had already decided that the Bourbons should return, but it was important to make sure that they recognize his own role. "I do not wish," he told Aimée de Coigny, one of his coterie, "to expose myself to a pardon, or to have to justify myself."[7] In his splendid new mansion on the Place de la Concorde,* he set about, with the aid of his women friends, the difficult task of repairing his links with the Pretender. When Louis XVIII, a refugee in England, heard of the attempt from Talleyrand's uncle, the future monarch exclaimed, "God be praised! Bonaparte must be close to his fall, for I am certain that when the Directory was near its own, your nephew wrote in similar terms to the victor of Italy!"[8]

Aimée de Coigny had become Talleyrand's liaison with the court of the Pretender through her lover Bruno de Boisgelin, a royalist who believed in an English style of monarchy and a parliament; exactly what Talleyrand himself had wanted in the Constituent days. Aimée herself, in spite of her lifelong habit of adopting the political preferences of the men in her life, when Montrond followed Talleyrand into Bonaparte's orbit,

---

* The property now of the United States government.

had joined her friend Mme de Staël in opposition to him; and when Napoleon divorced Josephine her resistance was confirmed. Once again, with Boisgelin, her intellectual independence gave way to her affections, but this time she was working against her own interests. As Church and "Victorian" morality returned with the Restoration, Aimée, like the other Merveilleuses, went out of fashion.

But it was Claire de Rémusat who was responsible for Talleyrand's next successful maneuver. He was determined to remain in Paris to play the most important role of his life, and in his ardent, almost hourly notes to his mistress (this one ends: "Goodbye my angel, burn this"), he spelled out one particular ruse. On the day of the Empress's departure from the Tuileries, he drove openly and slowly in his travel coach across Paris to one of the city's gates. By design, the captain of the National Guard there was M. de Rémusat, who asked to see his passport. Talleyrand's coach was turned around when he answered that he had none; then he went home to write the Regency Council that he had found the gate closed.

The question of who should now rule France would be settled by Talleyrand alone.

On the morning of April 1, 1814, the allied cavalry rode thirty abreast down the Champs-Elysées to the Tuileries, the first foreign armies to enter Paris since the Hundred Years' War in the fifteenth century. A deathly silence greeted this first contingent of the invaders.

There had been an unequal but heroic battle for Paris on the previous day. The Prussians were already shelling the capital and Cossacks were near the easternmost suburbs when Joseph Bonaparte, after briefly watching the fighting from the heights of Montmartre, decided to follow his family to Blois, first authorizing Marshal Marmont to sign the capitulation of Paris.

When Tsar Alexander arrived that evening, it was decided that he should stay at Talleyrand's residence. He had been on his way to the Elysée, but an anonymous letter (it has been suggested that its author was Talleyrand) warned him that the mansion was mined. Talks started immediately on Napoleon's successor. The Tsar himself was open-minded. He believed the Bourbons were too unpopular, too little known even, to be returned to the throne, "as unknown in the France of 1814," as Chateaubriand expressed it, "as the family of the Emperor of China." He himself was willing to accept a regency by Marie Louise, and naturally assumed that this was the wish of her father, the Emperor of Austria. Talleyrand, however, assured him that France would welcome the Bourbons and required only to be certain of a constitution; the new king, Louis XVIII, could then be invited to return from his present exile in England, once the Senate had produced this charter. Meanwhile a provisional government was to be set up with Talleyrand at its head.

The following day Caulaincourt as Napoleon's envoy arrived at the Talleyrand mansion. It resembled, he found, the residence of a king in exile, with the staircase and rooms crowded with monarchists, liberals, constitutionalists and the entourages of the Russian and Prussian sovereigns. Since it was both the seat of the provisional government and the Tsar's headquarters it was guarded day and night by Cossacks sleeping on straw in the courtyard.

The Emperor, Caulaincourt reported, had arrived in Fontainebleau and was ready to abdicate in favor of his son. The Tsar still hesitated and might have accepted these conditions, but Talleyrand assured him that a regency would simply mean Napoleon's swift return and, the Tsar added privately to his old friend Caulaincourt, it was Austria, more than any of the other allies, that was opposed to the Emperor's terms.

Against overwhelming odds Napoleon had fought some of the most brilliant battles of his career, but in his final retreat, riding ahead of his army, he could get no nearer to Paris than Fontainebleau, forty miles south of the capital. There he learned that by Joseph's orders the city had capitulated that morning. "What treachery!" he stormed, ". . . if I had only arrived four hours earlier!"[9] He began by attempting to order a new campaign—his army, at least 50,000 strong, was only four days' march away and 100,000 men were still stationed in the occupied countries. When the generals he summoned pronounced the situation hopeless, his new energy deserted him and he seemed detached from reality. "He appeared tired and lethargic," reported Constant. "His spirits went up and down, and on the same day he would be immensely sad, and the next moment whistling." Napoleon's ambition abandoned him; he attempted suicide with poison but was thwarted in the attempt by the age of the medicine.

Caulaincourt returned from Paris once more with the information that the Senate had produced a somewhat revised version of the Constitution of 1791 and that as soon as Louis XVIII had accepted it—and recovered from an exceptionally severe attack of gout—he would return to France and his throne. Although the Senate, also, had voted Napoleon's deposition, he still could not decide to abdicate and began bargaining on the size of the income he was insisting upon. He seems to have hoped that an appeal from Marie Louise to her father might grant him better terms; Caulaincourt, however, remonstrated: "I despair when I see you being the dupe of your confidence in your father-in-law's feelings."

Finally, on April 11, Napoleon agreed to abdicate unconditionally, whereupon the Tsar proposed that Napoleon be named sovereign of the island of Elba and Marie Louise duchess of Parma in Italy. It was he again who insisted that the former Emperor be accorded the large revenues he was asking for himself and for all his family.

Of all those who owed Napoleon everything, it appeared that only Caulaincourt, the Beauharnais, Josephine and Marie Louise remained loyal. Most of the marshals had deserted, as had Roustam the Mameluke, who for thirteen years had slept on the floor outside his door; Constant would follow later.

At Blois, most of the Empress's attendants left her to return to Paris. Joseph and Jérôme Bonaparte tried to bully her into surrendering to the first Austrian corps she could find, claiming that this was their only hope of safety. Jérôme went further and threatened to have her taken by force to the Austrian lines. Her jewelry was removed by royalist envoys sent to bring back the national Treasury; even the necklace she wore was taken off her neck. "I would be braver, calmer, if I were sharing your fate," she wrote her husband, "consoling you for all your reverses."[10] His answer was to write that she must pay a million francs each from the Treasury to Madame Mère, Louis, Jérôme, Pauline and Elisa; and take two million francs for herself and the King of Rome. She paid them all, then they too abandoned her. Madame Mère and Uncle Fesch set off for Rome immediately, Joseph for Switzerland.

Napoleon's letters to Marie Louise continued to be evasive: "You can come here if you like . . . you could stay there."[11] Her distraught letters showed immense affection and courage, particularly for a woman who, passive all her life, had obeyed only two men, one of whom was now doing everything possible to keep her from her husband. "You must," she wrote to Napoleon, "send someone to tell me what to do."[12] But he sent no instruction, nor mentioned his abdication. Marie Louise continued to write daily: "No one loves you as much as your faithful Louise,"[13] and she added that she wanted first to see her father and then accompany her husband to Elba.

When at last Napoleon sent a troop of Guards cavalry to fetch her, they found when they reached Blois that the Austrian net had closed in on her. "They have made me leave," Marie Louise wrote him, "orders have been given to prevent me from joining you, and even to resort to force if necessary. I am in deadly anxiety on your behalf. I think we are being duped, but I shall take a firm line with my father."[14] And after an interview with the Emperor of Austria she wrote that she had been dealt the worst blow: "He will not allow me to join you now, or see you, or travel with you to Elba. . . . He insisted on two months first in Austria, then on to Parma and that I could see you there."[15]

After Marie Louise had been taken under escort to the palace at Compiègne, and the Tsar and the King of Prussia came to pay their respects, they were astonished to find her bathed in tears. They had expected to find her relieved to be delivered from the Ogre. The Austrian plot developed further. One of her former ladies was said to have sent for both Constant and Roustam, and urged them to detail all Napoleon's liaisons since her marriage. She remained firm, however, and as she crossed the French border wrote in her diary that she was determined to join her husband in exile.

Marie Louise has been almost universally condemned for her conduct, yet she appears to have behaved irreproachably until once again her father made all her decisions for her. Surrounded by traitors, she alone attempted to reach Napoleon. Her letters to him throughout this period are as pressing and affectionate as those from Malmaison.

As he was about to leave Fontainebleau, Napoleon wrote Marie Louise that this would mean he would not hear from her for several days: "Have courage, keep up the honor of your rank and of my destiny."[16] And to Josephine: "They have betrayed me," he wrote. "Yes, all of them except our dear Eugène, so worthy of you and of me. . . . Adieu, my dear Josephine. Resign yourself as I am doing and never forget one who has never forgotten and will never forget you. P.S. I expect to hear from you when I reach Elba. I am far from being in good health."[17]

Before leaving for Elba in April, Napoleon summoned the Old

Guard for an emotional farewell, one of the great set pieces of Napoleonic iconography. After delivering one of his inspired speeches to the men lined up in the palace courtyard, he embraced their general and called for the standard of the First Regiment of Grenadiers; as he kissed the flag the troops could not hold back their tears; then, walking rapidly to his carriage, he drove off escorted by the commissioners of the allied powers and by General Bertrand, former marshal of the Palace. The Guard, recorded one of them, burned their flags and then, so as not to be separated from them, swallowed the ashes.

Josephine was at Navarre when she learned that a provisional government had been set up under the presidency of Talleyrand and that Napoleon had abdicated unconditionally. Caulaincourt came to see her and dwelt on Napoleon's advice that she should appeal to the Tsar for help. (Napoleon's memory of his relationship with Alexander had been under review and he was seen at Fontainebleau to drink to his health.)

Josephine first sent to Italy for Eugène to hurry to Paris. It was important, she said, for all of their futures that he come quickly, leaving his wife and children in Munich. As usual, she depended on his support in all the perilous moments of her life.

As she had done so often during and after the days of the Revolution, Josephine took up her pen. She wrote to Talleyrand: "We are broken-hearted. . . . I await the Senate's decision and I place my situation and that of my children in your hands. . . . I shall follow your advice with confidence."[18] Talleyrand, who saw that Josephine could be useful to the new King, when he returned to France, wrote to reassure her and to tell her that out of the fortune guaranteed to the imperial family, her own annuity would be one million francs, with 400,000 pledged for Hortense.

The King returned to Paris on May 4, the day on which Napoleon was stepping ashore at Elba; an uncharismatic figure, enormously fat, he could not, owing to his debilitating gout, walk without being supported on either side. His entry into Paris was saluted with delirious applause. "It is quite incomprehensible," declared one onlooker. "Here is a man whom only yesterday they did not know, and already they are full of enthusiasm for him!" Parisian enthusiasm was, of course, principally for the hope of peace. There was some coolness in the workmen's suburbs, but in the center of town the Bourbon lilies were worn in women's hats, and bed sheets (termed "white banners" for the occasion) floated from every window.

From the time of the allies' entry into Paris, a difference was made between the Beauharnais and the Bonapartes. Louis XVIII's position was felt to be fragile; the civilian population was divided and the army openly hostile, but all parties could claim Josephine. She was considered a link between the two Frances and a useful tool for isolating the Bonapartes— the one card they could all play safely.

From Paris, Metternich sent messengers to Navarre; so did the Tsar, who encouraged Josephine to return to Malmaison and dispatched Russian troops to guard her there. Initially, Parisians had simply been relieved to find there would be no pillaging and had summoned up little enthusiasm for this conqueror. Few wanted the overthrow of the Empire and many, even the ultra-royalists, were humiliated by the foreign occupation. But now Tsar Alexander had become Paris's hero, enjoying public acclaim and showing himself everywhere in an ostentatiously simple uniform, contrasting with those of his general staff. He went around Paris on foot, "stopping at every moment to speak to the people nearest him." Parisians marveled at the blond giant's magnanimous gestures. He was a model of tact. His Cossacks were camped along the Champs-Elysées, peacefully eating, singing and repairing their clothes and shoes; when he heard that their horses, tethered to the trees along the avenue, were destroying them by eating the bark, he gave orders for the damage to be paid for.

As soon as Josephine and Hortense arrived at Malmaison they found a message from the Russian Emperor; he wished to come pay his respects that day. Alexander was immediately enchanted by Josephine and still more by Hortense. He visited them daily, and interceded with the authorities for titles and revenues for them and for Eugène. He offered Josephine a palace in St. Petersburg, although he feared that the climate there "would be too rigorous"[19] for her; Hortense, at his insistence, was awarded the title of Duchesse de Saint Leu. Following his lead, Louis XVIII upon his return congratulated Eugène "on all the good his mother had done in France" and for "the zeal she had shown in attempting to save the life of the Duc d'Enghien."[20]

. . .

It became fashionable for distinguished foreigners to visit Malmaison; the house was far more crowded now than at any time since the divorce. All the foreign princes were impressed by Josephine's dignity; her feeling for Napoleon was evident. She and Hortense conducted the King of Prussia, the Russian grand dukes, her old admirer the Prince of Mecklenburg and all the allied sovereigns on tours of the greenhouses, the menagerie and the gardens. Only the Emperor of Austria wrote a polite note to say he would not visit her for fear of causing her pain. "But it is not *me* he has dethroned," she reminded her visitors, "it's his daughter!"

On the first day of the Tsar's visit, Josephine ordered over six thousand francs' worth of white muslin dresses, in spite of the reduction in her income. She was reverting to her old expedients of adapting to new power by cultivating influential new friends, the means by which she had survived the separation from her first husband, the Revolution and the days of Thermidor. She has been criticized for the opportunism she showed now—as well as for the purchase of those new dresses—and been accused of disloyalty in entertaining the enemy occupying France. Yet Napoleon himself, at a time when the Bonaparte brothers were threatening to force Marie Louise to give herself up to the Austrian army and imploring her to take them with her, had sent Caulaincourt to tell her "to put her trust in the Tsar." There were those who felt that Josephine lost some dignity by receiving the Tsar so often and by asking him to intercede for material benefits for herself and her children. Conceivably it was still more important for the woman, rather than for the former Empress, to be given this confirmation of her continuing seductiveness.

She did not abandon "Bonaparte," however. Indeed there is no doubt that she would have, as she claimed to one of her ladies, Georgette Ducrest, and to her doctor, "driven straight through occupied Paris to Fontainebleau, never again to be parted" from Napoleon, had she still been Empress of the French. But in spite of her social life and the flattery of those in power, Josephine confided to Hortense's reader: "Sometimes I feel so melancholy that I could die of despair; I cannot be reconciled to Bonaparte's fate."[21] And to another friend: "I don't know what is the matter with me, but sometimes I feel sad enough to die."[22] She worried ceaselessly about Napoleon, "fallen from so much grandeur, relegated to an island, abandoned by France."[23] By this time she had heard that he was to be sent to Elba, and Hortense's reader had been told that in Paris "it is said that when he left Fontainebleau, Napoleon had exclaimed: 'Josephine was right, my parting from her has brought me bad luck.' "[24]

Josephine could become flustered and angry at the slightest sign that she might be thought to utter a disloyal word. Mme de Staël, back from exile at last, was one of her many visitors. When she questioned Josephine on "whether she still loved Napoleon" Josephine left her without a word, confiding to one of her friends afterwards: "Do you know that Mme de Staël had the effrontery to ask whether I still loved the Emperor? I, who never ceased to love him during his good fortune, how could I love him less ardently now?"[25]

The Tsar was disturbed when Josephine caught cold while out driving in mid-May with him and Hortense. Her doctor said it was nothing, and she rejected Alexander's offer of a second opinion by his physician because she said: "It would hurt the feelings of my own doctor." On May 24 she was still chilled and feverish. Hortense implored her mother not to come downstairs to a dinner given at Malmaison for the Russian and Prussian sovereigns. Josephine not only dined with her guests but then, after opening the ball with the Tsar, took a long walk through the gardens with him to smell the scent, she said, of the lilac and the lilies of the valley.

She was still, the next day, showing visitors her gallery of paintings and the new black cygnets on the lake, though her doctor had applied mustard plasters the previous night for her inflamed throat and congested chest. She lingered for a few more days. On the last night, when her children were both out of the room, her attendant believed she heard her whisper: "Bonaparte ... Elba ... the King of Rome."[26]

She could not speak at all on the morning of the twenty-ninth. Hortense was too affected to stay in her mother's bedroom and so Josephine died in Eugène's arms, "going," he said, "as gently and as sweetly to meet death as she had met life."[27]

Neither of Josephine's children had thought immediately of sending the news of her death to Napoleon. When he learned of it in a French journal brought to Elba, he stayed locked in his room for two days, "refusing to see anyone but the Grand Marshal."[28]

. . .

By March 1815, Napoleon had been on Elba for ten months; once again, the British fleet was unable to contain him. On March 15, he slipped the naval cordon, landed on the French coast and was driving north with a handful of guardsmen. The crowds, as Napoleon proceeded through Provence, were almost as hostile as they had been when they attacked him on his journey south to Elba, when, haunted by his old fear of the mob, he had had to resort to a humiliating disguise. All this was changed after an encounter just south of Grenoble, one to be forever celebrated in Napoleonic legend. When a battalion sent by Louis XVIII to block his march appeared, Napoleon stepped forward, threw open his coat and declaimed: "Soldiers, if there is one among you who wishes to kill his Emperor, he can do so!" He was answered by shouts of *"Vive l'Empereur!"* [29]

His progress became increasingly triumphant from that day on until he reached Paris on March 20. In the capital there were cheers but principally apathy; cafés closed, the streets were empty.

At the Tuileries the white Bourbon flag had been blown from its mast by the strong March wind. Beds were unmade, ovens still warm after the King's hasty departure that morning. In the courtyard a shouting, cheering crowd greeted the former Emperor, pulled him from his traveling coach and half carried him shoulder high up the grand staircase.

The palace was already filling up with Bonapartist generals and officers on half pay (most of the marshals, except for Ney and Soult had left with the Bourbons or retired). Of the imperial cabinet only Fouché appeared and of the family, Hortense and Lucien. Marie Louise was not even mentioned. Fortunée Hamelin was there and several of the mistresses, including Duchâtel, Mlle George and Walewska, all in court dress. The company had discovered while they waited that the royal lilies on the Tuileries carpets had been simply glued on over the imperial bees, and they had been on all fours ripping off the offending emblems.

This was to be one of Napoleon's last triumphant days. "Even as he was carried upstairs," one observer noted, "there reigned as much anxiety as joy on the faces of his generals and his former ministers. . . . Hardly was he seated than words like "constitution" and "liberty" rang in his ear . . . a bitter pill which he swallowed with fairly good grace." [30]

. . .

After his return from Elba one of Napoleon's first questions to his physician, Dr. Corvisart, had been, "Why did you let my poor Josephine die?" "Sire," was the answer, "I believe she died of a broken heart."[31] Although the autopsy had revealed pneumonia and a "gangrenous angina," Napoleon readily believed Josephine's own doctor's similar diagnosis: "That *bonne* Josephine! She really loved me, didn't she?" "Oh yes, Sire, I heard her say that were she still Empress of the French, she would have crossed Paris in a coach and eight, her household in full livery, to have joined you in Fontainebleau, never to leave you." "She would have done it, Monsieur, she was capable of doing it."[32]

Two days after his return, Napoleon told Hortense that he wanted to visit Malmaison. She could not desert her stepfather now, although she had described to Eugène his return from Elba as "news which is going to place our poor France in a pitiful state."[33] It had required some courage to join him at the Tuileries; she ran not only the risk of his recriminations, but also, in the event of the return of the Bourbons, the loss of her annuity; and there had been sarcastic references to the title conferred on her by Louis XVIII.

At Malmaison, Napoleon went alone upstairs to the room where Josephine had died; when he returned Hortense saw that his eyes were wet with tears.

At the news of Napoleon's approach there had been a diaspora of turncoat marshals and courtiers. Germaine de Staël took the road to Switzerland. Claire de Rémusat burned the diaries she had kept of her days at the Consular and imperial courts; twenty years later she was to reconstitute them from memory.

Thérésia de Caraman Chimay, formerly Tallien, wrote to her husband in Brussels, attempting to describe the mood in the capital. "Everyone I know has gone. It is strange to see people in the street, some wearing the white and some the tricolor cockade, without exchanging a word, appearing neither shocked nor surprised by these different signs of their adherence. Only bunches of violets [a Bonapartist symbol] indicate the loyalties of those who wear them. . . . It is as though Parisians were watching a play of which they knew the outcome and which would cost them personally nothing."[34]

It could not be said that the Bourbons' departure was mourned by the mass of Parisians. Napoleon could only be sure of the army and what he termed "the Paris rabble," both of whom had remained cool toward the King. But fear of conscription gripped almost every family. Napoleon soon realized that at Elba he had been misled by reports of the warmth of the welcome he could expect, by tales of old soldiers grumbling in cafés, of the new king's tactless insistence that the tricolor flag—emblem of so many victories—be discarded in favor of the Bourbon white. But he noted that there were more cries of "down with priests" and "the guillotine for the aristocrats" than of cheers for the Emperor. "They have let me come, just as they have let the other fellow go," he said. Rather than become a "crowned Robespierre"[35] he was willing to give some liberal color to his regime. At Elba he had decided that "it was not the coalition of sovereigns, but "liberal ideas" that had overthrown him and that "if freedom of the press and a parliamentary government are necessary to the French" they could have them.[36]

Although Joseph Fouché had been appointed Louis XVIII's minister of police, he agreed now to fulfill the same post again for Napoleon. The Emperor instructed him to invite Benjamin Constant, an icon of the liberals, to help draft a new constitution. The one drawn up was approved by a referendum; it pleased neither Bonapartists nor liberals. Reluctantly, the Emperor accepted an assembly with two chambers, a free press and the abolition of censorship. The problem of liberal opposition, he believed, was solved; at St. Helena he admitted that he "intended to send the Chambers packing, once I was victorious and safe."[37]

The Tuileries Palace was soon considered too pompous for the constitutional monarch the Emperor was to become, and he moved into the Elysée mansion, his former gift to Josephine. With an eye to her propaganda value, Napoleon urged Fouché to invite Mme de Staël to return to France; Napoleon's need to claim the adherence of his "liberal" prize was obvious. Both Barras and Lafayette were offered posts in the new government; Lafayette accepted, though he wrote to U.S. President Thomas Jefferson that, but for Napoleon, war might still be averted.[38]

Since September a Congress had been in session in Vienna, assembled to conclude a treaty that would establish a solid peace in Europe.

Upon learning of Napoleon's escape from Elba the four great powers issued a unanimous declaration of war not against France but only, it was emphasized, against Napoleon in person, outlawing him for breaking the peace. England, Russia, Austria and Prussia each undertook to contribute a contingent of fifty thousand men in the field until peace was restored to Europe. It was Talleyrand, representing his country at the Congress, who took the lead in uniting the statesmen of the four powers against Napoleon and inspired the joint declaration.

Unknown to Napoleon, Fouché was as determined as Talleyrand that France should not again be torn by civil war and that the Emperor must go. Privately he confided "the man is even more demented than when he left for Elba; he will not last four months,"[39] and having decided that the Bourbons must be brought back he remained in touch with the King in exile in the Low Countries and with Talleyrand and Metternich in Vienna. (Cambacérès recorded that during those weeks Fouché was receiving so many expressions of affection from Talleyrand "that he was naturally terrified.")[40]

By the beginning of June the allied armies were poised to invade the country from the north, the east and the southeast. In the Emperor's entourage it was noted that his old resolve had been succeeded by a sort of indifference, even resignation. The French army's best hope was to attack immediately. Wellington's troops in Brussels numbered only ten thousand; it was imperative to strike before the Dutch and Belgian levies could join him and General Blücher's Prussians. Napoleon hesitated however, appeared to undergo another attack of indecisiveness and seemed reluctant to start on this campaign. On June 12, Thérésia wrote her husband: "The Emperor left at four this afternoon. The rain has never stopped and all our flowers have rotted in the bud." The rain continued in the northeast and covered the fields around Brussels with mud.

When Napoleon set out he was in excellent spirits, confident in his plan for defeating Wellington and Blücher separately, and with the best army he had commanded since Austerlitz; only the former high command was missing. The majority of the marshals had sworn an oath of allegiance to Louis XVIII; Ney and Soult, however, who had first done so had now rallied to the former Emperor. On his way to Belgium, Napoleon traveled in a newly armored traveling coach. A victory bulletin and his state robes accompanied him; a million francs' worth of diamonds were sewn into his coat.

On June 18 a few miles south of Brussels the two armies faced each other along hedgeless fields planted in corn, close to the village of Waterloo. It was clear that the coming battle would decide the fate of Europe. Napoleon was optimistic after a long night's sleep. Wellington had hurriedly deployed his Anglo-Dutch-Belgian forces; some of his officers had left a ball in Brussels only at three that morning and had not taken the time to change their clothes. Blücher, almost a day's march away, had not yet arrived.

All through that day the battle raged, its outcome doubtful until the late afternoon. At six-thirty Blücher and his Prussians arrived to support the allied forces. At 7:30, Napoleon, who had been holding the Imperial Guard in reserve, launched them in an attempt to splinter the allied line. Its now sparse battallions met the fire of the English in front, of the King's German Legion on their flank and of the Hanoverians behind. Suddenly, above the clamor of drums beating, bands playing and the roar of artillery a terrifying cry swept the battlefield: "The Guard is falling back!" Such a thing had never happened before. Three sparse Old Guard battallions attempted in vain to cover the retreat.

As darkness fell on the smoke-covered field, Napoleon was escorted to his traveling coach by Marshals Soult and Ney and Generals Bertrand, Gourgaud and Flahaut; abandoning the debris of his army, he raced back to Paris, issuing on his way the last of his bulletins; the battle, he claimed, had been won at Waterloo "until a sudden wave of panic terror swept the entire field of battle." He arrived at the Elysée at dawn and was helped from his carriage by Caulaincourt. At first, he was almost speechless, his nerve paralyzed. Although he had lost yet another great army, "he spoke of his situation with astonishing calm and complete detachment,"[41] noted Constant.

Once more, as in the retreat from Moscow and again at Fontainebleau, he took refuge in fantasy. First he spoke of leading a national resistance to the invader. This the Chambers ignored, but at Fouché's urging they insisted, for the sake of the country, on the Emperor's abdication; the allied powers had refused to negotiate as long as he remained in power. Napoleon hesitated for several days, attempted to bargain for a regency for Marie Louise and the King of Rome.* Then as soon as he signed a second abdication he suggested to Fouché, now president of a new provisional government, that he himself be made a member of that body.

The minister's answer was that he would have him arrested unless he left the country immediately. His continued presence in Paris was an obstacle to any peace treaty and a danger to himself. British and Prussian forces were marching, unresisted, on the capital, and General Blücher was known to have threatened to capture Napoleon Bonaparte and to have him shot in the same circumstances and in the same place as Enghien at Vincennes.

The former Emperor remained undecided as to whether to surrender to the British—he admired their constitution, was the unexpected reason he gave—or to sail for the New World. At his request Fouché ordered two frigates to be fitted out at the port of Rochefort, procured passports for America for him and his suite and told Napoleon that if he left immediately he had a good chance of running the British blockade. Since Fouché also informed Wellington of Napoleon's port of departure he appears to have been determined to be rid of the Emperor on any terms.

Still Napoleon delayed, in turn optimistic and apathetic. Finally, after just one hundred days in France, he sent word to Hortense to meet him at Malmaison. His mother, Walewska and her son and his boy by Denuelle received the same summons. On June 25 he drove out of the Elysée by a garden gate, up the Champs-Elysées for the last time and under the still unfinished Arc de Triomphe.

As he entered the park at Malmaison, Napoleon's first words were: "My poor Josephine! I can see her now, walking along one of the paths and picking the roses she loved so well. . . . We never really had any quarrels except about her debts."[42] And later he said to Hortense: "She was the most alluring, the most glamorous creature I have ever known, a woman in the true sense of the word, volatile, spirited and with the kindest heart in the world."[43]

Everything in the house recalled the early days of their long complicity. Frescoes from the rue de la Victoire were piled in the attic, Jose-

---

* The Emperor's letters to Marie Louise in Parma were being intercepted in Vienna. In any case she was by now subjugated by her chamberlain Neipperg, who in turn was a tool of Metternich, a man determined to separate young Napoleon from his mother.

phine's tenacious perfume still clung to her tented bedroom, to the endless closets of dresses, linens, hats and shawls. The swan, her emblem adopted in the heady Italian summer, was everywhere; the birds sailing on the lake were reflected on carpets, on upholstery and, with wings deployed, supporting the bed on which she died. Light as swansdown, the court trains laid away were froths of tulle, spangles and air.

After spending five days at Malmaison, Napoleon received an urgent message from Fouché directing him to leave immediately. The Prussian advance guard was already at Versailles; a column sent by Blücher to capture Napoleon dead or alive had been thwarted by Davout's order to blow up of the bridge nearest to Malmaison.

There were tearful farewells—Napoleon refused Walewska's offer to accompany him into exile and then stepped into a yellow carriage with no armorial bearings waiting for him at the gate with a mounted escort. Driving fast and by side roads, he reached Rochefort on the Atlantic coast by July 2. There he was joined by some of the officers who had elected to share his exile, by the Bertrands and by Joseph Bonaparte and his family. There were arguments as to their destination. While Napoleon hesitated for several days, Joseph was for forcing the tightening British blockade and proceeding to America.

On July 16 (Louis XVIII had returned to Paris a full week earlier to be greeted by "delirious enthusiasm") the former Emperor decided to embark on a British vessel. He had considered and turned down Joseph's offer of changing places with him (their resemblance was striking) and escaping to live as a gentlemen farmer in the New World. But he would prefer, he decided, a scene more in keeping with classical tradition and with his own legend. He presented himself to the British ship's captain in full uniform, wearing the grand cordon of the Legion of Honor, and followed by his officers, sixty servants and a large amount of silver from the Elysée. And in a letter to be forwarded to the prince regent in London, he wrote that he was throwing himself on the "hospitality of the British people."*

---

* Napoleon's companions had, it seemed, counted on being "installed in some comfortable country house"; one of the officers had even been heard to inquire what decorations they might expect."[44]

Only after boarding H.M.S. *Bellerophon* with his suite did Napoleon learn that he would not be permitted to land in Britain, but as a prisoner of war of the allies he would be transferred to another ship that would take him to his definitive exile.

One lady who watched Napoleon transfer ship off Plymouth on August 9 was transfixed. "I have seen Bonaparte distinctly," she wrote to a friend, "I was quite close to him for above three minutes . . . he resembles no human being I have ever seen. . . . He is apart from the rest of mankind. . . . He has not the least of a military air nor yet of a royal one, but a *something* greater than either, more imposing, more extraordinary than any creature I have ever seen. . . . He seems quite inaccessible to human tenderness or human distress—still he is wonderful! . . . Madame Bertrand did really attempt to throw herself into the sea.* . . . During the removal of Napoleon the most awful silence prevailed, you could have heard a pin drop in the sea."[45]

On board the ship sailing to St. Helena, the "little island" mentioned in his copy book at Auxonne, Napoleon's apparent serenity never altered. By the time he had dictated several chapters of his *Mémoires* during the ten-week passage, his companions noted an extraordinary change in him, a new exhilaration. He had recognized that he was about to make his one lasting conquest, the Napoleonic legend.

---

* When Fanny Bertrand learned that their destination was an island lost in the South Atlantic, she had attempted to throw herself overboard.

EPILOGUE

AFTER SERVING THE REVOLUTION, THE DIRECTORY, THE CONSULATE AND
the Empire, Fouché and Talleyrand were now the two guiding spirits of
the government of Louis XVIII.

Immediately before the Bourbon Restoration, the agents of Charles-
Maurice de Talleyrand, His Serene Highness the Prince of Bénévent,
were instructed to destroy every record in the Archives and more particularly any letters written by him on the subject of the Duc d'Enghien.
Because of Talleyrand's role in restoring the King to the throne and in
establishing peace at the Congress of Vienna, Louis had felt obliged to
take him on as Minister of Foreign Affairs.

When British gazettes reached St. Helena late in 1816 with news of
Talleyrand's very brief retirement, Napoleon commented: "It was he who
suggested the business of the Duc d'Enghien. I believe," he added, "that
there was a time when Talleyrand was truly attached to me." Then he
added the Prince's name to the familiar comment: "If I had only hanged
two men," he repeated, "Talleyrand and Fouché, I would still be on the
throne today."[1]

Within a few years Talleyrand and Napoleon's place in history were
transposed, as Talleyrand's role of Europe's peacemaker was eclipsed by a
growing Napoleonic cult.

Joseph Fouché, Duc d'Otrante, was as responsible as Talleyrand for the
return of the Bourbons. It was he, who on June 24, 1815, secretly working
for the return of Louis XVIII, threatened Napoleon with arrest if he

remained in Paris after Waterloo; he who effectively delivered him to the British.

Two weeks later the regicide accompanied Talleyrand to an audience with the king. Chateaubriand immortalized the scene in his *Mémoires*:

> Suddenly a door opened; silently, in came vice leaning on the arm of crime, Monsieur de Talleyrand supported by Monsieur Fouché; this infernal vision passed slowly before me and disappeared into the king's room. Fouché had come to swear faith and allegiance to his lord; on his knees, the loyal regicide placed the hands which had destroyed Louis XVI into the hands of the brother of the martyred king, and the godless bishop stood surety for that oath.[2]

Fouché was retained for a time as Minister of Police of the Bourbon king and was then sent into exile. In Trieste, the former priest, under the Terror the brutal murderer of thousands and whose blasphemous excesses had sickened Lyons, now assented to the baptism and religious education of his children. A widower, he married the young, impoverished daughter of one of those aristocratic families in whose houses he had always been so surprisingly welcome.

The Bonapartes dispersed. Napoleon's mother and several of his brothers and sisters lived in Rome under the protection of the long-suffering Pope. Only Joseph and his millions (twenty million by Napoleon's calculation, as well as some of the Spanish crown jewels pocketed when he fled from Madrid)[3] emigrated to the New World and lived in semiroyal state in Bordentown, New Jersey.

Elisa, the Murats (Murat himself died before a firing squad after attempting to regain the kingdom of Naples), Joseph and Lucien and most of the marshals, were monsters of ingratitude to the fallen Emperor.

Eugène de Beauharnais lived with his adoring family in his father-in-law's kingdom of Bavaria; Hortense retired to Switzerland, writing her memoirs and firing the imagination of her son Louis Napoleon with tales of the Empire.

Madame Mère and Pauline made some efforts to remain in communication with the prisoner of St. Helena (both had visited him at Elba), but none of Napoleon's extended family was more loyal than the royal consorts. Catherine of Würtemberg, Jérôme's devoted wife, refused her father's invitation to return to his court, preferring exile with the former king of Westphalia. With the exception of the other royal wife, Eugène's Augusta, she was one of the few members of the imperial family to remain faithful.

Although almost everyone who had figured in Napoleon's early life was rewarded, the Emperor was given little chance to make amends to Désirée. In spite of Napoleon, and, ironically, because she had produced a son (the Swedish crown would not have been offered to Bernadotte had he had no heir), Désirée acquired a legitimate throne.

Bernadotte's revenge for Julie's and Désirée's unwitting roles at Brumaire was unexpectedly appropriate. In 1810, the King of Sweden and the parliamentary delegates unanimously proposed to General Bernadotte that he be named Crown Prince of Sweden, and eventually succeed their childless king. Bernadotte consulted his wife, knowing that the imperial police opened all his family's correspondence and that, when Désirée and her sister Mme Joseph Bonaparte discussed the offer, the Emperor would be placed in the position of being unable to refuse his consent. This Napoleon was forced to give with the utmost reluctance.

Désirée was another matter. The adaptability of Josephine, of Napoleon and of all the Bonapartes was not for the Clary sisters. They adored each other, and felt immense affection for one another's husbands. Unconscious of how they had been used at Brumaire, without interest in the thrones of Naples, Spain and Sweden acquired by their husbands, they remained unimpressed by the honors and titles showered upon them, alarmed only by prospects of partings or of dissension in their immediate family. Barbaric foreign countries were a terrible trial to them both. From Hamburg, when Bernadotte was governor of the port, Désirée wrote her brother in Marseilles to send her artichokes and bottles of olive oil. "Here we only eat so as not to starve . . . the desserts, above all, are pitiful," she complained; and from Sweden the southerner continued to plead for barrels of olives and pickles, and to dream of the pears growing in her Paris garden.

Nothing could have exceeded her despair when she realized that

Bernadotte's acceptance of the Swedish crown meant leaving her sister Julie, leaving France. "I thought," she explained, "it was just another country of which we had only to take the title" and, after a first unfortunate visit to Sweden, filled with complaints of the cold and of homesickness, she spent increasingly long periods in Paris. At a moment of great tension between Napoleon and Bernadotte, the Emperor relayed to her what amounted to an order to leave the country. This she simply ignored. Neither awe nor a trace of sentiment toward Napoleon remained.

Napoleon's long-held resentments remained especially violent against the joyful crowd which had greeted him at the Chaumière, and Thérésia Tallien and Paul Barras were, in particular, victims of his unabating anger.

The entire Merveilleuse connection was outlawed after Brumaire, although Aimée de Coigny was still seen as the Tuileries in the early days of the Consulate. Her liberal opinions were outraged by the proclamation of the Life Consulate and by "Bonaparte's warmaking." The First Consul had particularly disliked her friendship with Josephine; he feared her frankness, her lack of hypocrisy and her indifference to public opinion, and she was never invited to the imperial court.

Of all the wild Merveilleuses, Fortunée Hamelin remained to the last unalterable—daring and witty, her style unchanged when fashion demanded it, her affections immutable, her friendships with former lovers and her loyalty to Napoleon lifelong.

Although Napoleon, oblivious to the crucial advice she had given him on the night of his return from Egypt, decreed she was not to be invited to the new Tuileries court, her cult of the First Consul and Emperor remained as enthusiastic as before Brumaire.

Throughout the Empire the salon of this unreconstructed Merveilleuse continued to be a center of entertainment for the worlds of finance, of the army and even of the Tuileries courtiers. According to Chateaubriand, her conversation was "the most graceful and brilliant imaginable," having "the two qualities which are most characteristic of France: nobility and lightness of touch."[4]

Upon his return to Paris from exile, Chateaubriand had become Fortunée's ardent admirer and was one of the many who owed her their protection from Bonaparte's police. Chateaubriand wrote to her in 1823:

"To you alone, I owe not to have been shot or imprisoned at Vincennes by Bonaparte. . . . I am ready to pay my debt of gratitude."[5] Not a word of this gratitude, however, appeared in his *Mémoires d'outre-tombe,* a source of bitter disappointment to Fortunée. This omission was probably Mme Récamier's supreme revenge for the Montrond episode in the Chaumière days; for all her generosity and lack of envy, Fortunée's biting witticisms at Juliette's expense had never ceased, and one of the pleasures of acquiring Chateaubriand as a lover had been that of winning him for a time from Juliette Récamier. Exiled for her role when Napoleon returned from Elba (her house had been one of the main centers of Bonapartist plotting), Fortunée was back in Paris two years later, with a passport furnished by Casimir de Montrond. It was he who was with her when she died.

Montrond himself survived a succession of brushes with Fouché's police throughout the Empire. His epigrams against the Bonaparte family and his echoes of Talleyrand's warnings of the imminent fall of the Empire were all repeated to Napoleon, who at one point ordered his arrest, only to find that Casimir had already departed for a rendezvous in the country with Laure d'Abrantès.

There was never any break with Talleyrand; Montrond continued to be his private secretary and his intermediary with foreign powers for bribes for treaties. At Talleyrand's death, Montrond was said to have shed the only tears he had ever known.

The sin of "immorality" evoked in Thérésia could hardly be ascribed to Juliette Récamier, another of the Chaumière circle. The childlike beauty was never connected with any scandal, but she was ostracized for other reasons. As First Consul, Bonaparte desired the woman—never totally discouraging admirers, never rewarding them—who he knew had rejected Lucien Bonaparte's passionate advances. It would have pleased him to be successful where his brother and so many others had failed.

Juliette's hostility toward Napoleon was evident from the day in 1803 when Germaine de Staël, her closest friend, was arrested and then exiled. She guessed at the time the implication in the Emperor's offer—or rather command—that she accept the position of lady-in-waiting to Josephine, as well as all the dangers of refusing it. Napoleon's opportunity for revenge came when the banker Jacques Récamier, in temporary straits, requested a moderate loan from the Bank of France. The request was relayed, as were all financial matters, to the Emperor, campaigning in Germany. "I am not Mme Récamier's lover" was Napoleon's answer to a plea for help to the bank from one of his marshals. The request was turned down, and the Récamier bank went into bankruptcy; it was said that M. Récamier himself might have preferred his wife to be more accommodating.

Paris understood that the Emperor's revenge had resulted in Juliette's exile and the ruin of her husband's bank, and a large part of Parisian society, including half the Tuileries court, lined up to bid her farewell on the day before the house went on the block.

When Napoleon heard the following year that Juliette had left Paris to stay with Mme de Staël in Switzerland, he issued an order that Mme Récamier be banished to "within a distance of at least forty leagues from Paris." She returned only after the Emperor's downfall.

Mme de Staël's own case was different, though she too had been present at the Chaumière in that seminal summer.

In exile Napoleon referred to Coppet, Germaine's Swiss property as "a veritable arsenal directed against me."[6] But he had always, he said, known "the influence of coteries in Paris," and he realized now what a useful ally she could have been.

Coppet had indeed become a little center of resistance crowded with distinguished persons from every country in Europe. Even twenty-four hours spent there was enough for any visitor to be considered suspect by the Emperor's police.

Nothing in her long exile could diminish Germaine de Staël's nostalgia for "the little stream of the rue du Bac." From 1802 until the Emperor's exile Germaine was forbidden to come closer to Paris than forty leagues. Once, in 1807, in order to oversee the printing of one of her books, she spent several days in hiding in the capital, venturing out only at night. Inevitably Napoleon heard of it and from the depths of Poland issued an order to his minister of police to "get that whore de Staël out of Paris."

Her cries and protests, her letters to her friends Joseph Bonaparte and Fouché, the immense moral authority she acquired by her writing, could not overcome Napoleon's obduracy. It was as though the full weight of his misogyny fell on this woman.

The Emperor was clear about his reasons. In one of Germaine's many attempts to be permitted to return to Paris she sent her son Auguste to plead her case with the Emperor. Napoleon told him that he knew that Mme de Staël would talk too much, open her salon to dissidents, and that he would be forced to send her to prison. "This would do me some harm in public opinion, so tell your mother that as long as I live she will not return to Paris. She would go everywhere, make jokes . . . she might not think that important, but *I* think it very important. I take *everything* seriously."[7]

In what she called "the infernal peace of Coppet" Germaine de Staël's life continued with the same intensity. In her forties, her company was as fatiguing as ever, her capacity for love and friendship as vigorous. Since she was unwilling to give up any former lovers and pursued new ones with all the ardor of her youth, life at Coppet was never anything but turbulent. With every door open to family, to casual visitors and to lovers, her intellectual vitality undiminished, her conversation unceasing, carrying from room to room her writing tablet, she published innumerable books and pamphlets during those years. She continued to take the same interest in politics, literature and philosophy. Her interest in liberalism in France remained to the end; she never, her son-in-law Victor de Broglie wrote, rejected "all the illusions of the men of 1789."[8]

In Paris once again after Napoleon's exile to Elba, her attitude to the Bourbons was neutral, but her anguish at France's defeat and her dread of a foreign military occupation inhibited the rejoicing expected of her.

At the news of Napoleon's landing from Elba, Germaine again took the road to Switzerland; once there she resisted the Emperor's hints, conveyed through Fouché, that she might, under certain conditions, be allowed to return to Paris. She did not know that he still referred to her as "that whore," nor that Benjamin Constant was reading him some of her more ardent love letters in order to entertain him.

When Germaine finally retuned to Paris after Napoleon's definitive exile to St. Helena, she found that her distress at the military occupation of the capital was more powerful than her pleasure at once more living in Paris. Her depression was visible in spite of her ceaseless entertaining. Her salon became once more the meeting place of crowned heads and distinguished persons of all parties and nationalities; one of her coups was a conference she arranged there between the Tsar and Lafayette. She irritated both the Tsar and Wellington by ceaselessly pressing them for an end to the military occupation of the country and for a liberal parliament.

She spent increasing periods of time at Coppet, which had become "the Estates-General of European opinion."[9] Even Byron paid her a visit there, though dreading "her terrible good intentions."[10] When, referring to his own domestic scandal, he quoted from her *Delphine:* "A man must know how to defy public opinion, a woman how to comply with it," the new Germaine answered: "One must not be at war with everyone. I tried it in my youth, but it was not a success."[11]

Until the day of her death in Paris in 1817, Germaine de Staël kept open house, "receiving all day and all night" and fighting her physical suffering, wrote her son-in-law, "with an heroic impetuosity."[12]

As for the man to whom Napoleon owed the most, Paul Barras was furiously obsessed with the ingratitude of the Bonapartes. He was spied-upon, gout-ridden and without funds; his relatives were persecuted and his loans to Mme Bonaparte never repaid.

In the *Mémorial,* his official autobiography, Napoleon would establish Paul Barras's reputation as the lazy, venal and homosexual head of a corrupt and ineffectual state. Charges of General Bonaparte's rape of the Republic, of Barras's liaison with Josephine and of the dowry of the Army of Italy were to be silenced.

Accused of venality as well as of immorality, the former Director was credited with a fabulous accumulation of riches, although he had refused to accept any part of the 100,000 francs accorded each departing member of the Directory. He also declined the pay of a retired lieutenant general on the grounds that he belonged to the Army of the Republic and had no wish to be paid by a government which had overthrown that republic.

The charges of venality were particularly inconsistent when compared with the vast fortunes accumulated by Talleyrand and many other officials under the Empire; still more so when contrasted with the financial burden imposed on the country by the Bonaparte family, the marshals and the Consular and imperial ministers, all of whom lived in a state requiring a yearly expenditure of hundreds of millions of francs. Josephine alone cost the nation several million francs a year.

There was also the upkeep and constant redecoration of the Emperor's forty-four palaces, in France and in the vassal countries. The nation paid, too, for the princely households not only of Josephine and Napoleon, but also of each member of his family—chamberlains, ladies-in-waiting, chaplains, equerries, ushers, readers, masters of the horse—all of whom were permanently employed in the great Bonaparte town and country houses.

Because Barras was consumed by bitterness and ever hoping for revenge, his distorted and reedited *Mémoires* are more informed by this hate than by any desire to record history. He remained an attentive and well-informed observer of the Consulate and Empire, particularly sarcastic on the subject of court protocol and titles. After his eviction from Grosbois, he became the recipient of offensively worded orders; he was forbidden to take the waters at Aix "because members of the imperial family may be there," and after eight years of living at his family home in Provence, he received an order of exile to Rome "without delaying either in Turin or in Florence since the two Princesses, sisters of the Emperor, reside in these cities. Should you refuse to go," the order added, "you would be imprisoned in solitary confinement in the Château d'If,"* and he was warned not to mention the nature of these orders. He did, of course, and complained of them loudly in Rome, a city he found little to his liking, and Thérésia was called upon to supply him with books not obtainable in that city such as the *Dictionary of Atheists*, Mme de Staël's best-seller *Corinne* and "other works of a bawdy nature."

Barras returned to Paris after the downfall of the Empire, and after his return from Elba, Napoleon through Fouché offered him a number of prestigious posts. The minister of police was shocked by Barras's impolitic refusal, and by his references to the coup d'état that ended the Directory. He insisted upon calling the 18 Brumaire "that revolutionary day which made of the French Republic an absolute monarchy, disguised by the charlatanism of a Consulate and an Empire," language still moderate compared with that of Napoleon's own family and his marshals.

Upon his return to Restoration Paris after Napoleon's defeat, Barras spent his last years in a "cottage" near his former country house in the rue de Chaillot. After thirty years of marriage, his wife came to look after him; still an ardent royalist, however, she refused to sit at his dinner table, shocked by the republican tone of the conversation.

With inverted snobbishness, the authentic vicomte insisted on the continuance of all republican forms, rebuking anyone referring to his

---

* The celebrated fortress prison of the "Man in the Iron Mask."

constant visitor Thérésia as Princesse de Chimay, calling her only "Mme Tallien, *ci-devant,*"* and himself "Citizen General." It was a form, too, of making fun of all the parvenu "imperial highnesses" and "excellencies" washed up by the Empire. His conversation was said to be Voltairian, caustic and atheistic, and delivered in a strong Provençal accent.

It was known to the police of King Charles X, successor of Louis XVIII that, in spite of the systematic destruction by Napoleon of all correspondence between them, Barras still retained mountains of letters protesting devotion and gratitude from the Bonaparte and Beauharnais families. Furthermore, the Bourbon kings could never be certain whether there was substance to the gossip linking Barras to the fate of the child Louis XVII; his papers, they were said to fear, might contain revelations proving both brothers usurpers of the throne. Consequently his health was so closely watched that when he died in 1829, the seals on his papers were broken within hours and the files removed.

To his last visitor Barras confided, between laughter and fits of coughing, that he had played one last trick on the government. He had sent all his papers to his executor Rousselin† and had just sealed thirty cartons for the police to find. "And do you know what is in them? All my laundry bills since 1793!"

In exile Napoleon could sometimes form an objective assessment of Barras. Questioned at St. Helena on the events of Vendémiaire, he answered: "That victory was due to Barras."[13] But on another occasion he remembered their relationship quite differently. "It has been said that I owed a great deal to Barras on 13 Vendémiaire, but that is not correct . . . it was I who had him named commander in chief. . . . Perhaps he had known me at the siege of Toulon, I don't remember . . . I visited him a few times in Paris when I arrived there as a general of artillery on half pay . . . I was influential in having him named a Director . . . I was a far more important person than Barras, who was only one out of three or four hundred deputies, whereas I was general in chief of the Army of the Interior."[14]

He arranged certain other aspects of their relationship too, deter-

---

* Neither could Barras's near-destitute guest Tallien bring himself to use Thérésia's title. " 'Princesse de Chimères' [Princess of Make-Believe] would be more like it," he would mutter.

† Rousselin de St. Albin was to add his own prejudiced and contradictory essays to Barras's *Mémoires.*

mined to distance Josephine from the Director. "Josephine," he told Bertrand, "only met Barras after she had known me. I was present when they were introduced to each other."[15]

Napoleon's recollection of his relationships with both Talliens was equally imprecise. Hortense remembered that Napoleon told her during the Hundred Days that he had no wish to see Tallien, "the man who had left Egypt for France, who had deserted without even warning me!"[16] But at St. Helena, Napoleon recollected that he asked Jean-Lambert, after his return from Elba, "how it happened that I never did anything for you?" Tallien's reply, according to Napoleon, was: "You saved France at Brumaire, but it was I who destroyed the hydra at Thermidor. . . . If only you had stood by my wife she would not have abandoned me." "I should have made him Duke of Thermidor," Napoleon concluded.[17] He had forgotten, or chosen to forget, that his orders to his ministers had been not to give any post to this witness of his own abandonment of the army in Egypt.

In 1801, Tallien had been on his way back to France when his frigate was captured by the British, and in London he found himself a hero for the last time. As the Man of Thermidor and the executioner of Robespierre, he was feted by both Whigs and Tories. By 1802 he was back in France, arrested, and all his papers removed by the police.

Talleyrand persuaded the Emperor in the coronation year of 1804 to give Tallien a consulate in Spain. During the war there the Spaniards removed not only Joseph Bonaparte from his throne, but also Tallien from his consulate. He returned to Paris, his face covered with scabs, with one eye lost from a disease contracted in Egypt.

He was too much aware of his repulsive appearance to visit his daughter at her school, though he constantly urged Thérésia to do so. Josephine, after Brumaire, had ceased to see her goddaughter Thermidor Rose Tallien, though she continued to pay for her education, and Tallien's letters to his former wife were full of worry about the child, now known as Josephine, and the effect upon her future of the probable imperial divorce.

Until the day of the coup of Brumaire, Napoleon remained outwardly Thérésia Tallien's friend. Once in power he turned on her, forbade her presence near his person or his court and struck at her through her husband. The contempt with which the vindictive Emperor treated her added to the drama of her declining years. Deeply in love with her husband, Joseph de Chimay, she was aware that his neglect of her stemmed directly from the dishonor in which she was held at the court in Paris.

At St. Helena, Napoleon placed the blame of the Bonapartes' abandonment of their friend on Josephine. "If Josephine had received Mme Tallien, it would probably have greatly influenced her fate," he conceded. It was she who refused his advice to receive the Princesse de Chimay, he maintained, forgetting his savage letter on the subject: "Mme Tallien had been very pretty," he argued, "and there was a time when all the admiration had been for her and Mme Bonaparte was only second, and Josephine claimed that it would remind her of a time in her life which she would rather forget."[18]

When Count Joseph de Caraman-Chimay, "gentle, modest, cold and silent,"[19] emigrated during the Revolution, he took with him the memory of Thérésia, glimpsed briefly at a post relay during her flight from Bordeaux into the trap of Paris. He never forgot that apparition, and when he returned to Paris he "loved her silently"[20] for a time, meeting her at the dissident houses of the resistant aristocracy and at Mme de Staël's receptions. In 1804 he notified his father of his intention to marry her.*

The Marquis de Caraman, Grand Cross of the Order of St. Louis, ex-commanding general of the First Division of the Army of Condé, brother of a guillotined lady-in-waiting of Marie Antoinette, indignantly refused his assent. The woman, he pointed out, had been married to the regicide and Septembrist Tallien, one of the men who had sent Joseph's own mother to prison and his aunt to the scaffold.

Though Thérésia's life was now devoted exclusively to her family, to religion and to good works, she was nevertheless sacrificed to the "Victorian" moral climate inaugurated by First Consul Bonaparte and exacerbated by the return of the Bourbons, a new era summed up by one returning emigré as "no more flirting, no sentimentality, no godlessness, no more sparkling wit, no more easy relationships, no more

---

* The date and the circumstances of the breakup of Thérésia's relationship with Ouvrard are unknown.

joy."[21] No more joy might indeed have been applied to Thérésia's married life.

She could still not appear in public without arousing offensive curiosity. In 1814 she had visited the Louvre Museum with some of her children by four different fathers. They had attracted a mob and were forced to leave in haste.

But it was Napoleon's vindictiveness that ruined her life. After the Treaty of 1815, which awarded the principality of Chimay to Holland, Joseph, who had acceded to this title, was made chamberlain to the sovereign in Brussels. It was less than fifteen years, as Thérésia would tell her children, since "although never crowned a Queen, for years I lived in a whirlwind not unlike that which surrounds a throne."[22] Now she was forced to watch her husband and sons drive off to court functions without her, as the Princesse de Chimay's lurid past excluded her from the new court where much would have been overlooked had the Tuileries been less implacable.

When the Chimays' son Joseph married a young woman whose claims to be Napoleon's illegitimate daughter were well established, Thérésia could be seen, fat and resigned, knitting socks for little Valentine de Chimay, the grandchild of General Bonaparte and of Mme Tallien.

The blood of Merveilleuses and of terrorists, of crowned heads and of revolutionary generals, and of the other actors in the Napoleonic drama was mixed in countless improbable alliances.

Talleyrand's blood was mingled with Hortense's,* Josephine's with Tsar Alexander's,† Jérôme Bonaparte's with the ancient dynasties of Saxe-Coburg and Orléans‡ so that the present head of the house of Bonaparte, Prince Napoleon, whose forebear was Jérôme, is also a descendant of the emperors of Austria and Russia, the kings of Spain, England, Poland and

---

* Duc de Morny, half-brother of Napoleon, and son of Hortense and Talleyrand's son Charles de Flahaut.

† By the marriage of one of Eugène's sons.

‡ Clementine of Belgium, great-grandchild of Louis Philippe, married Victor Bonaparte, grandson of Jérôme.

Prussia, and a cousin of the head of the royal house of France, the Comte de Paris.

The blood of General Bonaparte's "little fiancée," Désirée Clary, was mingled with Josephine's when Eugène's daughter married Désirée's son Oscar, Crown Prince of Sweden. Their descendants are the kings of Norway, Sweden and Belgium, the queens of Denmark and Greece and the Grand Duke of Luxembourg; their cousins are pretenders to the thrones of Brazil and Portugal.

The King of Rome, "Napoleon II," was raised in Vienna as an Austrian archduke and died there of tuberculosis at the age of twenty-one. He seldom saw his mother, who reigned over an Italian duchy and was as dependent on her second and third husbands as she once had been on Napoleon. Unaware of how Marie Louise had been duped into abandoning both him and his father, he commented: "My mother is kind but weak, she was not the wife my father deserved."[23] His death put an end to the Bonapartist party's hopes of a direct legitimate descendant of Napoleon, whose only living male posterity was by one of his two illegitimate sons.

At St. Helena, Napoleon tacitly recognized four illegitimate children: Napoléone, born to Mme de Montholon shortly after her departure from St. Helena; Emilie de Pellapra; Eléonore Denuelle's son Charles Léon and Alexandre Walewski.

After Waterloo, during his last visit to Malmaison, the Emperor sent for thirteen-year-old Charles Léon. (Eléonore Denuelle had asked permission to call their son "Napoleon." "Only half the name," was his response.[24]) The boy's resemblance to his father was already so remarkable that in later years people would turn and stare at him in the street. His reputation was detestable. His cousin Napoleon III, so generous to all other members of the Bonaparte family, would always refuse to see him. In spite of the Emperor's financial assistance to the self-styled count, this oldest son of Napoleon spent all his fortune in gaming houses and brothels and died a beggar. Like his father, his grandfather Carlo Buonaparte and other members of the Bonaparte family, he also died of stomach cancer.

Very different was the fate of Marie Walewska's son. After becoming by decree a French citizen, he first joined the Foreign Legion, became a fashionable Parisian figure and was given several diplomatic missions by his cousin Napoleon III, Emperor of the French. Courteous, subtle and cultivated he proved to be an excellent minister of foreign affairs and then ambassador to London. He was prematurely fat like many of the Bonapartes and somewhat pompous. Palmerston found only one fault in him: a total lack of humor.

Walewski's only living descendants—and alone with Charles Léon's, the only direct living posterity of Napoleon I—are by his legitimized son by the great French actress Rachel.

Although Napoleon's efforts to found a dynasty came to nothing, Josephine herself, with the assistance of Bonaparte's "little fiancée" Désirée, has as much claim as Queen Victoria to be the "grandmother of Europe." Her blood flows through the veins of all the reigning monarchs of Europe, save only the British.

Her own legend was born almost immediately after her death, fostered by the Bourbons hoping to benefit from her popularity. Royalists portrayed a barely recognizable Josephine. Fervently religious and a protector of the legitimate throne, she was said in entirely apocryphal dying words to have wished prosperity to the Bourbon king. As Paul Barras noted: "Since her death, that woman has acquired a whole package of virtues."

Louis XVIII took every opportunity to praise her; her "elegant simplicity"[25] was contrasted with the pretentiousness of the imperial family. "Deeply unhappy during her husband's reign," wrote one royalist, "she took refuge from his brutalities and his rejection in botanical lore. Alone, in the midst of those ostentatious Bonapartes, she understood the French people."[26]

In recently occupied France, her role of faithful spouse was exalted; unlike "the foreigner," she would have followed her husband into exile. She was seen "as a feminine reflection of the national need, a figure akin to a medieval Virgin of Mercy protecting suffering Christianity beneath her mantle."[27]

With the accession in midcentury of her grandson Napoleon III, Emperor of the French, son of Hortense and of Louis Bonaparte, another Josephine would emerge. Once again she was *Notre Dame des Victoires,* the army's icon, Napoleon I's true consort, consecrated as one of the rays of Napoleon I's ascending star.

Her legend grew with the publication of some of his love letters to her, although, with the increasing prudery of Restoration France, Hortense had not only expurgated large sections of these letters but entirely omitted, or else redated, the incendiary ones written before the marriage, as well as the agonized ones from Italy.

It became known that Napoleon II, son of Marie Louise and Napoleon, had declared: "Had Josephine been my mother, my father would not be buried at St. Helena and I would not be languishing in Vienna."[28] And in a final burst of hagiography it was common in contemporary prints to enshrine together a surprising trio: Napoleon I, Josephine and the King of Rome.

There were still, however, in the mid-nineteenth century men like Senator Thibaudeau who were writing of the Empress he had known at the Tuileries: "What grace! What majesty! Yet for me she would always be Barras's mistress, the woman who by her trafficking with army contractors was responsible for the death by hunger of so many of our men."[29] And there were some discreet smiles when Napoleon III, announcing his forthcoming marriage, described his bride as "gracious and kind, she will, I am certain, recall the virtues of Empress Josephine."

After the collapse of the Second Empire in 1870 there was to be at least one more reversal of opinion on Josephine, led by the more fervent Bonapartist historians. The Directory and everyone connected with it became a target for the censorious nineteenth-century biographers of Napoleon I (whose reverence sometimes moved them to capitalize his pronouns), who were almost unanimous in their savage attacks on his Empress. She is barely mentioned in the *Mémorial,* and Napoleon's cynical comments on her were not read until the deciphering of General Bertrand's diary in the mid-twentieth century.

More temperate appraisals and a recognition of Josephine's true gifts of kindness and generosity and of her role as consort have reinstated her as a central icon of French history.

It was a royalist lady who, at the news of Josephine's death, commented: "What an interesting woman she was; what tact, what a good heart, what a sense of proportion and taste in all she did. She even had the good taste to die at the right moment!" Echoed by Chancellor Pasquier's: "She had the good luck, denied by the author of her destiny, to die at the right time."[30]

. . .

But what would Napoleon's legend have been had he died at the "right time," without the exile that produced what has been described as "the most captivating and skilled of apologies"?[31]

Over thirty persons accompanied Napoleon into exile. They were General Count Emmanuel de Las Cases and his son; Baron Gaspard Gourgaud; Count Tristan de Montholon, his wife and young child; and Count Henri Gratien Bertrand, former grand marshal of the Tuileries court, his wife Fanny and their two children. Each of these families had brought a couple of domestics. Napoleon himself was served by a maître d'hôtel, three valets (Louis Marchand, replacing Constant, was to be yet another memorialist of the St. Helena days), a chaplain, a doctor, an usher, a footman, two chefs, Pierron the pastry cook, a coachman and a groom. Each of the four generals was to publish diaries which would established the Napoleonic legend.

The daily routine was organized with Napoleonic thoroughness even before the former Emperor had moved into his final accommodation or the officers were provided with their own quarters. Dictation, or rather his unending monologue, never ceased, starting each morning as he sat under an arbor in the garden of his temporary hosts. Meanwhile Marchand and the other valets were setting out the family portraits framed in diamonds, the Sèvres porcelain dinner service picturing French victories and the silver gilt set of toilet articles. A billiard table was installed and the Emperor's metal camp bed, curtained in green taffeta; shelves were built for the library of two thousand books Napoleon had brought with him and that were to be replenished regularly.

From the start the strictest etiquette was observed by the little company on the volcanic island in the Atlantic. Dinner was lit by the imperial candelabra and served by menservants in the Tuileries livery of green coats with silver lace. The four officers wore military uniform and their wives formal evening dress, their gowns as harshly criticized by the Emperor as though they were all still at court.

The day, at least until Napoleon's health started to fail, followed an unchanging pattern. After his valets had rubbed him down with eau de cologne and dressed him, the Emperor (he was known to his retinue by no other name), pacing as he dictated, took up with each officer in turn the history of his military campaigns, of his foreign and domestic policy, and of the political philosophy illuminating them. Napoleon seemed to his companions almost relieved by the change in his circumstances. He had left France at the very nadir of his reputation, compared most often to Attila and Genghis Khan. He had bequeathed a memory of death and pillaging throughout Europe, of a France invaded, dismembered and reduced in size since the Directory. With the chance now of presenting his life and achievements in his own words, he foresaw that he would win this last battle, the one that would fix the judgment of posterity. "There is," he had once written, "no immortality but the memory that is left in the minds of men."[32]

Las Cases's *Mémorial*, Napoleon's official biography, would be the first and the most influential of the St. Helena memoirs. In that lofty, philosophical testimonial there is nothing ignoble; the tone is generous and exalted. A Napoleonic legend was forged in the powerful *Mémorial* in which the man who had sacrificed three million French lives in wars of conquest claimed to have fought only to lay the foundations of liberty in Europe. His totalitarian government, like his wars, had been forced on him by reactionary states. As the son of the Revolution he had taken over the Republic at Brumaire only, he maintained, in the interests of democracy.

Above all he was a peacemaker. His wars had been necessary "to ensure the universal peace and the general good I contemplated."[33] Had he won the final victory, a community of sovereigns would have led to a European union with common laws and a common currency.

The ruler who had broken with the liberal "ideologues" referred to the "irresistible rise" of liberal ideas.[34] The man who had written "uprooting the German national spirit . . . is the chief aim of my policy"[35] proclaimed that his wish to fulfill the national aspirations of the peoples of Europe was another motive for his wars. With these claims he appealed to the two main currents of the nineteenth century—nationalism and liberalism—both of which he had suppressed as Emperor.

When Las Cases's *Mémorial* was published in France in 1823, two years after Napoleon's death, it burst on a country at peace, yearning for the days of military glory and for a time of patriotic exaltation, when bread

was cheap and the employment market was not swamped by the demo-
bilized Grand Army.

There was an almost universal emotional response to the *Mémorial's* publication, an intense reaction to its accents of lofty idealism
only heightened by Las Cases's description of the cruel living conditions
on St. Helena, of the calvary of the half-famished former Emperor and
the insolence of the island's governor. (Napoleon did, indeed, often refer to himself as Jesus Christ and to the conditions of his exile as his
Passion.)

The ruler who, as Chateaubriand expressed it, had "hated the people so cordially" was transformed into a "people's Napoleon" and became, mysteriously, a symbol of liberty. His name would be invoked
during the French revolutions of 1830 and 1848; it was the Napoleonic
cult inaugurated by the *Mémorial* which would help to sweep his
nephew Louis Napoleon to the throne in midcentury.

The *Mémorial* struck a chord too in the new romantic movement.
For the great writers of the nineteenth century—Hugo, Balzac, Pushkin,
Byron, Dumas, Chateaubriand—Napoleon became the romantic hero
incarnate. Stendhal, who had once protested the Emperor's suppression of
liberty, had his hero in *The Red and the Black* praise the *Mémorial* as "the
guide of my life, the object of my ecstatic admiration." The Emperor's
battles—even the retreat from Moscow—became subjects for sentimental
ballads as they had never been during the Empire.

After Las Cases had left the island, bearing with him the noble *Mémorial* in all its grandeur, the Emperor continued to dictate for hours,
sometimes almost simultaneously, to each of the three remaining officers. They could hardly keep pace, even so, with the transcription of his
monologue. Until the final deterioration in his health it could almost be
said that for six years Napoleon seldom ceased to speak. Unable to shut
off his ceaseless intellectual activity, sometimes he would not allow the
little company to retire to their own quarters until well after midnight
while his soliloquy continued from behind the drawn green curtains of
his camp bed.

The hours of dictation grew more erratic once the Emperor became
ill in his last two years. From the first, he suspected that he was "dying of

the same disease" that had killed his father.* Still on some days he continued to "empty the different drawers of my brain," as he expressed it. With his prodigious memory he reviewed every action, relived every battle and every aspect of his campaigns, his views on the marshals, on his family, on ancient history, on religious faith (he "did not believe that Jesus Christ had ever existed,"[36] but was equally certain that Mohammed had), on psychology, on military techniques. His true claims to greatness, however, the Civil Code and the impressive achievements of his administration, were seldom mentioned.

Both Montholon and Gourgaud would publish their own memoirs after Napoleon's death, but it was devoted Bertrand's faithful account of the events of the day and of every word uttered by his hero that gives the most vivid picture both of Napoleon's mind and of the life on the island.

When he retired to his own quarters late at night, General Bertrand wrote in a private shorthand, decoded only in the 1950s, a dispassionate record of the Emperor's comments: on men and events not covered by the official dictation; of the quarrels and jealousies of the little court, of the weather, the picnics, the varying quality of the champagne and burgundies at their dinner table; the news in the British gazettes received from London; of the state of Fanny Bertrand's health, and above all that of Napoleon's. In the last years he records every pitiful instance of the Emperor's vomitings, his blisterings and his purges.

Through Bertrand we learn much of the carefully orchestrated propaganda emanating from St. Helena, of the distortion of facts and events, of the cynicism of Napoleon's private comments on the French people, on religion and on morality ("morality is for the upper classes, the gallows for the rabble"[37]).

The diary is written entirely in the third person; Bertrand refers to himself always as "the Grand Marshal." He does not permit himself—nor apparently feel—the slightest criticism of the Emperor. His loyalty survives even tests like Napoleon's rage against his own devoted wife.

Fanny Bertrand was a daughter of Laure de La Touche de Longpré, that nemesis of Josephine de Beauharnais's first marriage. After Albine de Montholon returned to France with her baby, Napoléone, a daughter popularly considered to be the Emperor's, Fanny had refused to follow the

---

* Napoleon's postmortem would reveal a chronic inflammation of the stomach lining and an ulcerated liver. Lucien, Pauline and Caroline Bonaparte were all to die of cancerous ulcers.

other general's wife into Napoleon's bed. Bertrand was violently upbraided by his Emperor for failing to convince Fanny that this was her duty, and in the same level voice in which he records Napoleon's reflections on cuirasses for the infantry, Bertrand's almost nightly entries read: "His Majesty informed the Grand Marshal that the whole island knows that Mme Bertrand is a whore and that she sleeps in every ditch with the English staff officers."[38]

Although in these conversations with Bertrand, Napoleon often contradicts and even ridicules many of his pronouncements made in the official biographies and invents a number of scenes and even letters, we are left constantly exhilarated by the incisiveness of his views, even by the contradictions, and by his merciless clairvoyance as he meditates on battles and treaties and on the administration of his armies. And above all, as he evaluates people and events.

When he judges himself and his errors, there is no self-pity. He was a realist about himself. His "own undoing," he believed, was "too much ambition and a passionate nature," and he repeated to Gourgaud what he had said in the imperial days: "I like only those people who are useful to me—but only as long as they are useful,"[39] and to Bertrand: "contempt for men is the sentiment which dominates me."[40]

There was no more talk of world peace, but a reminder of his acknowledgment in 1813 that "what my enemies call general peace is my own destruction";[41] he said nothing to correct what he admitted during the Hundred Days: "I wanted to rule the world and in order to do this I needed unlimited power. . . . I needed world dictatorship."[42]

He had few regrets. These ranged from the fact that he should have paid more attention to political salons, to the harm done him by the weakness he had shown toward his family, and to the more radical: "I regret that I did not terrorize the country upon my return from Elba."[43]

There were some surprisingly petty irrelevancies. Napoleon could not keep away from the subject of the Bernadottes not, as might have been expected, because the former marshal had swung Sweden into an alliance with Russia during the last campaign, but absurdly—and inaccurately, and to Désirée's irritation—because he repeatedly claimed he was the godfather of her son. Among his least successful predictions were that the commoner Bernadotte would never reign, nor would his son Oscar find it possible to marry into any illustrious family.

Napoleon, the fatalist and historian, could not resist returning often to the "what-ifs," the events and battles that might have changed history. Had he given another general than Grouchy the command at Waterloo, "Blücher would not have arrived in time to 'save Wellington from defeat.' "[44] Had he had Talleyrand and Fouché hanged, the outcome of the Hundred Days would have been different.

Thanks to Bertrand's nightly entries we hear Napoleon organizing some of the legends. "I was a liberal ruler," he told Bertrand, and it was "Talleyrand and Fouché who insisted on censorship, on strangling the press and persecuting dissidents."[45] We hear him trying out several versions of the Egyptian campaign. In the official *Mémorial* he rejects the accusation that he had abandoned his army there. "I only obeyed France's appeal to return to save her."[46] To Gourgaud he asserted that the army's subsequent defeat in Egypt by the British was the Alsatian General Kléber's fault ("He was German, not French, and unlike me he did not love the Revolution.")[47] But he was more candid with Bertrand: "The expedition was useful to my ulterior projects," he declared. "France had to be beaten [while he was in Egypt], I needed a victorious return to reach my goal."[48]

With Bertrand, Napoleon could be objective about the two pivotal dates of his rise to power. "The day of Vendémiaire was due to Barras," he admitted, and still more surprisingly: "I do not think that the Republic would have been lost without my intervention at Brumaire."[49]

He returned obsessively to the harm caused him by the Austrian marriage and still more to what he asserted was Josephine's responsibility for the Russian campaign. "The Empress Josephine's indiscretion"—her supposed gossiping about his impotence, which reached the Tsar's mother— had changed all their destinies, he maintained.

Although the Austrian alliance, he continued, had seemed most likely to consolidate the Empire, and was generally considered by his ministers as his political masterpiece, it had caused him to lose his throne. It was now clear to him that the Austrians had only agreed to the marriage to give themselves a breathing space before joining another coalition against him. It was Josephine's indiscretion, therefore, that he was certain had "changed the destinies of the world" because had the Russian marriage taken place there would have been no Russian expedition; "the Russians do not abandon their family's allies."[50] He produced a new version of the scene at Erfurt. There, he said, to his astonishment the Tsar had offered to give him his sister's hand in marriage. "It was *his* suggestion. I answered that I had no intention of divorcing and that I loved my wife."[51]

In the *Mémorial* there are noble appeals to the King of Rome and sometimes to Marie Louise, but few references to Josephine. However, in the many hours of intimate conversation with Bertrand and with Gourgaud, Napoleon spoke often of his wives and mistresses.

"I have never loved, really loved, except perhaps Josephine—a little— and at that, because I was twenty-seven when I met her." He had married her, he said, because she led him to believe she owned a fortune, but when he went to inquire he found it was not true. "I really did love her but I did not esteem her, she was too much of a liar, but she had a certain irresistible something. . . ." And then, after a few erotic recollections he continued: "I esteemed Marie Louise far more, though perhaps I loved her less than Josephine, whose conduct was not exactly regular. But she was very attached to me and I liked the fact that she never wanted to leave me."[52]

After reading some apocryphal memoirs on Josephine, Napoleon told Bertrand that he could correct some of its errors. Her lover had not been the one named in the book, but "a little officer on Berthier's staff called Charles."[53] Furthermore Josephine, in spite of what was often said, had never tried to intercede for Enghien. "She was never interested in anyone besides herself, never asked for anything, not even for her son [exactly what he had once admired]. . . . At the Army of Italy I opened her letters—as you know that is something I often do—and learned that she was sending bills of exchange of three or four thousand écus to pay her debts. She was stealing from me . . . she was like that all her life, always debts, always hiding them, always denying them."[54]

He described Josephine when he first knew her to General Gourgaud as "at that time one of the most agreeable women, full of graceful charm—a woman in the fullest meaning of the term. . . . Her first reaction was always to say no, to gain time to think. . . . Not necessarily a lie, but more of a precaution, a defensive measure. She lied almost continually, but cleverly."[55] Later he asked the general: "I suppose it is true that she cuckolded me?" Gourgaud could only answer: "So they say, Sire."[56]

After describing to Gourgaud his first night with Marie Louise, Napoleon added that although he had been fond of his second wife he believed he had loved Josephine more, "that was natural, we had started out together, and then she was *une vraie femme,* the one I had chosen myself. . . . She was as much a liar as Marie was truthful. . . . I would never have left her had she been able to have a child."[57]

His views on the women in his life soured progressively. Even Walewska, when he learned of her remarriage, was excoriated. Napoleon's companions knew that word had reached him of Marie Louise's open liaison with the man Metternich had placed in charge of her as her chamberlain, but he never changed his instruction: after his death his heart in a sealed casket should be carried to her in Parma.

To the end he continued to be obsessed by his place in history and urged his companions to publish their memoirs as soon as they returned to France. He had few doubts, however, of the giant legend he would leave. His link to immortality was secure. "My destiny is the opposite of other men's," he had pointed out to Las Cases. "Other men are lowered by their downfall, my own raises me to infinite heights. Every day strips me of my tyrant's skin and of my ferocity!"[58] "I shall survive!" he assured Bertrand, and with implacable lucidity he had the last word: "Those who belittle me will find that they have belittled themselves."[59]

At the end of April 1821, a week before Napoleon died, he seemed to see Josephine before dawn. "She would not kiss me," he told Montholon, "she slipped away at the moment I was about to take her in my arms. . . . She hadn't changed, always the same, still completely devoted to me. She told me we were about to see each other again, never more to part." Bertrand thought that the Emperor's last words were "Who retreats? . . . at the head of the army!" Montholon believed he heard him murmur "Josephine."

ENDNOTES

Foreword

1. Stendhal, *Mémoires sur Napoléon,* from the 1818 preface.

Chapter 1. Come with Both Your Daughters, but Hurry

1. Pichevin, *L'Impératrice Joséphine.*
2. Masson, *Joséphine de Beauharnais.*
3. Ibid.
4. Ibid.
5. Ibid.
6. Ibid.
7. Ibid.
8. Aubenas, *Histoire de l'Impératrice Joséphine.*

Chapter 2. The Vilest of Creatures

1. Masson, *Joséphine de Beauharnais.*
2. Bouillé, *Souvenirs.*
3. Hanoteau, *Le Ménage Beauharnais.*
4. Masson, *Joséphine de Beauharnais.*
5. Bouillé, *Souvenirs.*
6. Montgaillard, *Souvenirs.*
7. Hanoteau, *Le Ménage Beauharnais.*
8. Walpole, *Correspondence.*
9. Herold, *Mistress to an Age.*
10. Letter to Jacques Necker, December 1803.
11. Ibid.
12. Morris, *A Diary of the French Revolution.*
13. La Tour du Pin, *Mémoires d'une femme de cinquante ans.*
14. Hanoteau, *Le Ménage Beauharnais.*
15. Ibid.
16. Babeau, *Paris en 1789.*
17. Hanoteau, *Le Ménage Beauharnais.*
18. Ibid.
19. Ibid.
20. Ibid.
21. Ibid.
22. Ibid.
23. Ibid.
24. Archives Nationales, Paris.

25. Masson, *Joséphine de Beauharnais.*

26. Archives Nationales, Paris.

27. Masson, *Joséphine de Beauharnais.*

28. Hanoteau, *Le Ménage Beauharnais.*

29. Constant, L., *Mémoires.*

30. Masson, *Joséphine de Beauharnais.*

31. Aubenas, *Histoire de l'Impératrice Joséphine.*

32. Ibid.

33. Rémusat, *Mémoires.*

34. Hortense, *Mémoires.*

35. Quoted in Janssens, *Joséphine de Beauharnais et son temps.*

Chapter 3. I Am an Amériquaine

1. Orieux, *Talleyrand.*

2. Rémusat, *Mémoires.*

3. Rice, *Thomas Jefferson's Paris.*

4. Masson, *Joséphine de Beauharnais.*

5. Brinton, *A Decade of Revolution.*

6. Frénilly, *Souvenirs.*

7. Hanoteau, *Le Ménage Beauharnais.*

8. Ibid.

9. Morris, *Diary of the French Revolution.*

10. Herold, *Mistress to an Age.*

11. Ibid.

12. Hanoteau, *Le Ménage Beauharnais.*

13. Frénilly, *Souvenirs.*

14. Lezay-Marnesia, *Souvenirs.*

15. Norvins, *Histoire de Napoléon.*

16. Herold, *Mistress to an Age.*

17. Thiébault, *Mémoires.*

18. Herold, *Mistress to an Age.*

19. Bluche, *Septembre 1792.*

20. Rémusat, *Mémoires.*

21. Lezay-Marnesia, *Souvenirs.*

22. Williams, *Souvenirs.*

23. Morris, *Diary and Letters.*

24. Furet and Richet, *La Révolution française.*

25. Masson, *Joséphine de Beauharnais.*

26. Ibid.

27. Ibid.

28. Ibid.

29. Rémusat, *Mémoires.*

30. Hortense, *Mémoires.*

31. Rémusat, *Mémoires.*

32. Masson, *Joséphine de Beauharnais.*

33. Ibid.

34. Ibid.

35. Hortense, *Mémoires.*

Chapter 4. Thermidor

1. Eliot, *Journal of My life.*

2. Castelot, *Joséphine.*

3. Sorel, *Le convent des Carmes.*

4. Blanc, *La denière lettre.*

5. Ibid.

6. Masson, *Joséphine de Beauharnais.*

7. Ibid.

8. Castelot, *Joséphine.*

9. Masson, *Joséphine de Beauharnais.*

10. Michelet, *Histoire de la Révolution française.*

11. Barras, *Mémoires.*

12. Ibid.

13. Michelet, *Histoire de la Révolution française.*

Chapter 5. At the Chaumière

1. Chevallier and Pincemaille, *L'Impératrice Joséphine.*

2. Castelot, *Joséphine.*

3. Ibid.

4. Mercier, *Le nouveau tableau de Paris.*

5. Ibid.

6. Ibid.

7. Ibid.

8. Ibid.

9. Frénilly, *Souvenirs.*

10. Ibid.

11. Ibid.

12. Pasquier, *Mémoires.*

13. Ibid.

14. Espinchal, *Journal d'emigration.*

15. Kotzebue, *Souvenirs.*

16. Gay, *Salons célèbres.*

17. Abrantès, *Mémoires.*

18. Kotzebue, *Souvenirs.*

19. Mercier, *Le nouveau tableau de Paris.*

20. Kotzebue, *Souvenirs.*

21. Chevallier and Pincemaille, *L'Impératrice Joséphine*

22. Castelot, *Joséphine.*

Chapter 6. A Transcendental Republican

1. Bertrand, *Cahiers.*

2. Bourrienne, *Mémoires.*

3. Bertrand, *Cahiers.*

4. Chuquet, *La Jeunesse de Napoléon.*

5. Bertrand, *Cahiers.*

6. Ibid.

7. Bourrienne, *Mémoires.*

8. Stendhal, *Mémoires.*

9. Bonaparte, J., *Mémoires.*

10. Bertrand, *Cahiers.*

11. Castelot, *Bonaparte.*

12. Bertrand, *Cahiers.*

13. Bordonove, *Napoléon.*

14. Brinton, *A Decade of Revolution.*

15. Castelot, *Bonaparte.*

16. Quoted in Savant, *Tel fut Napoléon.*

17. Joseph Bonaparte, *Mémoires.*

18. Estré, *Bonaparte.*

19. Herold, *The Mind of Napoleon.*

20. Bertrand, *Cahiers.*

21. Savant, *Tel fut Napoléon.*

22. Abrantès, *Mémoires.*

23. Girod de l'Ain, *Désirée Clary.*

24. Abrantès, *Mémoires.*

25. Swedish Royal Archives.

26. Chastenay, *Mémoires.*

27. Ibid.

Chapter 7. I Knew Only Barras

1. Madelin, *La Révolution.*

2. Abrantès, *Mémoires.*

3. *Correspondance de Napoléon Ier.*

4. Mercier, *Le nouveau tableau de Paris.*

5. Bertrand, *Cahiers.*

6. Barras, *Mémoires.*

7. *Correspondance de Napoléon Ier.*

8. Espinchal, *Journal d'emigration.*

9. Berry, *Voyages.*

10. Meister, *Souvenirs.*

11. Mallet du Pan, *Mémoires.*

12. Orieux, *Talleyrand.*

13. Alméras, *Barras et son temps.*

Chapter 8. Better Times Will Come

1. Quoted in Herold, *The Mind of Napoleon.*

2. *Correspondance de Napoléon Ier.*

3. Rémusat, *Mémoires.*

4. Swedish Royal Archives.

5. Ibid.

6. Ibid.

7. Ibid.

8. Ibid.

9. Abrantès, *Mémoires.*

10. Bertrand, *Cahiers.*

11. Ouvrard, *Mémoires.*

12. Tulard, *Napoléon ou le mythe du saveur.*

13. Abrantès, *Mémoires.*

14. Ibid.

15. Ibid.

16. Ibid.

17. Ouvrard, *Mémoires.*

18. Gay, *Salons célèbres.*

19. Swedish Royal Archives.

20. *Correspondance de Napoléon Ier.*

21. Ibid.

22. Lacretelle, *Histoire de la Révolution française.*

23. *Correspondance de Napoléon Ier.*

24. Herold, *The Mind of Napoleon.*

25. Swedish Royal Archives.

26. *Correspondance de Napoléon Ier.*

Chapter 9. The Folly at No.6

1. Chastenay, *Mémoires.*

2. Pasquier, *Mémoires.*

3. Gavoty, *Les amoureux de l'Impératrice Joséphine.*

4. Segur, *Mémoires.*

5. Barras, *Mémoires.*

6. Mossiker, *Napoleon and Josephine.*

7. Broglie, *Mémoires.*

8. Berry, *Voyages.*

9. Forneron, *Histoire générale.*

10. Ibid.

11. Ibid.

12. Berry, *Voyages*.

13. Mercier, *Le nouveau tableau de Paris*.

Chapter 10. General Vendémiaire

1. Bertrand, *Cahiers*.
2. Madelin, *La Révolution*.
3. Bertrand, *Cahiers*.
4. Abrantès, *Mémoires*.
5. Thiébault, *Mémoires*.
6. Carlyle, *The French Revolution*.
7. Ibid.
8. Fain, *Mémoires*.
9. Abrantès, *Mémoires*.
10. Ibid.
11. Bourrienne, *Mémoires*.
12. Ibid.
13. Barras, *Mémoires*.
14. Poniatowski, *Talleyrand et le Directoire*.
15. Masson, *Joséphine de Beauharnais*.
16. Savant, *Tel fut Barras*.
17. Ibid.
18. Masson, *Joséphine de Beauharnais*.
19. Chastenay, *Mémoires*.
20. Alméras, *Barras et sen temps*.

Chapter 11. To Destiny!

1. Bourgeat, *Napoléon: Lettres à Joséphine*.
2. Tulard, *Lettres d'amour à Joséphine*.
3. Gourgaud, *Journal*.
4. Ibid.
5. Tulard, *Lettres d'amour à Joséphine*.
6. Las Cases, *Mémorial*.
7. Ibid.
8. Gourgaud, *Mémoires*.
9. Bertrand, *Cahiers*.
10. Rémusat, *Mémoires*.
11. Ibid.
12. Marmont, *Mémoires*.
13. Ibid.
14. Bertrand, *Cahiers*.
15. Ibid.
16. Chuquet, *La Jeunesse de Napoléon*.
17. Ibid.
18. Gourgaud, *Mémoires*.
19. Bertrand, *Cahiers*.
20. Ibid.
21. Tulard, *Lettres d'amour à Joséphine*.
22. Barras, *Mémoires*.
23. Tulard, *Napoléon*.
24. Marmont, *Mémoires*.
25. Chardigny, *L'Homme Napoléon*.
26. Bertrand, *Cahiers*.
27. Rémusat, *Mémoires*.
28. Barras, *Mémoires*.
29. Masson, *Joséphine de Beauharnais*.
30. Barras, *Mémoires*.
31. Gourgaud, *Mémoires*.
32. Ouvrard, *Mémoires*.
33. Barras, *Mémoires*.
34. Ibid.

35. Montgaillard, *Souvenirs.*

36. Lacretelle, *Mémoires.*

37. Savant, *Napoléon et Joséphine.*

38. Gohier, *Mémoires.*

39. Gay, *Salons célèbres.*

40. Frénilly, *Souvenirs.*

Chapter 12. A Kind of Radiance

1. Las Cases, *Mémorial.*

2. Marmont, *Mémoires.*

3. Ibid.

4. Ibid.

5. Ibid.

6. Ibid.

7. Ibid.

8. Arnault, *Mémoires.*

9. Bonaparte, J., *Mémoires.*

10. Castelot, *Joséphine.*

11. Marmont, *Mémoires.*

12. Hamelin, *Douze ans de ma vie.*

13. Ibid.

14. Hastier, *Le grand amour de Joséphine.*

15. Abrantès, *Mémoires.*

16. Arnault, *Mémoires.*

17. Ibid.

18. Abrantès, *Mémoires.*

19. Merimée, *Correspondance générale.*

20. Barras, *Mémoires.*

21. Arnault, *Mémoires.*

22. Abrantès, *Mémoires.*

23. Ibid.

24. Bertrand, *Cahiers.*

25. Savant, *Napoléon et Joséphine.*

26. Marmont, *Mémoires.*

27. Masson, *Madame Bonaparte.*

28. Savant, *Napoléon et Joséphine.*

29. Coston, *Biographie.*

30. Ibid.

31. Savant, *Napoléon et Joséphine.*

32. Ibid.

33. Merimée, *Correspondance générale.*

34. Savant, *Napoléon et Joséphine.*

35. Abrantès, *Mémoires.*

36. Rémusat, *Mémoires.*

37. Lacretelle, *Mémoires.*

38. Savant, *Napoléon et Joséphine.*

39. Ibid.

40. Ibid.

41. Masson, *Madame Bonaparte.*

42. Arnault, *Mémoires.*

Chapter 13. Grandeur, Hope and Joy

1. Hamelin, *Douze ans de ma vie.*

2. Savant, *Napoléon et Joséphine.*

3. Ibid.

4. Ibid.

5. Ibid.

6. Mossiker, *Napoleon and Josephine.*

7. Hamelin, *Douze ans de ma vie.*

8. Ibid.

9. Ibid.

10. Aubenas, *Histoire de l'Impératrice Joséphine.*

11. Masson, *Madame Bonaparte.*

12. Ibid.

13. Ibid.

14. Savant, *Napoléon et Joséphine.*

15. Ibid.

16. Castelot, *Bonaparte.*

17. Ibid.

18. Arnault, *Souvenirs.*

19. Rémusat, *Mémoires.*

20. *Correspondance de Napoléon Ier.*

21. Swedish Royal Archives.

22. Marmont, *Mémoires.*

23. Arnault, *Souvenirs.*

24. Ivray, *La Lombardie.*

25. Coston, *Biographie.*

26. Colbert, *Traditions et Souvenirs.*

27. Miot de Melito, *Mémoires.*

28. Ibid.

29. Ibid.

30. Ibid.

Chapter 14. Farewell, General and Peacemaker!

1. Orieux, *Talleyrand.*

2. Ibid.

3. Herold, *Mistress to an Age.*

4. Ibid.

5. Ibid.

6. Ibid.

7. Barras, *Mémoires.*

8. Ibid.

9. Staël, *Sur l'influence des passions.*

10. Bourrienne, *Mémoires.*

11. Miot de Melito, *Mémoires.*

12. Bourrienne, *Mémoires.*

13. Ibid.

14. Bessand-Massenet, *Quand la France attendait Bonaparte.*

15. Poniatowski, *Talleyrand et le Directoire.*

16. Fonds Masson, Bibliothèque Thiers.

17. Unpublished letter, Fonds Masson, Bibliothèque Thiers.

18. Fonds Masson, Bibliothèque Thiers.

19. Soboul, *La Ier République.*

20. Las Cases, *Mémorial.*

21. Poniatowski, *Talleyrand et le Directoire.*

22. Miot de Melito, *Mémoires.*

23. Marmont, *Mémoires.*

24. Abrantès, *Mémoires.*

Chapter 15. Son and Hero of the Revolution

1. Talleyrand, *Mémoires.*

2. Bertrand, *Cahiers.*

3. Marmont, *Mémoires.*

4. Hortense, *Mémoires.*

5. Thiébault, *Mémoires.*

6. Mallet du Pan, *Mémoires.*

7. Wagener, *Madame Récamier.*

8. Poniatowski, *Talleyrand et le Directoire.*

9. Girardin, *Mémoires.*

10. Herold, *Mistress to an Age.*

11. Poniatowski, *Talleyrand et le Directoire.*

12. Bertrand, *Cahiers.*

13. Girardin, *Mémoires.*

14. Correspondence of Bernardin de St. Pierre, Fonds Masson, Bibliothèque Thiers.

15. Bonaparte, L., *Mémoires.*

16. Guillemin, *Madame de Staël.*

17. Hastier, *Le grand amour de Joséphine.*

18. Barras, *Mémoires.*

19. Carnot, *Mémoires.*

20. Hastier, *Le grand amour de Joséphine.*

21. Bertrand, *Cahiers.*

22. Ibid.

23. La Tour du Pin, *Mémoires.*

24. Hastier, *Le grand amour de Joséphine.*

25. Furet and Richet, *La Révolution française.*

26. Bourrienne, *Mémoires.*

27. Reubell, *Mémoires.*

28. Abrantès, *Mémoires.*

29. Herold, *Bonaparte in Egypt.*

30. Bourrienne, *Mémoires.*

31. Abrantès, *Mémoires.*

32. Bourrienne, *Mémoires.*

Chapter 16. There Is Nothing Left for Me

1. Masson, *Madame Bonaparte.*

2. Ibid.

3. Ibid.

4. Ibid.

5. Ibid.

6. Bourrienne, *Mémoires.*

7. Ibid.

8. Herold, *Bonaparte in Egypt.*

9. Bourrienne, *Mémoires.*

10. Masson, *Madame Bonaparte.*

11. Ibid.

12. Abrantès, *Mémoires.*

13. Masson, *Madame Bonaparte.*

14. Ibid.

15. Ibid.

16. Bourrienne, *Mémoires.*

17. Rémusat, *Mémoires.*

18. Herold, *The Mind of Napoleon.*

19. Herold, *Bonaparte in Egypt.*

20. Millet, *Souvenirs.*

21. Bourrienne, *Mémoires.*

22. Herold, *Bonaparte in Egypt.*

Chapter 17. There's Your Man

1. Mossiker, *Napoleon and Josephine.*

2. Chimay, *Madame Tallien.*

3. Bonaparte, J., *Mémoires.*

4. Masson, *Madame Bonaparte.*

5. Ibid.

6. Ibid.

7. Rémusat, *Mémoires.*

8. Abrantès, *Mémoires.*

9. Mossiker, *Napoleon and Josephine.*

10. Rémusat, *Mémoires.*

11. Masson, *Madame Bonaparte.*

12. Ibid.

13. Constant, B., *Mémoire.*

14. Vandal, *L'Avènement de Bonaparte.*

15. Bertrand, *Cahiers.*

16. Gohier, *Mémoires.*

17. Masson, *Madame Bonaparte.*

18. Letter from Charles de Constant to Charles Nauroy (Bibliothèque Nationale.

19. Mossiker, *Napoleon and Josephine.*

20. Ibid.

Chapter 18. The Fruit Is Ripe

1. Castelot, *Bonaparte.*

2. Las Cases, *Mémorial.*

3. Bourrienne, *Mémoires.*

4. Gohier, *Mémoires.*

5. Castelot, *Bonaparte.*

6. Gohier, *Mémoires.*

7. Roederer, *Journal.*

8. Vandal, *L'Avènement de Bonaparte.*

9. Bourrienne, *Mémoires.*

10. Ibid.

11. Arnault, *Souvenirs.*

12. Ibid.

13. Rémusat, *Mémoires.*

14. Arnault, *Souvenirs.*

15. Bertrand, *Cahiers.*

16. Bourrienne, *Mémoires.*

17. Ibid.

Chapter 19. Into the Hands of Vultures

1. Vandal, *L'Avènement de Bonaparte.*

2. Bourrienne, *Mémoires.*

3. Vandal, *L'Avènement de Bonaparte.*

4. Castelot, *Bonaparte.*

5. Bertrand, *Cahiers.*

6. Bourrienne, *Mémoires.*

7. Bainville, *Le 18 Brumaire.*

8. Vandal, *L'Avènement de Bonaparte.*

9. Ibid.

10. Abrantès, *Mémoires.*

11. Ibid.

12. Vandal, *L'Avènement de Bonaparte.*

Chapter 20. "A Republican Simplicity"

1. Roederer, *Journal.*

2. Vandal, *L'Avènement de Bonaparte.*

3. Hyde de Neuville, *Mémoires et Souvenirs.*

4. Ibid.

5. Bourrienne, *Mémoires.*

6. Hortense, *Mémoires.*

7. Bourrienne, *Mémoires.*

8. Abrantès, *Mémoires.*

9. Rémusat, *Mémoires.*

10. Abrantès, *Mémoires.*

11. Russell, *Paris.*

12. Rémusat, *Mémoires.*

13. Ibid.

14. Abrantès, *Mémoires.*

15. Gourgaud, *Journal.*

Chapter 21. He Is a Comet

1. Bourrienne, *Mémoires.*

2. Yorke, *Paris et la France.*

3. Bourrienne, *Mémoires.*

4. Hortense, *Mémoires.*

5. Ibid.

6. Vandal, *L'Avènement de Bonaparte.*

7. Ibid.

8. Masson, *Madama Bonaparte.*

9. Bourrienne, *Mémoires.*

10. Ibid.

11. Molé, *Mémoires.*

12. Madelin, *La Révolution.*

13. Bondonove, *Napoléon.*

14. Castelot, *Joséphine.*

15. Masson, *Madame Bonaparte.*

16. Bertrand, *Cahiers.*

17. Hastier, *Le grand amour de Joséphine.*

18. Ibid.

19. Savant, *Tel fut Bonaparte.*

20. Ibid.

21. Pasquier, *Mémoires.*

22. Bertrand, *Cahiers.*

23. Bourrienne, *Mémoires.*

24. Delay, *Avant Mémoire.*

25. Bourgeat, *Napoléan: Lettres à Joséphine.*

26. Bonaparte, L., *Mémoires.*

27. Lamothe-Langon, *Les après-diners de Cambacérès.*

28. Cambacérès's oration to the Senate.

29. Rémusat, *Mémoires.*

30. Abrantès, *Mémoires.*

31. Hortense, *Mémoires.*

Chapter 22. A Comfortable Woman

1. Yorke, *Letters from France.*

2. Ibid.

3. Kotzebue, *Souvenirs.*

4. Quoted in Knapton, *Empress Josephine.*

5. Yorke, *Letters from France.*

6. Kotzebue, *Souvenirs.*

7. Berry, *Voyages.*

8. Kotzebue, *Souvenirs.*

9. Berry, *Voyages.*

10. Ibid.

11. Greatheed, *An Englishman in Paris.*

12. Reichardt, *Un Hiver à Paris.*

13. Foster, *Letters.*

14. Yorke, *Letters from France.*

15. Bessborough, *Letters of Lord Gower.*

16. Greatheed, *An Englishman in Paris.*

17. Herold, *Mistress to an Age.*

18. Bessborough, *Letters of Lord Gower.*

19. Berry, *Voyages.*
20. Trotter, *Memoirs.*
21. Bourrienne, *Mémoires.*

10. Roederer, *Journal.*
11. Rémusat, *Mémoires.*
12. Abrantès, *Mémoires.*
13. Bertrand, *Cahiers.*

Chapter 23. Saint Napoleon

1. Poniatowski, *Talleyrand et le Consulat.*
2. Gaubert, *Le Sacre de Napoléon Ier.*
3. Masson, *Madame Bonaparte.*
4. Gourgaud, *Mémoires.*
5. Mounier, *Souvenirs.*
6. Masson, *Madame Bonaparte.*
7. Bertrand, *Cahiers.*
8. Ibid.
9. Mossiker, *Napoleon and Josephine.*
10. Constant, L., *Mémoires.*
11. Bibliothéque Nationale.
12. Greatheed, *An Englishman in Paris.*
13. Bertrand, *Cahiers.*

Chapter 24. Citizen Emperor

1. Lamothe-Langon, *Les après-diners de Cambacérès.*
2. Rémusat, *Mémoires.*
3. Gaubert, *le Sacre de Napoléon Ier.*
4. Masson, *Madame Bonaparte.*
5. Savant, *Napoléon et Joséphine.*
6. Bertrand, *Cahiers.*
7. Vaudey, *Souvenirs.*
8. Savant, *Napoléon et Joséphine.*
9. Rémusat, *Mémoires.*

Chapter 25. Proof of My Affection

1. Thiard, *Souvenirs.*
2. Rémusat, *Mémoires.*
3. Frénilly, *Souvenirs.*
4. Boigne, *Mémoires.*
5. Rémusat, *Mémoires.*
6. Abrantès, *Mémoires.*
7. Rémusat, *Mémoires.*
8. Quoted in Gaubert, *Le Sacre de Napoléon Ier.*
9. Rémusat, *Mémoires.*
10. Gaubert, *Le Sacre de Napoléon Ier.*
11. Bertrand, *Cahiers.*
12. Yorke, *Letters from France.*

Chapter 26. The Sun of Austerlitz

1. Hanoteau, *Les Beauharnais et l'Empereur.*
2. Constant, L., *Mémoires.*
3. Horne, *Napoleon: Master of Europe.*
4. Ibid.
5. Bourgeat, *Napoléon: Lettres à Joséphine.*
6. Ibid.
7. Castelot, *Napoléon.*

8. Ibid.

9. *Correspondance de Napoléon Ier.*

10. Bourgeat, *Napoléon: Lettres à José-phine.*

11. Ibid.

12. Castelot, *Joséphine.*

13. Talleyrand, *Mémoires.*

14. Savant, *Tel fut Napoléon.*

Chapter 27. One of the Rays of His Star

1. Rémusat, *Mémoires.*

2. Herold, *The Age of Napoleon.*

3. Guerrini, *Napoléon et Paris.*

4. Rémusat, *Mémoires.*

5. Méneval, *L'Impératrice Joséphine.*

6. Ibid.

7. Masson, *Joséphine, impératrice et reine.*

8. Letters at Malmaison Museum, quoted in Chevallier and Pince-maille, *L'Impératrice Joséphine.*

9. Méneval, *L'Impératrice Joséphine.*

10. Rémusat, *Mémoires.*

11. Abrantès, *Mémoires.*

12. Masson, *Joséphine, impératrice et reine.*

13. Constant, L., *Mémoires.*

14. Avrillon, *Mémoires.*

15. Abrantès, *Mémoires.*

16. Gay, *Salons célèbres.*

Chapter 28. I Saw Only You

1. Rémusat, *Mémoires.*

2. Ibid.

3. Archives Nationales, Paris.

4. Ibid.

5. Ibid.

6. Savant, *Napoléon et Joséphine.*

7. Ibid.

8. Archives Nationales, Paris.

9. Ibid.

10. Ibid.

11. Ibid.

12. Ibid.

13. Ibid.

14. Ibid.

15. Ibid.

16. Walewski Archives.

17. Ibid.

18. Ibid.

19. Ibid.

20. Gourgaud, *Mémoires.*

21. Walewski Archives.

22. Masson, *Joséphine, impératrice et reine.*

23. Ibid.

24. Archives Nationales, Paris.

25. Ibid.

26. Ibid.

27. Castelot, *Napoléon.*

28. Archives Nationales, Paris.

29. Hanoteau, *Les Beauharnais et l'Empereur.*

30. Archives Nationales, Paris.

31. Ibid.

32. Savant, *Napoléon et Joséphine.*

33. Unpublished letter, Fonds Masson, Bibliothèque Thiers.

34. Ibid.

35. Archives Nationales, Paris.

36. Bourgeat, *Napoléon: Lettres à Joséphine.*

37. Rémusat, *Mémoires.*

38. Bourgeat, *Napoléon: Lettres à Joséphine.*

39. Ibid.

40. Ibid.

41. Castelot, *Napoléon.*

Chapter 29. Our Extraordinary Destiny

1. Talleyrand, *Mémoires.*

2. Fouché, *Mémoires.*

3. Rémusat, *Mémoires.*

4. Ibid.

5. Fouché, *Mémoires.*

6. Bourgeat, *Napoléon: Lettres à Joséphine.*

7. Ibid.

8. Rémusat, *Mémoires.*

9. Talleyrand, *Mémoires.*

Chapter 30. Simply Perfect to Me

1. Hanoteau, *Les Beauharnais et l'Empereur.*

2. Ibid.

3. Talleyrand, *Mémoires.*

4. Rémusat, *Mémoires.*

5. Bertrand, *Cahiers.*

6. Constant, L., *Mémoires.*

7. Hanoteau, *Les Beauharnais et l'Empereur.*

8. Talleyrand, *Mémoires.*

9. Ibid.

10. Holland, *Mémoires.*

11. Bertrand, *Cahiers.*

12. Caulaincourt, *Mémoires.*

13. Ibid.

14. Ibid.

15. Savant, *Napoléon et Joséphine.*

16. Constant, L., *Mémoires.*

17. Hortense, *Mèmoires.*

18. Savant, *Napoléon et Joséphine.*

19. Thiébault, *Mémoires.*

20. Castelot, *Napoléon.*

21. Pasquier, *Mémoires.*

22. Fouché, *Mémoires.*

Chapter 31. L'Enfant de Wagram

1. *Correspondance de Napoléon Ier.*

2. Walewski Archives.

3. Rémusat, *Mémoires.*

4. Caulaincourt, *Mémoires.*

5. Ibid.

6. *Correspondance de Napoléon Ier.*

7. Savant, *Napoléon et Joséphine.*

8. Ibid.

9. Méneval, *L'Impératrice Joséphine.*

10. Bausset, *Mémoires.*

11. Hortense, *Mémoires.*

12. Ibid.

13. Ibid.
14. Ibid.
15. Abrantès, *Mémoires.*
16. Pasquier, *Mémoires.*
17. Masson, *Joséphine répudiée.*
18. Ibid.
19. Normand, *Telle fut Joséphine.*

20. Constant, L., *Mémoires.*
21. Beugnot, *Mémoires.*
22. Nicolson, *Napoleon 1812.*
23. Ibid.
24. Ibid.
25. Caulaincourt, *Mémoires.*
26. Colonel de Fezensac, quoted in Brett-James, *1812.*

Chapter 32. An Elegant Equality

1. Castelot, *Joséphine.*
2. Ibid.
3. Bourgeat, *Napoléon: Lettres à Joséphine.*
4. Gourgaud, *Mémoires.*
5. Martineau, *Marie-Louise.*
6. Ibid.
7. Bourgeat, *Napoléon: Lettres à Joséphine.*
8. Rémusat, *Mémoires.*
9. Hortense, *Mémoires.*
10. Martineau, *Marie-Louise.*
11. Ibid.
12. Ibid.
13. Bertrand, *Cahiers.*
14. Masson, *L'Impératrice Marie-Louise.*
15. Frénilly, *Souvenirs.*
16. Bourgeat, *Napoléon: Lettres à Joséphine.*
17. Castelot, *Joséphine.*
18. Abrantès, *Mémoires.*
19. Chastenay, *Mémoires.*

Chapter 33. The Beginning of the End

1. Bordonove, *Napoléon.*
2. Avrillon, *Mémoires.*
3. Marmont, *Mémoires.*
4. Martineau, *Marie-Louise.*
5. Ibid.
6. Bourgeat, *Napoléon: Lettres à Joséphine.*
7. Orieux, *Talleyrand.*
8. Ibid.
9. Bordonove, *Napoléon.*
10. Martineau, *Marie-Louise.*
11. Ibid.
12. Ibid.
13. Ibid.
14. Ibid.
15. Ibid.
16. Bourgeat, *Napoléon: Lettres à Joséphine.*
17. Ibid.
18. Fonds Masson, Bibliothèque Thiers.
19. Mossiker, *Napoleon and Josephine.*
20. Castelot, *Joséphine.*

21. Cochelet, *Mémoires*, quoted in Mossiker, *Napoleon and Josephine*.

22. Ducrest, *Mémoires*.

23. Ibid.

24. Cochelet, *Mémoires*, quoted in Mossiker, *Napoleon and Josephine*.

25. Knapton, *Empress Josephine*.

26. Mossiker, *Napoleon and Josephine*.

27. Ibid.

28. Masson, *Joséphine répudiée*.

29. Cronin, *Napoleon*.

30. Broglie, *Mémoires*.

31. Castelot, *Joséphine*.

32. Ibid.

33. Hortense, *Mémoires*.

34. Chimay, *Madame Tallien*.

35. Herold, *The Age of Napoleon*.

36. Bertrand, *Cahiers*.

37. Gourgaud, *Mémoires*.

38. Herold, *The Age of Napoleon*.

39. Bordonove, *Napoléon*.

40. Lamothe-Langon, Les après-diners de Cambacérès.

41. Constant, L., *Mémoires*.

42. Hortense, *Mémoires*.

43. Ibid.

44. Bordonove, *Napoléon*.

45. Lady Charlotte Fitzgerald, quoted in Brett-James, *The Hundred Days*.

Epilogue

1. Bertrand, *Cahiers*.

2. Chateaubriand, *Mémoires d'Outre-tombe*.

3. Bertrand, *Cahiers*.

4. Chateaubriand, *Mémoires d'Outre-tombe*.

5. Ibid.

6. Bertrand, *Cahiers*.

7. Lang, *Une vie d'orages*.

8. Broglie, *Mémoires*.

9. Lang, *Une vie d'orages*.

10. Ibid.

11. Ibid.

12. Broglie, *Mémoires*.

13. Bertrand, *Cahiers*.

14. Ibid.

15. Ibid.

16. Ibid.

17. Ibid.

18. Ibid.

19. Chimay, *Madame Tallien*.

20. Ibid.

21. Forneron, *Mémoires*.

22. Castelnau, *Madame Tallien*.

23. Martineau, *Marie-Louise*.

24. Chevallier and Pincemaille, *L'Impératrice Joséphine*.

25. Ibid.

26. Ibid.

27. Ibid.

28. Martineau, *Marie-Louise*.

29. Beugnot, *Mémoires*.

30. Pasquier, *Mémoires*.

31. Herold, *The Age of Napoleon*.

32. Letter to Jérôme Bonaparte, 1804, quoted in Herold, *The Mind of Napoleon.*

33. Las Cases, *Mémorial.*

34. Ibid.

35. Ibid.

36. Bertrand, *Cahiers.*

37. Ibid.

38. Ibid.

39. Gourgaud, *Mémoires.*

40. Bertrand, *Cahiers.*

41. Fain, *Mémoires.*

42. Constant, B., *Mémoire.*

43. Bertrand, *Cahiers.*

44. Ibid.

45. Ibid.

46. Las Cases, *Mémorial.*

47. Gourgaud, *Mémoires.*

48. Bertrand, *Cahiers.*

49. Ibid.

50. Ibid.

51. Ibid.

52. Gourgaud, *Mémoires.*

53. Bertrand, *Cahiers.*

54. Ibid.

55. Gourgaud, *Mémoires.*

56. Ibid.

57. Ibid.

58. Las Cases, *Mémorial.*

59. Bertrand, *Cahiers.*

Selected Bibliography

Abrantès, Duchesse d'. *Mémoires.* 4 vols. Paris: Albin Michel, n.d.

Alméras, Henri. *Barras et son temps.* Paris: Albin Michel, n.d.

———. *La Vie parisienne sous la Révolution et le Directoire.* Paris: Albin Michel, n.d.

———. *La Vie parisienne sous le Consulat et l'Empire.* Paris: Albin Michel, n.d.

Arnault, Antoine V. *Souvenirs d'un Sexagénaire.* Paris, 1833.

Aronson, Theo. *Napoleon and Josephine.* London: John Murray, 1990.

Aubert, Raymond. *Journal d'un bourgeois de Paris sous la Révolution.* Paris: France-Empire, 1974.

Audiger, M. G. *Souvenirs et anecdotes sur les comités révolutionnaires 1793–1795.* Paris: Auguste Mie, 1830.

Avrillon, Mademoiselle. *Mémoires de Mademoiselle Avrillon.* Paris: Mercure de France, 1969.

Babeau, Albert, *Paris en 1789.* Paris: Ed. Albin Michel, 1989.

Baczko, Bronislaw. *Comment sortir de la Terreur.* Paris: Gallimard, 1989.

Bainville, Jacques. *Le 18 Brumaire.* Paris: Hachette, 1925.

Barnett, Corelli. *Bonaparte.* London: Allen and Unwin, 1978.

Barras, Paul. *Mémoires de Barras, membre du Directoire.* 3 vols. Paris: Hachette, 1895.

Barthou, Louis. *Le neuf Thermidor.* Paris: Hachette, 1926.

Bausset, Louis François Joseph, Baron de. *Mémoires anecdotiques sur l'interieur du palais et sur quelque évènements de l'Empire.* Paris: Baudoin Frères, 1827–29.

Bertin, Ernest. *La Société du Consulat et de l'Empire.* Paris: Hachette, 1890.

Bertrand, Général. *Cahiers de Sainte Hélène.* Paris: Albin Michel, 1951–59.

Berry, Mary. *Voyages de Miss Berry à Paris, 1782–1836, traduits par Mme la Duchesse de Broglie.* Paris: A. Roblot, 1905.

Bessand-Massenet, Pierre. *La Fin d'une société.* Paris: Plon, 1952.

———. *Les Deux France.* Paris: Plon, n.d.

———. *Quand la France attendait Bonaparte 1794–1800.* Paris: Perrin, 1978.

Bessborough, Countess of. *Letters to Lord Gower.* Private correspondence, edited by Castalia, Countess Granville. London: John Murry, 1917

Beugnot, Comte. *Mémoires du Comte Beugnot, 1779–1785.* Paris: Hachette, 1959.

Bibesco, Princesse. *Lettres d'une fille de Napoléon.* Paris: Flammarion, 1933.

Bizardel, Yvon. *Les Américains à Paris pendant la Révolution française.* Paris: Calmann-Levy, 1972.

Blanc, Olivier. *La dernière lettre.* Paris: Robert Laffont, 1984.

Bluche, Frédéric. *Septembre 1792, logique d'un massacre.* Paris: Ed. Robert Laffont, 1986.

Boigne, Comtesse de. *Mémoires.* Paris: Mercure de France, 1971.

Bonaparte, Lucien. *Mémoires de Lucien Bonaparte, Prince Canino, écrits par lui-même.* Paris: Gosselin, 1836.

Bonsal, Stephen. *The Cause of Liberty.* London: Michael Joseph, 1947.

Bord, Gustave, and Louis Bigard. *La Maison du "Dix-huit Brumaire."* Paris: Hachette, 1930.

Bordonove, Georges. *Napoléon.* Paris: Pygmalion, 1978.

Bouillé, Louis-Amour, Marquis de. *Souvenirs pour servir aux mémoires de ma vie et de mon temps.* Paris: P. Picard, 1906–11.

Bouloiseau, Marc. *Le Comité de salut public 1793–1795.* Paris: Presses Universitaires de France, 1962.

Bourgeat, J., ed. *Napoléon: Lettres à Joséphine.* Paris: Guy Le Prat, 1941.

Bourrienne, Louis-Antoine. *Mémoires.* 5 vols. Paris: Garnier, n.d.

Brault, Eliane. *La Franc-maçonnerie et l'emancipation des femmes.* Paris: Dervy, 1953.

Bredin, Jean-Denis. *Sieyès, La clé de la Révolution française.* Paris: Fallois, 1988.

Brett-James, Antony. *1812.* New York: St. Martin's Press, 1966.

Brinton, Crane. *The Anatomy of Revolution.* New York: Vintage, 1965.

———. *A Decade of Revolution.* New York: Harper and Row, 1963.

Broglie, Victor Duc de. *Souvenirs, 1785–1870.* Paris: C. Lévy, 1886.

Bryant, Arthur. *The Age of Elegance 1812–1822.* London: Collins, 1950.

Cabanis, José. *Le Sacre de Napoleon*. Paris: Gallimard, 1970.

Carlyle, Thomas. *The French Revolution*. London: James Fraser, 1839.

Castelnau, Jacques. *Madame Tallien*. Paris: Hachette, 1937.

————. *Les Grands jours de la Convention 1792–1793*. Paris: Hachette, 1950.

Castelot, André. *Bonaparte*. Paris: Académique Perrin, 1967.

Caulaincourt, Louis de, Duc de Vicence. *Mémoires*. Paris: Plon, 1933.

Challamel, Augustin. *Les Clubs contre révolutionnaires*. Paris: Editions L. Cerf, 1895.

Chanson, P. *Lafayette et Napoléon*. Lyon-Paris: Les Editions de Lyon, 1958.

Chardigny, Louis. *L'Homme Napoléon*. Paris: Perrin, 1987.

Chastenay, Comtesse Victorine de. *Mémoires*. Paris: Plon, 1896.

Chateaubriand, René de. *Mémoires d'outretombe*. Paris: Editions du Centenaire, Flammarion, 1948.

Chevallier, Bernard, and Christophe Pincemaille. *L'Impératrice Joséphine*. Paris: Presses de la Renaissance, 1988.

Chimay, Princesse de. *Madame Tallien*. Paris: Plon, 1936.

Chuquet, Arthur. *La Jeunesse de Napoléon*. 3 vols. Paris: Collin, 1897.

Cobb, Richard. *Death in Paris, 1795–1801*. Oxford: Oxford University Press, 1978.

————. *The People's Armies*. New Haven: Yale University Press, 1987.

————. *Terreur et subsistances 1793–1795*. Paris: Clavreuil, 1964.

Cobban, Alfred. *The Social Interpretation of the French Revolution*. New York: Cambridge University Press, 1964.

Coignet, Capitaine. *Les cahiers du capitaine Coignet, publiés d'après le manuscrit original par Loredan* (1776–1850). Paris: Hachette, 1883.

Colbert, Marquis Auguste de. *Traditions et souvenirs touchant le temps et la vie du Général Auguste Colbert par le Marquis de Colbert*. Paris: Didot Frères, 1863–73.

Cole, Hubert. *Josephine*. New York: Viking, 1963.

Constant, Benjamin. *Mémoire sur les cent jours*. Paris: Beschut, 1820, 1822.

Constant, Louis. *Mémoires de Constant, premier valet de chambre de Napoléon Ier*. Paris: Albin Michel, 1909.

Cooper, Alfred Duff. *Talleyrand*. London: Jonathan Cape, 1932.

Correspondance de Napoléon Ier rassemblée dans les ouvrages publiés par les soins de Napoléon III (1858–69).

Coston, Baron François Gilbert de. *Biographie des premières années de Napoléon Bonaparte.* Paris et Valence: Marc Aurèle Frères, 1840.

Cronin, Vincent. *Napoleon.* London: William Collins and Sons, 1971.

Dauban, C. A. *La Démagogie en 1793 à Paris.* Paris: Plon, 1868.

———. *Paris en 1794 et en 1795.* Paris: Plon, 1868.

Davout, Maréchal Louis-Nicolas, Duc d'Auerstädt et Prince d'Eckmühl. *Correspondance.* Paris: Plon-Nourrit, 1885.

Despatys, Baron. *La Révolution, la Terreur, le Directoire 1791–1799.* Paris: Plon, 1909.

Diaz-Plaja, Fernando. *Teresa Cabarrus.* Barcelona: Olimpo, 1943.

Doyle, William. *The Oxford History of the French Revolution.* Oxford: Oxford University Press, 1989.

Ducrest, Georgette. *Mémoires sur l'Impératrice Joséphine.* 3 vols. Paris: L'Advocat Libraire, 1828.

Espinchal, Comte H. d'. *Journal d'emigration.* Paris : Perrin, 1912.

Estré, Henry d'. *Bonaparte, Les Années obscures.* Paris: Plon, 1942.

Fain, Baron. *Mémoires.* Paris: Plon-Nourrit, 1908.

Fauville, Henri. *La France de Bonaparte vue par les visiteurs anglais.* Aix-en-Provence: Edisud, 1989.

Faÿ, Bernard. *L'Esprit révolutionnaire en France et aux Etats-Unis.* Paris: Edouard Champion, 1925.

Fezensac, R. P., Duc de Montesquiou Fezensac. *Journal de la campagne de Russie en 1812.* Tours: A. Mame, 1849.

Fisher, H. A. L. *A History of Europe.* New York: Houghton Mifflin, 1936.

Forneron, H. *Histoire générale des emigrés.* 3 vols. Paris: E. Plon, Nourrit, 1884.

Fort, Bernadette. *Fictions of the French Revolution.* Evanston, Ill.: Northwestern University Press, 1991.

Fouché, Joseph. *Mémoires.* Paris: Tournon et Nouvelles, 1957.

Frénilly, Baron de. *Souvenirs du Baron de Frénilly.* Paris: Plon-Nourrit, 1909.

Furet, François, and Denis Richet. *La Révolution française.* Paris: Librairie Arthème Fayard, 1973.

Gallet, Michel. *Paris Domestic Architecture of the 18th Century.* London: Barrie & Jenkins, 1972.

Gaubert, Henri. *Le Sacre de Napoléon Ier.* Paris: Flammarion, 1964.

Gavoty, André. *Les amoureux de l'Impératrice Joséphine.* Paris: Librairie Arthème Fayard, 1961.

Gaxotte, Pierre. *Paris au XVIIIᵉ siècle.* Paris: B. Arthaud, 1968.

Gay, Sophie. *Salons célèbres.* Paris: Michel Lévy, 1864.

Gayot, André. *Fortunée Hamelin.* Paris: Emile-Paul, n.d.

Gershoy, Leo. *The Era of the French Revolution 1789–1799.* Princeton: Van Nostrand, 1957.

Girardin, Stanislas de, Vicomte d'Ermenonville. *Mémoires.* Paris: Moutardier, 1829.

Girod de l'Ain, Gabriel. *Désirée Clary.* Paris: Hachette, 1959.

Godechot, Jacques. *The Counter-Revolution, Doctrine and Action 1789–1804.* London: Routledge and Kegan Paul, 1972.

Goncourt, E. and J. *Histoire de la Société française pendant le Directoire.* Paris: l'Acádemie Goncourt, n.d.

Gourgaud, General Gaspard. *Journal inédit de 1815 á 1818.* Paris: Flammarion, 1899.

Greatheed, Bertie G. *An Englishman in Paris, 1803.* London: Geoffrey Bles, 1953.

Gronow, Captain. *The Reminiscences and Recollections of Captain Gronow.* London: The Bodley Head, 1964.

Guerrini, Maurice. *Napoléon et Paris.* Paris: P. Tequi, 1967.

Guillemin, Henri. *Madame de Staël, Benjamin Constant et Napoléon.* Paris: Plon, 1959.

Hamelin, Antoine R. *Douze ans de ma vie. Revue de Paris,* November 1926 and January 1927.

Hampson, Norman. *A Cultural History of the French Revolution.* London: Routledge and Kegan Paul, 1963.

Hanoteau, Jean. *Le Ménage Beauharnais.* Paris: Plon, 1935.

Harten, Elke, and Hans-Christian Harten. *Femmes, culture et révolution.* Paris: Des Femmes pour l'Edition Française, 1989.

Hastier, Louis. *Le grand amour de Joséphine.* Paris: Corea Buchet/Chastel, n.d.

Héricault, C. d'. *La Révolution de Thermidor.* Paris: Didier, 1876.

Herold, J. Christopher. *The Age of Napoleon.* Middlesex, England: Penguin Books, n.d.

———. *The Mind of Napoleon.* Translated by J. Christopher Herold. New York: Columbia University Press, 1955.

———. *Mistress to an Age: A Life of Madame de Staël.* New York: Bobbs-Merrill, 1958.

————. *Bonaparte in Egypt*. London: Hamish Hamilton, 1962.

Holland, Henry Edward Fox, Fourth Baron. *Journal, 1818–1830*. London: Thornton Butterworth, 1923.

Honour, Hugh. *Neo-Classicism*. Middlesex, England: Penguin Books, 1968.

Horne, Alistair. *Napoleon: Master of Europe 1805–1807*. London: Butter and Tanner, 1979.

Hortense, Reine. *Mémoires de la reine Hortense, publiés par le prince Napoléon*. Paris: Plon, n.d. (Déposé Bibliothèque Nationale, 1928.)

Hyde de Neuville, Baron Jean Guillaume. *Mémoires et souvenirs, publiés par la Vicomtesse de Bardennet*. Paris: Plon-Nourrit, 1888, 1890, 1892.

Ivray, Jehan d'. *La Lombardie au temps de Bonaparte*. Paris: 1919.

Janssens, Jacques. *Joséphine de Beauharnais et son temps*. Paris: Berger-Levrault, 1963.

Kelly, Linda. *Women of the French Revolution*. London: Hamish Hamilton, 1987.

Knapton, Ernest John. *Empress Josephine*. Cambridge: Harvard University Press, 1963.

Kotzebue, Auguste. *Souvenirs de Paris en 1804*. 2 vols. Paris: Chaignieau Aîné, 1805.

Kunstler, Charles. *La Vie privée de l'Impératrice Joséphine*. Paris: Hachette, 1939.

Lachouque, Commandant H. *Bonaparte et la cour consulaire*. Paris: Bloud and Gay, 1958.

Lachouque, Henri, and Anne S. K. Brown. *The Anatomy of Glory: Napoleon and His Guard*. London: Lund Humphries, 1961.

Lacretelle, Jean-Charles-Dominique de. *Histoire de la révolution Française*. Paris: Treuttel et Würtz, 1821–26.

Lamothe-Langon, Comte de. *Les après-dîners de Cambacérès*. Paris: Editions Fournier-Valdes, 1946.

Las Cases, Emmanuel, Comte de. *Mémorial de Sainte Hélène*. Paris: Pleïade, 1948.

La Tour du Pin, Marquise de. *Mémoires d'une femme de cinquante ans*. Paris: Chapelot, 1914.

Laver, James. *The Age of Illusion, Manners and Morals, 1750–1848*. New York: McKay, 1972.

Lees-Milne, James. *The Age of Adam*. London: B. T. Batsford, 1947.

Lefebvre, G. *Les Thermidoriens*. Paris: Armand Colin, 1937.

Lezay-Marnesia, M de. *Souvenirs*. Blois: Dezairs, 1857.

Lucas-Dubreton, J. *Le Culte de Napoléon, 1815–1848*. Paris: Albin Michel, 1960.

Lurie, Alison. *The Language of Clothes*. New York: Random House, 1981.

MacDonell, A. G. *Napoleon and His Marshals*. New York: Macmillan, 1934.

Madelin, Louis. *La Révolution*. Paris: Hachette, 1938.

Mallet du Pan, Jacques. *Mémoires et correspondance pour servir à l'histoire de la révolution française*. Paris: Amyot et Cherbulliez, 1851.

———. *Mémoires et Correspondance de Mallet du Pan*. 2 vols. Paris: Crapelet, 1851.

Mansel, Philip. *The Court of France 1789–1830*. Cambridge, Mass.: Cambridge University Press, 1988.

Marbot, Baron de. *Mémoires du Général Baron de Marbot*. 3 vols. Paris: Plon, 1898.

Markham, Felix. *Napoleon*. London: Weidenfeld and Nicolson, 1963.

Marmont, Auguste, Frédéric, Duc de Raguse. *Mémoires*. Paris: Perrotin, 1857.

Marquiset, Alfred. *Une Merveilleuse, Fortunée Hamelin*. Paris: Honoré Champion, 1909.

Martin, Kingsley. *French Thought in the Eighteenth Century*. London: Turnstile Press, 1954.

Martineau, Gilbert. *Marie-Louise*. Paris: France-Empire, 1985.

Masson, Frédéric. *Josephine Impératrice et Reine*. Paris: Sociéte d'Editions Littéraires et Artistiques, 1907.

———. *Joséphine répudiée*. Paris: Société d'Editions Littéraires et Artistiques, Librairie Paul Ollendorff, n.d.

———. *Joséphine de Beauharnais*. Paris: Paul Ollendorf, 1899.

———. *L'Impératrice Marie-Louise*. Paris: Société d'Editions Littéraires et Artistiques, n.d.

———. *Madame Bonaparte*. Paris: Albin Michel, n.d.

Mathiez, Albert. *La Réaction Thermidorienne*. Paris: Armand Colin, 1929.

Mavor, Elizabeth. *The Grand Tours of Katherine Wilmot France 1801–3 and Russia 1805–7*. London: Weidenfeld and Nicolson, 1992.

Meister, H. *Souvenirs de mon dernier voyage à Paris, 1795*. Zurich: Ebez, Orell, Gessner, Fussli, 1797.

Méneval J. E., Baron de. *L'impératrice Joséphine d'après les témoinages de ses principaux historiens*. Paris: C. Lévy, 1910.

Mercier, Sébastien. *Le Nouveau Tableau de Paris*. 6 vols. Paris: Fuchs, Pougens, Cramer, n.d.

Merimée, Prosper. *Correspondance générale*. Paris: 1955.

Michelet, *Histoire de la Révolution française*. Paris: Bibliothèque de la Pléiade, 1952.

Miot de Mélito, Comte A. F. *Mémoires du Comte Miot de Mélito.* 3 vols. Paris: Michel Levy, 1873.

Mitchell, S. *A Family Lawsuit: The Romantic Story of Elizabeth Patterson and Jerome Bonaparte.* New York: Farrar, Straus and Cudahy, 1958.

Molé, Mathien. *Souvenirs d'un témoin 1791–1803.* Geneva: Milieu du Monde, 1943.

Montgaillard, J. G. M., Rocques, Comte de. *Mémoires diplomatiques extraits des Archives du Ministère de l'Intérieur, avec introduction et notes par Clément de Lacroix.* Paris: Paul Ollendorf, 1895.

Montholon, Général Comte Jean-François-Charles-Tristan. *Récits de la captivité de l'Empereur à Sainte Hélène.* Paris: Paulin, 1847.

Morris, Gouverneur. *A Diary of the French Revolution 1789–93.* London: George G. Harrap, 1939.

Mossiker, Frances. *Napoleon and Josephine: The Biography of a Marriage.* New York: Simon and Schuster, 1964.

Mounier, Baron C. P. E. *Souvenirs.* Paris: Paul Ollendorf, 1896.

Napoleon, Joseph. *Mémoires et correspondance du roi Joseph par le Baron du Casse* (*1856–69*).

Nicolson, Nigel. *Napoleon 1812.* London: Weidenfeld and Nicolson, 1985.

Normand, Suzanne. *Telle fut Joséphine.* Paris: Editions de Sud, 1962.

Norvins, M. de. *Histoire de Napoléon.* Paris: A. Thoisnier-Desplaces, 1839.

Ollivier, Albert. *Le Dix-huit Brumaire.* Paris: Gallimard, 1959.

Oman, Carola. *Napoleon's Viceroy, E. de Beauharnais.* London: Hodder and Stoughton, 1966.

Orieux, Jean. *Talleyrand.* Paris: Flammarion, 1970.

Ouvrard, G. J. *Mémoires sur sa vie.* Paris: Moutardier, 1826.

Ozouf, Mona. *La Fête révolutionnaire 1789–1799.* Paris: Gallimard, 1976.

Palewski, Gaston. *Le Miroir de Talleyrand, Lettres inédites à la Duchesse de Courlande pendant le Congrès de Vienne.* Paris: Perrin, 1976.

Palmer, Arnold. *Moveable Feasts.* London: Oxford University Press, 1952.

Papillard, François. *Cambacérès.* Paris: Hachette, 1961.

Pasquier, Chancelier. *Mémoires.* 2 vols. Paris: Plon, 1894.

Pichevin, René. *L'Impératrice Joséphine.* Paris: P. E. Blondel-La Rougery, 1909.

Plutarch. *The Female Revolutionary.* 3 vols. London: J. Murray, 1808.

Poniatowski, Michel. *Talleyrand aux Etats Unis, 1794–1796.* Paris: Presses de la Cité, 1967.

————. *Talleyrand et le Consulat.* Paris: Perrin, 1954.

————. *Talleyrand et le Directoire.* Paris: Académique Perrin, 1982.

Reichardt, J. F. *Un Hiver à Paris sous le Consulat.* Paris: E. Plon, Nourrit, 1896.

————. *Un Prussien en France en 1792.* Paris: Perin, 1892.

Rémusat, Madame de. *Mémoires, 1802–1808.* 3 vols. Edited by Calman Lévy. Paris: Michel Lévy, 1893.

Reubell, Jean-François. *La diplomatie du Directoire et de Bonaparte d'après les papiers inédits de Reubell.* Paris: Bernard Nabonne, 1951.

Rheinardt, E. A. *L'Impératrice Joséphine.* Paris: Grasset, n.d.

Rice, Howard C., Jr. *Thomas Jefferson's Paris.* Princeton, NJ: Princeton University Press, 1976.

Richardson, Frank. *Napoleon, Bi-Sexual Emperor.* London: William Kimber, 1977.

Rigotard, Jean. *La Police parisienne de Napoléon.* Paris: Tallandier, 1990.

Robiquet, J. *La Vie quotidienne au temps de Napoléon.* Paris: Hachette, 1943.

Rocquain, F. *L'Esprit révolutionnaire avant la Révolution 1715–1789.* Paris: Plon, 1878.

Roederer, Comte Pierre-Louis. *Journal.* Paris: H. Daragon, 1909.

Rudé, George. *The French Revolution.* London: Weidenfeld and Nicolson, 1988.

Russell, John. *Paris.* New York: Abrams, 1983.

Saint-Amand, Imbert de. *La Citoyenne Bonaparte.* Paris: Libraire de la Société des Gens de Lettres, 1883.

Saint Bris, Gonzague. *Les Aiglons dispersés.* Paris: Jean-Claude Lattes, 1993.

Sainte-Croix de la Ronçière, G. de. *Joséphine.* Paris: Chez L'Auteur, 1934.

Saurel, Louis. *Le Jour où finit la Terreur.* Paris: Robert Laffont, 1962.

Savant, Jean. *Napoléon et Joséphine.* Paris: Club du Meilleur Livre, 1955.

————. *Cahiers.* Paris: L'Académie Nationale d'Histoire, 1972.

Schumann, Maurice. *Qui a tué le Duc d'Enghien?* Paris: Perrin, 1984.

Sédillot, René. *Le Coût de la Révolution française.* Paris: Perrin, 1987.

Simiot, Bernard. *De quoi vivait Bonaparte.* Paris: Albin Michel, 1992.

Six, George. *Les Généraux de la Révolution et de l'Empire.* Paris: Bordas, 1947.

Soboul, A. *La Ière République.* Paris: C. Lévy, 1968.

Sorel, A. *Le couvent des Carmes pendant la Terreur.* Paris: Didier, 1864.

Staël, Germaine de. *Sur l'influence des passions sur le bonheur des hommes et des nations.* Paris: Oeuvres complètes, Treuttel et Würtz, 1820–21.

Stendhal. *Mémoires sur Napoléon*. Paris: Ancienne Honoré Champion, 1929.

Thiard, A. T. M. de, Comte de Bissy. *Souvenirs diplomatiques et militaires du Général Thiard, chambellan de Napoléon Ier*. Paris: Flammarion, 1900.

Thibaudeau, A. C. *Mémoires sur la Convention et le Directoire*. 2 vols. Paris: Baudouin, 1824.

Thiébault, General Paul. *Mémoires publiés sous les auspices de sa fille Mlle Claire Thiébault et d'après le manuscrit original par F. Calmettes*. Paris: 1894–1910.

Thiry, Jean. *L'Aube du Consulat*. Paris: Berger-Levrault, 1948.

Tomalin, Claire. *The Life and Death of Mary Wollstonecraft*. London: Weidenfeld and Nicolson, 1974.

Trahard, Pierre. *La Sensibilité révolutionnaire 1789–94*. Paris: Boivin, 1936.

Trotter, John Bernard. *Memoirs of the latter years of C. J. Fox*. London: Printed for Richard Phillips, 1811.

Tulard, Jean. *Napoléon ou le mythe du saveur*. Paris: Fayard, 1977.

Tulard, Jean, ed. *Napoléon: Lettres d'amour à Joséphine*. Paris: Fayard, 1981.

Vandal, Albert. *L'Avènement de Bonaparte*. 2 vols. Paris: Plon-Nourrit, 1902.

Vaudey, Madame de. *Souvenirs du Directoire et de l'Empire par Madame la Baronne de Vaudey*. Paris: Imprimerie de Cosson, 1848.

Wagener, Françoise. *Madame Récamier*. Paris: Jean-Claude Lattes, 1986.

Walpole, Horace. *Correspondence*. Edited by Wilmarth S. Lewis. New Haven: Yale, 1948.

Williams, Helen Maria. *Souvenirs de la Révolution française*. Paris: Dondey Dupré, 1827.

Yalom, Marilyn. *Blood Sisters*. New York: Basic Books, 1993.

Yorke, Henry Redhead. *Paris et la France sous le Consulat*. Paris: Perrin, 1921.

INDEX